MARCUS AND NARCISSA WHITMAN AND THE OPENING OF OLD OREGON

VOLUME 1

DR. MARCUS WHITMAN
A painting by Drury Haight based on a Paul Kane sketch believed to be, by strong circumstantial evidence, an authentic likeness of Dr. Whitman.

Marcus and Narcissa Whitman and the Opening of Old Oregon
By Clifford M. Drury in Two Volumes
Volume 1

Copyright © 1986, 1994, 2014
Discover Your Northwest
New Edition 2014

Published by
Discover Your Northwest
164 South Jackson Street, Seattle WA 98104
DiscoverNW.org

ISBN 978-0-914019-67-1
Two Volume Set ISBN 978-0-914019-66-4
Printed in the USA

All rights reserved. No part of this publication may be reproduced or transmitted in any form or by any means, electronic or mechanical, including photocopy, recording, digital reproduction, or any information storage and retrieval system, without permission in writing from the publisher.

On September 15, 1985, Robert M. Drury, son of the author, signed an agreement to relinquish all rights, privileges, and investment in the books, together with all rights and privileges of the copyright, to Discover Your Northwest (formerly the Pacific Northwest National Parks and Forests Association). We continue to acknowledge and thank Mr. Drury for this lasting and important contribution to the history of the Northwest.

Discover Your Northwest is a 501_c3 nonprofit corporation. Our purpose is to provide for the enhanced enjoyment and understanding of visitors to public lands in our areas of operation in Washington, Oregon, Montana, Idaho, and California.

Book and Cover Design by Ben Nechanicky
Portraits on front cover:
Tomahas by Paul Kane; *Narcissa Prentiss Whitman, Dr. Marcus Whitman* by Drury Haight from Paul Kane sketches; *Tiloukaikt* by Paul Kane
Painting on back cover: *Whitman Mission* by William Henry Jackson, courtesy William Henry Jackson Collection, Oregon Trail Museum at Scotts Bluff National Monument

MARCUS AND NARCISSA WHITMAN AND THE OPENING OF OLD OREGON

VOLUME 1

CLIFFORD M. DRURY

DISCOVER YOUR NORTHWEST
SEATTLE, WASHINGTON

To My Wife

MIRIAM

Who has given invaluable
assistance in the preparation
of the manuscript

FOREWORD

Marcus and Narcissa Whitman and the Opening of Old Oregon is the most important book in existence, at least for the park rangers at Whitman Mission National Historic Site. It is the first book the rangers consult for detailed answers to questions from visitors. When I arrived at Whitman Mission National Historic Site in 1983, the first thing I read was this two-volume work, and since then, I have encouraged every new employee at the park to read it. There is no better way for park staff to prepare for visitors' questions than by reading Dr. Drury's work.

In 1973, Arthur Clark and Co. had published Dr. Clifford Drury's two volume set, *Marcus and Narcissa Whitman and the Opening of Old Oregon*. They decided not to republish the work in 1985, and returned all rights to the Dr. Clifford Drury estate. As a tribute to his recently deceased father, Robert Drury decided to donate the work in 1986 to the Pacific Northwest National Parks and Forests Association (now Discover Your Northwest) during the 150th anniversary of the Whitmans' arrival in the Pacific Northwest. Discover Your Northwest is a non-profit cooperating association working in partnership with several public lands agencies. It operates bookstores at visitor centers on National Park Service, U.S. Forest Service, Bureau of Reclamation, and Army Corps of Engineers sites across the Pacific Northwest. As a cooperating association, income remaining after operating expenses is used for enhanced visitor services and educational programs at host agency locations.

Robert Drury wrote a wonderful foreword to the cooperating association's edition of the book, and it follows in this edition. Once all copies of the intial printing were sold, Discover Your Northwest and Whitman Mission National Historic Site were faced with a challenge—how to bring these volumes into the 21st century and keep the work in print for future generations in a cost-effective manner. Through persistent and patient hard work that goal has been realized. What is still considered to be the most important reference on the Whitmans is available once again, and will remain so for the foreseeable future.

Many people have made this new, digitally-based edition possible. Discover Your Northwest's staff made significant contributions, especially Ben Nechanicky and Mark McKay, with the support and encouragement of Jim Adams, executive director. The Whitman Mission National Historic Site staff spent many hours on the project. Rick Laughlin proofread the entire book after it was digitized and corrected many errors that the optical scanning process introduced. Renee Rusler compiled the list of illustrations and suggested captions. She and David Borges were able to locate most of the illustrations used in the original work. Renee also led the way toward correcting and updating the index. The entire staff of the park's division of interpretation and resource management suggested additional illustrations and captions.

Dr. Clifford Drury's text is not modified from 1973, except for minor corrections that we feel he would have changed himself. Most illustrations and captions are the same, except those that were obviously outdated. We updated the outdoor photographs of the Great Grave and the Whitman Memorial Shaft to replace images that were over 25 years old.

You, the reader, have the product of many people's effort in your hands. This edition is the result of a true partnership between Discover Your Northwest and the National Park Service staff at Whitman Mission National Historic Site. They have created something that will benefit both organizations for many years to come; and more importantly, something that will enhance the public's understanding of the American settlement of the Pacific Northwest. We hope you will enjoy this work, appreciate our historical heritage, and support the preservation of our natural and cultural resources. If you have not visited Whitman Mission National Historic Site, we invite you to see us, either in person or through our website.

Roger Trick
Chief, Interpretation & Resources Management
Whitman Mission National Historic Site
June, 2012

FOREWORD TO THE PREVIOUS EDITION

In August of 1985, a graduate student in history who was planning to write a doctoral dissertation on Dr. Clifford Drury's work as a historian said in a letter to me, "I stand in awe of his scholarship." In reply I mentioned that I, too, stand in awe of his scholarship. It was expended over a 49 year period of time, recording and interpreting the work of Marcus and Narcissa Whitman, Presbyterians, and the other Presbyterian and Congregational missionaries of the Oregon Mission of the American Board of Commissioners for Foreign Missions, who settled in what is now Eastern Washington and Northern Idaho in 1836 and 1838. My father's second book on the Old Oregon missionaries was *Marcus Whitman, M. D., Pioneer and Martyr*, published in 1937. This first edition was extensively revised and enlarged in a two volume set, *Marcus and Narcissa Whitman and the Opening of Old Oregon*, published in 1973. It was his greatest and most significant work, a definitive history unlikely to be superceded, and which is now reprinted in this set by the Whitman Mission National Historic Site Branch of the Pacific Northwest National Parks and Forests Association. Altogether, there were twelve volumes published about the missionaries of the Oregon Mission, from 1936 through 1976, and I have counted 24 pamphlet and journal articles in my father's, *My Road from Yesterday—an Autobiography*, directly relating to these missionaries. Of course all of this written material is closely interrelated. The written legacy of careful scholarship is a permanent testimony to the gifts and work of Dr. Clifford M. Drury in this specialized area of American Westward expansion and missionary history.

In the summer of 1934 he taught a Bible class for the Presbyterian Nez Perces at Talmaks, their summer camp in the foothills of the Bitter Root Mountains in North Central Idaho. It was there that his interest was awakened in the work of the original Presbyterian missionaries to the Nez Perce and other nearby Indian tribes. Although only nine years old, I still remember the earnest discussion and questions my father had with several at Talmak on these missionaries. Discussion was soon translated into action, with research first made into the lives and work of the Rev, and Mrs. Henry Harmon Spalding, then the Whitmans. I remember taking field trips with my father where he sought out material for books and articles he would write. He had the necessary qualifications for all his many labors in this field: boundless energy and enthusiasm for his subjects; a doctoral dissertation in history; an ability to collect, sort out, evaluate and organize an extensive and complex array of information from many sources; and a drive to write and carry through to publication the carefully organized results of his labors. He did not have an outstanding voice for public speaking, but he was able to hold and increase the interest of his audiences because of his enthusiasm for the Old Oregon missionaries, his knowledge of almost all of the known facts of their lives and legacy, and his personal charisma. He seemed to be always on the go, studying research material, lecturing, writing, etc., and it comes as no surprise to those who knew him that he found it difficult to relax.

Dr. Clifford M. Drury was born on an Iowa farm near Early, Iowa, on November 7, 1897. He had a farm and small town background through his college years. He graduated from Buena Vista College in Storm Lake, Iowa, in 1918. After a brief period in the Army, and other activities in Iowa, he studied at the San Francisco Theological Seminary in San Anselmo, California, where he graduated in 1922. Also in that year, he married Miriam Leyrer and was ordained as a minister of the Presbyterian Church. The years 1923 to 1927 were spent in China where he was pastor of the interdenominational American Community Church in Shanghai. The academic year 1927–1928 was spent at the University of Edinburgh in Scotland where he worked on his doctorate. A pastorate in Moscow, Idaho, was accepted and in this decade to 1938, the first two works on Old Oregon missionaries were published. The years from 1938 to his retirement in 1963 were very busy and productive, first as Professor of Church History at the San Francisco Theological Seminary, then as Chaplain in the United States Navy during the war years, then back to his Church History Professor position. Sixteen books were published during these years, including a six volume narrative and statistical set, *History of the Chaplain Corps*. The retirement years, November, 1963, to near the time of his death on April 18, 1984, in Pasadena, California, were also busy and productive, with part-time teaching at the interdenominational Fuller Theological Seminary, with eight published books and his last book, *My Road from Yesterday—an Autobiography*, in the process of being published.

The Whitman Mission National Historic Site is a registered historic site with the United Presbyterian Church in the U.S.A. This recognition was given to the Whitman Mission National Historic Site by the Presbyterian Historical Society in 1983. Many of the details of the Whitman Missionaries and their mission were first made known to the pubic through the books and articles of Dr. Clifford M. Drury, and it is fitting that his great contributions be remembered during the 150th anniversary of the Whitmans' arrival in the Walla Walla Valley. The Sesquicentennial planned for 1986 will be a special year designed and proclaimed by Walla Walla County and City, and by the City of College Place, to be a year of special celebrations honoring the Whitmans' many contributions and the history of the Walla Walla Valley.

Robert M. Drury
Kansas City, KS
October, 1985

CONTENTS OF VOLUME I

ACKNOWLEDGMENTS, SOURCES, AND ABBREVIATIONS xiii
IN APPRECIATION xv
INTRODUCTION xvii

I. WHITMAN VOLUNTEERS FOR OREGON 3
   THE AMERICAN BOARD; SAMUEL PARKER; OREGON INDIANS IN THE RED
   RIVER MISSION SCHOOL; NEZ PERCE DELEGATION TO ST. LOUIS; SPOKANE
   GARRY; METHODISTS SEND JASON LEE TO OLD OREGON; SAMUEL PARKER
   APPOINTED; MARCUS WHITMAN AND NARCISSA PRENTISS VOLUNTEER.

II. WHITMAN'S FIRST EIGHTEEN YEARS, 1802–1820 45
    ANCESTRY, BIRTH, AND EARLY YEARS; TEN YEARS IN MASSACHUSETTS.

III. WHITMAN'S MEDICAL TRAINING 57
     RIDING WITH DR. BRYANT; WHITMAN'S FIRST TERM AT MEDICAL COLLEGE;
     WHITMAN IN CANADA; WHITMAN RETURNS TO MEDICAL COLLEGE.

IV. THREE YEARS AT WHEELER, 1832–1835 71
    THE CHOLERA EPIDEMIC; WHITMAN COMMISSIONED BY THE AMERICAN BOARD;
    PARKER'S APPEAL FOR MISSIONARIES; WHITMAN LEAVES FOR THE ROCKIES.

V. EARLY LIFE OF NARCISSA PRENTISS, 1808–1835 89
   ANCESTRY AND EARLY LIFE; THE CHURCH AT PRATTSBURG; HER EDUCATION;
   SHE REJECTS SPALDING'S PROPOSAL; "ARE FEMALES WANTED"; MARCUS AND
   NARCISSA ENGAGED; NARCISSA APPLIES FOR APPOINTMENT.

VI. WHITMAN'S FIRST JOURNEY TO THE ROCKIES, 1835 111
    HIS OFFICIAL COMMISSION; DIFFERENCES OF WHITMAN AND PARKER; HOS-
    TILITY OF THE MEN OF THE CARAVAN; CHOLERA STRIKES; FROM BELLEVUE TO
    THE RENDEZVOUS; AT THE RENDEZVOUS; WHITMAN AND PARKER SEPARATE;
    "WE COULD CROSS THE MOUNTAINS WITH A WAGON."

VII. MARCUS AND NARCISSA ARE MARRIED, 1836 149
     THE SEARCH FOR ASSOCIATES; HENRY H. SPALDING; ELIZA HART SPALDING;
     SPALDING'S UNFORTUNATE REMARK; "WE WANT YOU FOR OREGON"; THEIR
     PERSONAL APPEARANCE; MARCUS AND NARCISSA ARE MARRIED.

VIII. FIRST WHITE WOMEN TO CROSS THE ROCKIES, 1836 171
      OFFICIAL PASSPORTS FOR OREGON; FINAL INSTRUCTIONS FROM THE BOARD;
      FROM NARCISSA'S LETTERS; WILLIAM H. GRAY; TRAVEL OUTFIT ASSEMBLED;
      ON THE MARCH; THROUGH SOUTH PASS, JULY 4, 1836.

IX. FROM THE RENDEZVOUS TO FORT VANCOUVER 203
   AT THE RENDEZVOUS; TO FORT BOISE; NARCISSA'S DIARY; TO FORT VANCOUVER; THE MISSIONARIES AT FORT VANCOUVER.

X. WAIILATPU, 1836–1837 241
   MISSION SITE SELECTED; SPALDING SELECTS LAPWAI; WOMEN RETURN TO WALLA WALLA; FIRST HOUSE AT WAIILATPU; FOOD SUPPLIES; GRAY RETURNS TO THE STATES; AGRICULTURE AND EVANGELIZATION BEGIN AT WAIILATPU; THREE CAYUSE CHIEFS; ALICE CLARISSA BORN; TRIALS AND TRIUMPHS.

XI. THE VERSATILE DOCTOR, 1837–1838 271
   WHITMAN, THE DOCTOR, FARMER, AND MISSIONARY TEACHER; ELIZA SPALDING BORN; FIRST ADOBE HOUSE; LEE VISITS WHITMAN AND SPALDING.

XII. JASON LEE AND OREGON COLONIZATION 307
   LIEUTENANT SLACUM VISITS OREGON; BOUNDARY ISSUE; METHODIST REENFORCEMENTS; LEE LEAVES FOR NEW YORK; WHITMAN AND SPALDING ASK FOR MORE MISSIONARIES; METHODISTS RECEIVE A GOVERNMENT SUBSIDY; THE LAUSANNE REENFORCEMENT; REACTION OF THE HUDSON'S BAY COMPANY.

XIII. A YEAR OF ADJUSTMENTS, 1838–1839 333
   FINANCIAL MATTERS; FIRST PRESBYTERIAN CHURCH OF OREGON; REENFORCEMENT OF 1838; ASA BOWEN SMITH; "A STRANGE COMPANY OF MISSIONARIES"; COLUMBIA MATERNAL ASSOCIATION; TSHIMAKAIN SELECTION; COMING OF ROMAN CATHOLIC MISSIONARIES; WHITMAN'S SECOND HOUSE; GROWING DISSENTION IN THE MISSION; ALICE CLARISSA DROWNED; RECONCILIATION.

XIV. FOURTH YEAR OF THE OREGON MISSION, 1839–1840 401
   GRAY DEMANDS A SEPARATE STATION; INDEPENDENT MISSIONARIES ARRIVE; FIRST NATIVE CONVERTS; THOMAS J. FARNHAM; EMIGRANT HOUSE ERECTED; SPALDING CRITICIZED; MORE MISSIONARIES; ARRIVAL OF FATHER DESMET.

XV. FIFTH YEAR OF THE OREGON MISSION, 1840–1841 437
   CRITICAL LETTERS AGAINST SPALDING; FIRST WAGONS OVER THE BLUE MOUNTAINS; INDIAN TROUBLES; PROPOSAL TO SELL OUT TO THE METHODISTS; MUNGER INSANE; SMITHS AND ROGERS LEAVE; POLITICAL DEVELOPMENTS; THE WILKES EXPEDITION.

XVI. THE MISSION IN CRISIS, 1841–1842 479
   RED RIVER MIGRATION; WAR, DIPLOMACY, OR EMIGRATION; WHITMAN'S LIFE THREATENED; MORE DISSENTION IN THE MISSION; AMERICAN BOARD DISMISSES SPALDING; ROMAN CATHOLIC ACTIVITIES; ELIJAH WHITE AND THE 1842 EMIGRATION; GRAY RESIGNS; WHITMAN LEAVES FOR THE EAST.

Illustrations in Volume I

Marcus Whitman	Inside Front
Silhouettes of the HBC Officials	39
Rabbit-Skin-Leggins	40
No-Horns-on-his Head	40
Red River Mission School	41
Spokane Garry	42
Drawing of Deformed Head	42
Samuel Parker	43
William H. Gray	200
Oregon Trail Map	201
South Pass Monument	201
Ft. Vancouver, 1845	237
Fort Walla Walla	238
Council Lodge made of Woven Mats	238
Map of the Old Oregon Missions and Trails	397
Letter of Narcissa Whitman	398
Whitman House by Paul Kane	433
W.H. Jackson Painting of the Whitman Mission	433
Floor Plan of the Whitman Home	434
An 1884 Drawing of the Whitman Mission	435

Acknowledgments, Sources, and Abbreviations

Acknowledgment is made to Caxton Printers, Ltd., Caldwell, Idaho, for permission to use some of the material appearing originally in my *Marcus Whitman, M.D., Pioneer and Martyr*, which they published in 1937 and which is now out-of-print. Most of those listed under "Acknowledgments" in that volume are now deceased, but my feeling of gratitude to them for their help continues.

A major source of information used in the writing of this work is the letters and diaries of Marcus and Narcissa Whitman. Appendix I lists 302 such items. Other source materials, especially those in manuscript form, have been found in the following libraries or depositories of historical materials (abbreviations indicated in parentheses are used in endnotes):

American Board of Commissioners for Foreign Missions (A.B.C.F.M.) archives on deposit in Houghton Library, Harvard University, Cambridge, Massachusetts. (Coll. A.) These archives contain about one million words of the correspondence of the members of the Board's Oregon Mission, especially for the years 1835–50.

Bancroft Library, University of California, Berkeley. (Coll. B.)

Eastern Washington State Historical Society, Spokane, Washington, which contains most of the author's notes used in the writing of his eight books already published on the history of the Oregon Mission of the American Board, together with materials used in the preparation of the manuscript for the present volumes. (Coll. E.W.S.H.S.)

Hawaiian Mission Children's Society, Honolulu, Hawaii. (Coll. H.) The reference to "Children" is to the descendants of the original band of American Board missionaries who served in the Hawaiian Islands, then called Sandwich Islands.

Hudson's Bay Company (H.B.C.) archives were still in London when consulted by the author in the summer of 1966. (HBC Arch.) These are to be moved to Montreal, Canada.

Huntington Library and Art Gallery, San Marino, California.
Library of Congress and National Archives, Washington, D.C.
Oregon Historical Society (O.H.S.) Portland, Oregon. (Coll. o.)
Oregon State Archives, Salem, Oregon.
Presbyterian Historical Society, Philadelphia, Pennsylvania.
Roman Catholic Archdiocesan Archives, Seattle, Washington.
San Francisco Theological Seminary, San Anselmo, California.
Washington State University, Pullman, Washington. (Coll. Wn.)
Washington State Historical Society, Tacoma, Washington. (Coll. W.S.H.S.)
Whitman College, Walla Walla, Washington. (Coll. W.)
Yale University, Beinecke Rare Book and Manuscript Library, New Haven, Connecticut, which has the Coe Collection of Western Americana. (Coll. Y.)

Abbreviations used for Serial Publications

O.H.Q.—Oregon Historical Quarterly

P.H.Q.—Pacific Historical Quarterly

P.H.R.—Pacific Historical Review

P.N.Q.—Pacific Northwest Quarterly

T.O.P.A.—Transactions of the Oregon Pioneer Association

W.C.Q.—Whitman College Quarterly

W.H.Q.—Washington Historical Quarterly

Abbreviations used for Books.

See Bibliography for further information about these titles.

F.W.W.—Drury, *First White Women over the Rockies*

O.P.—Hulbert and Hulbert, *Overland to the Pacific*. Vols. V-VIII inclusive contain much of Whitman's correspondence with the American Board.

Other acknowledgments will be given in endnotes and in captions under illustrations.

In Appreciation

No work of this magnitude could ever have been written without the cooperation and often enthusiastic assistance of many persons scattered all the way from London, England, to Honolulu, Hawaii, and extending over a period of nearly forty years. I wish to express my appreciation to the American Philosophical Society of Philadelphia for a grant of $1,000.00 given in 1966 to help cover expenses of travel to London for the purpose of doing research in the archives of the Hudson's Bay Company.

Among the many individuals who have helped in many varied ways, I wish to give special mention to the following:

To the owner, who wishes to remain anonymous, of the John Mix Stanley paintings of two of the Cayuse Indians who took part in the Whitman massacre for his consent for me to use reproductions as illustrations in this work;

Andy Dagosta, Pasadena, California, for the map he drew of the trails in Old Oregon used by the missionaries;

The late father W. L. Davis, S.J., Gonzaga University, Spokane, Washington, who kindly made available hitherto unpublished diaries of early Roman Catholic Oregon missionaries;

Dr. Herman J. Deutsch, retired Professor of American History, Washington State University, Pullman, who wrote the Introduction for my biography of Henry Harmon Spalding, published in 1936, and who has gone over the present manuscript twice in the course of its preparation for publication;

Rev. Drury Haight, Pasadena, California, who painted the portraits from the Kane sketches believed to be of Marcus and Narcissa Whitman;

Father Edward J. Kowrach, St. Anne's Church, Medical Lake, Washington, for an English translation of Father Pascal Ricard's journal of 1847;

Robert E. Moody, Rushville, New York, whose cooperation in gathering material and in reading portions of my manuscript dates back to 1935;

Mrs. H. W. (Celista) Platz, Seattle, Washington, for a copy of the 56-page manuscript of her grandmother, Catherine Sager Pringle, with its excellent account of life in the Whitman home and of the massacre; Walter Alden Richards, Burbank, California, for helpful suggestions in the preparation of the manuscript;

Dr. Albert W. Thompson, retired Professor of Foreign Languages and Dean Emeritus, College of Sciences and Arts, Washington State University, Pullman, who has gone over my manuscript twice and whose comments have been invaluable;

Ross Woodbridge, Pittsford, New York, who has generously shared with me the results of his intensive researches into the Whitman story;

The Superintendents and Historians of the Whitman Mission National Historic Site for pictures and information about the mission;

The librarians of Whitman College (especially to Lawrence L. Dodd, Curator of Manuscripts & Special Collections), Oregon Historical Society, Houghton Library at Harvard University, and other libraries who have so generously given of their time to answer my numerous inquiries;

And finally — to Arthur H. Clark, Jr., Paul Galleher, and members of their staff whose assistance in preparation of the manuscript for publication is deeply appreciated.

To many, many others who have assisted, some of whom will be mentioned in footnotes, my deepest thanks.

Clifford M. Drury

INTRODUCTION

Here is the story of the Whitmans—Marcus and Narcissa—who played prominent roles in the history of Old Oregon during those critical years, 1836–47. The Whitmans and the Rev. and Mrs. Henry H. Spalding, all residents of New York State, were sent in 1836 to the Pacific Northwest as appointees of the American Board of Commissioners for Foreign Missions to evangelize the natives. The Whitmans settled among the Cayuse Indians near present-day Walla Walla, Washington, and the Spaldings among the Nez Perces near what is now Lewiston, Idaho.

Both Whitman, who was a Presbyterian elder and a physician, and Spalding, a Presbyterian minister, were convinced that the natives had to be civilized before they could be evangelized. Although neither of the two tribes—the Cayuses and the Nez Perces—were nomadic, they were highly mobile as they found it necessary to spend months of each year traveling in search of wild game, fish, or roots. Both Whitman and Spalding saw the necessity of inducing the Indians to take up farming and be settled so that a consistent program of education and evangelization could be conducted.

The missionaries also realized that, with the inevitable coming of the white man into the Old Oregon country, the natives would have to adjust to the new culture which would be thrust upon them or perish. The eleven years spent by the Whitmans at Waiilatpu were years of transition and upheavel for the Cayuses. Marcus and Narcissa faced more problems and more dangers than did the Spaldings or any of the other missionaries who served in Old Oregon because their station, Waiilatpu, became an outpost on the Oregon Trail.

Although Whitman's primary responsibility was to do all that he could to evangelize and civilize the natives, he also became involved in the political future of the Old Oregon country. In 1818 the United States and Great Britain signed a Treaty of Joint Occupation which temporarily postponed settlement of their respective claims to the vast territory lying north of the 42nd parallel (which was then the Mexican border), west of the Continental Divide, and extending northward to Alaska.

After being on the field for about two years, Whitman was alerted by the pioneer Methodist missionary to the Willamette Valley in Oregon, the Rev. Jason Lee, as to the importance of having the Oregon boundary fixed at a line far enough north to give the United States the lower Columbia River country and the Puget Sound area. Both Lee and Whitman became convinced that the most effective way for the United States to establish its sovereignty over this part of Old Oregon was through American emigration.

Dr. Whitman made three notable contributions to the opening of the Oregon country for American settlement:

1. He saw the feasibility of taking white American women over the Continental Divide while on an exploring tour to the Rockies in the summer of 1835. The successful crossing of the Rockies through South Pass by Mrs. Whitman and Mrs. Spalding on July 4, 1836, unlocked the mountain gateway for men who wanted to take their families with them to Oregon. Where women could go riding horseback on side-saddles, other women and children could follow in covered wagons.

2. Whitman's stubborn persistence made it possible in 1836 to take the first wheeled vehicle across a long section of the Oregon Trail extending from the Green River Rendezvous in the Rockies to Fort Boise. Where one wagon had gone, others could follow.

3. He was responsible in leading the first great Oregon emigration of about one thousand people in 1843 from Fort Hail into the Columbia River Valley.

These three history-making achievements combined to encourage thousands of Americans to make the overland trek to Oregon after 1843. The decisive factor in the establishment of the boundary with Great Britain in 1846 at the 49th was the numerical superiority of American settlers in Old Oregon over those of British citizenship.

Whitman served his country even in his tragic death on November 29, 1847. When the news of the Whitman massacre, which took the lives of fourteen people, reached Washington, D.C., Congress, hitherto dilatory, was moved to pass legislation making Oregon a territory of the United States.

A New Biography Needed

Three reasons called for this completely new biography of Dr. Whitman and not just a reprint of my *Marcus Whitman, M.D., Pioneer of Old Oregon* which appeared in 1937. In the first place, the earlier edition has long been out of print and second-hand copies are now in great demand.

Secondly much new information bearing on the lives of the Whitmans and the history of the Oregon Mission has been discovered or has been made available to me since 1937. This included materials located in the archives of the Hudson's Bay Company which I had the opportunity to examine in London, England, in the summer of 1966. In my first Whitman book, I used 222 letters written by either Marcus or Narcissa Whitman. Since then I have located eighty additional letters. Journals of two Roman Catholic missionaries who opened stations in the vicinity of Waiilatpu shortly before the massacre have been found. New illustrative materials in the form of sketches, paintings, or photographs have been discovered. Such unused sources, plus many more, called for a more detailed study of the Whitmans than has hitherto been made.

Finally, since I have continued my researches and writings in the history of the Oregon Mission of the American Board for nearly forty years, I now feel better qualified to evaluate the services rendered by the Whitmans to the natives, to the immigrants, and to the nation than ever before. With but one exception, I have found no reason to change any of the basic conclusions regarding Whitman's activities at Waiilatpu as set forth in the 1937 edition. That one exception deals with Whitman's interest in opening Oregon for American settlement. On the basis of new documentary evidence, I have in this work given more attention to the significant role that Whitman played in the opening of Old Oregon to American settlement.

This new work is not only a biography of Marcus and Narcissa Whitman, it is also a history of the Oregon Mission of the American Board. It will also be a source book for the history of the Old Oregon country during the mission period, 1835–47.

In making quotations from original sources as letters and diaries, I have for the sake of clarity introduced punctuation and have modernized some of the archaic spellings.

Clifford M. Drury
Pasadena, California
February, 1973

If I never do more than to have been one of the first to take white women across the mountains and prevent the disaster and reaction which would have occurred by the breaking up of the present [1843] emigration, and establishing the first wagon road across to the border of the Columbia River, I am satisfied.

Marcus Whitman from Fort Walla Walla, November 1, 1843, to Secretary David Greene, Boston.

[CHAPTER ONE]

WHITMAN VOLUNTEERS FOR OREGON

No seer could possibly have foretold a connection between a missionary meeting held in a small one-room country church at Wheeler, Steuben Country, New York, on a raw November evening in 1834, and the action taken by Congress in August 1848 which made Old Oregon[1] a territory of the United States. The fact that these two events were related is clearly evident from contemporary documents. The one who tied them together during that span of fourteen years was Dr. Marcus Whitman and this is the story of what happened.

First, let us look at that small and at the time rather insignificant meeting held in the Presbyterian Church of Wheeler—its locale, the speaker, his message, and especially the key person in the audience, Dr. Whitman. About midway along the tier of New York counties bordering on Pennsylvania is Steuben County with Bath as its county seat. The town or township of Wheeler, in the central part of the county, and the village of Wheeler, received their names from one of the original settlers, who is reported to have been one of the patriots who took part in the Boston tea party of 1773.[2]

The village of Wheeler is located about nine miles north of Bath and seven miles south of Prattsburg. It had a population of not more than twenty-five families when Dr. Whitman settled there early in 1832. His medical practice took him throughout the township, including such neighboring places as Prattsburg. Roads were poor and carriages expensive. People, especially men, usually traveled on horseback. The discovery of Dr. Whitman's saddlebags in the attic of an old house in Wheeler in 1936 gave mute evidence of his method of travel.[3]

When Dr. Whitman first settled at Wheeler, he lived in the home of Thomas Aulls, one of the elders of the Presbyterian Church. This church had been organized in 1824 with twenty-three charter members, but at the time of Whitman's arrival in 1832, was practically defunct. It had no building, no pastor, and no Sunday services. Whitman took an immediate interest in reviving the congregation. Under his initiative, a building, which measured 32 x 40 feet, was erected; it was dedicated on January 10, 1833. The church was reorganized with nine members. Whitman was elected a trustee on December 29, 1832, and joined the church on the following February 10 by letter of transfer from the Congregational Church of his home town, Rushville, New York. He was ordained an elder on Sunday, June 1, 1834.[4] The church records, still extant, show that he was active in the Sunday school, in temperance work, in the local branch of the American Bible Society, and in the official boards of the church. He was a generous contributor to the church's budget and to special needs, as the following minute in one of the record books testifies: "Recd. fifteen dollars from Doctor Whitman to pay M. H. Brown for balance due on stove & pipe for Meeting House."

The revitalized congregation called the Rev. James H. Hotchkin, 1771–1851, who had served as pastor of the Prattsburg Presbyterian Church from 1809 to 1830, to become its pastor in February 1833.[5] His salary was paid in part by the American Home Missionary Society, the domestic counterpart of the American Board of Commissioners for Foreign Missions, as the little congregation was not strong enough to be self-supporting.

Both of these mission boards enjoyed the support of the Congregational and Presbyterian denominations at that time. While at Prattsburg, Hotchkin had received into the church Narcissa Prentiss, who in 1836 was to become Mrs. Marcus Whitman, and Henry Harmon Spalding, who was destined to be associated with the Whitmans in the Oregon Mission of the American Board throughout its eleven-year history. Thus Hotchkin had the distinction of serving as the pastor of three of the most important members of that Mission.

Sometime during the latter part of November 1834, the Rev. Samuel Parker, 1779–1866, visited Wheeler and spoke before a small gathering in the Presbyterian Church in behalf of a proposed mission to far-away Oregon. Parker, who had visited St. Louis during the summer of 1834 on an exploring mission for the American Board, was then sent by the Board to tour western New York in order to solicit funds and recruit missionaries for the projected mission.

But of all places to visit for such purposes, could there have been a more unpromising place than Wheeler? Financially, the little congregation was still struggling to pay for its new building and to raise its share of its pastor's salary. As for finding someone in that small community who would volunteer to go to Oregon as a missionary—who would have dared suggest such a possibility? Yet this is exactly what happened.

It may be that bad weather had prompted Parker to lay over for a day or two in Wheeler, since he commented in a letter to his family dated December 5 on "the very bad state of the roads."[6] Moreover, Parker and Hotchkin were old friends. Each had served Presbyterian churches in the same general area for about twenty years and each had a connection with the American Board. Parker was then one of its agents and Hotchkin had been made an honorary member.

Parker had a thrilling story to tell. His enthusiasm for the proposed mission to Oregon was contagious. As a result, there in that small rural church at Wheeler, where Parker first met Whitman, a decision was made which had far-reaching consequences. Dr. Marcus Whitman volunteered to go as a missionary to Oregon! A few days later, on Tuesday, December 2, 1834, Whitman wrote to the American Board in Boston: "I have had an interview with the Rev. Samuel Parker upon the subject of Missions and have determined to offer myself to the Am. Board to accompany him on his Mission or beyond the Rocky Mountains."[7]

THE AMERICAN BOARD OF COMMISSIONERS FOR FOREIGN MISSIONS

The American Board played so important a role in the life of Marcus Whitman that a brief review of its early history and its objectives is necessary. During the first ten or fifteen years of the nineteenth century, a spiritual awakening pulsated through the nation, which resulted, among other things, in the rise of camp meetings on the western frontier, for example in Kentucky, and in the establishment of theological seminaries and mission boards in the East.

Such institutions of higher learning as Harvard, Yale, and Princeton, which had been founded primarily for the training of a Protestant ministry, had by 1800 become secularized. As a result such denominations as the Congregational and Presbyterian found it necessary for their continued existence to establish theological seminaries. Andover Theological Seminary, founded at Andover, Massachusetts, by the Congregationalists in 1808, was the first institution of this kind in America. Two years later the Presbyterians established their first seminary at Princeton, New Jersey.

Another result of the spiritual awakening which swept through the New England states during the early years of the nineteenth century was the establishment of the American Board of Commissioners for Foreign Missions in 1810. This arose out of an incident which took place on the campus of Williams College in northwestern Massachusetts in 1806. According to a commonly accepted story, the anti-religious feeling was so strong in the college that the Christian students found it best to retreat to a nearby grove in order to find privacy for their devotions. The leader of this band was the dynamic Samuel J. Mills, later active in such organizations as the American Colonization Society and the American Bible Society. He became one of the founders of the African Republic of Liberia.

One day in August 1806, five students at Williams College under the leadership of Mills met in the grove to discuss the proposition that the great commission of Jesus to go into all the world and preach the gospel to every creature was binding upon their generation. At that time there was not a single denominational foreign mission board in the United States. A sudden thunderstorm interrupted the prayer meeting and sent the five young men scurrying for cover. Unable to reach the shelter of a college building, they took refuge in the lee side of a haystack where they continued their discussions. There, under the leadership of Mills, the group solemnly dedicated themselves to the cause of foreign missions. They accepted the proposition that the great commission was binding upon them.

Several of these students, including Mills, enrolled at Andover Theological Seminary where they continued to crusade in the cause of foreign missions. Others, such as Adoniram Judson, who in 1812 was to become the founder of the Baptist Mission in Burma, joined them. The zeal of this group induced the Congregational Association of Massachusetts to establish in 1810 the American Board of Commissioners for Foreign Missions, often referred to as the A.B.C.F.M. Other Congregational Associations soon joined, and in 1812 the Presbyterians began their cooperation with the Board.

Thus from the incident of a prayer meeting held in a haystack came the germinal idea that resulted in the founding of the first foreign missionary board in the United States. The site of the haystack on the campus of Williams College is now marked by a pedestaled monument bearing a globe and the inscription: "The Field is the World. Birthplace of American Foreign Missions, 1806."

Since work with any non-English speaking people in the United States was classified as being foreign missions by most Protestant denominations throughout the nineteenth century, it was logical that the newly organized American Board should have become interested in the American Indians. The Board began its Indian work in 1816 when a few missionaries were sent to the Cherokees. Beginnings of missionary work with five other tribes had been made before Parker urged the Board to send him on an exploring tour to Old Oregon.

Samuel Parker

Samuel Parker was the connecting link between Marcus Whitman and the American Board and also between Whitman and Old Oregon. Parker was born April 28, 1779, at Ashfield, a village in the Berkshires of western Massachusetts, about twenty-five miles southeast of Williamstown, the site of Williams College.[8] His education was somewhat delayed; he was not graduated from Williams College until 1806, when he was twenty-seven years old.

Although a fellow student of Samuel J. Mills, there is no record of him being on the campus at the time of the haystack prayer meeting. After teaching school for a year, Parker began his theological studies under the tutelage of a Congregational minister and was licensed in 1806. He then served as an itinerant home missionary in the western part of New York State; this took him into such counties as Steuben, Allegany, and Cattaraugus which he was to revisit in the late fall and early winter of 1834.

Parker was a member of the first senior class at Andover Theological Seminary, 1810–11, but it does not appear that he was graduated. His associations at Andover with such enthusiasts for foreign Mission as Mills and Judson may have accounted for his lifelong interest in this aspect of Christian endeavor which was then beginning to challenge the attention of the Protestant churches.

Parker was ordained by the Congregational Church at Danby, Tompkins County, New York, in December 1812 when he was thirty-three years old. Later he became a Presbyterian minister, but throughout his life felt free to serve churches of either denomination. In 1812 he became pastor of the Congregational Church in Danby where he remained for fourteen years. He was married in 1815 to Miss Jerusha Lord; to this union three children were born—Jerusha, Samuel J., and Henry.

In 1882, the son, Samuel J. Parker, M.D., then sixty-four years old, wrote an article of about 75,000 words in answer to the question: "By whom were the missions of Dr. Whitman and others established and what was the influence of this movement on the history of the United States?"[9] In it he gave the following description of his father: "...a man some five feet six or eight inches high; blue eyes, slightly sandy hair, a little over weight, but not fleshy; and with mild features, light complexion... He was not an eloquent speaker in the pulpit; but earnest... He was an active man."[10]

Parker resigned his pastorate at Danby in 1826 and during the following eight years moved frequently from one church or position to another. In 1830 he built a house, which is still standing, at 404 East Seneca Street in Ithaca, New York. For a time Parker taught school in that city. During the early part of 1832, he accepted a call to be pastor of the Congregational Church in Middlefield, in west central Massachusetts. While living there, the March 1, 1833, issue of the *Christian Advocate* and *Journal and Zion's Herald*,[11] a Methodist paper published in New York, came to his attention. This carried what Parker considered to be a truly amazing account of a pilgrimage made by four Indians "from west of the Rocky Mountains" to St. Louis to get information about the Christian religion and possibly, also, some missionaries.

THE WISE MEN FROM THE WEST

Nearly one-half of the front page of the *Christian Advocate*, a periodical with the page size of the *New York Times*, was devoted to a feature article under the caption: "The Flat-Head Indians." The heart of the report was a letter from William Walker written from Upper Sandusky, Ohio, on January 19, 1833, to Gabriel P. Disosway, a Methodist merchant in New York City. Walker, who was part Wyandot Indian and also a Methodist, had visited St. Louis in the fall of 1831 to discuss with General William Clark, then in charge of Indian affairs west of the Mississippi River, the possible exchange of some land the Wyandots held in Ohio for a new location in the Indian Territory.[12] This was the Clark who with Meriwether Lewis had made the exploring tour into the Pacific Northwest in 1805–06.

According to Walker's letter, while in Clark's office, "…he informed me that three chiefs from the Flat-Head nation were in his house, and were quite sick, and that one (the fourth) had died a few days ago. They were from the west of the Rocky Mountains." Prompted by curiosity, Walker stepped into the room where the sick men were staying. He was attracted by the deformed skull of one of the Indians and sketched his picture showing the wedge-shaped malformation.

Walker's letter continues: "Gen. C. related to me the object of their mission… It appeared that some white men had penetrated into their country, and happened to be a spectator at one of their religious ceremonies, which they scrupulously perform at stated periods. He informed them that their mode of worshipping the supreme Being was radically wrong, and instead of being acceptable and pleasing, it was displeasing to him; he also informed them that the white people away toward the rising of the sun had been put in possession of the true mode of worshipping the great Spirit. *They had a book* containing directions how to conduct themselves in order to enjoy his favor and hold converse with him; and with this guide, no one need go astray."[13]

After returning to his home in Upper Sandusky, Walker, for some reason, waited for more than a year before writing to Disosway. He enclosed a copy of the drawing he had made of the Indian's deformed head. Disosway was so moved by the letter and the drawing that on February 18, 1833, he forwarded both to the editor of the Methodist *Christian Advocate* with comments of his own. This was the basis of the article which captured the attention of Samuel Parker.

Both the letter from Walker to Disosway and the latter's letter to the editor contained references to the Indians as being from west of the Rockies. Parker saw a parallel between the New Testament story of the wise men from the East who traveled westward seeking the Christ child and this delegation from the West going eastward to St. Louis to get the "book" which would tell them how to obtain the Great Spirit's favor. In a letter addressed to the American Board, dated April 10, 1833, Parker wrote: "Since I saw... what was stated under the head 'The Wise Men from the West,' I have asked myself the question, am I doing my duty with reference to those who are perishing without the gospel... ?"[14] Actually the *Christian Advocate* carried no such caption. In Parker's imagination, "The Flat-Head Indians" became "The Wise Men from the West."

OREGON INDIANS IN THE RED RIVER MISSION SCHOOL

Since the publication of the Walker-Disosway article in the *Christian Advocate* was directly responsible for both the Methodist Missionary Society and the American Board to send missionaries across the Rockies into Old Oregon in 1834 and 1835–38, we can well ask: What were the circumstances which inspired the Nez Perce Indians to make the journey to St. Louis to inquire about the white man's religion?

In 1812 the Hudson's Bay Company settled a colony of Scottish families at Red River where Winnipeg, Canada, is now. There followed many retired employees of the Company, then referred to as "servants," with their native wives and half-breed children. Most of the Scotsmen were Presbyterians, but the "servants," being French Canadians, were Roman Catholics. In 1821 the Anglican Church Missionary Society of London, with the approval of the Governing Committee of the Hudson's Bay Company, sent the Rev. John West, an Anglican, to the Red River colony. West has the distinction of being the first Protestant clergyman to settle in what is now western Canada.

Shortly after his arrival, West began to agitate for the establishment of a school for Indian youth.[15] In this project he had the enthusiastic support of two important members of the Company's Governing Committee in London, Nicholas Garry and Benjamin Harrison. As a result, the Church Missionary Society on January 27, 1822, authorized the establishment of the North-West American Mission at Red River with West as its superintendent. West returned to England in September

1823 and was succeeded by two more Anglicans, the Rev. David T. Jones and the Rev. William Cochran, both of whom were to play minor roles in the early history of Protestant missions in Old Oregon.

One of the most influential officials of the Hudson's Bay Company was Governor George Simpson, 1787–1860, who was knighted by Queen Victoria in 1841. Beginning in 1820, when Simpson was only thirty-three years old, and continuing for nearly forty years, he was the all-powerful administrator of a great commercial empire in what is now western Canada and the Pacific Northwest.

A second important Company official was Dr. John McLoughlin, 1784–1857, who in 1824 was appointed to take charge of the newly established Columbia Department. McLoughlin was both a physician and a fur trader. He was a handsome man, standing six feet four inches and wearing his white hair long so that it touched his shoulders. Deeply religious, Dr. McLoughlin was a man of great moral integrity.

When Simpson first heard of the Rev. John West's desire to establish a school for Indian youth at Red River, he expressed his disapproval. Writing to Andrew Colvile, a member of the Governing Committee of the Hudson's Bay Company in London, Simpson on May 20, 1822, ridiculed the proposal by saying that West "...takes a very sanguine view of this scheme which is to diffuse Christian Knowledge among the natives from the shores of the Pacific to those of [Hudson's] Bay." Simpson prophesied that the project "will be attended with little other good than filling the pockets and bellies of some hungry missionaries and schoolmasters and rearing the Indians in habits of indolence... I have always remarked that an enlightened Indian is good for nothing."[16]

In the early summer of 1824, when Governor Simpson was preparing to make his first journey into the Oregon country, he received a communication from the Church Missionary Society asking him to find some Indian boys from west of the Rockies who could be sent to the Red River Mission school. By this time Simpson had become aware of the great interest that Benjamin Harrison and others of the Company's London Committee were taking in the proposed school. Even though Simpson two years earlier had ridiculed the idea of trying to educate the natives, he was above all else a practical man. He was under orders, and if his superiors in London wished him to find some Indian boys in Oregon and take them back to Red River to be educated, this he would do.

In a letter addressed to Harrison on August 1, 1824, Simpson wrote: "While in the Columbia I shall endeavour to procure a few children... for the Missionary Society School."[17] And at about the same time, Simpson wrote to West and gave him the same assurance. Simpson had made a complete about-face.

Dr. John McLoughlin accompanied Simpson on his journey into Oregon in the spring and summer of 1824. McLoughlin was then ready to assume the duties of Chief Factor of the Columbia Department of the Hudson's Bay Company to which he had been appointed. The two men arrived at Fort George [present-day Astoria, Oregon] on the south bank of the Columbia River on November 8, 1824. Since the Company then had reason to believe that all territory south of the Columbia would probably come under the jurisdiction of the United States, both Simpson and McLoughlin felt that the site for a new trading post should be selected on the north bank of the river. Hence Fort Vancouver was established in a beautiful location near the mouth of the Willamette River. There McLoughlin remained when Simpson returned to Canada the following spring.

As Chief Factor at Fort Vancouver, located about one hundred miles from the mouth of the Columbia River, McLoughlin ruled Old Oregon as an uncrowned king from 1825 to his retirement in 1846. The establishment and continuation of both the Protestant and Roman Catholic missions in Old Oregon would have been impossible without the help of the Hudson's Bay Company and Dr. McLoughlin's sympathetic cooperation.

Before leaving Fort George to return to Red River, Simpson wrote a letter of some two thousand words on March 10, 1825, to Benjamin Harrison in London.[18] Whatever his private views regarding the wisdom of educating Indian boys may have been at that time, certainly this letter betrays no contrary spirit. Indeed, Simpson discreetly played the role of an advance agent for an evangelistic missionary society. "No part of North America that I have visited," he wrote, "presents advantages and facilities towards civilization equal to this coast; the population is numerous, settled in villages, peaceable and well disposed... the missionary society could not therefore fail of success if the subject were taken up with that interest which it merits and fit and proper persons selected for the mission." Simpson even suggested some places along the lower Columbia where stations could well be established and figured out the approximate cost for each missionary per annum.

There is no hint in this letter from Simpson to Harrison that American missionaries might ever preempt the territory. Simpson apparently assumed that just as the Hudson's Bay Company was enjoying exclusive privileges of the fur trade along the Columbia, an English missionary society would inherit the same favored position. Simpson had not forgotten his promise to take some Indian boys from the Oregon country back to the Red River Mission school. He told Harrison that he had tried to find some lads from the Chinook tribe but those suggested were "too young and delicate" for the long and difficult journey, so he had refused to take them.

On his way up the Columbia, Simpson stopped at the Company's Spokane House, a post which had been established in 1810 by the North West Company and which was closed in 1826 when Fort Colville was built.[19] The site of Spokane House is on the Spokane River, ten miles to the northwest of the present city of Spokane, Washington. There Simpson met Alexander Ross who had just returned from leading an expedition into the Snake River country in behalf of the Hudson's Bay Company. Simpson had offered Ross the position of teacher in the Red River Mission school at a salary of £100 per annum which offer Ross had accepted. He returned with Simpson that summer to Red River.

Ross in his *Fur Hunters of the Far West* tells how Simpson induced two chiefs of the Spokane area to let their sons go with him to the mission school. At first the proposal was rejected with scorn. According to Ross, one chief asked Simpson if they "were looked upon as dogs—willing to give up their children to go they knew not whither."[20] Simpson pointed out that the boys would be placed in the care of a "Minister of Religion to learn how to know and serve God." A chief of the Spokane tribe and another of the Kootenai (or Kutenais) each agreed to let a son go. According to Ross, one of the chiefs said: "We have given you our hearts—our children are our hearts; but bring them back again to us before they become white men—we wish to see them once more Indians..." Ross added: "They were about ten or twelve years old, both fine promising youths of equal age."

A surprising entry appears in Simpson's Journal for April 12, 1825, written while on his way eastward over the mountains: "Baptized the Indian boys, they are Sons of the Principal Spokan and Coutonais War

Chiefs, men of great Weight and consequence in this part of the Country; they are named Coutonais Pelly and Spokane Garry." [21] What did Simpson mean by writing that he had baptized the two Indian boys? Possibly he meant that he was christening them, giving them names. In each case he attached to the name of the tribe from which the individual came the last name of an important Hudson's Bay Company official, thus setting a precedent which was followed in later years when other Oregon Indians were sent to the Red River school. John Henry Pelly had served as Governor of the Hudson's Bay Company from 1822 to 1852, and Nicholas Garry as Deputy Governor from 1822 to 1835.

The ecclesiastical records of the Red River Mission, now in the archives of the Hudson's Bay Company, show that "Kootaney Pelly, an Indian boy of the Kootaney Nation" was baptized by the Rev. David T. Jones on June 24, 1827, and on the same day, "Spokan Garry, an Indian boy of the Spokan tribe." These were the first natives, not only from the Old Oregon country but also from the entire Pacific Coast of what is now the United States, to receive baptism by a Protestant minister. The fact that Jones administered this sacrament indicated that either Simpson had not formally done so, or, if he had indeed baptized the boys, the act was not recognized by the Anglican clergy.

In 1828 Governor Simpson made a second journey into the Oregon country. The following is recorded in regard to a speech he made to the Indians at Kamloops in what is now British Columbia in that year: "He, of course addressed them, and at some length, adverted to the propriety of behaving well among themselves, and exhorted them never to be guilty of theft, murder, or of any inhuman deeds towards the whites. To strengthen this argument, he produced, read, and translated to them two letters sent by the Indians at the Red River Settlement Missionary School to their parents at Spokan and the Kootanais country." [22]

From this we learn that Spokane Garry and Kootenay Pelly had each written a letter to his parents, and that Simpson was carrying them. It seems highly probable that the practical minded Simpson had not only suggested that the fifteen-year-old boys write such letters, but also told them what to say about how their people should treat white men.

The two lads made good progress at the school and by 1829 were able to read, write, and speak English fairly well. They returned to the Spokane country by going with the westward bound Hudson's Bay express, as the overland caravan was called, in the summer of 1829. The two youths, then about sixteen years old, carried back an enthusiastic report of their experiences at the mission school. Commenting on this, a western historian, J. Orin Oliphant, wrote: "Pelly and Garry were cast for a role deeply significant: they were to receive at the Red River an education that would serve as a *linguistic key* to open the door for the entrance of Christianity among their tribes." [23] No doubt their return, after an absence of four years, created a great sensation in their respective tribes. Spokane Garry seems to have exerted the greater influence.

The archives of the Hudson's Bay Company contain only a few fragmented sections of what was once an extensive series of journals of each of the Company's forts in the Old Oregon country. The only extant part of the Fort Colville journal covers the period April 12, 1830, to April 3, 1831. During this time Francis Heron was Chief Trader. His journal entry for April 14, 1830, carries the following reference to Spokane Garry: "Last evening all the Indian Chiefs about the place were admitted into the Gentlemen's Mess Hall and a speech was made to them, repeated by Spokane Garry in a satisfactory manner. The chiefs of the following nations were present: Spokain, Nez Perces, Coeur d'Alenes, Kootenais, Penderails, Cinq Pois [or San Poils], & Kettle Falls." [24] This is the first known instance of any of the Indian boys who had been educated at the Red River Mission school being used as an interpreter. The significance was noted by Heron.

When Spokane Gary and Kootenai Pelly returned to Red River in the spring of 1830 with the Company's eastbound express, five more Indian youths from four different tribes accompanied them.[25] As was the case with Spokane Garry and Kootenai Pelly, each of the five was given the name of a Hudson's Bay official. The eldest of the group was Nez Perce Ellice [later written as Ellis], age nineteen or twenty.[26] He was named after Edward Ellice, a member of the Company's Governing Committee in London, 1824–27. The other four were probably Cayuse Halket, age eleven, named after John Halket, also a member of the London Committee, 1829–48; San Poils Harrison, age eleven, a namesake of Benjamin Harrison, who served as Deputy Governor, 1835–39; Spokane Berens, age eleven, named after Joseph Berens, Jr., Governor of the Company, 1812–22; and Cayuse Pitt, age unknown, named after another Company official, Thomas Pitt. Other Oregon Indians may have been sent to the mission school after 1830 but only these seven had any direct or indirect influence on the Nez Perce delegation which visited St. Louis in the fall of 1831.[27]

These seven came from five tribes and from three different linguistic groups. The Spokanes and San Poils spoke Salishan languages; the Nez Perces a Sahaptin tongue. The Cayuses had originally belonged to a different linguistic stock, but were already forsaking their own language for Nez Perce at the time of first contact with white men. The Kootenai language was quite different from any of these. Surely this diversification of tribes and languages among the seven youths sent to the Red River school was not accidental. Here again we see the guiding hand of profit-conscious Simpson who realized the value of having interpreters in as many different Oregon tribes as possible.

From various documented sources, such as the mission school's baptismal and burial records, the ages of six of the seven youths mentioned above can fairly well be determined at the time of their first departure for the school. Four of the seven died while at Red River but the causes of their deaths are unknown. The dates of their burials are: Kootenai Pelly, April 6, 1831; San Poils Harrison, January 18, 1832; Spokane Berens, July 21, 1834; and Cayuse Halket, February 1, 1837.[28]

The fact that these four died while at the school was not forgotten by the Indians of Old Oregon. As will be mentioned later, the death of Cayuse Halket became a subject of controversy between the Cayuse Indians and Dr. Whitman in 1845. The three youths who lived to return to their respective tribes (not including Halket and Pelly who returned to Oregon for a time and then went back to Red River) were Cayuse Pitt, Nez Perce Ellis, and Spokane Garry.

Little is known about Cayuse Pitt. Three references to his being back with his people have been found in the correspondence of Dr. McLoughlin for 1836, 1837, and 1838.[29] Narcissa Whitman, writing to her sister Jane on February 2, 1842, stated: "A young Nez Perce [sic] that had been to the Red River school died last summer."

The two educated at the mission school, who later played important roles in their respective tribes, were Nez Perce Ellis and Spokane Garry. Ellis remained at the school for about four years, long enough to acquire a good command of English. He was appointed the first Head Chief of the Nez Perces in 1842 by Dr. Elijah White, the first Indian Agent to be assigned to Oregon by the United States Government. The important role that Spokane Garry played in the establishment of Protestant missions in Old Oregon will subsequently be told.

THE 1831 NEZ PERCE DELEGATION TO ST. LOUIS

The delegation of four Indians from west of the Rockies who visited St. Louis in the fall of 1831 were Nez Perces (one half-Nez Perce and half-Flathead) and not Flathead Indians as mistakenly identified by General Clark. The Flathead Indians, from what is now western Montana, made two attempts to send delegations of their people to St. Louis to obtain information about the white man's religion before 1831. This is evident from a letter sent by Father Pierre Jean DeSmet, the pioneer Catholic missionary to the Flatheads. He wrote to the Hon. J. C. Spencer on March 4, 1843: "It is now about 24 years since the Indian nation of the Flat-heads acquired a slight knowledge of the civil institutions of Christianity through the means of four poor Iroquois Indians[30] who had wandered beyond the Rocky Mountains. Anxious to obtain instructions, they sent about 20 years ago [i.e., in 1823] a deputation of three of their chiefs to St. Louis. They were carried off by sickness. As their Deputies did not return, they appointed five others who were massacred in passing through the territory of the Sioux. In 1834 a third delegation arrived, an Iroquois accompanied it... In 1839 they deputed other missioners to communicate their wishes. It was on this occasion that I was requested to accompany the deputies on their return.[31]

Father DeSmet traveled widely through the Old Oregon country during 1840–46 and, in the fall of 1841, founded St. Mary's Mission for the Flatheads in the Bitter Root River Valley.

At least three of the 1831 delegation were Nez Perces as is evident from the following facts: (1) The first Indian to die in St. Louis and to be buried by the Catholic priests on October 31, 1831, is listed in the cathedral records as being a Nez Perce;[32] (2) The two survivors were passengers on a steamer which left St. Louis on March 26, 1832, for the ascent of the Missouri as far as the mouth of the Yellowstone River. Aboard was the artist, George Catlin, who painted their portraits. Catlin called them Nez Perces.[33] The second Indian who died in St. Louis, who was buried on November 17, 1831, is identified in the cathedral records as being a Flathead. However, a strong Nez Perce tradition claims that his mother was a Flathead and his father a Nez Perce.[34]

There is a direct connection between the Oregon youths who attended the Red River Mission school and the Nez Perce delegation to St. Louis of 1831. The Walker-Disosway correspondence, which appeared in the March 1, 1833, issue of the *Christian Advocate*, undoubtedly provided the initial stimulus for the sending of the first missionaries into the Old Oregon country. This news-story, however, has been subject to much adverse criticism. As early as 1844, two of the Methodist missions to Old Oregon—Rev. Daniel Lee and Rev. Joseph H. Frost—called Walker's account "high-wrought."[35] Writing in 1850, the Methodist bishop, Osmon C. Baker, called it "in a high degree, apocryphal."[36] And as late as 1950, the author of the *History of Methodist Missions* referred to the *Christian Advocate* account as being "a highly romanticized, largely fictitious account of a comparatively simple event."[37] We need, therefore, to examine the Walker-Disosway account carefully.

The fact that four Indians from west of the Rockies visited General Clark in St. Louis in the fall of 1831 is indisputable. They had accompanied the Rocky Mountain Fur Company's caravan when it returned from the 1831 Rendezvous held in the Rockies to St. Louis.[38] The caravan was under the command of Lucian Fontanelle, a Roman Catholic, who took a special interest in the four Indians and evidently had taken them to the Roman Catholic Cathedral in St. Louis where he had introduced them to some of the priests. According to Walker's letter to Disosway, he called on Clark sometime between the deaths of the first and the second Indian.

On December 31, 1831, Joseph Rosati, Bishop of St. Louis, in a letter to a Catholic publication in Lyons, France, referred to the presence of the "four Indians, who live on the other side of the Rocky Mountains," in St. Louis for the purpose of seeing General Clark. Bishop Rosati reported that the four had visited the Catholic Church "and appeared to be exceedingly well pleased with it; unfortunately there was no one who understood their language."[39] When all became ill, they were visited by one or more of the priests, who reported that the Indians made the sign of the cross, an indication that they knew something of the Christian faith. Bishop Rosati made no mention of any request that the four might have made for missionaries or for the Bible.

There are two aspects of Walker's report which may have been embellished. The first is the drawing of the deformed head of one of the Indians that appeared in the *March 1, 1833*, issue of the *Christian Advocate*. In the early days of the history of Old Oregon, some of the natives along the Columbia River would depress the foreheads of newly born infants by tying a board over the forehead in such a manner as to make the upper part of the skull wedge-shaped. "You may form some idea of the shape of their heads," wrote Walker, "from the rough sketch I have made with the pen, though I confess I have drawn too long a proboscis for a flat-head." Before sending Walker's letter to the editor of the *Christian Advocate*, Disosway redrew the sketch. He explained: "From the outlines of the face in Mr. Walker's communication, I have endeavored to sketch a Flat Head for the purpose of illustrating more clearly this strange custom. The dotted lines will show the usual rotundity of a human head." Since we do not have Walker's original sketch, we cannot know how much Disosway altered it.

A second possible embellishment to be found in the Walker letter is in his statement regarding the extent of religious instruction that Clark gave the four Indians. Walker, who was a devout Methodist and well informed on doctrine, was no doubt aware that Clark was an Episcopalian. According to Walker, Clark gave the inquiring natives: "A succinct history of man, from his creation down to the advent of the Saviour; explaining to them all the moral precepts contained in the Bible, expounding to them the decalogue. Informed them of the advent of the Saviour, his life, precepts, his death, resurrection, ascension, and the relation he now stands to man as a mediator—that he will judge the world, etc." How could Clark have given this outline of Christian theology to the Indians if there was no one in St. Louis who understood their language, as Bishop Rosati said? In all fairness to Walker, let it be said that Clark's interpreter may have been unknown to the bishop.

Spokane Garry, the Connecting Link

After the errors have been corrected and the myths exposed, there remains a body of well-documented facts in the story of the Nez Perce delegation of 1831. Ample evidence is available to prove that Spokane Garry, the twelve-year-old boy who went to the Red River Mission school in 1825 and who returned to his people in 1829, was the connecting link between the school and the delegation. The first to give a contemporary account of the Indians' explanation as to why the four Nez Perces went to St. Louis was the Rev. Asa B. Smith, a member of the 1838 reenforcement of the American Board for its Oregon Mission. Asa and his wife Sarah opened a station at Kamiah, in the upper Clearwater River Valley, in May 1839 where Asa studied the language under the tutelage of an intelligent native called Lawyer.

Smith's letter to the American Board dated August 27, 1839, contains the following: "I have recently been making inquiries of the natives concerning the origin of their notions concerning the christian religion & of the object of those who went to the States as it was said, in search of Christian teachers... About ten years ago a young Spokan, who goes by the name of Spokan Garry, who had been at the Red River School, returned. My teacher, the Lawyer, saw him & learned from him respecting the Sabbath & some other things which he had heard at the school. This was the first time he had heard about the Sabbath & it was called by them *Halahpawit*. He returned & communicated what he had heard to his people. Soon after wh[ich] six individuals set out for the States, in search as he says of Christian teachers. Two of this number turned back in the mountains & the other four went on & arrived at St. Louis when two died, one died soon after having left that place & one alone returned to tell the Story & he is now dead."[40]

Since Lawyer referred to the return of Spokane Garry as having taken place "about ten years ago," this confirms the 1829 date of Garry's first return from the Red River school. Since Lawyer is reported to have had a Flathead mother and a Nez Perce father, he was bilingual and could, therefore, communicate directly with Spokane Garry. Although Heron, in the entry made in the Fort Colville journal for April 14, 1830, quoted above, did not mention by name any of the chiefs present that day, he did indicate that there was at least one from the Nez Perce tribe. In all probability that one was Lawyer. Spokane Garry, and not Kootenai Pelly, served as the interpreter for Heron at the April 1830 meeting with the chiefs as he was able to speak the language understood by five of the seven tribes represented. How natural it would have been for the sixteen or seventeen-year-old Garry to demonstrate to those present how much he had learned at the mission school by reading from the white man's Bible.[41]

Although the primary inspiration for the departure of the Nez Perce delegation to St. Louis in 1831 to get information about the white man's religion seems to have come from Lawyer's contact with Spokane Garry, yet the Nez Perces could have learned something about Christianity from one or more of the following four sources before Garry's return in 1829 from the mission school.

In the first place, several of the early explorers, trappers, or traders who were in the Old Oregon country prior to 1830 are known to have carried their Bibles with their guns. Among these were David Thompson, who established a trading post on Lake Pend Oreille in what is now northern Idaho in 1809, and Jedediah Smith, who spent a month, November 26 to December 20, 1824, at Flathead Post in what is now western Montana. It may be assumed that such Christian men would have spoken of their religious faith to the natives as opportunities afforded.

Secondly, many of the Indians of Old Oregon, including the Nez Perces, had contacts with American trappers and traders beginning about 1824, some of whom must have been Christians. They, too, could have told the natives about the white man's religion.

Thirdly, most of the "gentlemen" or officers of the Hudson's Bay Company, who served at the several forts or trading posts along the Columbia River after 1824, were Anglicans or Presbyterians, although a few were Roman Catholics. Most of the employees or "servants" of the Company were Roman Catholics.

Writing in her diary on January 2, 1837, Narcissa Whitman commented: "The Cayuses as well as the Nez Perces are very strict in attending to their worship which they have regularly every morning at day break & eve at twilight and once on the Sab[bath]. They sing & repeat a form of prayers very devoutly after which the Chief gives them a talk. The tunes & prayers were taught them by a Roman Catholic trader. Indeed their worship was commenced by him." Narcissa referred to Pierre Pambrun, a half-breed French Canadian, who had been placed in charge of Fort Walla Walla, a Hudson's Bay Company's post, as early as 1832.[42] And finally, some of the Roman Catholic Iroquois Indians, who had been taken into the Old Oregon country as early as 1818 by fur traders, could have passed on information about their faith to the Oregon Indians.

Several travelers who visited the Pacific Northwest before the arrival of the missionaries reported that some of the natives observed Sunday by remaining in camp and not engaging in hunting. This emphasis on Sunday observance indicates a Protestant rather than a Roman Catholic influence. It is significant that, in his conversation with A. B. Smith, Lawyer stated he first learned about the Sabbath from Spokane Garry. The importance of observing Sunday would have been stressed at the Red River Mission as this was under the sponsorship of the Church Missionary Society, an evangelical organization within the Anglican communion.

Another interesting entry in the Fort Colville journal, mentioned previously, reflects the influence that Garry and Pelly had upon the Indians of that locality. Under date of January 11, 1831, which was at least eight months after these two, together with the five other Indian boys, had left with the eastbound Hudson's Bay express for Red River, the following entry was made: "The Indians on the ground formally renounced in full council their ancient superstitions, doctrines, such as conjuration, medicine &c. and acknowledged themselves to be, and ever to continue, true and faithful Christians." [43]

Since Francis Heron, then in charge of Fort Colville, hailed from North Ireland and was a Protestant, it is likely that he was a Presbyterian. The question can be asked: Could such an amazing action have been taken by the natives in "full council" had not Spokane Garry and Kootenai Pelly, both sons of prominent chiefs, first told them about the white man's religion?

The fact that five more Indian youths from the Oregon country accompanied Garry and Pelly on their return journey to the mission school in the spring of 1830 also reflects the extent of the influence that the two had made upon their own and adjoining tribes.[44] Contemporary testimony from the Rev. David T. Jones of the Red River Mission confirms this judgment. The following is a quotation from one of his letters written sometime during the first months of 1831: "In the Summer of 1839, two Youths from over the Rocky Mountains—Kootemey and Spogan—went to visit their friends and relatives; and returned again... bringing with them five more Boys for education, all of whom are Chief's Sons, of much importance in their ways. This shows, evidently, the confidence placed by the natives there in the good faith of the White People, and also the value which they attach to Christian instruction." According to Jones, the impression that Garry and Pelly made upon their own and neighboring tribes "seems to have been very great."

Even though he made this report to the Church Missionary Society in London with understandable jubilance, yet he added a word of caution: "Of course, this will be evanescent for want of a permanent and definitive system of instruction."[45]

The question has been asked: If Lawyer heard Spokane Garry at Fort Colville on April 14, 1830, why did the Nez Perces wait more than a year before sending a delegation to St. Louis? The simple answer is that Lawyer did not have enough time to return to his home, consult with other leaders of his tribe, select a deputation, and for them to get to the Rendezvous in time to go with the returning caravan to St. Louis.

Walker in his letter to Disosway stated that "a national council" had been held by the Indians at which time the four chiefs were selected "to proceed to St. Louis to see their great father, Gen. Clarke, to inquire of him, having no doubt but he would tell them the whole truth about it." This account is confirmed by a statement made to the author by Corbett Lawyer, a grandson of Chief Lawyer, to the effect that Nez Perce tradition holds that those who went to St. Louis had been selected in the spring of 1831 when the Flatheads and the Nez Perces were camped together in the buffalo country of what is now western Montana.[46]

According to a statement made by Lucien Fontanelle, who was in charge of the caravan which escorted the Nez Perce delegation to St. Louis in the summer of 1831, four Nez Perces and three Flatheads composed the original party but that one Nez Perce and two Flatheads turned back.[47]

And still another question has been asked: If curiosity regarding the white man's religion had been aroused by Garry and Pelly, who had spent about four years in the Red River Mission school, why did not the Nez Perce delegation go to Red River for the information they wanted rather than to St. Louis?

Among the explanations given to account for the Indians' choice of St. Louis is that made by Thomas E. Jessett: "It is my opinion that they were seeking the Church of England Mission at the Red River but got lost and were diverted by American trappers to St. Louis."[48]

The logical answer, however, to this question is that the Nez Perces were accustomed to travel by horseback and not by canoe. A journey to Red River would have meant going most of the way by water. Moreover, the Hudson's Bay Company was not inclined to take passengers with them on their overland express, so it was not likely that the Indian delegation could have gone that way even if they had so desired.[49]

It should also be noted that the Nez Perces and Flatheads had much closer relationships with the American fur traders in the buffalo country and at the Rendezvous than with those of the Hudson's Bay Company. And finally, as stated by Walker, the Nez Perces remembered William Clark, who with Meriwether Lewis had visited their country nearly thirty years previously, and they wanted to see him. His headquarters were in St. Louis. It was most logical, therefore, for the Indian delegation to head for St. Louis rather than for Red River.

Some have also asked: If the Nez Perce delegation's visit to St. Louis was so important, why did not General Clark make note of it in his writings?[50] An indirect reference to the visit of the Indians has been located in General Clark's writings. In his "1830 Report on the Fur Trade" written from his St. Louis office on November 20, 1831, Clark stated: "Yet surrounded as I am by hundreds of Indians, some emigrating from the North East, & for whom a home is to be provided here others from *West of the Rocky Mountains visiting me*."[51] William Walker came from Sandusky, Ohio, or from the "North East" seeking a home for the Wyandots somewhere west of the Mississippi. The reference to the Indians coming from west of the Rockies could well apply to the Nez Perces.

PROTESTANT CHURCHES STIRRED BY THE NEZ PERCE APPEAL

Dr. Ray Billington, who is today one of the best known authorities on the history of the American frontier, wrote: "In all American history no single letter accomplished such impossible wonders as that penned on January 19, 1833, by an educated Wyandot Indian named William Walker to his friend, Gabriel P. Disosway, a New York merchant interested in the Methodist Missionary Society. For that letter set off a chain reaction of events which added the Pacific Northwest to the United States."[52] The whole westward thrust of the Protestant missionary movement into the Old Oregon country was inspired by the Walker-Disosway article in the March 1, 1833, issue of the *Christian Advocate*.

The dramatic appeal of the Nez Perce delegation stirred the imaginations of the Protestants of New England, that seedbed of so many altruistic and benevolent movements. Never before had a delegation visited the United States from a non-Christian land or people, then referred to as "pagan" or "heathen," asking for missionaries and the Bible. But here was a party of four Indians who had made the long journey from beyond the Rocky Mountains to St. Louis for that express purpose! The incident pricked the consciences of many church members. Writing from St. Louis on April 17, 1833, the Rev. A. M'Allister, a Methodist minister, commented: "How ominous this visit of the Cho-pin-nish [i.e. Nez Perces] and Flat Head Indians! How loud the call to the missionary spirit of the age!" [53]

The article in the *Christian Advocate* was reprinted or reviewed in several other religious publications. Letters of inquiry were sent to clergymen and others in St. Louis asking if the incident were true and if so, requesting more details. On May 10, 1833, the *Christian Advocate* featured the story for the second time and reprinted the sketch of the dying Indian's deformed head. Along with this article were letters from three St. Louis residents which confirmed the essential facts of Walker's report. One of the writers, the Rev. E. W. Sehon, in his letter of April 16 stated: "Gen. Clark informed me that the publication which appeared in the Advocate was correct." [54]

Sehon inquired of General Clark regarding the reasons why the Indians had made such a long journey. "He informed me," Sehon wrote, "the cause of their visit was the following: Two of their number had received an education at some Jesuitical school [sic] in Montreal, Canada, had returned to their tribe, and endeavored as far as possible to instruct their brethren how the whites approached the Great Spirit." Here is a clear reference to Spokane Garry and Kootenai Pelly but Clark was mistaken when he said that they had attended some "Jesuitical school in Montreal." [55]

So great was the impact of the Walker-Disosway article in the *Christian Advocate* that within the seven years, 1834–40, the Methodist Missionary Society and the American Board sent ninety-one men, women, and children to Old Oregon. When the five couples, who went out to Oregon in 1839 and 1840 on an independent basis, are added to this number, the total including children, but not counting those born in Oregon, comes to 101.

By a curious coincidence this number almost equaled the passenger list of the *Mayflower* which carried 102 Pilgrims to Cape Cod in 1620.

Indeed the parallel was not lost upon many New Englanders of that generation, as several references may be found in the missionary literature of that period to the new "Plymouth Colony" on the Pacific Coast. The influence of that small band of Protestant missionaries on the religious, social, economic, and political history of Old Oregon was deep and lasting. In this unfolding drama, Dr. Marcus Whitman was destined to play an important role.

THE METHODISTS SEND JASON LEE TO OLD OREGON

The first denomination to respond to the Nez Perce appeal was the Methodist Epicopal Church. In 1834 it sent the Rev. Jason Lee; his nephew, the Rev. Daniel Lee; a schoolteacher, Cyrus Shepard; and two hired laymen, Philip L. Edwards and Courtney M. Walker, overland to Oregon. Altogether the Methodist Missionary Society, during the years 1834–39, sent seventy-five men, women, and children to its Oregon Mission. With the exception of the first party in 1834, all went by sea around Cape Horn.[56]

Jason Lee was appointed "missionary to the Flathead Indians" on July 17, 1833. Because of ignorance on the part of the Missionary Society regarding the location and names of western tribes, the term "Flathead Mission" was used by the Methodists until October 1835 when it became the "Oregon Mission." Jason and Daniel Lee spent the winter of 1833–34 making preparations for their westward journey. Fortunately for them, the explorer and fur trader, Nathaniel J. Wyeth, returned to his home in Cambridge, Massachusetts, in November 1833 after making his first journey to the Rockies. Since he was planning to return to the mountains in 1834, he invited the Lees to accompany him that far. Thus the first party of Protestant missionaries to go overland to Oregon was assured of protection and a qualified guide for the first part of their journey.

Wyeth (called Captain since he was in charge of his caravan), the mission party and a company of about sixty men with some two hundred horses, mules, and cattle left Liberty, Missouri, on April 26, 1834. The animals belonging to the missionaries included ten horses, four mules, two cows, and a bull.[57] The Wyeth caravan traveled independently of that of the American Fur Company although each was bound for the annual Rendezvous to be held that year on the Green River, a few miles to the west of South Pass in the Continental Divide. South Pass, first opened in 1824, became in time the great gateway to Oregon and also to northern California. The Wyeth party rode through the pass on June 15.

Because of the shortage of grass, the Rendezvous that year was shifted to Ham's Fork, a tributary of Green River. On July 2, Captain Wyeth and his men, together with the mission party, left the Rendezvous for the Snake River country. On the 14th, Wyeth selected a site, near present-day Pocatello, Idaho, where he established a trading post called Fort Hall. Two years later the Hudson's Bay Company would secure title to this fort. There at Fort Hall, on Sunday, July 27, Jason Lee conducted the first Protestant service ever held by an ordained missionary in the vast interior of the Old Oregon country.

The Lee party left Fort Hall on July 30 and traveled with Thomas McKay and his Hudson's Bay Company's brigade to Fort Walla Walla on the Columbia River, where they arrived on September 1. The distance from Liberty, Missouri, to Walla Walla was about 1,900 miles. The missionaries continued their journey down the Columbia River and arrived at Fort Vancouver on September 15, where they were warmly welcomed by Dr. McLoughlin. The brig, *May Dacre*, which carried supplies for the mission around Cape Horn, arrived in the Columbia the following day. The timing was perfect.

The Methodist Missionary Society had commissioned Jason Lee and his associates to open a mission among the Flatheads or Nez Perces, but on the recommendation of Dr. McLoughlin, they selected a site for their work at French Prairie on the Willamette River about sixty miles up from where it emptied into the Columbia. Here a log house was erected, into which they moved on October 29. The Methodist Society sent out by ship a reenforcement of twelve and another of seven, both with women and children, in 1837. In 1838 Jason Lee returned to the States by the overland route in order to get still more reenforcements. On his way East, he visited the Whitmans and the Spaldings at their stations in the upper Columbia River Valley. The significance of that visit will be told in a later chapter.

Samuel Parker and the American Board

Although the Methodist Church was the first to send missionaries to Oregon, actually the first person who offered to go in response to the Nez Perce appeal was the Rev. Samuel Parker, then pastor of a Congregational church at Middlefield, Massachusetts. Deeply moved by the article in the *Christian Advocate* about the "Flatheads," Parker in a letter to the American Board dated April 10, 1833, wrote: "From my first entering the ministry, I think I have had some of the missionary spirit... and I have come to the conclusion to offer myself to go beyond the Rocky Mountains to establish a mission among the Flathead Indians, or some other tribe."

The missionary spirit to which Parker had been exposed while a student at Williams College and at Andover Theological Seminary was now asserting itself. The more he thought about it, the more determined he became. He became convinced that God had called him to go to Oregon as a missionary.

Parker's Application Rejected

Within the structure of the American Board at that time was, which we might today call an Executive Committee, the Prudential Committee. The very name suggests the caution with which the Board spent its limited funds. Parker's surprising offer to go as a missionary to Oregon was referred to this Committee. In his letter of application, Parker suggested the possibility of making an exploration trip and then "after a few years to return to my family, who will reside in Ithaca where I have a house." In reply one of the secretaries of the Board, writing on April 15, inquired as to Parker's age and the number and ages of his children. He also asked: "Have you conferred with your wife, & what are her feelings on the subject?"

Making allowance for the slowness of the mails in those days, we note that Parker lost no time in replying. Writing on April 27, he stated that he was fifty-four years old. He had a daughter, sixteen; a son, fourteen; and another son, ten. As far as his wife's attitude was concerned, he wrote: "She, as well as myself, thinks the object an important one, and although it will require much self-denial, yet we are willing, committing ourselves to God, our Redeemer, to meet it."

Parker's letter arrived at the Board's offices in Boston on May 3, just before a scheduled meeting of the Prudential Committee, and, therefore received prompt attention. A reply was written by the Rev. David Greene, 1797–1866, an assistant secretary in charge of the Board's Indian work. Judging by his letter to Parker of May 4, there was much shaking of heads by members of the Committee when they learned of his age and his family responsibilities. The oldest missionary ever appointed by the Board up to that time, according to Greene, was ten years younger than Parker. Greene asked: How could one of his age hope to acquire a strange language? Having a wife and three children was a serious objection. Kindly but firmly, Greene told Parker that the Board could not appoint him.

PARKER WINS APPOINTMENT BY THE AMERICAN BOARD

A common characteristic of a visionary is persistence. Certainly this was true of Samuel Parker. Replying to Greene's letter on May 17, Parker sought to answer the various objections which had been raised. He stressed his conviction that this was God's will. "I think the call for the gospel beyond the Rocky Mountains," he wrote, "is a plain intimation of providence." He stated that he was ready to serve without salary, provided the Board would give his family four or five hundred dollars a year for their support during his absence, and he urged a reconsideration of his application.

Greene replied on August 21 and reaffirmed the decision of the Prudential Committee. His appointment was not expedient. Moreover, a new factor had entered the case. "The Methodists have long since claimed this field," wrote Greene, "and it is reported that their missionaries are about proceeding to their labors." From this it is evident that the American Board was aware of Jason Lee's appointment. Greene explained that the Prudential Committee was guided by the principle of comity and therefore did not wish to enter any mission field occupied or about to be occupied by another denomination. Actually this argument was not valid; the Oregon country was so vast and there were so many different Indian tribes in it, that the presence of one church would mean no real competition or overlapping for another. Undoubtedly the Board felt that Parker was too old to be appointed for such a distant and unknown field.

Parker resigned his church in Middlefield sometime during the summer of 1833 and moved his family to their Ithaca home. He accepted a position as a schoolteacher for that fall and following winter. Monday, January 6, 1834, was observed by the First Presbyterian Church of Ithaca as a day of fasting and prayer. Parker was present at one of the meetings held in the church's session house. In a letter to the Board dated January 16, Parker told what happened. "My strong feelings on the subject of the West again arose. I proposed to the church and those present that day, and others in this village and town who might be disposed to join them, should furnish the men... and support a missionary station beyond the Rocky Mountains." Parker spoke with such conviction and enthusiasm that those present appointed a committee of five to see what could be done. "Three young men," wrote Parker, "of fervent piety, good talents, and acquirements, and of more than ordinary promise offer themselves for the work." He informed the Board that he had no doubt but that the full amount of money needed to support the mission could be raised. He then asked: "Will the Board accept our offer." [58]

As secretary Greene happened to be out of the city when Parker's letter arrived, he did not reply until February 20. Since Parker had raised the money and had found volunteers to go with him, the Board reluctantly reconsidered his application for an appointment and authorized him to proceed with his plans to go on an exploring tour to Oregon under the Board's auspices. Later the Board agreed to pay $450.00 annually for the support of Parker's family for one or two years. Instead of finding three assistants, Parker succeeded in enlisting only two—the Rev. John Dunbar and Samuel Allis, Jr., both Presbyterians.

THE PAWNEE INDIAN MISSION FOUNDED

Both the American Board and Samuel Parker were ignorant as to how a mission party could travel hundreds of miles across the plains and the mountains to Oregon and not be molested by thieving or even hostile Indians. Seemingly, they had no information about the necessity of traveling under the protection of some fur company's caravan. Jason Lee was better informed. He and his associates were on the frontier in plenty of time to leave with the Wyeth party on April 26, 1834. Parker and his two companions did not leave Ithaca until May 5,[59] and did not arrive in St. Louis until the 23rd, nearly a month after both the Wyeth party and the Fur Company's caravan had left for the Rendezvous. In a letter written to Greene from St. Louis on May 27, Parker bemoaned the fact that they were "too late to go with any safety to the Oregon Territory that year."

After some consultations in St. Louis with Major John Dougherty, U.S. Indian Agent for the Pawnee, Oto, and Omaha Indian tribes, it was decided that Dunbar and Allis should begin mission work with the Pawnees in what is now Nebraska while Parker would return East for reenforcements and make a second attempt the next year to go to Oregon.

Just when Parker arrived back in Ithaca is not known. Since the archives of the American Board do not contain any letters from him for the fall of 1834, it seems probable that Parker journeyed to Boston in order to make a personal report to Secretary Greene. The Board's *Annual Report* for 1834 carried a brief notice of Parker's return and about his intention to find new associates and make another attempt to go to Oregon the following year. "This," the *Report* stated, "has been approved by the Committee." Evidently the assurance of continued financial support from the Ithaca church and Parker's unbounded enthusiasm induced the Prudential Committee, somewhat against its better judgment, to rescind its former action and to endorse Parker's second attempt to go to Oregon. According to this 1834 *Report*, the Board spent $471.01 that year to cover the expenses of Parker, Dunbar, and Allis "on their exploring tour to the Indians west of the State of Missouri" [see Appendix 2]. Undoubtedly all or most of this money came from the First Presbyterian Church of Ithaca.

Marcus Whitman and Narcissa Prentiss Volunteer for Oregon

Heartened by the action of the Prudential Committee, Parker turned enthusiastically to his task of raising more money and finding associates for his Oregon mission. Actually, judging by the receipts of the Board which were credited to him, Parker was much more concerned about finding someone to go with him to Oregon than he was in raising money. Surprisingly, instead of visiting the larger churches in the cities where larger gifts could possibly be secured, Parker made a tour during the fall of 1834 in the counties of Steuben, Allegany, and Cattaraugus in western New York. Reporting to the Board on December 24, 1834, Parker frankly stated: "...almost all the churches in the counties are small and feeble, and are assisted by the H.M.S." [60]

One reason why Parker turned to this area was that there he was on familiar territory. They were the counties where he had begun his ministry after his licensure in 1808 as an itinerant home missionary. He knew the churches, many of the people, and some of the pastors. Another factor worked to Parker's advantage. Throughout the history of Protestantism in the United States, the small rural churches have always been a fruitful source for the recruitment of ministers and missionaries. So it was that late in November 1834, Parker drove his horses, hitched to a light wagon, over muddy roads into the little crossroads village of Wheeler where he was welcomed by his old friend, the Rev. James H. Hotchkin, pastor of its small Presbyterian church. Thus the stage was set for an event which took place in that one-room country church which was destined to have far-reaching effects in later years in distant Oregon.

Although we have no copy of the message Parker delivered in Wheeler, we need but little imagination to summarize what he had to say. Drawing upon the several articles which had appeared in the *Christian Advocate*, Parker retold the story of the visit of the four Nez Perces to St. Louis in the fall of 1831. He surely told of his own visit to St. Louis during the previous summer where, possibly, he had had an opportunity to interview General Clark. Although Parker may never have heard of the Red River Mission school, or of Spokane Garry, or of Chief Lawyer, yet he had enough documented facts to present a moving appeal. Dr. Marcus Whitman, who heard Parker speak that evening, was stirred. When Parker climaxed his address with a plea for someone to go with him to Oregon the following spring, Whitman volunteered.

After leaving Wheeler, Parker traveled about forty-five miles west to a little settlement on the Genesee River then called Amity but now known as Belmont. There Parker repeated his message in the Presbyterian Church and made another plea for missionaries. Somewhat to his surprise, Narcissa Prentiss, daughter of judge and Mrs. Stephen Prentiss, offered herself. Since the American Board then rarely sent "unmarried females" into the foreign mission field, and since work with the American Indians was then considered to be a part of foreign missions, it appears that Parker gave her little encouragement.

Writing to his family on December 5, Parker reported: "My labours have been fatiguing owing to the very bad state of the roads. My success has been as good as I expected. The collections, though small, have been greater than have ever been taken up on any other application of like nature. I have found some missionaries. Dr. Whitman of Wheeler, Steuben County, New York, has agreed to offer himself to the Board to go beyond the mountains. He has no family. Two ladies offer themselves, one a daughter of judge Prentiss of Amity..." [61]

We often need the perspective of time before we can appreciate the significance of events which at the time of their occurrence may appear to be insignificant. So it was with the Rev. James H. Hotchkin when his most influential layman decided to go as a missionary to the Indians of Oregon. According to the requirements of the American Home Missionary Society, which subsidized Hotchkin's salary, he had to submit a quarterly report of his work. The only reference to Whitman located in these reports is the following which appeared in the one dated January 12, 1835: "...one of our elders expects shortly to leave us to join the company of Missionaries to go beyond the Rocky Mountains." When Hotchkin submitted his report for the summer months of July, August, and September, 1835, when Whitman was with Parker on their journey to the Rockies, he wrote: "Nothing has occured in the congregation during the quarter." [62]

Whitman returned in the fall of 1835 bringing with him two Nez Perce youths and some thrilling news. He and Parker had met a large party of Nez Perces at the Rendezvous in the Rockies and had found them eager for missionaries. Jason Lee and his associates had by-passed that tribe and had settled in the Willamette Valley. Whitman had observed that it was possible to take women over the Rockies, hence he could return, be married to Narcissa Prentiss to whom he was engaged, and take her with him to Oregon.

Another married couple would have to be found to go with them. Parker and Whitman had separated at the Rendezvous—Parker to continue with the Nez Perces on an exploring tour of Oregon; Whitman to return home for reenforcements and then to go out to the Rockies again in the summer of 1836.

The significance of these important events seems to have escaped the attention of Whitman's pastor at Wheeler. In his quarterly report dated January 7, 1836, Hotchkin, commenting on the events of the previous fall, wrote: "Nothing peculiar has taken place."

CHAPTER ONE *Whitman Volunteers for Oregon* 33

CHAPTER I ENDNOTES

1 The term "Old Oregon" is commonly used to indicate the area which lies west of the Continental Divide and north of the present-day California-Oregon border. Prior to 1846 this 42nd parallel was the Mexican border. Following the settlement of the border question with Great Britain in 1846, the states of Washington, Oregon, Idaho, and the western parts of Montana and Wyoming were carved out of Old Oregon. Unless otherwise stated in the text of this work, the use of the name "Oregon" refers to Old Oregon as here defined.

2 From a letter to the author dated April 6, 1969, from Harold G. Shults of Prattsburg, N.Y.

3 These saddlebags are now in the Presbyterian Historical Society, Philadelphia.

4 See article by S. W. Pratt, "The Making of Whitman," *Sunset Magazine*, vol. XXIII (August 1909), pp. 185–8, and his original notes in Coll. Wn. Pratt, who belonged to an old Prattsburg family, made a special effort to interview people who knew the Whitmans and the Spaldings. Several of his articles appeared in local newspapers in New York State. He is also the author of *History of the Presbyterian Church of Prattsburg*, 1876.

5 Hotchkin, *History of the Purchase and Settlement of Western New York*, gives much information about the Presbyterian churches of Wheeler and Prattsburg.

6 *W.C.Q.*, II (October 1898), p. 12.

7 Whitman Letter #5. Hereafter all references to Whitman letters listed in Appendix I will be by number in brackets inserted in the text, unless such letters are identified by date when written.

8 *W.C.Q.*, II (October 1898), pp. 3 ff. contains a biographical sketch of Parker by Myron Eells. See also article by Henry Parker, *Church at Home and Abroad*, March 1895, and manuscripts by Dr. Samuel J. Parker mentioned below in fn. 9.

9 Original ms. in Cornell University Library, Ithaca, N.Y. Dr. Parker made copies for Yale University Library; Bancroft Library, University of California, Berkeley; and the University of Washington Library, Seattle. Myron Eells made a copy for Whitman College, Walla Walla, Wash. These copies do not agree with each other. In his old age, Dr. Parker displayed a bitter anti-Hudson's Bay Company and also an anti-Roman Catholic attitude; hence his writings must be critically examined for accuracy. Many of his comments about the Whitmans and his father are reliable since, as a seventeen-year-old youth, he met Marcus and Narcissa Whitman shortly after their marriage in February 1836 and also had access to his father's papers.

10 Parker ms., Ithaca.

11 Hereafter referred to as the *Christian Advocate*.

12 Francis Haines, "The Nez Perce Delegation to St. Louis in 1831," *P.H.R.*, VI (1937), pp. 71–8, maintained that Walker was not in St. Louis at the time of the visit of the four Indians and that he was "spinning a traveller's yarn" in his letter to Disosway. J. Orin Oliphant, "Francis Haines and William Walker, a Critique," *P.H.R.*, XIV (1945), pp. 211–16, answered Haines. The November 25, 1831, issue of the *Christian Advocate* mentioned the fact that Walker headed a delegation of six Wyandotes who went that fall to see Gen. Clark in St. Louis.

13 The letters of Walker and Disosway have been reprinted in Hulbert, *O.P.*, V: 87 ff. The italics used here are the author's.

14 Hulbert, *O.P.*, VI:212. The old files of the American Board, referred to as Coll. A., are in Houghton Library, Harvard University.

15 For further information about the Red River school see Tucker, *Rainbow in the North*; Drury, "Oregon Indians in the Red River School," *P.H.R.* VII (1938): 55 ff; Oliphant, "George Simpson and Oregon Missions," *ibid.*, VI (1937): 237 ff; Jessett, "Anglicanism Among the Indians of Washington Territory," *P.N.Q.*, XLII (1951): 224 ff; and Jessett, "Christian Missions to the Indians of Oregon," Church History, XXVIII (June 1959): 147 ff.

16 Frederick Merk (ed.), *Fur Trade and Empire: George Simpson's Journal*, Cambridge, 1931, p. 138.

17 HBC Arch., D/4/3.

18 *Ibid.*

19 The North West Company and the Hudson's Bay Company joined in 1821 under the name of the latter. Fort Colville was named after Andrew Colvile, a member of the London Committee of the H.B.C. He spelled his name with only one "l" in the last syllable.

20 Alexander Ross, *Fur Hunters of the Far West*, 2nd edition, London, 1855, II: 156.

21 See fn. 16.

22 Malcolm McLeod (ed.) Peace River. A Canoe Voyage from Hudson's Bay to Pacific, by the late Sir George Simpson, in 1828. Journal of the late Chief Factor, Archibald McDonald who Accompanied him. Ottawa, 1872, p. 34. The quotation is from McDonald's Journal. McDonald was placed in charge of Fort Colville in 1836.

23 *P.H.Q.*, VI (1937):238.

24 HBC Arch., B/45/a/1.

25 Tucker, *Rainbow in the North*, p. 70. Josephy, *The Nez Perce Indians*, p. 89, states that the party with the Indian boys left the Spokane country for Red River on April 30, 1830.

26 Allen, *Ten Years in Oregon*, p. 185, claims that Ellis was thirty-two years old in 1842 when he was made Head Chief of the Nez Perces.

27 Other Indian boys from Old Oregon mentioned as having been sent to the Red River school include William Collins of the Kootenais: see article by Dr. Wm. McKay, *Oregon Churchman*, Dec. 15, 1873; Boyd, *History of the Synod of Washington*, p. 231; Lewis, "The Case of Spokane Gary," *Spokane Historical Society Bulletin*, January 1917, p. 13, mentions a Jim Lion of the Nez Perces. Possibly these names refer to Indian boys sent to the Red River school after 1831.

28 HBC Arch., Records of the Mission School. Tucker, *Rainbow in the North*, pp. 73-4, states that Cayuse Halket "visited his friends on the Columbia River in 1834, but not being able to reconcile himself to their mode of life, he returned to reside with Mr. Cochran" at the mission school. William McKay, in the *Oregon Churchman*, December 15, 1873, wrote: "While Halket was among his people, he frequently held services, according to the Episcopal form among them." Writing in his old age on July 14, 1892, to Mrs. Eva Emory Dye, McKay made extravagant claims for Halket: "He held services every Sabbath on the Church of England form of worship and taught them the Christian Religion and sung hymns to them." Location of the original letter is unknown, if still extant. A friend of Mrs. Dye's gave the author a copy. McKay's evaluation of what a fifteen-year-old boy was able to do to evangelize the Cayuse tribe is very questionable. The Whitmans made no reference to this in any of their letters.

29 HBC Arch., McLoughlin to Pambrun, Nov. 2, 1836; April 14, 1837; and March 28, 1838. Nothing was said in any of these letters of any effort Pitt was making to spread Christianity among his people.

30 Catholic Iroquois Indians are known to have been employed by fur traders and taken into the Old Oregon country as early as 1818. Josephy, *The Nez Perce Indians*, p. 55.

31 Original in Office of Indian Affairs, Oregon Superintendency, 1842–80, National Archives, Washington, D.C.

32 Drury, *Spalding*, p. 74, gives the text of the burial records.

33 Original paintings are in the Smithsonian Institution, Washington, D.C. See illustrations in this volume. George Catlin, *North American Indians*, Edinburgh, 1926, pp. 123 ff.

34 McBeth, *The Nez Perces Since Lewis and Clark*, pp. 30 ff. Miss McBeth, who was for many years a missionary among the Nez Perces and knew their traditions, wrote of the Indian whose sketch was drawn by Walker: "Ka-ou-pu (Man of the Morning or Daylight) . . . His mother was a Flathead, his father a Nez Perce."

35 Lee and Frost, *Ten Years in Oregon*, p. 110.

36 William Sprague, *Annals of the American Pulpit*, New York, 1866–69, VII:794, in an article by Bishop Baker about Jason Lee.

37 Barclay, *History of Methodist Missions*, II:203. See also Appendix 3 of this work.

38 The caravan carrying supplies from the States would meet the trappers at some agreed upon place in the Rockies each summer from 1824 to 1839, called the Rendezvous. Most of these gatherings were held west of the Continental Divide. There the supplies would be exchanged for furs. The Rocky Mountain Fur Company was dissolved in 1834. Thereafter the caravans were sent out by the American Fur Company. See W. J. Ghent, *The Early Far West*, New York, 1936, pp. 20 ff, for a discussion of the fur companies and the annual Rendezvous.

39 *Hulbert, O.P.*, VI:87.

40 Drury, *Spalding and Smith*, pp. 106 ff.

41 While gathering material for my biography of Henry Harmon Spalding, I visited the granddaughter of Spokane Garry, Mrs. Joe Nozer, at Worley, Idaho, on August 23, 1935. She showed me her grandfather's Bible, his Anglican prayer book, a New Testament, and a small pamphlet with hymns in an Indian language. The Bible, octavo in size, was published by the British and Foreign Bible Society in 1804. Later, I discovered in the records of the Red River Mission a reference to a shipment of Bibles from this Society to the school. In Spokane Garry's Bible was an original letter from H. H. Spalding to Garry dated March 28, 1874. This letter is now in Coll. Wn. The discovery of Spokane Garry's Bible gives further confirmation to the account that Lawyer gave Smith.

42 Since Mrs. Whitman was writing about four months after she and her husband had arrived in Oregon, this comment shows that the natives had been following these practices long before they came. See also, Washington Irving, *Adventures of Captain Bonneville*, New York, 1837, III:7; W. A. Ferris, *Life in the Rocky Mountains*, Salt Lake City, 1940, p. 75; N. J. Wyeth, *Correspondence and Journals*, Eugene, Oregon, 1899, p. 192; Parker, *Journal of an Exploring Tour*, contains many references to the Nez Perces observing Sunday; and Elliott's article, "Religion Among the Flatheads," *O.H.Q.*, XXXVII (1936), pp. 1–8.

43 HBC Arch., B/45/a/1. The action of the Indian council was premature and futile. Old customs and superstitions continued as the missionaries who settled among them in 1839 testified. See Drury, *Walker*. The action taken by the council, however, is an indication of how some of the natives felt.

44 Garry returned to his people during the summer of 1831, following the death of Pelly on April 6 of that year. For a time Garry was zealous in his efforts to civilize and evangelize his people. However, the task was too much for an eighteen-year-old youth. According to W. S. Lewis, "The Case of Spokane Garry," in *Spokane Historical Society*, Bulletin, No. 1, p. 16: "Spokane Garry himself gradually abandoned his efforts at religious teaching, and when pressed for the reason, gruffly stated that he had quit because the other Indians 'jawed' him so much about it." When the Walkers and Eellses settled among the Spokanes in the spring of 1839, they were keenly disappointed by Garry's refusal to cooperate.

45 Oliphant in *P.H.Q.*, vi (1937):243, quoting from the *Church Missionary Record*, London, November 1831, p. 232.

46 See Drury, *Spalding*, pp. 72 ff, for further details about the Nez Perce delegation.

47 Whitman letter #11. Whitman, on his first journey to the Rockies with the caravan of the American Fur Company in 1835, inquired of Fontanelle regarding the personnel of the Nez Perce delegation.

48 Jessett in *Church History*, XXVII (1959): 150. Jessett stresses the Anglican influence of the Red River Mission on the Oregon Indians who studied there, and claims that when these youths returned to their respective tribes, they introduced Anglican forms of worship among the natives. Jessett maintains that this is the reason why Garry was reluctant to cooperate with the Congregational missionaries who opened a station among the Spokanes under the auspices of the American Board in 1839.

49 The Rev. Jason Lee applied for passage across Canada with the Hudson's Bay Express of 1838. McLoughlin denied the request by writing from Fort Vancouver on February 12, 1838: "It is not in our power to do ourselves the pleasure to accommodate you with a passage across the mountains." HBC Arch., B/231/b.

50 Josephy, *The Nez Perce Indians*, p. 102: "The episode seems not to have been of unusual significance to the busy Indian superintendent."

51 While searching through the files of the Department of Indian Affairs in National Archives, Washington, D.C., in the summer of 1946, I found General Clark's report. This was published in *O.H.Q.*, XLVIII (1947): 33 ff.

52 From "A Letter to the Editor that Got Unexpected Results," *Together*, a Methodist periodical published in Chicago, November 1959.

53 Hulbert,*O.P.*,V:111.

54 *Ibid.*

55 The Jesuit order was dissolved by Pope Clement XIV in 1773. The Jesuits did not begin their work in Canada again until 1842.

56 Barclay, *History of Methodist Missions*, II:200 ff. gives a detailed history of the Oregon Mission of the Methodist Church.

57 Although Robert Campbell, an American fur trader, had driven an ox or a cow over the Rockies to the Green River Rendezvous in 1833, the Lee party was the first to take cattle all the way to the Pacific Coast. Jason Lee's Diary appeared in *O.H.Q.*, XVII (1916).

58 A white marble tablet in the vestibule of the First Presbyterian Church of Ithaca, New York, bears the statement that there on January 6, 1834, "this Church resolved to send and support the Oregon Mission of Rev. Samuel Parker." A monument to Parker and Whitman was dedicated on the church's property on May 12, 1935.

59 The day that Parker, Dunbar, and Allis sailed from Ithaca on a Cayuga Lake steamer, Parker's two sons, ages ten and fourteen, watched their departure. They then erected a pile of stones on the spot which were later cemented together into what was called the "Pilar of Faith." This monument, now at 227 Willard Way, Ithaca, once bore an explanatory plaque which has been stolen.

60 The initials stand for the American Home Missionary Society, a parallel organization to the A.B.C.F.M. The files of the A.H.M.S. are in Hammond Library, Chicago Theological Seminary.

61 *W.C.Q.*, II (Oct. 1898): pp. 12–3.

62 A.H.M.S. files, Chicago Theological Seminary.

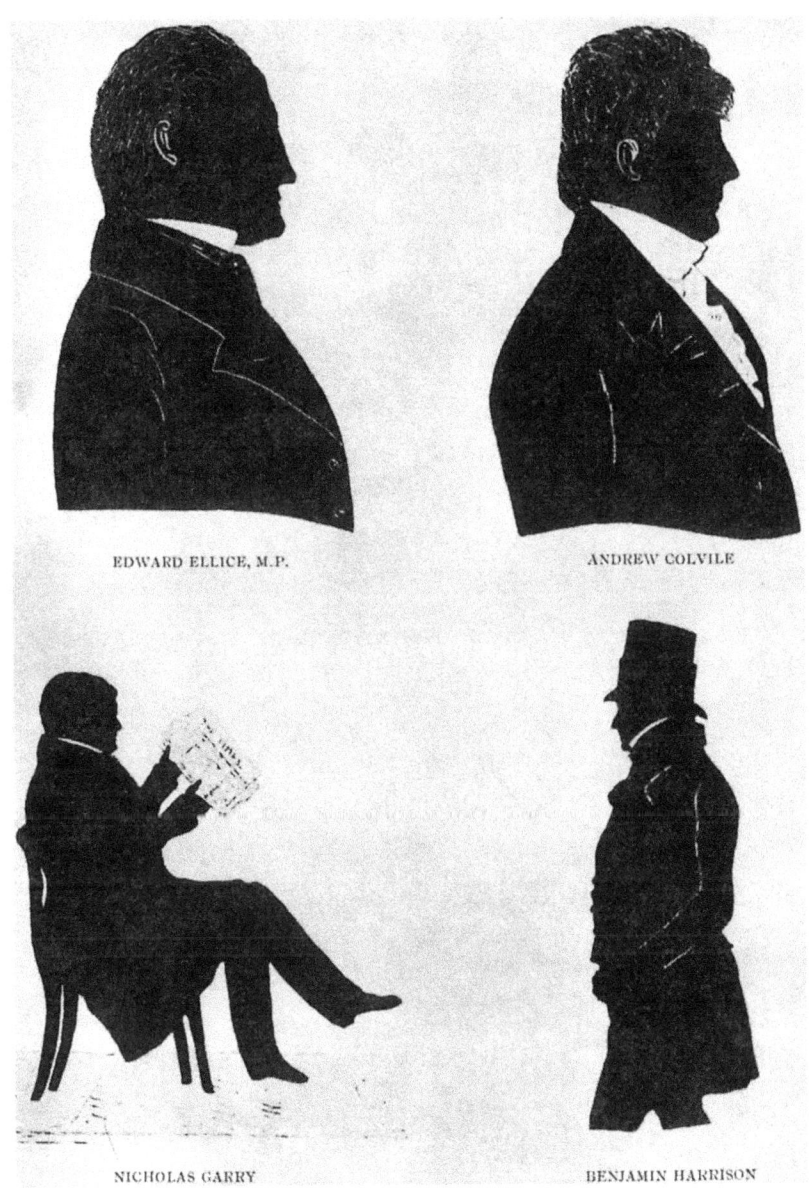

FOUR HUDSON'S BAY COMPANY OFFICIALS
All figure in the activities of the Company in Oregon. Nez Perce Ellice (or Ellis) was named after Edward Ellice, Spokane Garry after Nicholas Garry. Fort Colvile (later Colville) was named after Andrew Colvile, and Harrison was prominent in founding the Red River School. From an old restaurant near the Bank of England; undated but evidently taken from life. Courtesy, Hudson's Bay Company, London.

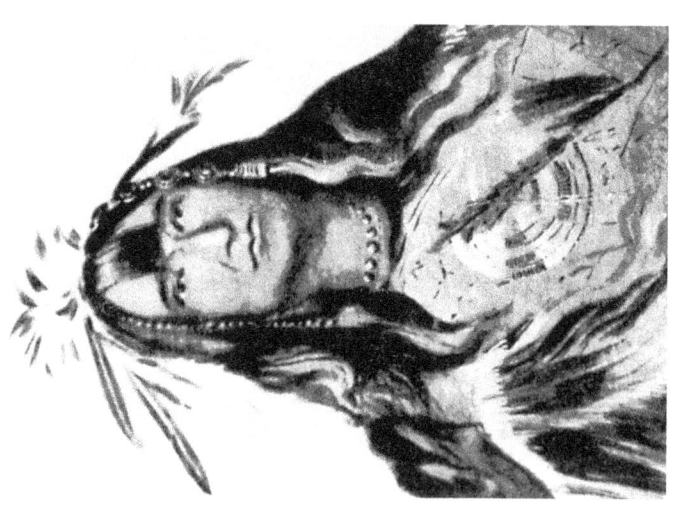

RABBIT-SKIN-LEGGINS AND NO-HORNS-ON-HIS-HEAD

Two Nez Perce members of the Indian delegation to St. Louis in 1831. Paintings by George Catlin. Courtesy, The Smithsonian Institution, Washington, D.C.

THE RED RIVER MISSION SCHOOL

Located near present Winnipeg, Canada. The seven Oregon Indian boys taken east by the Hudson's Bay Company, attended this school, and here the first natives from west of the Rockies received Protestant Baptism. From West, *Substance of a Journal*, p. 155.

SPOKANE GARRY
Educated at Red River Mission School beginning in 1825, he returned in 1829 to his tribe and preached Christianity. He then went to the School one more year. Photograph taken about 1860. Courtesy, Canadian Public Archives; from North American Boundary Commission Records.

KA-OU-PU OR PAUL
From the drawing of G. P. Disosway copied from the original of William Walker and reproduced in *Christian Advocate*, March 1, 1833. Ka-ou-pu was a member of the Nez Perce delegation to St. Louis in 1831, where he sickened and died in November 1831, after being christened Paul by the Roman Catholics. From *Christian Advocate* and *Journal and Zion's Herald*, New York.

SAMUEL PARKER
Parker recruited both Marcus and Narcissa for the Oregon Mission. He traveled with Marcus on their first trip into the Mountains, 1835. From J. A. Miller, *Presbyterianism in Steuben*, Angelica, N.Y., 1897.

[CHAPTER TWO]

WHITMAN'S FIRST EIGHTEEN YEARS
1802–1820

All of the six missionaries who were involved in the founding of the Oregon Mission of the American Board—namely, Samuel Parker, Marcus and Narcissa Whitman, Henry and Eliza Spalding, and William H. Gray—came from western New York. The first four of these came from a comparatively small triangular area in the Finger Lake district of the State. Samuel Parker lived at Ithaca, located at the southern end of Cayuga Lake. About forty miles to the west lay Prattsburg (originally spelled Prattsburgh), the birthplace of Narcissa Prentiss who became Mrs. Whitman. Nearby is Wheeler where Henry Harmon Spalding was born. About twenty-five miles north by east of Prattsburg is Rushville, which now straddles the boundary separating Yates and Ontario counties, the birthplace of Marcus Whitman. Eliza Hart, who married Henry H. Spalding, came from Holland Patent which is about ten miles north of Utica, New York. William H. Gray was living in Utica when he volunteered to go to Oregon.

Ancestry, Birth, and Early Years

Marcus Whitman belonged to the seventh generation of the descendants of John Whitman who arrived in the Massachusetts Bay Colony sometime prior to December 1638. It is believed that John Whitman came from Norfolk, England, where the family name was originally spelled Whiteman.¹

Samuel Lincoln, an ancestor of Abraham Lincoln, came to the same New England colony, also from Norfolk, in 1637, or at about the same time as did John Whitman. One of Samuel's sons, Mordecai, married a granddaughter of John Whitman. Their son, another Mordecai, was the great-great-grandfather of Abraham Lincoln. This means that the martyred pioneer missionary of Old Oregon and the martyred President were both descendants of John Whitman.

Beza Whitman, 1773–1810, the father of Marcus, and a younger half-brother, Freedom Whitman, settled at Cummington, a small village in the heart of the Berkshires of western Massachusetts in 1795. In the adjacent town² of Windsor lived the family of Hezekiah and Alice Green.³ Like the Whitmans, the Green family had long been in America. Hezekiah was of the sixth generation of the descendants of Thomas Green who migrated to Massachusetts from England about 1636. Beza Whitman had not been at Cummington long before he fell in love with Alice Green, 1777–1857, the youngest child of Hezekiah and Alice Green. They were married on March 9, 1797, and their first-born, a son named Augustus, arrived on January 7, 1798.⁴

Following the Revolutionary War, a restless urge for more fertile lands sent many New Englanders into western New York and into what was then called the Connecticut Western Reserve, which included what is now northeastern Ohio. About 1796, Henry Green, 1763–1849, an older brother of Alice, the wife of Beza Whitman, moved from Windsor to Ontario County, New York, and became one of the early settlers of Naples.

He moved in 1799 to a place called Federal Hollow. There, Henry Green, later known as Captain Green, operated a sawmill and gristmill on a stream called West River which empties into the southern end of Canandaigua Lake. Henry was so impressed with the opportunities of western New York that he persuaded his sister Alice and her husband to migrate thither.

Sometime early in 1799, Beza loaded his worldly goods onto an ox-drawn wagon and headed for Ontario County. His wife, carrying their year-old son Augustus, rode horseback. The family settled first at Canandaigua. There on August 16 of that year, their second son, Erastus, was born, and died the following October 16. Shortly afterwards,

Beza and Alice moved to Federal Hollow where they occupied a log cabin which shortly before had been vacated by the Henry Green family. There the Whitmans began life anew. According to a local tradition, a bear raided Beza's pigpen one night, an incident which throws light upon the primitive conditions then existing in that frontier community.

There in that humble cabin on September 4, 1802, a third son was born to Beza and Alice Whitman. They called him Marcus. Why that name? Possibly because Beza had a cousin, James Whitman of Belchertown, Massachusetts, who had a six-year-old son named Marcus. It may be that a friendship between the two Whitman families suggested this name to Beza and Alice.

In 1818, at the suggestion of the doctor in Federal Hollow, Ira Bryant, the name of the settlement was changed to Rushville in order to honor Dr. Benjamin Rush, a Revolutionary War patriot and one of the signers of the Declaration of Independence. In order to avoid confusion, the name Rushville will hereafter be used to indicate the birthplace of Marcus Whitman, even though the change of name did not occur until he was about sixteen years old.

Beza was an industrious worker. He built a tannery on West River and plied his trade as a shoemaker.[5] He so prospered that sometime before 1807, he was able to build a frame house which was used as an inn as well as a home.[6] Courthouse records at Canandaigua show that Beza purchased forty acres of land about half-a-mile south of Rushville in December 1809 for $450.00. Two other sons and a daughter came to the Whitman home in Rushville following the birth of Marcus. They were Samuel, 1804–1875; Henry, 1806–1854; and Alice (Mrs. Wisewell), 1808–1887.

We know very little about the early life of Marcus. A niece of his, Mary Alice Wisewell, gives us the following glimpse into the Whitman home: "His parents lived in a log house -the country was new and wild, and as his father was a tanner and currier, his mother being lonely often used to go and sit with her husband in the little shop opposite the house, binding shoes. Having left him [i.e., Marcus] a baby in his cradle one evening, she was much startled to find on her return that a log had fallen from the fireplace and had burned the lower end of the cradle, and that he was nearly suffocated by the smoke."[7]

Only one reference has been found in the 175 letters Marcus Whitman is known to have written [see Appendix 1] of any boyhood experiences. In his letter of April 13, 1846, to Secretary Greene, Whitman wrote: "I was accustomed to tend a carding machine when I was a boy." A carding machine was used in the preparation of wool for spinning. We may safely assume that the kind of life Marcus lived during the first eight years of his life in Rushville was an important preparation for his later experiences as a missionary to the Indians in Old Oregon where living conditions were even more primitive than in western New York.

From such information as is available, Marcus resembled his mother. The Rev. S. W. Pratt, D.D., who served in 1907 as Moderator of the Presbyterian Synod of New York, once wrote: "Marcus was said to have derived much of his vigor and energy and resoluteness from his mother, who was physically very strong and untiring, weaving for her household, making cheese and performing other industrial duties. She had no patience with laziness... She never spent any time in sentiment, but abounded in deeds." [8]

As a missionary doctor in Old Oregon, Whitman was remembered as having these same characteristics of "vigor and energy." In a letter which a Methodist missionary, the Rev. H. K. W. Perkins, wrote to a sister of Narcissa's on October 19, 1849, we find the following appraisal of Dr. Whitman: "He could never stop to parley. It was always yes or no... he was always at work" [See Appendix 6]. As was the mother, so was the son.

TEN YEARS IN MASSACHUSETTS

Sorrow came to the Whitman home in Rushville on April 7, 1810, when Beza Whitman died in his thirty-seventh year. He was buried in the Baldwin Corners cemetery near the village, where one can still read on the brown sandstone marker the following epitaph, so characteristic of that period:

> Stop here my friend and think on me
> I once was in the world like the
> This is a call aloud to the
> Prepare for Death and follow me

The widow was left with five children all under twelve years of age. The financial burden was too great for her slender resources, so she turned to relatives for help. In the fall of that year Marcus, then only eight years old, was sent to live with his late father's half-brother, Freedom Whitman, at Cummington, Massachusetts. Thus Marcus suffered a double tragedy. He was not only bereft of his father, but was also separated from his mother, his brothers, and his younger sister. However, in the slight of events which stemmed from his residence at Cummington and nearby Plainfield, it is most likely that Marcus Whitman would never have gone to Old Oregon as a medical missionary had he remained in Rushville.

In Whitman's first letter to the American Board, dated June 3, 1834, he summarized his early life as follows: "My Father died when I was about seven years old and I was sent to reside with my Father's brother in Massachusetts where I received my early education and religious instruction. My Grand Father (for he resided in the same family) and Uncle were both pious & gave me constant religious instruction and care. I was under their care mostly for ten years." In the ecclesiastical terminology of that generation, "pious" meant what the word "religious" now implies. Uncle Freedom and Grandfather Samuel, both devout Baptists, left an indelible impression upon young Marcus.[9]

Marcus lived with his relatives in Cummington for five years, 1810–15. The village is located in the northwest corner of Hampshire County, about twenty miles south of the Vermont border and on the eastern slope of the beautiful Berkshire Hills. After this range enters Vermont, the highlands are known as the Green Mountains. About six miles north of Cummington is Plainfield where Marcus lived for the next five years. Near Plairifield is West Mountain which rises 2,160 feet above sea level and is the highest point in the county. Running through the valley is Mill Creek on which, in those days, several mills were located. There in those villages of Cummington and Plainfield, surrounded by hills, forests, water, and farm lands, Marcus spent ten years of his youth, 1810–20.

At the time Marcus arrived in Cummington, a youth six years older than he, by the name of William Cullen Bryant, was living in the same village. The Bryant home, a large rambling structure of three stories, is still standing, and visitors are shown a room on the third floor where, in 1811, Bryant, then only seventeen years old, wrote the well-known poem "Thanatopsis." In this poem, for the first time in published American literature, the word "Oregon" is used.

> *Take the wings*
> *Of morning, pierce the Barcan wilderness,*
> *Or lose thyself in the continuous woods*
> *Where rolls the Oregon, and hears no sound,*
> *Save his own dashings...*

The Oregon! This was the name by which the "River of the West" was then called. Evidently this name was unknown to Captain Robert Gray who discovered the river in 1792 and named it after his ship, the Columbia. Bryant, on the other hand, had never heard of Captain Gray's discovery when he wrote his "Thanatopsis." The question raises: How did that seventeen-year-old youth in Cummington, Massachusetts, learn in 1811 about a mighty river some 3,000 miles to the west called the Oregon? The most plausible answer is that Bryant had access to Jonathan Carver's *Travels Through the Interior Parts of North America in the Years 1766, 1767, and 1768* which had been published in London in 1778. Carver had spent the winter of 1766–7 with some Sioux Indians near present-day Minneapolis and, during the following year, made another exploring trip, this time penetrating into what is now western Canada. In his book Carver made mention of a river which flowed into the Pacific Ocean which he called the "Origan" and also the "Oregon." Much has been written on the origin of this name.[10] For our story, it is sufficient to indicate that in all probability Carver's work was the source of the word "Oregon" in "Thanatopsis." Even though Bryant was six years older than Whitman, the two attended the same school in Plainfield at the same time; hence it is altogether possible that Bryant told Whitman about that mysterious river far to the west which flowed into the Pacific Ocean and which, in time, gave its name to that vast territory, in what is now the Pacific Northwest, first known as Old Oregon.

Marcus returned to Rushvile in 1815 to visit his mother and relatives. He had changed so much during his five-year absence that his mother did not know him. His niece, Alice Whitman Wisewell, tells the story: "When thirteen years old, he unexpectedly returned home for a visit of three weeks. Coming in at evening, he went up to his mother and reached out his hand, saying, 'How do you do, Mother?'—and she drew back thinking herself no mother to him. This so grieved him that he burst into tears. My mother says that it was during this visit that she first saw him [i.e., her brother] to know him—being six years younger."[11]

During the five years Marcus had been away from Rushville, his mother in 1811 had married Calvin Loomis, 1766–1840. To this marriage, the second for each, three children were born—Erastus, 1813;[12] Oren Green, 1841–81; and Luther, 1816–17. Calvin Loomis continued the business activities which Beza Whitman had been conducting: the tannery, the shoeshop, and the tavern. Thus when Marcus returned to his home, he found it necessary to become acquainted with a stepfather and a baby half-brother.

FIVE YEARS AT PLAINFIELD

After returning to Massachusetts, Marcus went to Plainfield where he lived in the home of Colonel John Packard.[13] The change of residence from his Uncle's home in Cummington was made because Marcus was to attend the school in Plainfield taught by the pastor of the local Congregational Church, the Rev. Moses Hallock, and the Packard home was located about a mile from the school. Colonel Packard, a charter member of the Plainfield church and one of its deacons, was a man of considerable influence in both the community and the church.[14]

Here Marcus lived from 1815 to 1820 when he passed from his thirteenth to his eighteenth year. These were the years of adolescence, the critical teen-age period when every normal boy looks forward to the future and dreams of what he will do when he reaches man's estate.

References to the activities of Marcus during these formative years are almost non-existent. The *Hampshire Gazette* of Northampton, Massachusetts, in its issue of July 22, 1884, carried the following about Whitman: "He is distinctly remembered by some of his associates, as an energetic youth, possessing a good mind, and good principles." The *Gazette* also reported the following incident: "By his daring, promptness, and skill, when a large boy, he saved another boy on the point of drowning from a watery grave."

The center of the Plainfield community was the Congregational Church and this became a dominant force in molding the character of young Whitman. A characteristic of the religious life of New England of that generation was the strict emphasis placed on the observance of Sunday, or the Sabbath as it was then called. Here we see the influence of Puritanism which took root in England before 1600 and which left a deep impression upon the evangelical churches of both England and

New England for several generations. In Whitman's day, the proper observance of the Sabbath was one of the most important outward signs of being a Christian. Strictly speaking, the Sabbath is Saturday, the holy day of the Jewish faith, but for the Puritans, Sabbath was the same as Sunday. The misuse of this term continued in Protestant circles in the United States until the early 1900s.

The records of the Plainfield church show how strictly Sunday was observed. Sabbath began at sundown on Saturday and continued until sundown on Sunday. Such innocent pleasures as boating or even loitering on a river bank were strictly forbidden. In 1800 the Plainfield church acquired a 650 pound bell and when this sounded on Sunday, be it morning or evening, all were reminded to go to church. Woe unto him who absented himself without good reason. All this explains why Whitman and his associates in the Oregon Mission laid such emphasis on the importance of Sabbath observance.

The Plainfield Congregational Church erected a building shortly after its organization in 1786 which measured 42½ x 55½ feet. The building contained forty-four box pews on the main floor and nineteen in the gallery. The pew occupied by Colonel Packard and his family, and therefore also by Marcus Whitman, was located in the southwest corner of the main floor.[15] During the "long prayer," it was customary for the congregation to stand. The seats in the pews were hinged and when the people stood, these were lifted up in order to give more room. When the "Amen" was pronounced, the seats all fell back into place with a bang and clatter that would astonish a present-day congregation.

THE INFLUENCE OF THE REV. MOSES HALLOCK

Marcus Whitman was highly favored during his adolescent years in having the scholarly Rev. Moses Hallock for both his teacher and his minister. Hallock was called to the pulpit of the Plainfield Congregational Church in 1792. He was then thirty-two years old, an ex-Revolutionary War soldier, and a graduate of Yale in the class of 1788. He served the Plainfield church for thirty-seven years, dying in 1887.

Shortly after his installation as pastor of the church, Hallock opened a school which he conducted with great effectiveness until 1824. More than three hundred students, of whom thirty were girls, studied under his direction. A few boarded in his home. The non-boarding students, including Marcus, paid a dollar a week for some meals, perhaps the noon luncheon, and for tuition. Hallock's school was established a year after the founding of Williams College, thirty miles distant. One hundred and thirty-two of Hallock's students are reported to have gone to college, most of them at nearby Williams College.

Several of Hallock's students later became well-known. Among these were William Cullen Bryant from nearby Cummington and John Brown of Harper's Ferry fame. Bryant has left for us the following account of his experiences as a student in Hallock's academy: "I was early at my task in the morning, and kept on until bed-time; at night I dreamed of Greek, and my first thought in the morning was of my lesson for the day. At the end of two calendar months, I knew the Greek Testament from end to end almost as if it had been English." [16]

John Brown's contact with the Hallock school was of short duration; the exact time is not known. In 1818, Brown, whose home was in Hudson, Ohio, decided to study for the ministry. Since Hallock was a relative of Brown's mother, it was natural for the young man to go to Plainfield to study. Brown was two years older than Whitman; in all probability the two were students in Hallock's school at the same time, as Whitman did not return to Rushville until 1820. Brown's well-known concern with the slavery issue, came long after he left Plainfield. Whitman's letters mention slavery only once or twice. He was too far removed in distant Old Oregon after 1836 to be involved.

The strong religious influence which Moses Hallock exercised over the young men who were his students is evident in the number who entered the ministry or who became missionaries. Fifty out of 304 students, including two of his own sons, became ministers, and seven became missionaries.[17] The Plainfield church started a Sunday school in May 1819. Since the American Sunday School Union, as a national organization, was not established until 1824, it is to the credit of the Plainfield church that it adopted this means of Christian education so early. Marcus, then in his seventeenth year, enrolled in a class taught by Deacon James Richards. Commenting on his interest in the Sunday school movement, Whitman in his letter to the American Board dated June 3, 1834, wrote: "I have attended as a schollar, teacher or Superintendent ever since."

All three of Deacon Richards' sons entered the ministry, two of whom became foreign missionaries. James Richards, Jr., after completing his work in Hallock's school, went to Williams College. He was one of the five young men who took part in the haystack prayer meeting held in August 1806, to which reference has already been made. James, Jr., was one of the first appointees of the newly organized American Board of Commissioners for Foreign Missions and was sent as its pioneer missionary to Ceylon. How logical to suppose that Deacon Richards would have told the boys in his Sunday school class about his son in a faraway "heathen" land. Another son, William, who was a couple of years older than Marcus, was a member of a party of missionaries sent by the Board to Hawaii in 1822.

In 1819 the religious revival that swept through many New England communities came to Plainfield. Evangelistic meetings were popular, and when extended over several days or weeks were called "protracted meetings." Among those at Plainfield who felt a spiritual quickening was Marcus Whitman. In a letter of June 3, 1834, to the Board, he wrote: "I attended the administrations of Rev. Moses Hallock at which time I was awakened to a sense of my sin and danger and brought by Divine grace to rely on the Lord Jesus for pardon and salvation."

Even though Marcus had what could be called a conversion experience, he did not join the church in Plainfield. Possibly he found himself caught between conflicting loyalties. His uncle and grandfather in Cummington were Baptists. Denominational distinctions were so sharply drawn then that the records of the Congregational Church in Plainfield show that some members had been dismissed for holding "the Baptist error." Possibly Whitman decided, under the circumstances, to postpone joining a church until he returned to Rushville.

The same influences that molded William Cullen Bryant into one of America's most articulate poets in the expression of his Christian faith; which contributed to the iron resolve of John Brown to be faithful unto death for his convictions; which sent James Richards, Jr., and his brother to the foreign mission field; also moved the heart of Marcus Whitman. He too would be a minister. "My preliminary education," he wrote in his first letter to the Board, "consists of the English branches with some knowledge of Latin and some little of Greek." As a student in Hallock's school, Marcus had received the classical education then required of young men who planned to enter the ministry.

The ten years that Marcus Whitman spent in Massachusetts were the decisive years of his life. There he had the good fortune to come under the influence of such active Christian men as his uncle and grandfather, John Packard, Deacon Richards, and especially the Rev. Moses Hallock. Home, church, and school combined to give young Marcus Whitman a strong Christian faith which gave direction to his life. He resolved to live to serve his fellowmen and his first choice was the Gospel ministry. It seems safe to say that if Marcus Whitman had never gone to Massachusetts, he never would have gone to Old Oregon.

CHAPTER 2 ENDNOTES

1 Charles H. Farnham, *History of the Descendants of John Whitman*, New Haven, 1889, provided genealogical information for this section.

2 The word "town" is used in New York State and in New England to indicate a township. In other parts of the United States, a town is a village.

3 Samuel S. Greene, *Genealogical Sketch of the Descendants of Thomas Green*, Boston, 1858.

4 From entry in the Whitman family Bible, now in Coll. W.

5 Little is known about Beza Whitman. Coll. W contains a receipt in his handwriting.

6 Information supplied by Robert Moody of Rushville. This house remained standing until about 1905.

7 Wisewell letter, Coll. W. See Drury, *Whitman*, following p. 24 for pictures of the sister and brothers of Marcus Whitman.

8 *Sunset Magazine*, XXIII(August 1909), p. 186. Also, Drury, *Whitman*, pp. 25–6 for an account of the discovery of what is believed to be a picture of Whitman's mother and for a reproduction of the photograph.

9 Nahum Mitchell in his *History of Bridgewater, Mass.*, Boston, 1840, states that Samuel Whitman "was plunged," i.e., baptized by immersion, when over ninety years of age. Samuel and his son Freedom were charter members of a Baptist Church established in Cummington on May 29, 1821.

10 Several accounts of the origin of the name "Oregon" are to be found in various issues of the *O.H.Q.*; Bancroft, *Oregon*, I:17 ff; *The Record*, Washington State University, Pullman, p. 27; and George R. Stewart, *Names on the Land*, New York, 1945, pp. 153 ff.

11 Wisewell letter, Coll. W. This letter, written during the lifetime of the author, was dictated by her to her daughter. It gives us, therefore, authentic glimpses into the early life of Marcus Whitman.

12 The name Erastus had also been given to Mrs. Beza Whitman's second son who also died in infancy. In that generation, it was quite customary for parents to use the same name a second time if the first child had died.

13 The original John Packard house, now known as the Laurens Seely home, is still standing and is occupied. The house has been remodeled.

14 Charles N. Dyer, *History of the Town of Plainfield*, Northampton, 1891, p. 93. Dyer gives much detailed information about the church and its pastor, Moses Hallock.

15 *Ibid.*, p. 7.

16 W. A. Bradley, *Wm. Cullen Bryant*, New York, 1905, pp. 22–3.

17 Dyer, *op. cit.* For some reason Dyer did not include the name of Marcus Whitman as being one of the missionaries, although in that day work with the American Indians was usually classified as foreign missions.

[CHAPTER THREE]

WHITMAN'S MEDICAL TRAINING

Marcus Whitman returned to Rushville in 1820, when he was eighteen years old, with the hope that his family would approve his plans to study for the ministry. To his great disappointment, they did not. His niece, Mary Alice Wisewell, commented: "His heart was set on studying for the ministry, but he was opposed by his brothers who thought his limited means would compel him to be a charity scholar, and persuaded him against his will to take up the study of medicine. My mother says many a time she has seen the big tears on his face as he thought of his disappointment in his course of life."[1]

Both the Congregational and the Presbyterian denominations, with which Whitman had contacts, frowned upon an uneducated ministry. Both churches required a full four-year college course followed by three years in a theological seminary. A few exceptions to this general rule were occasionally made and some scholarship aid was available. Seven years in college and seminary were expensive and it is evident that the Whitman family could offer little or no financial assistance to Marcus in the fulfillment of his cherished dream.

In addition to the financial problem, another influence was his mother's unsympathetic attitude. In Whitman's first letter to the American Board, he wrote: "My Mother is living and professes a hope but is not attracted to any church." Beza and Alice Whitman were not among the charter members of the Congregational Church of Rushville when it was organized in 1802, even though they were then living in Rushville, nor did they join later.[2] On the other hand, Captain Henry Green, Mrs. Whitman's brother, was one of the organizers and later became a deacon. Other Whitman relatives also were members. Many years later, Marcus was to write from the Missouri frontier to his mother, on May 27, 1843: "I feel most desirous to know that my Dear Mother has determined to live the rest of her days witnessing a good profession of godliness. What keeps you from this? Is it that you are not a sinner, or if not that, is it that there is no Saviour of sinners, or is it that you have not too long refused & neglected to love & obey him. Has not his forbearance & his mercy been very long expended towards you?"

In spite of his deep disappointment, Marcus was obedient to the wishes of his family. For the next three years, until he attained his majority in 1823, he lived in his mother's home and rendered such assistance as he could in his stepfather's business, the tannery and shoeshop.

When Marcus returned to his home, he learned that the village Congregational Church had in 1814 united with the Presbytery of Geneva and that it was then being served by the Rev. Joseph Merrill, a Presbyterian. In order to meet the spiritual needs of the expanding frontier, the Congregational Association of Connecticut and the Presbyterian General Assembly had adopted a Plan of Union in 1801. According to this agreement, members and ministers of both denominations cooperated in small communities. Both ministers and congregations moved rather freely back and forth in their regional denominational affiliations. Such congregations were often called "half-and-half" or "Presbygational" churches. Although the Rushville church retained its membership in the Presbytery of Geneva until 1855 and often had Presbyterian pastors, it retained its local Congregational polity. The church still continues its Congregational affiliations and hence will be referred to as such in this book. The Plan of Union accounts in part for the cooperation of the Congregational and Presbyterian Churches in the American Board.

The Rushville congregation erected a new brick "meeting house" in 1818. This building served the community until it was burned on the night of January 31, 1971, as the result of an incendiary fire. A new, and somewhat smaller sanctuary, in the same architectural style, has been erected on the same site. Unfortunately, the minutes of the church for its early years have been lost, but in a record book kept by Samuel Whitman, a brother of Marcus, we find the following: "Nov. 1870. Fifty years this Month Since I Profest to love God and to love his People. Brother Marcus Whitman Profest to love God the same time. S. Whitman."[3] This confirms Whitman's statement in his first letter to the American Board: "I did not unite with the Church until I returned to Rushville, (my native place)."

Merrill was followed in the pastorate of the Rushville church by the Rev. David Page in May 1821. Both of these men were graduates of Dartmouth College. According to one report, Marcus continued his Latin studies under Page. The history of the Rushville church, written for its centennial in 1902, states that upon his return to his home, Marcus "immediately interested himself in the welfare of the church by conducting sunrise prayer meetings with two other young men." The church's extant Sunday school records list Marcus as a teacher in 1822 and again in 1823. He taught a class of boys whose ages ranged from eight to sixteen.

The Rushville church was not without missionary enthusiasm although at that time the foreign missionary movement had touched but few American churches. On October 23, 1819, the brig *Thaddeus* sailed from New York with a party of seven missionaries and their wives, all appointees of the American Board, to begin missionary work in the Hawaiian Islands, then known as the Sandwich Islands. The party reached Hawaii, the largest of the Islands, on March 20, 1820, and Honolulu on April 19. Among those pioneer missionaries was Elisha Loomis, 1799–1836, of Rushville. Loomis was a printer and took with him a printing press valued at $450.00. He was helpful in reducing the native language to writing and in printing the Gospel of Matthew in that tongue. Because of his wife's ill health, he returned to Rushville in 1827.

Loomis had left Rushville before Whitman returned to his home in 1820, yet it is possible that the two knew each other as young boys. Certainly, they were friendly after Loomis returned from the Islands, because when Whitman sent in a list of references to the American Board in the summer of 1834, he included the name of Elisha Loomis, "former Missionary Printer to the Sandwich Islands" [Letter 4]. In 1838 the Hawaiian Mission sent a small printing press to the Oregon Mission, and it is possible that this was one of the presses which Loomis had used during his residence in the Islands.

In tracing out the reasons for Whitman's interest in foreign mission, we should not overlook the possible influence of Elisha Loomis. There is evidence that Whitman was in Rushville at times during 1827, the year that Loomis returned from the Islands. Possibly the two met again then and that Whitman spent hours listening to the wonderful tales that Loomis could have told of the far-away islands set in the warm Pacific where the natives had accepted Christianity with great eagerness. If such a surmise be true, then this would have awakened in Whitman the old longing to be a minister and perhaps go as a missionary to the "benighted heathens" in some distant land.

Riding with Dr. Bryant

Marcus Whitman celebrated his twenty-first birthday on September 4, 1823. He was then free to follow his own inclinations. Frustrated in his plan to enter the ministry, Marcus turned his attention to the medical profession as a promising field for altruistic service. In that generation, training to be a doctor did not demand the extensive educational background which is now required. A medical course was short and comparatively inexpensive. All that was needed as basic preparation was a fair literary education and this Whitman had. Indeed, he was much better prepared than the average medical student as he had studied both Latin and Greek. In those days when a young man aspired to be a doctor, he usually began his studies under some local physician, who would take the student with him when visiting his patients. In a colloquialism of the time, this was referred to as "riding with the Doctor." From the meager evidence available, it appears that Marcus Whitman began riding with Dr. Ira Bryant, Rushville's doctor, sometime in the fall of 1823.

Dr. Ira Bryant, 1786–1840, reported to have been a distant cousin of William Cullen Bryant, had settled in Rushville sometime prior to 1818 and practiced his profession there until his death. In his letter of application to the American Board, Whitman wrote: "In my profession I studied and practiced regularly with a good physician" [Letter 3]. Whitman did not indicate how long he had ridden with Dr. Bryant. Since he entered a medical school in the fall of 1825 and received a license to practice medicine the next spring, the assumption is that he must have had at least two years experience with Dr. Bryant.

One of Whitman's boyhood playmates, later a schoolmate, was Jonathan Pratt, Jr., 1801–1880. In the summer of 1936, while searching for material bearing on the life of Marcus Whitman, I called on Carleton Pratt, the son of Jonathan, at his home in Hopewell near Rushville. With me was Robert Moody of Rushville. In his old age, Carleton Pratt was sick and infirm. Shortly before we called, he had sold an antique desk which had once been used by his father. The contents of the drawers had been dumped on the floor when the desk was taken away, and this debris was still there at the time of our visit.

Looking through the papers, we found two letters written by Marcus to Jonathan in 1827 and 1828. These are the oldest Whitman letters known. Jonathan's diary was also discovered covering the period, with irregular entries, from January 1, 1824, to May 2, 1828. The name of Marcus Whitman does not appear, but twice the initial letters "M.W." are given which seem to refer to him. Since both Marcus and Jonathan were riding with Dr. Bryant at the same time during parts of 1824 and 1825, the experiences which Jonathan records throw light upon some obscure years in the life of Marcus. The old Pratt home burned on November 19, 1936, and Carleton Pratt lost his life in the fire. The Whitman source material there discovered was rescued none too soon.[4]

From the documents found in the Pratt home, we learn that Augustus Whitman on November 10, 1823, had signed a letter recommending Jonathan to be a school-teacher. It appears that Jonathan alternated between teaching school and riding with Dr. Bryant. There is evidence that Marcus Whitman did the same. In 1845 Newton Gilbert, 1818–1879, of Rushville migrated to Oregon and called on the Whitmans at their mission station at Waiilatpu. Writing shortly after that visit, Whitman referred to Gilbert as being "formerly my day & Sabbath School Schollar" [Letter 178].

On July 17, 1936, Mrs. Isaac Lee Patterson of Portland, Oregon, wrote to me saying: "When I was a young girl, my grandmother, Lavina Lindsley, born in Middlesex, New York, told me several times that she had been to school to Marcus Whitman."[5] There is also evidence that Marcus, in addition to teaching school for a time, assisted his brother Henry in the operation of a sawmill.[6] Here he learned a skill which was of great value to him after he had arrived in Old Oregon.

On April 4, 1824, Jonathan Pratt noted in his diary: "Saturday finished Anatomy & was pleased to get through for I found a great part of it verry [sic] dry study, but think of the different parts of which it is composed, viz. Muscles, Bloodvessels, Lymphatics and Nerves, that the Muscles is the most perplexing. When shall I get through my studies; two long years (if I live) before I can attend a course of medical lectures, one course of which being three months will complete my studies." Here Jonathan clearly states that a medical student was expected to study two years under a local physician and then take a three months' course in a medical school before receiving his license. This was the program followed by Marcus Whitman.

WHITMAN'S FIRST TERM AT THE MEDICAL COLLEGE

Having completed his two-year period of riding with Dr. Bryant, Whitman was ready for the medical college. He enrolled in the College of Physicians and Surgeons of the Western District of New York at Fairfield, Herkimer County, New York, on or before October 3, 1825, when he was about a month past his twenty-third birthday.[7] At that time this school was one of the best medical colleges in the nation, having some distinguished teachers on its faculty, including Doctors Westel Willoughby, Joseph White, T. Romeyn Beck, James Hadley, and James McNaughton.[8] According to the custom of the school, the students paid their tuition by buying tickets of admission to the lectures of the individual professors. Among the extant documents regarding Whitman's medical training is the ticket given by Dr. Willoughby to Marcus Whitman October 3, 1825, upon the payment of ten dollars as tuition for "Lectures on Midwifery."[9]

The Fairfield College of Physicians and Surgeons grew out of an academy which had been established at Fairfield in 1802. The Medical College was chartered in 1812 and continued until 1839; during this time 555 students were graduated. The academy continued alongside the medical department. In 1839 the academy was reorganized as Fairfield Seminary and conducted on a coeducational basis until 1891 when it became a military academy for eleven years. Of the five buildings which once stood on the campus, only the chapel remains and it is now deserted and in a dilapidated condition.[10]

Dr. Willoughby, one of the founders of the Medical College, served as its head for nearly thirty years. Under his leadership the school reached a peak enrolment of 217 in 1833–34.[11] In the sixteen-week session of 1825–26, when Whitman was a student, 130 were enrolled. The Fairfield Medical College was a most logical choice for Whitman as it was nearer to his home than any other institution of this kind. Moreover, the costs were reasonable. The catalog for 1825–26 advertised: "The whole expense for Tickets, Board, Wood, during a course, not to exceed 100 dollars." The cost of the tuition tickets for the courses offered that term amounted to $54.00. Although textbooks were available to students on a rental basis, the catalog recommended that the students "furnish themselves with some of the most approved works on each branch of instruction, as a sufficient number of copies may not be at hand to supply a large class."[12]

Among the graduates and faculty members of the Medical College were several who won fame. Asa Gray, 1810–1888, received his M.D. from Fairfield in 1831 and afterwards lectured there on botany. Possibly Whitman, when he returned for a second term in the fall of 1831, had an opportunity to become acquainted with Gray. Daniel Brainard, once a student at Fairfield, founded Rush Medical College in Chicago with a faculty consisting almost entirely of Fairfield men in 1837. One of these professors was Dr. W. S. Davis, who organized the American Medical Association in 1847. Many of the former students of Fairfield served as doctors in the Civil War and many went West to become doctors in frontier communities.

The late Dr. F. C. Waite, for many years a member of the Medical Faculty of Western Reserve University, Cleveland, Ohio, and a recognized medical historian, summarized the importance of the Fairfield Medical College in a letter to me dated in July 1935: "I say advisedly and with much familiarity with all the medical schools of that period that *no other school in the United States* could have trained Whitman for the work he was to do as a frontier physician as could Fairfield, for that was the purpose of the school, namely, to train men for frontier work."[13]

The popular prejudice against the use of human bodies for dissection by medical students was still strong in the days of Whitman's preparation. Sometimes the students would resort to robbing graves for newly buried bodies. This practice was referred to as "resurrection." The public naturally resented such indignities and oftentimes the medical schools as well as individual students became involved in trouble over the practice. The Trustees of the Fairfield College in 1819 took the following action against any student who should be guilty "of digging up or in removing from any cemetery or burying ground any dead human body to be used as an anatomical subject in said College, he shall forthwith be dismissed from the College."[14]

The New York State Legislature, by act of March 30, 1820, gave to Fairfield

College the bodies of convicts dying in the Auburn State Prison which were not claimed by relatives or friends. Dissection of a human body was, therefore, dependent upon the success of the faculty in securing an occasional cadaver. Even so, Fairfield College was the only medical school in New York State at that time where cadavers could legally be studied. Anatomy was largely taught by lectures, accompanied by charts or demonstrations on a skeleton. One of the buildings on the campus was called the laboratory, but in spite of the name, the students had virtually no laboratory facilities as we now know them.

Since the College was located in a village which had fewer than two thousand inhabitants, there was no hospital or clinic nearby in which the students could gain practical experience. Usually not more than one of the faculty members lived in Fairfield. The others came from a distance, often from New York City, to give a series of lectures extending over several days before returning to their homes. In all probability, William H. Gray, who later was associated with Marcus Whitman in the Oregon Mission, was a fifteen-year-old youth living in Fairfield when Whitman was a student at the Medical College in 1825–26. No evidence, however, has been found that the two ever met at that time.

THE NEXT FIVE YEARS, 1826–1831

Students who completed a sixteen-week session at Fairfield Medical College were qualified to be licensed to practice medicine. New York State had no licensing medical board before 1841, so the only license a doctor could have in Whitman's day was that issued by that county medical society which would receive him. Whitman finished his term at Fairfield on January 23, 1826, and on the following May 9th was licensed to practice medicine within the State of New York by the Herkimer County Medical Society.[15] Since the Medical College at Fairfield was located in Herkimer County and since Dr. Willoughby, one of Whitman's professors, was then president of the Society, it was logical that Whitman should have applied to that body for licensure.

By courtesy such a license as that granted to Whitman was usually accepted anywhere in the United States or Canada. Although licensed physicians did not have the Doctor of Medicine degree, they were usually called "Doctor."

The M.D. degree could then have been earned by taking a second sixteen-week course at some recognized medical school. It has been estimated that not more than one-half of the medical students of that period ever returned to a school to complete the requirements for the degree. Some practical difficulties discouraged a student from going back to the same institution from which he had been graduated. To do so meant that he would be listening to the same lectures that he had once heard, unless there had been changes in the faculty. Those who coveted the M.D. degree often attended a different school or waited several years until some changes had been made in the faculty or the curriculum of the school where they had first studied. There were no graduate courses in American medical schools until after the Civil War.

The next authenticated dates in Whitman's life are found in the correspondence that he had with Jonathan Pratt who, after winning his licensure, opened an office at Sugargrove, Warren County, Pennsylvania, in the fall of 1826. In the following August, Pratt complained in his diary about his ill health. Sometime during the latter part of that month or during the first part of September, Pratt wrote to Whitman begging him to take over his practice at Sugargrove for a short time. In Whitman's reply, dated September 11, 1827 (the oldest Whitman letter extant), he indicated that he was still looking for a place to settle where he could practice medicine. Just what he had been doing during the sixteen months after completing his work at Fairfield is not known. Whitman wrote: "Friend Jonathan: I received your letter yesterday; it probably lay in the office several days, I being absent to the east. I have been making preparation for going into practice: had calculated to go westward but not as soon as you require, but as your health is so ill & you wish me to come and assist you, I will endeavor to get ready the latter part of this or by Monday of next week. I wish you to stay till I come. I have a horse and probably shall ride..."

The authors of a history of Warren County included a chapter dealing with the early doctors who practiced at Sugargrove and mentioned Dr. Jonathan Pratt. They stated that he was followed by "another bachelor physician, Dr. Marcus Whitman." [16] Pratt in his diary tells of his return to Sugargrove on December 13 of that year. Hence it may be assumed that Whitman practiced medicine in Sugargrove for about two months when he was substituting for his friend who needed a vacation.

The reference to Whitman being a bachelor raises the interesting question: Why was he not married by 1827 when he was twenty-five years old? He and Narcissa Prentiss were not married until February 1836 when he was in his thirty-fourth year. Why the long delay in getting married?

According to a surprising family tradition among the descendants of Thomas Saunders, a pioneer resident of Rushville, Whitman was married sometime in the 1820s to Miss Persia Saunders.[17] Such a report is erroneous as Persia's tombstone in the French Cemetery at Rushville gives her maiden name and the dates: Born, July 12, 1807, and died, March 28, 1830. It is possible that Marcus and Persia were engaged and that her ill health delayed a marriage. With the passing of many years, the memory of an engagement might have become the tradition of a marriage. The possible romance ending by the death of the young lady may have been the reason Whitman did not marry during his twenties.

WHITMAN IN CANADA

Following Whitman's return from Sugargrove, he visited Upper Canada[18] in search of a promising community. He called on a former classmate, Dr. James Hunter,[19] who was practicing in the Niagara Peninsula. In Whitman's second letter to Pratt, also written from Rushville, dated February 5, 1828, he reported: "I had a good journey with some exceptions but found it necessary to stay longer than I expected in Canada. I found my friend well and ready to assist me as far as I could wish. I intend going to Canada but as to what particular place I shall occupy, I do not know, or whether I shall take license this spring or go into copartnership with Hunter. I intend to return to Canada in a few days. As to the prospects in Canada, I cannot say precisely but I think they are better than at Sugargrove."

After due investigation, Whitman selected a village called St. Anne in Gainsboro township, located about twenty-five miles west of Niagara Falls. The 1829 census of Upper Canada shows that the County of Lincoln, in which Gainsboro and the present County of Welland were located, then had a population of less than twenty thousand. Whitman was licensed by the Upper Canada Medical Board in July 1829.[20] He was listed as being from "Niagara District." It is evident that Whitman had been practising his profession in Canada for more than a year before he received this official permission.

Whitman Returns to the Medical College

During the spring and summer of 1830, Whitman passed through a period of uncertainty, as he debated whether he should give up medicine and study for the ministry. Ten years earlier, when he returned to Rushville from Plainfield, he had dreamed of becoming a minister. Circumstances, probably largely financial, had directed him into medicine. Now, when he was twenty-eight years old, he seriously considered changing his profession. What was the reason for this discontent? Perhaps he had been engaged to Persia Saunders so that her death on March 28 of that year was a contributing factor to this yearning to follow through with his youthful dream.

This we know: Whitman was back in Rushville in the fall of 1830, for he reunited with the Congregational Church there on November 6 by letter from "the Presbyterian Church in Gainsboro, Upper Canada." Thus Whitman's residence in Canada did not extend to much more than two years if indeed it was that long. Whitman's pastor at Rushville when he rejoined was the Rev. Joseph Brackett, 1781–1832, under whose direction he began his theological studies. In his letter to the American Board dated June 27, 1834, Whitman summarized what had happened: "In the fall of 1830 I gave up the practice of my profession and entered upon a course of study preparatory to the ministry."

Little is known of Whitman's activities for the year following his return to Rushville. We learn that he studied theology for a time and that he suffered from ill health. Of this he wrote in his letter to the Board of June 27: "I had not continued long [in the studies] when for want of active exercise I found my health become impaired by a pain in the left side which I attributed to an inflammation of the spleen. I immediately resorted to remedies with apparently full relief, resumed study so soon that it caused a return of the pain & again I used remedies with partial relief. Then I used exercise & continued it for a number of months when I found I was not able to study & returned to the practice of my profession."

The question arises: If his health prevented his continuing his theological studies, how was he able to return to his medical practice? It may be that Whitman had come to realize that it was not wise for him at his age to change his profession and spend years in study to meet the educational requirements for the ministry of either the Congregational or the Presbyterian Churches. So he decided to return to the Medical College at Fairfield for another sixteen weeks' course and thus earn his M.D. degree.

When Whitman reenrolled at the College in the fall of 1831, he found that the institution then ranked third in size among the medical schools of the country with 205 students in attendance.[21] During his five-year absence, one of his former professors, Dr. White, had retired and had been succeeded by Dr. John Delamater, an eminent physician and a successful teacher.[22] On the whole Whitman was highly favored in being able to study under some of the best medical professors of that generation.

Whitman returned to Fairfield with a new zest for learning that often comes after one has been away from an academic schedule for several years. Now he had definitely and finally dismissed the idea of being a minister. With more maturity and several years of practical experience, he was receptive for further instruction.

The records of the Board of Trustees of the Medical College give the thesis subjects of each of the thirty-nine graduates of the class of January 1832.[23] Whitman wrote on "Caloric."[24] The term was then used to denote "some subtle influence that causes the heat of the body." Strange as it may seem to us today, the doctors of that generation failed to appreciate the importance of fever in the diagnosis of disease. Since we do not have a copy of Whitman's thesis, we are unable to learn just how far he was probing into this important subject. The very choice of such a topic for investigation indicates that he felt that there was some connection between fever, or "caloric," and disease.

The minutes of the Board of Trustees of the Medical College for January 24, 1832, contain the following: "After the reading of the Theses by the candidates for graduation, and it being certified by the Registrar that they had individually complied with the requirements of the Laws of this state and the ordinances of the college, it was resolved that they be recommended to the Regents of the [State] University for the Degree of Doctor of Medicine."

Thereafter Marcus Whitman could rightfully, and not merely by courtesy, be called Doctor Whitman. He was a well-trained physician, and much better qualified than the average doctor of his day. His academic work had been preceded by a two-year apprenticeship, riding with a country doctor. He had studied under eminent professors. He had spent several years practicing medicine in frontier communities, having been licensed in both New York State and in Canada. Finally he had earned the M.D. degree which was granted by the University of the State of New York. Thus at the age of twenty-nine, Dr. Marcus Whitman found himself equipped for his life's work, but the stage on which he was to play a major role was not then ready for his entrance.

CHAPTER 3 ENDNOTES

1 Wisewell letter, Coll. W.

2 *Centennial Celebration*, 1902, Rushville Congregational Church.

3 Original record book now owned by Mrs. W. Merle Wheaton of Cohocton, N.Y.

4 See Appendix 1 for location of Whitman letters 1 & 2. The Pratt diary is in Coll. Wn.

5 This Levina Lindsley, a married woman, is not to be confused with the Levina Linsley of Prattsburg to whom H. H. Spalding is reported to have been engaged. See Drury, *Spalding*, p. 39. The reported dates of birth, 1810 and 1799, also indicate two different women.

6 Eells, *Marcus Whitman*, p. 23.

7 Mowry, *Marcus Whitman*, p. 62, erroneously states that Whitman attended the Berkshire Medical Institution at Pittsfield, Mass.

8 Drury, Whitman, gives pictures of six of Whitman's professors at Fairfield and copies of pages from the catalog of the Medical College. Most of the information concerning Whitman's medical education used in this chapter was furnished by the late Dr. F. C. Waite.

9 Original ticket in Coll. B. See picture in Drury, *Whitman*, p. 44.

10 Thomas C. O'Donnell, Tip of the Hill, Boonville, N.Y., 1953, gives a history of the Medical College and of the Academy.

11 *Transactions of the Medical Society of the State of New York*, Vol. IV, p. 160.

12 A copy of the catalog is in the New York State Library, Albany. Photostat copy in Coll. Wn.

13 Dr. Waite in a letter to me dated July 1935. The file of my correspondence with him, together with other papers, has been deposited in the Eastern Washington State Historical Society, Spokane.

14 Information supplied by Dr. Waite.

15 Original certificate owned by Mrs. Dudley Voorhees, Middlesex, N.Y. See Drury, *Whitman*, p. 53.

16 J. S. Shenck and W. S. Rann, *History of Warren County, Syracuse*, 1887, p. 435.

17 Persia was pronounced Per-sigh-a, with the accent on the second syllable. This tradition was called to my attention by A. L. Saunders of Canton, Ill. The tombstone dates were supplied by Robert Moody of Rushville.

18 Canada was divided into Lower Canada and Upper Canada by the Ottawa River. The Province of Ontario is in Upper Canada.

19 Hunter was registered in the 1825–26 term at Fairfield as being from Niagara, Upper Canada.

20 William Canniff, *The Medical Profession in Upper Canada, Toronto*, 1894, p. 56.

21 Waite, "The Medical Education of Marcus Whitman," *O.H.Q.*, XXVII (1936): 192 ff.

22 See Waite's article on Dr. Delamater, *Bulletin of the Cleveland Academy of Medicine*, May 1930.

23 Dr. Waite discovered the original records in 1935 in the New York State Library, Albany.

24 See picture of page with name of Whitman's thesis in Drury, *Whitman*, p. 53.

[CHAPTER FOUR]

THREE YEARS AT WHEELER
1832–1835

On a large granite boulder at a crossroads in the village of Wheeler, New York, is a memorial plaque which states that the medical office of Dr. Marcus Whitman once stood at that place. The two-story building was constructed out of heavy hand-hewn timbers covered on the outside with boards. According to a local tradition, Whitman used the building as both his home and office. Just why Whitman selected Wheeler as the place where he would practice medicine after receiving his M.D. degree is not known. According to a census taken in 1835, Wheeler township had about 1,600 people scattered over more than forty-six square miles. Possibly the town had no doctor before he arrived. The fact that Wheeler was within forty miles of Rushville might also have been an attraction.

About two miles south of Wheeler is another marker along the roadside which states that Henry H. Spalding was born near that place on November 26, 1803. How strange that these two, who were to be so closely associated for eleven years in the Oregon Mission of the American Board, should each have had contacts with the little village of Wheeler. In 1832, when Whitman settled in Wheeler, Spalding was a senior in Western Reserve College at Hudson, Ohio.

Whitman's practice was largely in the country. The only practical way for him to visit his patients was on horseback. In such communities in those days, a doctor might ride ten or fifteen miles to see a patient and then find upon his return home a call to go a similar distance in another direction. If a doctor could keep up his practice by owning but one horse, it was evident that his calls were not numerous and consequently he could not be a popular or competent doctor. Such a man was called a "one-horse doctor" and the term came to be used to imply mediocrity.

Whitman's methods, medicines, and instruments, like those of other doctors of his generation, were as primitive as the community in which he lived. He had no fever thermometer, for doctors then did not appreciate its importance, as has been mentioned in the preceding chapter. Since very few stethoscopes were then in use, it is doubtful if Whitman had one. A set of amputating knives cost about fifty dollars. Whitman probably secured a set together with some surgical saws early in his professional career. The doctor in that day was also the dentist and with the aid of a turnkey would extract teeth, sometimes leaving a splinter of a tooth in the jaw. The cost of such a service was usually ten cents for each tooth.

It may be that Dr. Whitman did not have any obstetrical forceps, because his professor of obstetrics, Dr. Westel Willoughby, was much opposed to their use. The germ theory of disease was unknown and, of course, the wonderful antibiotics so common today were then in the future. Such a precaution as boiling instruments to sterilize them before use was not common practice. The properties of a weak solution of lye or of iodine as disinfectants were somewhat appreciated, although the real reason for their effectiveness was unknown. Usually doctors would merely wipe their instruments clean after use and put them away. Suppuration was commonly thought to be essential to healing and much was said about "laudable pus" until as late as 1870.

Because of a common belief that disease was caused by an excess of blood, the doctors of that generation often bled their patients. This was a remedy which had been practiced for centuries even on patients who had suffered an accident. Rarely, however, do we read of Whitman following this custom.[1] Anesthesia with its merciful power to produce unconsciousness was then unknown. In amputation cases, the patient might be made drunk; be stupefied with heavy doses of opium; or be held by strong men and bonds while the doctor worked as fast as he could. Some surgeons boasted that they could amputate an arm in three minutes and a leg in five. Sometimes an ordinary carpenter's fine-toothed saw was used if the operating surgeon lacked a surgical saw.

The doctor of that generation had to be his own apothecary as only the largest towns had drug stores. Very few medicines were given in liquid form. The doctor would buy his drugs in bulk in crude form and then pulverize them with a hand mortar. He had to know how to manufacture his own pills. Inventories of drugs used in Whitman's day show that a good doctor would have about fifty different kinds. Great reliance was placed on calomel, a compound of mercury and chlorine, which was an effective purgative. When Whitman rode his district, he must have carried with him a variety of the most used drugs in his saddlebags. Thus he was able to supply the medicine needed at the time he called on his patients.

False teeth were only for the wealthy, and even so, were ill-fitting and uncomfortable. Spectacles were available for those who needed them, but these were fitted by the trial and error method, usually with no consideration of the fact that one eye might be out of adjustment with the other. Thus a pair of spectacles often did more harm than good. Sometimes the same pair would be used by several members of the family.

Considering the medical conditions of Whitman's generation, we need not wonder that a medical student could be licensed after riding for a couple of years with some doctor and then attending a medical college for sixteen weeks. By that time he had learned about all that could be taught. The fact that Whitman returned to the medical college for a second term means that he was better prepared than the average doctor of his day.

The business side of a doctor's practice is of interest. He usually received a fee of twenty-five cents for a call in his office, including any medicine prescribed. The fee was doubled if the doctor had to make a house call within a five-mile radius. Beyond that distance, there was an extra charge of six and one-fourth cents for each mile. An obstetrical case would cost from two to five dollars. The usual fee for amputating a leg was ten dollars.[2]

In spite of the limitations and handicaps under which Whitman worked, as compared with modern-day conditions, we know that he was favored, as every successful physician should be, with a personality which inspired confidence. The people of Wheeler and vicinity grew to love him. After he had practiced medicine in the community for three years, word was spread abroad that he was planning to go to Oregon as a medical missionary. In Parker's letter of January 1, 1835, to the American Board, we may read: "I am afraid that the people in Wheeler and the vicinity on account of their [being] unwilling to spare one whom they so highly esteem as a physician and Christian will dissuade him from offering himself." In 1869, some thirty-five years after Whitman's appointment, an elder of the Wheeler church wrote to the New School[3] Presbyterian Board of Home Missions protesting the fact that so important a person in the local church and community had been sent as a missionary to Oregon. "Dr. Whitman was an elder in our church," the unnamed correspondent wrote, "and a very good and useful member, practiced medicine all over the town. Everybody liked him and he had great influence over the inhabitants."[4]

The Cholera Epidemic

Little did Marcus Whitman suspect, as he rode the byways of Steuben County during 1832, 1833, and 1834, that he was preparing himself for a special emergency which was to arise when he and Samuel Parker were on the western Missouri frontier in 1835. The emergency dated back to the introduction of the dreaded Asiatic cholera into the United States in 1832.

During World War I, Spanish influenza spread from city to city, from nation to nation, and across oceans with terrifying rapidity, leaving in its wake millions of newly made graves. A century earlier, or, to be exact, in 1817, a similar epidemic, Asiatic cholera, originating in Bengal, India, began its deadly march around the world. Transportation was slower then, but the march once begun never stopped even though at times it was delayed. It swept across Russia and Poland and reached Berlin by the summer of 1831. There the epidemic claimed seven thousand lives. By November of that year it had reached Scotland. In February 1832, the dread disease appeared in London and by March was in Liverpool. In June the cholera crossed the Atlantic in a boat from Belfast bound for Quebec and within a week, cholera was found in Montreal. From there it spread southward through the waterways down to New

York, and across the state along the Erie Canal to the Great Lakes. Cases were reported in Detroit on July 5, and soldiers going to the Black Hawk War carried the disease to Chicago. Continuing its relentless march, the epidemic moved southward along the Mississippi River and by mid-September was in New Orleans.

The terror of the people was nearly as dreadful as the disease itself. They had reason to be afraid, for the epidemic struck with fearful rapidity. Oftentimes people left their homes in the morning, apparently in the best of health, only to be dead before sundown. From the records of reliable contemporary physicians, we learn that not more than one-third of the cases recovered in 1832. In following years, as the doctors learned more about the disease, they were able to save more of their patients.

Among Dr. Whitman's contemporaries was the Rev. Joel Wakeman, 1809–1889, whose personal reminiscences of both Marcus and Narcissa appeared in a Prattsburgh, New York newspaper in 1893 and again in 1898. One of his unpublished manuscripts, written sometime after 1890 in his old age, is entitled "The Fearful Scourge of 1832." In this he wrote: "No summer in the history of the American people has ever equaled 1832 for excitement and general prostration of all enterprise. Every newspaper was freighted with the number of the dead and dying in the city—every breeze that swept by our doors, brought rumors (and often greatly exaggerated rumors) of the rapid increase of the scourge in the villages and inland towns... The plague was bad; so exceedingly bad that the present generation can form no adequate conception of its fearful ravages. Merchants were afraid to travel to the cities to buy goods. Because of the lack of knowledge about disease germs, all kinds of foolish superstitions swept the country. Some thought that food was responsible for the disease and for a time melons, cucumbers, green corn, and other vegetables were rejected, and even in some place their sale was forbidden by law." [5]

People fled in fear from the infected areas. It was noticed that many of the towns inland from the routes of travel escaped the contagion and to these many of the refugees went. Some towns of five thousand or more located in the midst of the contagion lost half of their population in a single day because of the precipitous flight of their residents.

Methods of Treatment

The helplessness of the physicians was almost as great as the terror of the people. Marcus Whitman, who had received his M.D. degree in January of that year, had been given no instruction whatsoever upon the subject of cholera in the Medical College. Ordinary remedies had no effect. Many physicians resorted to that old, old panacea of bloodletting, but this only left the unfortunate patient less able to combat the disease.

A few doctors began to make some astute observations. They noticed that deaths were prevalent among the lower strata of society, especially among those who lived along rivers and canals. These people were careless about their toilet facilities. Frequently they took their drinking water from these waterways which had been polluted but, not knowing anything about germs, this did not concern them. It was also observed that those addicted to intoxicating liquors were most prone to contract the disease. This, we now know, was due to the fact that the saloons were usually along the water fronts and the customers were provided with drinking water dipped up from the most convenient river or canal.

Slowly the doctors came to some basic convictions. They advised cleanliness, isolation for the sick, and the use of copperas and chloride of lime in drains, cesspools, and outbuildings. Members of the famed medical society of the University of Edinburgh studied the problem and issued a pamphlet with their recommendations for the prevention and treatment of the disease. This pamphlet was brought to the United States and its contents reprinted in some of the country's newspapers. It was not then unusual to see a doctor using a country newspaper as the latest authority on how to treat Asiatic cholera.

Wheeler was sufficiently distant from the Erie Canal to avoid the major impact of the epidemic and yet it was near enough to bring fear to the hearts of the people. Dr. F. C. Waite, the medical historian, writing in January 1936, commented: "From what we know of Marcus Whitman, we cannot imagine that he did other than get all the information he could about the symptoms and treatment of cholera. He had an education both preliminary and professional much above the average. Moreover he was ambitious to learn. Otherwise he would not have returned to the medical college for further instruction after four years of practice."

The cholera epidemic lasted for about three years. The fact that Whitman learned to recognize the symptoms and was acquainted with the most approved methods to prevent its spread and to minister to the afflicted proved to be of inestimable value in the spring of 1835 when he and Parker were on their exploring tour to the Rockies with the caravan of the American Fur Company. This story belongs to a later chapter.

WHITMAN MEETS THE PRENTISS FAMILY

Living in nearby Prattsburg, when Dr. Whitman was in Wheeler, was the family of Judge Stephen Prentiss. He and his wife were the parents of nine children, four boys and five girls. Their third child and eldest daughter was Narcissa, and their second daughter was Jane. Whitman's professional and church interests often took him to Prattsburg where one day he attended a prayer meeting in the Prentiss home. Years later, in a letter addressed to Jane, May 17, 1842, Marcus refreshed her memory of their first meeting: "I was just telling Narcissa what an interest I had taken in yourself ever since I was introduced to you at your father's house... at the close of a prayer meeting. That was my first introduction to the family. From that moment my heart has been towards the family. But you smile, I suppose, and say it was Narcissa; no, it was Jane; Narcissa was in Butler. I presume you will have no recollection of the introduction; if so, let it rest on my recollection, which is vivid." Butler was in Wayne County, about seventy-five miles to the north where Narcissa may have been teaching school.

We have no evidence that Marcus and Narcissa met before the Prentiss family moved to nearby Amity in Allegany County in June 1834, yet in light of later events, it appears that they had become acquainted. Marcus was sufficiently well acquainted with the pastor of the Prattsburg church, the Rev. George Rudd, to request his endorsement upon the application he sent to the American Board in December 1834. This common interest in the Presbyterian Church and the proximity of Wheeler to Prattsburg would certainly have been favorable to the forming of a friendship between Marcus and Narcissa.

WHITMAN REJECTED BY THE AMERICAN BOARD

When we read the many references made by Whitman's later associates to his great physical strength and endurance, we are surprised to learn that when he first applied for an appointment under the American Board, he was rejected because of ill health. Nearly a year before Whitman heard Parker make his plea for missionaries to go with him to Old Oregon in the Wheeler Presbyterian Church, he had been considering offering his services to the American Board to go as a medical missionary to some tribe of American Indians. Evidently Whitman had never forgotten his youthful ambition to be a minister, and being a medical missionary to some Indian tribe appealed to him as a good substitute.

Sometime during April 1834, Whitman visited his mother in Rush-vile. While there he discussed with the Rev. Henry P. Strong, then pastor of the local Congregational Church, his idea of being a medical missionary to the Indians. Strong endorsed the proposal and, on April 25, took the initiative and wrote to the American Board, thus bringing to its attention for the first time the name of Dr. Marcus Whitman: "I write at this time to make known to you the request of Doct. Marcus Whitman. He is a young man of about 30 or 35 years of age, of solid, judicious mind, of, as I hope & believe, more than ordinary piety and perseverance, a regular bred Physician. He has practiced several years with good success & credit. He is, in my opinion, well qualified to act as a Missionary Physician: & altho I know not that he thinks of it, yet I think he might, if thought expedient, after a time be ordained to advantage. *He has formerly been in poor health*, but is now better, & thinks a station with some of our western Indians would be useful to him. He has thought of being a missionary for some time past, & I think him better qualified to do good in that capacity than most young men with whom I am acquainted. He would be glad to hear from you, as, should he go, he would have some worldly concerns to arrange."[6]

Since the secretaries of the Board were having difficulty finding qualified persons to go as missionaries to the American Indians, they were immediately interested. Secretary B. B. Wisner, then in charge of Indian missions under the Board, wrote to Strong on May 1: "Your account of him is so far satisfactory as to induce me to request you to suggest to him to address me a letter in which he shall give some account of himself, his parentage, education, religious history, views and feelings on the missionary subject &c, &c. We wish also to be informed whether he is married; and if he is, whether he has children, and if so, how many; if not married, whether he expects to be. We shall be glad to receive a communication."

Upon receipt of this letter, Strong wrote to Whitman informing him of what the Board wished to know. In his first letter to the Board, dated June 3, 1834, Whitman gave a brief review of his life, mentioning such facts as his residence in Massachusetts, his studies under Moses Hallock, the Sunday school class he had attended which was taught by Deacon Pichards, and his joining the church at Rushville. He referred to the "constant religious instruction" he had received from his "pious" grandfather and uncle at Cummington. Theologically, Whitman was an orthodox Calvinist.

Regarding his views on the missionary cause, Whitman wrote: "I regard the Heathen[7] as not having retained the knowledge of the true God and as perishing as described by St. Paul... I am willing to go to any field of usefulness at the direction of the A. Board. I will cooperate as Physician, Teacher or Agriculturalist so far as I may be able, if required. I am not married and I have no present arrangement upon that subject. Yet I think I should wish to take a wife, if the service of the Board would admit."

Whitman's letter was satisfactory in all respects save one—he made no reference to his health. On June 14, Wisner answered Whitman's letter and mentioned the fact that Strong had reported that he had been in poor health. Wisner wrote: "Now good health and good constitution are very important prerequisites for missionary service; for if a man in this civilized and Christian society needs to take great care... what would be likely to be the case with him among savages & pagans & all the privations and perplexities of missionary service? Please write, as soon as practicable, and give us your history as to health."

Wisner also asked: "What should you think of going to the Marquesas Islands [in the South Pacific]? We are now in need of a physician for that mission." Wisner recommended that Whitman be married should he be appointed, "if you can get a good missionary wife." On that same June 14, Wisner wrote to Strong and mentioned the fact that Whitman in his letter of application had made no reference to his health which was "a very important point." Wisner asked about Whitman's "talents and mental improvements." He wanted to know if Whitman had "the ability to appear respectable among sensible and respectable people, and to make a general good impression, to acquire the respect of others, and to get and keep an influence over others?"

As has been stated in the previous chapter, Whitman answered Wisner's inquiries about his health in his letter of June 27. He then explained how he had suffered from what he thought was "an inflammation of the spleen," which led him to give up the practice of medicine for a time. After studying theology for several months and finding that his health had not improved, Whitman returned to his practice of medicine. In further explanation, he wrote: "I have not been for any length of time without a slight pain & for the last two or three weeks there has been an agravation of pain & soreness so that I have used remedies & shall have to use more still... " Whitman stated that he felt able to work in a temperate climate but had "some fears of a hot climate." Therefore, he was unwilling to accept an appointment for the Marquesian Islands. He closed his letter by saying: "I have some lands in possession which I should wish to sell & considerable business to settle if the Board should approve of me.[8] It shall be done as soon as I am notified to that effect."

Whitman's letter was dated June 27 but postmarked at Wheeler on the 30th. It took five days for the letter to be carried from Wheeler to Boston. Wisner was puzzled as to what to say in reply and waited nearly two weeks before writing. In his letter to Whitman dated July 17, Wisner wrote: "I have hardly known what answer to return to it [i.e., Whitman's letter of June 27]. Millions of heathen are perishing for lack of the knowledge of the Gospel... and you are willing and desirous to go... But your health is such that you think you cannot go to a warm climate & in such climates are the *immense* majority of heathen. Among no others have we any mission except among the Indians... & among these we have no demand for a physician at this time. Indeed it seems doubtful whether your health is such as to justify your going on a mission at all." And there the matter rested.

On August 12, 1824, Strong wrote a belated reply to Wisner's letter of inquiry of June 14. Part of the delay in writing, he explained was due to illness. Strong then gave the following recommendation for Whitman: "I find that his talents are above mediocrity, his mental improvement respectable, in his profession above ordinary Physicians; in appearance, among respectable people, rather forbidding at first, but makes a good impression & retains influence, will be a pleasant missionary companion, cooperates well with others. Upon the whole, his acquaintance with the world is respectable & his friends think he will do well as a missionary."

Strong's recommendation came too late as the Board had already decided not to appoint Whitman for the time being. Some good, however, came out of the correspondence as all of the preliminary investigations regarding Whitman's fitness to be appointed, provided his health improved, had been made. Thus, when Whitman's name was again brought to the Board's attention in the following December, quick action was possible.

WHITMAN COMMISSIONED BY THE AMERICAN BOARD

By 1834 the American Board was experiencing great difficulty in finding suitable missionaries who were willing to go to the American Indians. This problem is clearly outlined in a letter that Secretary David Greene wrote on September 10, 1834, to the Rev. Cyrus Kingsbury, then one of the Board's missionaries to the Indians in what is now Oklahoma. After stating that "very few candidates for missionary service are willing to go among the Indians," Greene wrote: "They had rather learn a language spoken by tens of millions & live among a dense and settled population, have daily access to thousands, & think that the fruits of their labors will be felt by large nations and through future generations, than to spend their lives in what they apprehend will be almost fruitless toil in reclaiming small tribes of sparsely settled migrators and nearly inaccessible men, who are wasting away and seemed devoted to extinction. Men of talent and energy, and of other missionary qualifications, are not disposed to engage in such a field..." [9]

PARKER'S APPEAL FOR MISSIONARIES

During 1834 events were taking place elsewhere which, before the end of the year, were to have a life-changing effect on Marcus Whitman. Samuel Parker, who left his two companions, John Dunbar and Samuel Allis, on the Missouri frontier to open a mission among the Pawnee Indians, returned to his home in Ithaca, New York, sometime during the first part of July. During the first week of August, Parker visited the headquarters of the American Board to report on his trip to St. Louis. The Prudential Committee was so favorably impressed with the outlook that it approved his proposal to look for associates and make a second effort to go to the Rockies in 1835.

Parker was directed to act as an agent for the Board "in such parts of the State of New York, and in such manner as shall seem best by the Rev. Chauncey Eddy, Genl. Agent for the Board of that State;"[10] to seek volunteers for a proposed mission in Oregon; and to raise money. "In looking for suitable persons to be missionaries or teachers," wrote Wisner to Parker on August 7, "you will exercise great discretion, being well satisfied that they are qualified for the service, and so circumstanced that they may and ought to be engaged in it, before you bring the subject to them."

When Parker spoke in the Wheeler Presbyterian Church on an evening late in November 1834 on the appeal of "the Wise Men from the West," he unwittingly brought to a focus the unfulfilled dreams and aspirations of Marcus Whitman. Parker's appeal for missionaries opened a door for Whitman. This was exactly what he had long wanted to do. The fact that Parker's destination happened to be Old Oregon was incidental. Whitman was ready to accept any invitation which might have come from any western Indian tribe. We can only imagine the conversation which took place that November evening after Parker had spoken. Whitman's eagerness to be accepted by the Board was matched by Parker's desire to have someone go with him to the Rockies the next spring. Parker urged Whitman to make immediate application to the American Board for an appointment and suggested that he solicit testimonials from the pastors of the churches in Wheeler, Prattsburg, and Rushville to be sent with his letter.

WHITMAN REAPPLIES TO THE BOARD

Whitman lost no time in getting the needed testimonials. He turned first to his pastor, the Rev. J. H. Hotchkin, who on November 27 wrote: "I hereby certify that I have been intimately acquainted with him for about two years past... he is a member in good standing, and a Ruling Elder in said church, highly esteemed as a Christian of hopeful piety, and possessing in a good degree the spirit of active benevolence. In his medical profession, he has deservedly been held in estimation, and has a good share of practice." Hotchkin heartily recommended his appointment. Three of the elders of the Wheeler church added their signatures to the testimonial with the statement that they "most cordially" concurred in the opinions of their pastor.

Whitman then rode to Prattsburg where on Saturday, the 29th, he secured the endorsement of the Rev. George R. Rudd. Whitman then hastened on to Rushville where, on December 1, the Rev. H. P. Strong added his testimonial. Strong wrote: "I have simply to say as before, that the most judicious friends of Missions think him well qualified for the undertaking." Having collected these endorsements, Whitman wrote to the Board on December 2 and asked to be appointed to go with Parker on his mission "beyond the Rocky Mountains." "My health is so much restored," he wrote, "that I think it will offer no impediment. I find no sensible inconvenience from my former difficultys and think I shall not [suffer] from the climate or labour of such a Mission." This letter with the accompanying testimonials was received by the Board on December 9.[11]

In the meantime Parker wrote to his family on December 5 saying that he had found Dr. Whitman, but for some reason he did not notify the Board until the 17th of that month. Writing then from Dansville, New York, he said: "Doct. Whitman... whom I saw a few weeks since made up his mind to offer himself... He has the name of being a good physician and a devoted Christian. I think there can be no doubt in this case." After Parker's return to Ithaca, he wrote a second time about Whitman's offer on December 25: "His general reputation is regard to all the particulars required and into which I have made particular inquiry, I think places his case beyond any particular doubt. He wishes to accompany me in my expected tour."

The Prudential Committee met in Boston on January 6, 1835, at which time Whitman's application for an appointment was reconsidered. Since his health had evidently been improved, there was no longer any hesitancy to give him a commission to go with Parker that spring on an exploring tour to the Rockies. Writing to Whitman on January 7, Secretary Greene reported the action of the Prudential Committee and stated that Parker would be conferring with him "respecting the time of starting, the kind of outfit which will be required, and other topics connected with the undertaking." As will be noted later, few persons were less qualified to give advice on such matters than Samuel Parker.

Greene in his letter to Whitman of January 7 gave the following wise advice: "On such a tour as this, as well as in your missionary labors among any of the wandering tribes of our continent, great patience, fortitude, & perseverance are necessary. You must be willing to encounter hardships, dangers, self-denials in almost every shape & discouragements without being moved by them from your purpose. Nothing but an unquenchable desire to do good to the souls of the Indians, originating and cherished by a supreme love to Christ and firm faith in the promises, can sustain you and carry you through."

Secretary Wisner, who had been in charge of the Board's Indian Mission and the first to correspond with Whitman, died on February 9, 1835. He was succeeded by his assistant, the Rev. David Greene, who, throughout the history of the Oregon Mission was in charge of that field. No one can read his letters to the missionaries without being impressed with his good judgment and wise advice.[12] Through his correspondence, Greene played a significant role in the history of the Oregon Mission of the American Board.

Although the Board made a grant of $450.00 a year to Parker for the support of his family during his absence while on his exploring tours, no allowances for a salary for either him or for Whitman were made. This was true of all missionaries who joined the Oregon Mission. They received necessary travel and living expenses, and that was all. After getting settled in their respective stations in the Old Oregon wilderness, they were expected to be self-supporting. Naturally the time and energy spent on farming and looking after their livestock meant that less could be done in learning the language and in civilizing and evangelizing the natives. More will be said later about this fundamental weakness in the Board's policies.

WHITMAN LEAVES FOR THE ROCKIES

After receiving Greene's letter of January 7 with the news of his appointment, Whitman went to Ithaca to see Parker and to make plans for their exploring tour. Upon his arrival at Parker's home, he was disappointed to learn that no one else had been found to go with them. Whitman was also disappointed in discovering how indefinite Parker was as to the objectives of their prospective exploring tour.

After returning to his home in Wheeler, Whitman wrote to Greene on February 2 and asked for more instructions regarding the "intentions of the committee as to the extent and design of our commission."

Whitman also told Greene that he planned to start on his long horseback ride to St. Louis on February 16, provided he had received a reply by that date. Whitman asked that Greene send his reply to him at Rushville which indicates that he was planning to spend some time there with his relatives before leaving for the West. He reassurred Greene regarding his health by writing: "My health is generally good."

Parker was planning to go by stage to Pittsburgh and then by river steamer to St. Louis, taking with him some of Whitman's baggage. The two men planned to meet in St. Louis on or about April 1. They would then have plenty of time to assemble their outfit and be ready to leave with the caravan of the American Fur Company from the western frontier of Missouri in early May.

Two documents are extant from the days when Whitman was closing out his business affairs and getting ready to leave for the Rockies.[13] Each is dated February 5, 1835. One is a receipt for eleven dollars signed by Whitman and given to the father of a boy whom he had treated for an attack of scarlet fever. The second is a church letter given Whitman by the Rev. James H. Hotchkin. This was the first letter of transfer of membership given to a church member who expected to join a Protestant church somewhere west of the Rocky Mountains. After reviewing the circumstances which had led Whitman to request such a certificate, Hotchkin stated: "He is hereby on his request [dismissed] from his particular relation to the church of Wheeler, and affectionately recommended to the christian regard of any of God's people wherever he may travel and to the fellowship and communion of any particular church wherever God in his providence may cast his lot."

Replying to Whitman's request for more definite instructions, Greene on February 9 wrote to Whitman directing his letter, as requested, to Rushville. Greene wrote: "Respecting the object, extent & nature of your tour, you can learn from communications addressed to Mr. Parker last year or the present; especially from two long letters of instructions written to him last spring." Parker had left the letters with Dunbar in the summer of 1834; hence Whitman had not been able to see them. Greene, however, summarized what had been written: "The object of the Com. is to learn as fully as possible the conditions & character of the remote & secluded tribes, that they may more effectually call upon the Christian church to furnish them the men & the means in other respects for giving them the gospel." Greene promised to forward Whitman's official commission certifying his appointment as a missionary of the American Board to him at St. Louis.

Whitman received Greene's letter on Thursday, February 19, which was several days later than Whitman had planned for his departure for St. Louis. After bidding his mother and other relatives farewell, he mounted his horse and started on the long ride westward. He spent the week-end at Amity, New York, where Narcissa Prentiss was then living with her parents. There Whitman was a guest in the home of the Rev. and Mrs. Oliver S. Powell. Powell was pastor of the Amity Presbyterian Church in which the Prentiss family were members. During that week-end Marcus Whitman and Narcissa Prentiss became engaged.

When Whitman resumed his travels on Monday, his cup of happiness was full and running over. Although his youthful dream of becoming a minister had not been realized, now he had found an acceptable substitute in his appointment as a medical missionary. Adventure, travel, Christian service, and the lure of the unknown, lay before him. He would return as soon as possible to claim his bride. No doubt he found it difficult to leave Narcissa so soon after becoming engaged, but a high sense of duty bade him go.

Greene's letter of February 9, 1835, notifying Whitman of his appointment by the American Board was the cue which called for his entry into the great drama then taking place on a national scale involving the destiny of Old Oregon.

Chapter 4 Endnotes

1 After carefully checking the letters and diaries of the members of the Oregon Mission for references to bleeding, I was able to find only three instances where Whitman followed this practice.

2 F. C. Waite, "The Equipment of a Country Doctor in Northern Ohio in 1822," *Ohio State Medical Journal*, July 1936.

3 The Presbyterian Church divided into two parts in 1837 known as the Old School and the New School. Each of these branches divided over the slavery issue. The two Southern branches united in 1861 to become what is now the Presbyterian Church in the United States. The two Northern branches joined in 1869 to become the Presbyterian Church in the United States of America.

4 *Presbyterian Monthly*, New York, iv (December 1869):272.

5 Wakeman ms., Coll. Wn.

6 Hulbert, *O.P.* V:244 ff, gives the correspondence of the American Board with Strong and Whitman regarding the latter's appointment. The italics in this quotation are the author's.

7 In the commonly used ecclesiastical terminology of that day, non-Christians were referred to as "heathens" or "pagans." Such terms did not then carry any derogatory meanings.

8 S. W. Pratt wrote: "About this time Whitman bought a farm of 150 acres on the Pultenay Estate, lying about midway between Wheeler and Prattsburg . . . on this he built a log house where he dwelt for a time." Pratt ms., Coll. Wn.

9 Hulbert, *O.P.*, V:266. The Rev. A. B. Smith, who went out to Old Oregon in 1838 as an appointee of the American Board, emphasized in his letters to the Board this same observation. See Drury, *Spalding and Smith*, p. 109, and *passim*.

10 Eddy's office was in Utica, New York.

11 The secretaries of the American Board were accustomed to note on letters received the date of arrival and also when answered.

12 Some of Greene's letters to Whitman and other members of the Oregon Mission have been included in Hulbert, *O.P.*

13 Both documents in Coll. W.

[CHAPTER FIVE]

EARLY LIFE OF NARCISSA PRENTISS
1808–1835

Narcissa Prentiss, who became Mrs. Marcus Whitman, is one of the best-known and most-loved characters in the history of the Pacific Northwest. This is due in part to the fact that we know so much about her. Most of the 126 letters and diaries which she wrote, originals or copies of which have been located, have been published.[1] Since these writings were meant for her loved ones and not for the general public, they reveal for us her inner feelings, her hopes and fears, her joys and sorrows. Narcissa was a keen observer and has left us vivid accounts of her travels and her life at the Waiilatpu mission station in Old Oregon. Finally the fact that she suffered a martyr's death along with her husband at the hands of a small band of Cayuse Indians on November 29, 1847, has given her an added claim to fame.

In addition to Narcissa's writings, we have the reminiscences and writings of others who knew her. Fortunately for all interested in the history of the Oregon Mission of the American Board, the Board kept the correspondence received from its missionaries. These letters, estimated to contain about one million words, are now on deposit in Houghton Library, Harvard University. With but rare exceptions, all of the letters to the Board written from Oregon were by the male members of the Mission. As will be explained later, the wives of the Oregon missionaries were not permitted to vote in their business meetings, hence it was not to be expected that they would be writing to the Board.

The reminiscences of those who knew Narcissa when she was a young woman at Prattsburg show her to have been vivacious, attractive, gregarious, idealistic, and sentimentally religious.

NARCISSA'S ANCESTRY AND EARLY LIFE

Narcissa was the eldest daughter and the third child of Stephen and Clarissa Prentiss, who settled in Prattsburg, Steuben County, New York, about 1805. Her descent can be traced to Henry Prentice,[2] who migrated from England and settled at Cambridge, Massachusetts, prior to 1640. The line of descent from Henry through two Solomons and three Stephens is as follows:

Solomon (1646–1719)
Solomon (1673–1758)
Stephen (1719–)
Stephen (1744–1831)
Stephen (1777–1862)

Born at Grafton, Massachusetts, Stephen Prentiss, the father of Narcissa, apparently moved with his family while still a small boy to Walpole, New Hampshire. This Stephen was there when the first and second Federal censuses were taken in 1790 and 1800. In his early twenties, Stephen migrated to Onondaga County in western New York where he married Clarissa Ward on January 3, 1803. Evidence indicates that the second Stephen Prentiss changed the spelling of the family name from Prentice to Prentiss.[3] It appears that the change was also made in collateral branches of the family.

About two years after their marriage, Stephen and Clarissa settled in Prattsburg (originally spelled Prattsburgh), a village named after the Pratt family who were the first owners of the land and among the first settlers. Captain Joel Pratt[4] secured title to the whole township in which the village of Prattsburg is located and, in order to obtain settlers, granted favorable terms to desirable people. The fact that Stephen and Clarissa named their second-born Harvey Pratt is indicative of their respect for the Captain.

Stephen Prentiss and his family were among the earliest settlers in the whole county. The same primitive conditions existed here as at Rushville, about twenty-five miles by the road to the north. Roads were almost non-existent. There were no schools or churches. People lived in log cabins on small clearings. For a time Stephen farmed on West Hill near Prattsburg, but soon began operating a sawmill and a gristmill on the banks of the little stream which flows through Prattsburg. Stephen was a carpenter and joiner and, no doubt, used lumber from his mill to build houses for the growing community.

According to a local tradition, Stephen erected a house for his family which is still standing in Prattsburg, although not on its original site. The house measures 22 x 32 feet, is a story and a half high, thus providing bedrooms upstairs, with windows at the gable ends. The house was purchased in 1936 by interested Presbyterians when it was in danger of being razed because of its dilapidated condition. It has been restored and is now being maintained as an historic site.

It was in that unpretentious home that Narcissa was born on Monday, March 14, 1808. Narcissa is such an uncommon name that we wonder why it was chosen. Since some girls are named after flowers, as Violet and Rose, perhaps she was given the feminine form of Narcissus, i.e., Narcissa.

She had two older brothers, Stephen Turner, born in 1804, and Harvey Pratt, 1805. Six more children followed Narcissa—Jonas Galusha, 1810; Jane Abigail, 1811; Mary Ann, 1813; Clarissa, 1815; Harriet, 1818; and Edward Warren, 1820. How a family with so many children, ranging in ages from an infant to teen-agers, was able to live in such a small house without such modern conveniences as inside running water and an indoor toilet is hard to imagine. Without doubt, Narcissa, as the eldest of the girls, was obliged to accept many responsibilities in the home as soon as she was able to do so. As can be noted in her correspondence, Narcissa felt especially close to her two younger sisters, Jane and Harriet. Jane never married. Harriet married John Jackson and the couple made their home in Oberlin, Ohio; they became the parents of a daughter who was named Narcissa Whitman.[5]

NARCISSA'S FATHER, STEPHEN PRENTISS

The Rev. Joel Wakeman, to whom reference has already been made, has given us the following description of Narcissa's father in his reminiscences: "In the early spring of 1832, I became a resident of Prattsburg. I very soon made the acquaintance of Judge Stephen Prentiss, the father of Narcissa, who was then engaged in erecting the Presbyterian parsonage... He was an architect, a master builder, and followed that occupation as he had calls... He was quite tall, finely proportioned, a little inclined to corpulency... He was remarkably reticent for a man of his intelligence and standing... and it was a rare thing for him to indulge in laughter." [6]

Courthouse records at Bath show that Stephen Prentiss bought eleven acres of land in 1810 for $200.00 and a year later paid $100.00 for another ten acres, both plots being in the vicinity of Prattsburg. Stephen served at least one term as County Supervisor beginning in 1824 and for a time was Probate Judge, thus meriting the title of Judge. Narcissa was proud of this position and when she addressed letters to her father, she usually included the title: "Hon. Stephen Prentiss."

Drunkenness was not a serious problem on the American frontier in the decades immediately following the Revolutionary War, hence the churches were slow to promote temperance. One of the results of the spiritual awakening which swept the country during the first two decades of the nineteenth century was the founding of a number of such interdenominational organizations as missionary societies, Bible societies, anti-slavery societies, and temperance societies. Until the church began to prick the consciences of its members on the evils of drinking, good church members and even ministers imbibed strong liquor without the disapproval of the community. Hence it was not thought unbecoming for Judge Prentiss to run a distillery along with his mills.

The Rev. Levi Fay Waldo, a descendant of an old Prattsburg family and a relative of the Prentiss family, wrote in his reminiscences: "From my earliest recollection he was always known as Judge Prentiss, having served one term as County or Probate Judge. He carried on his business about one-half mile southeast of the public square, where he had a sawmill, a gristmill, and a distillery... My uncle, Prentiss Fay, a most excellent Christian man, worked for his uncle in the distillery, where I am told they kept the Bible depository and held mid-week prayer meetings." [7]

In 1825 or 1826 a temperance lecturer spoke in Prattsburg. Judge Prentiss attended the meeting and, according to Wakeman, left in anger "feeling that he had been personally abused and insulted." At a later date, Prentiss gave up the distillery because he became fearful of the effects of drinking on his sons. "If I remember correctly," wrote Wakeman, "the good old parson [i.e. Hotchkin] embraced the reform at that time, and also the merchant that presented him occasionally with five gallons of rum."[8]

Narcissa's Mother, Clarissa Prentiss

Wakeman, who also knew Narcissa's mother, has given us the following description of her: "Mrs. Clarissa Prentiss, the wife and mother, was quite tall and fleshy and queenly in her deportment. She was intelligent, gifted in conversation, and possessed great weight of Christian character. Her influence was potent in her family and the community. She was remarkably sedate, never excited, always master of the occasion whatever occurred. She also, like unto her husband, seldom laughed. As familiar as I was in the family, I do not remember of ever seeing her laugh."[9]

In church circles of that generation, seriousness of mien was a sign of piety. Undue laughter was considered ungodly, especially on Sunday. This attitude was a part of the Puritan inheritance which both Stephen and Clarissa had received. Narcissa resembled her mother more than she did her father. She too was "queenly in her deportment" and "gifted in conversation," but in one respect she differed from both her parents: Narcissa had a sense of humor. Her large family of adopted children at the Whitman mission in Old Oregon remembered how often she sang and laughed.

The Church at Prattsburg

Captain Joel Pratt's nephew, Jared Pratt, settled at what became Prattsburg with his family in 1800. The Captain and his family followed a few years later. The Pratts were devout Congregationalists as were most of the pioneer settlers of that community. In order that a church might be established with sufficient financial resources, Captain Pratt required every purchaser of one hundred acres of land to pay fifteen dollars annually to the church. A Congregational Church was organized on June 26, 1804, and like the Congregational Church of Rushville, came under the Congregational-Presbyterian Plan of Union. In 1809 the Rev. James H. Hotchkin, a Congregational minister, became the church's second pastor. The church thrived under his ministry and had 240 members when he resigned in 1830. Both the pastor and the church joined the local presbytery, although the church, as did the one in Rushville, retained the Congregational form of government. In Narcissa's first letter to the American Board, dated February 23, 1835, she said: "I... united with the Congregational church in that place [i.e., Prattsburg]."

Because of complications arising out of the Plan of Union which had been adopted by the Congregational and Presbyterian Churches in 1801, some ministers and some congregations on the frontier were caught in a period of indecision, not knowing which way to go. The Rev. James H. Hotchkin, who was pastor of the Prattsburg church when Narcissa Prentiss and Henry Spalding were members, was a New School Presbyterian. The church, however, followed Congregational polity in its local government and did not vote to be fully Presbyterian until 1839. In view of this final decision, this church will hereafter be referred to as being Presbyterian, although in fact it was "Presbygational."

Church Life in Prattsburg

A rectangular meeting house, 22 x 32 feet, was erected in Prattsburg in 1807. This was the same size as the Prentiss home, and, no doubt, Stephen Prentiss was the builder. Two years later, about the time that Hotchkin became pastor, an eighteen-foot addition was built at one end. The church thrived under the ministry of the new pastor. In 1820 the building was enlarged again when the rectangular structure was sawn into two parts, from end to end, through the middle and the two sections separated by eleven feet. The intervening space was then built up anew, thus giving an auditorium 33 x 50 feet. This building satisfied the needs of the congregation for about seven years; then it was razed, and a more spacious structure was erected in 1828.

The reminiscences of two men who remembered the old Prattsburg church are extant. S. W. Pratt wrote: "This church was never, either in its exterior or interior appointments, much of a feast to the lover of fair architectural proportions. Painting never adorned it."[10] Joel Wakeman commented: "The old church with its naked floor, box pews, tallow candles, and the old oval pulpit, elevated eight feet above the floor and perched up against the wall like a robin's nest," was the center of the community. The church had a "circular gallery."[11] Since the church was unheated, the women in wintertime took with them small charcoal burning foot-warmers. The men bore the cold as best they could while the pastor preached wearing a heavy overcoat and mittens.

In that plain unpainted wooden building, lighted in the evenings by tallow candles, the Spirit of God moved the hearts of the people. The members of the church took their religion seriously. Sunday, or Sabbath, observance was one of the main outward signs of their faith. Since Sunday began at sundown on Saturday, the Prattsburg Church on October 11, 1808, voted: "That the members of the church will not attend raisings or other similar associations on Saturday in the afternoon."[12] The reference to "raisings" was to gatherings of neighbors who met to help one of their number raise logs for a log cabin. These were popular social events on the raw frontier and, if liquor was available, sometimes degenerated into a raucous party. Hence the church forbade raisings on Saturday afternoon for fear that such might violate the decorum which was supposed to be observed with the coming of the Sabbath at sundown.

Narcissa's mother took the lead in the religious interests of her home. She joined the Prattsburg Church in 1807 but her husband did not do so until 1817.[13] Waldo recalled the interest the Prentiss family took in music. "Judge Prentiss and all his family were singers," he wrote. "My earliest recollections of him are as choir leader, setting the tone with an old-fashioned pitch pipe, and now and then giving it a toot between the stanzas to make sure that they were keeping up to the pitch."

However, the minutes of the church show that judge Prentiss was not always directing the choir for the Sunday services. According to an item dated April 14, 1828, Judge Prentiss was asked to explain why he had absented himself from the Presbyterian Church in order to worship with the Methodists. The record states: "His reasons were: he was best edified in attending with the Methodists, and was not wholly pleased with the administration in this church particularly with respect to discipline."[14]

Possibly the reference to the "discipline" of the Presbyterian Church is to an action taken by the Presbytery of Bath on August 28, 1828, in regard to Freemasonry. The Presbytery, moved no doubt by the strong anti-Masonic agitation of that time in western New York, declared that

CHAPTER FIVE *Early Life of Narcissa Prentiss, 1808–1835*

Freemasonry was "hostile" to the interests of the Church of Christ," and called upon all members of churches within its jurisdiction to "abandon the institution." Although we do not have positive proof that Judge Prentiss was a Mason, circumstantial evidence supports the theory. The Methodists were more lenient and permitted their members to belong to the lodge. Therefore, on May 5, 1829, Judge Prentiss joined the Methodist Church of Prattsburg and for more than eighteen months the church affiliations of the Prentiss family were divided. Then, according to the records of the Presbyterian Church, the judge on January 19, 1831, confessed his "fault" and was received back into the Presbyterian fold.

NARCISSA AND THE CHURCH

The very first entry in the record of baptisms of the Prattsburg Church is the following: "Lord's Day, July 17th, 1808, Baptized by Rev. Solomon Allen Willis... Narcissa Prentiss, daughter of Stephen Prentiss." Since the Prattsburg Church at that time had no resident minister, a Congregational pastor from a nearby town was asked to officiate. Two baby boys were baptized at the same time. Narcissa was then a little over four months old. She grew up under the ministry of the Rev. James H. Hotchkin who has been described as being: "An admirable specimen of the clergy of the olden time... was educated, correct, dignified, genial, orthodox; and when he fell a-preaching or a-praying, kept straight on to the end of his subject, without the slightest regard to the whims of his congregation, or the tokens of passing time." [15]

Writing in his old age, Hotchkin gave the following account of a religious revival which was experienced in the Prattsburg church during the winter of 1818–19, and which reached a climax in February: "The first Sabbath in that month was a day of unusual solemnity. At an appointed weekly meeting, the house of worship was filled to overflowing... Individuals were seen trembling on their seats, and the silent tear trickling down their cheeks... Nothing was heard but the voice of the speaker imparting instructions, addressing exhortation to the assembly, or lifting up the prayer unto God. More than thirty, it is believed, were born again during that eventful week." [16] Hotchkin tells that all the converts won in this revival were received into the church on the first Sunday of the following June. On that June 6, 1819, "fifty-nine individuals stood before a great congregation" and made their public confession of faith. People came from neighboring towns for the occasion. Since the attendance was too large for the seating capacity of the church, the meeting was held out-of-doors in a grove of trees, perhaps on the village commons. The weather was perfect. Hotchkin took for his text, Isaiah 53:11: "He shall see of the travail of his soul, and shall be satisfied." The text reveals the joy Hotchkin felt upon that auspicious occasion.

Among the new members welcomed that day was golden-haired Narcissa Prentiss, then eleven years old. Her two older brothers, Stephen and Harvey, were with her. By an interesting coincidence a revival was held about the same time in Plainfield, Massachusetts, where Marcus Whitman also experienced a spiritual awakening. About five years later, when Narcissa was nearly sixteen, she had another religious experience which led her to give herself to the missionary cause. Of this she wrote in her first letter to the American Board: "I frequently desired to go to the heathen but only half-heartedly and it was not till the first Monday of Jan. 1824 that I felt to consecrate myself without reserve to the Missionary work waiting the leadings of Providence concerning me." This must have been an impressive experience since Narcissa, eleven years later, was able to recall the exact day it had occurred.

Years later, Catherine Sager, one of the orphaned children raised by the Whitmans at their mission station, asked her foster mother what had led her to want to be a missionary. Narcissa replied by saying that she had been deeply moved by reading the life of Harriet Boardman, a pioneer American Board missionary to India.[17] Once while writing to her sister Harriet from her mission station in Old Oregon, Narcissa asked: "What books do you read? Do you comfort Ma by reading to her such books as Dwight's Theology, Dodridge's Rise and Progress, Milner's Church History, etc., as Narcissa used to do in her younger days?" [Letter 81]. The works here mentioned were then required reading by candidates for the ministry. No doubt Narcissa had borrowed the books from her pastor's library. Any person who dips into such writings today finds them heavy reading. But those were serious-minded days.

Repeatedly in the reminiscences of those who knew Narcissa come references to her singing. Levi Fay Waldo, a Prattsburg boy who became a Congregational minister, wrote: "She seems to have been peculiarly gifted in speech, and especially in prayer and song. I well remember her clear sweet voice, as a leading soprano, in the old church at home."[18] And Wakeman wrote: "Her voice was an important factor in the social prayer meeting and missionary concerts that were held monthly in those days."[19] The word "concert" was then commonly applied to a prayer meeting when people joined in concerted prayer.

Years later in distant Oregon, natives sometimes traveled many miles just to hear Narcissa Whitman sing. In a letter to her mother dated March 30, 1847, she wrote: "While I was at Vancouver, one Indian woman came a great distance with her daughter, as she said, to hear me sing with the children." The Cayuse Indians at Waiilatpu felt the charm of that same voice, so much so that Narcissa wrote: "I was not aware that singing was a qualification of so much importance to a missionary" [Letter 40].

Wakeman tells of a revival which occurred in Prattsburg in the summer and fall of 1832 during the ministry of the Rev. George R. Rudd, who followed Hotchkin as pastor of the Prattsburg Church in 1830. During the summer months, sunrise prayer meetings were held in which the Prentiss family took an active part. Of Narcissa's participation, Wakeman wrote: "No one devoted more time in personal efforts to win souls to Christ than Narcissa. There are some still living who can trace their first serious impressions to her charming singing and tender appeals to yield to the overtures of mercy... She had a clear, strong voice, and by cultivation it was under perfect control and as sweet and musical as a chime of bells."

A good index of the vitality of the Prattsburg Church, which played so important a role in the life of Narcissa Prentiss, is the long list of sons and daughters of the church who entered full-time Christian service. Up to 1876 the church boasted of having sent twenty-six men into the ministry and "not far from a score of ministers' wives have also gone out from this church."[20] Most of this number belonged to Narcissa's generation. As will be noted, Henry H. Spalding, who was born in Wheeler, November 26, 1803, spent his boyhood in a foster home near Prattsburg. He was a member of the Prattsburg Church and attended the same academy as did Narcissa. He is numbered among the twenty-six young men who entered the ministry.

With a growing family, Stephen Prentiss found that the house in which his older children, including Narcissa, had been born had become too small. At some unknown date, he either bought or built "a large two story frame house" located on the west side of the village square. The Prentiss home became the center for many happy gatherings of young people. Narcissa was vivacious and popular. Sometimes her mother would say: "I wish Narcissa would not always have so much company." Years later when Narcissa found her Oregon home crowded with guests, she felt moved to write: "It is well for me now that I have had so much experience in waiting upon company, and I can do it when necessary without considering it a great task" [Letter 78J.

Narcissa's Education

Throughout the centuries the Christian church has been the mother of schools, and this has been especially true of Congregationalism and Presbyterianism. The pioneers of Prattsburg were as much concerned about having proper educational facilities as they were in having a church. As early as 1812 a school was built next to the church. Advanced pupils were taken into the home of the pastor, James H. Hotchkin. As the population of the town increased, a movement was launched in 1823 to raise money through voluntary gifts and taxes to build an academy. Stephen Prentiss was one of the most active promoters of the project and became a member of the first Board of Trustees. The school was called Franklin Academy in honor of Benjamin Franklin. A building 32 x 54 feet, two stories high, "surmounted with a cupola and belfry," was opened in 1824. It stood next to the church. At first the academy was only for boys but when the building was enlarged in 1827 by adding rooms at either end of the original structure, a "female department" was opened.

The records of Franklin Academy and Collegiate Institute show that Narcissa was a student there for the term ending April 6, 1828, when thirty-four boys and twenty-eight girls were enrolled. The tuition fee was $6.00 for a term of twenty-one weeks. Another tuition record for the term ending September 28, 1831, lists the names of fifty-four young men, including Henry H. Spalding, and forty-six young women, including Narcissa Prentiss. Thus for at least one term Henry and Narcissa were fellow students. He would have been twenty-eight and she, twenty-three.

Narcissa Rejects Spalding's Proposal for Marriage

In a letter to her father dated October 10, 1840, and written from her mission station at Waiilatpu, Narcissa said: "The man who came with us is one who never ought to have come. My dear husband has suffered more from him in consequence of his wicked jealousy, and his great pique towards me, than can be known in this world." The context of the remark clearly indicates that she was referring to Spalding. Light on the reason for this comment is found in a letter that Narcissa's sister, Harriet, wrote on January 11, 1893, to an Oregon author, Mrs. Eva Emery Dye. Regarding Spalding, Harriet wrote: "He was a student when a young man in Franklin Academy, Prattsburg, the place of our nativity, and he wished to make Narcissa his wife, and her refusal of him caused the wicked feeling he cherished towards them both." [21] The consequences of Narcissa's rejection of Henry's proposal for marriage were far-reaching, as shall be noted later.

Narcissa Teaches School

Extant records do not permit us to reconstruct with accuracy the events in Narcissa's life from April 1828, when she completed her work in Franklin Academy, and June 1834 when the Prentiss family moved to Amity in Allegany County which adjoins Steuben County on the west. Waldo stated that Narcissa studied in Mrs. Emma Willard's famous "Female Seminary" at Troy, New York, but did not indicate when nor for how long.[22] Mrs. Willard, 1787–1870, had founded her school in 1821; it soon attracted students from all parts of the East. Within fifty years more than 13,000 young women had studied there.[23] The school specialized in the training of teachers; it was what we would now call a normal school. Mrs. Willard, a woman of commanding personality, left a deep impression upon the girls who studied under her direction. She wrote on many subjects, was interested in such reform mevements as temperance, and was the author of "Rocked in the Cradle of the Deep."

After completing such training as was available, Narcissa, according to Wakeman, "taught district schools several years with marked success." [24] One of her former pupils, O. P. Fay, writing his reminiscences for a Prattsburg newspaper in 1898, stated: "I well remember Marcus Whitman's wife, Narcissa Prentiss; she taught our district school when I was quite a lad, and she seemed to me then as a woman of rare abilities, with qualifications sufficient to teach in any academy instead of a common school... She had a class in natural philosophy [term then used to designate a science course] and wanted to start one in chemistry also, but that was more than we could venture to try until we had graduated in philosophy. She taught the best school of any teacher in our district." [25] For a time Narcissa taught a kindergarten in Bath, and Marcus, in a letter to Jane Prentiss, refers to Narcissa teaching in Butler[26] [Letter 109].

This is all that is known of the background of Narcissa Prentiss who, on February 18, 1836, was married to Dr. Marcus Whitman. From the information available, we see her as an attractive light auburn-haired young woman, well educated for her generation, highly literate in her writings, one who loved to entertain company, an able school teacher, and above all one deeply religious who dreamed of being some day a missionary. If contemporary accounts show her to have been rather sentimental in her religious beliefs and activities, let us remember that this was characteristic of church life of her time. Narcissa's later letters, written from her lonely mission station in Old Oregon, carry frequent nostalgic references to the "melting seasons" [i.e., when people would weep for their sins] which were characteristic of the revival meetings held in the Prattsburg church.

Although often dreaming of being a missionary, Narcissa had little opportunity to know what such a career entailed, especially among the American Indians. The foreign missionary work of the church was still too new for objective appraisals to have been made. Such books about missionary activities as were available often gave an unrealistic and idealized picture. No doubt Narcissa's best source of information was the American Board's official publication, the *Missionary Herald*. An examination of the file of this magazine for the years 1820–36 reveals the fact that very little information was given about work with the American Indians. Thus Narcissa, when she did offer to go as a missionary to the Indians of Old Oregon, was woefully uninformed.

Are Females Wanted?

Wakeman tells us that the residents of Prattsburg were troubled in the spring of 1834 when they learned that the Prentiss family was to move to Amity. The residence of twenty-eight or more years was to be terminated. We are not told why Judge Prentiss decided to move, but perhaps it was because Amity was a new community where a number of houses were to be erected. Prentiss, as a carpenter, may have been attracted by these business opportunities. Amity, now known as Belmont, lies about forty miles southwest of Prattsburg.

A Presbyterian Church had been organized at Amity on January 30, 1833. For nine years, the small congregation held its services in a log schoolhouse. During the years 1833–35, the Rev. Samuel May served as a part-time pastor. On April 27, 1834, the Prattsburg church granted letters of dismissal to Stephen and Clarissa Prentiss and to their children, Jonas G., Narcissa, Clarissa, Harriet, and Edward, "to join the Presbyterian Church in Amity, N.Y." In the early spring of 1835, the Rev. Oliver S. Powell, a brother-in-law, became pastor of the Amity church. For a time both the Mays and the Powells seriously considered going to Old Oregon as missionaries.

In the latter part of November 1834, the Rev. Samuel Parker arrived in Amity to make his appeal for missionaries and money for his proposed Oregon mission. If Wheeler had been an unlikely place to find an associate to go with him to Oregon, Amity was even more so. At a meeting held in the log schoolhouse, Parker repeated the message he had given at Wheeler. He told about the long trip "the Wise Men from the West" had made to St. Louis to get the white man's Bible. He told of his trip to St. Louis during the preceding summer and of his intention to go to the Rockies in the spring of 1835. He explained how the American Board had authorized him to find associates, and no doubt told of his visit to Wheeler where Dr. Whitman had volunteered.

Narcissa Prentiss was present that evening when Parker spoke. His appeal for missionaries found her in as receptive a mood as Marcus Whitman had been. For years she too had considered the possibility of going to some foreign land as a missionary and was, therefore, prepared to respond to the appeal that Parker made. After the meeting, Narcissa asked Parker: "Is there a place for an unmarried female in my Lord's vineyard?"

Parker was not sure about the designs of Providence, and was doubtful about the readiness of the Board to appoint a single woman as a missionary. The foreign missionary program of all American Protestant denominations was still so new that their mission boards failed to appreciate the value of unmarried women. Parker was looking for men and was unprepared to find a young woman responding to his appeal. In a letter to the American Board dated December 17, 1834, he asked: "Are females wanted? A Miss Narcissa Prentiss of Amity is very anxious to go to the heathen. Her education is good—piety conspicuous—her influence is good. She will offer herself if needed."

From Amity Parker drove a few miles to the west and repeated his message in the Presbyterian Church of Cuba where another single woman offered to go, a Miss McCoy. On January 1, 1835, Parker again wrote to the Board and explained why he had been cautious in giving either Miss Prentiss or Miss McCoy any hope of an appointment. He wrote: "I think I said nothing about their going among the Indians, or to any particular part of the world, but only that they would offer themselves if their services were needed. I recollect that I told them if they offered themselves, it must be to go anywhere the Board should choose."

Secretary Greene, replying to Parker's letter of December 17, wrote on the 24th: "I don't think we have missions among the Indians where unmarried females are valuable just now." Parker must have been rather discouraging in the advice he gave to the two young women, as Greene, in his letter to Parker of January 7, 1835, stated that neither had made application for an appointment. So the matter rested with Narcissa until Marcus Whitman spent the week-end of February 22 with the Powells at Amity—and then everything was changed.

MARCUS AND NARCISSA BECOME ENGAGED

As has been stated in the preceding chapter, when Whitman received Greene's letter of January 7, 1835, telling him of his appointment as an "Assistant Missionary" to accompany Samuel Parker on his exploring tour to the Rockies, he rode to Ithaca to consult with Parker regarding their plans. While visiting Parker, Whitman learned that Narcissa Prentiss of Amity had also volunteered to go to Oregon as a missionary. According to Samuel J. Parker, Jr., his father at that time suggested to Whitman that he call on Narcissa and propose marriage.[27] There seems to be no doubt but that by this time Marcus knew Narcissa. Their common interest in church activities could have brought them together after Whitman's first visit in the Prentiss home in Prattsburg.

Parker's suggestion struck a responsive chord in Whitman's heart for he had long been thinking about getting married. In his letter of June 3, 1834, to the Board he had written: "I think I should wish to take a wife, if the service of the Board would admit." It is easy to imagine Whitman reasoning that if both he and Narcissa Prentiss were offering their services to the American Board to go as missionaries to the Indians of Oregon, then Providence might be intending that they go as husband and wife.

In all probability Marcus wrote to Narcissa telling her of his appointment and of his intention to start overland for St. Louis on February 9, and that it would not be out of his way to call on her should she welcome the visit. There is some evidence to indicate that Parker also wrote to Narcissa telling her of possible developments. If such suppositions be valid, then there would have been time for Narcissa to have replied. Whatever was the background, this we know—Whitman had made definite plans to visit Amity and call on Narcissa before he left Rushville on January 19.

After his return from Ithaca, Whitman closed out his business affairs at Wheeler and then went to Rushvile to say farewell to his mother and other relatives and to await final instructions from Greene. The expected letter, dated February 9, was received on Thursday, the 19th. Whitman left that day for Amity where he arrived sometime on the following Saturday and was received as a guest in the Powell home.

Just why Narcissa was not married when she was approaching her twenty-seventh birthday is not known. By the standards of that generation, she was already considered to be an old maid. From the descriptions given by her contemporaries of her attractiveness and accomplishments, we may safely assume that she had had proposals for marriage but had rejected them, including that of Henry H. Spalding.

We do not have any account of Whitman's visit to Amity or just how or when he asked Narcissa to be his wife. After her marriage in February 1836, Narcissa explained to Mrs. Parker: "We had to make love somewhat abruptly and must do our courtship now we are married."[28] Undoubtedly their common desire to be missionaries to the Indians of Oregon was a bond which drew them together. To them, a kindly Providence had brought them together; God had called them to be husband and wife to serve in the same field.

After becoming engaged sometime during that week-end of February 22, Marcus and Narcissa had to make some quick and important decisions. Marcus encouraged Narcissa to make immediate application to the Board for an appointment. The two discussed the question as to when they might be married. Since the Powells had received word of their appointment by the American Board to the Pawnee Mission and were planning to leave that spring for their field, Marcus and Narcissa discussed the possibility of her traveling to the Missouri frontier with them. Then as soon as Marcus returned from his exploring journey to the Rockies, they could be married. Everything, however, was indefinite. For the time being, it was enough to know that they loved each other and that someday they would be married.

NARCISSA PRENTISS APPOINTED BY THE AMERICAN BOARD

On Monday morning, February 23, Marcus mounted his horse and headed for St. Louis. On that same day Narcissa sent the following letter of application to the American Board:

Dear Brethren:

Permit an unworthy sister to address you. Having found favour of the Lord and desiring to live for the conversion of the world, I now offer myself to the American Board to be employed in their service among the heathen, if counted worthy. As it is requested of me to make some statements concerning myself, I shall endeavour to be as brief as possible, knowing the value of your time, especially now under the late *afflictive bereavement*. [29]

My native place is Prattsburg, Steuben County. I was born March 14, A.D. 1808. In the beginning of the year 1819 a precious revival of religion was witnessed in Prattsburg. I became a subject of the work, united with the Congregational church in that place and remained a member of it fifteen years. My advantages for acquiring an education have been good, having been situated near Franklin Academy—and most of the time when not attending school have been engaged in teaching. My last effort in teaching was an Infant School in which I took great delight. My brothers and sisters, nine in number, with our parents, have all united with the same church. In June last we removed to Amity, Allegheny County, where we now reside.

In relation to my feelings upon the subject of mission, I will say but little. From my conversion I have felt a particular interest for the salvation of the heathen, and an increasing desire for information on the subject and have not neglected to gratify that desire: but from time to time, with peculiar feelings, greeted the arrival of the Missionary Herald.[30] I frequently desired to go to the heathen but only half-heartedly—and it was not till the first Monday of Jan. 1824 that I felt to consecrate myself without reserve to the Missionary work waiting the leadings of Providence concerning me.

Feeling it more my privilege than duty to labour for the conversion of the heathen, I respectfully submit myself to your direction and subscribe,

Your unworthy sister in the Lord,

Narcissa Prentiss.

This, the first of Narcissa's extant letters, was written in a clear hand on pale green paper. On the back of the letter are three short testimonials. The Rev. Samuel W. May, who signed himself, "Minister of Angelica," wrote: "Having been acquainted for some time with Miss Narcissa Prentiss—I therefore most cheerfully recommend her to your Board as well qualified for usefulness in instructing the heathen in the way to Heaven." The Rev. William Bridgman, pastor of the Cuba Presbyterian Church, wrote: "...from a personal acquaintance with Miss Prentiss, I do consider her well qualified for usefulness in that station." And the Rev. Oliver S. Powell stated: "I fully concur in the above recommendations... I am happy in the prospect of having so efficient a fellow labourer in the missionary service."

Powell then added the following illuminating footnotes: "As it is probable that Miss Prentiss will hereafter become the companion of Doct. Marcus Whitman (should he be established missionary beyond the Rocky Mts.) it may be proper to add that he expressed a desire that she might accompany us on our mission as it will be a field of usefulness & an opportunity for [her] becoming acquainted with the labors of a missionary." In other words, Powell was suggesting that Narcissa also be assigned to the Pawnee Mission until Whitman would be able to return from his exploring tour.

A few weeks after Whitman had left for St. Louis, Mrs. Powell discovered that she was pregnant. Under the circumstances, the Powells felt that for the time being it would not be wise for them to undertake missionary work. Narcissa hastened to inform Marcus of the new developments. On April 30, 1835, Marcus replied writing from Liberty, Missouri: "I had not given up the hope that you would have been able to come on with Mr. Powell until I received your letter. I regret very much that he did not come... Had I known one half as much of the trip as I now do, when I left you, I should have been entirely willing, if not anxious, that you should have accompanied me."

The original copy of this letter is not known to be extant. A copy appeared in Mowry's *Marcus Whitman*. Mowry stated that Narcissa had written on the margin of the letter: "Mr. Parker said I could go just as well as not. N. Prentiss."[31] This is a puzzling statement. Did Narcissa, at the time she heard Parker speak in her church, then discuss with him the possibility of her going with the Powells to the Pawnees? Or could it be that Parker wrote to Narcissa from Ithaca, after talking with Whitman, and suggested the possibility of the two getting married and for her to go then with Marcus to the Missouri frontier. If so, then it was Marcus who prudently urged a delay. He wanted to see if it were wise to take a wife on such a long journey not only to the Missouri frontier but also across the plains to the Rockies.

Narcissa's letter of application with its several endorsements was sent to Parker, who, on March 5, forwarded it to the Board with a letter of his own. He wrote: "I enclose Miss Narcissa Prentiss' offer of herself to become a missionary. I have for some time been acquainted with Judge Prentiss' family. Their standing as intelligent Christians in public estimation is *good*. Narcissa's education, talents, person, disposition, conciliatory manners, and sound judgment promise well for usefullness in a mission field."

Acting upon Narcissa's letter of application together with the testimonials and the information that she and Marcus Whitman were engaged, the Prudential Committee of the Board approved her appointment on March 18, 1835. In the letter of notification sent to her, nothing was said about her destination. It seemed to have been understood that she was to wait until Marcus had returned.

Chapter 5 Endnotes

1 See Appendix I for list of letters written by Narcissa Whitman.

2 W.C.Q. I (1897):8:27 ff, contains an article on the Prentiss Family by the Rev. Levi Fay Waldo, who was once a resident of Prattsburg.

3 C. F. J. Binney, *History and Genealogy of the Prentice or Prentiss Family*, 2nd ed., Boston, 1883, p. 75, claims that Stephen was born at Walpole, N.H. Ross Woodbridge, drew my attention to *Vital Records of Grafton, Massachusetts*, p. 106, which states that this Stephen Prentiss was born at Grafton, Mass. He has also provided information from tombstones found in the old cemetery at Walpole regarding the change of the spelling of the family name. Warren Prentiss, a great-nephew of Narcissa Prentiss Whitman, of Palos Verdes Peninsula, Calif., has also supplied genealogical information about the Prentiss family.

4 Joel Pratt had a brother Jared, who was an ancestor of the Mormon Apostles, Orson and Parley P. Pratt.

5 Sometime before 1891, Harriet Prentiss Jackson gave a collection of letters written by her sister Narcissa to the Oregon Historical Society in Portland. Most of these were published in the 1891 and 1893 issues of the *Transactions of the Oregon Pioneer Association*. See Appendix I.

6 Wakeman ms., Coll. Wn. Copy in *Prattsburg News*, Jan. 20, 1898. See Drury, *Whitman*, p. 72 for picture of the manse built by Prentiss.

7 *W.C.Q.*, I(1897) 3:26.

8 Wakeman ms., Coll. Wn.

9 *Ibid.*

10 S. W. Pratt, *History of the Presbyterian Church of Prattsburg*, 1876, pp. 5–6.

11 Wakeman ms., Coll. Wn.

12 James A. Miller, *Presbyterianism in Steuben and Allegany*, Angelica, N.Y., 1897, p. 54.

13 From original Prattsburg Presbyterian Church records.

14 *Ibid.*

15 Miller, op. cit., p. 69.

16 J H. Hotchkin published his *A History of the Purchase and Settlement of Western New York, and of the Rise, Progress, and present state of the Presbyterian Church in that Section*, in New York in 1848. The quotation here given is from p. 465.

17 See article by Catherine Sager Pringle in Mary Osborn Douthit (ed.) *Souvenir of Western Women*, Portland, 1905. No copy of a life of Harriet Boardman, either in book, pamphelt, or magazine article form, has been located.

18 *W.C.Q.*, II (1898):1:38. Waldo was a Congregational minister in Canon City, Cob., at the time he wrote his memories of Narcissa Whitman. He also stated: "She could offer up the finest petition to the Throne of Grace of any person I ever heard in my life."

19 Wakeman ms., Coll. Wn. *Prattsburg News*, August 10, 1893.

20 *Prattsburg News*, January 27, 1898. Among the members of the church who became a Presbyterian minister was David Mailin, who served as pastor of a prominent church in Philadelphia. Later, out in Old Oregon, Narcissa was to give his name to a forlorn lad, half-Spanish and half-Indian, whom the Whitmans took into their home.

21 Original letter in Coll. O. While gathering material for my Spalding book, I consulted with Miss Charlotte Howe of Prattsburg, who was well informed on the town's history. She strongly rejected the idea that Spalding was a rejected suitor of Narcissa's and asked for proof. At that time I was unaware of Harriet's letter. Having discovered the letter before my *Marcus Whitman* was published, I made a correction in that book. See p. 84.

22 *W.C.Q.*, II (1898):1:39.

23 A. W. Fairbanks, *Emma Willard and her Pupils*, New York, 1898, makes no mention of her students before 1843, hence no record of Narcissa Prentiss.

24 *Prattsburg News*, January 27, 1898.

25 *Ibid.*, January 16, 1898.

26 See Drury, *Whitman*, p. 85, for details about Narcissa's "infant school" at Bath.

27 Parker ms., Cornell University Library.

28 W.C.Q., II (1898):3:13.

29 Italics indicate words underlined in the original letter. The reference is to the death of Secretary B. B. Wisner which was mentioned in Greene's letter to Whitman of February 9, 1835, which Marcus showed to Narcissa.

30 The Board's official publication, the *Missionary Herald*, included in each of its monthly issues extracts from letters received from its missionaries. During the period of the Oregon Mission, 183–47, lengthy extracts from the Oregon missionaries were published.

31 *Op. cit.*, p. 56.

[CHAPTER SIX]

WHITMAN'S FIRST JOURNEY TO THE ROCKIES
1835

When Marcus Whitman left Amity on that Monday morning, February 23, 1835, he was making his first entry as an actor on the Old Oregon stage. For more than twelve years, or until his tragic death on November 29, 1847, he was destined to play a leading role in the stirring events which were to take place in the Pacific Northwest. Whitman made three journeys across the plains to the Rockies. This, the first, came in 1835. He retraced the route with his wife and the Spaldings in 1836, and again with the first great wagon train to go to Oregon in 1843.

Upon the advice of Parker, Whitman drew on the American Board for $100.00 for expenses. After his arrival at Liberty, Missouri, Whitman wrote to the Board on May 13 saying in part: "...I have expended in the following manner: about $30 expenses of traveling to St. Louis, seven dollars lost from my pocket with my wallet; sixty-one of the remainder I have expended for some additional clothing & articles of goods & medicines to carry with us, & in part to pay expenses." This indicates that the actual travel costs of the thirty-seven days horseback ride from Amity to St. Louis was less than one dollar a day.

Since Whitman had informed Greene of his desire to visit relatives and friends in Ohio and Illinois [Letter 6], we can trace in some detail the approximate route he followed. After leaving Amity, he rode west until he came to the Buffalo-Cleveland highway. In all probability Whitman reached Erie, Pennsylvania, before Sunday, March 1. Since he was loath to travel on Sunday, he probably spent the day resting and in attending church. From Erie, Whitman rode to Kirkland, Ohio. There he must have seen the new Mormon temple then being erected; it is still standing. In 1835 the growing cult of Mormonism was a main topic of conversation throughout the area.

At Kirkland, Whitman turned to the left and rode seven miles south to the small crossroads community of Chester, about ten miles south of Cleveland, where he visited a number of relatives and friends. Within a few years after Whitman's return to Rushville from Plainfield, Massachusetts, a migration had begun to the Western Reserve in northeastern Ohio. It had caught up many of the people he had known in Cummington and Plainfield. Among those who had migrated were Freedom Whitman and his wife; two of Beza Whitman's sisters and their families; and Colonel and Mrs. John Packard.[1] No wonder that Whitman, on his westward journey in 1835, took time to call on his relatives and friends at Chester whom he had not seen for about fifteen years. After leaving Chester, Whitman rode westward to Danville, Illinois, which is about 125 miles south of Chicago, where he was a guest in the home of his brother Samuel.[2] In that home was a five-year-old boy named Perrin Beza, the son of Samuel, who had been named after his two grandfathers; we shall hear of him later.

WHITMAN'S OFFICIAL COMMISSION

Whitman received at St. Louis a communication from Secretary Greene which contained his official commission, dated February 17, 1835, and the Board's final instructions. The commission was a certificate, which measures about eight by ten inches, with an engraved picture in top center.[3] The illustration epitomized the Board's philosophy of foreign missions. In the center of the picture is a sailing ship presumably arriving in some foreign port with the morning sun appearing above the distant horizon. In the foreground are some palm trees which suggest a tropical climate. On either side of the harbor are buildings, including some which represent Hindu temples. In the immediate foreground is a group of forty or more natives who, with outstretched arms, appear to be welcoming the arrival of the Christian missionaries supposedly aboard the ship. Beneath the picture is the verse from Isaiah 9:2 (King James version): "The people that walked in darkness have seen a great light: they that dwell in the land of the shadow of death, upon them hath the light shined."

After the printed inscription: "This is to certify that" comes the penned statement: "Doct. Marcus Whitman is an assistant missionary to the Indian tribes West of the State of Missouri." Whitman was not commissioned as a "missionary," for that classification was then reserved for ordained men. Instead he was called an "assistant missionary." The January 1838 issue of the *Missionary Herald* listed him as "Physician" and in following years as "Physician and Catechist." The wives of the missionaries of the American Board were not then officially commissioned.

Differences Arise Between Whitman And Parker

Whitman arrived in St. Louis on April 1, whereas Parker, who had left Ithaca on March 14 traveling by stage to Pittsburgh and from there by river boat, did not arrive until the 4th. The two men called upon the officials of the American Fur Company and secured permission to travel with the Company's caravan across the plains and the Rockies to the Rendezvous, which was to be held that year on the Green River in what is now western Wyoming. The caravan was to be under the command of Lucien Fontenelle,[4] 1800–1840. Whitman and Parker left St. Louis on April 8 on the steamboat Siam for Liberty on the western Missouri frontier, near present-day Kansas City. The boat trip between these two points was usually made in seven or eight days, but this time because of an accident, the Siam took two weeks.

Since the Fur Company's caravan was not to leave Liberty until May 14, Whitman and Parker had about three weeks in which to purchase their animals, assemble equipment, and complete other necessary arrangements. At first Whitman deferred to Parker's judgment regarding what should be purchased. This was to be expected, as Parker was fifty-six years old and Whitman, thirty-three. Moreover, Parker was the one who had initiated and promoted the exploring mission. He had already made one journey to St. Louis and was presumably better informed on what was needed for overland travel.

Differences of opinion, however, soon arose between the two men over what should be purchased. Parker, who knew from personal experience the difficulty of raising money for missions, was far too parsimonious. Whitman turned to Fontenelle for advice. None of Whitman's contemporary letters reveal the extent of the differences of opinion between him and Parker over this question. Several years later, when Whitman learned of some criticisms that Parker had passed on to the Board regarding the costs of the Oregon Mission, he was moved to write a long and revealing letter in which he gave some sharp criticisms of Parker [Letter 62].

Writing to Greene on May 10, 1839, Whitman frankly stated: "...as you introduce Rev. Samuel Parker as authority for supposing we might have saved expense, I will venture to make a few statements respecting his policy in this Country, & in his general tour of exploring. When he joined me at St. Louis, I thought he must know all that was required for our journey as he had been out before & made inquiry, so that I committed all arrangements to him. He said that our personal baggage must not exceed fifty pounds & in this he wished to include everything necessary to be carried, viz clothing, stationary, books, Medicines, Instruments, Ammunition, Goods for trading supplies, &c, &c. We made our arrangements accordingly, as near as possible. In the purchase of animals, he limited us to one apiece for riding, & one for packing which we bought. Mr. P. took one to ride to Fort Leavenworth about thirty miles, & injured his [i.e., the horse's] back so that he was unfit for the journey. He then sold him & bought another. Fearing the consequences of such an accident when we might be remote from the means of other supplies, I tried to persuade him to purchase another animal, but to no effect, & so we started with but three to cross the Rocky Mountains. One mule was to pack all the provisions necessary to take on that long route, including the above items of clothing, &c., besides cooking furniture, bedding, tent, axe, &c One of the items taken was Samuel Parker's saddle case which is now at Whitman College. This is a cylindrical leather bag, approximately 22½" long by 10½" in diameter and is marked on one end: "Rev. S. Parker, Ithaca." [5]

While still at Liberty, Whitman and Parker met the Rev. Moses Merrill, a Baptist missionary who had established a mission among the Oto Indians on the north bank of the Platte River about eight miles west of Bellevue in 1834. Merrill had gone to Liberty with an ox drawn wagon for supplies and was planning to return with Fontenelle. Bellevue lay on the west bank of the Missouri about twenty miles south of present-day

Omaha, Nebraska. Fontenelle, with between fifty and sixty men, about two hundred horses and mules, six wagons, and three ox teams, left Liberty for Bellevue on Thursday morning, May 14. Previously Fontenelle had shipped some of his supplies by boat up the Missouri River.

Whitman, in his letter of May 10, 1839, told Greene of unhappy experiences with Parker which took place at the very beginning of their overland travels: "Mr. P. obtained leave to put a small supply of provisions into Mr. Fontenelle's wagon. And now for the task of packing; a thing I had never seen done, & had no example before me, as the company was to go up to Bellevue before arranging their packs... This task I performed alone in the streets of Liberty, & after putting all but our provisions on the poor old mule, I started alone, but did not go far before all was in disorder & needed a repacking, a scene often occurring & for which I was as often blamed by Mr. P. for my unskillful management."

Experience is needed to tie a miscellaneous assortment of items on the back of an animal and have them remain securely in place when it is trotting or even walking. This Whitman lacked at first but in time he became an expert packer. Whitman's account continues: "It was not long before we found Mr. F. did not wish to take the trouble of our provisions, & we were forced to put them into Mr. Merrill's wagon, although he was obliged with a loaded ox team to keep up with Mr. F. with [his] mules & empty wagons. In order to do this, I assisted him in taking out his boxes at every bad place & carrying them on our backs or else lifting at the wheels in the mud &c."

Hostility of the Men of the Caravan

The unwillingness of Fontenelle to permit the missionaries to place some of their supplies in his empty wagons boded ill for their future relationships. The caravan had hardly started before Whitman became aware that the rough and ungodly men of Fontenelle's company did not appreciate the presence of missionaries and emphatically expressed their displeasure. Whitman wrote: "Very evident tokens gave us to understand that our company was not agreeable, such as the throwing of rotten eggs at me." He added: "In order to remedy this, I used to labour with extreme exertion with Mr. F's men in crossing rivers, making rafts & bridges, &c. In this way we reached Bellevue. I found I was very much exhausted in health, having been an invalid for some years previous."

Parker, in his *Journal of an Exploring Tour Beyond the Rocky Mountains*, likewise referred to the hostility of the men of the caravan, who "so disliked the restraints which our presence imposed upon them that, as they afterwards confessed, they had plotted our death & intended on the first convenient occasion to put this purpose into execution." [6] Since the caravan was traveling rather slowly over the two hundred mile stretch which separated Liberty from Bellevue, the three missionaries decided to remain in camp over Sunday, May 24. When the men of the caravan learned of this, they took great offense.

Parker described what happened: "After our arrangements were made for the night, one of the desperadoes came to our tent with a basin of alcohol, and stated that they had taken offense of our refusing to travel with them on the Sabbath... and concluded to pass it over, if we would take a friendly drink with them. This of course we declined. He said the men were highly displeased, and he could not say what would be the result—giving us to understand that if we refused their terms of reconciliation, our lives would be in danger. We still refused. He then said if we would put the basin to our lips and wet them, they would accept that as satisfaction. But his arguments and threats not availing to shake our temperance principles, he went away, but as we afterwards learned without giving up the purpose of revenge on some other occasion." [7]

Parker recorded a second incident in which some of the men of the caravan expressed their dislike of the missionaries and especially their disapproval "because we did not travel with them on the sabbath." After the caravan had crossed a stream where a raft had been needed, some of the men tried to dismantle the raft and set it adrift before the three missionaries could use it. "Providentially," wrote Parker, "it did not drift far before it lodged against a tree, and, without much loss of time, we repaired it and passed over." [8]

Whitman's Journal

Whitman began a journal on May 14, the day the caravan left Liberty. He kept it with more or less regularity until October 26 when he was back at Cantonment Leavenworth after his journey to the Rockies.

Whitman took the original manuscript of this journal with him to Rushville where, it appears, he copied and enlarged it and then sent the revised version with a letter dated December 17 to the American Board.[9] A comparison of the original with the revised copy shows that Whitman made many changes, mostly of a minor nature, as the following extracts illustrate. The streams mentioned empty into the east side of the Missouri River.

Original Journal

[May] 24. The Sabbath. Rested in company with Rev. Roses Merrill. How refreshing is the rest of the Sabbath and how delightful is social worship in this uncultivated prairie. Mr. Fontanell's men went on.

25th. Started and crossed the big Tarkoo with raft. Came up with Mr. Fontanell at evening.

27. Spent the day in crossing the River on the raft.

28th. Made a raft and crossed the west branch of the Nishnabotna. Mr. Fronsa [Fontenelle] has waggons which he crosses on the raft. We swim our animals over. The water was rising so fast we had great difficulty to get off the bottom before crossing.

29th. Made a bridge over the five barrel creek. [Now Keg Creek.]

30th. Bridged the Maraguim [Mosquito] creek and crossed the Missouri and came to Bellevue. We stopped at the government agency under the hospitality of Mr. Merrill. The Brethren Dunbar and

American Board Copy

24. The Sabbath. We rested in company with Mr. Merrill. Mr. Fontanelle's men went on. How refreshing is the Sabbath and how delightful social worship in this uncultivated prairie. I bled myself for the pain in my side which is quite severe.[10]

30. We arrived at Bellevue after a very fatigueing journey. The rains were excessive and the streams high. Most of them had to be bridged or crossed by rafts. We put up with Mr. Merrill at the agency. Messrs. Dunbar and Allis are waiting for Maj. Dockerty [John Dougherty], agent for the Pawnees. They speak encouragingly of their reception among the Pawnees.

31st. Sabbath. Mr. Parker preached in Mr. Merrill's house in the morning & in the evening prayer meeting.

1st June. Attended concert[11] with Mr. Merrill's family and the Brethren of the Pawnee mission. How blessed is the consideration of union and concert in such a cause.

Allis of the Pawnee mission are here awaiting the arrival of Maj. Dockerty, agent for the Pawnees. They speak encourageingly of their reception among the Pawnees.

10 June. I was called to visit one of Mr. Fontanell's men sick with Cholera. Spent much of the night with him.

11th. Patient much relieved.

10. I was called to visit one of Mr. Fontanelle's men sick with cholera. Spent much of the night with him.

11th. Patient much relieved.

Parker, in his *Journal*, commented on their drinking water: "The water of all this portion of country, especially of the Missouri river, and its large tributaries, are very turbid, owing to the nature of the soil over which they pass. A pail full of water, standing half an hour at the seasons of freshets, will deposit three-eighths of an inch of sediment; and yet the water, when settled, appears to be of good quality." One of the difficulties which the missionaries encountered while traveling at that season of the year across the rolling prairies lush with the new growth of grass was the lack of wood for fuel. Parker wrote: "Our mode of living, from day to day, had already necessarily become uniform. Dry bread and bacon constituted our breakfast, dinner and supper. The bacon we cooked, when we could obtain wood for fire; but when out of sight of land,' that is, when nothing but green grass could be seen, we eat our bacon without cooking." [12]

Whitman found the sixteen-day trip from Liberty to Bellevue a gruelling experience. Although the caravan once traveled twenty miles in one day, yet because of heavy rains and swollen streams, it averaged about thirteen miles. Wherever a rushing torrent could not be forded by a wagon, either a bridge had to be built or a raft constructed, so that the wagons could be taken across. All this took time. Whitman and Parker had a small conical tent which provided some protection at night but, like the men of the caravan, they had to sleep on the wet ground.

Whitman quickly discovered that Parker was more of a liability than a help on the trail. It is difficult to imagine any two men with more opposite qualifications for a journey across the plains and the mountains in those days than Marcus Whitman and Samuel Parker. Whitman was the practical type, eager to do his share of work and more. He was an out-of-doors man, rugged, likeable, and adjustable to the circumstances of his environment. Parker was an older man. At fifty-six he never should have ventured on such an expedition. His disposition was more suited for the study than for the rough life of western travel. He was tactless, fussy, and dogmatic. Parker let Whitman do most of the work in packing, setting up camp, and preparing the meals. Perhaps Parker was standing on protocol. After all, he had the status of being a "missionary" of the American Board; Whitman was only an "assistant missionary."

William H. Gray, who went out to Oregon in 1836 with the Whitman-Spalding party, characterized Parker as follows: "Mr. Parker was inclined to self-applause, requiring his full share of ministerial approbation or respect... was rather fastidious."[13]

Another characterization of Parker is found in a letter that W. G. Rae, an official of the Hudson's Bay Company, wrote from Fort Nez Perce (the early name for Fort Walla Walla), on March 20, 1836: "There is a Missionary there [referring to Fort Vancouver] from the United States of the presbyterian persuasion who sends us all to Hell—honest man—with as little ceremony as I would (at this moment for I am very hungry) drive a rump steak into my bread basket. Parker is the Worthy's name—and I must do him the justice to say he deals as plainly with the high as the low—in this respect I find no fault but altogether I think however good his motives—that he goes much too bluntly..."[14]

Becoming aware of the unfriendly attitude of the men of the caravan towards him and Parker, Whitman became concerned. How would it be possible for the two to cross the plains and the mountains unless they had the goodwill and the cooperation of Fontenelle and his men? Since he had become engaged to Narcissa Prentiss, Whitman was naturally taking note of travel conditions to see if it would be possible to take a white woman across the country to Oregon. If he were to get married and if at least one other married couple would join them, they would have to travel under the protection of the Fur Company's caravan after leaving the Missouri frontier. Whitman knew that if he and Parker could not win the respect of the men of the caravan, it would be impossible for any mission party with women to contemplate an overland journey to Oregon the following year.

Alert to the problem, Whitman overexerted himself in helping the men of the caravan get their wagons over the swollen streams. He felt that this was one way of overcoming the growing hostility which was being shown, but he paid a heavy price. Writing in his journal on May 20, Whitman confessed: "Much afflicted with pain in my side which is much aggravated by fatigue." On June 15, two weeks after the caravan had arrived at Bellevue, he again mentioned his ill health: "I have been quite sick yesterday and today." All such discouragements and afflictions, combined with the continued hostility of the men and the liability of Parker's attitude, made the outlook bleak. Whitman began to wonder if it would be possible for him and Parker to complete their projected exploring tour.

THE DREAD CHOLERA STRIKES

A couplet from Shakespeare's *Julius Caesar* is here applicable:

There is a tide in the affairs of men,
Which, taken at the flood, leads on to fortune.

At Bellevue, in a sudden and unexpected way, the tide turned for Whitman when the dread cholera struck down some of the men of the caravan. As has been stated, Asiatic cholera was brought from Ireland to the Atlantic states in June 1832, and within a few months had spread across the country to St. Louis. The disease had reappeared with lessened virulence in 1833, but was worse in 1834. In some mysterious way, the deadly germs contaminated the drinking water used by Fontenelle and his men when they were encamped at Bellevue in June 1835.

Whitman's journal tells the story. On June 16, he wrote: "My health is improved. Went to see a man for whom I was called last night but was unable to go. Found him in a hopeless collapse of cholera. Another case, the man laying on the bank of the river and in the evening exposed to a severe shower, soon after which he died." On the 19th Whitman wrote: "There have been several new cases of cholera each day and one death last night. Mr. Fontanelle is sick with cholera."

On June 21, in a letter to Narcissa, Whitman wrote: "For the last twelve days have been attending upon Mr. Fontanelle's men; the cholera has raged severely among them; three only have died. Mr. Fontanelle is sick with it himself, but now convalescent. He has a house and farm half a mile below here, where his men have been, some encamped, and some in his buildings. It is not strange that they should have the cholera because of their intemperance, their sunken and filthy situation."

Although we have no evidence that Whitman had actually treated a case of cholera while practicing medicine at Wheeler, it is evident that he had been close enough to the Erie Canal and other focal points of infection to become informed about the symptoms of the disease and the best ways to treat it. He had learned that contagion was connected with intemperance and lack of cleanliness. He knew the importance of good clean drinking water, and he knew the most appropriate medication to be used. When Fontenelle called upon Whitman for help, Whitman at once recommended that the men be moved from the low bottom lands bordering the river, where the water supply had evidently become polluted, to "a clean, healthy situation" on higher ground. This stopped the spread of the disease.

Looking back on those days, Parker commented in his *Journal*: "Three of the company died; and several others barely survived, through the blessing of God upon the assiduous attentions of Doct. Whitman, my associate, and the free use of powerful medicines. And, had it not been for his successful practice, the men would have dispersed, and the caravan would have failed of going to the place of rendezvous. This was plainly seen and frankly acknowledged." [15]

After the death of the three men, all others who had been stricken, including Fontenelle, recovered. A magical change of attitude towards the missionaries took place. There were no more throwing of rotten eggs at them, no more taunts because of their temperance principles, and no more harassments. Dr. Whitman became the most respected man in the caravan. Parker was tolerated for Whitman's sake. Both Whitman and Parker viewed the cholera epidemic, as far as they were concerned, as being providential. "The medical skill of the Doctor," wrote Parker, "converted those [who had been hostile] into permanent friends."

Four years later, Whitman in a letter to Greene likewise stressed the providential aspects of the epidemic by writing: "At this place the Lord had a great change for us, for the Cholera appearing in camp, my aid was greatly sought. Mr. F. himself being one of the subjects of the disease and recovering (as also most of his men), he showed his gratitude, as well as all other persons concerned in the company, by bestowing upon us every favor in his power" [Letter 62].

What if there had been no cholera outbreak at Bellevue: Would the two missionaries have been able to continue their exploring tour to the Rockies that summer? What if Whitman had been a minister and not a doctor? Would he have been able to overcome the hostility of the company and so win the friendship of Fontenelle that it was possible for the mission party of the following year, which included two women, to travel with the caravan to the Rendezvous? This is doubtful. From all available evidence, it is safe to conclude that Whitman's skill as a doctor in dealing with the cholera epidemic at Bellevue made possible the establishment of the Oregon Mission of the American Board in 1836.

From Bellevue to the Rendezvous

The friction which had arisen between Whitman and Parker during the trek from Liberty to Bellevue threatened to end their missionary tour at the latter place. Whitman insisted on buying another mule and hiring a man to help in packing and unpacking. Parker was opposed to such extra costs. His determination to keep the expenses of the exploring tour to a minimum may have reflected some promise that he had made to Secretary Greene, whom he had seen in Boston in the fall of 1834.

Whitman, knowing that they would have to carry enough food for at least three weeks, until they arrived at the buffalo range, in addition to other equipment and supplies, continued to insist on the absolute necessity of having a second pack animal. In his letter of May 1839, Whitman gave Greene the following details: "After much entreaty I received for a reply, *You* may purchase one if *you* will take the *responsibility*.' I replied, *No*, Mr. P. not under such circumstances. In such a situation I cannot go any farther.' After that he reluctantly consented to buy one, but would not hire a man to assist in packing, although we were repeatedly urged to do it." It is evident that Fontenelle was one who recommended that the two missionaries hire a packer.

Whitman faced the eight-week journey to the Rendezvous with a heavy heart as he realized that most if not all of the labor connected with packing and unpacking, setting up camp and preparing meals, would devolve upon him. On June 22, the day he and Parker left Bellevue, Whitman wrote in his journal: "My health is feeble," and then bravely added, "but I am not discouraged."

After being delayed by the cholera outbreak for a full three weeks, Fontenelle was eager to be on his way even though some of his men were not fully recovered. On Sunday, June 21, he moved the caravan a short distance out of Bellevue into the prairie. The trail that he planned to follow paralleled somewhat the north bank of the Platte River to its forks, about three hundred miles west of Bellevue, and then up the North Fork to Fort Laramie. This trading post, located at the mouth of Laramie Creek, was founded only the year before, 1834, and is not to be confused with present-day Laramie, Wyoming, which lies about eighty miles to the southwest.[16]

The buffalo range began in the vicinity of what is now North Platte, Nebraska, at the forks of the Platte, which was a good three weeks march from Bellevue. The long delay at Bellevue had meant a serious depletion of Fontenelle's food supplies, hence the urgency to be on their way and get to the buffalo range as soon as possible. After reaching buffalo, the men would live almost exclusively on meat.

Having conscientious scruples about traveling on Sunday unless it was absolutely necessary, Whitman and Parker remained in camp at Bellevue on the day that Fontenelle left. Both men knew, however, that as soon as the caravan entered the Indian country, they would have to stay with it on Sundays as well as other days of the week for safety's sake. On Monday, June 22, the two men started their westward march and easily caught up with the caravan before evening.

Parker, like Whitman, made rough notes along the way which became the basis for the report he submitted to the Board on June 25, 1835.[17] He used both these rough notes and his report in the writing of his *Journal of an Exploring Tour* which was first published in 1838. A comparison of Whitman's journal and his letters, written shortly after his return to *Rushville* in the fall of 1835, with Parker's writings reveals some striking differences in their respective attitudes toward the objectives of their tour.

Whitman was the practical person, mindful of his engagement to Narcissa Prentiss and concerned with the problems involved in taking her together with one or more other married couples across the prairies and over the Rockies to Oregon. He saw the importance of establishing a good rapport with the leaders of the American Fur Company's caravan. He also wanted to make sure that the hardships of horseback travel, when the women would be riding on side-saddles, would not be too much for them to endure. Of course Indian women had crossed the mountains but they, like the Indian men, rode astride. The Spanish, in what is now southwestern United States, had taken their wives over the Continental Divide but they too may have ridden astride. Certainly the mountains in the south were not as rugged as those north of what was then the Mexican border. Whitman knew that no white woman had ever crossed those rugged and little known mountains which lay north of the border. Was such an endeavor feasible? This he wanted to investigate.

Parker, on the other hand, had no such concern in mind. He was not planning to establish any particular mission. He was on an exploring tour and was viewing the whole scene on a grand scale. He had an observant eye and an inquiring mind. He gathered a myriad of facts regarding the physical features of the country, its geology, fauna, flora, climate, the customs of the Indians, and the activities of the fur companies. Although of great value to Americans interested in Oregon, Parker's explorations and published journal proved to be of little use to the American Board or to its Oregon missionaries.

The combined testimony of Whitman and Parker through their respective accounts give us some vivid descriptions of the experiences and hardships endured on the trail. At the end of their first day's ride after leaving Bellevue, Parker noted: "In the afternoon we had to ride in a heavy, cold rain, in consequence of which I became much chilled. We overtook the caravan, and encamped on a high prairie, where we could find but little wood, and it was difficult to make a fire. We had for supper coarse bread made of corn, and some bacon. The change from the comforts to the bare necessities of life was trying... On the 23d, the storm still continued, and we did not remove our encampment." [18]

Fontenelle got the caravan on the march again about noon on the 24th but before the men could make camp in the late afternoon, they were drenched with another heavy rain. Whitman wrote that evening in his journal after they had made camp during the storm: "The water ran across our tent like a brook, so that we could not lay down until late, and then cover ourselves with wet blankets." [19]

The caravan made slow progress partly because of the inclement weather and also due to the difficulties involved in taking six heavily loaded wagons over the soggy prairie. The Elkhorn River was crossed on the 26th in a boat made by covering one of the wagon boxes with buffalo skins. The Loup Fork of the Platte was forded on July 1, and on the 4th, the caravan arrived at a large Pawnee Indian village and camped near it. "We were invited to three feasts," wrote Whitman, "two of boiled corn, and one of dryed buffalo meat." [20] Here Whitman and Parker met Allis and Dunbar, who had gone out to the frontier with Parker the preceding year, and who were then traveling with the Pawnee Indians. There on the prairie of what is now eastern Nebraska, Whitman became aware of some of the problems and difficulties which missionaries faced in trying to evangelize roving bands of Indians. These were problems which he would have to face later in Old Oregon.

"How solitary is the situation of Messrs. Dunbar and Allis," he wrote in his journal, "each with different bands."

Whitman's ill health continued. He referred to it in his journal for July 7 and on the 13th wrote: "I have had dysentery for several days so that it was with great difficulty I could travel with the company." Parker, however, made no reference to this in his journal. Four years later when Whitman was stung by Parker's criticism, he wrote to Greene saying: "Soon after passing the Pawnees, I was taken sick with a painful bowel complaint. Being often obliged to stop, I fell in the rear of camp, & was unable to overtake them again until they had long been encamped for I was too weak to ride faster than a walk. I must have failed by the way had it not been for one of the Companies Clerks who kindly kept me company & assisted me in mounting & dismounting.

"Before I was able to stand, I was obliged to do our cooking or else do without eating, for I do not recollect that Mr. P. ever got a meal during my sickness either for himself or me, but went to eat with Mr. F. & it was only by the favour of his cook that I obtained a little food occasionally. During this time, Mr. P. was obliged to pack the animals, which task he found himself very unskilllfull & poorly able to perform. I write thus to show how unfit it was for us to be without an experienced servant" [Letter 62].

Parker in his June 1837 report to the Board gave the following account of their "Mode of travelling:" "At break of day the call is made, out, out, gear up your mules.' We get on our way about sunrise, travel on until about the middle of the day and stop for breakfast[21]—our horses and mules are turned out for about two hours to feed upon the prairies, under guard. In the afternoon we travel until about two hours sun, when we encamp for the night—the animals are again turned out until near dark, when they are taken up and staked out with twelve or fifteen feet of rope, in a hollow square, formed by the river on one side—three wagons on one side, extending back to the river, and three on the opposite side, and the packs in the rear. Guards are placed around the square, relieved every two hours during the night. This is done to keep hostile Indians from falling upon us by surprise, or from stealing our horses." [22] He also wrote: "We were permitted, by favor, to pitch our tent next to the river, half way between the two wings, which made our situation a little more retired." [23] Here we see clear evidence of Fontenelle's appreciation of Whitman in assigning a man to help during his illness and in giving the missionaries a favored camping site.

The first buffalo was killed on July 13, a little over three weeks after the caravan had left Bellevue. By this time the men were almost out of food. After reaching the buffalo range, the men lived almost exclusively on buffalo meat. On July 20, Parker noted in his journal that he had participated in a buffalo hunt and that he had shot and wounded one.[24] Although Parker did not so indicate, we can assume that another person killed the animal. There is no evidence that Whitman ever took part in a buffalo hunt. He was by conviction opposed to the use of force and would not engage in hunting wild animals unless the demand for food required it. He took no pleasure in seeing the buffalo killed and let others shoot what were necessary to provide food for the caravan.

The caravan arrived at Fort Laramie on July 20, which was about two-thirds of the way from Liberty to the Rendezvous. Here the wagons were left and the baggage transferred to pack animals. At this point, Thomas Fitzpatrick[25] relieved Fontenelle as captain of the caravan.

Before parting company with Fontenelle, Whitman asked for his bill for giving the two missionaries protection while crossing the plains from Bellevue. According to Parker, Fontenelle refused to even think of making such a charge and told Whitman: "If any one is indebted, it is myself, for you have saved my life, and the lives of my men." [26] In a letter to Andrew Drips, one of the partners in the American Fur Company who was awaiting the arrival of the caravan at the Rendezvous, Fontenelle recommended that special care and attention be given to Whitman and

Parker and to "...the Doctor particularly. He has been of great service to us." [27] Fontenelle praised Whitman to Fitzpatrick. During the journey from Fort Laramie to the Rendezvous, a friendship grew up between Whitman and Fitzpatrick which proved to be of great value the next year when the mission party of five, including two women, crossed the plains and the Rockies with the caravan then under Fitzpatrick's command.

The caravan started out on the last segment of its journey on August 1. The trail followed the south bank of the North Fork of the Platte until it crossed the river at a point a few miles southwest of present-day Casper, Wyoming, whence it followed the north bank of the Sweetwater River to the summit of the Rockies. The caravan passed that great landmark on the Oregon Trail, Independence Rock, on August 7, and rode through South Pass on the 10th.

The Pass, which became the great mountain gateway to Old Oregon, lies at an elevation of about 7,550 feet. The ascent is so gradual that the exact summit can be located only with difficulty. Parker that day wrote in his journal: "It [i.e., the Pass] varies in width from two to fifteen miles... Though there are some elevations and depressions in this valley, yet comparatively speaking, it is level." Then with prophetic insight, Parker added: "There would be no difficulty in the way of constructing a rail-road from the Atlantic to the Pacific ocean." [28]

AT THE 1835 RENDEZVOUS

Books could be written about the way changing fashions in men's and women's clothing have affected the economy and even the history of our country. For several centuries the beautiful fur of the beaver has been an important item of dress and adornment both in America and abroad. Since the European species of beaver became almost extinct in the 17th century, the fur of the American species, *Castor canadensis*, was in great demand. When it became known that vast numbers of these animals were to be found in the Rocky Mountains of both Canada and the United States, several fur companies were organized which vied with each other in the scramble for the rich rewards found in the sale of beaver pelts. Sometimes the rivalry of these contending companies led to violence and even to bloodshed.

In Canada the Hudson's Bay Company, which had been chartered in 1670, secured exclusive rights to the fur trade of Old Oregon when it absorbed the North West Company in 1821. The Hudson's Bay Company had its Canadian headquarters at Lachine, nine miles from Montreal. The Company partitioned British America into four great departments. The Columbia Department covered the Columbia River Valley and, after 1825, the Pacific slope of what is now Canada, then called New Caledonia. Fort Vancouver, located on the north bank of the Columbia River near the mouth of the Willamette River, became the headquarters of the Columbia Department. The furs collected at that place were sent by sea to the Orient or to England.

The American Fur Company, chartered in 1808 by John Jacob Astor, was organized to compete with the great fur companies of Canada. Branch headquarters were established in St. Louis in 1822. The history of the American fur companies is complex during the third and fourth decades of the 19th century. For our purpose it is sufficient to say that Astor retired from the fur trade in 1834 and by 1835 the American Fur Company was supreme in the mountain fur trade.[29] Since the Americans did not have the advantage enjoyed by the British of being able to ship their furs to various markets by sea, they had to carry their furs out of the Rockies on pack animals. In order to collect the pelts from the hundreds of trappers which the several American fur companies employed, annual gatherings were held during the midsummer at some previously appointed place in the Rockies called the Rendezvous. Sixteen of these gatherings took place beginning in 1825 and ending with a small, unsponsored gathering of trappers in 1840. During the peak years in the history of the American Fur Company, 1835–38, annual caravans consisting of several hundred pack animals loaded with supplies from civilization and under the care of fifty or sixty men would leave the Missouri frontier as early in May as conditions permitted for the mountains. At the Rendezvous the supplies would be traded for furs which would then be taken back to St. Louis.

Most of the Rendezvous were held west of the Continental Divide, the favorite place being on Green River, a tributary of the Colorado, near what is now Daniel, Wyoming.[30] Here was a well watered meadow, some twelve miles long and about ten miles wide. This provided an ideal pasture to accommodate large herds of horses. Sometimes as many as five thousand Indians would be present; if each Indian had two horses, this would mean ten thousand animals. In addition were the horses and mules belonging to the trappers and to the Fur Company's caravan. Thus a large meadow was a necessity. The location on Green River was one of surpassing beauty. To the east was the imposing Wind River range with Fremont Peak rising to a height of 13,700 feet. Although the Rendezvous was an event unique to the American fur trade, the Hudson's Bay Company would often send small parties to these gatherings from their trading posts in the Columbia River Valley.

The Indians who attended the Rendezvous came from such still friendly tribes as the Shoshones or Snakes, the Bannocks, the Nez Perces, the Cayuses, the Flatheads, and sometimes the Utes. Most of the trappers, also called mountain men,[31] had a native wife—sometimes more than one. The Rendezvous was the great social event of the year for these men. Most of the year, they had lived in lonely isolation, but now with their wives and half-breed children, they assembled not only to trade their pelts for supplies but also to celebrate. The Hudson's Bay Company tried to prevent the bartering of liquor to the Indians or to the mountain men for furs, but the American companies had no such scruples. Large quantities of whisky were carried by the caravans to the Rendezvous in barrels especially made to fit over the curvature of a horse's back. For some ten days or two weeks, there would be intermingled with business dealings—drinking, carousing, horse racing, gambling, philandering, and fighting.

A vivid description of the Rendezvous of 1884 held on Ham's Fork of Green River has been given us by the naturalist, John K. Townsend, who wrote from personal observation. With particular reference to the mountain men, he wrote: "These people with their obstreperous mirth; their whooping, and howling, and quarreling, added to the mounted Indians who are constantly dashing into and through our camp, yelling like fiends; the barking and baying of savage wolf-dogs, and the incessant crackling of rifles and carbines render our camp a perfect bedlam." He also commented on the "jargon of drunken traders... the swearing and screaming of our own men, who are scarcely less savage than the rest, being heated by the detestable liquor which circulates freely among them."[32]

All trading was done on a barter basis. Beaver pelts were valued from five to eight dollars each, depending upon size and quality. Prices for the goods brought from the States were high. Townsend wrote that tobacco which sold for ten cents a pound in Philadelphia brought $2.00 at the Rendezvous. Whiskey sold for $2.00 a pint even when diluted; three awls brought fifty cents; and a blanket $25.00.[33]

For nearly two decades after 1815, the fashionable headpiece for men was the high beaver hat with a crown of varying shape and a narrow rolling brim. But when Prince Albert of England in the early 1830s preferred the silk hat to the beaver hat, this doomed the beaver trade. Perhaps the change came just in time to save the Rocky Mountain beaver from the fate of its European cousin. Only about two hundred trappers attended the 1835 Rendezvous and their supply of pelts was smaller than that of the previous year. The beaver trade had already started to decline.

By another of those coincidences of history, which the devout Christian might call the providence of God, the Fur Company's caravans were still crossing the plains during the summers of 1835, 1836, and 1838, thus providing protection for the missionaries of the American Board who traveled to Old Oregon during those years. Without such protection in hostile Indian country east of the Rockies, there might have been no Oregon Mission of the American Board.

The 1835 caravan with Whitman and Parker finally arrived at the Green River Rendezvous on Wednesday, August 12, about a month behind schedule. It was greeted with uproarious enthusiasm by the impatient trappers and by about 2,000 Indians [Letter 11]. The weather at that altitude was already beginning to turn cold. Parker noted that the thermometer stood at 24° on the morning of the 11th. Even before the trading for furs and supplies could begin, the casks of whiskey had to be opened and the carousing began. Both Whitman and Parker were dismayed to see the demoralizing effects of the liquor traffic, not only upon the mountain men, but upon the Indians as well. The hard life of the trappers took a terrific toll. Parker reported that the attrition rate among them amounted to about one-third each year.[34]

Upon Whitman's return to the States, he wrote to Greene on December 28 and gave considerable information as to the extent of the liquor traffic. "All the present regulations upon this point are disregarded or evaded," he said, "and I fear all further regulations will be equally ineffectual." Whitman sensed the fact that the hesitancy of some of the officials of the American Fur Company, including Fontenelle, to extend a cordial welcome to the missionaries was the feeling that "our object would always be regarded as opposed to their interests." In this letter to Greene, Whitman suggested that perhaps the American Board could lay pressure on the Government to take some steps to curb the evil, but warned: "You are aware of the delicacy of this subject to one who is liable to be exposed to opposition of Traders."

At the Rendezvous Whitman and Parker were introduced to the buckskin dress worn by the Indians and whites alike. The day came when Whitman likewise wore buckskin. The fringes below the neck across the back, at the bottom of the jacket, at the end of the sleeves and trouser legs were not just for ornament but rather to facilitate the draining of water. Water drains better from points than from a straight edge; this may he the reason why our Creator gave us eyelashes.

Dr. Whitman's Operation

Among the colorful characters at the 1835 Rendezvous was Jim Bridger, one of the most famous of the mountain men. He had been a member of a trappers' party which had a skirmish with the Blackfeet Indians at Pierre's Hole[35] on July 18, 1832 in what is now known as Teton Basin in Idaho near the Wyoming border. A few days later Bridger was in another skirmish with the Blackfeet at which time he was wounded, receiving an arrowhead in his back. Incidentally, it is evident which way Bridger was going when the arrow struck.

The three-inch arrowhead remained in Bridger's back for three years until Whitman removed it on August 13, 1835. Parker described the operation: "It was a difficult operation, because the arrow was hooked at the point by striking a large bone and a cartilaginous substance had grown around it. The Doctor pursued the operation with great selfpossession and perseverance; and his patient manifested equal firmness."[36] This operation, perhaps the first ever to be performed by an American-trained physician west of the Rockies, came eleven years before the blessed effects of anesthesia were first demonstrated in the United States.[37]

Parker's account continues: "The Doctor also extracted another arrow from the shoulder of one of the hunters, which had been there two years and a half. His reputation becoming favorably established, calls for medical and surgical aid were almost incessant."[38] Even some of the

Indians sought his help. Here was a medicine man greater than they had ever seen, whose skill was magic in their eyes. Whitman carried back with him to the States a stone arrowhead taken from some Indian's body which the author saw in the summer of 1955 when he visited its owner who lived near Rushville.

Due attention has never been given to the important connection between Whitman's medical and surgical ability and the founding of the Oregon Mission of the American Board. We find several instances in the history of Protestant foreign missions where some land hostile to the introduction of Christianity has been opened because of the skill of a missionary doctor. This was true of Korea where a missionary doctor performed a successful operation on a member of the royal family and, as a result, the land was opened to Christian missionaries. So may it be said of Old Oregon.

The fact that Whitman saved the caravan of 1835 at Bellevue prepared the way for the mission party of 1836, which included women, to cross the plains in safety. Now at the Rendezvous, Whitman in his open-air clinic won the respect and admiration of mountain men and Indians alike. Friendships were begun which continued through the remaining years of Whitman's life. Two mountain men whom Whitman first met at the Rendezvous of 1835 were Jim Bridger and Joe Meek; each of them in later years sent a half-breed daughter to the Whitman mission to be cared for and educated. Moreover, the reputation that Whitman gained among the natives was an important factor in the warm welcome given the members of the 1836 mission party by both the Cayuse and Nez Perce Indians.

WHITMAN AND PARKER SEPARATE

On Sunday, August 16, Whitman and Parker met with the principal men of the Nez Perce and Flathead tribes and explained the object of their visit. A French Canadian mountain man, Charles Compo, who had a Nez Perce wife, may have been their interpreter. Without a doubt, references were made to the Nez Perce delegation which had gone with Fontenelle to St. Louis four years earlier. When Whitman sent the journal of his overland travels to Greene, he gave Fontenelle's account of the delegation, and quoted him as saying that the Indians went "to gain religious knowledge" [Letter 11].

Whitman and Parker asked the Indians if they had met the Jason Lee party which passed through the Rockies the previous year. They replied that "they never heard of the Methodist missionaries." It may be that the two men misunderstood what the Indians said; we do have evidence that Lee met with some of the Cayuses and some Nez Perces at the Rendezvous of 1834 and also later at Fort Walla Walla. A Scottish adventurer, Sir William Drummond Stewart, who had traveled with the Wyeth party and the Lees to the Willamette Valley the previous year, was present at the 1835 Rendezvous. He told Whitman that on the advice of Dr. John McLoughlin, Chief Factor of the Hudson's Bay Company at Fort Vancouver, the Methodist missionaries had decided to settle in the Willamette Valley. Hence, the Nez Perce field was still open for Protestant missionaries, free of any denominational competition.

Whitman wrote in his journal on August 16: "We had a talk with the chiefs of the Flathead and Napiersas [i.e., Nez Perce] tribes, in which they expressed great pleasure in seeing us and strong desires to be taught. Little Chief of the Flatheads said he was greatly rejoiced when he heard there was a teacher from the Almighty and a physician coming among them;... He had been told some things he said about the worship of God but he did not practice them. But now, if a teacher would come among them, he and his children (meaning all over whom he had authority) would obey all he should say."

Parker reported: "The first chief of the Nez Perces, Tai-quin-su-watish, arose and said, He had heard from white men a little about God, which had only gone into his ears; he wished to know enough to have it go down into his heart, to influence his life, and to teach his people.' Others spoke to the same import, and they all made as many promises as we could desire."[39]

Tai-quin-su-watish, known to Whitman and Spalding as Tack-en-sua-tis, was nicknamed Rotten Belly by the trappers. This unsavory title was due to a severe stomach wound he had received in the Battle of Pierre's Hole. The nickname continued long after the festering wound had healed. Chief Tackensuatis was to be one of the most enthusiastic friends of the missionaries during the first years of the Oregon Mission of the American Board, but later his attitude changed.

Whitman and Parker were deeply stirred by the earnestness and sincerity of the Indians and by their evident eagerness for Christian teaching. All that they learned in this conference confirmed the Walker-Disosway report which had appeared in the March 1, 1833, issue of the New York *Christian Advocate*. Following their conference with the chiefs of the Flathead and Nez Perce tribes on Sunday, August 16, Whitman wrote in his journal: "After mutual conversation and prayer with reference to these tribes, and being satisfied there were no missionaries of any denomination among them, I said to Mr. Parker if we had another associate with us, I should like to return home and, if the Board should approve, come out next year with others to establish a mission among them."

Much to Whitman's surprise, Parker gave immediate approval to the suggestion that Whitman return for associates while he continued on the exploring tour. Knowing Parker's ineptitude in packing and the fact that he was then in his fifty-seventh year, Whitman at first was skeptical of the wisdom of having him continue the tour alone. Parker insisted that it would be perfectly safe for him to travel with the Nez Perce Indians to their homeland. Whitman asked what the people in the States would say if some accident befell him. Parker replied: "I told him to give himself no uneasiness upon this subject, for we could not go safely together without divine protection, and with it, I could go alone."[40] This was a courageous attitude to take. All honor to him!

William H. Gray, who went out to Oregon with the Whitman-Spalding party in 1836, in his *History of Oregon*, suggested that a subdued friction had developed between the two men which made Parker desirous of going his own way alone. Gray wrote: "The peculiarities of Messrs. Parker and Whitman were such, that, when they had reached the rendezvous on Green River... they agreed to separate; not because Dr. Whitman was not willing and anxious to continue the exploring expedition in company with Mr. Parker, but because Mr. P. could not put up' with the off-hand, careless, and, as he thought, slovenly manner in which Dr. Whitman was inclined to travel."[41]

Perhaps the most important factor which induced Whitman to consent to Parker's daring proposal to separate was his desire to return home, be married, find associates, and lead a mission party to Oregon in the spring and summer of 1836. Whitman was convinced that travel conditions across the plains and even over the Rockies presented no serious obstacle for women.

In his report to Greene, he wrote: "There were 20 wagons at one time from St. Louis at the place where the company rendezvoused last summer" [Letter 11]. Realizing that nearly 2,000 miles separated the Missouri frontier from Fort Walla Walla and being fully aware that custom then demanded white women should ride on side-saddles rather than astride, Whitman reasoned that wherever a wagon could go, a woman could go. If she grew weary riding side-saddle, let her ride in the wagon. Being thus convinced that it was indeed feasible for women to cross the Rockies if a light wagon could be taken along, Whitman was eager to return home and get married. Whitman's immediate concern was for the safety and comfort of Parker should he continue with the exploring project with the Indians.

Whitman and Parker met with the Nez Perces on Monday, the 17th of August. Since the Flatheads were not included in the consultations of that day, this indicates that the two men had decided that it was best, in view of the slender resources of the American Board, to limit their attention to one tribe. Regarding this meeting, Whitman informed the Board: "They expressed great satisfaction that I should return and see if others would come and live among them and teach them and readily promised the necessary escort to Mr. Parker, together with assistance to pack and drive his animals" [Letter 11].

Parker gives confirming testimony in his journal: "They were much pleased and promised to assist me, and to send a convoy with me from their country to Fort Walla Walla on the Columbia River. They selected one of their principal young men for my particular assistant, as long as I should have need of him, who was called Kentuc; and I engaged a *voyageur*, who understood English, and also the Nez Perce language sufficiently well to interpret common business, and some of the plain truths of our holy religion, to go with me while I should continue with these tribes."[42]

Kentuc (or Kentucky) was a fun-loving young Nez Perce who was so named by the trappers because of his efforts to sing a popular ballad "The Hunters of Kentucky."[43] The voyageur was Charles Compo. Satisfied with the arrangements that had been made with the Indians for Parker's welfare, Whitman gave his final consent to the plan. Since the Nez Perces were eager to be on their way, the missionaries found that they had but four days in which to prepare for their separation.

Letters had to be written by Parker for Whitman to carry back to the States. Whitman turned over to Parker both of their pack animals with most of the camping equipment, keeping only his riding horse and the barest essentials. Needing a pack animal, he made inquiry and found that a good horse at the Rendezvous sold for $100.00, which was more than he felt justified in asking the Board to pay. He finally bought a decrepit animal for $5.00 but, as he later explained to Greene, the horse "was a disgrace to any man to pack on account of his extreme sore back" [Letter 62]. A mitigating factor was the lightness of Whitman's pack.

Criticism has sometimes been made that the missionaries forced themselves upon the Cayuse and Nez Perce Indians. Contemporary evidence is all to the contrary. The Protestant thrust into the Old Oregon country came as the result of the appeal made by the Nez Perce delegation to St. Louis in 1831. Both Whitman and Parker in their respective journals and letters, when commenting on their experiences at the 1835 Rendezvous, testified as to the eagerness of the Indians for missionaries.

Nothing was said by the natives regarding land for mission sites. This was apparently something that all took for granted. Since at that time the Indians knew nothing about the white man's custom of securing legal titles to certain parcels of land, this simply was not an issue. In general the Indians promised to do all that they could to induce the missionaries to settle among them. Whitman received assurances that if he found associates and brought them to the 1836 Rendezvous, the Nez Perces would escort them to Fort Walla Walla.

WHITMAN SELECTS TWO NEZ PERCE BOYS TO RETURN WITH HIM

At the August 17 meeting with the Nez Perces, Whitman suggested that he take back to the States with him a Nez Perce lad by the name of Tack-i-too-tis or Tack-it-ton-i-tis whom he renamed Richard. After some discussion regarding the advantages of giving the youth some education and a chance to learn the English language, the boy's father consented. Whitman later explained to Greene: "My reason for taking him is that he can speak the English language a little and by being with white people he will soon speak so as to interpret or assist in learning his language" [Letter 11].

Three days later another Nez Perce chief begged Whitman to take his son, Ais, also. "The father said," wrote Whitman, "he had but one more son, but he was willing to part with this one that he might be taught the religion of the whites or the Christian religion." Whitman was doubtful of the wisdom of taking two Indian boys back to the States with him, but Parker urged him to do so and suggested that the second lad could stay with his family in Ithaca. Finally being convinced that it would prove helpful in the future to have two boys who could speak English and who would have some knowledge of Christianity, Whitman consented. Ais was renamed John.

An interesting parallel can be drawn between the sending of Spokane Garry and Kootenai Pelly to the Red River Mission school in 1825 and Whitman's taking the two Nez Perce boys, Richard and John, with him to the States in 1835. In both instances the boys were sent to a school where they would learn English with the expectation of being used later as interpreters, and also with the hope that they would be taught the Christian religion.

Before Whitman and Parker parted, they witnessed a duel fought by two mountain men, Kit Carson and a French bully called Shunar. Parker tells the story and thus introduces for the first time in the literature of the West the name of Kit Carson. The two men fought with pistols, each being on horseback. Both fired almost simultaneously. Shunar's bullet passed over Carson's head. According to Parker: "C's ball entered S's hand, came out at the wrist, and passed through the arm above the elbow." [44] As Carson was reloading preparing to fire again, Shunar begged for his life and the duel was over. The savage incident gave Whitman another patient.

On Friday, August 21, the Nez Perces moved their camp three miles, thus beginning their homeward march. Whitman went along and spent the night with Parker. The next morning the two men parted, never to meet again. With a heavy heart Whitman returned to the Rendezvous. That day he wrote in his journal: "Mr. Parker went on this morning, after we had unitedly sought the blessing and guidance of God. He went on with firmness. I regretted exceedingly to see him go alone, but so we have decided, hoping more fully to advance the cause of our divine master." Whitman's return meant that a mission could be established in Oregon at least a year earlier than would have been possible had he continued with Parker.

The Return Journey

The caravan loaded with a year's harvest of furs left the Rendezvous for Fort Laramie under Fitzpatrick's leadership on August 27. With the caravan were some eighty-five mountain men who were returning to civilization.[45] Among these was Robert Newell who later played an important role in Oregon's history.[46] He bore the nickname "Doc" because of some skill he had in minor surgery and in the use of a few simple remedies. A friendship developed between Newell and Whitman on this eastward journey. Five years later a son born to Newell and his Nez Perce wife, was named Marcus Whitman. Here is further evidence of the favorable impression that Whitman made on his contemporaries.

The returning caravan arrived at Fort Laramie on September 8 where Fontenelle took over the command from Fitzpatrick. By September 3, the caravan was in the buffalo country, and a halt of three days was called in order for the men to kill buffalo and dry the meat for the remainder of the journey. On or about October 10, Whitman left the caravan and rode on ahead to a trading post conducted by Jean Pierre Cabanné about ten miles above present-day Omaha.[47] There he had the pleasure of meeting Dunbar and Allis with whom he spent a Sunday before continuing to Bellevue. Both Dunbar and Allis were engaged to be married and they asked Whitman to escort their fiancées to Liberty the next spring. This he promised to do.

Having made previous arrangements with Fontenelle, Whitman left his horses and those belonging to the Indian boys to be wintered with the Fur Company's animals on the Missouri bottom lands near Bellevue. Through the courtesy of Cabanné, free passage was given to Whitman and the boys on a boat which left Bellevue on October 20 for St. Louis. The boat arrived at Fort Leavenworth on the 26th, where Whitman met Colonel Henry Dodge and received confirming information from him about the feasibility of taking wagons over the Rockies [Letter 11].

Whitman and the Indian boys landed in St. Louis on November 4. Here the letters Parker had written to the Board and to his family, which Whitman had carried, were forwarded. Whitman wrote to Greene on the 7th and told him of the decision that he and Parker had made at the Rendezvous to separate—Parker to continue on his exploring tour and he to return for associates. Whitman stressed the friendly attitude of the

Indians, reporting that the Nez Perces were "remarkably well disposed and exceedingly anxious to receive instruction."

He further stated: "They say they have always been unhappy since they have become informed of the religion of the whites; they do not understand it. It has only reached their ears; they wish it to affect their most vital parts. They are very much inclined to follow any advice given them by the whites and are ready to adopt anything that is taught them as religion." Whitman expressed the hope that he could "return with others... next spring, if the Board should approve of it" [Letter 13].

In the closing paragraph of the report sent to Greene from Rushville on December 17, Whitman mentioned receiving contributions for the Board from an individual in Cincinnati and the Presbyterian Church at Erie, Pennsylvania. From such references we are able to trace out the route of his return journey. He traveled by river boat from St. Louis to Cincinnati; thence by stage to Cleveland; and then by boat or stage to Erie. Since there was in that day no means of rapid communication, Marcus had no way of sending advance word to Narcissa of his coming. When he arrived at Amity, he learned that the Prentiss family had moved about six miles to the north to a small village called Angelica. Judging by the time it took Whitman to go to St. Louis in the early spring of that year, he could hardly have arrived in Angelica before December 10, 1835.

No record remains of the joy that both Marcus and Narcissa felt on their meeting again. He had much to tell, and she was eager to listen. We can assume that he told about the cholera epidemic and of the assurances given by the American Fur Company for the safe conduct across the plains and the Rockies of any mission party, including women, which he might bring out in 1836. No doubt Marcus told about the great herds of buffalo which at times moved like dark clouds hugging the landscape. He surely would have mentioned the gentle approach to the Continental Divide through South Pass. The Rockies were not nearly as formidable as some had said. And what a topic for conversation—the buckskin clad mountain men and the thousands of Indians at the Rendezvous! No doubt he mentioned such men as Jim Bridger, Joe Meek, Kit Carson, and Doe Newell and perhaps he showed Narcissa the stone arrowhead he had extracted from an Indian which he had carried back as a souvenir.

A high point of his report to Narcissa would have been a description of the enthusiastic reception given to him and Parker by the Nez Perces. The Indians were eager for missionaries. The very presence of the two Indian boys, Richard and John, doubly emphasized this point. And finally Marcus would certainly have told how wheeled vehicles could be taken over the Rockies. He would have assured Narcissa and her parents that it was perfectly feasible for women to cross the Rockies, for wherever a wagon could go, a woman could go. There was then no valid reason why the two should not be married and go out to Oregon the next year with at least one other couple. Little imagination is needed to conjure up the thrilling stories Marcus was able to tell of his great adventure.

We know practically nothing of what Narcissa was able to tell Marcus regarding her experiences during their nine-month separation. She no doubt told of sending in her letter of application to the American Board on February 23, the day that Marcus had left for St. Louis. She would have been able to report that she had received notice of her appointment and that Secretary Greene had discreetly stated in his letter to her of March 19: "The particular tribe for whom you may labour & your location cannot of coarse be stated definitely at present."[48] After Marcus had explained the possibilities and the difficulties of women crossing the Rockies, Narcissa unhesitatingly indicated her readiness to be married and go with him to Oregon.

Realizing that it would be unwise for Narcissa to be the only woman in whatever mission party might be assembled, the next problem to be faced was that of finding at least one other couple to go with them. Among the possible candidates, Narcissa suggested the names of Henry and Eliza Spalding. Although we do not know whether Marcus at that time knew the Rev. Henry H. Spalding, we know that Narcissa did. As has been stated, Henry and Narcissa had grown up in Prattsburg, and had attended the same church and the same academy at the same time. Henry had proposed marriage and had been rejected. Later, Henry had married Eliza Hart and the two had been appointed by the American Board to be missionaries among the Osage Indians at a station near what is now Emporia, Kansas. Their departure had been delayed in 1835 because of the expected birth of a child. A stillborn baby girl was born to the Spaldings at Prattsburg on October 24 shortly before Marcus' return from the Rockies.[49] No doubt Narcissa knew of this.

The urgency of finding associates prompted Whitman to write to Spalding to see if he would be willing to change his destination and go with him and Narcissa to Oregon, provided the Board would give its consent. Although Whitman was taking the initiative in looking for associates, yet at the same time he was expecting the Board to help in the search.

After a short visit with Narcissa at Angelica, Whitman hastened on to Rushville. Mrs. Mary Alice Wisewell Caulkins, a daughter of Whitman's only sister, has described how her uncle with the two Indian boys arrived at his mother's home late on a Saturday evening, perhaps December 12. The family had retired for the night. Mrs. Caulkins wrote: "His mother, then Mrs. Loomis, hearing a noise, recognized his step and ran in her nightclothes to meet him."[50]

The household was soon aroused. The fire in the fireplace was stirred up. All present listened with rapt attention to the marvelous tales of adventure which Marcus had to relate. Mrs. Caulkins also wrote of an incident which took place the next morning: "A brother, Augustus, lived only across the street, but the Sabbath was so strictly observed that there was no communication between the two families on that day, so Augustus and his family were already in church without knowing that Marcus was in town." When Marcus and the two Indian boys unexpectedly entered the church, sixteen-year-old Deborah Whitman broke the decorum of the meeting by suddenly jumping up and crying out: "Why, there's Uncle Marcus!"[51]

When Whitman agreed to take the two Nez Perce boys back to the States with him, Parker had suggested that one be left with his family in Ithaca. After a short visit with relatives in Rushville, Whitman took Richard and John to Ithaca. In his reminiscences of his father, Samuel J. Parker, M.D., wrote: "My recollections are that one day late in the fall of 1835, he came to my father's house... and there was at the door the two Indian boys; that he said he had been a few days with his brother's family at Rushville; and that the Indian boys could not bear to be separated."[52] Even though Mrs. Parker had two sons living with her then—Samuel, seventeen, and Henry, thirteen—who could help take care of the Indian boys, she viewed the responsibility with considerable misgivings. Samuel J. remembered that several days were spent in consulting with members of the Ithaca Presbyterian Church, who no doubt promised to help, before Mrs. Parker consented to receive the boys into her home.

In his reminiscences, Samuel J. told of how the Nez Perces were always suspicious of all strangers, and especially those who might be carrying guns. Among the incidents related are the following: "...and what was amusing, these Indian boys were ever on the look-out for being murdered. As one day they came home on the most rapid run, having seen a codger' with a gun just above Spring St. and another [time] while four or five of us were sporting on skates... a man with a gun hunting partridges, sent them off like the wind; into the cliffs of the creek, while we skated undisturbed."

The Indian boys attended a school taught by Miss Emeline Palmer, who was engaged to Samuel Allis and who planned to go out to the Missouri frontier the next spring. She took a special interest in the lads. The strangeness of their environment and language difficulties brought problems. Sometime in January, Whitman returned to Ithaca and took Richard back to Rushville where, perhaps, he was placed in the home of his brother Augustus.

In Whitman's letter to Greene written from Rushville on December 17, he reported the presence of the boys. Replying on the 30th, Greene wrote: "I think you will have cause to regret that you brought the two Indian boys with you. Our whole experience is against such a measure. The boys will probably be ruined by the attention they will receive They can hardly fail to occasion considerable expense." [53] Here is a good example of Greene's straightforwardness in speaking his mind. As will be shown later, the two boys were of great help to the mission party on their westward journey the following summer. However, the high hopes of Whitman regarding the usefulness of the boys in the mission were not realized after their arrival in Old Oregon.

"We Could Cross the Mountains with a Wagon"

As has been stated, when Whitman wrote to Greene from St. Louis on November 7, 1835, he expressed his hope of finding associates and going out to Oregon the following spring if this met the approval of the Board. Although Whitman had said nothing in this letter of his desire to get married and take his wife with him over the Rockies, Greene was able to read between the lines. He replied on December 8 and asked: "Have you carefully ascertained & weighed the difficulties in the way of conducting females to those remote & desolate regions and comfortably sustaining families there?... How are annual supplies to be obtained with such certainty that a family may safely depend upon them." [54]

David Greene was a hard-headed New Englander, a Yale graduate, and a Board career man, to whom the difficulties of escorting women over the Rockies to Oregon and sustaining a family in such "remote & desolate regions" seemed insurmountable. Yet he was willing to accept Whitman's judgment. "You are better able to judge than we," he wrote. "If there is no obstacle here, we will send as many suitable persons as can be found." The final decision as to the feasibility and advisability of taking women over the Rockies and establishing homes in the Oregon wilderness was Whitman's. In making the decision to venture forward, Whitman was assuming a degree of cooperation from the natives which at that time was untested and unpredictable.

Even before receiving Greene's letter of December 8, Whitman had anticipated the questions which might be asked regarding the feasibility of taking women over the Rockies. Before mailing the journal of his travels to Greene, Whitman added a 2,000 word appendix in which he passed on important information about various western Indian tribes and commented especially on travel conditions. He answered three questions which he felt members of the Board would surely ask: (1) What protection was available for a mission party while crossing through hostile Indian territory? (2) What food supplies would be available to the members of a mission party while en route and after their arrival in Oregon? And (3) was it feasible to take women on a 1,900 mile trip after leaving the Missouri frontier across the plains and over the Rockies when they would have to ride on side-saddles most of the way?

Regarding protection for a mission party, he wrote: "I have every assurance [of traveling with the caravan] from Mr. Fontenelle if we should go out with him next year." Whitman did not seem to be concerned about the need for protection for the part of the journey which stretched from the Rendezvous to Fort Walla Walla.

Regarding food supplies, he explained: "Our subsistence would be such as we should take from the settlements to last us to Buffalo [i.e., the buffalo range]. We could take flour besides to last us in part to our destination. The Company would furnish us with meat from their hunters after we reach Buffalo... We could drive cows and other cattle without much if any expense and I would advise to take enough so that in case of necessity we might kill some for beef after we arrived at our destination." He added that after their arrival in Oregon, they could purchase supplies from the Hudson's Bay Company with drafts on the American Board. Whitman knew that the Jason Lee party had driven a small band of cattle to Oregon in 1834.

As to the feasibility of taking women, Whitman wrote: "We could cross the mountains with a wagon." The implication was clear: Wagons could be taken for the convenience of women should they grow weary riding on side-saddles.

What a contrast between Parker's report of his exploring tour and Whitman's factual and illuminating analysis of travel conditions. Parker looked into the future and prophesied that the day would come when a railroad would cross the Rockies. Whitman, considering the problems of the present, saw the possibility of taking wagons thus making it feasible for women to ride horseback over the mountains. In Whitman, the Board had unknowingly chosen a man well qualified to observe travel conditions and to make sound judgments regarding certain practical problems which a party of missionaries going overland to Oregon would have to face.

Whitman sent his journal with an accompanying letter to the Board from Rushville on December 17. Again he referred to the possibility of taking a wagon: "If you see fit to send [a] mission to the other side of the mountains, we can go as far as the Black Hills [i.e., Fort Laramie] with a wagon for the convenience of females and from that to rendezvous." For a third time, in his letter to Greene of December 28, 1835, he repeated the reference to a wagon: "We should go as far as the Black Hills with a wagon."

Greene, in his letter to Whitman dated December 30, frankly stated that the Board had found it difficult to recruit men willing to work in mission fields in America. Somehow the glamor of going overseas was more appealing. He wrote: "The patient, enduring, contented, unostentatious [person] whose love for God and the souls of men vents itself out, making no noise and never having their names heard of—these are the persons wanted for such a service." [55]

Oregon was then so far away and so isolated, that the prospect of making a journey of six months or more was frightening, especially for women. Mail service was spasmodic and uncertain. After their arrival on the field, the missionaries discovered that it usually took two years for a letter to be sent by sailing ship around Cape Horn to the States and for a reply to be received. Moreover, some candidates for the mission field questioned the wisdom of spending a lifetime working with a tribe having only a few hundred or possibly a few thousand members, and learning their language, when the same effort could be spent on some foreign field as China or India where the people were settled in cities and where millions spoke the same tongue. This issue was raised by the Rev. A. B. Smith, a member of the 1838 reenforcement to the Oregon Mission who settled among the Nez Perces in the upper Clearwater Valley. He came to the point where he deeply regretted his decision to go to the Nez Perces and wrote to Greene saying how much he wished he had gone to Siam.[56]

The year 1835 came to a close with Whitman engaged in doing what Parker had been doing just a year before—looking for missionaries, and especially for at least one married couple, who would be willing to go with him and Narcissa to Oregon. There was more urgency in Whitman's search than in Parker's—Whitman had promised to return the two Indian boys to their fathers in the summer of 1836. Since he wanted to be on his way to the Missouri frontier by the middle of February, Whitman had but six weeks to find some qualified couple who would accept his assurance that it was indeed possible for women to cross the Rockies

CHAPTER 6 ENDNOTES

1 The late Dr. F. C. Waite and I visited the Chester County cemetery in the summer of 1935 where we found the tombstones of many of Whitman's relatives and friends whom he had known in Massachusetts. John Packard's tombstone states that he died April 11, 1843.

2 *W.C.Q.*, II (1898):2:33, quotes Perrin Whitman as saying that his parents were then living at Deerfield, Ill. Samuel Whitman's record book (see fn. 3, Chapter Three) clearly states that he was living at Danville and not Deerfield.

3 Original certificate is in Coll. W. See picture in Drury, *Whitman*, p. 88.

4 For the sake of clarity and consistency, corrections have occasionally been made in quotations taken from Whitman's writings. Fontenelle's name, for instance, has a variety of spellings. Whitman and others of his day usually spelled wagon with a double "g"–"waggon."

5 Whitman College has no record as to the history of this item except that it was presented to the college in October 1949 by George A. Taber of Reading, Mass., who claimed that it was owned by Dr. Whitman. The inscription on the bag clearly indicates that it had once belonged to Parker.

6 *Op. cit.*, 5th ed., p. 46. Unless otherwise noted, all quotations from Parker's *Journal* will be from the 5th edition.

7 *Ibid.*, p. 46.

8 *Ibid.*, p. 37.

9 See notation Letter 11, Appendix 1, regarding location of the two versions of Whitman's journal.

10 This is one of the few references to bleeding found in Whitman's writings.

11 The word "concert" was often used by Christians of Whitman's day to indicate a prayer meeting, or "a concert of prayer."

12 Parker, *op. cit.*, p. 39.

13 Gray, *Oregon*, p. 107.

14 G. P. Glazebrook (ed.), *The Hargrave Correspondence*, Publications of the Champlain Society, Toronto, 1938, XXIV:235.

15 Parker, *op. cit.*, p. 46.

16 Fort Laramie was sometimes called Fort William after the fur trader, William Sublette.

17 Samuel J. Parker, M.D., in his manuscript in Coll. B, stated that his father used two notebooks on the trail: "One that he carried in his pocket, quite small, made of sheets of paper cut, and sewed together with thread. 2nd. A red spotted paper-covered note-book… that he wrote fuller in and kept in his valise as he travelled." All efforts to locate either or both of these notebooks have failed.

18 Parker, Journal, p. 47.

19 Hulbert, *O.P.*, VI: 150 ff.

20 *Ibid.*, p. 152.

21 The Fur Company's caravan usually made two camps or marches a day. The morning march was usually shorter than that of the afternoon. This meant two meals a day.

22 Hulbert, *O.P.*, VI:96.

23 Parker, *Journal*, p. 52.

24 *Ibid.*, p. 61.

25 Fitzpatrick had been one of the exploring party that discovered South Pass in March 1824. He was known as "Broken Hand." See L. R. Hafen and W. J. Ghent, *Broken Hand, Life Story of Thomas Fitzpatrick*, Denver, 1931.

26 Parker, *Journal*, p. 72.

27 Hafen, *Mountain Men*, v:95, quoting from Fontenelle's letter of August 1, 1835, in Drips Papers, Missouri Historical Society.

28 Parker, *Journal*, p. 77. Parker died in 1866, three years before the first transcontinental railroad was completed but near enough to know that his prophecy would be fulfilled.

29 See W. J. Ghent, *The Early Far West*, New York, 1936, and Bernard DeVoto, *Across the Wide Missouri*, Boston, 1948, for detailed information about the American fur companies and the Rendezvous.

30 Only three of the Rendezvous were held for the full or partial period at some site east of the Continental Divide—1829, 1830, and 1838.

31 See L. R. Hafen (ed.), *Mountain Men and the Fur Trade*, 10 vols., Clark Co., Glendale, Calif., 1965–72. All of the mountain men mentioned in this work have biographical sketches in this set. The first reference that the author has been able to find which calls the trappers "mountain men" is in the diary of Mrs. Cushing Eells, April 30, 1838. See Drury, *F.W.W.*, II:75.

32 J. K. Townsend, *Sporting Excursions in the Rocky Mountains*, London, 1840, I:123.

33 C. W. Ebberts ms., Coll. B., pp. 8–9.

34 Parker, *Journal*, p. 189.

35 The term "hole" was used by the trappers to designate a part of a valley.

36 Parker, *Journal*, pp. 80–1.

37 The use of ether was first demonstrated in this country in Boston in 1846.

38 Parker, in the first edition of his *Journal*, p. 77, wrote that calls for Dr. Whitman's services "were constant every hour of the day."

39 Parker to Greene, Aug. 17, 1835. Coll. A.

40 Parker, *Journal*, p. 82.

41 Op cit., p. 108.

42 Parker, *Journal*, p. 83.

43 Josephy, *The Nez Perce Indians*, p. 125.

44 Parker, *Journal*, p. 84.

45 Hafen, *Mountain Men*, I:148.

46 Dorothy O. Johansen (ed.), *Robert Newell's Memoranda*, p. 33.

47 Hulbert, *O.P.*, VI:158.

48 *Ibid.*, p. 142.

49 From Spalding's family Bible, Pacific University, Forest Grove, Ore.

50 Mrs. Caulkins ms., Coll. Wn.

51 Nixon, *How Marcus Whitman Saved Oregon* gives a different version of the incident, claiming that it was Whitman's mother who exclaimed: "Well, well, there is Marcus Whitman." Mowry in his *Marcus Whitman* and other writers have followed Nixon. The account given by the niece seems to be the true story.

52 Parker ms., Cornell University Library, Ithaca, N.Y.

53 Hulbert, *O.P.*, VI: 177.

54 *Ibid.*, p. 170.

55 Ibid., p. 176.

56 Drury, *Spalding and Smith*, p. 109.

[CHAPTER SEVEN]

MARCUS AND NARCISSA ARE MARRIED 1836

Sometime during the summer of 1835, Judge and Mrs. Prentiss with four of their children had moved from Amity to Angelica, about six miles to the north. The records of the Presbyterian Church of Angelica show that on Sunday, September 27, 1835: "Stephen Prentiss and Clarissa his wife, Narcissa, Clarissa, Harriet, R., and Edward W., their children," were received into the church.[1]

Narcissa with characteristic enthusiasm gave herself to the activities of the church, which then numbered about 135 members. She sang in the choir and taught a class of girls in the Sunday school. Included in the church's membership was William Geiger, Jr., of whom we shall hear more later.

Judge Prentiss was elected an elder in the Angelica church on January 21, 1836, and was ordained to that office on Thursday evening, February 18, just before the marriage service was conducted for his daughter Narcissa and Marcus Whitman. An indication of the interest that Stephen Prentiss took in the church is the fact that he and his pastor, the Rev. Leverett Hull, were commissioners to the Presbyterian General Assembly which met in Philadelphia in May 1836.

Writing to Sarah Hull, the wife of the pastor, in the spring of 1835, Narcissa expressed her deep concern about the proposed Oregon Mission.[2]

Narcissa referred to some "obstacles" which had arisen which threatened the founding of an Oregon Mission. She asked her friend: "What can be the obstacles which the Board of Missions speak of? Is it want of funds or missionaries? Or is it the want of faith and prayer in the churches?" Narcissa then recalled the Nez Perce appeal of 1831: "Surely the obstacles cannot be with the Indians, whom they have sent over to us and invited us to carry them the Word of Life." Out of touch with Marcus who was then on his long trek to the Rockies, Narcissa was dreaming, planning, and praying for that Oregon Mission of which she wanted to be a part. Again quoting from her letter: "I can say, notwithstanding the clouds of darkness that overshadow the future, and the obstacles that roll up before the mind like waves of the sea, that I am permitted to believe that a mission will be established there soon, at least before many years shall have passed away."

The Search for Associates

Whitman's major concern after his return from the Rockies was to find at least one married couple to go with him and Narcissa to Oregon in the spring of 1836. As previously stated, Narcissa had told Marcus about the plans of Henry and Eliza Spalding to go as missionaries to the Osage Indians. Whitman had written to Spalding to see if they would consent to a change of destination and go with him and Narcissa to Oregon. When Whitman mailed his journal to Greene from Rushville on December 17, he reported: "I received a letter yesterday from H. H. Spalding saying that he would be ready to accompany me across the mountains if the Board would approve of it."

For a time Whitman's heart was at ease as he felt that the Board would consent to a reassignment for the Spaldings. Greene had been informed that Mrs. Spalding was expecting to give birth to a child in October 1835. Whitman, however, had failed to tell him that the child was stillborn, perhaps assuming that Spalding would have passed on this information. This failure to keep Greene posted almost canceled any hope of a mission party going out to Oregon in 1836.

A letter from Greene dated December 8 reached Whitman at Rushvile after he had mailed his journal. The slowness of the mails of that day added to the complexities of the problem. Greene put the burden of finding associates on Whitman's shoulders. "Before taking measures to obtain associates," he wrote, "you had better confer with our agent, Mr. Eddy, who may have some person in mind." The reference is to the Rev. Chauncey Eddy, to whom reference has already been made.[3] Greene then gave the names of several possible candidates, including those of the Rev., and Mrs. Oliver S. Powell, in whose home Whitman was a guest at the time he became engaged to Narcissa.

The month of December 1835 passed with the Board making no definite appointments for the Oregon Mission. Whitman was still waiting for confirmation from the Board as to a change of destination for the Spaldings.

The Prudential Committee of the Board met in Boston on January 5, and the next day Greene wrote to Whitman notifying him that the Committee had authorized him to return to Oregon with his wife, another married couple and three single men—preferably a teacher, a farmer, and a "mechanic"—if such could be found. The term "mechanic" was then used to indicate a craftsman, such as a carpenter, or even a laborer. Greene definitely stated: "But families of children cannot be taken." He added that should an Oregon Mission party be sent, the fiancées of Dunbar and Allis would accompany them to Council Bluffs and that in all probability Dr. Benedict Satterlee, who had been appointed to the Pawnee Mission, would also go along. No mention was made of Spalding in this letter.

On this same day, January 5, Whitman again wrote to Greene and again brought up the name of Spalding. He reminded Greene that Spalding had indicated his willingness to go to Oregon and also mentioned the fact that the Powells had a baby, which meant that they could not be appointed. Greene, replying on January 15, explained why nothing had been said about the Spaldings. "The same object," he wrote, "we suppose to he against Mr. and Mrs. Spalding which you mention in the case of Mr. Powell."

A week later Greene again wrote to Whitman informing him that other prospective candidates for the Oregon Mission had for various reasons withdrawn their names from consideration. Then came the following comment about Spalding: "I do not know where to look for a missionary to accompany you, unless Mr. Spaulding[4] should go. His child (as I understand he has one) will be a hinderance; and it seems to me that no person with an infant child should go to such a work."

Here, seemingly, was a modification of Greene's former statement that no couple with a child would be appointed. Then followed a most significant comment on Spalding's personality which fell like a thin shadow on things to come: "Besides I have some doubt whether his temperament will fit him for intercourse with the traders and travellers in that region." Actually, as later events proved, Spalding's problem was not to be with traders and travelers but rather with his own coworkers in the mission. Greene did have a favorable word: "As to labouriousness, self-denial, energy and perseverance, I presume few men are better qualified than he."[5]

Matters were rapidly approaching a crisis. Whitman had given the most solemn assurances to the fathers of the two Indian boys that he would bring them to the 1836 Rendezvous and he had also promised to meet Parker there at that time. The month of January was about gone with nothing definite accomplished. If there were to be an Oregon Mission established that year, the party should be on its way within a month.

Whitman's letter to Greene of January 29, in reply to Greene's letter of the 22nd, was filled with discouraging news. Whitman confessed that all his efforts to find someone to go with him and Narcissa had failed. "I wrote Mr. Eddy some time since," he stated, "and have been in constant expectation of an answer, but do not receive it. We ought to leave for St. Louis by 25th Feb. or at the furtherest the 1st March."

Whitman clarified the status of the Spaldings by writing: "Your allusion to Mr. Spalding is not correct; they lost their child by death some time since. They expect to be at Prattsburg where I can see him if desired." Whitman was still hoping that Greene would have success in finding someone, for he wrote: "I should like to know your success and intention as soon as possible."

In his letter to Whitman of the previous December 30, Greene had listed some of the qualifications needed by any who aspired to be a missionary to the Indians, including: "Much apparent zeal for the conversion of the Indians, strong professions of devotedness to the cause of Christ, and readiness to encounter hardship and danger... and such I hope you may find the finger of Providence pointing to." Replying to Whitman's letter of January 29, Greene on February 5 rather reluctantly admitted that "the finger of Providence" was pointing to Henry H.

Spalding. One by one all other possible candidates had been eliminated. The Spaldings were already under appointment to go to the Osage Indians, but had indicated a willingness to change their destination. The need for some immediate decision prompted Greene to give a half-hearted consent, for he wrote: "I know not who will accompany you unless Mr. Spalding should." Before receiving Greene's letter, Whitman on February 6, wrote to a brother-in-law of Samuel Parker, Harley Lord, in whose Ithaca home John, one of the Nez Perce boys, was living, and said: "The present prospect is poor for going next spring. Our only other method is to have the destination of Rev. H. H. Spalding changed from the Osages to the Nez Perces." [6]

Henry Harmon Spalding

Henry Harmon Spalding was born out of wedlock in a log cabin near Wheeler, Steuben County, New York, on November 26, 1803.[7] He was therefore, nearly fifteen months younger than Marcus Whitman. Abandoned by his mother when a babe only fourteen months old and reared in a foster home, Henry had a hard time. Years later, the Rev. James Hotchkin, who was once his pastor, stated that Spalding had been "inured to hardship from infancy." [8]

Little is known of the first seventeen years of Spalding's life. In his old age, Spalding returned to Wheeler and was invited to occupy the pulpit in the Presbyterian Church on a Sunday in May 1871. Some of his old friends and neighbors were present. Great emotions swept over him as he looked into the faces of gray-haired men and women who had known him in his youth. The intervening years rolled away, and he saw himself with self-pitying eyes in his own yesterdays.

The next day he wrote to his wife, the second Mrs. Spalding, and in this letter pulled aside the veil which had shrouded those first seventeen years: "Some mates of those school days were present, grayheaded men and women. What memories! The place where I was born and the place where my unfeeling mother gave me (but 14 months old) to a stranger and saw her child no more, and the place where I was brought up by an adopted mother, and where I was kicked out, and the brook and the willow and the hill where I fished and played and tumbled with other children,... and the hills and the bottoms where I gathered chestnuts and butternuts and the road I took when he kicked me out after whipping my mother and me, to a neighbor, sad, destitute, 17, crying, a cast off bastard wishing myself dead! What emotions!"[9]

The forlorn lad, with the odious epithet "bastard," which an infuriated foster father had shouted at him, ringing in his ears, took the road to Prattsburg. There he found shelter in the home of Ezra Rice, a schoolteacher, where he remained for the next four years, 1820–24. Of these years Spalding wrote in his diary: "[I] worked for my board and room and went to a common school which he taught."[10] His opportunities for an education were limited; he noted in his diary that when he was twenty-one he could read only with difficulty and could laboriously "write after a copy."

Henry enrolled in the newly opened Franklin Academy in Prattsburg in the summer of 1825 when he was twenty-two years old. In the autobiographical note that he wrote in the beginning of his diary, he made mention of his "bashfulness" when called upon to speak before some school audience. Using modern psychological terms, might we not call this an inferiority complex? And how could it have been otherwise when one remembers his background? He was five or six years older than his classmates. He was without doubt clad in the plainest of clothing. He was at this time living in the home of a farmer three miles from the village, where he worked for his board and room, and walked back and forth to school. He was, as he described himself, "worse than an orphan."

Henry was a student at the academy at irregular intervals from the summer of 1825 to the early fall of 1831. Sometimes he interrupted his studies in order to make some money by teaching country schools, especially during the winter months. We must admire his tenacity in his struggle for an education against great odds. He was baptized and received into the membership of the Prattsburg Presbyterian Church on October 2, 1825, when he was twenty-two. During the winter of 1828–29, Henry decided to enter the ministry. At that time Franklin Academy was prepared to give the first two years of college work, so Henry returned to the academy. With scholarship aid from the American Education Society,[11] Henry enrolled in Western Reserve College at Hudson, Ohio, in the fall of 1831. He was graduated from that institution with an A.B. degree in 1833.

Eliza Hart Spalding

Sometime during 1830, Spalding began corresponding with Eliza Hart, who at that time was living with her parents, Captain and Mrs. Levi Hart, at Holland Patent, near Utica, New York, and about 140 miles northeast of Prattsburg. Eliza was born at Kensington, later called Berlin, Connecticut, on August 11, 1807. She was, therefore, about four years younger than Henry and about eight months older than Narcissa.

Henry and Eliza had not met before they began writing to each other on the recommendation of a mutual friend. They first met in the fall of 1831 shortly before he left for college in Ohio. Another year passed with the two depending upon the mails for their courtship. Henry visited Eliza again in the fall of 1832, at which time it appears that they became engaged.

Eliza was deeply religious. She joined the Presbyterian Church of Holland Patent on August 15, 1826, when nineteen years old. William H. Gray, who went out to Oregon with the Whitman–Spalding party in 1836, wrote his impressions of Eliza as he remembered her at their first meeting: "She was above medium height, slender in form, with coarse features, dark brown hair, blue eyes, rather dark complexion, coarse voice, of a serious turn of mind, and quick in understanding language." [12]

Little is known about Eliza's youth and education. She is reported to have attended a female seminary in Clinton, New York, and to have taught school for a time.[13] She had some ability in painting and learned the common skills needed in a pioneer home of her generation including spinning and weaving. Eliza attended a school at Hudson, Ohio, 1832–33 while Henry was taking his last year of college work at Western Reserve College. The two were married in Hudson on October 13, 1833, and left soon afterwards for Lane Theological Seminary, a New School Presbyterian institution located in Walnut Hills, Cincinnati, where they spent the next two years.

Henry found Eliza to be a devoted and faithful helpmate. Since the Presbyterian Church at that time frowned upon seminary students getting married, Henry was disqualified from receiving further scholarship aid. He and Eliza opened a boarding house at Walnut Hills for other students and provided board and room for $3.00 a week. Henry bought a cow which supplied milk for their table. He also worked in a printing establishment thus learning a trade which proved of value to him in Old Oregon.

Eliza Spalding is pictured in several fictional accounts of the Oregon Mission as being poorly educated and of a weak character. The contrary is the case. She was the best educated of the six women who were in the Oregon Mission. Confirming evidence to support this judgment is found in the following quotation from a letter Eliza wrote to a sister from Walnut Hills on March 31, 1834: "I am now pursuing Greek and Hebrew studies. I take the same lessons that Mr. S. does in the Greek Testament, and in the Hebrew Bible. I am quite pleased with these studies, but find the Greek Grammar rather perplexing. I generally attend Dr. [Lyman] Beecher's lectures on Theology, Saturdays, from the hours of ten to twelve, which are very interesting and profitable."[14] Perhaps no one in the Oregon Mission acquired the native language more quickly than she.

Spalding Appointed by the American Board

Hoping to secure a teacher's position under the Government with the Choctaw Indians, Henry decided to leave the Seminary in May 1835 at the end of his second year and one year before completing the full theological course. Due application was made for such an appointment. In the expectation of receiving favorable word, Henry and Eliza returned to Holland Patent to make preparations for leaving for their new work. Captain Hart gave the couple a light Dearborn wagon and other items valued at $120.00.[15] This is the much publicized wagon which Whitman and Spalding took with them over the Rockies and as far west as Fort Boise in 1836, but of this more will be said later.

In a letter dated March 20, 1888, to the Rev. Myron Eells,[16] the Rev. J. S. Griffin[17] wrote: "Touching the question of wagons from the East to this coast... I will say, that on the 5th day of July, 1835, in the town of Holland Patent... I worked with H. H. Spalding on the barn floor of his father-in-law, a Mr. Hart, in putting the top on a small wagon, when he was soon to leave for the west to engage in Indian Missions."[18] From this we know that this became a covered wagon.

Perrin Whitman, who saw the remains of the wagon at Fort Boise in the fall of 1843, wrote: "It had been one of the old fashioned Deerborn wagons, with wooden springs from one axle to another made out of hard wood... The bed was of a dark brown color, and the wheels were yellow with blue stripes. It was as a light two horse wagon." [19]

Several weeks passed after Spalding sent in his application for a government appointment without any reply being received. Spalding was becoming increasingly worried as he had been so confident that the appointment would be forthcoming. During the latter part of July 1835, the Spaldings loaded their few possessions on their wagon and drove to Prattsburg. Still more days passed without any word from the government. Spalding then wrote to the American Board and offered to go to "any part of that portion of the vineyard of Christ over which the Lord has appointed you stewards." [20]

In order to hasten consideration by the Board of his application, Spalding asked several who knew him to send in testimonials. Among these was Artemas Bullard, field agent of the Presbyterian Foreign Missionary Society who, in a letter dated August 14, made the following penetrating comment: "I consider Mr. S. a man of ardent piety. His mental powers are not remarkable, though decent... Few men are willing to labor more abundantly or endure more fatigue, or make greater sacrifices than he... He can turn his hand to almost any kind of handy work. Is not remarkable for judgment and common sense, though not particularly deficient. Is sometimes too much inclined to denounce or censure those who are not as zealous and ardent as himself... On the whole I expect in his proper place he will make a good missionary. His wife is highly respected and beloved in a large circle of friends on Walnut Hill and in Cincinnati." [21]

Greene replied to Spalding's letter of application on August 14. The Board was in urgent need of men for its Indian missions and welcomed his interest. Greene advised Spalding to be ordained "as if you were appointed" and said that the Prudential Committee would act on his application at its next meeting. Spalding met with the Presbytery of Bath and, after being examined and found qualified, was ordained to the ministry on August 27, 1835. Sometime that fall, Spalding was notified that the Board had appointed him to the Boudinot station among the Osage Indians on the Neosho River in what is now eastern Kansas. The notification of their assignment came too late for the Spaldings to go to their field in the fall of 1835. Eliza was pregnant and gave birth at Prattsburg to the stillborn baby girl on October 24. Following her confinement, Eliza was seriously ill for several weeks. Sometime during the week of December 10, Spalding received word from Whitman asking if he and his wife would be willing to change their destination from the Osage to the Nez Perce Indians. Whitman, while at Rushville, received a letter from Spalding on December 16 in which Spalding stated their willingness to go to Oregon should the Board approve.

Spalding's Unfortunate Remark

Spalding wrote to Greene from Holland Patent on December 28, 1835: "If the Board and Dr. Whitman wish me to go to the Rocky Mountains with him, I am ready. Act your pleasure." Evidently the Spaldings had returned to Eliza's parental home for a few weeks before leaving for their mission field, wherever that might be. Greene, still unaware of the death of the Spalding baby, replied on January 2: "It does not seem to me desirable that yr destination should be changed to the Rocky Mountain Indians at this time unless you strongly desire it." [22] Greene evidently felt that the Spaldings might go to the Osage Indians with an infant but should not attempt taking one with them on the long and hazardous journey over the Rockies to Oregon. Spalding was not told why the Board was reluctant to approve a change of destination for him.

The Spaldings returned to Prattsburg during the first week of February 1836 where they spent several days before leaving for their Osage Indian station. Since some of Spalding's Prattsburg friends knew that he had been under consideration to go with the Whitmans to Oregon, the questions naturally arose: Why was Whitman still looking for associates? Why were the Spaldings not going to Oregon? Circumstantial evidence suggests that Spalding was put on the defensive. His pride had been touched. Some explanation was needed, so one day in a public assembly—perhaps in a church service—he said: "I do not want to go into the same mission with Narcissa Prentiss as I question her judgment." [23] Such a statement reflected a latent feeling of resentment or possibly even of hostility on Spalding's part towards Narcissa. He could not forget that he had been a rejected suitor.

Some have wondered why Whitman ever induced Spalding to join him in the Oregon Mission project. A writer in the *American Heritage* called this a "baffling" detail and characterized Spalding as being "a man of touchy pride and smoldering resentments." [24] The most plausible answer to this question is that Whitman had no other choice. After an extensive search for associates, with one after another possible candidate being eliminated for various reasons, Whitman had to take whomever he could find who was willing to go with him and Narcissa to Oregon. Time was running out. He had promised to return the Indian boys to their fathers and to meet Parker at the 1836 Rendezvous; and he had assured the Nez Perces that he would return with associates in 1836 and open a mission among them. Possibly Whitman had not heard of Spalding's unfortunate remark, or, if he had heard, had failed to appreciate its full significance. The fact that Narcissa was the one who first suggested Spalding's name, even though he was a rejected suitor, shows that she harbored no ill will towards him. Perhaps she felt that since Henry had married Eliza Hart, his memory of a broken romance would not be an obstacle.

"We Want You for Oregon"

Greene's letter of February 5, in which a reluctant approval was given for Whitman to see if Spalding would consent going to Oregon, reached Whitman on the 12th. Whitman felt that the urgency of the occasion called for immediate action. He decided to ride at once to Prattsburg, where he understood the Spaldings were then staying, and make a personal appeal. From circumstantial evidence, it appears that Whitman arrived in Prattsburg either on Friday afternoon, the 12th, or early the next morning. To his great disappointment, he learned that the Spaldings had left for Howard, a village about twenty miles to the southwest of Prattsburg, where Spalding had a speaking appointment on Sunday in the Presbyterian Church there.

A winter storm had laid a thick blanket of snow over the land making travel difficult. Because of the snow, Spalding had to put runners on his wagon, thus converting it into a sleigh.

Whitman set out from Prattsburg in pursuit of the Spaldings and overtook them on the road shortly before they arrived at Howard with the hail: "We want you for Oregon." [25] Whitman continued with them into the village where Spalding engaged a room in the inn.[26] There Whitman presented his plea. He reviewed the course of events and explained how Greene had been reluctant to assign them to Oregon because he thought that their child had lived.

Whitman stressed the argument of need. Unless he could find a clergyman to go with him and Narcissa, there would be no Oregon Mission founded that year.

This struck a responsive chord in the hearts of both Henry and Eliza. They were not afraid of the journey, having been satisfied by what Whitman told them regarding the feasibility of women crossing the Rockies. It is possible that Whitman referred to their wagon and urged them to take it with them. Henry was a little hesitant, because he felt that Eliza might not be physically strong enough to endure the long horseback ride, but she pluckily declared: "I like the command just as it stands, 'Go ye into all the world,' and no exceptions for poor health." [27] The three sought God's guidance in prayer.

Being assured of the willingness of the Spaldings to accompany him and Narcissa to Oregon, Whitman returned to Rushville on Monday, February 15, with a light heart. His Oregon Mission was assured! Yet in a letter that he wrote to Greene from Rushville that evening, we find a trace of apprehension: "I am willing to accompany Mr. Spalding as an associate, yet I know little of his peculiar adaptedness to that station." Whitman told Greene that the Spaldings would continue their journey to Cincinnati where they would await his arrival. He suggested that Greene write to him at that place and confirm the change of destination.

Writing to Greene from Jamestown, New York, on February 17, Spalding reviewed what had happened at Howard. "He says," Spalding wrote, "you are perfectly willing the destiny should be changed. He said all the other attempts to obtain a clergyman have failed and if I refused, the Mission to the Rocky Mountains must be abandoned, at least for the present... I felt it my duty to consent to his request." [28]

We have reason to believe that the Spaldings visited the Prentiss home in Angelica, which was about thirty miles to the west of Howard and along the route that they were following to Jamestown, New York, on their way to Pittsburgh. If so, they could have carried a letter from Marcus to Narcissa informing her of the developments and suggesting that she plan for their wedding that very week.

From a statement made by Narcissa in a letter she wrote to her father on October 10, 1840, it appears that Judge Prentiss had heard about Spalding's unfortunate remark about not wanting to go "into the same mission with Narcissa Prentiss," and had demanded an explanation.

Narcissa wrote: "This pretended settlement with father, before we started, was only an excuse, and from all we have seen and heard, both during the journey and since we have been here the same bitter feeling exists." The resentment which Henry Spalding harbored towards Narcissa Whitman was to have far-reaching consequences for the Oregon Mission of the American Board.

Their Personal Appearance

Before telling of the marriage of Marcus and Narcissa and of their departure for Oregon, it is fitting that mention should be made of the descriptions of their personal appearance which were made by their contemporaries. Until the discovery in the summer of 1968 of what appear to be authentic sketches of Marcus and Narcissa Whitman made by the Canadian artist, Paul Kane, regarding which more will be said later, we had to rely only upon these recollections of their contemporaries as to their personal appearance.

Joel Wakeman described Narcissa as follows: "She was of medium height, symmetrically formed, very graceful in her deportment and general carriage, slightly sandy complexion, a brilliant, sparkling eye, perculiarly so when engaged in animated conversation. She was not a beauty, and yet, when engaged in singing or conversation there was something in her appearance very attractive." [29] Levi Waldo, also drawing upon personal recollections, wrote: "She was a beautiful blonde, of fair form and well rounded features, dignified and stately, yet modest in her bearing, kindly and Christian in social life, honoring and gracing every station that she was called to fill." [30] In another account she was described as being "of slight build, a little above medium height, blue eyes, pretty, with beautiful blonde hair." [31] Others referred to her hair as being a golden or light colored auburn.[32] Narcissa weighed herself a few weeks after her marriage and in a letter to her sister Jane said that the scales registered 136 pounds [Letter 21]. Writing to her parents on October 9, 1844, Narcissa stated that she then weighed 167 pounds, "much higher than ever before in my life."

Several idealized portraits or sketches have been made of Narcissa, one of which by Mrs. Orville R. Allen hangs in Prentiss Hall at Whitman College. This is a lifesize study which shows her wearing a gray silk dress with flowing sleeves and a low neck line. The artist was guided by some hazy tradition that she wore such a dress and "fluffed up her hair" once when about to greet her husband upon his return from a trip.[33] According to Matilda Sager Delaney, who spent several years as a little girl in the Whitman mission home, Narcissa never had a silk dress. The sleeves, which the artist copied from a pair which once belong to Narcissa, were the only authentic part of the portrait.[34]

When the Rev. Oliver W. Nixon published his *How Marcus Whitman Saved Oregon* [see Appendix 4], he included idealized pictures of both Marcus and Narcissa. The first and second editions of this work give an imaginary picture of Narcissa without any explanation as to how it happened to have been drawn or by whom. A different drawing appeared in the third and subsequent editions with the following caption: "No authentic picture of Mrs. Whitman is in existence. This portrait of her has been drawn under the supervision of a gentleman familiar with her appearance and with suggestions from members of her family. It is considered a good likeness of her." However, when we compared this second Nixon picture with the Kane sketch, we see only slight similarities.

W. H. Gray, in his *History of Oregon*, has given us the following description of Narcissa: "...a lady of refined feelings and commanding appearance. She had very light hair, fresh complexion, and light blue eyes. Her features were large, her form full and round. At the time she arrived in the country [i.e., Oregon], she was considered a fine, noble-looking woman, affable and free to converse with all she met. Her conversation was animated and cheerful. Firmness in her was natural, and to some, especially the Indians, it was repulsive."[35] Gray's comment about the reaction of the Indians to her firmness, is confirmed in the appraisal given her by the Rev. H. K. W. Perkins [See Appendix 6].

The first two editions of Nixon's book also carried an idealized sketch of Marcus Whitman. Incredible to relate, he is there pictured as wearing the ministerial garb of 1870. A retouched picture of Whitman appeared in the third edition with this anachronism corrected but with Whitman wearing burnsides, unknown in 1836. Under this retouched sketch, Nixon stated: "Changes have been made under the supervision of the family, who now pronounce this a very correct likeness." Since this sketch, like that of Narcissa, was drawn some thirty-five years after Whitman had been killed, it can have no claim to accuracy. It certainly has no resemblance to the recently discovered sketch by Kane believed to be of Whitman.[36]

Gray in his *Oregon*, has given us the following description of Whitman: "He was above medium height; of spare habit; peculiar hair, a portion of each being white and a dark brown, so that it might be called iron-gray; deep blue eyes, and large mouth." [37]

Two members of the 1844 Oregon emigration spent some time working for Whitman at his mission station, each of whom has given us his reminiscences. Alanson Hinman, of whom further mention will be made, wrote: "He [was]... tall, with high cheek bones and prominent eyebrows, beneath which were grave kindly eyes of gray." [38] B. F. Nichols, who as an eighteen-year-old youth spent the winter of 1844–45 at Waiilatpu, wrote in 1897: "I think he was a man that would weigh about 175 pounds, being what we would call a raw-boned man. He was muscular and sineway, with broad shoulders, neck slightly bent forward... His eyes were blue, rather dark, I think; his hair was brown, his forehead massive and broad, and his nose, though not large, was straight and prominent. His cheekbones were high and prominent, and his mouth was nearer like General Grant's than any one else I know of, denoting firmness and determination." [39] Nichols also told of seeing Whitman walk into a corral and catch a three-year-old steer by the under jaw and near horn and throw it to the ground. "Bulldogging" steers is still practiced in western rodeos and indicates skill as well as great physical strength.

Several attempts have been made in recent years to create an idealized portrait of Marcus Whitman. One of the best known is that painted by Ernest Ralph Norling; it was presented by a group of physicians and surgeons of the Pacific Northwest to Whitman College in August 1936 at the time of the Whitman Centennial celebration. This is a life-size study and pictures Whitman with a beard and clad in buckskins. The two statues which have been made of Whitman, will be described in the last chapter of this work.

MARCUS AND NARCISSA ARE MARRIED

When Marcus sent word to Narcissa of his success in persuading the Spaldings to go with them to Oregon, she immediately planned for the marriage to be performed on Thursday evening, February 18. The time was opportune as a congregational meeting of the Angelica Presbyterian Church had been called for that evening when her father was to be ordained an elder. An audience would thus be on hand then for the wedding. Marcus had found it necessary to return to Rushville after seeing the Spaldings at Howard, but was able to arrive at Angelica by Wednesday, the 17th. Narcissa's bombazine wedding dress had already been made.[40]

According to the minute book of the Angelica church, after Judge Prentiss and two others were ordained as elders, the newly constituted session met and granted a letter of dismission "to our sister Narcissa Prentiss who is destined to the Mission beyond the Rocky Mountains." As will be stated, Narcissa presented this letter when the First Presbyterian Church of Oregon was organized on August 18, 1838.

In a letter to her parents written about two years after her marriage, Narcissa mentioned a communion service held just before her wedding. Judge Prentiss, as one of the newly-ordained elders, could have served the bread and the cup to his daughter and future son-in-law. Then came the exchange of vows when Marcus and Narcissa were made husband and wife.

According to the custom of the day, the minister then preached a sermon, which may have been addressed especially to the bridal couple. Of that sermon Narcissa later wrote: "Brother Hull, you know not how much good that sermon I heard you preach... the which you gave me, does me now in this desert land. O that I had more than one! I read it, meditate upon it in my solitary hours until the truth of it burns upon my heart and cheers my soul with its blessed promise" [Letter 37].

The dramatic events of the evening came to a climax with the singing of the following sentimental hymn[41] written by the Rev. Samuel F. Smith, the author of "America."

Yes, my native land! I love thee;

All thy scenes I love them well;

Friends, connections, happy country, Can I bid you all farewell?

Can I leave thee, can I leave thee,

Far in heathen lands to dwell?

Home!–thy joys are passing lovely

Joys no stranger-heart can tell;

Happy home!–'tis sure I love thee!

> Can I-can I say-Farewell?
>
> Can I leave thee, can I leave thee,
>
> Far in heathen lands to dwell?

One by one members of the choir and congregation found their throats constricted with emotion and their cheeks dampened with tears. Only a few, including Narcissa, sang the next stanza:

> Yes! I hasten gladly,
>
> From the scenes I love so well;
>
> Far away, ye billows! bear me;
>
> Lovely native land!-farewell!
>
> Pleased I leave thee, pleased I leave thee,
>
> Far in heathen lands to dwell.

Muffled sobs could be heard by the time the last stanza was reached. The sentiment of the hymn was too overpowering. Narcissa in her clear soprano voice, which Wakeman described as being "as sweet and musical as a chime of bells," sang the last stanza as a solo—a dramatic event which all present that evening never forgot.

> In the deserts let me labor,
>
> On the mountains let me tell,
>
> How he died-the blessed Saviour
>
> To redeem a world from hell!
>
> Let me hasten, let me hasten,
>
> Far in heathen lands to dwell.[42]

The next day the bridal couple left for Rushville and Ithaca to get Richard and John before leaving for St. Louis. Imagination alone must supply the details of their last farewells. No doubt all were aware that the parting might be final. Narcissa, like Eliza Spalding, was never to return.

From a reference in one of Narcissa's letters [#35], we know that the Whitmans spent Sunday, February 21 in Ithaca. Samuel J. Parker, M.D., years later recalled their visit: "Dr. Whitman made addresses in the churches; and Mrs. Whitman in the Sunday schools, especially the Presby. and the Dutch Reformed Churches."[43] Undoubtedly present in the latter church was Miss Mary Augusta Dix who, almost exactly two years later, was to marry William Henry Gray and leave at once with the 1838 reenforcement of the American Board for its Oregon Mission.

Following their visit in Ithaca, the Whitmans with at least one of the Nez Perce boys went to Rushville where final farewells had to be said again. Only a few scattered references in the Whitman letters throw light upon the events of those days. We read of Whitman speaking in the Congregational Church on Sunday, February 28. Narcissa, in her letter of March 31 to her sister Jane, wrote: "I had made for me in Brother Augustusí shoe store in Rushville, a pair of gentlemen's boots, and from him we supplied ourselves with what shoes we wanted." The women of the church presented Marcus with some shirts which he was tempted to leave behind as surplus baggage when arranging the packs before leaving the Missouri frontier. Narcissa, however, persuaded him to take them [Letter 26].

Nothing was said in any of the correspondence between the Board and the Whitmans and the Spaldings about a salary. Apparently the missionaries were content to receive traveling expenses and such funds as were needed to make their mission self-supporting. Likewise nothing was said about furloughs, retirement, or educational benefits for children. In simple faith, which many church leaders of today would call unrealistic and improvident, these devoted missionaries moved into their future, believing that the Lord would provide.

Whitman, like Spalding, made appeals for funds for the Board in a number of churches interested in their proposed mission. Writing to the Board on March 3, 1836, Whitman reported that he had received $26.00 from the Angelica church and $200.00 from the Rushville congregation. According to a financial report he submitted to the Board on September 5, the traveling expenses for himself, his wife, and the two Indian boys from Rushville to Cincinnati covering the dates March 3–18 were $185.11. Even such a modest sum might have included the cost of some supplies.

The Whitmans bade their loved ones and friends at Rushville farewell on Thursday, March 3, and started in private conveyance for Pittsburgh going by way of Elmira, New York, and Williamsport and Hollidaysburg, Pennsylvania. Near Williamsport, they overtook Dr. and Mrs. Benedict Satterlee and Miss Emeline Palmer, the fiancée of Samuel Allis, who were on their way to join the Pawnee Mission.[44] These three had left Ithaca on March 1 but, because of the ill health of Mrs. Satterlee, their travels had been interrupted. The mission party, now numbering seven, spent Sunday, March 6, in Williamsport where a local doctor was called to consult with Whitman and Satterlee regarding Mrs. Satterlee's condition.

In those days the American Board did not require a physical examination of its missionary candidates. This was not due to carelessness but rather to the current lack of medical knowledge. Dr. Satterlee had just completed his course at the Fairfield Medical College and presumably was as qualified as any physician could then be to diagnose his bride's physical condition. Her health, however, was so precarious by the time they reached Williamsport that there was some thought of sending her home [Letter 22]. A day's rest in an inn proved so beneficial that the doctors felt she could continue with the party.

The missionaries continued their journey by sleigh on Monday, March 7, and arrived at Pittsburgh the following Saturday. Had they been traveling a few weeks later, they could have taken the recently opened Allegheny Portage Railroad from Hollidaysburg to Pittsburgh, but this was closed during the winter months. The party took rooms in the Exchange Hotel.[45] On Sunday Marcus with the two Indian boys attended the East Liberty Presbyterian Church[46] where the boys created a sensation when their identities became known. Narcissa, suffering from a headache, remained in her room at the hotel [Letter 20]. Here, the following day, she spent her twenty-eighth birthday. The party secured passage down the Ohio River on the 127-ton steamboat, *Siam*, that left Pittsburgh Tuesday morning, the 15th. The vessel had been launched in 1835 and was the one which had carried Whitman and Parker up the Missouri River to Liberty that spring.

CHAPTER 7 ENDNOTES

1 I examined the original records of this church, now no longer in existence, in the summer of 1935.

2 Mowry, *Marcus Whitman*, pp. 65 ff. Whitman letter #10. Mowry gives no date or place of writing.

3 See fn. 10, Chapter Four.

4 Spalding spelled his name without the "u."

5 Hulbert, *O.P.*, printed some of the letters Greene sent to Whitman but did not include his letter of January 22, 1835, from which this quotation is taken. Copy is in Coll. A.

6 Parker ms., Coll. W.

7 Drury, *Spalding*, gives details about the early life of H. H. Spalding.

8 Hotchkin to the American Board, August 6, 1835, Coll. A.

9 Spalding to his wife, May 3, 1871, Coll. O.

10 Original diary in Coll. W.

11 Organized in 1815 to aid indigent students studying for the ministry, largely Congregational in its constituency but for a time included the Presbyterians.

12 Gray, *Oregon*, p. 110.

13 For more details regarding Eliza Spalding's early life, see Drury, *Spalding*.

14 Original letter is in the Presbyterian Historical Society, Philadelphia. Dr. Beecher was then President of Lane Theological Seminary.

15 Spalding reported this price to the American Board as the value of "sundries" given to him and his wife by "Capt. Hart for miss. to Flat Head Indians." See *Missionary Herald*, May 1836, p. 196. Capt. Hart did not know when he gave the wagon and other items to the Spaldings that they would be going to Oregon. He was much opposed to his daughter going so far away. Capt. Hart died Feb. 27, 1846, and in his will denied Eliza any of his property unless she returned home. Drury, *Spalding*, p. 317.

16 A son of the Rev. Cushing Eells who was a member of the 1838 reenforcement to the Oregon Mission.

17 Rev. J. S. Griffin and his wife went overland to Oregon in 1839 as independent missionaries.

18 Original letter in Coll. W.

19 *W.C.Q.*, II (1898):2:36.

20 Original, Coll. A.

21 *Ibid.*

22 Drury, *Spalding*, pp. 68-9.

23 Drury, *Spalding and Smith*, p. 294, quoting from an entry in Spalding's diary for July 9, 1840. See also Smith to Greene, September 3, 1840, Coll. A.; Gray to Greene, October 14, 1840; and Drury, *Whitman*, p. 119.

24 *Op. cit.*, August 1959, p. 44.

25 Spalding, *Senate Document*, p. 9.

26 A picture of the inn is in Drury, *Whitman*, p. 121. It was known as the Hamilton House and was torn down in the spring of 1919.

27 Spalding, *Senate Document*, p. 9.

28 Original, Coll. A.

29 *Prattsburg News*, January 27, 1898.

30 *W.C.Q.*, I (1897)3:20.

31 Description given to the author in 1935 by a resident of Rushville who recalled what her mother had told her.

32 Locks of Narcissa's hair, showing it to be blond with an auburn tinge, are in Colls. O., W., and Wn.

33 Portland, Ore., *Times Sun*, May 8, 1927. The portrait was dedicated May 16, 1927.

34 The late Mrs. Edmund Bowden of Seattle donated one of the sleeves to Whitman College.

35 *Op. Cit.*, p. 109.

36 The *Presbyterian Journal of History*, December 1932, published what it claimed to be a picture of Marcus Whitman from an "original ambrotype." Since the ambrotype process, which was a transparency on glass, was not discovered until 1851 and not patented until 1854, this claim is clearly unfounded. The picture may have been one of Whitman's namesakes.

37 *Op. Cit.*, p. 108.

38 *O.H.Q.*, II (1901):26.

39 *W.C.Q.*, I (1897):3:19.

40 Matilda Sager Delaney to Mrs. Bowden, March 26, 1928; copy in Coll. Wn: "Her best dress was a black bombazine—it was her wedding dress and her whole family wore black at her wedding."

41 Several tunes have been associated with this hymn including Newton, Wellwood, Smyrna, Latter Day, and Greenville. This was a favorite hymn used in that generation especially in farewell services for missionaries leaving for some distant land.

42 When I visited Angelica in the summer of 1935, an old lady whose grandparents were present at the wedding told me this story. See also *Magazine of American History*, September 1884, p. 193. The Angelica church burned in 1868. See references to the wedding in Whitman letters 19 and 44.

43 Parker ms., Cornell Uni.

44 Miss Esther Smith, the fiancée of John Dunbar, who was supposed to go out with this party was, for some reason, detained. Dunbar returned East the following winter and was then married. *Nebraska State Historical Society*, II:149.

45 I am indebted to Ross Woodbridge (see "In Appreciation") for this information. He found a record of the hotel's list of guests in the *Daily Pittsburg Gazette* for March 14, 1836.

46 While passing through Pittsburgh, the missionaries received a silver communion set from the East Liberty Presbyterian Church. The chalice, inscribed: "E. L. Pby. church," without its base, is now in the Presbyterian (Indian) Church of Spalding, Idaho.

[CHAPTER EIGHT]

FIRST WHITE WOMEN TO CROSS THE ROCKIES 1836

The day that Whitman-Satterlee party left Pittsburgh, March 15, 1836, Narcissa wrote her first travel letter which she addressed to her mother: "Dear, Dear Mother: —Your proposal concerning keeping a diary as I journey comes before my mind often. I have not found it practicable while traveling by land, although many events have passed which, if noted as they occurred, might have been interesting. We left Pittsburgh this morning at ten o'clock, and are sailing at the rate of thirteen miles an hour. It is delightful passing so rapidly down the waters of the beautiful river. The motion of the boat is very agreeable to me, except when writing. Our accommodations are good; we occupy a stateroom where we can be as retired as we wish" [Letter 20].

Four of these travel letters are extant, dated March 15 and 31, and June 3 and 27. Two are missing: May 15 and July 7.[1] Sometimes Narcissa made daily entries in these letters, thus making them more of a diary than just letters; at other times, she would summarize the events of a week or more. Narcissa was a gifted writer. Her letters and diary are filled with interesting anecdotes, vivid descriptions, with now and then a touch of humor. She was fully aware of the uniqueness of the experience which lay before her as twice in these letters, she referred to their travels as "an unheard of journey for females," as indeed it was.

The *Siam* took two days to go from Pittsburgh to Cincinnati, as the missionaries arrived there on Tuesday noon, the 17th. The Spaldings were eagerly awaiting their coming and for the first time Narcissa and Eliza met. Writing to her sister Jane on April 7, Narcissa commented: "Mrs. Spalding does not look nor feel quite healthy enough for our enterprise. Riding affects her differently from what it does me. Everyone who sees me compliments me as being the best able to endure the journey over the mountains from my looks. Sister S. is very resolute, no shrinking with her. She possesses good fortitude. I like her very much. She wears well on acquaintance. She is a very suitable person for Mr. Spalding, has the right temperament to match him. I think we shall get along very well together; we have so far."

Undoubtedly, a main subject for conversation when the two couples first met was the possible difficulties involved in taking white women over the Rockies. While passing through Pittsburgh, Spalding had opportunity to meet the famous painter of Indians who had been on an expedition to the far west in 1832 and who could, therefore, speak out of first-hand knowledge. We have Catlin's advice in Spalding's letter to the American Board dated March 2, 1836: "He says he would not attempt to take a white female into that country for the whole of Am; for two reasons. The first, the enthusiastic desire to see a white woman every where prevailing among the distant tribes, may terminate in unrestrained passion, consequently in her ruin... 2nd, the fatigues of the journey, he thinks, will destroy them. 1400 miles from the mouth of the Platte, on pack horses, rivers to swim, and every night to spend in the open air, hot suns and storms. The buffalo meat we can live on doubtless. But this like the other objections you see is supposed. No female has yet made the trip."

Henry and Eliza Spalding were as ready to undertake the venturesome journey as were Marcus and Narcissa Whitman.

To avoid traveling on Sunday, the Whitman-Spalding party stayed over in Cincinnati until the following Tuesday, March 22, when they resumed their voyage down the river to St. Louis on the *Junius*. Here is another example of the Puritanical emphasis on Sunday observance and the reluctance to travel on that day which was characteristic of American Protestantism of that generation.

Whitman and Spalding took advantage of the days spent in Cincinnati to buy some supplies for their overland journey, drawing upon the American Board for $200.00 for that purpose. On Sunday the mission party, now enlarged to nine, attended the Presbyterian Church where they heard Dr. Lyman Beecher preach. Narcissa, in her diary-letter begun on March 15, said that after their short sojourn in the city, they "felt strengthened and comforted as we left... to pursue our journey into the wilderness."

The missionaries had expected to reach St. Louis before the following Sunday, but Saturday night found them still eighty-nine miles from their destination. The steamer, as was sometimes the custom of the river boats at that time, tied up for the night. On Sunday morning the party disembarked at Chester, Illinois, again to avoid traveling on that day. After spending the day with a small group of Christians found in that village, the mission party was fortunate in being able to secure passage on another steamer, the *Majestic*, which was passing up the river Monday morning on its way to St. Louis. Delayed by fog, the vessel did not tie up at a wharf in the city until Tuesday afternoon, March 29.

As soon as he was able, Whitman went to the post office to see if any mail had arrived for him or for others in the party. He found letters from Greene and the War Department, but nothing from loved ones. Narcissa expressed her deep disappointment by writing in her diary: "Husband has been to the Office expecting to find letters from dear, dear friends at home but finds none. Why have they not written, seeing it is the very last, last time they will have to cheer my heart with intelligence from home, home, sweet home, and the friends I love." Here we see a homesick Narcissa. After thus opening her heart, she added words which she underlined: "But I am not sad."

The day after their arrival in St. Louis, the Whitmans and the Spaldings visited the new Catholic Cathedral. This venerable and historic building stands today on the west central side of the recently established Jefferson National Memorial. Started in 1831 and dedicated in 1834, the Cathedral had been in the course of construction when the Nez Perce delegation visited St. Louis in the winter of 1831–32. The older building, which the Indians had visited, might still have been standing when the Whitmans and Spaldings were there. Had they known about the contacts the Oregon Indians had with the Catholic clergy in St. Louis, they would no doubt have shown keen interest in the first Cathedral.

CHAPTER EIGHT *First White Women to Cross the Rockies, 1836* **173**

The Whitmans were met in St. Louis by an old acquaintance of Narcissa's, the Rev. Milton Kimball, a Presbyterian minister and a field agent of the American Board. In the course of showing them the sights of the city, he took them to the new Cathedral at a time when an Archbishop was conducting High Mass. The strange ritual, the unfamiliar Latin chants, the richly embroidered vestments, the candles, and the incense all left an unfavorable impression on the missionaries. This may have been the first time any of them had ever witnessed a Roman Catholic service.

We must remember that the Whitmans and the Spaldings were heirs to the strong anti-Catholic feeling common to Protestantism in the United States in that generation.[2] Describing her reactions, Narcissa in a letter to her sister Jane, dated March 31, wrote: "While sitting there and beholding this idolatry, I thot of the whited seplucher which indeed appeared beautiful to men but within was full of dead men's bones and all uncleanness" [Matt. 23:27]. And Eliza wrote that same day in her diary: "...the unpleasant sensations we experienced on witnessing their heartless forms and ceremonies, induced us soon to leave, rejoicing that we had never been left to embrace such delusions."[3]

We should remember that Narcissa was writing in the privacy of a family letter and not for publication; Eliza was confiding her thoughts to her diary meant only for herself. The comments of the two women no doubt reflected their husbands' attitudes towards Roman Catholicism.

OFFICIAL GOVERNMENT PERMIT TO RESIDE IN OREGON

While at Cincinnati, Spalding had received a letter from Greene dated February 25 giving the Board's official consent for the change of destination for the Spaldings.[4] Greene wrote: "I have written to the Secretary of War for letters of introduction & permits to enter & reside in the Indian country, which I have requested him to forward to St. Louis for yourself & Dr. Whitman." Old Oregon was then a semi-foreign land with both the United States and Great Britain exercising joint occupancy under the Treaty of 1818, so the permits which Greene requested of the War Department were called passports in the official records.

We have no evidence that Greene had requested such a permit for Samuel Parker nor is there evidence that the Methodist Church had requested such for Jason Lee and his associates. Certainly the mountain men who were trapping beaver on both sides of the Continental Divide never bothered about asking for such a document. The initiative in securing passports for the missionaries of the American Board seems to have been taken by Greene early in January 1836 when it became apparent that a mission party would be going to Oregon that spring. In reply to Greene's request, Lewis Cass, who served as Secretary of War 1831–36, wrote on January 20 that the War Department approved "the design of the Board," and that permission for Whitman and his associates to live among the Indians of Oregon was granted.[5]

When Greene learned that Spalding had consented to accompany Whitman to Oregon, he wrote again to Secretary Cass asking for another permit in which Spalding would be mentioned. According to the custom of the time, no reference was made to their wives. This revised passport, dated "War Department, Office of Indian Affairs, March 2, 1836," was in the Post Office in St. Louis when Whitman called for his mail on March 29. The document reads as follows:

> THE AMERICAN BOARD OF FOREIGN MISSIONS HAVE APPRISED THE DEPARTMENT THAT THEY HAVE APPOINTED DOCTOR MARCUS WHITMAN AND REV. HENRY SPALDING, LATE OF THE STATE OF NEW YORK, TO BE MISSIONARIES AND TEACHERS TO *RESIDE* IN THE INDIAN COUNTRY AMONG THE FLAT HEAD AND NEZ PERCE INDIANS.
>
> APPROVING THE DESIGN OF THE BOARD THOSE GENTLEMEN ARE *PERMITTED TO RESIDE IN THE COUNTRY*, AND I RECOMMEND THEM TO THE OFFICERS OF THE ARMY OF THE UNITED STATES, TO THE INDIAN AGENTS AND TO THE CITIZENS GENERALLY AND *I REQUEST FOR THEM SUCH ATTENTION AND AID AS WILL FACILITATE THE ACCOMPLISHMENTS OF THEIR OBJECTS, AND PROTECTION SHOULD CIRCUMSTANCES REQUIRE IT.*[6]

Here is the United States Government's official permission for the missionaries to travel through Indian country and to live among the natives in Oregon for the purpose of establishing mission stations. This passport gave the promise of protection by the U.S. Army and Indian Agents "should circumstances require it." Not one of the several memorials sent to Congress by the American residents of the Willamette Valley, beginning in 1838, refers to this promise of the Government to protect its citizens in Oregon. Evidently the writers of these memorials were unaware of the passport and the promises therein contained.

Final Instructions from Greene

Among the letters Whitman received at St. Louis was one from Greene dated March 4, 1836. In his final instructions, he gave some sound advice. Greene first dealt with the associations that the missionaries would have with "traders, agents, &c," and wrote: "Let your conduct be unblameable, exemplary & free from the appearance of evil. Do not feel it necessary to be the forward reprover of everything wrong among this class of persons, remembering that your business is almost exclusively with the Indians. While you are strict & uncompromising as to yr. own principles & conduct, do not be harsh & dictatorial to others. Do them good & be kind to all as you have opportunity. Let Christian love shine brightly in all that you do."

A second subject was "The Sabbath." "Keep it strictly," Greene urged, "and let the Indians & all others see that you do so. Make the distinction between that and other days as broad and obvious as you can... You must introduce the Sabbath, explain its meaning, design & use. You must fix the standard of its sacredness."[7] Here is a reflection of the Puritan movement which was strong in England and Scotland beginning shortly before the reign of Elizabeth I. All saints days and special holy days were eliminated from the calendar, and emphasis was placed on keeping the Sabbath, as Sunday was then called. To this day the observance of Christmas and Easter in most Presbyterian churches in Scotland is minimized. Christmas is a family day, and every Sunday "a day of resurrection."

It was a matter of great concern to the missionaries that Sunday was never observed by the caravan of the American Fur Company, with which they were to travel while crossing the plains. Their diaries and letters are sprinkled with comments which reflect their distress. If they traveled with the caravan on Sunday, they would be breaking one of the ten commandments: "Remember the Sabbath Day to keep it holy." If they remained in camp, they might be robbed or even killed by hostile Indians. The dilemma was real and most distressing. When the American Board's 1838 reenforcement to the Oregon Mission paused for a few days in Cincinnati, a member of the party asked Dr. Lyman Beecher what he would do when conscience clashed with caution. "Well," replied the practical theologian, "if I were to cross the Atlantic, I certainly would not jump overboard when Saturday night came."[8]

A third word of advice from Greene urged the missionaries to concentrate on benefiting the Indians. "Avoid all secular and political interference with any class of men. Engage in no trading not absolutely necessary for obtaining the necessaries of life for yr-selves and families... Let all yr worldly and secular concerns be as limited and compact as yr circumstances will permit." Wise advice! The Methodist Mission in the Willamette Valley came under the severe censure of the Hudson's Bay Company because of its business activities, but such criticism was never directed to the Oregon Mission of the American Board. Writing to the Governors of the Hudson's Bay Company in London on October 18, 1838, James Douglas, later to become a Chief Factor of Fort Vancouver, expressed his fears regarding the intentions of the Methodist missionaries to engage in trade. "My remarks apply solely to the Methodists," he wrote, "and have no reference to the Calvinist missionaries who voluntarily came forward and pledged themselves not to trade furs." [9]

"Live near to God," urged Greene in his concluding remarks. "May yr mission be as life from the dead to the benighted tribes of the remote west." On the whole, this was a good letter, filled with wise and kindly counsel.

From Narcissa's Letters

To Narcissa Whitman, the journey from her home in New York State to far-away Old Oregon was a thrilling and a wonderful experience. Her letters, more than those of any other member of the mission parties of 1836 or 1838, reveal the excitement of the West and the first impressions of an alert observer of the wonders along the route.

After telling of her impressions of the Roman Catholic Mass, Narcissa mentioned the fact that Elijah Lovejoy, the well-known editor of an abolitionist paper then being published in St. Louis, had called at the boat and had invited the Whitmans to dine with him. Marcus talked with him but Narcissa happened to be absent at the time. The Whitmans were unable to accept Lovejoy's invitation. "He wished to know when we were married," Narcissa wrote, "because he designed to publish it in the Observer." The April 7 issue of Lovejoy's paper reported the marriage of Marcus and Narcissa and noted that they had passed through St. Louis en route "to the Bored Nose [i.e., Nez Percé or Pierced Nose] Indians." [10]

Under date of March 30, Narcissa wrote in her journal-letter: "I think I should like to whisper in Mother's ear many things which I cannot write. If I could only see her in her room for one half hour. This much, Dear Mother, I have one of the kindest Husbands and the very best every way." Then Narcissa added a special message for her father: "Tell Father by the side of his calomel, he has a quarter of a pound of lobelia and a large quantity of Cayenne which will answer my purpose better than some of the apothecary medicines."

The average reader of today will miss the significance of the reference that Narcissa here made to lobelia and cayenne pepper, but to those acquainted with America's medical history, those words stand out like words on a telegram. They are the code words for Thomsonianism, a medical cult founded by Samuel Thomson, an illiterate New Hampshire farmer, in 1808. Thomson strongly opposed the use of epsom salts and calomel, and the practice of bleeding. These were the favorite remedies of the regular physicians whom Thomson called "mineral murderers." He maintained that all medicines except those of vegetable origin were poisonous. His treatment called for the patient to take a drink made from the herb *lobelia inflata*, which acted as a powerful emetic. Hence the regular doctors called the Thomsonian practitioners "puke-doctors." After inducing vomiting, Thomson would make the patient perspire by having him take "hot-drops" prepared by a patented formula, the principal ingredient being cayenne pepper.[11]

Since Judge Prentiss was a Thomsonian, it appears that Narcissa, out of respect for his views, was inclined to follow the same remedies when needed. Yet she had married one of the "mineral murderers." The fact that Marcus was willing to take with them to Oregon a small quantity of lobelia and cayenne pepper, "by side of his calomel," reveals his tolerant spirit. Since no further reference to these items appear in later letters of the Whitmans, we may assume that Narcissa gave up her father's medical theories and accepted those of her husband.

St. Louis to Liberty

The mission party secured accommodations on the *Chariton* which left St. Louis "immediately after dinner" on Thursday, March 31, for Liberty, Missouri. At twilight the steamer moved out of the wide sweep of the Mississippi and entered the narrower channel of the Missouri

River. The moon shone in all its brightness making night navigation possible. The newly-wedded couple of six weeks found the scene exhilerating. "It was a beautiful evening," wrote Narcissa to Jane. "My husband and myself went upon the top of the boat to take a commanding view of the scenery. How majestic, how grand was the scene. The meeting of two such great waters. 'Surely how admirable are thy works, O Lord of Hosts!' I could have dwelt upon the scene still longer with pleasure but Brother Spalding called us to prayers and we left beholding the works of God for his immediate worship." The Spaldings had been married nearly three years and by that time Henry evidently had more religion than romance in his soul.

On April 1, the wide-eyed and excited Narcissa wrote: "My eyes are satiated with the same beautiful scenery all along the coasts of this mighty river so peculiar to this western country. One year ago today since my husband first arrived in St. Louis on his exploring route to the mountains. We are one week earlier passing up the river this spring than he was last year." Whenever the boat stopped to take on fuel for the wood-burning engine, Marcus and Narcissa would go ashore where they "rambled considerably in pursuit of new objects."

The vessel stopped at Jefferson City, the half-way point to Liberty, on Saturday evening and continued on its way on Sunday. With troubled consciences the missionaries stayed aboard. There was no other choice. The three hundred mile journey from St. Louis ended on Thursday, April 7, when the party disembarked at Liberty on a raw spring morning with the thermometer registering 24° at nine o'clock. Liberty was about halfway between their homes in New York State and Fort Walla Walla on the Columbia River. So far they had traveled most of the way in comparative ease on river steamers. Nineteen hundred miles of prairie, mountain, and desert stretched before them. The most trying part of their journey lay ahead.

Again turning to Narcissa's letter to her sister, we read: "I have such a good place to shelter, under my husband's wings. He is so excellent. I love to confide in his judgment and act under him. He is just like Mother in telling me my failings. He does it in such a way that I like to have him, for it gives me a chance to improve. Jane, if you want to be happy, get a good husband and be a missionary… The way looks pleasant notwithstanding we are now near encountering the difficulties of *an unheard of journey for females.*"[12]

Before leaving St. Louis, Whitman had learned that the American Fur Company was planning to ship some of its personnel and supplies to Bellevue on the steamer *Diana*. This boat was scheduled to sail from St. Louis a couple of weeks after the *Chariton*, on which the missionaries had booked passage to Liberty. Whitman requested permission for his party to board the *Diana* at Liberty and thus be taken to Bellevue. The request was granted, thus giving Whitman and Spalding about two weeks at Liberty in which to complete arrangements for their overland journey, including the buying of horses, mules, cows, and supplies.

Members of the mission party were delighted to receive some mail at Liberty. Narcissa got a letter from her brother-in-law, the Rev. Lyman Judson, who had married her sister Mary Ann. This was the only letter she received from any member of her family for nearly two and a half years.

William Henry Gray

Whitman received a letter from Greene at St. Louis dated March 9, when the mission party was already one week on its way to Pittsburg. It brought the good news that a single man had been appointed to go with them, William Henry Gray. Greene wrote: "Since I wrote you last, our Com. have appointed a Mr. Gray, a good teacher, cabinet maker and house-joiner, from Utica, to yr mission, and instructed him, if when he receives our letter he shall think he can overtake you before you leave the frontier, he may start after you. He is highly recommended, and we hope that he will make a valuable assistant. He said that he would be ready to start in two days after receiving his appointment. We hope that he may overtake you."[13]

Gray caught up with the mission party at Liberty on April 19, and announced that he had been appointed by the American Board to go with them to Oregon as a mechanic. The Whitmans and the Spaldings welcomed him with enthusiasm. Since Gray became such a controversial figure in the Oregon Mission, it is well to review briefly the circumstances leading up to his appointment and something of his qualifications.

Gray was born at Fairfield, New York, on September 8, 1810, and was possibly living there when Whitman was a student at the Fairfield Medical College, 1825–6. It is altogether possible that the two attended the same church during that winter and had other social contacts, never dreaming of their future associations in Old Oregon.

Following the death of his father in 1826, Gray became an apprentice to a cabinetmaker at Springfield, Otsego County, New York, where he remained until he was twenty-one, when he moved to Utica. Judging by the letters of recommendation received by the American Board and some extant letters that he wrote, Gray's education was limited. He was described, in one of the letters of recommendation, as being "an extremely dull scholar." Gray joined the Presbyterian Church in Utica in November 1831. His brother John was a Presbyterian minister who hoped that William would also enter the ministry.

Gray was ambitious, always striving for a status in life higher than that for which he was qualified. In the fall of 1835, he aspired to be a doctor and "commenced riding with a practising physician" in Utica, who likewise found Gray to be very "dull." [14] It so happened that Gray boarded at the same place in Utica where the Rev. Chauncey Eddy, a field agent of the American Board, was also taking his meals. As has been stated, as early as December 8, 1835, Greene had suggested to Whitman that he get in touch with Eddy about possible associates for the Oregon Mission. Evidently Whitman had delayed in doing so until in desperation, for fear that he would not find someone, he wrote to Eddy sometime during the early part of February. Eddy, who had a favorable impression of Gray, asked him on February 15 if he would be interested in joining Whitman and going to Oregon as a missionary. This happened to be the very day that Whitman wrote to Greene to report his success in finding the Spaldings.

Gray's response to Eddy's question was immediate. He declared himself ready to go on two days' notice, "or less if necessary." The Rev. Ira Pettibone, pastor of the church of which Gray was a member, sent a testimonial to the Board which carried the endorsement of two of his elders. The following extracts from Pettibone's letter are most revealing:

> We think him possessed of ardent piety... He has a tolerable share of what may be called common sense... He evinces an unusual share of perseverance; and a confidence in his own abilities *to a fault*... His literary acquisitions are slender owing to the fact that he is a *slow scholar*... He is a skillful mechanic... He has good health and a firm constitution. [And then Pettibone added the following:]

Brother Gray has by no means the qualifications that we think desirable for such a station but perhaps as many are combined in him as in any young man of our acquaintance who is willing to go.

The Prudential Committee of the Board acted in haste on Gray's application sometime after February 25 and before March 9.[15] Gray must have received word of his appointment sometime during the first week of March and left at once for Liberty. He is reported to have been engaged to a young lady in Utica at the time, but there seems to have been no problem in postponing the marriage.

The suddenness with which Gray decided to go as a missionary to Oregon reflects his impulsive nature, while at the same time the haste in which the Board acted reveals the urgency it felt to recruit additional workers for the Oregon Mission. Secretary Greene, whose letters show him to have been a man of sound judgment, must have had some qualms of conscience when he approved the appointment of one who had such doubtful recommendations as Gray. Yet was it not better to send one with mediocre qualifications than none at all?

Travel Outfit Assembled

The Whitmans and the Spaldings were greatly encouraged with Gray's arrival. Providence, they thought, had smiled on them again. During the twelve days at Liberty, before Gray arrived, Whitman and Spalding had been busy buying animals and assembling their equipment. On September 5, 1836, the three men submitted a financial report to the Board; from this we are able to obtain a good idea of the outfit they assembled for their overland journey.

The report, made out in Whitman's handwriting, lists total expenditures at $3,063.96. A large farm wagon was purchased to carry the heavier baggage over the first part of their journey. Spalding's light wagon was reserved for the women's use if needed and for some lighter items of supplies. Twelve horses, six mules, and seventeen head of cattle, including four fresh milk cows, were purchased. Whitman's judgment as to what was needed prevailed and this time he was not hampered by the negative vote of a Parker.

Whitman's itemized account follows: "Traveling & Provisions—$590.98; Labor—$275.75; Saddlery & Harness—$267.73; Cattle—$118.00;

Indian goods to trade for horses & provisions—$225.25; Horses & Mules—$926.00; Tools & Furniture—$219.03; Guns & Ammunition—$91.44; Clothing—$208.05; Books & Stationery—$74.57; Seeds—$7.17; Medicines & Instruments—$28.39; Incidentals—$35.20." The supplies included a tin plate, knife, fork, and cup for each person. Narcissa wrote of the women having rubber life preservers, "so that, if we fall into the water we shall not drown" [Letter 21]. Possibly these were purchased in Cincinnati before the party embarked on their voyage down the river. There is no reference to the women keeping these items after they left Liberty, Missouri.

More than one-third of the total cost of their outfit went for horses, mules, and cattle, including four milk cows. Writing to Greene on May 5, Whitman explained: "Our expenses have been much worse than I expected, horses and cattle cost over $1,000.00." Marcus gave Narcissa the choice of a horse or a mule to ride. She chose the horse. Richard, who was inclined to judge the value of a riding animal by its speed, took one look at the mule and exclaimed: "That very bad mule, can't catch buffalo" [Letter 21]. Side-saddles were purchased for the women. This permitted the left foot to remain in the stirrup while the right leg rested over a hook on the saddle.

While the men were busy assembling their livestock and equipment, Narcissa and Eliza were making a tent. Of this Narcissa wrote: "It is made of bed ticking in conical form, large enough for us all to sleep under, viz Mr. Spalding and wife, Dr. Whitman and wife, Mr. Gray, Richard Takahtoo-ah-tis, and John Ais—quite a little family, raised with a center pole and fastened down with pegs, covering a large circle. There we shall live, eat and sleep for the summer to come at least, perhaps longer." Whitman and Parker had used a small conical tent the previous year. Perhaps this shape was selected in imitation of an Indian tepee.

Narcissa's account continues: "We five spread our India Rubber cloth on the ground, then our blankets and encamp for the night. We take plenty of Mackinaw blankets which answers for our bed and bedding. When we journey, we place them over our saddles and ride on them" [Letter 21].

Both Whitman and Spalding, and likewise the four ministers of the 1838 reenforcement, were loath to carry guns, feeling that to do so was inconsistent with their role as missionaries. No indication has been found in the diaries or letters that any of these six men joined in a buffalo hunt. As has been stated, Parker mentioned doing so on only one occasion. However, Whitman purchased guns and ammunition for his party, either because the American Fur Company insisted that all men traveling with its caravan be armed in case of an Indian attack, or for the use of men hired to hunt buffalo for food.

Whitman hired a young man by the name of Dulin to assist with the packing and the care of the animals and also welcomed to their party a young Nez Perce by the name of Samuel Temoni, who for some reason had visited the white man's country and was then returning to his people. Shortly after the mission party had left Liberty, a redhaired, nineteen-year-old youth from New Haven, Connecticut, Miles Goodyear, attached himself to the party.[16] Thus their number grew to ten five missionaries, three Nez Perces, and two hired men. Dulin left the party at the Rendezvous but Goodyear continued to Fort Hall.

On Thursday, April 21, Samuel Allis arrived at Liberty, having descended the Missouri River by boat from Bellevue. On the following Saturday, he was married to Miss Emeline Palmer, the Rev. H. H. Spalding officiating.[17]

The Mission Party Almost Left Behind

Whitman had arranged with the American Fur Company in St. Louis for himself and the two women to be taken from Liberty to Bellevue on the Company's boat, *Diana*. Plans were made at Liberty for Spalding, Gray, the two hired men, and the Nez Perces to go overland with two wagons (including Spalding's) loaded with supplies and with the livestock. They were to proceed up the east bank of the Missouri River to a point opposite Fort Leavenworth, where there was a ferry, cross to the west bank and strike out in a northwesterly direction across the prairie to the Oto Agency on the north bank of the Platte River.

Whitman planned for the Spalding party to join the caravan of the Fur Company when it passed the Agency, which was located a few miles to the west of Bellevue. Only enough food was taken to carry them through to the buffalo range, with some additional items for the journey from the Rendezvous to Fort Walla Walla. Like the fur traders and trappers, the mission party expected to live on buffalo meat, either fresh or dried, for most of their journey. The Spalding-Gray party left Liberty on Wednesday, April 27.

Mrs. Satterlee, who had been ill ever since she left her home in Ithaca, died late Saturday night, April 30, at the age of twenty-three. Whitman performed an autopsy and discovered that she had succumbed to a lung disease of "long standing," undoubtedly tuberculosis. Just as the funeral service was about to be held on Sunday, May 1, the Fur Company's boat suddenly appeared on its voyage up the river. To the consternation and dismay of Whitman and the two women, the captain refused to stop. In response to Whitman's frantic appeals, the captain shouted back that he was loaded and could take no more passengers. Later Whitman learned that the captain had not been told of the arrangements made in St. Louis for the boat to pick up the three at Liberty and take them to Bellevue.

After the steamer had disappeared around a bend in the river, the missionaries returned to their sad duty of burying the earthly remains of Mrs. Satterlee. A new burden had suddenly been thrust upon Whitman's shoulders. He, more than any of the others, realized the absolute necessity for the protection of their small party while traveling through hostile Indian country. Unless he and the two women could get to the Oto Agency, about 300 miles distant, in time to join the Spalding party before the caravan passed, no Oregon Mission could be established that year.

Immediate plans had to be made to meet this emergency. Since Allis and Satterlee had planned to leave for Bellevue soon after Mrs. Satterlee's funeral, with their heavily loaded wagon, drawn by three yoke of oxen, Whitman decided that he and the women should travel with them. He hired a man with a wagon to take them to Fort Leavenworth. The mission party left Liberty on Tuesday, May 3. For a time Whitman was content to stay with Allis and Satterlee, but the progress being made by the oxen was too slow. Becoming impatient, Whitman sent Allis on ahead to overtake Spalding and request that the light wagon be returned for the convenience of the women. Allis caught up with Spalding near what is now the Kansas-Nebraska border and got the light wagon. Spalding, knowing that Whitman and the women would be following, continued on his way.

Since all of the heavy baggage had been placed in the wagons, including the tent, Whitman and the women had only their hand luggage and their bedding which they had expected to carry aboard the steamer. Until the light wagon returned with more camping equipment, the three were obliged to sleep in the open. This was a rough initiation into the rigors of prairie travel for the two women.

After the death of Mrs. Satterlee, Whitman became concerned about Eliza Spalding's health. "I have some fears," he confided in his letter of May 5 to Greene written at Leavenworth, "with respect to Mrs. Spalding's ability to stand the journey." He knew that once on the trail away from civilization, there could be no turning back. The exigencies of prairie travel of that day meant that the Fur Company's caravan could not tarry for any one who became too sick to be moved. The sick and infirm either kept up with the caravan by riding in a wagon or were left behind. No favours could be expected, even for missionary women; they ventured forth at their own risk.

At Fort Leavenworth, the man whom Whitman had hired to take them to that place, turned back. Fortunately Whitman was able to find another team and driver to carry them until they met Allis. In spite of the great need for haste, the three missionaries spent Sunday, May 8, at the Methodist Mission for the Kickapoo Indians near the fort. On Monday, they resumed their pursuit of Spalding, and on the 11th or 12th met Allis with the light wagon. The Whitman party caught up with Spalding some time before Saturday, the 14th, when they were within eighteen miles of the Oto Agency. Again the missionaries obeyed their consciences and remained in camp over Sunday. On that day the Fur Company's caravan left Bellevue, under the command of Captain Fitzpatrick, with whom Whitman had traveled the previous year.

While the missionaries were encamped on Sunday, the 15th, a messenger arrived from Major John Dougherty, the Indian Agent assigned to the Otoes. Dougherty's brother was seriously ill and the Major begged Whitman to attend the sick man as soon as possible. Whitman left early Monday morning with the assurance that the messenger would return and guide the mission party to a crossing of the Platte River near the Oto Agency where Whitman would meet them on Tuesday. After ministering to the sick man, Whitman rode several miles west of the Agency and caught up with Fitzpatrick and the caravan. He urged Fitzpatrick to wait a few days until the mission party could catch up. Fitzpatrick was friendly and indicated his willingness to have the missionaries travel with the caravan, but insisted on the necessity of pressing on. He felt that the mission party could overtake the caravan before it reached hostile Indian country. Whitman retrieved from Fitzpatrick the horses which had been left at Bellevue the previous fall.

When Whitman returned to the Platte River crossing on Tuesday, he found to his dismay that the Spalding party was not there. It did not arrive until the next day; the guide had got lost on the uninhabited prairie. This precipitated a new crisis; the caravan was moving further and further away with each passing day.

The spring rains had swollen the Platte River, and fording was impossible. Driving the livestock across was a simple matter. The real problem lay in getting the wagons and heavy baggage across. Fortunately, an Indian canoe was found large enough to carry about six hundred pounds. Narcissa wrote: "We stretched a rope across the river and pulled the goods over in the canoe without much difficulty" [Letter 26]. In this same letter to Whitman's brother, Augustus, Narcissa said: "Husband became so completely exhausted with swimming the river on Thursday, the 19th, that it was with difficulty that he made the shore the last time. Mr. Spalding was sick, our two hired men good for nothing." The crossing was not completed until Friday night.

Precious time was lost Saturday morning when one of the wagons had to be repaired. The missionaries were not able to resume their march until early afternoon. By that time they realized that they had too much baggage. Regretfully they gave many items to Dunbar and Allis. Spalding found it necessary to part with some of his treasured theological books. With the Fur Company's caravan four days in advance and knowing that unless they caught up with it before coming to the Pawnee Indian villages, it would not be safe to travel without escort, the mission party pressed on in haste. The outlook was bleak, and they faced the fact that they might have to turn back.

On the March

With Dunbar as their guide, they pushed westward along the north bank of the Platte River. They traveled all day Sunday, May 22, necessity making excuse for their troubled conscience, and they reached the Elkhorn River on Monday in time to cross it before dark. Mrs. Spalding in her diary tells of their using an Indian "skin canoe."[18] Here Dunbar left them, as another guide became available who was to stay with the party until they caught up with the caravan. On Tuesday, the 24th, the missionaries made a grueling march of sixty miles. The Whitmans and the Spaldings rode most of the day in the light wagon. Although the wooden springs had little resiliency, the couples found that sitting upon bundles of bedding made riding fairly comfortable. Gray was in the larger wagon. The Indian boys drove the cattle, while Dulin and Goodyear looked after the horses.

The missionaries tried to reach the Loup River by Tuesday night, but the cattle gave out about nine o'clock in the evening, when they were still at least five miles from their objective. In view of these circumstances, the Whitmans decided to remain with the Indian boys and the cattle in the open prairie, while Gray and the Spaldings would continue on to the river. Narcissa wrote: "Husb[and] had a cup tied to his saddle in which he milked what we wished to drink. This was our supper" [Letter 26]. Early in the morning they were on the march again and rode to the river before breakfast. To their great joy, they saw the caravan on the opposite bank.

It took the missionaries half a day to cross the Loup River, and on Wednesday afternoon they made another forced march in order to catch up with the caravan. They drove until one o'clock Thursday morning, when with thankful hearts they joined the sleeping caravan. The race had been won! Later the missionaries learned that the failure of the Company to take axle grease for their seven heavily loaded wagons had caused a delay of several days shortly after the caravan had started. Two fat oxen had to be slain in order to make the grease. It was this delay which permitted the mission party to catch up. Had it not been for this lack of axle grease, a great many aspects of the subsequent history of the Pacific Northwest would have been much different.

Whitman, in a letter dated June 4 to Narcissa's parents, wrote: "We then felt that we had been signally blessed, thanked God and took courage." The last five words of this quotation are taken from Acts 28:15 and refer to an experience of the Apostle Paul who, when being taken as a prisoner to Rome, met some friends who comforted him. Paul wrote that "he thanked God and took courage." Since Whitman referred to this text on subsequent occasions, we can believe that it was especially meaningful to him. The failure of the Company to take axle grease, which in turn caused a delay for the caravan, was accepted by the missionaries as evidence of God's protective care over them.

On Thursday the caravan, with the mission party in the rear, passed the first of the Pawnee villages where Narcissa and Eliza experienced for the first time the sensation of being objects of great curiosity by the Indians. They were no doubt the first white women that most if not all the Indians had ever seen. Narcissa wrote: "We especially were visited by them both at noon and night. We ladies were such a curiosity to them, they would come and stand around our tent —peep in and grin in astonishment to see such looking objects" [Letter 26].

In Narcissa's chatty letter of June 3 to members of her family, we find many fascinating wordpictures of her experiences such as the following: "I told you how many bipeds there was in our company, now for the quadrupeds, —14 horses and six mules and fifteen head of cattle. We milk four cows[19]... if you wish to see the camp in motion, look away ahead and see first the pilot and the Captain Fitzpatrick, just before him —next the pack animals, all mules loaded with great packs —soon after you will see the wagons and in the rear our company. We all cover quite a space. The pack mules always string along one after the other just like Indians."

This letter reflects an exuberant spirit. Narcissa, the bride, was thoroughly enjoying her unusual experiences and took pleasure in telling her family back in Angelica about them. "I wish I could describe to you how we live so that you can realize it," she wrote. "Our manner of living is far preferable to any in the States. I never was so contented and happy before. Neither have I enjoyed such health for years. In the morn as soon as the day breaks, the first that we hear is the word arise, arise. Then the mules set up such noise as you never heard which puts the whole camp in motion. We encamp in a large ring—baggage and men, tents and wagons on the outside and all the animals, except the cows [which] are fastened to pickets, within the circle. This arrangement is to accommodate the guard who stands regularly every night and day, also when we are in motion, to protect our animals from the approach of Indians who would steal them... We are ready to start, usually at six—travel till eleven, encamp, rest and feed, start again about two—travel until six or before if we come to a good tavern—then encamp for the night."

Narcissa made light of the discomforts of prairie travel. Reading between the lines of her letter, we find her joking, laughing, and singing.

"Our table is the ground," she wrote, "our table-cloth is an India rubber cloth, used when it rains as a cloak; our dishes are made of tin basins for tea cups, iron spoons and plates, each of us, and several pans for milk and to put our meat in when we wish to set it upon the table each one carries his own knife in a scabbard and it is always ready for use. When the table things [are] spread, after making our forks of sticks and helping ourselves to chairs, we gather around the table. Husband always provides my seat and in a way that you would laugh to see us. It is the fashion of all this country to imitate the Turks."

The missionaries took with them bread and some other perishable supplies which lasted for a few days, and then the women were obliged to bake bread over an open fire. Regarding their food, Narcissa wrote: "Let me assure you of this, we relish our food none the less for sitting on the ground while eating. We have tea and a plenty of milk which is a luxury in this country. Our milk has assisted us very much in making our bread since we have been journeying. While the fur company has felt the want of food, our milk has been of great service to us, but was considerable work to supply ten persons with bread three times a day... What little flour we have left we shall preserve for thickening our broth, which is excellent. I never saw anything like buffalo meat to satisfy hunger."

The caravan reached the eastern edge of the buffalo range on June 2 when the first buffalo was killed. The mission party had been obliged to live for twelve days, after leaving the Platte River crossing, on the food they had taken with them and the milk from their cows. After being supplied with buffalo meat, Whitman took over the job of cook. Writing on June 27, Narcissa praised her husband for the talent he had in cooking the meat in different ways. "We have had no bread since [reaching the buffalo range]" she wrote. "We have meat and tea in the morn and tea and meat at noon. All our variety consists in the different ways of cooking. I relish it well and it agrees with me. My health is excellent, so long as I have buffalo meat I do not wish anything else. Sister S. is affected by it considerably, has been quite sick." Whitman, writing to Greene from the Rendezvous on July 16, reported: "Mrs. Spalding has suffered considerably from change of diet but in the end, I am confident her health will be greatly improved by the journey."

When a buffalo was killed for meat, the hunter would take the tongue, which was considered a great delicacy, and the hump ribs. The rest of the carcas would be left to rot. Cornelius Rogers, one of the members of the 1838 reenforcement sent out to the Oregon Mission by the American Board, gave the following account of buffalo meat: "The meat is very sweet and easily cooked. Ten minutes boiling is enough, more will make it tough. The meat is sometimes 'jerked' by being dried in the sun or over a slow fire. In this state it can be kept for three or four days in the most sultry weather." [20] Since but few buffalo were to be found west of the Continental Divide, the missionaries were obliged to take some of the 'jerked' or dried meat with them on their westward journey across what is now southern Idaho.[21]

In her letter of June 3, Narcissa wrote: "Our fuel for cooking since we left timber (no timber except on the rivers) has been dried buffalo dung. We now find plenty of it and it answers a very good purpose, similar to the kind of coal used in Pennsylvania. (I suppose Harriet will make up a face at this, but if she was here she would be glad to have her supper cooked at any rate, in this scarce timber country)." On the treeless prairies, travelers used buffalo chips for fuel, often called them "prairie coal." A member of the Oregon emigration of 1852 noted in his diary that at first the women were most fastidious about picking up the chips and would wear gloves, but that passed and they "began gathering the buffalo chips with their bare hands." [22]

While on the march, the caravan averaged about twenty miles a day. Narcissa wrote: "It is astonishing how [well we] get along with our wagons where there are no roads. I think I may say [it is] easier traveling here than on any turnpike in the [States]" [Letter 26]. On the back page of this letter, Narcissa added a note for her sister-in-law, the wife of her husband's older brother, Augustus: "Now Sister Julia, between you and me, I just want to tell you how much trouble I have had with Marcus[23] two or three weeks past. He was under the impression that we had too much baggage and could not think of anything so easy to be dispensed with as his own wearing apparel, those shirts the Ladies made him just before we left home, his black suit and overcoat, these were the condemned articles, sell them he must as soon as he got to the fort [i.e., Laramie]. At first I could not believe him in earnest. All the reasons I could bring were of no avail, he still said he would get rid of them. I told him to sell all of mine too, I could do without them better than he could—indeed I did not wish to dress unless he could. I had already mended and repaired the coat he wears until it would not stay on him..." Narcissa succeeded in persuading her husband to keep the shirts and other items of clothing.

After joining the Fur Company's caravan on May 26th, the missionaries found it necessary to travel on Sunday to the great distress of their consciences. The following quotation from Eliza Spalding's diary for May 29 is typical of expressions found in the writings of her cornpardons: "This is the second Sabbath that has dawned upon us since we left Otoe... Oh, the blessed privilege of those who can every sabbath go to the house of God with the multitude who keep holy day, and do not feel themselves under the necessity of journeying on the Lord's holy Sabbath." [24]

The caravan reached Fort Laramie on Monday, June 13, which meant that it was about five weeks earlier than was the caravan of the preceding year. There it remained for eight days before leaving on Tuesday, June 14, for the Rendezvous on Green River. During this interval the women had an opportunity to wash their clothes. Narcissa noted that only three such opportunities came to them en route; once at Fort Laramie, again at the Rendezvous, and the third time at Fort Boise [Letter 29]. The mission party was not given rooms within the Fort but remained encamped outside. Eliza mentioned in her diary what a welcome sight it was just to see the walls of buildings again. A worship service was held at the Fort on Sunday, June 19, at which Spalding preached and some of the men of the caravan attended.

Through South Pass – July 4, 1836

Fitzpatrick left all of his wagons at the Fort and repacked the baggage on animals. Each mule was given a load weighing about 250 pounds and the horses a somewhat heavier pack. Whitman and Spalding left their big wagon and likewise arranged packs for the few animals they had, besides loading as much as possible on the light Dearborn wagon. This meant that the women, who had been alternating between riding horseback and riding in the wagon, would have to continue the trip on their side-saddles unless an emergency arose.

After leaving Fort Laramie on June 21, the caravan followed the south bank of the North Platte for about five days until it reached a crossing place near what is now Casper, Wyoming. Upon arriving there,

Fitzpatrick found the river too high to be forded so boats had to be made by stretching buffalo hides over a frame of willow branches. These were called "bull-boats" because only the skins taken from tough old buffalo bulls were used. The delay at the crossing included a Sunday, which permitted the missionaries to enjoy a day of rest and worship to their great satisfaction.

After crossing the river, the trail led along the north bank to the Sweetwater River which was then followed to the summit of the Rockies. The caravan paused for a short time at Independence Rock, that great landmark and register of the Oregon Trail. This isolated and monumental piece of granite is about 175 feet high, 2,100 feet long, and about a mile in circumference. This became a favorite camping spot for westward bound travelers, many of whom carved their names on the rock. According to Gray, "all the prominent persons" of the 1836 caravan cut their names on the south end of the rock.[25] If any member of the mission party did so, erosion has erased them, for no such inscriptions have been found.

July 4, 1836, was an epoch-making day in the history of the Pacific Northwest, for on that day Narcissa Whitman and Eliza Spalding rode through South Pass on the Continental Divide on their way to Old Oregon. They were the first white American women to do so and were seven years in advance of the first Oregon emigration wagon train of 1843. Narcissa and Eliza pioneered the way. What these two had been able to do riding side-saddles gave confidence to countless other women to follow in covered wagons.

Participants in some history-making incident are often unaware of its real significance at the time of the event. So it was with the Whitmans and the Spaldings as they rode over the Continental Divide on that July 4, in 1836. The only reference found in the contemporary writings of the members of the party is the following brief statement from Eliza's diary: "Crossed a ridge of land today; called the divide, which separates the waters that flow into the Atlantic from those that flow into the Pacific, and camped for the night on the head waters of the Colorado." [26] As far as Eliza Spalding was concerned, this was just another day of travel.

The editor of the *Missionary Herald*, in his report of the arrival of the mission party at Fort Vancouver in the October 1837 issue of his magazine, dismissed the significance of the crossing of the Rockies in a single sentence: "Mrs. Spalding and Mrs. Whitman are believed to be the first white women who have crossed the Rocky Mountains." Although the editor failed to appreciate the significance of the event, Senator Lewis F. Linn of Missouri did not. When he learned of what Mrs. Whitman and Mrs. Spalding had been able to accomplish, he arose in the U.S. Senate on June 6, 1838, and declared: "*Thus has vanished the great obstacle to a direct and facile communication between the Mississippi Valley and the Pacific Ocean.*"[27] The great Rocky Mountain barrier had been breached. The door to Old Oregon had been opened for women and children!

After Whitman's visit to Washington and Boston in 1843, of which more will be said later, he returned with the first great Oregon emigration of 1843 and was largely responsible for the success achieved by the emigrants in taking their wagons west of Fort Hall and over the Blue Mountains into the Columbia River Valley. Writing to Greene on November 1, 1843, shortly after his return to his mission station, Whitman proudly stated: "If I never do more than to have been one of the first to take white women across the Mountains & prevent the disaster & reaction which would have occurred by the breaking up of the present Emigration & establishing the first wagon road across to the borders of the Columbia River, I am satisfied." Here we see a recognition by Whitman, seven years after he and Spalding had taken their wives over the Rockies, of the great significance of that accomplishment.

The Whitman massacre of November 1847 naturally focused attention on the Whitmans and the past history of the Oregon Mission. A writer in the *Oregon Spectator* for February 5, 1848, using the pseudonym "Oregonian," drew attention to the fact that Mrs. Whitman and Mrs. Spalding "were the first white females that ventured to try the perils of a journey across the mountains, which, at that time, was considered presumptuous in the extreme, and doubtless has contributed to dispel the fears and remove the dread of a passage from the Mississippi to the Columbia, more than all other adventures." Here is the judgment of a contemporary. "Oregonian" further stated: "I have no fears in venturing the assertion, that the simple act of these two females, sustained by others who have followed them[28] on a similar enterprise, has contributed more to the present occupancy of Oregon than all the fine-spun speeches and high-sounding words that have yet issued from the executive branch at Washington."

Years later the eloquent but historically inaccurate H. H. Spalding wrote the following highly embellished account of the crossing of the Continental Divide as part of a Resolution adopted by the Pleasant Butte Baptist Church of Linn County, Oregon, on October 22, 1869: "At twelve o'clock on the 4th of July last, thirty-three years ago, two Protestant heroines, Mrs. Spalding and Mrs. Whitman, alighted from their horses, themselves in great weakness, at the dividing point on the Rocky Mountains, in the famous South Pass, and after returning profound thanks to Almighty God for his heavenly care of them thus far, and dedicating themselves anew to his holy cause, with the banner of the cross in one hand and the stars and stripes in the other, they stepped down, the first American women, into the Territory of Oregon, and took formal possession in the name of their Saviour and their country, in the name of American mothers and of the American church; and being immediately confronted by the British lion, they instantly bearded the royal beast in his lair. Honorable day! It sealed the fate of Great Britain on these shores." [29]

The late Dr. Grace Raymond Hebard, once Professor of Economies and Sociology at the University of Wyoming, has added further embellishments to the story. In an article published in the *Washington Historical Quarterly* for 1917, she quoted Mrs. Spalding as saying when she stood in South Pass: "It is a reality of a dream that after four months of painful journey I am alive and actually standing on the summit of the Rocky Mountains where the foot of a white woman has never before trod." [30]

A drawing in Nixon's *Whitman's Ride Through Savage Lands* pictures the missionaries kneeling in prayer by a covered wagon and an American flag flying from a nearby flagpole. A similar illustration in Myron Eell's *Marcus Whitman* shows Spalding holding the flag while the other members of the party are kneeling as in prayer.

If such a dramatic prayer meeting had ever been held, surely Narcissa or one of the three men would have referred to it in some of their writings. Not one of the mission party ever referred to having a United States flag on their journey. Only Eliza Spalding made reference to the pass, as has been stated, when she wrote: "Crossed a ridge of land today; called the divide." We must dismiss Spalding's account as being nothing more than the embellishment of an old man's fertile imagination. Since the missionaries were accustomed to hold daily devotions, it may be that when they met in worship on the evening of July 4, some mention was made of God's providence in bringing them safely over the Rockies. Such a meeting could have been the basis of Spalding's remarks made some thirty-three years later when memory and imagination became inseparably intertwined.

Eighty years after Narcissa Whitman and Eliza Spalding rode through South Pass, in June 1916, a patriotic citizen of Lander, Wyoming—Captain Herman G. Nickerson—placed an upright stone monument about three feet high at the summit of the pass along some of the ruts made by Oregon bound wagons. This monument bears the words:

NARCISSA PRENTISS WHITMAN. ELIZA HART SPALDING.
FIRST WHITE WOMEN TO CROSS THIS PASS. JULY 4, 1836.

Chapter 8 Endnotes

1 Drury, *F.W.W.*, vol. I contains copies of Narcissa's travel letters and her diary.

2 Ray A. Billington, *The Protestant Crusade, 1800–1860*, Quadrangle Books, Chicago, 1964, gives an excellent history of the rise and spread of the anti-Catholic sentiment in the United States. One of the most influential and outspoken critics of Roman Catholicism was Dr. Lyman Beecher, under whom the Spaldings had studied at Lane Theological Seminary, Cincinnati.

3 Drury, *F.W.W.*, I:186.

4 Hulbert, *O.P.*, VI:189.

5 Copy in Office of Indian Affairs, Letters Received, 1843, Schools, W-2091, National Archives.

6 From copy in Coll. H., sent by Spalding to Hiram Bingham, Sept. 19, 1836. Permits were likewise secured for members of the 1838 reenforcement to the Oregon Mission.

7 Hulbert, *O.P.*, VI:194.

8 Eells, *Father Eells*, p. 89.

9 HBC Arch., B/223/b/8a.

10 Lovejoy's printing establishment in St. Louis was destroyed by an anti-abolitionist mob about a month after the Whitmans were in the city. Lovejoy then moved to Alton, Illinois, where he continued to publish his *Observer*. On November 7, 1837, another mob destroyed his press and killed him.

11 See Drury, *Whitman*, pp. 134 ff, for more details about this medical cult.

12 Italics, the author's.

13 Hulbert, *O.P.*, VI:197. Greene directed this letter to Independence, Mo., which was about fifteen miles from Liberty.

14 Eddy to Greene, Coll. A. Hulbert, *O.P.*, VI:188 ff.

15 Gray's name was not included in Greene's letter to the Secretary of War dated Feb. 25, 1836, when Greene asked for a passport for Spalding.

16 Gray, *Oregon*, p. 113, claimed that Goodyear was only sixteen years old and that he was from Iowa. See Hafen, *Mountain Men*, II:179 ff., for a sketch of his life.

17 See article by Allis, "Forty Years among the Indians on the Eastern Borders of Nebraska," in *Transactions and Reports of the Nebraska State Historical Society, II* (1887): 133 ff. Reference to his marriage is on page 148. Allis, in a letter to the American Board, July 14, 1836, said: "I think it is a hasty step to take Females across the Mountains at present."

18 Drury, *F.W.W.*, I:190.

19 Jason Lee took a small band of cattle across the country to Oregon in 1834. So far as is known, the taking of cattle by Whitman and Spalding was the second time such was done.

20 From letter of Cornelius Rogers, July 3, 1838, in *Oregonian & Indians Advocate* December 1838, p. 35. Also, *P.N.Q.*, 56 (1965):4:159.

21 See article by G. M. Christman on "The Mountain Bison," *American West*, Palo Alto, Calif., VIII (1971):3:44 ff. The mountain bison was a different subspecies of that of the plains. One characteristic was that the mountain bison was larger. A herd of the mountain bison is in Yellowstone National Park.

22 *T.O.P.A.*, 1905, p. 441.

23 Here is one of the few instances in the letters of Narcissa when she referred to her husband by his first name. Usually she called him "husband" or "the Doctor." The same reticence to the use of Christian names is found in the writings of all members of the Oregon Mission. It was never "Henry" or "Eliza" but rather "Mr. Spalding" and "Mrs. Spalding."

24 Drury, *F.W.W.*, I:191.

25 Gray, *Oregon*, p. 118.

26 Drury, *F.W.W.*, I:193.

27 *25th Cong. 2nd Sess., Document No. 470*, Report of Sen. Linn on Senate Bill, No. 206. Italics, the author's.

28 "Oregonian's" reference to the women who followed Mrs. Whitman and Mrs. Spalding was to the four women who crossed the Rockies in 1838 as members of the American Board's reenforcement to the Oregon Mission and to the five wives of independent missionaries who went out to Old Oregon in 1839 and 1840. Altogether eleven women rode horseback through South Pass before the first great Oregon emigration went west in 1843.

29 Spalding, *Senate Document*, p. 75. A similar statement appeared in the Chicago *Advance*, Dec. 1, 1870, p. 11.

30 *Op. Cit.*, VIII (Jan. 1917): p. 30. Although Mrs. Hebard refers to Mrs. Spalding's diary, she gave no precise reference and this quotation has not been found. The author does not believe it is authentic.

WILLIAM HENRY GRAY
A member of the first Oregon party, 1836, of the American Board, Gray was to cause serious problems within the Mission. Courtesy, *Whitman College Quarterly*, June 1913.

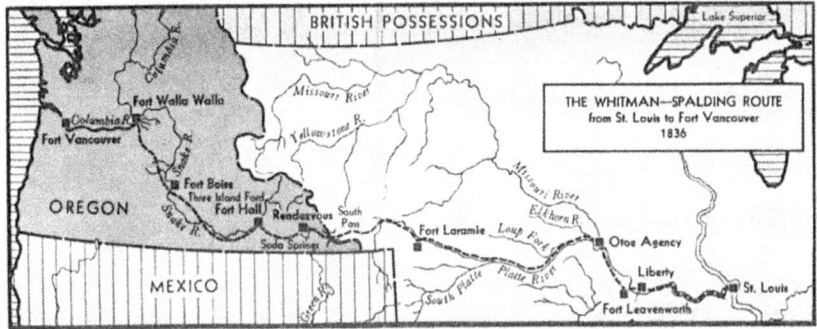

THE OREGON TRAIL, 1836
The route used by the Whitman-Spalding party on their first trip over the Rockies. By permission of the National Park Service, United States Department of the Interior.

SOUTH PASS MONUMENT
The monument at South Pass in Wyoming was erected in honor of the first white American women to cross the Continental Divide. Photo by C. M. Drury. By permission of the National Park Service, United States Department of the Interior.

[CHAPTER NINE]

FROM THE RENDEZVOUS TO FORT VANCOUVER

A messenger had been sent ahead from Independence Rock to the trappers and Indians who were impatiently awaiting the coming of the caravan at Green River to inform them when it was expected to arrive. The messenger also passed on the exciting news of the presence of missionaries, including women, with the caravan. Many of the trappers had not seen a white woman for years and it is doubtful if any of the Indians had ever seen one.

A self-appointed welcoming committee rode out to greet the incoming caravan and to give a mountain-style welcome to the missionaries. Gray tells what happened: "Two days before we arrived at our rendezvous and some two hours before we reached camp, the whole caravan was alarmed by the arrival of some ten Indians and four or five white men, whose dress and appearance could scarcely be distinguished from that of the Indians. As they came in sight over the hills, they all gave a yell, such as hunters and Indians only can give; whiz, whiz, came their balls over our heads..."[1] For a few minutes the missionaries were alarmed, thinking that they were about to be attacked by hostile Indians, but then their attention was directed to a white flag flying from a raised gun. As the welcoming party rode down one side of the caravan and up the other, they were greeted by wild shouts from the men of the caravan and by more firing of guns. Finally the excitement died down, and the missionaries were given a warm personal welcome.

After the mission party had made camp, two of the Indians were invited to join them for supper. They were Tackensuatis,[2] whom Whitman and Parker had met at the Rendezvous the previous year, and Ish-hol-hol-hoats-hoats, better known as Lawyer.[3] Chief Lawyer has already been mentioned, as it was he who had heard Spokane Garry read from his Bible and had carried back the story of what Garry had told of the white man's religion to the Nez Perces. As has been stated, Lawyer later told the Rev. A. B. Smith that he was the connecting link between Spokane Garry and the Nez Perce delegation which went to St. Louis in 1831 to get teachers and more information about Christianity.

Lawyer's exact age is unknown but circumstantial evidence places his birth in 1802, which was also the year in which Whitman was born. Since Lawyer had some knowledge of English, he was able to communicate directly with the missionaries. Gray, in his comments on the evening meal with the two Indians, wrote: "Of this feast, these sons of the wilderness partook with expressions of great satisfaction. The Lawyer, twenty-seven years after, spoke of it as the time when his heart became one with the *Suapies* (Americans)."[4]

One of the members of the welcoming committee was Kentuc, who had accompanied Parker on his exploring tour of the Pacific Northwest in 1835. He delivered a letter from Parker to Whitman dated May 10, 1836. Parker stated that "his way was hedged up" and hence he had decided not to return to the States by the overland route, but would return by sea.[5] This was a great disappointment to the Whitmans and the Spaldings, especially as Parker had left no directions and had given no advice regarding possible locations for mission stations.

Whitman was loath to write any letter of complaint regarding Parker, and it was not until he learned of Parker's criticism of him that Whitman on May 10, 1839, wrote to the American Board sharply criticizing Parker for many things that he did or did not do. In this letter we may read: "We cannot say how much good Mr. P's tour will do others, it has done us none, for instead of meeting us at Rendezvous as he agreed, he neglected even to write a single letter containing any information concerning the country, Indians, prospects, or advice of any kind whatever."

Parker spent the winter at Fort Vancouver as a non-paying guest of the Hudson's Bay Company. He visited the upper Columbia River country in the spring of 1836 going as far as Fort Colville. When he thought of the long journey overland, his heart failed him. "We cannot avoid the conclusion," wrote Whitman to Greene, "that he preferred to go home by way of England in the Company's ship as he said he had the offer of a free passage." Parker sailed from Fort Vancouver on June 12 for Hawaii. He was obliged to wait there until November 14 when he was able to obtain passage on a ship bound for New London, Connecticut.[6] During a wearisome voyage of five months around Cape Horn, when at times he had to subsist on salt meat, dried vegetables, and stale biscuits infested with weevils, Parker wished that he had returned overland. He landed at New London, on May 18, 1837, after an absence from the United States of two years and two months and after having traveled about 28,000 miles.

In 1838 Parker published the first edition of his *Journal of an Exploring Tour Beyond the Rocky Mountains* at Ithaca, New York. This book with its map of the Old Oregon country, one of the first to be made available to the public, became immensely popular, especially among those who dreamed of migrating to that far-away land. The *Journal* ran through five American and three European editions. Parker's son, Samuel J., estimated that at least ten thousand copies were sold in the United States and another four thousand abroad.

At the Rendezvous

Among those who took a leading part in giving the mission party such a boisterous welcome was twenty-six year-old Joseph L. Meek, 1810–1875, one of the most colorful of the mountain men.[7] Meek first went out to the Rockies in the spring of 1829 when only nineteen years old. Many of his fantastic adventures are told for us in Frances Fuller Victor's book, *River of the West*. Meek had been at the 1835 Rendezvous when he first met Whitman. He was especially impressed by Narcissa Whitman, who was not only in better health at the time than was Eliza Spalding, but who was also by nature more vivacious and sociable. Meek never lost an opportunity to be in her company. During the ride to the Green River Rendezvous after leaving the Big Sandy on the morning of July 5, Meek rode at Narcissa's side and regaled her with his "bar" (bear) stories.

The mission party escorted by Meek, Tackensuatis, Lawyer, Kentuc, and others, arrived at the Rendezvous on Wednesday evening, July 6. Gray tells us that about one hundred American trappers were there that year, about two hundred Nez Perces and Flatheads, and also several hundred Indians from other tribes including a few Cayuses.[8] All joined in giving the missionaries a heart-warming welcome. "As soon as I alighted from my horse," wrote Narcissa, "I was met by a company of native women, one after the other, shaking hands and saluting me with a most hearty kiss. They gave Sister Spalding the same salutation" [Letter 27].

The two white women were at once the center of a "gazing throng" as Narcissa described it. Tackensuatis and Lawyer brought their wives and introduced them. "It was truly pleasing," commented Narcissa, "to see the meeting of Richard and John with their friends. Richard was affected to tears, his father is not here but several of his band and brothers. When they met each took off his hat and shook hands as respectful as in civilized life." Both Richard and John remained with the mission party until it reached Fort Walla Walla.[9]

Whitman in his letter to Greene written from the Rendezvous said that the Indians "were greatly interested with our females, cattle, & wagon." They called the wagon a "land canoe." Although vivacious Narcissa made the greater impression of the two women on the white men, it was Eliza who appealed to the natives. Eliza was obliged to remain in the tent much of the time the party was at the Rendezvous because of illness,[10] but even so she began at once learning the Nez Perce language. Evidence indicates that she was the first among the missionaries to become proficient in the use of this tongue.

The mountain men were likewise attracted by the women. Gray noted: "The rough veteran mountain hunter would touch his hat in a manner absolutely ridiculous."[11] Some of the men manifested a sudden interest in religion and attended the morning and evening devotions of the missionaries. Hearing women's voices raised in song was a new and thrilling experience for a Rendezvous gathering. Some asked for Bibles; regarding this, Narcissa wrote: "This is a cause worth living for—Wherever we go we find opportunities of doing good—If we had packed one or two animals with bibles & testaments, we should have had abundant opportunity of disposing of them to the traders & trappers of the mountains who would have received them gratefully... We have given away all we have to spare."

Among the mountain men at the 1836 Rendezvous were two who turned author and in their respective books told of the impression the white women had made on both the trappers and the Indians. The first was Osborne Russell whose *Journal of a Trapper; or Nine Years in the Rocky Mountains, 1834–1843*, was published posthumously in 1914. Russell wrote: "The two ladies were gazed upon with wonder and astonishment by the rude Savages, they being the first white women ever seen by these Indians, the first that had ever penetrated into these wild and rocky regions." [12] According to Dr. George H. Atkinson, a pioneer Congregational minister in Portland, Oregon, Russell was "converted while reading his Bible in his lonely hunter's cabin in the Rocky Mountains." [13] It may be that he was one who received a Bible from the missionaries at the 1836 Rendezvous.

The second mountain man who turned author was Isaac P. Rose who, in 1884, published his *Four Years in the Rockies*, from which the following is taken: "Mrs. Whitman was a large, stately, fair skinned woman, with blue eyes and light, auburn, almost golden hair. Her manners were at once dignified and gracious. She was, both by nature and education, a lady, and had a lady's appreciation of all that was courageous and refined; yet not without an element of romance and heroism in her disposition strong enough to have impelled her to undertake a missionary's life in the wilderness. Mrs. Spalding, the other lady, was more delicate than her companion, yet equally earnest and zealous in the cause they had undertaken. The Indians would turn their gaze from the dark haired, dark eyed Mrs. Spalding to what was, to them, the more interesting golden hair and blue eyes of Mrs. Whitman, and they seemed to regard them both as beings of a superior nature." [14]

Whitman in his report to the American Board of his 1835 visit to the Rendezvous had given a summary of the different Indian tribes of the area and had mentioned "the Napiersas[15] [i.e., Nez Perces] and Kiusas [i.e., Cayuses]." Parker had visited the Cayuse Indians when at Fort Walla Walla in May 1836 and stated in his report to the Board that he had attempted to give them some instruction in the Christian religion. He wrote: "Here is a promising field for missionary labours." [16] In all probability Parker told the Cayuses of the possible coming of Whitman that summer with associates and may have suggested that a mission station might be established in their midst. If this were the case, then the Cayuses would have had time to send some of their number to the Rendezvous to make known their desires. There is no contemporary evidence that Parker ever promised the Cayuses any payment for land to be used as a mission station as has been claimed by some of Whitman's critics.

A strong spirit of rivalry developed at the Rendezvous between the Cayuses and the Nez Perces in regard as to where the missionaries were to settle. The members of each of these tribes had come to feel that they would reap many benefits if the missionaries would live with them. Of this Narcissa wrote: "This reminds me of a quarrel among the [Indian] women while... at Rendezvous. The Nez Perce women said we were going to live with them, and the Cayuses said, No, we were going to live with them. The contradiction was so sharp they nearly came to blows" [Letter 34].

It is well to emphasize the fact that the missionaries did not force themselves upon unwilling natives. Both the Cayuses and the Nez Perces were quick to promise full cooperation. Undoubtedly the Indians had mixed motives in their desire to have the missionaries settle among them. There is evidence of a sincere desire to learn more of the white man's religion. On the other hand, as A. B. Smith pointed out in a letter he wrote to the Board on August 27, 1839, regarding the Nez Perces: "They have manifested a great desire for missionaries, but there is no doubt but that much of this desire has been the hope of temporal gain."[17]

Whitman, in his letter to Greene written at the Rendezvous and dated July 16, 1836, stated that he and Spalding had decided to go through to Fort Walla Walla and thence to Fort Vancouver. This meant that the Flatheads would be by-passed in favor of the tribes that spoke the Nez Perce language, which included the Cayuses. Commenting on his decision to take women over the Rockies, Whitman wrote: "I see no reason to regret our choice of a journey by land." During their travels across the plains, they had enjoyed excellent weather. Whitman reported that they had had but one shower "that gave us any inconvenience." He said that Mrs. Spalding had suffered some from a change of diet but that his wife had endured the journey very well.

Spalding also wrote to the Board from the Rendezvous. In his letter of July 8, he reported: "We travelled 1,700 miles to Liberty mostly by water; 1,300 from Liberty to this place, all by land, and have yet 600 miles to make. Our living since we reached buffalo country, 300 miles from the mouth of the Platte, on the first of June, has been nothing but buffalo meat and the poorest kind of buffalo are very scarce this year."

Whitman, in his letter of July 16 to Greene, reported that when he was about to leave the Rendezvous, he went to Captain Fitzpatrick and asked for his bill to cover many favors received including the shoeing of the horses of the missionaries, supplies of meat, etc. Fitzpatrick then asked Dr. Whitman for his bill for medical services rendered to men of the caravan. Whitman replied: "I have no bill." "Then," said Fitzpatrick, "neither have I." Whitman wrote: "We have received nothing but favour and kindness from this company while with them." This incident is reminiscent of Fontenelle's attitude when Whitman parted company with him at Fort Laramie in July 1835, when Fontenelle also refused to submit a bill to Whitman. Surely there would have been no mission party with women going overland to Old Oregon in 1836, under the escort of the American Fur Company, had not the way been prepared by Whitman's medical services to the men of the 1835 caravan who had been stricken with cholera.

After having parted with the Fur Company's caravan, the mission party was faced with the serious question as to an escort for them from the Rendezvous to Fort Walla Walla. The Nez Perce Indians, as though fearful of losing their new-found friends, were eager for the missionaries to go with them by the northern route to Fort Walla Walla. This is what Parker had done in 1835, and it took him forty-five days to make the journey. This route was very mountainous. It crossed and recrossed the Continental Divide four times.[18] Whitman was warned by well-informed mountain men that it would be impossible to take the Dearborn wagon that way and also that such a trail would be most difficult if not impossible for the cattle.

The alternative route would be along the Snake River across the desert of what is now southern Idaho. Lawyer and Tackensuatis promised to accompany the mission party as far west as Soda Springs. Whitman and Spalding decided that with the help of their two Indian boys and Goodyear, they could make the journey in safety. Dulin who had been with them since leaving the frontier left them at the Rendezvous. John Hinds, a Negro, who was ill with "dropsy" joined the party in order to get medical help from Dr. Whitman [Letter 39]. As early as July 8, only two days after their arrival at the Rendezvous, Spalding in his letter to Greene stated that they had decided to take the Snake River route.

An unexpected and most welcome development came on July 12; a small party of Hudson's Bay men under the command of John L. McLeod and Thomas McKay arrived at the Rendezvous to take part in trading. The Company had purchased from Nathaniel J. Wyeth the fort which he had built in 1834, known as Fort Hall, near present-day Pocatello, Idaho. Wyeth was on his way back to the States and had traveled with McLeod and McKay to the Rendezvous. Parker, learning of the intention of the Hudson's Bay Company to acquire Fort Hall, had sent a second letter to Whitman by McLeod and McKay in which he advised the mission party to travel under their protection. The missionaries looked upon this as another token of divine favor and hastened to make their plans accordingly. On Thursday, July 14, they moved to the encampment of McLeod and McKay which was about ten miles from the main Rendezvous. Since the Nez Perces had also decided to travel with the Hudson's Bay Company's party as far as Fort Hall, they likewise moved their camp to be near McLeod.

Narcissa described the warm reception given them by the Hudson's Bay men: "On our arrival Mr. McL. came to meet us, led us to his tent & gave us a supper which consisted of steak (Antelope), broiled ham, biscuit & butter, tea and loaf sugar brought from Wallah Wallah. This we relished very much as we had not seen anything of the bread kind since the last of May. Especially sister Spalding who has found it quite difficult to eat meat [for] some time." McLeod gave his guests glowing accounts of the abundance of fresh vegetables and food supplies at Fort Walla Walla and Fort Vancouver. This was good news!

Years later, Spalding looked back upon the first meeting of the mission party with McLeod and McKay and remembered how "The shrewd McKay as he met our little party leaving Green River to join his camp said, referring to our ladies, 'There is something that Doct. McLoughlin cannot ship out of the country so easy.'" [19]

Although the contemporary writings of Whitman, Spalding, and Gray do not indicate that any of them appreciated the significance of their feat in taking the first white women over the Rockies, Tom McKay was one who did. As the stepson of Dr. John McLoughlin, he was well acquainted with the firmness with which the Doctor, as Chief Factor at Fort Vancouver, conducted the business of his company. Dr. McLoughlin could outbid, outsell, and outmaneuver any threatened rival in the fur trade. But larger issues were arising than those involved in the fur trade which would give the Hudson's Bay Company and the British Government increasing concern.

One of these issues was the location of the boundary in Old Oregon which would determine which part of that vast territory would come under the jurisdiction of the United States and which would go to Great Britain. Tom McKay saw in the presence of two white women at the Rendezvous, on the west side of the Continental Divide, a development which challenged England's dominance in Old Oregon.

> Only two white women at the Rendezvous! This was an epoch making event with far-reaching consequences for the political future of Old Oregon. Their very presence proved that the Rocky Mountains were no longer a barrier to American emigration. The two women riding horseback, on side-saddles, through South Pass had opened the mountain door to Old Oregon to countless thousands of women to follow. Where two women could go on horseback, other women could follow in covered wagons, ówives, mothers, sisters, and daughters. The coming of families meant the establishment of homes, schools, churches, and inevitably the formation of a civil government under the jurisdiction of the United States. In a flash all this was made clear to Tom McKay who saw that the focal point of competition between Great Britain and the United States was no longer to be centered in the fur trade but rather in the growth of a resident white population in Old Oregon. Hence the remark: "There is something that Doct. McLoughlin cannot ship out of the country so easy."

FROM THE RENDEZVOUS TO FORT BOISE

The Hudson's Bay party with the missionaries and some two hundred or more Nez Perces started for Fort Hall on Saturday, July 16. While crossing the plains, the Fur Company's caravan made two "camps" [i.e., marches] a day, stopping for a two-hour period at midday for rest and refreshment. The Indians, however, made but one camp a day. They did not stop after they got started in the morning until they were ready to camp for the night. McLeod, his men, and the mission party found it best to accommodate themselves to the Indians' custom although the women found it most trying and were glad to resume their former schedule after parting with the Indians at Fort Hall.

NARCISSA WHITMAN'S DIARY

After leaving the Rendezvous, the missionaries had no opportunity to send letters back to their homes until they arrived at Fort Vancouver. Narcissa, who had been writing a series of travel letters to her family, decided to keep a diary instead. Judging from the evidence, she first made rough notes along the way in a pocket notebook. After arriving at Fort Vancouver, she wrote the first draft of her diary from these notes and from memory. This first draft is so uniform in its writing and in the flow of ink, that it could not have been written at irregular intervals along the trail. Then Narcissa made a copy for her mother and also one for her husband's mother. Thus there are the rough notes, the original diary, and two copies, all extant.[20]

The copy that Narcissa sent to her parents was published in some local paper shortly after it had been received. This displeased her. Writing to her sister Jane on September 18, 1838, Narcissa said: "I regret you should have it printed, or any [part] of it, for it was never designed for public eye." Yet by a queer irony of fate, nothing written by a member of the Oregon Mission of the American Board has been reprinted as often as Narcissa's charming diary.[21]

NARCISSA TELLS THE STORY

Narcissa in her diary gives the following description of their travel experiences:

> We commenced our journey to Walla Walla July 18, 1836, under the protection of Mr. McLeod & his company... On the 19th did not move at all. 20th. Came twelve miles... over many steep & high mountains... the 22nd was a tedious day to us, we started about nine o'clock a.m., rode until half past four, p.m. Came twenty one miles. Had two short showers in the afternoon which cooled the air considerably. Before this the heat was oppressive. I thought of Mother's bread & butter many times as any hungry child would, but did not find it on the way. I fancy pork & potatoes would relish extremely well. Have been living on fresh meat

for two months exclusively. Am cloyed with it. I do not know how I shall endure this part of the journey.

On Sunday, July 23, Narcissa's thoughts turned to her home and to her parents. She wrote of praying for them: "Earnestly desired that God would bless them in their declining years, & smooth their passage to the tomb; that in the absence of their earthly comforts, he would fill their souls with his more immediate presence, so that they may never have cause to regret the sacrifice they have made for his Name Sake." Here she is referring to her departure from the family circle for Oregon.

On July 27, Narcissa wrote:

> Our cattle endure the journey remarkably well. They are a source of great comfort to us in this land of scarcity, they supply us with sufficient milk for our tea & coffee which is indeed a luxury... Have seen no buffalo since we left Rendezvous. Had no game of any kind except a few messes of Antelope which John's Father gave us. We have plenty of dry Buffalo meat which we purchased of the Indians & dry it is for me. I can scarcely eat it, it appears so filthy,[22] but it will keep us alive, and we ought to be thankful for it. We have had a few meals of fresh fish also, which relished well... Found no berries. Neither have I found any of Ma's bread. (Girls do not waste the bread, if you know how well I should relish even the dryest morsel, you would have every piece carefully.) Do not think I regret coming. No, far from it. I would not go back for a world. I am contented and happy notwithstanding I sometimes get very hungry and weary.

McLeod gave the missionaries some rice he had obtained at Fort Walla Walla; this was greatly appreciated.

Narcissa refers several times to the light wagon which Whitman was determined to take with him to his future mission station. As has been stated, this wagon was not the first to have been taken over the Continental Divide, but it was the first to have been taken across what is now southern Idaho as far west as Fort Boise. Narcissa repeatedly mentioned the great difficulties the men, and especially her husband, faced in their endeavors to take the wagon over terrain never before crossed by a wheeled vehicle. On July 25, she wrote:

Husband has had a tedious time with the wagon today. Got set in the creek this morning while crossing, was obliged to wade considerably in getting it out. After that in going between two mountains, on the side of one so steep that it was difficult for the horses to pass, the wagon was upset twice. Did not wonder at this at all. It was a greater wonder that it was not turning a somerset continually. It is not very grateful to my feelings to see him wear out with such excessive fatigue as I am obliged to... All the most difficult part of the way he has walked in his laborious attempt to take the wagon over.

On July 28 after traveling through some "very mountainous" country, Narcissa reported: "One of the axle trees of the wagon broke today. Was a little rejoiced, for we were in hopes they would leave it and have no more trouble with it. Our rejoycing was in vain, however, for they are making a cart of the hind wheels this afternoon & lashing the forward wheels to it, intending to take it through in some shape or other. They are so resolute & untiring in their efforts, they will probably succeed." This incident occurred two days before the party arrived at Soda Springs.

On July 30, the missionaries rode ten miles out of their way in order to see an unusual phenomenon of nature just west of present-day Soda Springs, Idaho. Here two springs, called Steamboat Springs and Beer Springs, emitted hot water heavily saturated with soda and some form of gas which killed birds and insects in the immediate vicinity. In recent times, these bubbling springs have been inundated by the Soda Point Reservoir.

After leaving the mountainous country, the trail entered a flat desert where the thermometer often rose above 100°. On August 2, Narcissa wrote: "Heat excessive. Truly I thought 'the Heavens over us were brass, & the earth iron under our feet'." Narcissa's quotation from Deuteronomy 28:23, so appropriate in describing the weather, reveals her thorough knowledge of the Bible.

The missionaries arrived at Fort Hall on Wednesday morning, August 3, where they were cordially welcomed by Captain Joseph Thing, the Hudson's Bay Company's official in charge. The fort was located on the south bank of the Snake River about twelve miles from what is now Pocatello, Idaho. Thing provided rooms in the fort for the two couples.

This was the first time that the Whitmans and the Spaldings had been able to sleep within a building since leaving the Missouri frontier.

Thing proudly showed his garden, which was the beginning of agriculture in what is now Idaho. His turnips were excellent; his corn had been frostbitten; his crop of peas and onions was not promising. That evening the missionaries had the pleasure of dining on "turnips & fried bread" as a supplement to their dried buffalo meat and for dessert, they had tea and stewed wild serviceberries. Narcissa noted: "We had stools to sit on."

Instead of following the Snake River across what is now southern Idaho, the Nez Perces with the few Cayuses who were traveling with them turned north at Fort Hall. "The whole tribe are exceedingly anxious to have us go with them, use every argument they can invent to prevail on us to do so, & not only arguments, but stratagem. We all think it not best." The missionaries were convinced that the route the Indians were planning to take would be longer and consume more time. "To go with them would take us two months or more," wrote Narcissa, "when now we expect to go to Walla Walla in twenty-five days, or be there by the first of September. When we get there, rest will be sweet to us." Chief Tackensuatis, his family, Kentuc, and a few other Indians decided to stay with the mission party.

One who did not remain with the missionaries was Miles Goodyear. According to Gray: "Miles Goodyear, the boy we picked up two days from Fort Leavenworth, who had been assigned to assist the Doctor, was determined, if the Doctor took his wagon any further, to leave the company. He was the only one that could be spared to assist in this wild, and, as all considered, crazy undertaking." Goodyear was given two horses and "the best outfit" the mission party could give him.[23]

The McLeod party with the Missionaries, their Indian helpers, and Hinds, left Fort Hall on Thursday, August 4, for Fort Boise.[24] Since they were no longer with the main body of the Nez Perces, they could travel at a more leisurely pace and make two camps a day. "I feel this to be a great mercy to us weak females," wrote Narcissa in her diary, "for it was more than we could well endure to travel during the heat of the day without refreshment."

Their trail led along the south bank of the Snake River which the missionaries had seen for the first time at Fort Hall. This tributary of the Columbia River is the seventh largest river in the United States in volume of water carried. On August 5 Narcissa wrote: "We came through several swamps & all the last part of the way we were so swarmed with musquetoes as to be scarcely able to see, especially while crossing the Portneuf [River] which we did just before we came into camp. It is the widest river I have forded on horseback. It seemed as if the cows would run mad for the musquetoes." [25]

Some indication of the dangers the women faced when riding sidesaddle, with only the left foot in the stirrup and with the right leg hooked over a horn on the saddle, is found in the following entry from Eliza's diary for August 6: "Yesterday my horse became unmanageable in consequence of stepping into a hornet's nest. I was thrown, and notwithstanding my foot remained a moment in the stirrup, and my body dragged for some distance, I received no serious injury." This was the second time that Eliza had had such an experience.[26]

Narcissa described the terrain over which they rode as being nothing more than a barren sandy desert were it not for the sage. "In some places," she noted, "it grows in bunches to the height of a man's head, & it is so stiff and hard as to be much in the way of our animals and wagon." Whitman, still determined to take the wagon with them, often found it difficult to get it either around or over the sage.

On Sunday evening, August 7, Narcissa wrote: "Came fifteen miles without seeing water, over a dry parched earth, covered with its native sage as parched as the earth itself. Heat excessive." Whitman later wrote: "Imagination can hardly equal the barrenness of the Snake River [country]" [Letter 31]. On Monday, the 8th, the missionaries were provided with some fresh elk meat, the first they had eaten, and on the 12th they got fresh salmon from some Indians at Salmon Falls. Narcissa wrote regarding the fish: "Had we been a few days earlier, we should not have been able to obtain any fish, for they had but just come up." Since the falls were too high for the salmon, this was the limit of their spawning run up the river.

There follows in Narcissa's diary for August 12, one of the most quoted passages of her writings, often referred to as the soliloquy to her trunk:

> Friday Eve. Dear Harriet, the little trunk you gave me has come with me so far & now I must leave it here alone. Poor little

trunk, I am sorry to leave thee. Thou must abide here alone & no more by this presence remind me of my Dear Harriet. Twenty miles below the Falls on Snake River. This shall be thy place of rest. Farewell little Trunk. I thank thee for thy faithful services & that I have been cheered by thy presence so long. Thus we scatter as we go along.

[Narcissa's entry for August 12 continues:] The hills are so steep and rocky that Husband thought it best to lighten the wagon as much as possible & take nothing but the wheels, leaving the box with my trunk. I regret leaving anything that came from home especially that trunk, but it is best. It would have been better for us not to have attempted to bring any baggage whatever, only what was necessary to use on the way. It costs so much labor, besides the expense of animals. If I were to make this journey again, I would make quite different preparations. To pack & unpack so many times & cross so many streams, where the packs frequently get wet, requires no small amount of labour, besides the injury done to the articles... The custom of the country is to possess nothing & then you will lose nothing while traveling. Farewell for the present.

On the next day, Narcissa wrote in her diary that McKay had "asked the privilege of taking the little trunk along so that my soliloquy about it last night was for nought." Possibly McKay later returned the trunk to her but nothing was said of this in her diary.

In order to take a shorter route to Fort Boise, McLeod decided to cross the Snake River at a place near present-day Glenns Ferry, Idaho. There several islands break the swift flow of the river making fording on horseback possible. Narcissa mentioned in her diary for August 13 that the crossing was made where there were two islands.[27] She wrote: "The packs are placed upon the top of the highest horses & in this way crossed without wetting. Two of the tallest horses were selected to carry Mrs. S. & myself over... The last branch we rode as much as a half-mile in crossing & against the current too, which made it hard for the horses, the water being up to their sides." Few men today would ever attempt such a crossing but the women accepted the experience, no doubt riding side-saddle, as matter-of-course. "I once thought," wrote Narcissa, "that crossing streams would be the most dreadful part of the journey. I can now cross the most difficult stream without the least fear."

Whitman had a most difficult time in getting the cart across the Snake River. Narcissa described the event: "Both the cart & the mules were capsized in the water and the mules entangled in the harness. Both the cart and mules turned upside down in the river." After a desperate struggle the cart and the mules were landed on the north bank. Here again we see Whitman's determination to take the wagon through at all cost.

After reaching the north bank of the river, McLeod and his men pushed on ahead of the missionaries who found their progress delayed by the cattle. The trail led in a northwesterly direction across the desert to the Boise River which was then followed to its mouth on the Snake River where Fort Boise was located. This fort had been established in the summer of 1834 by Thomas McKay, and he remained there after his return from the Rendezvous of 1836.

The mission party arrived at Fort Boise, which Narcissa called "Snake Fort," on Friday noon, August 19. On Saturday morning, she wrote in her diary: "Last night I put my clothes in water & this morning finished washing before breakfast. I find it not very agreeable to do such work in the middle of the day when I have no shelter to protect me from the sun's scorching rays. This is the third time I have washed since I left the states, or home either." McLeod, who was planning to escort the mission party to Fort Walla Walla, was ready to leave that Saturday but after finding the women busy with their washing kindly offered to wait until Monday. "This, I can assure you," wrote Narcissa, "was a favour for which we can never be too thankful for our souls need the rest of the Sab. as well as our bodies."

Whitman had to face some harsh realities at Fort Boise. Aware that the horses, which had been pulling the wagon reduced to a cart through the sage, were physically exhausted, and learning that the trail which lay before them over the Blue Mountains was far more difficult than any yet followed, he reluctantly decided to leave the wagon at the fort.[28] Even though Whitman failed to take the wagon through to the Columbia River, his accomplishment in getting it as far west as Fort Boise is worthy of acclaim. He had proved that it was possible for a wheeled vehicle to cross the desert which lay between the Rockies and the Blue Mountains.

A long section of what came to be the Oregon trail, stretching for some four hundred miles west of the Rendezvous, had been opened to vehicular traffic. Seven years later, when some one thousand Oregon-bound emigrants with their wagons were told at Fort Hall that it was impossible to take wagons any further west, it was Whitman who stepped forward and assured them that it could be done, as his experience had proven.

Time is needed to give perspective so that the significance of passing events can be appreciated. Even as members of the 1836 mission party had not at the time recognized the significance of white women crossing the Rockies, neither did they appreciate the importance of their feat in taking the wagon as far west as Fort Boise. Gray called it a "crazy undertaking." It was not until November 1843 that we find Whitman taking justifiable pride in the part he played in "establishing the first wagon road across to the border of the Columbia River" [Letter 142].

FROM FORT BOISE TO FORT VANCOUVER

The mission party crossed to the west bank of the Snake River on Monday morning, August 22. The women were taken over in a rude Indian canoe made out of rushes and willow branches. After crossing the river, the missionaries were in what is now eastern Oregon. Their trail led in a northerly direction. They crossed the Malheur River at noon on the 23rd and by the evening of the 24th had reached Burnt River. Nowhere along their entire journey had they encountered such mountainous and difficult terrain as along Burnt River. After crossing a divide, they came into Powder River Valley on the afternoon of the 26th. By this time McLeod was getting restless. Fort Walla Walla was about four days' march away. He suggested, since they were no longer in hostile Indian country, that he push on ahead with the Whitmans and Gray, leaving the Spaldings to follow with the cattle. Chief Tackensuatis was now able to guide the Spaldings. The tent was left with them as McLeod turned his tent over to the Whitmans. Narcissa's diary mentions many favors which McLeod extended to them. A good instance is recorded in her diary for August 27 when McLeod succeeded in shooting twenty-two wild ducks and gave nine of them to the Whitmans.

The trail led from Powder River over another divide into Grande Ronde Valley, which was a favorite place for a part of the Nez Perce tribe. On the 28th, Narcissa wrote: "We descended a very steep hill coming into Grande Ronde at the foot of which is a beautiful cluster of trees... Grande Ronde is indeed a beautiful place. It is a circular plain, surrounded with lofty mountains & has a beautiful stream coursing through it, skirted with timber, quite large timber." After traveling for so many weeks on the treeless prairies and the barren deserts, riding through forests was what Narcissa called, "a very agreeable change."

On Monday, August 29, while crossing the Blue Mountains, Narcissa gave the following vivid description of her experiences: "Before noon we began to descend one of the most terrible mountains for steepness & length I have yet seen. It was like winding stairs in its descent & in some places almost perpendicular. We were a long time descending it. The horses appeared to dread the hill as much as we did. They would turn & wind in a zigzag manner all the way down. The men usually walked but I could not get permission to, neither did I desire it much. We had no sooner gained the foot of the mountain when another more steep & dreadful was before us."

The Whitmans had an exciting experience late that afternoon. They rode out to a vantage point at about the 5,000 foot level where a beautiful landscape burst into view. Below them and somewhat to the right were the valleys of the Umatilla and Walla Walla Rivers. A little further away flowed the mighty Columbia. They were highly favored in having a clear day for they could see two hundred miles across what is now eastern Oregon to the snowy peaks of the Cascade Mountain Range. "It was beautiful," wrote Narcissa that evening. "Just as we gained the highest elevation & began to descend, the sun was dipping his disk behind the western horizon. Beyond the valley, we could see two distinct mountains, Mount Hood & Mount St. Helens. These lofty peaks were of a conical form & separate from each other by a considerable distance. Behind the former the sun was hiding part of his rays which gave us a more distinct view of this gigantic cone. The beauty of this extensive valley contrasted well with the rolling mountains behind us & at this hour of twilight was enchanting & quite diverted my mind from the fatigue under which I was labouring."

Tuesday, August 30, was spent in camp because of some difficulty McLeod had with some of his pack animals. Early the next morning, McLeod rode on ahead to notify those at Fort Walla Walla of the approach of the missionaries. On the 31st, the Whitmans rode about thirty miles over dry hills, which are now devoted to wheat fields, and camped for the night on Walla Walla River about eight miles from Fort Walla Walla. In the course of their travels that day, they rode past the site which was to become their home. Whitman did not then know that the mission party would have to go to Fort Vancouver for supplies. For the time being, Fort Walla Walla on the Columbia was considered to be the terminus of their travels as they felt sure that they would find a location somewhere near that place. The missionaries of the American Board arrived at Fort Walla Walla just two years to the day after the arrival of the Jason Lee party.

The site of Fort Walla Walla is now covered by the waters of the Columbia River which have been backed up by the McNary Dam, completed in December 1953. The fort was located on a sandy elevation on the east bank of the Columbia near the mouth of the Walla Walla River and was originally called Fort Nez Perce. At the time of the arrival of the 1836 mission party, a French Canadian, Pierre C. Pambrun, was the Hudson's Bay official in charge. Narcissa's account of their arrival at the fort in her diary for September 1 pulsates with the excitement she felt as they ended their long overland journey.

"September 1st, 1836. You can better imagine our feelings this morning than I can describe them. I could not realize that the end of our long journey was so near. We arose as soon as it was light, took a cup of coffee and eat of the duck we had given us last night, then dressed for Walla W. We started while it was yet early, for all were in haste to reach the desired haven." Marcus was riding an Indian pony which did not know how to pace as did the horse Narcissa was riding, so they had to gallop all the way to the fort. "The first appearance of civilization we saw," wrote Narcissa, "was the garden, two miles this side of the fort. The fatigues of the long journey seemed to be forgotten in the excitement of being so near the close."

Seeing the approach of the Whitmans and Gray, McLeod, Pambrun, and a naturalist who happened to be at the fort, John K. Townsend, rode forth to greet them. "After the usual introductions and salutatations," added Narcissa, "we entered the fort & were comfortably seated in cushioned armed chairs." They were served breakfast: "...fresh salmon, potatoes, tea, bread & butter." While at breakfast, a rooster placed himself on the door sill and crowed. Even such an insignificant incident stirred

Narcissa to write: "Now whether it was the sight of the first white female or out of compliment to the company, I know not... I was pleased with his appearance."

After breakfast the three missionaries were taken on a tour of the fort and the grounds. Narcissa mentioned seeing chickens, turkeys, pigeons, goats, and "the largest & fattest cattle & swine I ever saw." The Whitmans were given a room in the west bastion of the fort "full of port holes in the sides but no windows, & filled with fire arms." The room even had a "large cannon." Narcissa wrote that she was so pleased to be sheltered from the scorching sun that she paid no attention to the armaments.

Later in the morning, Pambrun treated his guests to some muskmelons. According to Narcissa, one was "eighteen inches in length." This was a real treat. Dinner was served at 4:00 p.m. The very fact that Narcissa listed the various items on the menu is an indication of how much she appreciated the change of diet: "...pork, potatoes, beets, cabbage, turnips, tea, bread & butter." The privations of the trail were over and they were back in civilization again. The missionaries met Mrs. Pambrun, a native woman, who spoke some French but very little English.

Townsend, who had gone out to Old Oregon with the Wyeth party and the Methodist missionaries in 1834, has given us the following in his journal under date of September 1, 1836: "I have had this evening some interesting conversation with our guests, the missionaries. They appear admirably qualified for the arduous duty to which they have devoted themselves, their minds being fully alive to the mortifications and trials incident to a residence among wild Indians, but they do not shrink from the task, believing it to be their religious duty to engage in this work. The ladies have borne the journey astonishingly; they look robust and healthy."[29] From this it is evident that Eliza Spalding's health was better at the end than it had been at the beginning of her overland journey.

On September 2, the day after their arrival at the fort, Narcissa noted in her diary that her husband had decided to go to Fort Vancouver, a six days' voyage by boat down the Columbia River. Whitman wanted to see Dr. McLoughlin. By this time he had learned that he would not be able to get all supplies needed at Fort Walla Walla and that he would have to get them at Fort Vancouver. Narcissa decided to go with him rather than remain at Walla Walla. McLeod and Townsend left for Vancouver the 3rd with heavily loaded boats. Since Pambrun was also planning to go to Vancouver a few days later, the Whitmans decided to travel with him.

The Spalding party with the pack animals and the cattle arrived at Fort Walla Walla on the afternoon of the 3rd. The Spaldings were given the same cordial welcome as had been extended to the Whitmans and Gray. Only eight head of the original herd of seventeen (including perhaps two calves born en route) cattle survived the long trek. Two had been butchered en route; two calves were lost; and five had to be left at Fort Boise because of their sore feet. The missionaries were glad to have these eight as they knew it was not the policy of the Hudson's Bay Company to sell cattle to settlers or to missionaries. Evidently the Company gave the missionaries five head to replace those left at Fort Boise, as Whitman, in a letter to Parker dated September 18, wrote: "We shall have five cows, seven heifers, and one bull." The missionaries had left the Missouri frontier with fourteen head of horses, including the two that Whitman had left the year before at Bellevue, and six mules. Eight of the horses were taken through. The letters of the missionaries do not tell the fate of the mules.

At Fort Walla Walla the missionaries met Charles Compo[30] who had served as Parker's interpreter the previous year. Compo complained to Whitman about the treatment he had received from Parker; he had given up his chances of trapping in the fall and winter of 1885–36 in order to go with Parker, and had received only $18.00 worth of Indian goods for his services. Whitman asked Greene: "How could so small a compensation be right?" [Letter 62]. Compo spent the winter with the Nez Perce Indians hoping to return to the Rendezvous with Parker in the spring of 1836. When Parker failed to make that journey, Compo entered the employ of the Hudson's Bay Company at Fort Walla Walla where he remained for two years.

The five missionaries left for Fort Vancouver with Pambrun on September 6. Gray described the boat which carried them down the Columbia as being "about 30 feet long and 8 wide in the center, coming to a point at each end, propelled by 5 oares and a stearsman, of sufficient depth to early 2,500 pounds."[31] A trip up or down the Columbia River in those days involved several portages because of dangerous rapids or falls.

This meant that all occupants of the boats would have to walk the length of the portage; in some places this exposed them to the flea infested terrain. This came as a surprise to Narcissa who in her diary tells of her unpleasant experiences. Once she had seated herself in the shade of a large rock when suddenly she became aware of insects crawling on her neck. She soon discovered that she was covered with thousands of fleas!

"Immediately," she wrote, "I cast my eyes upon my dress and to my astonishment found it was black with these creatures all making all possible speed to lay siege to my neck & ears. This sight made me almost frantic." Narcissa shouted for help but no one was within hearing at the time. She began climbing up the rocks and finally attracted her husband's attention. "I could not tell him," she wrote, "but showed him the cause of my distress. On opening the gathers in my dress around my waist, every plait was lined with them. Thus they had already laid themselves in ambush against a fresh attack. We brushed & shook & brushed for an hour, not stopping to kill them for that would have been impossible." After returning to the boat, the Whitmans learned that every one else in the party had been likewise afflicted. They found no relief until they were able to camp for the night and change their apparel.

On the evening of September 9, a day when the party remained in camp because of contrary winds, a band of Indians visited them. Narcissa noted: "Every head was flattened. These are the first I have seen so near as to be able to examine them." It was the picture of a deformed head said to be of one of the four Indians who had visited St. Louis in the fall of 1831, with the accompanying appeal for missionaries, which had attracted the attention of Samuel Parker when he read the March 1, 1833, issue of the New York *Christian Advocate*. Now the missionaries were seeing the custom in reality. Two days later while making the portage at the Cascades, Narcissa had a better opportunity to observe the flattening process. "I saw an infant here," she wrote, "whose head was in the pressing machine. This was a pitiful sight. Its mother took great satisfaction in unbinding & showing its naked head to us." The infant was only three weeks old and the bones of the skull were still pliable. Narcissa learned that the infant's head would usually be kept under pressure for three or more months. "There is a variety of shapes among them," she wrote. "Some are sharper [i.e., more wedge-shaped] than others. I saw a child about a year old whose head had been recently released from its pressure, as I suppose from its looks. All the back part of it was of a purple colour as if it had been sadly bruised."

The custom of flattening the heads of infants was common in that day in the lower Columbia River country, and there is evidence that a few of the natives in the upper country also practiced it. By 1836 the custom was beginning to die out.

AT FORT VANCOUVER

Pambrun's boat with the five missionary passengers arrived at Fort Vancouver on Monday morning, September 12. The first to greet them was the naturalist, J. K. Townsend, who escorted them to the main gate of the fort. Dr. McLoughlin and others, hearing of their arrival, hastened to greet them. He gave a warm welcome to the missionaries who had come to the end of a seven-months journey across the continent. Dr. McLoughlin was quick to appreciate the significance of the achievement of the women in crossing the Rockies and, according to Spalding, called upon "his powers of invention to confer upon them some title of honor due to their heroism." [32]

McLoughlin presented his wife, Margaret, to the missionaries. She was the daughter of a Swiss merchant in Canada and a Cree Indian woman and is described by those who knew her as being intelligent and capable. She was the widow of Alexander McKay,[33] when Dr. McLoughlin married her, and already the mother of four children including Tom McKay. Among those at Fort Vancouver at the time of the arrival of the mission party was twelve-year-old William McKay, son of Thomas, who later was sent East on the advice of Dr. Whitman to study at the Fairfield Medical College.

In the welcoming party was Sir James Douglas, Dr. McLoughlin's chief associate and later his successor, and Dr. William Frazer Tolmie, a young Scottish physician who had been sent to Fort Vancouver in 1833 to relieve Dr. McLoughlin of his medical cares. Douglas also had a half-breed wife. Another couple who was introduced to the missionaries were the Rev. and Mrs. Herbert Beaver, who had arrived from England on the *Neriade*, then in port, only six days before the arrival of the American Board missionaries. Beaver, an Anglican clergyman, was to be the chaplain of the Fort. Another English woman at the Fort was a Mrs. Capendel, the wife of one of the employees of the Company. "This is more than we expected," noted Narcissa in her diary, "that we should be privileged with the acquaintance & society of two English ladies."

Now that the "unheard of journey for females" was completed, what was the verdict of those who were directly involved? Was Marcus Whitman, the first who believed that such a journey for women was possible, to be censured for promoting so foolhardy an undertaking or was he to be commended for his sound judgment? Great risks were taken. Mrs. Satterlee, who had accompanied her husband to the Missouri frontier, had died at Liberty. Mrs. Spalding was ill several times along the way. After the trying experience of crossing the desert of what is now southern Idaho, Spalding wrote to Greene on September 20: "I can never advise females, notwithstanding, to venture a route over the mountains so long as a passage to this country is so easy by sea.

Narcissa agreed with Marcus in recommending the overland route. Writing to Mrs. Parker from Fort Vancouver on October 24, Narcissa said: "Do you ask whether I regret coming by land? I must answer no! *by no means*. If I were at home now, I would choose to come this way in preference to a seven months voyage" [Letter 35]. No one was better qualified to judge the relative merits of an overland journey as compared with a sea voyage than Samuel Parker, for he had gone both ways. In a letter to Elkanah Walker, who was thinking of taking his bride overland to Oregon, Parker on February 19, 1838, wrote: "By all means go across the continent by land. I would rather go across the continent three times than around the Cape once... A lady can go with far more comfort by land than by water." [34]

THE WOMEN AT FORT VANCOUVER

What a delightful place this [is]," wrote Narcissa in her diary. "What a contrast this to the rough barren sand plains through which we have so recently passed. Here we find fruit of every description, apples, peaches, grapes, pear, plum, & fig trees in abundance." In the extensive gardens, she saw: "...cucumbers, melons, beans, peas, beets, cabbages, tomatoes, and every kind of vegetable too numerous to be mentioned." The missionaries were taken on a tour of the barns and fields on the afternoon of September 14. Narcissa was greatly impressed. "They estimate their wheat crop at 4,000 bushels this year, peas, the same," she wrote. "Oats & barley between 15 & 1,700 bushels each. The potato & turnip fields are large and fine. Their cattle are numerous, estimated at 1,000 head in all their settlements, also sheep & goats, but the sheep are of an inferior kind. We find also hens, turkeys, pigeons, but no geese." The Company also had three hundred hogs.

They inspected the dairy where between fifty and sixty cows were being milked. The Company had a gristmill run by horse power at Vancouver and another powered by water at Fort Colville. Their storehouses were filled with all manner of merchandise. Regarding this Narcissa informed her family on November 1:

> The Company lets us have goods as cheap as can be afforded & cheaper probably than we can get them from the States. They only charge us a hundred per cent more than the prime cost, or England prices. All their goods are of the best quality & will be durable. Husband has obtained a good [heating] stove of Mr. Pambrun of W.W. & we take up enough sheet iron for the pipe. My tin ware has all been made within a week past of the first rate block tin. I have six large milk pans, coffee & tea pots, candle sticks & molds. Covered pails & a baker... and besides this the blacksmiths have all been employed in making our farming utensils &c... There are a few deficiencies in the cloth line. No provision is made for bedding except blankets & these are dear. No sheets, nothing for shirting except striped or calico. I have found a piece of bleach linen which I take for sheets, the only one in the store, price 75 cents per yard. We see now that it was not necessary to bring anything because we find all here [Letter 38].

Narcissa noted one exception—religious books and papers.

Dr. McLoughlin's hospitality to the two missionary couples knew no limits. He invited them to dine at his table along with his wife and daughter Maria. Others who were also included in that select circle were Sir James and his wife and possibly Dr. Tomie [Letter 26]. The Beavers were not so honored nor was Gray. Since protocol was an important aspect of the social life at Fort Vancouver, and since Gray was known to be the "mechanic" for the mission, Dr. McLoughlin did not consider him as having the same status as the two couples. Gray never forgot what he considered to be the discourteous treatment he had received at the Fort and this may have been the basis for his anti-Hudson's Bay Company attitude so evident in his book.³⁵ Dr. McLoughlin's dining-room furniture, including his china and some of his silver, are now on display in the McLoughlin house at Oregon City, Oregon. These items give evidence of a culture and an elegance that only the chief factor of an important trading post of the Company could afford.

Narcissa commented on the abundance and variety of food served. On September 23 she noted: "There is such a variety I know not where to begin. For breakfast we have coffee or coco. Salt Salmon & roast duck, wild & potatoes. When we have eaten our supply of them, our plates are changed & we make a finish on bread & butter. For dinner we have a greater variety. First we are always treated to a dish of soup, which is very good. Every kind of vegetable in use is taken & choped fine & put into water with a little rice & boiled to a soup." The menu always included a variety of vegetables and of meats— "roast duck... boiled pork... fresh Salmon..." Following the main course would come the dessert—a rice pudding or apple pie and fruit and cheese. "The gentlemen frequently drink toasts to each other," wrote Narcissa, "but never give us the opportunity of refusing for they know we belong to the teetotal Society." Undoubtedly many a glass was lifted by the gentlemen of the Company in honor of their guests and especially the two women. Never before had the Whitmans and the Spaldings been so well feasted and honored.

When Parker had spent the winter of 1835–36 at Fort Vancouver, he had been invited by Dr. McLoughlln to teach sacred music to the fifty or more half-breed children then enrolled in the school.³⁶ How natural, therefore, was it for Dr. McLoughlin to invite the two women to help in the school and especially for Narcissa to teach singing. Narcissa made three references in her diary to this experience. "I could employ all my time in writing, & work for myself if it were not for his [i.e., Dr. McLoughlin's] wishes," she once wrote. "I sing with the children every evening also, which is considered a favor." And again: "I sing about an hour every evening with the children, teaching them new tunes, at the request of Dr. McLoughlin." It is easy to believe that Dr. McLoughlin was present whenever possible for those informal concerts, for he, too, had succumbed to the charms of her sweet voice. At his invitation, Narcissa became a tutor for his daughter, Maria.

The Rev. Herbert Beaver, however, looked upon the presence of the women in the school as an infringement of his rights. So on September 30, a little more than two weeks after the mission party had arrived, Beaver addressed a note to Dr. McLoughlin protesting the introduction of "various systems of instructions" and asked if the school "is under my sole superintendence?"[37] Dr. McLoughlin replied the same day and firmly informed Beaver that the school was under "my direction." Even after receiving that clarification, Beaver wrote to "Mesdames Whitman and Spalding" on October 1 informing them that in England "it is unusual... for any person to take part, without his permission and request, in the parochial duties of the minister... He would, therefore, hope that after this explanation, the Ladies, whom he has thus presumed to address, will refrain from teaching, in any respect, the children of the School at Vancouver, over which he has charge in virtue of his office."

Dr. McLoughlin was incensed when he learned of this letter. He requested his chaplain to call at his office on Monday morning, October 3. Beaver replied that he preferred to conduct business by writing letters and not by a personal interview. At 1:00 p.m. that day, Dr. McLoughlin sent another note to Beaver in which he stated that he viewed the letter sent to the two missionary ladies as "a deliberate insult to the Honble. [i.e., Honorable] Company." McLoughlin was firm in stating that he expected "that necessary degree of deference to his wishes" from Chaplain Beaver that was required "from all other persons in the service under him."

Beaver replied with another note dated "half past two" on that Monday. He claimed that he was greatly surprised to learn that his letter to the women was taken as an insult. "He would gladly state," he wrote, "for their satisfaction, that not the slightest insult was intended."[38] There the matter rested.

The women at Dr. McLoughlin's insistence continued their work in the school. Beaver, who had been at Fort Vancouver for less than a month, found himself out of favor with the chief factor. He poured out his troubles in long letters to Benjamin Harrison, a member of the Governing Committee of the Company in London and one, as has been stated, who had been very influential in founding the Red River Mission school.

In Beaver's letter to Harrison dated November 15, 1836, we may read: "With respect to private treatment, I might have characterized it as insufferable by any person accustomed to the contrary; and I might have affirmed, in general, that no Englishman, no gentleman, no Christian, no clergyman, no married couple, could possibly remain here, without having their feelings daily outraged by every species of conduct offensive to their former habits." [39] Already Beaver regretted his appointment to Fort Vancouver and wished that he had returned to England on a vessel that had but shortly before sailed from Fort Vancouver. In spite of the appropriateness of his name for a fur-trading post, Chaplain Beaver was not a success at Vancouver. He and his wife returned to England in 1838.

The Men at Fort Vancouver

There is evidence which supports the theory that long before the mission party arrived at Fort Vancouver, Whitman and Spalding had agreed to establish separate stations. And so it was. The Whitman home at Waiilatpu, near Fort Walla Walla and among the Cayuses, was 120 miles from the Spalding station on the Clearwater River with the Nez Perces at a place called Lapwai, now known as Spalding, Idaho. Why did the two couples separate? Why, in view of the limited financial resources of the American Board, were two stations established, when common sense would dictate that they concentrate their energies in one station? Why should they have denied themselves the fellowship and support of each other when so far removed from civilization?

The answer to such questions seems to be that Henry, as has been stated, had proposed marriage to Narcissa and had been rejected. He had found a most loyal helpmate in Eliza Hart, but could never forget the humiliation and disappointment of being turned down by Narcissa. Possibly Whitman was aware of this when he begged the Spaldings to go with him and Narcissa to Old Oregon. If so, it may be that he felt that since Henry was married to Eliza, the old romance was no longer an issue. Narcissa's father was doubtful of the wisdom of his daughter going to the same mission with Henry Spalding but, after having had a personal interview with Spalding, withdrew his objection.

Spalding, however, could not forget, and difficulties arose between him and Whitman on their overland journey to Oregon. Gray in a letter to Greene dated October 14, 1840, stated that the two men had quarreled three times on their way across the country: "...at the Pawnee village, at Fort Boise on the Snake River, and at Walla Walla on the Columbia." Gray did not give the reasons for the disagreements. After the 1838 reenforcement arrived, Elkanah Walker asked Spalding why he had gone so far from Waiilatpu to establish a separate station. According to Gray, Spalding replied: "Do you suppose I would have come off here all alone, a hundred and twenty miles, if I could have lived with him and Mrs. Whitman?"[40]

The fact that the Whitmans and the Spaldings were sent to the same field by the same mission board did not mean that they were temperamentally suited to be bosom friends. Before they were missionaries, these four were human beings with the frailties to which we are all subject. Whitman and Spalding very wisely agreed, before they arrived at Fort Vancouver, to have separate stations even if this required some duplication of equipment and supplies. On the other hand, having two stations with work in two different tribes meant an expansion of their missionary influence.

In all probability Whitman and Spalding discussed with the Cayuse and Nez Perce Indians at the Rendezvous the desirability of having a station with each tribe. Narcissa noted in her diary for September 21, 1836, written at Vancouver: "Mr. Parker recommended a place on the Koos Kooske [Clearwater] river, six days ride above Walla W." This is the only known reference in the writings of the mission party of 1836 to any definite recommendation left by Parker to a possible site for a mission station. Parker had visited the upper Columbia River country in the spring of 1836. His reference to a six days' ride from Fort Walla Walla indicated the Kamiah country. It is possible that Parker left some verbal recommendations with Dr. McLoughlin, but Whitman claimed that Parker had left no written instructions. Evidence indicates that Whitman and Spalding, after consulting with Dr. McLoughlin, made their final decision to have the Whitmans settle among the Cayuses and the Spaldings among the Nez Perces when the two couples were at Fort Vancouver. Plans were then made accordingly.

After further consultation with Dr. McLoughlin, Whitman and Spalding decided that it would be wise for them to return with Gray to Fort Walla Walla, to select the sites, and possibly begin building while the women would remain at Fort Vancouver. Dr. McLoughlin expressed his willingness to sell supplies. A bill of goods amounting to £371-8-1 was purchased, which included household furniture, clothing, home and farming utensils, building supplies, Indian goods, books, stationery, and some provisions. Of this amount, Whitman assumed £188-7-2;

Spalding £172-13-1; and Gray £10-7-10 [Letter 42]. Gray's bill was the smallest as he was not planning to have a separate station and he was unmarried.

During the whole mission period of eleven years, 1836–47, financial transactions between the missionaries and the Hudson's Bay Company were on the basis of English currency. According to a letter that Henry Hill, Treasurer of the American Board wrote to Spalding on June 23, 1837, every £100 cost the Board about $540.00. When the cost of purchases made at Fort Vancouver in the fall of 1836 is added to the $3,273.96 incurred before the missionaries left the States, we find that the Board paid out nearly $6,000.00 to establish the Oregon Mission. This sum does not include the costs incurred by Parker on his exploring tour [See Appendix 2]. Dr. McLoughlin assured Whitman that the expenses incurred by the 1836 mission party in going to Oregon, covering a period of about seven months, were less than the cost would have been had they gone by sea [Letter 88].

Both Whitman and Spalding were generous in their expressions of appreciation for the assistance rendered to them by the Hudson's Bay Company. Whitman made special mention of the warm reception given them by Dr. McLoughlin [Letter 42]. Without the help of this Company, especially in making supplies available and indirectly in keeping the natives peaceful, it is doubtful whether the American Board would ever have been able to establish and maintain its Oregon Mission.[41]

The North West Company, as early as 1813, had imported Hawaiians, sometimes called Kanakas, into the Oregon country as laborers, as the local Indians could not be depended upon to do manual work.[42] The Hudson's Bay Company also found the Hawaiians useful and dependable. When Whitman inquired as to the possibility of getting such help, Dr. McLoughlin suggested that he write to the Rev. Hiram Bingham, head of the American Board's Mission in the Islands, and ask him to send some Hawaiians to aid in the Oregon Mission. McLoughlin also suggested that while writing, he ask Bingham for some sheep as it was contrary to the policy of the Company to sell any animals from their large flocks or herds. A letter was written to Bingham on September 19, 1836, which was signed by Whitman, Spalding, and Gray, asking for both Hawaiian laborers and some sheep.

On Wednesday, September 21, 1836, a heavily laden boat manned by eleven oarsmen left Fort Vancouver for Fort Walla Walla. Among the passengers, in addition to the three missionary men, were Pambrun and a Cayuse chief who had accompanied the mission party to Fort Vancouver. Spalding in a letter to Greene, which was begun on September 20, reported that before they left Fort Vancouver, Dr. McLoughlin had suggested that they seek God's guidance in prayer and joined his petitions with theirs. Narcissa and Eliza were reluctant to see their husbands leave. "One thing comforts me," wrote Narcissa, "they are as unwilling to leave us as we are to stay & would not, if it was possible for us to go now."

The boat party reached the Cascades on the Columbia on the 22nd where a portage was necessary. Another portage of about one-half mile was required at The Dalles. Indians native to the region were always willing to help carry the freight and the boats over the portage if given a little tobacco. Depending upon the size of the boat, from thirty to forty Indians were needed even when a boat was empty. The party arrived at Fort Walla Walla on October 2.

CHAPTER 9 ENDNOTES

1 *Op. cit.*, p. 118.

2 Tackensuatis was not the father of Richard as erroneously stated in Drury, *F.W.W.*, I:84.

3 See Drury, "I, the Lawyer," in *New York Westerners*, VII (May 1960), No. 1. Lawyer's name is spelled Hol-Lol-Sote-Tote on the Lawyer monument, Whitman College campus, Walla Walla. Lawyer served as Head Chief of the Nez Perces, 1849–71.

4 McBeth, *The Nez Perces Since Lewis and Clark*, p. 25, states that the word means "crowned ones" in reference to the hats which the white men wore. Other explanations are given in Josephy, *The Nez Perce Indians*, p. 38.

5 Spalding to American Board, July 6, 1836, Coll. A.

6 During the months in Hawaii, Parker gave an account of his explorations to the Rev. Hiram Bingham of the Hawaiian Mission, who wrote a series of articles on "The Introduction of the Gospel among the Aborigines of North America, West of the Rocky Mountains," which appeared in the *Hawaiian Spectator* beginning in 1838.

7 For sketch of the life of Joe Meek, see Hafen, *Mountain Men*, I:313 ff.

8 Gray, *Oregon*, p. 122.

9 For a time both youths were helpful as interpreters but on the whole, as Secretary Greene had prophesied, the experiment of taking the Indian boys East was not a success.

10 Gray, *Oregon*, pp. 118 & 123.

11 *Ibid.*, 123.

12 *Op. Cit.*, pp. 41 & 109. Drury, *F.W.W.*, I:68, and Drury, *Whitman*, 145, for references to some mountain men who sold packs of playing cards to unsuspecting natives who thought they were buying Bibles.

13 Mrs. Nancy Atkinson, *Biography of Rev. C. H. Atkinson*, Portland, 1893, p. 177. Russell became a charter member of the First Presbyterian Church of Oregon City, organized May 25, 1844.

14 James B. Marsh, *Four Years in the Rockies*, New Castle, Pa., 1884, p. 156.

15 Whitman's spelling of Nez Perce as "Napiersas" shows that he was trying to represent the French pronunciation which he had heard. The Anglicized pronunciation is now used—"Nez Purse." Hulbert, *O.P.*, VI: 162.

16 Hulbert, *O.P.*, VI: 117–8. This comment was made after Parker had visited the Cayuse country the second time, i.e., in May 1836.

17 Drury, *Spalding and Smith*, p. 107.

18 Stanley Davison, "Worker in God's Wilderness," *Montana*, Helena (Winter, 1957) has a map (p. 16) of the supposed route taken by the Nez Perces and Parker in 1835. See also Josephy, *The Nez Perce Indians*, pp. 134 ff., for description of the probable route.

19 Spalding ms. file, #201, p. 7, Coll. W.

20 The original notes made by Narcissa while traveling, and from which the diary was later written, are in private hands, but they have been seen by a historian who vouches for their authenticity. The first copy of Narcissa's diary, made from these notes, is in W.S.H.S. See Drury, *F.W.W.*, I:71 ff., for a comparison of Diary A., which was sent to Narcissa's mother, and Diary B., which was sent to her husband's mother. In my *Whitman*, p. 148, fn. 16, I stated that the diary in

W.S.H.S. was not an original. This opinion was based on a picture of the first page which had been published and which was not in Narcissa's handwriting. I was not then able to examine the original document. Since then, I have had this privilege, and am now convinced that, with the exception of the first page, the diary is authentic.

21 In addition to the publication of her diary referred to by Narcissa, the text has appeared in *T.O.P.A.*, 1891; *Chronicle Express*, Penn Yan, N.Y., beginning January 8, 1891; *O.H.Q.*, XXXVIII (1937) in an article by T. C. Elliott, "Coming of the White Women," and in Drury, *F.W.W.*, I.

22 All quotations from Narcissa's diary in this section have been taken from Drury, *F.W.W.*, I. Spalding to Greene, September 20, 1836, Coll. A., claimed that the dried buffalo meat was ". . . sour, mouldy, & full of all manner of filth, such as I would not have fed to a dog."

23 Gray, *Oregon*, p. 133; and Hafen, *Mountain Men*, II: 179 ff.

24 An excellent map of the Oregon Trail through what is now southern Idaho, with explanatory notes, is to be found in a pamphlet issued by the Department of Highways, State of Idaho, *Route of the Oregon Trail in Idaho*, 1968 & 1967.

25 The mosquitoes and flies are still extremely annoying in some of the places visited by the missionaries. I was at the site of the 1836 Rendezvous in July 1960 and found them as described by Narcissa. Horses were plagued by the horse fly, the deer fly, and the botfly. Some of the insects laid their eggs in the nostrils of the animals while others stung them in the tender spot back of the ankle, just above the hoof. Such attacks often made the animals half crazy.

26 Drury, *F.W.W.*, I:195, fn. 32.

27 The picture of the two-island crossing in Drury, *F.W.W.*, I:83, does not show the correct site. The probable location is shown in *Route of the Oregon Trail in Idaho*, p. 8.

28 Farnham, *Travels*, p. 142, mentions seeing the wagon at Fort Boise in 1839. Perrin Whitman, *W.C.Q.*, II (June 1898), p. 36, also refers to seeing it in 1843. Cannon, *Waiilatpu*, p. 25, states that the wagon had been used to move the effects of the Fort to a new location early in the 1860s. This is the last known reference to the famous wagon.

29 John K. Townsend, *Narrative of a Journey Across the Rocky Mountains*, in *Early Western Travels*, Cleveland, 1905, p. 355.

30 See chapter on Charles Compo, by Drury, in Hafen, *Mountain Men*, VIII: 87 ff.

31 Gray to Ambler, September 9, 1886, Coll. O.

32 Spalding to Greene, Sept. 20, 1886, Coll. A.

33 Alexander McKay lost his life on the ill-fated Tonquin which was blown up on the west coast of Vancouver Island in June 1811.

34 Drury, *Walker*, p. 62. For a more detailed discussion of the wisdom of taking women overland, see Drury, *F.W.W.*, I:114 ff., and III: 307 ff.

35 Gray, *Oregon*, p. 153, referring to himself: ". . . he was looked upon as a vagabond, and entitled to no place or encouragement . . . There was nothing but master and servant in the country." Gray was housed in "the quarters of the clerks." p. 149.

36 Parker, *Journal*, p. 171.

37 HBC Arch., B/223/b/ 14. See also *Reports and Letters of Herbert Beaver, 1836–1838*, Thomas E. Jessett (ed.), Champoeg Press, 1959.

38 Jessett, *op. cit.*, p. 12.

39 HBC Arch., A/ 11/69, folder 23. Jessett, pp. 19 ff.

40 Original letter, Coll. A.

41 Gray became critical of the Hudson's Bay Company. See ante fn., 35. Gray wrote in his *Oregon*, p. 158: "To the disgrace of most of the missionaries, this state of absolute dependence and submission to the Hudson's Bay Company was submitted to and encouraged."

42 The Hawaiians were also called Owyhees. A county in Idaho bears this name. Drury, *Spalding and Smith*, p. 152, quotes from a letter written by Smith on August 1, 1840, in which he states that one Hawaiian could do more work than four Indians, and one American more than four Hawaiians.

FORT VANCOUVER, 1845

The Hudson's Bay Company post, established 1825. Drawing used by permission of the National Park Service, United States Department of the Interior. Courtesy Whitman Mission National Historic Site.

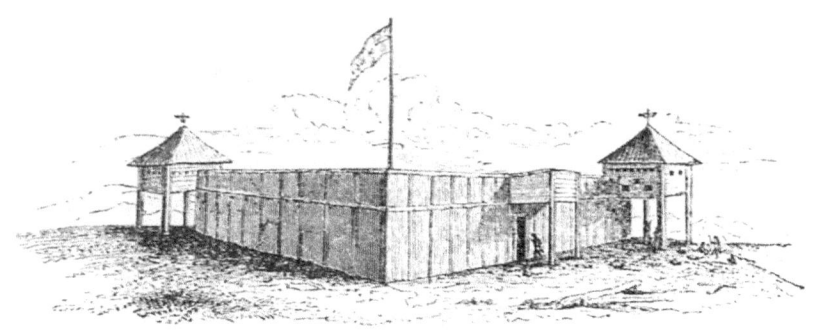

Fort Walla Walla

Sketch of Fort Walla Walla drawn in 1841 by a member of the Wilkes expedition. This was the Hudson's Bay Company fort located at the confluence of the Columbia and Walla Walla rivers. This was the Fort Walla Walla that the Whitmans interacted with. Later the U.S. Army would build another fort by the same name located in what is today the town of Walla Walla.

Council Lodge Made of Woven Mats

This tule lodge is typical of the type of housing used by the native peoples throughout the Columbia Plateau at the time of the Whitman's Arrival in the area in the 1830s. This photo was taken ca. 1900 by Major Lee Moorhouse. Provided by Whitman Mission National Historic Site, courtesy Smithsonian Institution.

[CHAPTER TEN]

WAIILATPU
1836–1837

The real history of the Oregon Mission of the American Board began with the arrival of Whitman, Spalding, and Gray at Fort Walla Walla on October 2, 1836. The preceding nine chapters of this book constitute the prelude of a new section which begins with this chapter.

Fort Walla Walla was located at one of the most important crossroads of Old Oregon. Before it rolled the mighty Columbia River, the largest in America, not in size of the area drained but rather in volume of water carried, as it flows several times faster than does the Mississippi. The Columbia provided the main artery of travel connecting Fort Vancouver with the Company's forts in what is now the State of Washington and with its activities east of the Canadian Rockies.

Each spring an express, which usually consisted of several bateaux or canoes manned by Indians of various tribes, French Canadians, or half-breeds, would leave Fort Vancouver and proceed up the Columbia stopping at the forts along the way—Walla Walla, Okanogan, and Colville. After reaching the waters of the upper Columbia, the men would cross the Continental Divide through Athabasca Pass which had an elevation of only 5,736 feet, being about 1,800 feet lower than the South Pass used by the Americans. The express would then continue eastward by the streams and lakes of Canada to Montreal. Although called an "express," it usually took the men six months to make the transcontinental journey. Another express would leave Montreal for Fort Vancouver about the same time. Occasionally a second express would be sent each way during the same year.

Fort Walla Walla was the main terminus of the overland section of the Oregon Trail, a trail stretching eastward over the Blue Mountains, through Grande Ronde Valley, and on to the Rendezvous and South Pass. A network of Indian trails branched out of Fort Walla Walla. One led into the Nez Perce country in the Clearwater Valley, another to the north into the Spokane country. Still other trails connected the Fort with the tribes of what is now central Washington and to The Dalles. Writing in the spring of 1840, Narcissa said: "We are emphatically [i.e., definitely] situated on the highway between the States and the Columbia River" [Letter 76]. By that date, Narcissa had realized that all who entered Old Oregon by the overland route would be passing their home—mountain men, Hudson's Bay Company's officials, explorers, adventurers, and immigrants. Within the next seven years the number arriving annually over the Oregon Trail would be numbered in the thousands.

When Whitman and Spalding agreed at Fort Vancouver for the former to settle among the Cayuses near Fort Walla Walla and the latter to go to the Nez Perces in the Clearwater Valley, neither could have appreciated the strategic importance of the proposed site for the Whitman station. The decision for the two couples to settle among tribes speaking the same language was of prime importance. The original language of the Cayuses had been very different from that of the Nez Perces, but at the time the Whitmans settled among them, the Cayuses were adopting the Nez Perce tongue.[1] Likewise, many of the Walla Walla and Umatilla Indians, neighbors to the Cayuses, knew the Nez Perce language because of intermarriage and trade relations. According to the best available estimates, the Cayuse tribe then numbered between three and four hundred; the Nez Perces between three and four thousand.[2]

Waiilatpu Selected

On Tuesday, October 4, Whitman, Spalding, Gray, and Pambrun set out to explore the Walla Walla[3] River Valley in search of a suitable site for the Whitman station. This river, which rises in the Blue Mountains, near what is now the Oregon-Washington border, is only about forty miles long. The four men followed its north bank, and on the 5th came to a place, about twenty-five miles east of Fort Walla Walla and about seven miles west of present-day Walla Walla, which Whitman felt was suitable for his station.

The site included about three hundred acres which lay in a triangular area between the Walla Walla River and its tributary, now known as Mill Creek. Their confluence marked the apex of a triangle with the base about eighty rods long stretching from the top of a sharp bend in Walla Walla River to Mill Creek. The streams were lined with cottonwood and birch trees; the soil appeared excellent. If Whitman then had in mind the possibility of future irrigation, he would have noted the favorable availability of water when he selected the site.

There is no contemporary evidence to indicate that Samuel Parker had recommended that particular location. Whitman reported that he found the Cayuses of the vicinity "very favorable" [Letter 32]. The site was near the favorite camping ground of Chief Umtippe. The acreage was covered with a coarse rye grass that grew in bunches sometimes higher than a man's head. The Indians called the general area Wy-eé-lat-poo,[4] "the place of the rye grass." The tall grass is still growing there on what is now the Whitman Mission National Historic Site.

On October 6 the men returned to Fort Walla Walla and on the 8th, Whitman wrote to Parker and told of the selection of a mission site among the Cayuses. "You are aware," he wrote, "of the importance of this place and its influence on the future civilization of the Indians; it is undoubtedly before the Willamette Valley or any point on the Columbia." Whitman was not then thinking about any incoming American population. His concern was with the Indians. In the light of later developments, his appraisal of the strategic importance of establishing a mission among the Cayuses was correct.

THE SPALDING MISSION LOCATED

Having selected the Waiilatpu site, Whitman and Spalding were ready to choose a location among the Nez Perces. Gray was given the responsibility of taking supplies out to Waiilatpu, while Whitman and Spalding visited the Clearwater[5] Valley in search of a suitable place for the Spalding mission. The Black, John Hinds, who had traveled with the mission party from the Rendezvous to Fort Walla Walla in order to receive medical care from Dr. Whitman, and who had remained at the fort while the missionaries went to Fort Vancouver, may have given some help to Gray.

On October 7, Chief Tackensuatis (whom Whitman usually referred to by his nickname, Rotten Belly) arrived at Walla Walla with a party of from twenty to thirty Nez Perces to escort the missionaries to his country. When the Nez Perces learned that Whitman had decided to settle among the Cayuses, they immediately protested. Whitman wrote: "The Nez Perces do not like my stopping with the Cayous; and say that the Nez Perces do not have difficulties with the white man as Cayous do and that we will see the difference"[6] [Letter 32]. No doubt it was Tackensuatis who gave this ominous warning. Prophetic words! Would that Whitman had heeded them.

Whitman and Spalding with their escort left Fort Walla Walla on Saturday, October 8, for the Nez Perce country. The company remained in camp over Sunday. The missionaries felt frustrated in not being able, for want of a good interpreter, to communicate with the Indians about Christianity. They were gratified, however, to note that the Nez Perces observed daily devotions and were quite willing to refrain from traveling on Sunday.

On Tuesday, the 11th, the party arrived at the confluence of the Snake and Clearwater Rivers, where Lewiston, Idaho, is now located. The next day they rode about ten miles up the Clearwater to the mouth of Lapwai[7] Creek which flows into the river from the south. Here was a fairly level plain large enough for cultivation and also having possibilities for irrigation. Spalding, however, was attracted by another site about two miles up Lapwai Creek at the foot of Thunder Mountain[8] where three springs were flowing. Finding the land suitable for cultivation, Spalding decided to locate there.

The geographical locations of Waiilatpu and Lapwai inevitably affected the subsequent outlook and activities of both Whitman and Spalding. Whitman deliberately chose to settle among a tribe numbering three hundred or more in order to capitalize on the "future importance of this place." His station was destined to become the first outpost on the Oregon Trail west of the Blue Mountains, so that in coming years much of his time and resources would be devoted to the immigrants. At the time Whitman selected Waiilatpu to be the site of his mission, neither he nor the Cayuse Indians ever dreamed that this would happen. For the present, the Indians were pleased with having won a degree of status by having one of the two missionary couples decide to live with them.

Spalding, on the other hand, elected to settle in the midst of a larger tribe far removed from the comings and goings of the white men on the Columbia River or on the Oregon Trail. Of all the Protestant missionaries who went to Old Oregon, no one had greater success in evangelizing and civilizing the natives than Henry Harmon Spalding, and no one of the missionary women was more loved by the Indians than his wife, Eliza. An important factor in Spalding's success was the enthusiasm with which he was welcomed by the Nez Perces. This was in sharp contract to the merely "very favorable" attitude of the Cayuses mentioned by Whitman [Letter 32]. No chief was more eager to have the missionaries settle among his people than Tackensuatis. "This is all my country," he said to Spalding as they rode into the Lapwai Valley. "Where you settle, I will settle. Only let me know what you want done, and it will be done." [9]

Whitman never enjoyed such wholehearted cooperation from the natives at Waiilatpu as Spalding received at Lapwai. It is true that within two years, Tackensuatis lost his enthusiasm for the white man's religion,[10] but at first Spalding benefited greatly from his assistance. Other Nez Perce chiefs, such as Timothy and Joseph, as will be indicated, came to Spalding's aid.

Having selected a site for the Spalding mission, the two missionaries began their 120 mile ride back to Waiilatpu, now without an Indian escort. Each of the two men was to ride that long trail which connected their two stations many times during the following eleven years. They arrived at Waiilatpu on October 14th, where they found Gray at work preparing logs for a house.[11] He was assisted by Charles Compo and the two Hawaiians who had been hired through the cooperation of Pambrun at Fort Walla Walla. Since both Whitman and Spalding realized the necessity of having a house erected at each station before winter came, they decided that it was best for Whitman to remain at Waiilatpu and work with Gray and for Spalding to go to Fort Vancouver to get the women. Upon their return, Gray could then go and help Spalding build his cabin.

THE WOMEN RETURN TO WALLA WALLA

Spalding was back at Fort Walla Walla in time to engage passage with the annual Hudson's Bay express from Montreal which arrived on Saturday, October 15. The express left on Sunday at 4:00 a.m. and made the voyage down the river in a record time of less than three days. Sails were hoisted on the boats to catch a favorable wind which accelerated their progress. The express arrived at Fort Vancouver on Thursday, the 18th, at 2:00 p.m.

Dr. McLoughlin was surprised to see Spalding back so soon. He had made the round trip in less than a month and was able to report that mission sites had been selected at Waiilatpu and at Lapwai. Spalding noted in a letter to Greene that he had traveled 1,200 miles after his arrival at Fort Walla Walla on September 8, and altogether 5,800 since February 1. "There is yet 425 miles to travel," he wrote, "before myself & wife reach our location." [12]

Dr. McLoughlin was disappointed to learn that the women desired to return with Spalding to Fort Walla Walla as soon as necessary arrangements could be made. "The Dr.," wrote Narcissa in her diary, "urges me to stay all winter. He is a very sympathetic man." Dr. McLoughlin was aware that Narcissa was then in the fifth month of her pregnancy and felt that the care she would have at Fort Vancouver would be much better for her than the privations and hardships attendant upon the establishment of a pioneer home during the late fall or winter. In spite of his repeated urgings, however, the women decided to return with Spalding.

Narcissa and Eliza had spent four happy weeks at Vancouver. Besides making three copies of her diary while at the fort, Narcissa wrote a number of letters, six of which are extant in either the original or printed form [Letters 33-38]. Some interesting sidelights on Oregon life as she saw it are found in these letters. Writing to her former pastor, the Rev. Leverett Hull, on October 25, she referred to a Cayuse boy who was then attending the Red River Mission school. "A young chief of the tribe and of considerable influence has been to school at a mission station on Red River, east of the mountains, [with] Mr. Cockran, missionary, and Mr. Jones, chaplain of the Hudson Bay Company... The Cayuse chief is still there. We expect his return next fall. In his former visits home he has exerted a good influence in favor of religion and we feel encouraged to think he will be of essential service to the mission."

No doubt Narcissa had received information about this youth, Cayuse Halket, from a letter that Spalding had brought from her husband. Cayuse Halket had been only eleven years old when sent to the mission school in 1830. He was a nephew of an important Cayuse chief called Tauitau (Tawatoe or Young Chief) [Letter 181b]. According to an historian of the Anglican Church in Canada: "Cayuse Halket is said to have been a pleasing, thoughtful lad who also came from beyond the Rocky Mountains; he returned there in 1834 but could not adjust to the life, and so came back and lived with Mr. Cochran."[13] He died at Red River on February 1, 1837, as will be noted. In October 1836, however, both Marcus and Narcissa were hoping that the young man would return to his people after being educated at the mission school and thus be able to assist them in missionary activities at Waiilatpu.

In the frank letter to her former pastor, Narcissa felt free to comment on her impressions of the Anglican services conducted at Fort Vancouver by the Rev. Herbert Beaver. She reported that he preached twice each Sunday and although she enjoyed the services, yet "to contrast it with the preaching at home, I find a great want of plainness and heart. He is a great way behind the times. The standard of piety is low with him and other professed Christians here. He seldom draws the line of distinction between the righteous and the wicked, and when he does it is so faintly that it is scarcely perceptible." She was critical even of the gentlemen of the Company who were Presbyterians. "Do not see much evidence of real piety among them," she wrote. "No family worship, no social prayer meetings; yet at the same time all think themselves Christians, safe enough; at least they appear so." She reported that a Roman Catholic priest was expected, as most of the servants of the Company were of that faith.

During her month's residence at the Fort, Narcissa was able to secure enough feathers from wild fowl to make a feather bed. Perhaps Eliza was able to do the same. Occasionally the women took horseback rides. One day Mrs. McLoughlin sought to persuade them to give up their sidesaddles and ride astride as did the native women. "We have never seen the necessity of changing our fashion," noted Narcissa in her diary. For her and Eliza, riding astride was immodest. We have no evidence to indicate that any of the six women connected with the Oregon Mission ever gave up her side-saddle during the eleven-year history of the Mission.[14]

Narcissa took advantage of the interlude of two weeks or more between Spalding's arrival on October 18 and her departure for the journey up the river to write letters which were to be carried to the States on a ship scheduled to leave soon from Fort Vancouver. At the end of the diary mailed to her parents, she wrote: "Husband is so filled with business that I must write for him, until he is less hurried in his business. (He is far away now, poor husband, three hundred miles. If I had wings I would fly. Adieu.)" Those words —"so filled with business"— aptly described Marcus Whitman. He was always an activist, giving himself unstintingly to many responsibilities.

Spalding took two weeks to assemble his supplies and load them into the two boats which Dr. McLoughlin so kindly provided. Eight of the oarsmen were Iroquois Indians. There is no evidence that any charge was made by the Hudson's Bay Company for this service. John McLeod, who was at Vancouver, decided to accompany the Spalding party to Fort Walla Walla. On Thursday noon, November 3, the two heavily loaded boats shoved off on their tedious journey up the Columbia against the swift current. McLeod and Mrs. Whitman were in one boat; the Spaldings were in the other.

An incident took place at the time of the departure of the boats from Vancouver which aroused the ire of Chaplain Beaver. In a letter dated November 15 and directed to Benjamin Harrison in London, Beaver told what happened: "When the missionaries went from the Fort the other day, I was shocked not at being present, but at hearing that the scholars, by command, had been paraded on the River beach, and sung there an hymn. Sacred music should only be used on solemn occasions, but it is made here a common entertainment of an evening, without the slightest religious feeling or purpose." [15] Completely ignoring how his chaplain might feel, Dr. McLoughlin had arranged for the school children to bid the missionaries Godspeed by singing some of the songs Narcissa had taught them.

The rainy season began before the Spalding party left Fort Vancouver. On their way up the Columbia, it rained steadily for three days, November 4-6. The women succeeded in keeping dry by staying under oilcloth. Narcissa has given the following description: "At night, when a great fire was made, our tents pitched and the cloth spread for tea, all was pleasant and comfortable. I rolled my bed and blankets in my India-rubber cloak, which preserved them quite well from the rain, so that nights I slept warm and comfortably as ever. My featherbed was of essential service to me in keeping my health this rainy voyage" [Letter 39].

They arrived at Fort Walla Walla on Sunday, November 13, after a disagreeable trip of ten days with rain falling nearly every day. Narcissa was disappointed not to see her husband at Walla Walla, but understood the reason for his absence when told that he and Gray were busy at Waiilatpu building a house. Whitman and Gray returned to Fort Walla Walla on Friday, the 18th, and all five were together for a religious service the following Sunday. This was the last time the five were together until after the arrival of the reenforcement in the early fall of 1838.

In the meantime a party of 125 Nez Perces, no doubt under the leadership of Tackensuatis, arrived at Fort Walla Walla to escort the Spaldings to Lapwai. Whereas Whitman had resolved to erect a suitable dwelling for his wife before taking her to Waiilatpu, the Spaldings were willing to live in an Indian tepee until a log cabin could be built. The Nez Perces were eager to do everything possible for their missionaries. Of this Spalding wrote to Greene: "They took entire direction of everything, pitched and struck our tent, saddled our horses, and gladly would have put victuals to our mouths, had we wished it. So eager were they to do all they could to make us comfortable. I was astonished at the ease with which they handled and packed our heavy bags and cases, the latter sixteen inches square, thirty inches long, and weighing usually 125 pounds each. Our effects loaded twenty horses."

If we estimate the average load for each horse to have been 250 pounds, the Spaldings must have taken with them about 5,000 pounds of goods and provisions. This included everything: clothing, farm utensils, furniture, books, building materials including glass, and some food supplies. Whitman must have transported a like quantity of goods to his station. A division of the cattle was made; Spalding took five cows, the bull, and two calves. Since we do not know whether the calves were born after the missionaries reported having thirteen head, we cannot tell whether Whitman received five or seven cows.

The Spaldings and Gray, with their Nez Perce escort, left Walla Walla on Tuesday, November 22, and arrived at Lapwai on the 29th. Narcissa and Eliza, each isolated in her own lonely home in the wilderness, were not to see each other for about a year. Whitman returned to

Waiilatpu to complete work on the house he was building while his wife remained at the Fort. At this time Whitman had no assistants except for the two Hawaiians.

John Hinds, the black man, died sometime during the last week of November. Of this Narcissa wrote on December 5: "Already death has entered our home, and laid one low." According to a commonly accepted theory, Whitman buried the body at the foot of the hill to the northeast of the mission house. Thus the little cemetery at Waiilatpu had its beginning even before actual missionary work for the Indians could begin.

Just as Dr. McLoughlin had asked Narcissa to teach English to his daughter, Maria, at Walla Walla Pambrun made a similar request for his wife and daughter, the latter of whom was also called Maria. This Narcissa was glad to do. "We consider it a very kind providence," she wrote, "to be situated near one family so interesting, and a native female that promises to be so much society for me. She is learning to speak the English language quite fast" [Letter 39].

THE FIRST HOUSE AT WAIILATPU

When Whitman arrived at Waiilatpu on October 14, after making the trip to Lapwai with Spalding, he was able to give his full time to the imperative task of building a suitable house before winter came.

Perhaps with the advice of both Gray and Spalding, a site was selected about one hundred feet north of the top of the horseshoe bend in the Walla Walla River. The location of the first mission house at that particular site proved to have been unfortunate; the land was too low and was flooded by the rising waters of the river late in the winter of 1837–38.

We do not have full details of the type of construction which Whitman intended to follow but it appears that he planned a hybrid combination of small logs and adobe bricks. According to Narcissa, her husband planned to erect a story-and-a-half house which would measure 30 x 36 feet [Letter 39]. A limited supply of logs suitable to be whipsawed into boards was available by cutting down some cottonwood trees which grew along the streams in the vicinity. Whipsawing was a slow and laborious process. A log would be propped up at an angle over a pit. A thin tapering whipsaw, about six feet long with handles on either end, would be used by two men, one in the pit and the other standing on top of the log. The resulting green cottonwood boards proved to be unsatisfactory as they warped when drying out. Later Whitman sent men into the foothills of the Blue Mountains where pine trees were available.

On their westward journey, the missionaries had observed the use of adobe bricks at such places as Fort Laramie, Fort Hall, and Fort Boise. These were made by mixing soil with grass or straw and, after shaping the material in a frame, letting them dry in the sun. Evidently Whitman planned to erect a wooden frame for his house and then fill in the wall spaces with either trimmed logs or adobe bricks.

Since Whitman came from New York State where a house was rarely built in those days without a cellar or basement, he naturally assumed that his house should have one. This would not only provide a convenient and safe place for storage but, also, the dirt excavated could be used to make adobe bricks.

A shallow basement, about four and one-half feet deep, was dug under the proposed building and the walls were lined with adobes which measured 5 x 7 x 10 inches. The bricks were laid according to the "header-stretcher method," two deep which gave a wall fourteen inches wide.[16] Just how high the basement walls were raised above the ground level is not known.

Because of the lateness of the season, the scarcity of building materials, and the lack of efficient assistants, Whitman found it necessary to abandon his plan to erect the house as originally planned and concentrate on a lean-to on the west side of the house, the frame of which had been erected. This lean-to measured twelve feet wide and ran the length of the thirty-six foot west wall of the house. A large adobe fireplace was placed in the center of the west wall of the lean-to with a window space on each side. The roof was made out of poles covered first with the long tough rye grass, over which five or six inches of dirt or sod were placed. As can well be imagined, this type of roof was not efficient in times of heavy rains; the moisture seeped through and great globules of mud would drop into the room below. Spalding, who was obliged to use the same type of roof for his home, once wrote: "Our mud roofs show us that the earth was made to drink the rain, not to shed it."

On Friday, December 9, 1836, Whitman returned to Fort Walla Walla for his wife. Late the next day Narcissa's "unheard of journey for females" came to an end when she alighted from her horse in front of the rudely constructed lean-to. Their wedding journey of nine months and about 2,500 miles, including the trip to Fort Vancouver, was over.

Narcissa began a letter to her mother on December 5, shortly before she left Fort Walla Walla, and from time to time added to it. On the 26th she described her arrival at Waiilatpu: "Where are we now?" she asked. "And who are we that we should be thus blessed of the Lord? I can scarcely realize that we are thus comfortably fixed & keeping house so soon after our marriage when considering what was then before us. We arrived here on the tenth, distance twenty-five miles from W.W.; found a house reared & the lean-to enclosed, a good chimney & fireplace & the floor laid. No windows or door except blankets. My heart truly leaped for joy as I alighted from my horse, entered and seated myself before a pleasant fire (for it was now night). It occurred to me that my dear Parents had made a similar beginning & perhaps more difficult one than ours." In her description of the lean-to, she stated: "The siding is made of split logs fitted into grooved posts, & the spaces filled with mud [i.e., adobe bricks]."

THE WHITMANS BEGIN HOUSEKEEPING

Although the Whitmans had ridden by Waiilatpu on their way to Fort Walla Walla on August 31, they then had no reason to be interested in the site. But now it was different. This was to be their home. The day after her arrival, Narcissa had an opportunity to survey her surroundings. About three hundred yards to the northeast of the lean-to was a cone-shaped hill a little more than one hundred feet high.[17] From the top of that elevation, Narcissa had an excellent view of the adjoinlug territory. She could trace the course of the Walla Walla River as it curled in a half loop around the south and west sides of the site her husband had selected. She could also see, about one-half mile to the west, the confluence of Mill Creek with the Walla Walla River. Fifteen or more miles to the south and east were the lower tree-covered slopes of the Blue Mountains, the upper levels of which were already covered with snow [Letter 39]. "It is indeed a lovely situation," she wrote to her mother.

On December 16, eighteen inches of snow fell, and remained on the ground for about six weeks [Letters 39 & 42]. Whitman's livestock had to paw through the snow to find forage. On that day Pambrun sent a table and some window sashes to the Whitmans. "I have taken the liberty to prime them," commented Narcissa, "and set some of the lights [i.e., window panes], & engaged in it thought a great deal about Father, how handily he used to do such work." The "lights" had been purchased from the Hudson's Bay Company; they measured about 7 x 8 inches and were only about one millimeter thick. Many fragments of such thin glass have been found in the archaeological diggings at Waiilatpu. The windows, each with twelve panes, were not ready to be placed until Saturday, December 24.

By December 26, enough additional boards had been sawed to make it possible for Whitman to erect two partitions in the lean-to, thus making a small room at either end. "My room is in the south end," Narcissa told her mother, "a small bedroom & pantry on the north end, and a very pleasant kitchen in the middle." The heating stove which the Whitmans got from Pambrun was placed in their bedroom. The central room was heated by the fireplace where Narcissa did her cooking.

In the various postscripts which Narcissa added to the letter begun on December 5, she commented on many incidental items of interest. Regarding the weather, she wrote on January 2, 1837: "I am spending my winter as comfortably as heart could wish, & have suffered less from excessive cold than in many winters previous in New York. Winters are not very severe here."

On February 18, the first anniversary of her marriage, Narcissa found her thoughts spanning the continent to her Angelica home. "One year since I have heard a lisp even of my beloved friends in Angelica," she wrote, "and who can tell how many are sleeping in their graves by this time. Ah! it would be like cold water to a thirsty soul indeed, to know how you all do." She seemed to have forgotten about receiving a letter from her brother-in-law, the Rev. Lyman Judson, at Liberty, Missouri. Perhaps because of the uncertainty as to how a letter should be addressed, Narcissa's family did not write until they heard from her. She had to wait until July 1838 before a letter from her home arrived at Waiilatpu.

In this February 18 postscript, she boasted of her comforts: "We have now 3 chairs & a bedstead & all our doors are made & hanging." Regarding the chairs, she wrote: "These are exceedingly comfortable although not of the finest order. My chairs, two of them are of my Husband's making; with deer skin bottoms woven as the fancy chairs of the States are & very durable. Our bedstead is made of rough boards & nailed to the wall, according to the fashion of the country." On this Narcissa was able to place her prized feather bed.

Narcissa listed other acquisitions: "You will scarcely think it possible that I should have such a convenience as a barrel to pound my clothes in for washing so soon, in this part of the world, & probably mine with Mrs. Pambrun are the only two this side of the Rocky Mountains." She even had a dog and a cat. "My dog," she explained, "was a present from Mr. McLeod." The many references to McLeod in her diary and letters indicate that he took a special interest in her and delighted to show such favors as he could. "These may appear small subjects to fill a letter with," she wrote, "but my object is to show you that people can live here, & as comfortably too as in many places east of the mountains."

Food Supplies

Until the first harvest was reaped, both the Whitmans and the Spaldings were dependent upon the Hudson's Bay Company and the Indians for food supplies. No reference in the writings of Whitman and Spalding has been found telling about either going out to hunt wild game. Whitman's letter to Greene of May 5, 1837, reports: "We feel we have passed a comfortable winter indeed; but still at my place we have eaten nine wild horses bought of the Indians at a cost of about $6. each in goods. We have had a tolerable supply of flour, corn, butter & a little pork & venison & a few potatoes. We are now getting fish in small quantity but soon expect to get plenty of salmon of which I hope to salt a good supply."

Narcissa in a letter to her family dated May 3, wrote: "The Indians have furnished us a little venison—barely enough for our own eating—but to supply our men and visitors, we have killed and eaten ten wild horses bought of the Indians. This will make you pity me, but you had better save your pity for more worthy subjects. I do not prefer it to other meat, but can eat it very well when we have nothing else." Two years later, Whitman informed Greene that up to that date—May 10,

1839—they had butchered and eaten "twenty-three or four horses since we have been here" [Letter 62]. Two of Whitman's cows calved the first part of February 1837; thus plenty of milk was then available.

Since there was so much that needed to be done, Whitman hired such transient labor as he could. He found the Hawaiians very satisfactory. One of them, Jack or John, stayed with the Whitmans for several years and will be mentioned later in this story. Regarding the possibility of using natives as laborers, Narcissa wrote that they did not "love to work well enough for us to place any dependence upon them." Occasionally Whitman was able to hire a mountain man who happened to pass that way [Letter 41]. Of course when such men were hired, extra food had to be provided, with Narcissa doing the cooking over an open fire in the fireplace.

W. H. GRAY RETURNS TO THE STATES

Although W. H. Gray had joined the mission as a mechanic [i.e., a craftsman] with the expectation that he would relieve both Whitman and Spalding of some of their secular duties such as building and farming, yet he was a great disappointment to both. Gray remained at Lapwai helping Spalding for only a month until December 28, 1836, when he left for Fort Walla Walla. On January 4 he rode out to Waiilatpu where he stayed for only four or five days helping Whitman hang some doors.[18] He then returned to the fort where he met Francis Ermatinger, one of the traders in the employ of the Hudson's Bay Company, who was on his way to Vancouver. Gray decided to go with him. While at Fort Vancouver the previous fall, Gray had written to Greene suggesting that he make an exploring trip for the Board.[19] Without waiting for official approval of such a plan, Gray made arrangements to go with Ermatinger through the Flathead country in the spring of 1837.

Gray returned to Walla Walla on March 14, and after another short visit with the Whitmans, left for Spokane Falls. If Gray consulted with Whitman about his intentions to visit the Flathead country, there is no evidence that Whitman approved. The failure of Gray to stay at Waiilatpu and help with the work of building and preparing the soil for spring planting must have been a keen disappointment to Whitman. It so happened that Spalding was at Spokane Falls on March 31 where he met Gray and then learned to his surprise that Gray was planning to return to the States to ask the American Board to send out a reenforcement for its Oregon Mission.

Gray was engaged to be married; this may have been another reason for his desire to return. Also, his restless nature and his inclination "to do good on his own hook,"[20] accounts for his independent action. Gray aspired to have a station of his own, such as both Whitman and Spalding had. He was unhappy to work in any subordinate capacity. In furtherance of his dream, he conceived a plan of driving a herd of horses to the Missouri frontier where they would be sold and the money used to buy cattle which would then be driven to Oregon in 1838. The Nez Perces, who had come to appreciate the value of American cattle, were attracted by Gray's proposal and promised to cooperate. Gray seems to have won a reluctant approval from Spalding for the plan. Gray then succeeded in persuading four Nez Perces to go with him, including Ellis, one of the young men who had studied at the Red River school. Also among the Nez Perces was one called The Hat. The Nez Perces offered to send some of their horses with Gray, hoping to get cattle in return.

Gray and his Indian companions with a band of horses left Spokane Falls with Ermatinger on April 5 for the Rendezvous. After reaching that place, Ellis and two of the Nez Perces, for some unknown reason, decided not to continue with Gray. They turned back taking their horses with them. Only The Hat stayed with Gray who, at the Rendezvous, persuaded a prominent Iroquois, Big Ignace, and four Flathead Indians to join his party.

BEGINNINGS OF AGRICULTURE AT WAIILATPU

While in Cincinnati in the early spring of 1836, Whitman and Spalding had purchased $7.00 worth of seeds to be taken with them. No doubt these were vegetable seeds. While at Fort Vancouver, Narcissa carefully saved all the seeds of the fruit that she ate. "This is a rule of Vancouver," she noted in her diary, and added: "I have got collected before me an assortment of garden seeds, which I take up with me, also, I intend taking some young sprouts of apple, peach & grapes, & some strawberry vines, etc., from the nursery here."

While still at Fort Vancouver, Whitman wrote to friends in the States asking for seeds of the locust, chestnut, and walnut trees. Narcissa added that she wanted seeds of the butternut tree as well [Letter 34]. To this day locust trees, which were not native to the Pacific Northwest, are growing on the mission sites at Waiilatpu and Lapwai.

With a practical eye on the duties of a housekeeper, Narcissa requested her relatives to send her some broom corn seed, which she called "another very important article for us housewives."[21] She explained that although they did take some seeds of this plant with them, they were afraid that the seeds would not do well and wanted a fresh supply. "They have nothing of the kind here," Narcissa wrote, "but use hemlock boughs for broom. Hemlock, I say, there is no such tree known here. It is balsam" [Letter 34].

Only seven Whitman letters written in 1837 have been located, and one of these is in a publication [See Appendix 1]. Only one of Whitman's letters to the Board is extant. This, containing some two thousand words, is dated May 5. Surely both Marcus and Narcissa wrote other letters which, for some reason, have been lost or destroyed. Because of the paucity of source material for 1837, we are unable to trace out in detail the story of what happened at Waiilatpu during that year.

Regarding his farm activities, Whitman wrote on May 5: "I began to plow the first week in March but was unable to do much on account of Mrs. Whitman's health." As will be told later, a baby girl was born on March 14. This important event naturally had caused some interruptions in Whitman's farming activities. His account to Greene continues: "My farm [work animals] consists of one yoke oxen belonging to one of the Cayuse Chiefs[22] & a yoke of bulls, one belonging to the Co & one to the mission both of which I have broken, two horses & four mules. With this team I am able to break the ground very well.[23] I have two acres of peas sowed, 9 acres of corn planted & intend to plant 3 more and have planted & intend to plant 2 acres of potatoes, in all 16 acres. If associates come, I think they will have little to fear for want of provision. I hope to obtain wheat for fall sowing."

From a letter written by Narcissa on April 11, 1838, we learn that her husband harvested about two hundred fifty bushels of potatoes and two hundred bushels of corn, besides an abundance of garden vegetables in the fall of 1837. Because of an expected demand by the Indians for pea and potato seed in the spring of 1838, Narcissa wrote that they refrained from eating peas and used potatoes only sparingly. By the summer and fall of 1838, the gardens and fields at both Waiilatpu and Lapwai were producing so abundantly that the food problem, except for beef, had been solved.

First Efforts at Evangelization

The experience of the American Board in Indian evangelism was so limited by 1836 that it could give but little guidance to the Whitmans and the Spaldings as to the best methods to be pursued in their endeavors to Christianize the Indians of Old Oregon. The American Board had established its first Indian mission in 1816 with the Cherokees. Work was begun on a limited basis with four other tribes before Dunbar and Allis were sent to the Pawnees in 1834.[24] Thus the Whitmans and the Spaldings were pioneers in Indian evangelism.

Such questions as to whether they could teach the Indians English and work through that language or learn the native language and use it for instructional purposes were unanswered. Were they to try to settle the natives on small farms or in villages before establishing schools and possibly churches, or should they follow the Indians in their migrations to find food and preach the Gospel as opportunities afforded? Which should have precedence—civilization or evangelization? The missionaries had to find answers to such perplexing questions through experience.

First came the immediate problem of acquiring the native language. The missionaries soon discovered that the Nez Perce tongue was extremely complex. A. B. Smith, a member of the 1838 reenforcement and the best linguist in the Oregon Mission, said that the tendency of the language to compound words was "beyond description."[25] He who had specialized in the study of Hebrew, Greek, and Latin found that the Nez Perce language had no resemblance whatever to these, and called it "unclassical and outlandish."[26]

In all probability Whitman had made a beginning in acquiring the language when he took the two Indian boys, Richard and John, east with him in 1835. No doubt members of the mission party picked up some words from these youths as they traveled westward in 1836. The high expectations entertained by Whitman in using the two boys as interpreters were never realized. John rejoined his family who lived near Lapwai. Writing on October 3, 1838, to Mrs. Parker, Narcissa said: "John is the same unassuming, humble, obedient lad that he was while at Ithaca... But he is not long for this world, if he is still alive.

Nearly one year ago he was taken with the most afflicting disease I ever saw—the swelling of the joints." Nothing more is known about John. According to Spalding, Richard ran away from Waiilatpu after taking "considerable property... He is a profane, gambling youth." [27]

Since the Nez Perce language had never been reduced to writing, the missionaries at first had no system of representing the sounds of the language, such as an alphabet, to aid them in learning the tongue. In Whitman's May 5, 1837, letter, he wrote: "A few Indians only wintered with us & did not afford us a very favorable opportunity for acquiring the language." Several years had to pass before the Whitmans had mastered the language sufficiently well for them to teach the doctrines of Christianity effectively, but by that time the natives had lost much of their enthusiasm for the white man's religion. It should be remembered that Whitman was a doctor and not trained as a minister or as an evangelist. His professional and secular duties were demanding, increasingly so as time passed, which left him little time for study or teaching.

An entry in Narcissa's letter of December 5, 1836, which has a postscript dated the following March 6, gives us this description of a meeting of natives held in her kitchen: "Sab. Eve. Today our congregation has increased very considerably in consequence of the arrival of a party of Indians during the past week. A strong desire is manifest in them all to understand the truth & to be taught. Last eve our room was full of men & boys, who came every eve to learn to sing. The whole tribe both men, women & children would like the same privilege if our room was larger & my health would admit so much singing. Indeed I should not attempt to sing with them, were it not for the assistance my Husband renders. You will recollect when he was in Angelica, he could not sing a single tune. Now he is able to sing several tunes & lead the school in them.[28] This saves me a great deal hard singing." We may assume that the Whitmans were teaching the natives to sing religious songs with English words which, of course, they could not understand. Possibly Richard or Compo, if present, could have served as interpreters.

For an indefinite period before the Whitmans settled at Waiilatpu, the Cayuse were accustomed to hold daily devotions after what they were told to be Christian forms of worship. Writing on January 2, 1837, Narcissa said: "The Cayuses as well as the Nez Perces are very strict in attending to their worship which they have regularly every morning at day break & eve at twilight and once on the Sab. They sing & repeat a form of prayers very devoutly after which the Chief gives them a talk. The tunes & prayers were taught them by a Roman Catholic trader. Indeed their worship was commenced by him" [Letter 39J. In all probability the Roman Catholic trader was Pierre Pambrun who had been placed in charge of Fort Walla Walla in 1832.[29] Whitman gives similar information in his letter of May 5, 1837: "The present worship of the Indians was established by the Traders of the Hudson Bay Co. & it consists of the singing a form of prayer[30] after which the Chief gives them a talk."

As has been noted in the first chapter of this book, some knowledge of Christianity was passed on to the various tribes living in the upper Columbia River country by the Oregon Indian boys who had been sent to the Red River Mission school. Two of these lads, Cayuse Halket and Cayuse Pitt, may have been partly responsible for the introduction of certain forms of Christian worship among their people.[31] When Samuel Parker traveled through the Nez Perce and Cayuse country in 1835 and 1836, he frequently held religious services, and since he had an interpreter, he was able to impart some information about Christianity. According to his journal, he camped along the Walla Walla River on May 18, 1836, "twenty-two miles" from Fort Walla Walla, which would have placed him near Waiilatpu. On the Sunday following, May 22, Parker held a religious service for the natives at Fort Walla Walla.

In Whitman's letter to Greene of May 5, 1837, he reviewed the little that they had been able to do in the way of giving religious instruction to the Indians. "We have made but little attempt to teach them," he wrote, "except to sing, with which they are much pleased & adopt in their worship which they have at the Chief's lodge night & morning & Sabbath afternoon. In the afternoon of Sabbath I assemble them for worship & instruction." Without a good interpreter, Whitman's efforts would have been almost useless. There is a pathetic touch in reading about the Indians singing the songs that the Whitmans had taught them without understanding the real meaning of the words.

Added to the language barrier was the fact that the Indians were semi-nomadic. The Cayuses, like their neighbors, the Nez Perces, were frequently on the move. They had to be in order to survive. At one time of the year they would go to the Columbia River or one of its tributaries for the salmon which were taken in great numbers and dried. At another season, some would migrate to the buffalo country in what is now Montana and Wyoming to hunt these animals for their meat and hides. Still again, they would gather on some upper prairie to dig for the onion-like tubor of the camas plant. This roving existence posed a great problem for the missionaries. How were they to teach and evangelize a people, as Spalding once wrote to Greene, "who were always on the wing?"

THE INDIANS IN A PERIOD OF RAPID CHANGE

The Whitmans and the Spaldings began their work with the natives of Old Oregon at a time of rapid change. Writing to Greene from the Rendezvous on July 8, 1836, Spalding said: "What is done for the poor Indians of this western world must be done soon. The only thing that can save them from annihilation is the introduction of civilization." He was dismayed to note how the great herds of buffalo on the western plains were being decimated. Here were real grounds for the grievances that the red man held against the white, by killing off the buffalo, the white man was also destroying age-old customs.

Although the Cayuses and the Nez Perces did not sense in 1836 and the years immediately following that their manner of life was destined to be replaced by the white man's civilization, this both Whitman and Spalding realized. Even if missionaries had never gone to Old Oregon, the natives would have had to face that inevitable period of transition. Both Whitman and Spalding were one in their commitment to do all within their power to civilize the natives. They were convinced that the Indians would be unable to preserve their old manner of life. They would have to adapt themselves to the white man's ways or perish.

In Whitman's letter to Greene of May 5, 1837, he reported that most of the Cayuses had returned from the mountains by early March "& for a time labored very hard to prepare ground to plant." By that time Whitman was at work breaking the virgin soil for his fields. Since he had but one plow, he was unable then to use it for the natives, but he was setting an example of how the earth could best be cultivated. "I had no means of assisting them," he wrote, "but by loaning hoes of which [I] had but fifteen but still they had succeeded in making a good beginning." After working a few weeks planting corn and potatoes, the Indians were off again, this time to the camas prairies. "They will return to hoe their corn in about four weeks," Whitman wrote. "I think there

CHAPTER TEN *Waiilatpu, 1836-1837* 261

can be no doubt of their readiness to adopt cultivation & when they have plenty of food, they will be little disposed to wander."

There is no evidence, as some have suggested, that the Indians turned reluctantly to farming. As soon as they appreciated the relative ease with which they could obtain food from the soil, as compared to the time-consuming treks into the buffalo country or elsewhere for food, they began to clamor for hoes and plows.

Again and again in the first letters that Whitman and Spalding wrote to the Board or to relatives or friends, we find them pleading for hoes and plows, especially the latter. Spalding, in his letter to Greene of September 11, 1838, summarized his philosophy of evangelism, which Whitman fully shared: "While we point them with one hand to the Lamb of God which taketh away the sins of the world, we believe it equally our duty to point with the other to the hoe, as the means of saving their famishing bodies from an untimely grave & furnishing the means of subsistence to future generations." [32] This emphasis on settling the natives on farms was in full harmony with the views of such an enlightened Indian Agent as Major John Dougherty, to whom reference has been made. As early as 1829 Dougherty was urging the government to encourage the Indians to take up farming.[33] Whitman had called on Dougherty at the Oto Indian Agency in May 1836, at which time, no doubt, this subject of settling the Indians had been discussed.

A few critics have accused the missionaries of taking part in the expropriation of the lands and resources of the Oregon Indians. The reverse is the case. No group of individuals did more to help the natives bridge the gap from a primitive, semi-nomadic life to a civilized, settled existence than did the missionaries. As far as the Cayuses and the Nez Perces were concerned, Whitman and Spalding introduced the hoe and the plow and taught the natives to plant vegetables, especially potatoes, wheat, and corn. They helped them obtain American cattle. They reduced the language to writing, and printed primers and other little books in the Nez Perce tongue on the first American press to be brought to the Pacific Coast. To civilize and educate the natives was a fundamental part of their endeavors to evangelize them. The Indians had to be settled before any consistent program of education could be conducted. They had to be able to read before they could appreciate the teachings of the Bible.

Whitman and Spalding never debated the question as to which should receive the major emphasis—to civilize or to evangelize. The two went together. And with all due respect to the activities of the Methodist missionaries, who established their work in the Willamette Valley in 1834, and to the Roman Catholic priests, who entered Old Oregon in 1838, no missionaries did so much for the improvement of the material welfare of the Cayuse and Nez Perce Indians as Marcus Whitman and Henry Spalding.

THREE CAYUSE CHIEFS

Narcissa, in a postscript dated January 2, 1837, to the letter to her mother which had been begun on the previous December 5, mentioned three Cayuse chiefs, each of whom was to play an important role in the unfolding drama which had begun to take place at Waiilatpu. They were Umtippe,[34] "Towerlooe" (Tauitai) or Young Chief, and Tiloukaikt. Umtippe was an old man when the Whitmans arrived and died sometime during the winter of 1840–41. The problems he caused remained as a source of irritation for the Whitmans long after he had died. Both Young Chief and Tiloukaikt lived throughout the eleven-year mission period.

In her note of January 2, Narcissa wrote: "We are on the lands of the Old Chief Umtippe who with a lodge[35] or two are now absent for a few days hunting deer. But a few of the Cayuses winter here... The Young Chief, Towerlooe, is of another family & is more properly the ruling chief. He is Uncle to the young Cayuse Halket now at Red River Mission whom we expect to return this fall & to whom the chieftainship belongs by inheritance. The old Chief Umtippe has been a savage creature in his day. His heart is still the same, full of all manner of hypocrisy, deceit and guile. He is a mortal beggar as all Indians are. If you ask a favour of him, sometimes it is granted or not, just as he feels; if granted it must be well paid for. A few days ago he took it into his head to require pay for teaching us the language & forbade his people from coming & talking with us for fear we should learn a few words from them." It should be noted that Narcissa did not claim that the avaricious Chief Umtippe asked payment for the land occupied by the mission but rather for such services as he or others had rendered in teaching the language. Upon the death of Umtippe, during the winter of 1840–41, Tiloukaikt succeeded to the leadership of the band living in the vicinity of Waiilatpu. When Narcissa mentioned Tiloukaikt in a note dated March 30, following the birth of her baby, she then called him "a friendly Indian" [Letter 39].

Alice Clarissa Whitman

On the evening of Narcissa's twenty-ninth birthday, March 14, 1837, a daughter was born to the Whitmans. They named her Alice after the mother and sister of Marcus, and Clarissa after the mother and a sister of Narcissa. She was the first white child to be born of white American parents in the Old Oregon country and the second girl of American parents on the whole Pacific Slope of what is now the United States.[36] I was sick but about two hours," Narcissa told her family. "She was born half past eight, so early in the evening that we all had time to get considerable rest that night" [Letter 40].

Anticipating the need for some assistance, the Whitmans had sent for Mrs. Pambrun, who arrived with two of her children about two weeks before the baby was born, but, according to Narcissa, she was not of much help. "She with my Husband dressed the babe," Narcissa wrote. "It would have made you smile to see them work over the little creature. Mrs. P. never saw one dressed before as we dress them having been accustomed to dress her own in the native style... Thus you see, Beloved Sisters, how the missionary does in heathen lands. No Mother, no sister, to relieve me of a single care, only an affectionate Husband, who as a physician & nurse exceeds all I ever knew."

Narcissa's confinement came at an exceedingly busy time for Marcus. He had started plowing the first week of March and felt the need to complete his planting. About this time, a party of Indians arrived who desired instruction as to how they could begin agriculture. Hoes, seed corn, and potatoes had to be distributed. Whitman then had to take time to show the natives how to prepare the soil and plant the seeds. A few days after the birth of the baby, Pambrun arrived to take his wife and family back to Fort Walla Walla. With him were Gray and Ermatinger who remained a few days at Waiilatpu before leaving for the Spokane country. Regarding her husband, Narcissa wrote: "He was excessively pressed with care and labour during the whole time of my confinement. Beside the attention I required of him, he had my washing & the cooking to do for the family."

Narcissa made a rapid recovery. Within a week she was up and carrying on the work of her home. Writing two weeks after her baby was born, Narcissa gave the following description of the child: "Her hair is a light brown... She is plump & large, holds her head up finely & looks about considerably. She weighs ten pounds." The proud and happy mother called her "a treasure invaluable" [Letter 40].

When the Pambruns returned to the fort on Saturday, the 24th, they left their twelve-year-old daughter, Maria, with the Whitmans to assist in the house work and to learn more English. On April 1, an Indian girl, possibly a half-breed, sixteen years old, arrived, who appeared no larger than an average American girl of twelve years. Narcissa named her Sarah Hull after the wife of the minister who had officiated at her wedding. "You have no idea," wrote Narcissa to her family, "how difficult it is to realize any benefit from those who do not understand you."

This practice of bestowing Bible names or the names of relatives and friends on natives, especially converts, was common to Protestant missionaries of that generation. The practice was followed by the missionaries of both the American Board and the Methodist Society at work in Oregon. Some of these New England surnames and Bible names continue among the Cayuses and Nez Perces to this day.

The Cayuses were tremendously interested in the birth of a white baby in their midst. On March 30, Narcissa wrote: "The Little Stranger is visited daily by the Chiefs & principal men in camp & the women throng the house continually waiting an opportunity to see her. Her whole appearance is so new to them. Her complexion, her size & dress & all excite a deal of wonder for they never raise a child here except they are lashed tight to a board & the girls' heads undergo the flattening process" [Letter 40]. In this same letter, she wrote "Tee-low-kiki [Tiloukaikt], a friendly Indian, called to see her the next day after she was born; Said she was a Cayuse Te-mi (Cayuse girl) because she was born on Cayuse wai-tis (Cayuse land). He told us her arrival was expected by all the people of the country... The whole tribe are highly pleased because we allow her to be called a Cayuse girl."

Narcissa made two additional references in her letters to the native custom of flattening the foreheads of some of their newly born infants. On May 3, she wrote: "The system of head-flattening exists among their people in a degree, but not to excess. The girls' heads only are flattened.

They consider it a peculiar mark of beauty and it makes them more acceptable in the sight of the men as wives. They raise but few of their children. Great numbers of them die" [Letter 41]. Narcissa was writing of the natives in the vicinity of Waiilatpu and not of the lower Columbia River country where the head-flattening custom was more prevalent.

In an hitherto unquoted letter of Narcissa's is found her third reference to this custom. Writing to Mrs. G. P. Judd of the American Board's Mission in Honolulu on September 1, 1837, she said: "Our babe has scarcely seen a sick day since she was born. She is now nearly six months old and weighs twenty-two pounds. I do not know as she is larger or heavier than children usually are at home, but the natives here are much surprised at her size and strength, and her rapid growth, which is very different from their children. Her clean, round, natural head is a striking contrast to their scurfy, ill shapen, flat heads, and they feel it so. It speaks louder than words, against their cruel, murderous system of flattening the heads of their infants. My heart bleeds for suffering infancy about me. O when will these mothers possess the feelings that belong to their endearing name?" [Letter 42a].

No reference has been found in any of Spalding's writings to the practice of head-flattening among the Nez Perces. Yet it seems that the custom must have been in vogue to some extent among these people, as one of the four Nez Perces who went to St. Louis in 1831 had such a deformed head, as shown in the drawing made by William Walker which was published in the New York *Christian Advocate*. By the time the Whitmans settled at Waiilatpu, the custom was dying out among the Cayuses. Alice Clarissa's "clean, round, natural head" was an eloquent and persuasive object lesson for them. It requires little imagination for us to believe that no Cayuse mother would willingly deform her baby's head after seeing Alice Clarissa. Here was one of the unexpected good results of the ministry of Marcus and Narcissa among the Cayuses.

TRIALS AND TRIUMPHS

Many of the trials experienced by the Whitmans during their first four months' residence at Waiilatpu foreshadowed greater difficulties which were to come. The language problem was more baffling and frustrating then they had expected. The Whitmans had no good teacher or interpreter. Richard, in whom Whitman had placed so much hope, proved to be unreliable. Chief Umtippe, whom Narcissa called a "mortal beggar," was demanding payment for any help given the missionaries in learning the language.

The winter of 1836-37 was unusually severe for that region; snow stayed on the ground for six weeks. For several weeks the Whitmans found it difficult to keep their house comfortably warm as they had nothing but blankets for windows and doors. For want of beef or wild game, the Whitmans had to turn to eating horse flesh. The failure of Gray to stay and help with the building and the farming must have been a great disappointment, yet there is no word of complaint on this subject in any of the extant letters of either of the Whitmans written during 1837.

Their trials, however, were more than offset by their accomplishments. In spite of many difficulties, a beginning had been made. Their house was gradually being made more comfortable. Both Marcus and Narcissa enjoyed good health. We hear less of Marcus' physical disability which had caused the American Board to reject his application in the spring of 1834. It has been conjectured that Whitman's trouble had been stomach ulcers which cleared up. This could have explained the pain he experienced in his left side. A beginning had been made in language study and agriculture. Some of the natives had shown a desire to be taught the principles of Christianity, and even though Chief Umtippe created some difficulties, the Indians, for the most part, were friendly and cooperative.

Completely removed from the protection that the United States could give in case of trouble, and living some twenty-five miles from Fort Walla Walla, the Whitmans had established their home in the wilderness in the midst of an uncivilized tribe where they were to live for several years without fear of physical harm. The coming of Alice Clarissa had established a bond of sympathy between the natives and the missionaries. The outlook was propitious.

CHAPTER 10 ENDNOTES

1 The original Cayuse language is now extinct. Deward E. Walker, Jr., states in his *Mutual Cross-Utilization of Economic Resources in the Plateau...*, Washington State University, Laboratory of Anthropology, Pullman, 1967, *Reports of Investigations, No. 41*: "Nez Perce was a *lingua franca* from the Bitterroots in the east to the Dalles-Celilo region in the west... " by the time these Indians had their first contacts with the white men. "The Nez Perces, Cayuse, and Palouse were so intermarried... it was virtually impossible to distinguish them particularly for the Nez Perces and Cayuse." Pp. 18 & 21.

2 The most reliable estimates of the numbers in the Nez Perce and Cayuse tribes were made by A. B. Smith in 1839 and 1840. See Drury, *Spalding and Smith*, pp. 109, 129, & 136.

3 Indian name for "little river."

4 The automatic guides, i.e., the little electronic speakers installed at several points on the grounds of the Whitman Mission National Historic Site, place the accent on the second syllable. According to an explanation given me personally by the late Dr. Stephen B. L. Penrose, President of Whitman College, Myron and Edwin Eells, sons of the Rev. Cushing Eells, differed as to the correct pronunciation of Waiilatpu. One placed the accent on the second syllable, and the other on the third. On March 30, 1837, Narcissa spelled the name "Wi-el-et-poo."

5 Lewis and Clark called the river Kooskooske, whereas the missionaries referred to it as the Clearwater, which is the name that prevailed.

6 Narcissa in her letter of October 24, 1836, wrote: "The Nez Perces are exceedingly anxious [for us] to have a location among them, Husband writes. Say they do not have difficulty with the whites as the Cayuses do & we will find it so."

7 Lapwai is usually explained as meaning "place of butterflies."

8 The hills along the Clearwater at Lapwai Creek rise to an elevation of about 2,600 feet above sea level, or about 1,800 feet above the river.

9 Drury, *Spalding*, p. 159.

10 Drury, *Spalding and Smith*, p. 127.

11 Possibly Gray was also making adobe bricks and such necessary items of furniture as chairs, stools, and tables, during the absence of Whitman from Waiilatpu.

12 Spalding to Greene from Fort Vancouver, Sept. 20, 1836, Coll. A. Spalding gave different figures at a later time. See Drury, *Spalding*, p. 162, where the total distance was estimated at 6,155 miles. The earlier figure is to be preferred.

13 T. C. Boon, The *Anglican Church from the Bay to the Rockies*, Toronto, 1962, p. 33.

14 Mrs. Elkanah Walker's side-saddle is in the museum of O.H.S., Portland. A picture of this saddle is in Drury, *F.W.W.*, II:68.

15 HBC Arch, A/11/69. Jessett, *Herbert Beaver*, p. 22. See Chapter Nine, fn. 37.

16 From archaeological findings, Whitman Mission National Historic Site.

17 A twenty-seven foot high granite shaft, including height of the base, now crowns the top of this hill as a memorial to the Whitmans.

18 Gray's *Journal*, *W.C.Q.*, June 1913.

19 Gray to Greene, Sept. 19, 1836. Coll. A.

20 From testimonial letter of Chauncey Eddy to Greene, Feb. 17, 1836. Coll. A.

21 Narcissa succeeded in getting some broom corn seeds, for on July 7, 1842, in a letter to Maria Pambrun, she wrote: "Our broom corn did not do well last year."

22 The Hudson's Bay Company would loan animals to natives or settlers on condition that the Company would receive any increase of stock and also be paid for any animal lost. Whitman letter 42.

23 Ordinarily a man with a two-horse team and a 16 inch plowshare can plow about three acres a day. Whitman with a yoke of oxen working in tough virgin soil studded with clumps of rye grass would have been fortunate to plow one acre a day.

24 Drury, *Presbyterian Panorama*, Philadelphia, 1952, pp. 59 ff., gives a summary of the beginnings of mission work by the American Board with the American Indians.

25 Drury, *Spalding and Smith*, pp. 104 & 138.

26 *Ibid.*, p. 180.

27 Drury, *Whitman*, p. 172, quoting from Spalding's letter to Parker of Feb. 11, 1837. See also Whitman letter 42. Josephy, *Nez Perce Indians*, p. 382, lists Richard as one of the Nez Perce chiefs who signed a treaty with the U.S. Government on Aug. 6, 1858. Yet Victor, *The Early Wars of Oregon*, p. 208, claims that he was killed during the Cayuse War of 1848. According to another account in the *Pacific Northwesterner*, Summer, 1958, p. 45, Richard was killed in the Steptoe campaign in May 1858.

28 Gray, *Oregon*, p. 109, states that one of Narcissa's "amusements" while crossing the country in the summer of 1836 was "to teach the Doctor to sing, which she did with considerable success."

29 Simpson, in his Character Book, HBC Arch., described Pambrun as being in 1832: "...about 45 years of age—17 years in the service; an active, steady, dapper little fellow." He had the rank of clerk when given charge of Fort Walla Walla; was promoted to chief trader in Nov. 1839; remained at the fort until his death on May 15, 1841.

30 No indication is given whether the songs and prayers taught to the Indians were in Latin, French, English, or Nez Perce.

31 See section, "Oregon Indians in the Red River Mission School," Chapter One, for information about Cayuse Halket.

32 See illustration in this work of Spalding holding a Bible in one hand and a hoe in the other—symbolic of his philosophy of Indian missions.

33 *Missouri Historical Review*, Vol. LXV (April 1971): pp. 252 ff.

34 Possible Umtippe was Tum-a-tap-um mentioned several times by Alexander Ross in his *The Fur Hunters of the Far West*, K. A. Spalding (ed.), Norman, Oklahoma, 1956. On page 123, we may read: "Notwithstanding reiterated professions of friendship, it was observed that his disposition was uncommonly selfish. He never opened his mouth but to insist on our goods being lavished on his numerous train of followers, without the hope of compensation. The more he received, the more his assurance increased, and his demands had no bounds."

35 A Cayuse Indian lodge was an oblong shelter made out of reed mats or skins supported by willow poles and large enough to accommodate several families, each with its own hearth.

36 The late Dr. John A. Hawgood of Birmingham, England, discovered the baptismal record of Isabelle Anna, daughter of Mr. and Mrs. Thomas O. Larkin, born on January 31, 1833, at Monterey, California, where Larkin was U.S. Consul. California was then a part of Mexico. The baby died in infancy. A son, Thomas O. Larkin, Jr., was born on April 13, 1834. Information received in a personal interview with Dr. Hawgood.

[CHAPTER ELEVEN]

THE VERSATILE DOCTOR
1837–1838

The Whitmans at Waiilatpu and the Spaldings at Lapwai carried on their work in their separate stations for about two years with but little outside help beyond that of a few Hawaiians and an occasional wandering mountain man. The restless Gray, who was supposed to assist in the secular affairs of the mission, had given only six weeks of his time to help Whitman and about four to aid Spalding before leaving for Fort Vancouver and then for the States. Both Whitman and Spalding were fully aware that the American Board expected them to be self-supporting, with the exception of a few basic staples which had to be imported. Such a policy meant that both men, and the associates who joined them in 1838, had to devote most of their time and energy to manual labor just to keep themselves and their families alive and fairly comfortable.

At Waiilatpu Whitman had to superintend or actually engage in such duties as farming, building fences to protect his crops, taking care of his animals, milking cows, butchering a horse when needed, sawing logs to make boards, making adobe bricks for the unfinished part of his house, plus a multitude of incidental duties connected with maintaining a home in the wilderness. Fortunately both Whitman and Spalding were versatile and energetic. Neither was afraid of work. Each had to be a jack-of-all-trades in order to survive. The multiplicity of such secular duties, however, made it difficult for either man to spend much time on language study and on those professional duties for which each was especially qualified. The marvel is that they were able to accomplish as much as they did in civilizing and evangelizing the natives under such restricting conditions. With infinite patience and devotion, the Whitmans and the Spaldings gave themselves, without expectation of any material reward, to ministering to a people of an entirely different culture—to semi-nomadic, "heathen" Indians.

Our chief source of information regarding the activities of the Whitmans during the two years from their arrival in Oregon to the fall of 1838 is their correspondence. After that date, their letters are supplemented by the letters and diaries of the 1838 reenforcement. During their eleven-year residence in Old Oregon, beginning with their arrival at the 1836 Rendezvous, the Whitmans wrote 275 letters which are extant either in original or in copy form. Only six original Whitman letters written during 1837 have been found, and an additional one which was published. For the eight-month period beginning January 1, 1838, and ending with the arrival of the reenforcement in the early fall of that year, thirteen Whitman letters are known of which four were written by Narcissa. Even though the source material for these months is scanty, we can glean considerable information from them regarding Whitman's activities as a doctor, a farmer, and a teacher.

WHITMAN, THE DOCTOR

Although Whitman was sent to Old Oregon as a missionary physician, we find that he rarely referred to his professional experiences in his letters. When writing to the Board, he would sometimes refer to the health of his wife or of his associates, but seldom would he mention the ailments of the natives. Here even Narcissa fails us. If the theory that her father was a Thomsonian is correct, then we can understand her hesitancy to say much about her husband's medical practice to members of her family. Under such circumstances the tactful thing would be to say nothing about a subject over which there was such pronounced disagreement. We do find, however, a few statements in Narcissa's letters which throw light upon the conditions her husband faced as a missionary doctor among superstitious natives.

Both the Cayuses and the Nez Perces had medicine men whom

they called *te-wats*. Like many medicine men of primitive peoples, they had, no doubt, some effective remedies. They also relied upon what the Whitmans considered to be sorcery, superstition, and deceit in trying to effect cures. A terrifying aspect of te-watism was their acceptance of the right of relatives of a deceased person to kill the te-wat if he were unable to cure his patient. This custom put Dr. Whitman constantly under threat of death and greatly restricted what he might otherwise have been able to accomplish.

In Narcissa's letter of May 2, 1837, she wrote that many of the Indians of their vicinity were ill "with an inflamation of the lungs." Many turned to Dr. Whitman for help. He was, in their eyes, a white te-wat of great renown, for had he not removed an arrowhead from the back of Jim Bridger at the Rendezvous of 1835? Among the afflicted was the wife of the irascible Chief Umtippe. Narcissa described what happened: "The old chief Umtippe's wife was quite sick and came near dying. For a season they were satisfied with my husband's attention, and were doing well; but when they would overeat themselves, or go into a relapse from unnecessary exposure, then they must have their te-wat doctors; say that the medicine was bad, and all was bad. Their te-wat is the same species of juggling as practiced by the Pawnees, which Mr. Dunbar describes,[1] playing the fool over them, and giving no medicine" [Letter 41].

"Umtippe got in a rage about his wife," wrote Narcissa, "and told my husband, while she was under his care, that if his wife died that night he should kill him. The contest has been sharp between him and the Indians, and husband was nearly sick with the excitement and care of them." Losing faith in Dr. Whitman, Umtippe sent for "the great Walla Walla te-wat," and thus Whitman was relieved of the responsibility if the woman died. The Walla Walla te-wat came and "after going through several incantations, and receiving a horse and a blanket or two, pronounced her well; but the next day she was the same again." Umtippe's rage was then directed against the te-wat and said "that he was bad and ought to be killed." Since Narcissa does not say whether the woman died or not, we may assume that she lived and that the te-wat's life was spared. A few weeks later Umtippe became ill. "Notwithstanding all his villainy," wrote Narcissa, "he came to my husband to be doctored. He was very sick, and we thought he would die; but the medicine given him soon relieved him."

A few days later, the grim superstition of the Indians wrought its vengeance on "the great Walla Walla te-wat." Narcissa wrote on May 2: "Last Saturday the war chief died at Walla Walla. He was a Cayuse and a relative of Umtippe; was sick but six days; employed the same Walla Walla tewat Umtippe sent for, but he died in his hands. The same day... a younger brother of Umtippe went to Walla Walla; arrived about twilight, and shot the te-wat dead. Thus they are avenged." Narcissa felt that as soon as some of the older chiefs died, no doubt including Umtippe, things would be different. She contrasted the older chiefs, who were "filled with so much war and bloodshed," with the younger men, who had "an eager desire to adopt the manners and customs of civilized life; but they are ruled by the chiefs, and feel themselves obliged to bow in subjection to them."

Introducing Chief Stickus

On Monday, May 1, 1837, another influential Cayuse chief called on Dr. Whitman and asked for medical attention. He was Stickus whom Narcissa called "an excellent Indian" and who lived with his band on the Umatilla River about twenty-five miles from Waiilatpu. The Whitmans took Stickus into their home where they could give him personal attention. In doing so they realized the risk they ran if he died. Writing late in the evening of the following Wednesday, Narcissa said: "He has been taking medicine, and it appears to have relieved him in a measure; but, because he is not all about immediately, he became exceedingly uneasy and restless and talks about the te-wats. He, with many other sensible ones in the tribe, and men of influence, too, are convinced that it is a deception, and not of God, and yet no doubt feel a great struggle in their minds to entirely renounce that in which they have so long had implicit confidence." The Whitmans found that customs generations old did not change quickly. They had to be patient, and they knew it was wise to exercise restraint.

Before Narcissa closed her letter, she made an appeal for additional workers, an appeal that comes again and again in the letters that she and Marcus wrote: "Who will come over and help us? Weak, frail nature cannot endure excessive care and anxiety any great length of time, without falling under it." She then made mention of her husband's health. "I refer more particularly to my husband. His labor this spring has affected his health considerably. His old complaint in his side affects him occasionally." There is no evidence that Whitman had any physical problems while crossing the country or during their first months' residence at Waiilatpu. Narcissa attributed the recurrence of his old trouble to excessive labor, hence the plea for assistants.

Narcissa's letter closes with the following postscript: "You are indebted to little Alice Clarissa's disposition for this sheet. I have no cradle yet, and she has lain in my lap all day; for she does not like to be where she cannot see her mother, long at a time. She receives many kisses for her grandparents, uncles and aunts, every day. She is now in bed with her father, sleeping sweetly. She is pleasant company for me, here alone. One o'clock [a.m.] and I retire, leave the sick Indian to himself the remainder of the night." Stickus recovered, and the Whitmans had no more loyal friend during their remaining ten and one-half years residence among the Cayuses than this chief. How different would have been the history of the Whitman mission had the locations of Stickus and Tiloukaikt been reversed.

WHITMAN, THE FARMER

Both Whitman and Spalding saw the necessity of teaching the Indians the arts of civilization for two compelling reasons. In the first place, their semi-nomadic type of life gave them a precarious livelihood. The buffalo east of the mountains were being decimated. The missionaries realized that the day was rapidly approaching when the wild game would not provide sufficient meat for the natives. Narcissa wrote: "We are anxious to give them the means of procuring their provisions in a more easy way, so that there may be less starving ones during the winter" [Letter 46]. Therefore, the necessity to teach the Indians how to cultivate the soil. There is evidence to indicate that the Cayuses were aware of this need and were ready to make an adjustment to the circumstances which were being forced upon them, as increasingly they were asking for plows. At the same time this necessity to change their pattern of living may have been one of the most serious grievances that the Indians harbored against the white men.

The second reason why the missionaries urged the natives to take up cultivating the soil was to induce them to give up their semi-nomadic habits and accept a settled life. This was necessary before any consistent program of education or religious instruction could be conducted.

Whitman found the soil and the climate at Waiilatpu admirably suited for agriculture. He began in the spring of 1837, with only one plow and fifteen hoes, the herculean task of cultivating sufficient land to provide for his needs and to teach the natives how to till the soil. Spalding was facing the same frustrating experience at Lapwai where he too lacked agricultural instruments. He tried to make a plow out of cedar wood, using large roots for the "chip and mold boards." [2] This, however, proved unsuccessful. Whitman saw a plow that Pambrun was using, made out of wood with an iron point, and wrote to McLoughlin requesting that at least one of like kind be made for him. McLoughlin, in a letter dated June 23, 1837, replied: "The plough you request will be made." [3] When Jason Lee visited Waiilatpu in the spring of 1838, he found several of these wooden plows with iron points in use, but they were not very satisfactory.

Whitman hesitated to ask the Board to send plows, as he was aware of its limited resources. Moreover, he knew that some members of the Board would question the wisdom of spending benevolence funds for such secular objects as plows. How could the infant American Board, founded in 1810, with a limited constituency and restricted income, afford to venture into the field of furnishing agricultural tools to whole tribes of Indians? In Whitman's letter to Greene of May 5, 1837, he stressed the importance of having plows and hoes, and suggested that if such were sent to the Hawaiian Islands, ships of the Hudson's Bay Company would carry them to the Columbia.

The planting season of 1838, when the Indians showed an increased desire for plows, added to Whitman's feeling of frustration. Writing to Greene on May 8 of that year, Whitman made the following plea for plows:

> We are now at an important crisis, & need men & means to carry out what has been so auspiciously begun & that there be no reaction. There is danger of this, for the want of facilities to accomplish our plans, & to induce the Indians to settle around us that we may teach them & their children without interruption. Even this year I am confident if we had had suitable ploughs & hoes that they would have raised [enough] corn & potatoes &c. to have detained a large number with us constantly. We shall labour under great disadvantage until such things can be sent.

I have thought best not to ask the Board for them fearing what reception it might meet with & so have written to several gentlemen of my acquaintance to send us fifty ploughs & three hundred hoes, & in case of failure I have ordered my Brother [i.e., Augustus Whitman] to appropriate two hundred dollars on my account to that object. But this is not enough, what are three hundred hoes & fifty ploughs? We ought to have at least seventy five or one hundred ploughs & six hundred hoes immediately to save this starving multitude from an untimely grave.

Whitman's willingness to contribute two hundred dollars from his personal funds left with his brother speaks eloquently of his faith in this cause. This sum amounted to more than a schoolteacher's pay for one year. Whitman's appeal to the Board continues: "If the Board cannot approve of such an expense, I do not see how they can afford to proceed without it, for it seems evident that without them we shall not see the Indians at our station for any considerable time. On the contrary, if we had them, it would not be long before we should see them located around us with houses, fields, gardens, hogs & cows, & their children enjoying the benefit of constant instruction, at far less expense to the Board then to take them into our families for that purpose. They are fond of ploughing."

Whitman had to wait two years before he learned of the result of this appeal. Then to his great satisfaction, he heard that a shipment of supplies from the Board had arrived at Fort Vancouver which included ten plows, "18 or 20 doz. hoes, two cook stoves," and many other items [Letter 76a]. In the same shipment were twenty-five plows donated by the Rushville Congregational Church [Letter 89]. The arrival of these thirty-five plows came after the spring planting of 1840, but in time for the sowing of fall wheat. Thus we see that four years elapsed after the Whitmans had settled at Waiilatpu before enough good plows were on hand for the Indians to make a beginning in cultivation.

In his letter of May 8, 1838, Whitman wrote: "Had I one doubt of the disposition of the Indians to cultivate, I would not thus write: but having seen them for two seasons breaking ground with hoes & sticks & having given them the trial of the plough, I feel an entire confidence in their disposition & ability... Several of them have already planted half to an acre of potatoes & have considerable fields of corn and peas."

Whitman had only sixteen acres under cultivation in 1837. This was increased to forty acres in 1838 including "six acres of potatoes, two & half of wheat," with peas, oats, and corn making up the balance. Much of what he raised had to be given to the Indians for seed. "This field is emphatically white for the harvest," he wrote, "although we bring the gospel as the first object, we cannot gain an assurance unless they are attracted & retained by the plough & hoe, & in this way even before the language is acquired you may have the people drawn around you & ready to hear your every instruction. And why should not this be our method of proceeding? Is it not what Paul meant when he said, ëI become all things unto all men,' that he accommodated himself to the circumstances of the People? Why then should we not take the best, & may I not say, the only way to win them to Christ?" Here was Whitman's philosophy of missions. Secretary Greene was inclined to begin with a sermon and end with the plow. Whitman and Spalding had the opposite emphasis-begin with the plow and end with the sermon.

At first it seems that no questions were raised by the natives regarding ownership or use of the land. Evidently Whitman had been invited by Umtippe to settle in his vicinity and there is no evidence that the chief asked for or received any compensation. Since the Indians were often absent from their home lands for months of each year, they had no sense of individual proprietary rights to any particular acreage. Not until the Cayuses had begun to cultivate the fields did the idea of private ownership of designated plots of land become a part of their thinking.

In his letter to Greene dated March 12, 1838, Whitman explained why the Indians, who did want to cultivate some land in the immediate vicinity of Waiilatpu, were eager for that particular location: "Their great fear is that other Indians will steal from them... & all are anxious to plant where I can watch their crops for, as they say, the Indians fear me but do not fear them." A revolutionary new idea had taken root: the private ownership of land. Later this was an issue which would cause trouble for Whitman, when Tiloukaikt demanded payment for the lands occupied by the mission.

Beginnings in Horticulture

While still at Fort Vancouver, Narcissa noted in her diary her intention to take some "sprouts of apple, peach & grape" with them when they made the return trip to Fort Walla Walla. We may assume that this is what happened for, soon after they moved to Waiilatpu, Whitman planted an orchard to the west of their house. We have record of Spalding sending fifty young apple trees to Whitman in February 1842.[4] Since it takes years for an apple orchard to become productive, we do not find many references in the writings of the missionaries to fruit being harvested at Waiilatpu. We do have evidence that the Whitmans were able to pick a few apples in the fall of 1846.[5] There is no evidence that any of the Cayuses took any special interest in planting fruit trees; some of the Nez Perces, however, did so.

Beginnings in Animal Husbandry

No record has been found of the division that Whitman and Spalding made of their horses and mules after their arrival in Old Oregon. In his letter to Greene dated July 8, 1840, Whitman stated that he had seventeen head of horses. The Cayuses had large herds of horses; consequently Whitman was able to buy from them for as low as $6.00 a head during the first five years that he lived at Waiilatpu, when he and his family were obliged to eat horseflesh. Spalding, in the inventory that he made of the Waiilatpu property owned at the time of the massacre, claimed that Whitman had forty-six horses of which number ten were broken to harness.[6] This means that Whitman had been able to use Cayuse horses, often called ponies, to pull plows.

When the missionaries first settled among the Old Oregon Indians, the natives had only two domesticated animals—the horse and the dog. Although Whitman made mention of one Cayuse chief who had secured some oxen from the Hudson's Bay Company, these were on loan only. The Company did not wish to encourage the natives to raise cattle. This, however, became the policy of Whitman and Spalding who, from the very beginning of their missionary work, looked upon cattle raising by the natives as one good method of inducing them to abandon their roving habits and settle down to farming.

After Whitman and Spalding had divided their small herd of cattle which survived the long overland trek, Whitman had either five or seven heifers or cows. For five years the Whitmans refrained from eating beef, wishing to build up their little herd. During these years, Whitman found it necessary to butcher thirty-two horses for food.[7] In his report of mission activities at Waiilatpu, written for Greene on July 6, 1840, Whitman said that he then had "...five cows, two one year-old heifers & three heifer calves. One pair oxen, two pair of steers, two yearling bulls & two bull calves, twenty in all." Not until the summer of 1841 did Whitman feel free to kill his first beef, "a steer four years old" which had been fattened on the luxurious grass of the region and which "gave us one hundred and forty-eight pounds of tried tallow" [Letter 100]. After that time, the necessity of killing horses for food diminished.

With the increase of their respective herds, both Whitman and Spalding occasionally parted with some of their cattle, giving or selling them to a few selected natives who they believed would prize them. We have no accurate figures as to how many head of cattle the Indians owned at the close of the mission period. Since the Nez Perces were several times more numerous than the Cayuses and also since they seem to have demonstrated a greater desire to adopt the white man's ways, we may assume that they had more cattle than the Cayuses. At the time of the Cayuse War, 1848–49, members of that tribe were reported to have had forty head of cattle.[8] It is possible that some of that number had been stolen from Oregon immigrants, or received through trading.

Following the great California cattle drive of 1837, when about six hundred head of Spanish cattle were driven into the Willamette Valley, cattle became more easily available to the Indians. The Methodist missionaries introduced some cattle into The Dalles area in 1838. The Spanish cattle were of inferior stock as compared to the American breed, being smaller; also the cows were poor in milk production.

Spalding, in his Waiilatpu inventory, stated that Whitman had 290 head of cattle in November 1847, including "100 milch cows; 80 young cattle; 11 yoke of oxen; 80 calves; and 8 beef cattle."[9] The fact that Whitman had one hundred milk cows does not mean that he was actually milking that many, rather these were breeding animals. We are not told just how Whitman was able to keep his live stock separate from that owned by the Indians before he was able to fence sufficient pasture land to keep them confined. Perhaps he had some system of identifying his stock by notching the ears of the young or by branding them. Whitman was handicapped in his efforts to erect rail fences at Waiilatpu because of the lack of nearby suitable timber.

Introduction of Hogs and Sheep

In a letter that Spalding wrote to Greene in the summer of 1837, he reported getting three hogs from the Hudson's Bay Company at Fort Colville.[10] Whitman, in a financial report submitted to the American Board dated March 27, 1838, stated that he had spent £10-3-6 for "Flour & Seeds & Hogs." He did not indicate how many were purchased or when, though it was probably in the summer of 1837. Writing on December 3, 1839, Whitman stated: "I killed four hogs which weighed 1,083 lbs." Narcissa wrote on November 6, 1841: "Seven hogs have been butchered today." In order to keep large quantities of freshly butchered meat, the Whitmans would have had to dry it, smoke it, or salt it down. As will be mentioned later, the Oregon Mission received large shipments of salt from their associates in the Hawaiian Islands.

More important than hogs for both the Whitmans and the Spaldings were sheep. Evidence is lacking as to whether the missionaries were able to induce the natives to raise these animals. The Indians were quick to see the value of cattle as they could be turned loose to graze on the fenceless prairies, but hogs and sheep had to be confined and watched. Moreover, sheep were often victims of marauding animals such as wolves and coyotes. This was a problem that the natives were not as well able to meet as the missionaries, who controlled the predatory animals by resorting to the use of poison.

While still at Fort Vancouver, Whitman, Spalding, and Gray had jointly signed a letter dated September 19, 1836, which was addressed to the Rev. Hiram Bingham, head of the Hawaiian Mission of the American Board, in which they requested that he send some sheep to them. No doubt Dr. McLoughlin had encouraged them to do this as he was forbidden by the policy of his Company to sell any from the large flock at the fort. "Any number from 50 to 200 would be acceptable," the men wrote. Bingham was in full sympathy with the project, but had to wait until he could secure transportation for the animals on a ship bound for Fort Vancouver. An opportunity came with the unexpected arrival in Honolulu, during the latter part of December 1836, of a ship bearing a party of twelve Methodist missionaries, including three men, five women, and four children, on their way to the Willamette Valley. The party had sailed from Boston the latter part of the previous July. The voyage around Cape Horn had taken five months. The Methodists had to wait in Honolulu for nearly four months before they secured passage on a vessel, the *Diana*, which was bound for the Columbia River. The missionaries consented to look after eight head of sheep which Bingham was ready to send to Oregon.

The *Diana*, with the first Methodist reenforcement for its Oregon Mission, dropped anchor at Fort Vancouver on May 28, 1837. Dr. McLoughlin notified Whitman that eight sheep had been left with him "but one of them died." McLoughlin replaced the dead sheep with a ram from his flock, but charged Whitman for it. He also reported that Bingham had sent seventy bags of salt and a contribution from the Hawaiian Christians of $79.87½.[11] The salt was a most welcome gift as it was needed to preserve fish and meat.

The first missionaries of the American Board had arrived in the Hawaiian Islands (then called the Sandwich Islands) in the early months of 1820 and met with immediate and rather fantastic success. By 1837 they claimed about five thousand converts and by 1853 the native church became both self-supporting and self-administering.[12] The first "foreign missionary" project of the infant Hawaiian Church was to contribute to the Oregon Mission of the American Board. The gifts made in 1837, although relatively small, were significant. Other gifts followed.

Mrs. Elkanah Walker, a member of the 1838 reenforcement for the Oregon Mission, wrote in her diary on May 17, 1839: "Mr. Bingham's church has made our mission a present of about 400 dollars." At other times the Hawaiian Christians sent kegs of sugar or molasses to Oregon. In May 1839 the Hawaiian Mission sent a small printing press to Oregon, of which mention will be made later. Many of the Hawaiians who entered the employ of the Hudson's Bay Company or of the Oregon Mission were Christians.

In August 1837, Dr. McLoughlin turned the eight sheep over to the interpreter stationed at Fort Walla Walla, who happened to be at Fort Vancouver, with instructions to deliver them to Whitman. Writing to Levi Chamberlain, the business agent of the Hawaiian Mission, on October 7, Whitman related a sad story: "From his negligence & injuring their legs with cords (they were brought in canoes), three died after reaching Walla Walla. Only one ewe is living." That lone ewe marked the beginning of the sheep and wool industry which once throve in what is now often called the Inland Empire of the Pacific Northwest.[13]

Whitman, eager to get more sheep, wrote to Chamberlain a second time on October 16 and asked him to send "fifteen or twenty sheep, all ewes except one or two rams." In this letter he also requested that two married Hawaiian men with their wives be sent. When Whitman began building at Waiilatpu, he had the assistance of two Hawaiians whom he had gotten through the Hudson's Bay Company, but difficulties arose because they were single. Whitman explained: "The Indians are constantly urging them to take some of their women, & one asked liberty of me to do so, a few days since. But I replied he had a wife at home & for that reason must not take one here." Whitman felt that if one or more couples could be sent at the same time as the sheep, they could care for the animals in transit. Another reason for wanting married couples was to have the women help Narcissa in her house work.

Acting on Whitman's request, Chamberlain sent six sheep to the Oregon Mission in the spring of 1838 and a married couple, Joseph and Maria Maki Whitman acknowledged the arrival of five of the six sheep (one died en route) in a letter to Chamberlain dated October 30, 1838. The Oregon Mission paid £12 sterling for the fare of the Hawaiian couple. Joseph and Maria proved to be excellent workers and were a much appreciated addition to the Whitman household.

The sheep throve in Oregon. Writing to his former mentor, Dr. Ira Bryant of Rushville, on May 24, 1841, Whitman reported: "The sheep belonging to the Mission breed twice a year & in some instances I think they have had lambs three times in twelve months." With such a rate of reproduction, the flocks increased at a surprising rate. Spalding reported having forty-one sheep in July 1841 and 150 in April 1846.[14] In August 1840 Spalding noted in his diary the completion of the building of a loom.[15] The inventory of the Lapwai station, compiled after the Whitman massacre, listed not only the loom but also two spinning wheels. Whitman reported having eighty sheep in April 1845 [Letter 170] and the Waiilatpu inventory listed ninety-two sheep and two spinning wheels. Since both Whitman and Spalding may have given or sold some sheep to the Indians, no accurate statistics regarding the increase of their flocks are available.

Whitman saw the possibilities of a booming sheep industry in the upper Columbia River country. Writing to A. B. Smith, after the latter had left the Oregon Mission and gone to Hawaii, on May 31, 1844,

Whitman described Oregon as: "A country where a man can winter a thousand sheep easier than he could feed half the number from a well stored barn in your own native Vermont." Whitman looked into the future and dreamed of the day when: "The wool grown here & manufactured in the country would be exchanged for domestick articles, the same as a trade with the Islands... no foreign fabricks can come in competition." [16] Today large woolen mills stand at Pendleton, Oregon, in fulfillment of Whitman's dreams.

Meeting the Threat of Marauding Animals

The introduction of sheep into the interior of Old Oregon back in the 1830s and 1840s had its difficulties and precipitated some serious complications, as will be noted. One of the members of the 1838 reenforcement to the Oregon Mission, the Rev. A. B. Smith, writing from Kamiah on September 3, 1840, critically commented: "He [i.e., Spalding] & Doct. W. were in such haste to introduce all the arts of civilization among the Indians at the very onset, they encumbered themselves with sheep; but the [Indian] camp was so full of dogs that the poor harmless sheep could have no peace but were in danger of being destroyed at once." Spalding tried to meet this threat by offering a reward for every dog killed but, according to Smith, this proved highly unpopular with the natives who liked their dogs.[17]

Another and a more serious threat to the sheep came from the marauding wolves and coyotes. Spalding made several references in his diary to wolves attacking and sometimes killing young cattle and even horses. The helpless sheep were easy victims. On October 2, 1839, Spalding wrote to Greene requesting: "A quantity of strycnia or Nux Vomica sufficient to kill 1,000 wolves." [18] We have no evidence to indicate how much of this poison, if any was sent by Greene. Whitman had to face the same problem as Spalding in protecting his sheep from marauding animals. Although no record has been found in any of Whitman's letters to Greene asking for poison, he may have received such from Spalding or from the Hudson's Bay Company. As will be noted later, the fact that Whitman did use poison to kill wolves became the basis for certain serious charges made at the time of the massacre.

Other Innovations

In addition to the introduction of cattle, hogs, and sheep, the Whitmans and the Spaldings had poultry. Writing to his friend and former mentor, Dr. Ira Bryant, on May 24, 1841, Whitman listed some of the improvements made at Waiilatpu which included "some out houses as Corn Cribs, & Granary, Harness House, Smoke & hen houses, double back houses."[19] The reference to hen houses indicates the presence of poultry, and Narcissa once wrote of having a few turkeys. Spalding informed Greene in September 1838 of having forty hens. Neither of the inventories of property lost or destroyed at Waiilatpu or at Lapwai following the massacre, however, mentioned poultry.[20] We do not know to what extent, if any, the natives were encouraged to raise chickens but with the Indians' fondness of dogs, we doubt that this experiment proved successful.[21]

Whitman, The Missionary Teacher

The task of establishing a home in the primeval wilderness was so tremendous that we marvel how Whitman found time to learn the language and to conduct a school for the natives or to give any instruction in the basic truths of the Christian religion. As a doctor he had a major responsibility to minister to the physical ailments of his associates and, as far as possible, those of the natives. He was not expected to perform the duties of an ordained minister, yet as a conscientious Christian, he felt an obligation to do all that he could to educate and to evangelize the natives. In this he had the wholehearted cooperation of Narcissa.

By the fall of 1837, the Whitmans felt that they had sufficient mastery of the language to begin a school. Writing on April 11, 1838, Narcissa said: "We have had a school for them about four months past, & much of the time our kitchen has been crowded & all seem very much attached." By that time Spalding had made a beginning in reducing the Nez Perce language to writing and had submitted a manuscript primer of seventy-two pages to the Whitmans for their approval. Narcissa copied this primer before it was sent to the Hawaiian Mission to be printed. Whitman knew that a printing press was there because his friend, Elisha Loomis of Rushville, had taken one out to the Islands in 1820. The primer was never published in full, only a few proof sheets were run off, as it was discovered that Spalding's transcription of the language was incorrect.

In Whitman's letter of March 12, 1838, to Greene, we find the following account of his method of religious instruction: "We have two meetings for Indians on the Sabbath & in the evening what we call a sabbath school for the children & youth. The attention on religious instruction is good & solemn. Worship is strictly maintained in the principal lodges morning & evening. Lately I have been explaining the ten Commandments & our saviour's first & great commandment to which they listen with great attention & from their inquiries I think they understand them." [22]

A reference to Cayuse Halket is found in this letter: "The young Cayuse who had been about seven years at the Mission School at Red River died about a year since just as he was about to return to his people." As previously stated, Cayuse Halket was buried at Red River on February 1, 1837. "We had looked for his return with much interest," wrote Whitman, "as he had been home on a visit & behaved very well.[23] But Providence has removed him from either good or harm in his life any further than his people remember his good advice." If Cayuse Halket had been active or effective in any endeavor to introduce Christianity among his people, as some have suggested,[24] surely Whitman would have mentioned it. Whitman dismissed the youth's influence simply by saying that he had "behaved very well," and had given some good advice.

The news of Cayuse Halket's death was carried to Oregon by the Hudson's Bay Company's westbound express of 1837. Dr. McLoughlin was disturbed, as is shown in a letter he wrote to Spalding on November 27, 1837: "In my opinion, Indians ought never to be taken from their lands to a Civilized Country, as they will see so many things new to them, that they may form very mistaken opinions, and if any thing happens to displease them, they may give those who take them there an immensity of trouble. You see the return we get for sending the young Cayuse Chief to be educated at Red River, now that he is dead, his Relations, at least some of them, give it out that we killed him." [25]

Narcissa in her letter of April 11, 1838, also commented on their endeavors to teach Christianity. She wrote: "For several Sabbaths past, our worship with them has been very interesting. All seem to manifest a deep interest in the instruction given them. Some feel almost to blame us for telling them about eternal realities. One said that it was good when they knew nothing but to hunt, eat, drink, and sleep; now it is bad." Here is the age-old question: Is it better to live in ignorance of the divine law and be content, or to have an enlightened conscience and be discontented?

Narcissa wrote especially about the children. "There are many very interesting children," she commented, "both among the Nez Perces and Cayuses. We have generally given names to those that have attended school. One boy about ten years old, we have given the name of Edward,- a bright, active boy, and loves his book." We shall hear more about this Edward, who evidently had been named after one of Narcissa's brothers. He was a son of Chief Tiloukaikt and was also known as Shu-ma-hici. His portrait, painted by John Mix Stanley in October 1847, is reproduced as an illustration in volume two of this work.

In this letter of Narcissa's of April 11, we find another reference to Umtippe. "The old chief, Umtippe, who threatened my husband's life last spring, is especially changed," she wrote, "particularly in his deportment to us, and about the house." Narcissa stressed the fact that "becoming familiar with the language" had made instruction much more effective. Interpreters were never satisfactory, especially when dealing with theological terms. Later on, in a letter dated May 10, 1838, Narcissa wrote: "Under date of April 11th, I spoke of old Umtippe's appearance. He seems to be declining fast. Last Saturday he came here, he said, on purpose to spend the Sabbath. Said he had had recently three fainting turns, and felt that he could not live a great while. He had been very wicked, and did not know where his soul would go when he died - was lost about it." The Rev. Jason Lee happened to be at Waiilatpu that week-end and was invited to speak at the Indians' worship service. Of course an interpreter was needed and perhaps Whitman was able to serve in that capacity. Lee's words made a deep impression on Umtippe. "Never can a person manifest a greater change," wrote Narcissa. "That selfish, wicked, cunning and troublesome old chief, now so still and quiet, so attentive to the truth, and grateful for favors now given! Surely nought but the spirit of God has done this."

One of the problems that the missionaries experienced when trying to convert the Indians was that of getting them to understand Calvinistic doctrines. To the missionaries, becoming a Christian meant not only that one should show penitence for sins committed but also have an understanding of what it meant to accept Jesus Christ and his forgiveness. This was the faith in which the missionaries had been reared and it was natural for them to make these requirements of their would-be converts. Turning again to Narcissa's letter of April 11, 1838, we read: "We are not yet satisfied how much he [i.e., Chief Umtippe] understands of the atonement, or whether he has any correct views of salvation through Jesus Christ. But this we do know, that God is able by his spirit to take what little truth we are able to give, and impress it upon the hearts and consciences of the most benighted minds."

The doctrine of the atonement of Christ, often puzzling to informed Christians, was doubly so to the Cayuses who were hearing about it for the first time from the Whitmans. "To hold up before them the atonement," wrote Narcissa to the American Board missionaries in Honolulu, "and [say] that their sins bore a part in crucifying the Lord of glory; they say, 'It is another saying; we never heard it before; we do not understand it'."[26] Here is one reason why the Roman Catholic missionaries were able to baptize Oregon Indians by the hundreds, while the Protestants had so few whom they felt were qualified for church membership; their standards were too difficult.

Although Narcissa, in her letter of May 10, 1838, reported that old Chief Umtippe was in failing health and might die at any time, he lived for more than two years after she wrote. In a letter to Greene dated March 28, 1841, Whitman stated: "The old chief Cut Lip died last winter, which has removed a very troublesome cause." In all probability Cut Up, also referred to in some contemporary writings as Split Lip, was none other than Umtippe.[27] Evidently Tiloukaikt took over the chieftainship of the band living in the vicinity of Waiilatpu before Umtippe died. Whitman, in his letter to Greene of November 11, 1841, mentions a brother of Umtippe, Waptash-tak-mahl, five times. This subchief of the Waiilatpu band of Indians, was also called Feathercap or Tamsucky.[28]

To the missionaries, the Indians acted like children in many respects. They were dutiful and obedient at times, and again petulent and threatening. In his letter to Greene of March 12, 1838, Whitman wrote that the Indians "were much more friendly & accommodating than last year, but still I need not tell you we have many perverse dispositions to encounter." The Cayuse men considered manual work to be beneath their dignity and were even fearful that the missionaries would make their children work if sent to school. "Gratitude," wrote Narcissa, "has no place in their hearts" [Letter 46]. On the other hand, she also told of their respect for the white man's property: "I have let my clothes remain out over night, feeling just as sale in doing it as I used to in Prattsburg" [Letter 40]. Later, however, the extent of the family wash became a controversial issue as the Indians looked with envious eyes upon what they considered an excessive amount of clothing owned by the Whitman household.

Eliza Spalding Born

Whitman's letter to Greene of March 12, 1838, and Narcissa's letter to her parents written two days later, tell of their visit during the previous November to the Spaldings at Lapwai when their baby girl was born. This was the first time that Narcissa and Eliza had seen each other after they had parted at Fort Walla Walla on November 22, 1836. Realizing that the Whitmans would be taking their eight-month-old daughter with them, Spalding sent three of his Indians with a "leather lodge" [i.e., a buffalo skin tepee], to Waiilatpu for their use. With that convenience, wrote Whitman, "we could have a fire at night & be secure from the weather although doomed to suffer some from smoke."

After boarding up the windows, locking the doors, and giving a trusted Hawaiian precise directions for the care of the animals, including the sheep, the Whitmans left for Lapwai on Tuesday noon, November 7, 1837. Whitman had a second Hawaiian man go with them. They traveled only ten miles the first afternoon which would have taken them a little beyond present day Walla Walla. The Whitmans felt "obliged to make all possible speed," as Narcissa explained, because of a late start. On Wednesday, the 8th, they rode nearly thirty miles and camped on the Touchet River, a tributary of the Walla Walla River, in the vicinity of what is now Dayton, Washington. They were following an old Indian trail which connected the Walla Walla Valley with the Clearwater. Lewis and Clark had gone that way in the spring of 1806 on their return trip to the States from their winter's camp south of what is now Astoria, Oregon.

Riding side-saddle while holding a lively child was no easy task for Narcissa and, no doubt, Marcus shared the responsibility part of the way. Narcissa wrote that they got very tired before they stopped to camp on Wednesday. It started raining that night and continued until noon the next day, so they moved only six miles on Thursday. When they awoke on Friday morning, they found two inches of snow on the ground. Whitman wrote: "We made a long day's ride & encamped on waters emptying into Snake River." This would have been the Tucannon River or its tributary, Pataha Creek. On Friday they encountered both snow and rain until two o'clock in the afternoon. On Saturday morning, after going over a high divide, the Whitmans arrived at Chief Timothy's lodge at Alpowa[29] Creek, where they found a note from Spalding urging them to press on with all possible speed. Timothy was one of Spalding's first converts and was without doubt the most faithful and sincere of native Christians.

Narcissa gives the following account of their experiences on Saturday, the 11th:

> We rode all day in the wind and rain and came to the Snake river about the middle of the afternoon and thought to stop, but it cleared away, and after making a fire and warming a little, we started again and came to the crossing place, and when the sun went down, it found me sitting by the root of a large tree on stones with my babe in my arms, watching by moonlight the movements in crossing our baggage and horses. This was the only piece of wood in sight and with a few bunches of wild sage, a fire was made against it to warm me while waiting to cross. Soon I was seated in a canoe with my babe and landed safely across [Letter 44].

The Whitmans were then at the confluence of the Snake and Clearwater Rivers, the site of present-day Lewiston, Idaho, and about twelve miles from Lapwai. Since the next day was Sunday and there was "a good moon," as Narcissa described it, they felt an urgency to keep traveling. After some deliberation, Narcissa claimed that she was "too much fatigued," so they camped for the night. On Sunday morning, the 12th, the Whitmans rode on to Lapwai, but left the Hawaiian and the three Indian helpers with the baggage and the other animals to follow on Monday morning. "It was with no common emotion," wrote Whitman, "that we met after a years absence & so far as Mrs. Spalding was concerned, the year was spent without seeing any civilized friends after Brother Gray left the December previous. We found Brother Spalding situated under better circumstances than we could expect from his single-handed situation" [Letter 43].

The Spalding baby, a girl, arrived on Wednesday morning, November 15. She was the first white child to have been born in what is now the State of Idaho and the first born of white American parents in Old Oregon who lived to maturity.[30] She was named Eliza after her mother. On Sunday, November 26, Spalding baptized his daughter and Alice Clarissa, and administered the sacrament of the Lord's Supper. Narcissa referred to this as "a blessing which we have not enjoyed since we sat at the table with our beloved friends in Angelica on the eve of our marriage." This was the first time that the missionaries had been able to use the silver communion set received from the East Liberty Presbyterian Church of Pittsburgh, Pennsylvania, while on their westward journey.[31]

Whitman reported to Greene: "We prolonged our visit for Mrs. Spalding's recovery, as in a former sickness she had a protracted and tedious recovery." Eliza had some difficulty in nursing her baby for lack of milk. "Little Alice Clarissa," wrote Narcissa, "has been very much favored; she has had enough to spare most of the time." The weather continued cold with snow on the ground. Narcissa felt appalled as she contemplated the long journey by horseback to Waiilatpu. It was so difficult under such conditions to care for a child still in the diaper stage. The Whitmans, therefore, decided to return by canoe, going down the Clearwater to the Snake, and thence down the Snake and the Columbia Rivers to Fort Walla Walla. A suitable dug-out canoe was made available, and Spalding induced some of his Indians to man the little boat. Whitman was impressed with the friendliness of the Nez Perces at Lapwai, whom he found much more cooperative than the Cayuses at Waiilatpu.

The Return Trip by Canoe

After turning their horses and some of their baggage over to the faithful Hawaiian and the three Indians who were to take the overland route back to Waiilatpu, the Whitmans with their little girl embarked in their log canoe on Saturday, December 2, for their return trip. They camped that night at the confluence of the Clearwater and the Snake Rivers. One wonders why they left the Spaldings on Saturday rather than waiting over another Sunday until Monday. The presence of a large encampment of Nez Perces at the mouth of the Clearwater might have been the reason. Whitman informed Greene that the Indians there were "very attentive to religious instruction as all the Indians do in this section."

The return trip took four and a half days, not counting the Sunday spent with the Indians. The river was low and navigation was dangerous in some places. Once they had to portage. "We had a tedious journey home," wrote Narcissa, "almost every night were obliged to clear away the snow to find a place to camp upon." They arrived at Fort Walla Walla on Thursday, December 7th, and after spending the night there, left for Waiilatpu the next morning. Narcissa wrote that Alice Clarissa "rode with her father all the way from Walla Walla (twenty-five miles) and we only stopped once to nurse and change her, which she did not relish quite so well as to be moving" [Letter 44]. No wonder the child objected; having a diaper changed out-of-doors in a snow storm was not a pleasant experience. "It was some time after dark before we reached home," wrote Narcissa, "and [we] were not a little rejoiced to see it again." To their relief, they found everything safe and in good condition.

The Whitmans had been gone from November 7 to December 8; it had taken the doctor a month to make one professional call. During the eleven-year history of the Oregon Mission, sixteen children were born to five of the six missionary wives.[32] With but few exceptions, Dr. Whitman was the attending physician. An inordinate amount of time was spent in making long horseback rides and in waiting for the babies to arrive. Mrs. Elkanah Walker gave birth to four children and Mrs. Cushing Eells to two while the two families lived at Tshimakain near present-day Spokane, Washington, about 140 miles from Waiilatpu. Whitman was present at four of these deliveries. On a fifth occasion he arrived a few days late; Mrs. Walker met him at the door with her baby in her arms.[33] The total distance covered on these five journeys was more than 1,400 miles, nearly one-half the distance across the United States, and the elapsed time in travel and in waiting amounted to about one hundred days.

The First Adobe House

When Whitman began building at Waiilatpu on October 14, 1836, he ambitiously planned a story-and-a-half building, 30 x 86 feet, similar in style to the salt-box house common in New England. As has been stated, he found it necessary to abandon work on what had been started and to concentrate on the erection of a lean-to on the west side of the house, which measured 12 x 36 feet. Just when Whitman was able to complete the construction of the main part of his house is not known, as there is a hiatus in the extant Whitman correspondence to the Board from May 5, 1837, to March 12, 1838. In his March 12 letter, Whitman mentioned some window sash which Spalding had made for him and which he evidently took back to Waiilatpu on his return trip from Lapwai in December 1837. Possibly the Whitmans moved into their enlarged quarters sometime during the early part of 1838.

Some incidental descriptions of the Whitman home are found in the writings of members of the 1838 reenforcement who arrived at Waiilatpu on August 29, 1838. Mrs. Cushing Eells commented: "Dr. W's house... is built of adobe... I can not describe its appearance as I can not compare it with anything I ever saw. There are doors and windows, but they are of the roughest kind; the boards being sawed by hand and put together by no carpenter, but by one who knew nothing about such work, as is evident from its appearance... The furniture is very primitive.[34] The bedsteads are boards nailed to the side of the house, sink fashion, then some blankets and husks made the bed; but it is good compared with traveling accommodations."[35] Mrs. Elkanah Walker mentions the house having "three large rooms, two bedrooms," but she does not indicate whether this included the three rooms in the lean-to. We have no accurate information regarding the floor plan of the main house.

In the latter part of December 1837, a warm wind (known in that region as a chinook) melted the snow on the Blue Mountains so rapidly and in such quantities that the Walla Walla River overflowed its banks. Narcissa tells what happened:

> On the eve of the 28th, the waters entered our cellar; the walls settled; the props gave way one after another; & for the whole night we were in the utmost anxiety, fearing the consequences

to our whole house. Soon after dark our men & Indians went to work dipping out the water & throwing earth against the walls & continued all night long. In great mercy to us our house was preserved to us standing, although the wall is materially injured... We were obliged for several days & nights in succession to keep the water bailed out.[36]

On May 8, 1838, Whitman reported another flooding: "A second rise in March has so far damaged my house that I shall be obliged to build again this summer as the present one will not answer to finish. I intend to build of dobies again with projecting roof & without a cellar[37] on a place where I think there is no danger." During the winter of 1837–38, Whitman sent the Hawaiians to the foothills of the Blue Mountains to saw some pine boards. With the prospect of building a new house on higher ground, the need for lumber was imperative.

The Whitman Household

A new house was needed also for an expanding family. Mention has been made of Maria Pambrun and the Indian girl, Sarah Hull, who were received into the Whitman home in the spring of 1837. Just how long Maria remained is not known. Sarah lived with the Whitmans until her death on August 11, 1838. Just where she stayed when the Whitmans made their trip to Lapwai in the late fall of 1837 is not known. Sarah quickly learned enough English to be of real assistance to Narcissa and perhaps she was able to help both of the Whitmans learn the Nez Perce language.

Following the Whitmans' return from Lapwai, Mungo Mevway, a lad twelve or thirteen years old, the son of an Hawaiian father and a native woman, was also received into the Whitman home. He had been sent by Dr. McLoughlin from Fort Vancouver [Letters 54 & 42c]. Mungo remained with the Whitmans until October 1841, when he went to live with the Walkers at Tshimakain. There, a year or so later, he married a Spokane girl. His name frequently appears in the writings of the missionaries.

Each of the three men whom the Whitmans met at the 1836 Rendezvous—Tom McKay, Joe Meek, and Jim Bridger—sent a half-breed daughter to live in the Whitman home and be educated. The first to be received was the teen-ager, Margaret McKay, who arrived at Waiilatpu during the winter of 1837–38. Narcissa wrote: "She is a good girl, for one who has had so few advantages, and renders me much assistance in my domestic labors." As will be told later, the Meek and Bridger girls came in 1840 and 1841.

Whitman had two single Hawaiians working for him from the fall of 1836 to the spring of 1838. Sometime in the spring of 1838, Charles Compo, the French Canadian mountain man, who had served as interpreter and guide for Samuel Parker, moved with his Nez Perce wife and infant son from Fort Walla Walla to Waiilatpu and entered Whitman's employ. Both of the Whitmans made favorable mention of him in their 1838 letters.

Writing to her sister, Mary Ann, on September 25, Narcissa said: "Charles Compo... came here and put himself under our protection, and went to cultivating land here, and assisting my husband in his cares. He is an excellent man, and we feel as if the Lord had sent him here. Husband left him in charge when he went to Mr. S's, having got all the crops in..." And in her letter to Mrs. Parker: "We have employed him to take charge of the farm, etc., and find him very faithful and trusty. His superior knowledge of the language makes him truly a helper in our work. He has been a regular attendant upon our family social and Sabbath worship" [Letter 52]. Compo, born in Canada, had been reared as a Roman Catholic. He evidently had some connection with either the Hudson's Bay Company or some American fur company before entering Parker's employ in 1835. There is no evidence to indicate where Compo and his family lived at Waiilatpu, perhaps in his own lodge.

From the very beginning of Waiilatpu, the Whitman mission virtually became a convalescent home or hospital. The Black, John Hinds, had accompanied the Whitman-Spalding party from the 1836 Rendezvous to Fort Walla Walla in order to get medical help from Dr. Whitman. He followed Whitman to Waiilatpu, where he died during the last week of November 1836. In Whitman's letter of March 12, 1838, he mentioned a sick half-breed boy whom Dr. McLoughlin had sent from Fort Vancouver for "medical aid."

On June 28, 1838, Joseph and Maria Maki arrived at Waiilatpu, both being members of the mission church in Honolulu. With them was a single Hawaiian, referred to as Jack, who worked for either the Whitmans or the Spaldings for several years. The Makies were the only

Hawaiian couple to be sent to the Oregon Mission; the others were single men. The Whitmans were delighted to have a married couple, who were Christians, in their home. "You cannot imagine," wrote Narcissa, "how it strengthened our hearts to hear them pray, notwithstanding we could not understand a single word" [Letter 54].

Joseph and Maria proved to be most dependable. Thus with their own baby; the four Indian or half-breed children; and four, or possibly five, Hawaiians; the Whitman household numbered eleven or twelve, not including the Compo family. Moreover, the Whitmans were confident that Gray would be returning that fall with a reenforcement. There was indeed a need for a larger house. Although Whitman, in his letter to Greene of May 8, 1838, mentioned his intention to rebuild on higher ground, little was actually done in this regard during the summer of 1838 with the possible exception of having some boards cut.

WILLIAM CAMERON MCKAY

During the first part of March 1838, Tom McKay, who was on his way to Fort Hall to get some furs from the Hudson's Bay Company, stopped at Waiilatpu to see his daughter, Margaret, and his friends, the Whitmans. With him were his three sons, William, John, and Alexander. McKay told the Whitmans of two other visitors who would be following him to Fort Walla Walla. The first was Dr. John McLoughlin who would be traveling with the Company's eastbound express to Montreal. From thence he expected to visit Boston and New York before sailing for England. Dr. McLoughlin was expected to arrive at Walla Walla the latter part of March. McKay, who wanted his son, William Cameron, 1824–1892, to be a physician, had made arrangements for him to accompany Dr. McLoughlin to Scotland, where relatives had promised to assist the lad financially in getting an education.

The second expected visitor would be the Rev. Jason Lee who, according to McKay, would probably arrive at Walla Walla the first part of April. Lee was going East by the overland route in order to get reenforcements for his mission. McKay had already made arrangements for Lee to take the two younger sons to the States and place them in Lee's Alma Mater, Wilbraham Academy, in Massachusetts.[38]

Tom McKay and his children were indirectly related to Dr. McLoughlin as the doctor had married Alexander McKay's widow,

Margaret, the mother of Tom. Margaret was a half-breed. Tom married a native woman; therefore his children had five-eighths Indian blood. Tom's son, William, had been one of those who witnessed the arrival of the Whitmans and Spaldings at Fort Vancouver on September 12, 1836, and no doubt was thrilled to see his step-grandfather welcome the white women to the fort. He and his brothers and sister had been in the school when Narcissa taught the children to sing some of her favorite religious songs.

On February 21, 1885, nearly fifty years later, Dr. W. C. McKay recalled: "When Dr. Whitman learned what the plans were for my future, he protested and earnestly urged my father to send me to the United States and make ëan American' of me. He said this country would certainly belong to the United States in a few years, and I would succeed better here if I was educated in the States, and became an American in thought and feeling." When McKay explained that he was financially unable to pay the costs of keeping three boys in eastern schools, Whitman offered to give "a draft on the missionary board which he represented and taking from my father the equivalent in property needed at the mission." [39]

Tom McKay had to make a critical decision there at Waiilatpu. Should his son go with Dr. McLoughlin to Scotland and become a Britisher in training and outlook, or go with Jason Lee to the States and become an American? Although the British Government did not officially assert any claim to the Oregon country to the south and east of the Columbia River after signing the joint Occupation Treaty with the United States in 1818; nevertheless the Hudson's Bay Company continued to look with longing eyes for many years on all of Old Oregon. Two of the Company's forts on the Columbia—Walla Walla and Colville—were on the east bank of the river and Fort Boise and Fort Hall were far in the interior of Old Oregon. By 1838 the Company, beginning to face realities, felt it wise to concentrate its efforts on retaining the area to the north and west of the Columbia River.

McKay, as a step-son of Dr. McLoughlin, would have been aware of the apprehension felt by his Company over the growing American influence in Oregon. As has been stated, it was he who, when he first saw Narcissa Whitman and Eliza Spalding at the 1836 Rendezvous, said: "There is something that Doct. McLoughlin cannot ship out of the country so easy." McKay finally accepted Whitman's reasoning and decided to send his son William to the academy connected with the Medical School at Fairfield, New York, where Whitman had studied. William was to be an American!

McKay took his three sons with him to Fort Hall. Jason Lee, who followed McKay, arrived at Fort Hall on June 12 and took the three boys with him to the States. After spending several years in the academy at Fairfield, William transferred to Geneva College where he was a student in 1841–42. He then followed one of his teachers to a new medical school at Willoughby, Ohio, where he apparently remained until he returned to Oregon in the latter part of 1843.

Tom McKay moved to the Willamette Valley in 1839 and threw his lot in with the Americans.[40] In this incident, in which we find Whitman urging Tom McKay to send his son to a school in the States to be educated, we see the first indication of Whitman's convictions regarding the future of Old Oregon. He was convinced that the lower Columbia River Valley was to be a part of the United States!

Dr. McLoughlin Visits Walla Walla

Dr. McLoughlin arrived at Fort Walla Walla on March 28, 1838, en route to London. Since he had been delayed in his travels, he sent advance word to the Whitmans, saying that he would be unable to go out to Waiilatpu and requesting that they meet him at the fort. A heavy rain on the morning of the 28th prevented Narcissa and her little girl from going, but Marcus made the trip and met with Dr. McLoughlin that evening.

Letters between Old Oregon and the States were carried by one of three routes: (1) by a voyage of nine months or more around South America via Honolulu; (2) by some trusted traveler who planned to cross to the States over the Oregon Trail, or (3) by the Hudson's Bay Company's express across Canada. The Company was cooperative in its willingness to carry mail, and both the Whitmans and the Spaldings took advantage of the opportunity to send letters with Dr. McLoughlin.[41]

Dr. McLoughlin had previously informed Whitman and Spalding of his hope to call at the headquarters of the American Board in Boston; therefore, Spalding wrote a letter of introduction to Secretary Greene on March 12, which Whitman also signed. They mentioned with deep appreciation the "numerous favors" extended to them by Dr. McLoughlin and others in the Hudson's Bay Company. On the same day, Whitman wrote to Greene: "We cannot speak too highly of his kindness to us since we have been in this country." Dr. McLoughlin replied on March 29, modestly stating: "You put too high a value on the little I have done."[42]

This exchange of letters indicates the good feeling which existed between the Company and the Whitmans and the Spaldings. Beginning in 1838, the Company's officials at Fort Vancouver began to doubt the designs of the Methodist missionaries in the Willamette Valley. They suspected them of wishing to engage in trade and to promote American colonization. Thus there was a growing coolness towards the Methodist missionaries not shown to those under the American Board.

Jason Lee Visits the Whitmans and the Spaldings

On Friday, April 13, 1838, the Rev. Jason Lee arrived at Fort Walla Walla on his way to the States to get reenforcements for the Methodist Mission in the Willamette Valley. The next day he rode out to Waiilatpu, where he met the Whitmans for the first time. He described their meeting in his diary: "Dr. Whitman met us and conducted us to the house. Mrs. Whitman met us at the door, and I soon found myself seated and engaged in earnest and familiar conversation as if we were old acquaintances."[43] On the following day, Sunday, the 15th, Lee preached to the Indians with Whitman interpreting. Chief Umtippe attended this service.

Lee was favorably impressed with the progress the Cayuse Indians had made in cultivating the land. On the 16th he noted in his diary: "Visited the In[dian]'s farms and was surprised that they had done so much in the absence of almost every tool necessary to do with. Some had two or three acres, wheat, peas, corn & potatoes." Of Lee's visit, Narcissa wrote: "Our visit with him has been a refreshing one. He is the first Christian brother that has visited us since Mr. Gray left last March, 1837."[44]

Lee left for Lapwai on Thursday, April 19, and spent the week-end with the Spaldings, whom he also met for the first time. More will be told of this visit in a subsequent chapter. Lee started back to Waiilatpu with Spalding on Monday morning, the 23rd, and for some reason the two felt the necessity of riding 140 miles to Fort Walla Walla in two days.

In a letter to his nephew, the Rev. Daniel Lee, dated from the fort on April 25, Lee commented: "Both the Kioose and the Nez Perces are doing a great deal in cultivation, the former with wooden ploughs with a little bit of iron nailed upon them, and hoes, and the latter with hoes alone. Some of the Nez Perces came to the Doctor's for potatoes to plant, a distance of 300 mil. [i.e., for the round trip]. I was astonished to see the industry of these Indians. The fact is they are starving, and they will be forced to work their land." [45]

Regarding his visit to Lapwai, Lee wrote: "They [i.e., the Nez Perces] expressed a great joy at seeing me, and several made very sensible speeches, and all seemed anxious to be taught. But still he [Spalding] has his troubles with them. The truth is they are *Indians*; though they are certainly superior to those upon the Willamette, and though his things are much exposed as they can be, they steal nothing from him."

Lee felt that Whitman and Spalding had been able to accomplish more in civilizing and evangelizing the Indians by having two stations than could have been possible if they had stayed together. Yet, he doubted the wisdom of the separation. "It was rather a rash measure," he wrote, "to put themselves so entirely into the hands of the Indians where there was no absolute necessity for it." Evidently Lee was not told the real reason for the separation.

"LET THEM FEEL THE LASH"

In his letter of April 25, 1838, to his nephew, Lee made the surprising statement: "Both Mr. W. & Mr. S. use highhanded measures with their people, and when they deserve it, let them feel the *lash*." [46] Lee was mistaken in believing that Whitman ever used or ordered the use of the whip, but was correct in stating that Spalding did. Whitman was a pacifist and consistently refrained from using force to discipline the natives. Not one reference to Whitman using the whip himself or ordering the chiefs to use it on the natives has been found, even in the statements of his critics.

Spalding's diary contains at least two references to Indians being whipped, evidently on his orders. On January 9, 1839, he wrote: "Williams wife left him last night." Williams was a mountain man who had been married by Spalding to a Nez Perce woman. She was so mistreated by her husband that she left him, but it was not Williams, but the woman who was punished. Spalding wrote: "Williams wife is whiped, 70 lashes. Indians come nigh whipping him."[47] The second diary entry is for August 19, 1841: "Cause three children to be whiped for stealing corn." Since Lee visited Lapwai in 1838, before the above entries were made, it seems evident that Spalding had been ordering offenders to be punished by the lash on earlier occasions.

Only one reference has been found of Spalding himself using the whip on an Indian and then he was forced to do so by other Nez Perces.[48] The very fact, however, that he consented to such humiliating punishment as that inflicted on the wife of Williams seems reprehensible. We should, however, place such incidents in the context of that generation.

In a country where there were no prisons or law-enforcing agencies, the white man adopted the lash as a quick and effective way to punish wrongdoers and to inculcate respect for the rights of others. Long before the missionaries settled among the Indians of Old Oregon, the Hudson's Bay Company had authorized the use of the lash on Indian offenders. In a letter to Greene dated May 5, 1837, Whitman wrote: "A system of punishment for crimes established by the traders has done much good."

Although Whitman did not specify that the Hudson's Bay Company approved the use of the lash, we do find evidence of this in a letter Dr. McLoughlin wrote to Spalding on November 28, 1837. Dr. McLoughlin was unhappy over the attitude of Ellis and Garry who, after their return from the Red River Mission school, said they had been taught that it was wrong to whip wrongdoers. McLoughlin wrote: "You see the return that Ellice is making us for the expense we have been upon him and you know how Garry has acted. When he came [back] he found that the chiefs were in the habit of flogging, at our suggesting, those who stole, &c., and by which in a great measure they had put a stop to those evil practices, and made their followers live more correctly than before. In the same way as Ellice, who told the Chiefs we misled them, that Mr. Johns[49] had told him it was wrong to flog on any account... and they consequently gave over [i.e., up] flogging and last year the Cayuse Chief told me that he now saw they were wrong in giving up flogging, as the young men would not attend to anything."[50] We therefore see that the Hudson's Bay Company and the Indians themselves were using the lash before the missionaries arrived. This throws new light on Lee's hasty statement that both Whitman and Spalding used "highhanded measures with their people."

The lash was commonly used at the Roman Catholic missions in California during the mission period as a means of enforcing discipline. Flogging was a common punishment in the United States Navy until it was abolished by Act of Congress on September 28, 1850. As will be mentioned later, Indian Agent Elijah White in the late fall of 1842 induced the Nez Perces and the Cayuses to accept a code of laws. Four of the eleven articles specifically listed a penalty of from twenty-five to fifty lashes for each offense.[51]

MADAME DORION

Among the visitors who called on the Whitmans in the spring of 1838 was Madame Dorion, the heroine of Washington Irving's *Astoria*. Of this visit Narcissa wrote: "Saturday [i.e., April 14] Mrs. Pambrun came with her three daughters, Maria, Ada, & Harriet, also two daughters & a son of an Iowa [Indian], the old woman spoken of in Washington Irving's *Astoria* (Perhaps Father has not seen the book, it contains a more just representation of this country than any other written previous.)[52] She is now the wife of a Frenchman now residing at the Fort. She was here with the rest & spent the Sabbath & left today. Mr. Lee arriving at Walla Walla on Friday came with them [Letter 46].

Pierre Dorion, with his wife and their two little boys, had been a member of a trapping party working along the Snake River in January 1814 when attacked by Indians. All of the men were killed. Madame Dorion managed to escape with her boys and two horses. She had a limited amount of provisions and a few buffalo robes and blankets. She fled into the Blue Mountains where alone, hundreds of miles from friends, she managed to keep herself and her children alive through the winter months. She killed the horses and smoked the meat. With their hides and the buffalo robes, she constructed a rude shelter. She had no guns, only knives. As soon as possible in the spring, she continued her journey towards the Columbia River and was found by some Walla Walla Indians who adopted her and the little boys into their tribe. This is the story to which Narcissa referred; it is told in more detail by Washington Irving.

Madame Dorion later married John Toupin, a French Canadian, who became the interpreter at Fort Walla Walla. In July 1841, Father A. M. A. Blanchet, one of the pioneer Roman Catholic missionaries to Old Oregon, blessed a relationship which had existed since 1824.

Narcissa's letters show that life at Waiilatpu was not dull; interesting guests were coming and going; Tom McKay and his four children, Madame Dorion and her three daughters, Jason Lee and the two Indian boys he was taking to the States, and Pierre Pambrun, his wife, and their children. These were but the forerunners of many more who, during the following years, were to visit the Whitman mission, some to spend months or even years there.

CHAPTER 11 ENDNOTES

1 *Kansas Historical Society Collections*, XIV:706; Hulbert, *O.P.*, VII: 10.

2 Drury, *Spalding*, p. 168.

3 HBC Arch., B/223/b/17.

4 Drury, *Spalding and Smith*, p. 329. On Oct. 13, 1936, in company with the late Dr. Arthur H. Limouze, Secretary of the Presbyterian Board of National Missions, I visited the site of Spalding's first home at Lapwai. We there found a shoot growing out of an old apple tree trunk, perhaps one that Spalding had planted, on which were some apples identified as the Gentian, a fall apple common in New York State a century ago.

5 Drury, *F.W.W.*, II:302, with reference to diary of Mrs. Elkanah Walker, Oct. 2, 1846, where she refers to receiving three apples from the Whitman orchard. She wrote: "They . . . are very nice."

6 Following the Whitman massacre of 1847, Spalding compiled an inventory of property lost or abandoned at Lapwai. This was published in Drury, *Spalding and Smith*, pp. 359 ff. A similar inventory was compiled for property lost or abandoned at Waiilatpu which appeared in Richardson, *The Whitman Mission*, pp. 149 ff.

7 Palmer, *Journal of Travels*, p. 57.

8 Victor, *Early Indian Wars of Oregon*, p. 211.

9 Richardson, *The Whitman Mission*, p. 153.

10 Drury, *Spalding*, p. 178. Although Spalding, in the inventory he compiled for Lapwai, listed thirty-one hogs, he made no mention of hogs in the similar inventory compiled for Waiilatpu. This was probably an oversight.

11 HBC Arch., B/223/b/17, letters of Dr. McLoughlin to Whitman of June 23 and August 3, 1837, and letter of September 27 to Spalding. *The Hawaiian Spectator, Vol. I (1838)*, p. 331, quotes from a letter of Dr. Whitman's for Oct. 5, 1837: "The donation of salt, by the King and his sister, gave us much satisfaction, as a token of respect for the servants of the Lord Jesus."

12 Drury, *Presbyterian Panorama*, pp. 57 ff. The Hawaiian Evangelical Association organized in 1853, took over the administration of the former activities of the American Board in the Islands.

13 For years Idaho ranked first among the states of the Union in the production of wool and mutton.

14 Drury, *Spalding*, pp. 269 & 315. W. D. Breckenridge, a member of the Wilkes Expedition, visited Lapwai in June 1841 and wrote in his journal for the 25th: "He [i.e., Spalding] showed me a Yewe that had 7 lambs in one year, viz: 2 in the early part of January, 3 in June, and 2 in Decr. Yewes breed with him twice every year. He showed me also 38 sheep the off spring of two Yewes in three years." *W.H.Q.*, XXII (Jan. 1931), p. 51.

15 Drury, *Spalding and Smith*, p. 320.

16 Whitman, in this letter, believed that the Pacific Northwest would become a great wool producing and manufacturing country. Here was an activity which the white men, and not the Indians, would control.

17 Drury, *Spalding and Smith*, p. 174.

18 *Ibid.*, p. 268.

19 Archaeological excavations at Waiilatpu indicate that double toilets or "back houses" were at the east end to the "T" of the main mission house. The excavations of the pits revealed a large number of artifacts, such as broken dishes, etc., which had been discarded there.

20 Drury, *Spalding and Smith*, pp. 265 and 359 give evidence that Spalding had chickens at Lapwai.

21 Drury, *F.W.W.*, II contains many references to the difficulties the missionaries at Tshimakain had raising chickens because of the tendency of the Indian dogs to kill them. See index in that volume.

22 Whitman, in this letter, refers to a former communication to Greene which he had written in the fall of 1837 in which he had given an account of his evangelistic work. Evidently this letter was lost in transit as it is not now in Coll. A.

23 Two dates have been given as to the time of Cayuse Halket's visit to his people. Wm. McKay in Boyd's *History of the Synod of Washington*, p. 231, suggested 1831. Tucker in *Rainbow in the North*, p. 74, more accurately gives 1834.

24 See Chapter One, fn. 29.

25 HBC Arch., B/223/b/18.f.9.

26 *Hawaiian Spectator*, I:332 quoting from an undated letter of Narcissa's but written before the end of 1837.

27 Brouillet, *House Document*, p. 18. Brouillet claimed that the mission site at Waiilatpu belonged to three chiefs: "Splitted Lip or Tomtipi [Umtippe], Red Cloak or Waptashtakamal, and Pilankaikt [Tiloukaikt]."

28 Hulbert, *O.P.*, VII:248, quoting from Whitman's letter of Nov. 11, 1841, identifies Waptashtakmahl with Feather Cap. Cannon, *Waiilatpu*, p. 103, states that Feathercap belonged to Tiloukaikt's camp and was also known as Tamsucky. The variety of names given to the same individual makes positive identification difficult.

29 Timothy named his camping site Halahpawit or Alpowa which means "Sabbath rest" in the Nez Perce tongue. The very name is evidence of Timothy's desire to keep Sunday as a day of rest. Alpowa is about twelve miles west of Lewiston, Idaho, on the road leading to Walla Walla.

30 Mrs. Eliza Spalding Warren died at Coeur d'Alene, Idaho, June 21, 1919.

31 See Chapter Seven, fn. 45.

32 See Drury, *F.W.W.*, I:22, for list of the children of the missionaries with their birthdays.

33 *Ibid.*, II:265. The baby was born Feb. 10, 1844. Dr. Whitman arrived on the 22nd. Rev. and Mrs. Elkanah Walker and the Rev. and Mrs. Cushing Eells were members of the 1838 reenforcement to the Oregon Mission.

34 Narcissa in a letter to her parents, April 11, 1838, told of Pambrun sending her a rocking chair, and also a little chair for her daughter.

35 Drury, *F.W.W.*, II: 116.

36 *Ibid.*, I:132. This quotation was not included when the rest of the letter was published in *T.O.P.A.*, 1891, pp. 101 ff. See below, fn. 44.

37 Archaeological excavations at Waiilatpu show that there was a cellar beneath one of the rooms in the long arm of the "T" shaped mission house.

38 Brosnan, *Jason Lee*, p. 107.

39 Dr. W. C. McKay's reminiscences appeared in Boyd, *History of the Synod of Washington*, pp. 280 ff., also in *T.O.P.A.*, 1889, 91 ff.

40 Larsell, "Development of Medical Education in the Pacific Northwest," *O.H.Q.*, XXVII (1926), 65 ff.; see also chapter on Tom McKay in Hafen, *Mountain Men*, VI: 259 ff.

41 Whitman, Letter 89, stated: "We write you twice & sometimes three times a year, once in the fall by the Islands & in the spring by Canada & by the American Rendezvous." In Letter 42c he wrote: "The American traders will not forward letters coming this way." Dr. McLoughlin, writing to Spalding on April 14, 1837, stated: "I am of opinion the Hudson's Bay Company would agree to bring any dispatches for you by the Express from Canada and for this your correspondents have only to send their letters (forty letters could come) to Hudson's Bay Company's office at Montreal, or rather Lachine." HBC Arch., 2/228/b/17.

42 Original in Coll. A.

43 *O.H.Q.*, XVII (1916), 417 ff. Lee, who had been at Fort Vancouver during the week before the Whitman-Spalding party arrived, had left to return to his station on Sept. 10th, not knowing that the American Board missionaries would arrive two days later.

44 About 1,400 words of this letter (No. 46) were omitted when it was published in *T.O.P.A.*, 1891, pp. 101 ff. Although the letter was dated April 11, 1838, it contains some entries under later dates.

45 Brosnan, *Jason Lee*, p. 95.

46 *Ibid.*

47 Drury, *Spalding and Smith*, pp. 173 & 252.

48 Brouillet, *House Document*, p. 20, quoting John Toupin who claimed that the Indians told Spalding: "Whip him, or if not, we will put you in his place and whip you."

49 A reference to the Rev. David T. Jones, one of the clergyman at the Red River Mission School when the Old Oregon Indian boys were there.

50 HBC Arch., B/223/b/18, fo. 9-9d.

51 See below, Chapter XVII, "Laws of the Nez Perces."

52 This work appeared in Philadelphia in 1836. Just how or when Narcissa got to read this book is not known.

[CHAPTER TWELVE]

JASON LEE AND OREGON COLONIZATION

Since both Great Britain and the United States laid claim to Old Oregon and were unable to agree as to the location of the boundary line, they signed a Treaty of Joint Occupancy on October 20, 1818, which was subject for reconsideration if an agreement had not been reached within ten years.[1] During the following twenty-eight years, 1818–1846, the two powers found themselves engaged in a contest for title. The main question was—where was the dividing line to be drawn? The Hudson's Bay Company, the unofficial arm of the British Government, wanted it at the Columbia River. The United States, having become aware by 1839 of the strategic and economic importance of Puget Sound for naval and commercial harbors, insisted upon a more northern line.

During these critical years, 1838–1846, the debate over the location of the boundary was carried on in many circles; in the British Parliament and in the halls of Congress; in diplomatic conferences and in the press; in the councils of the Hudson's Bay Company and in its Oregon trading posts; and especially after 1838 in the embryonic American settlements along the Willamette and Columbia Rivers. Both the Protestant and Roman Catholic missionaries in Old Oregon were drawn into the controversy.

A question which has perplexed scholars, who have studied the life of the Rev. Jason Lee, is whether he became more interested in colonizing the Willamette Valley with Americans than in evangelizing the natives. His interest in American colonization was linked with his desire to have the United States extend its jurisdiction over a large part of Old Oregon. After weighing the evidence, the historian H. H. Bancroft was convinced that after 1838 we must "regard Jason Lee less as a missionary than as an American colonizer." Cornelius Brosnan, an authority on Lee, took the opposite point of view; he insisted that the reenforcement sent out by the Methodist Missionary Society in 1839, consisting of fifty men, women, and children, "was not primarily a colonizing enterprise, but distinctly a missionary expedition." [2]

The question can be restated: Did Jason Lee ride East in 1838 to save Oregon for the United States, or was he primarily interested in securing a missionary reenforcement to assist in evangelizing and civilizing the rapidly diminishing tribes in the lower Columbia River basin? Instead of accepting the now discredited theory of Whitman riding East in 1842 to save Oregon, might it not be possible that Lee was the one who made such a ride in 1838? Let the facts speak for themselves.

LIEUTENANT WILLIAM A. SLACUM, U.S.N., VISITS OREGON

Our review of background events must begin with a Boston schoolteacher and Oregon enthusiast, Hall Jackson Kelley, who as early as 1829 founded a society to promote an American settlement in the disputed Columbia River country. He repeatedly presented memorials to Congress and made numerous appeals to prospective settlers, all for the purpose of insuring the extension of United States jurisdiction over a part of Old Oregon.

In 1833 Kelley started out for Oregon via New Orleans, Vera Cruz, thence across Mexico to San Diego, California. There he met and joined forces with an American trapper and explorer, Ewing Young.[3] These two, with sixteen men and a band of from eighty to one hundred horses, worked their way north into Oregon, arriving in the Willamette Valley in October 1834. Kelley called on the Lees at their mission near what is now Salem, Oregon.

Unfortunately for Kelley and Young, Governor José Figueroa of

California wrote to Dr. McLoughlin accusing the men of being horse thieves. The large band of horses which they drove into Oregon lent some credence to the report. On the basis of this information, McLoughlin gave the men a cool reception at Fort Vancouver and also refused to extend to them the privileges of trade. Later McLoughlin learned that the report sent by Governor Figueroa was false, but the damage had been done. Both Kelley and Young harbored a deep hostility against Dr. McLoughlin and the Hudson's Bay Company. Young settled in the Willamette Valley, but Kelley returned to the States in 1835.

When Kelley got back to Boston, he wrote an account of his visit to Oregon which was published in a government document.[4] Kelley claimed that the few American settlers in Oregon were suffering from the monopolistic practices of the Hudson's Bay Company. He was most critical of Dr. McLoughlin and claimed that the Company was flagrantly violating the terms of the 1818 Treaty of Joint Occupation.[5] This outburst against the Hudson's Bay Company only corroborated similar reports which had been coming to the attention of the United States Government.

President Andrew Jackson, who is remembered for his expansionist policies, directed John Forsyth, Secretary of State, to send someone to Oregon to investigate. Forsyth commissioned Lieut. William A. Slacum, then a purser in the U.S. Navy, "to proceed to the Northwest Coast of America and to the River Oregon [i.e., Columbia], by such means as he should find best, and there ascertain the truth of Kelley's story."[6]

Slacum began his journey on June 1, 1836. He crossed Mexico and after some delays was able to sail from La Paz on October 10 for Honolulu. Although Slacum might have secured passage to the Columbia River on a Hudson's Bay Company's vessel, he felt it wise to be independent. He chartered the American brig, *Loriot*, for $700.00 a month and set sail for Oregon on October 24 taking with him a small cargo of items for the Indian trade. When Slacum arrived at Fort Vancouver on January 2, 1837, he was politely received by Dr. McLoughlin, who naturally inquired as to the object of his visit. Since he had so little cargo, it was evident that his main objective in visiting Oregon was not trade. Slacum said that he was on a private fact-finding expedition. Dr. McLoughlin was not fooled. To him Slacum was a spy, a government agent of the United States.

For some thirty years after the return of the Lewis and Clark party from the Pacific Coast, the United States Government had remained strangely indifferent to its rights to the Old Oregon country. With the single exception of United States Commissioner, J. B. Provost, who visited Oregon in 1818 to receive back Fort George (Astoria), which had been sold to the British by the Americans in 1813 because of the War of 1812, Slacum was the first government official to visit the Pacific Northwest after Lewis and Clark.

Some of the early reports on Oregon indicated that the country was not favorable for colonization. Wilson P. Hunt, who had led the overland expedition to the Pacific Coast sponsored by John Jacob Astor in 1810–12, stated in a memorandum to a member of Congress, the Hon. Edward Bates, dated February 15, 1828: "The nature of the country on the N.W. coast is such as *forever* to prevent agriculture."[7] So Slacum was really sent on a mission of rediscovery.

Slacum remained at Fort Vancouver from January 2 to the 10th. McLoughlin cooperated fully in supplying information about the activities of the Company and its resources. Slacum then called on Jason Lee at its mission, near present-day Salem, Oregon, where he arrived on the 14th. Slacum spent about two weeks in the Willamette Valley, largely if not exclusively in Lee's company, and in his official report stated that he had called on all of the thirty American settlers.[8] He listened with sympathetic ears to the many complaints made by the Americans against the monopolistic practices of the Hudson's Bay Company. Especially objectionable was the refusal of the Company to sell cattle to the settlers even though the Company's herds at Fort Vancouver numbered over a thousand head. It was well known that cattle could be purchased in California for $3.00 a head.

Under the leadership of Lee, and with Slacum's enthusiastic backstage endorsement, a meeting of the settlers was held at Champoeg with forty-one present, including thirteen French Canadians, former servants of the Hudson's Bay Company. At that time[9] the Willamette Cattle Company was formed with all forty-one men signing the Articles of Agreement. Slacum offered to take a party to California on his ship to buy cattle which could then be driven into the Willamette Valley. Out of their meager financial resources, the settlers pledged $900.00. Jason Lee invested $400.00 for the Methodist Mission and Slacum added another $500.00, which probably came from some government funds placed at his disposal by President Jackson.[10] With a $1,800.00 on hand, the newly organized company expected to buy about six hundred head of Spanish cattle.

After Slacum had returned to Fort Vancouver and had told Dr. McLoughlin what the settlers had done, McLoughlin, much to Slacum's surprise, asked to be included in the project and contributed $900.00. This act of Dr. McLoughlin's indicates that he was not in sympathy with the Company's refusal to sell cattle, a policy which had been dictated by his superiors. Strange to say, Slacum made no mention of McLoughlin's contribution in his official report to Congress, thus revealing Slacum's bias against the Hudson's Bay Company.

Lee accompanied Slacum back to Fort Vancouver and conducted a farewell service for the departing cattlemen aboard the *Loriot* on January 21. The cattle drive was an outstanding success. Evidently some additional funds had been raised as about eight hundred head of cattle were purchased at $3.00 each and forty horses at $12.00 a head. The drive ended in mid-October. Nearly two hundred head of cattle were lost along the trail. These losses, together with other expenses, brought the final cost per head upon delivery in Oregon to $7.67. The success of this cattle drive of 1837 opened a new era in Oregon's history. It made the settlers, as far as cattle were concerned, independent of the Company's stranglehold on a basic element in Oregon's economy.

When Slacum returned to the States, he carried with him a petition, addressed to the United States Congress and signed by the American settlers in the Willamette Valley. The Americans begged that Congress would "recognize them in their helpless and defenceless state, and extend to them the protection of its laws, as being, or desiring to become citizens."[11] The last clause may have had reference to some French Canadians who had also signed with the Americans. This was the first of several petitions forwarded to Congress by Americans living in the Valley, each of which asked for the establishment of their government's jurisdiction in Oregon. Actually, any unilateral establishment of such an authority was not possible under the joint Occupation Treaty of 1818. The boundary issue had to be settled first.

The Oregon Boundary Issue

The location of the boundary which would separate that part of Old Oregon which would come under the jurisdiction of the United States from that which would be under the British flag, was becoming increasingly controversial by 1837. The British Government wanted the Columbia River to be the boundary. A variation of this proposal is to be found in a letter Governor Simpson wrote to Dr. McLoughlin on June 21, 1843, in which he suggested that the boundary start from the summit of the Rockies at the 49° parallel, continue south to the route followed by Lewis and Clark, then down the Clearwater, the Snake, and the Columbia Rivers to the Pacific Ocean.[12] Such a dividing line would have given to Great Britain a large slice of what is now northwestern Montana, all of the panhandle of what is now northern Idaho, and all but the southeastern corner of what is now Washington.

Slacum, as a Navy officer, was quick to see the strategic value of having Puget Sound as a part of the United States. "I beg leave to call your attention to the topography of 'Pugitt's sound'," he wrote in his report, "and urge, in the most earnest manner, that this point should never be abandoned. If the United States claim, as I hope they ever will, at least as far as 49 degrees north latitude, running due west from the 'Lake of the Woods,' on the above parallel, we shall take in Pugitt's Sound. In a military point of view, it is of the highest importance to the United States."[13]

Slacum also pointed out that it was the policy of the Hudson's Bay Company to encourage their retired servants to settle on the Cowlitz River "as it lies to the north of the Columbia." Slacum explained: "The reason he [i.e., McLoughlin] assigns is, that the north side of the Columbia River will belong to the Hudson's Bay Company." Feeling that such an attitude posed a threat to American rights, Slacum wrote: "If one side of the river is claimed, with the same propriety they might claim both sides." To Slacum, the establishment of the border at the 49° parallel was vital to the best interests of the United States of Puget Sound as providing harbors for the Navy and for commercial shipping. It was the only good harbor site along the whole Pacific Coast north of San Francisco Bay.

But how was that goal to be achieved? By war? That was unthinkable. The alternative was by diplomacy, but before diplomacy could be effective, there had to be a good bargaining base. To Slacum the trump card for the Americans would be the presence of a large colony of its citizens in Old Oregon.

Reasoning backwards from events which took place after Slacum left Oregon, we can conclude that Slacum convinced Lee of the importance of increasing the number of American citizens in Oregon. There was no other person so strategically situated as Lee to promote such a project. Judging by evidence, which will be given subsequently, Slacum assured Lee that the United States Government would subsidize the cost of chartering a ship to carry a company of settlers, who could be called missionaries, to Oregon.

Since such a move would arouse the suspicions of the British Government, Slacum no doubt stressed the need for secrecy. Instead of advertising the political advantages of having more Americans settle in the Willamette Valley, the emphasis could be placed on the missionary aspects. Those recruited could go out under the auspices of the Methodist Missionary Society. As to personnel, let the emphasis be on farmers, mechanics, and artisans, rather than on ordained men.

Bancroft, in his *Oregon* (p. 166), suggests that Lee might have been dreaming of being a colonizer for Oregon when he met Kelley late in 1834, but the evidence for this theory is not strong. "There can be little doubt," wrote Bancroft, "that the scheme took form on being encouraged by Slacum to look for the support of government in sustaining American supremacy south of the Columbia." No doubt Slacum urged Lee to return to the States with him in order to get the reenforcement as soon as possible. Lee, however, felt that he could not leave at that time. He had but three assistants—Daniel Lee, Cyrus Shepard, and Philip P. Edwards.[14] Lee may have assured Slacum that if a reenforcement for his mission arrived in 1837, he would leave for the States the following spring.

Arrival of Methodist Reenforcements

Two parties of Methodist missionaries reached Oregon in 1837, both having come by sea. The first with twelve persons arrived in May; the second with seven, the following September. The combined personnel included five men, seven women, and seven children. In the first group was Dr. Elijah P. White, the first physician to join the Willamette Mission. After serving for three years, because of serious difficulties with Jason Lee, Dr. White withdrew from the Methodist Mission and returned to the States. In the second reenforcement was the Rev. Henry Kirk White Perkins who, shortly after his arrival in Oregon, married Miss Elvira Johnson, a member of the first party. The couple was assigned to the Methodist station at The Dalles, also called Waskopum.

In Slacum's report to Congress, he stated that the total Indian population of the Willamette Valley was only 1,200, including the membership of five tribes. Slacum said that disease had "swept off no less than 5,000 to 6,000 souls" since 1829.[15] The Methodist reenforcements, including that which reached Oregon aboard the *Lausanne* in May 1840, brought the total number of men, women, and children sent out by the Methodist Missionary Society to about seventy-five, of which number fifty were adults. If the Indian population had remained constant and if all adults worked in the Willamette Valley, there would have been one adult missionary for every twenty-four natives! Actually, several stations were opened outside of the Valley, such as the one at The Dalles where there were more than a thousand Indians. But even so, the overconcentration of missionaries for so few natives, who were rapidly dying off, shows that the primary emphasis of the Methodists had become one of colonization and not Indian evangelization.

Lee Leaves for New York

After the arrival of the reenforcements of 1837, Lee felt that it would be possible for him to leave for the East in the spring of 1838. It is not known to what extent he shared with his colleagues any assurance given him by Slacum that the government would subsidize the chartering of a ship to carry a large reenforcement to Old Oregon. Contemporary Methodist records merely indicate that the Oregon missionaries felt a reenforcement was desired in order to reach untouched tribes and that laymen were needed to relieve ministers of secular duties.[16]

Before leaving for the States, Lee with the assistance of P. L. Edwards and David Leslie (a member of the second reenforcement), prepared a memorial to be submitted to Congress. This was the second appeal to be drawn up by residents of the Willamette Valley, the first having been carried East by Slacum. Lee called a meeting of the settlers for March 16, 1838, at the Methodist Mission when the memorial was presented for their approval.

The document adopted was another plea for the United States Government "to take formal and speedy possession" of Oregon. It did not specify where the boundary line was to be placed. The memorialists pointed out that the harmonious relationships then existing between the little colony of American settlers and the Hudson's Bay Company might not continue if the settlement increased in population. The Americans claimed that they were living in a land without law. They stressed the need for some official government authority in Oregon "to secure the execution of all laws affecting Indian trade and the intercourse of white men with the Indians." The memorial was signed by all nine male members of the Methodist Mission, eighteen American settlers, and nine French Canadians. Lee carried this memorial with him on his journey to the States.[17]

On March 26, 1838, Lee bade farewell to his wife[18] and associates and left for Fort Walla Walla. With him were P. L. Edwards, who had gone out to Oregon with the Lee party in 1834; F. Y. Young, who was returning to his home in the States;[19] and two Indian boys named Thomas Adams and William Brooks, whom he was taking with him as prime exhibits of the work of the Methodist Mission school.[20]

WHITMAN AND SPALDING REQUEST 220 ADDITIONAL WORKERS

On Saturday, April 14, 1838, the day after arriving at Fort Walla Walla, Lee rode out to Waiilatpu to see the Whitmans. There he remained for five days before starting for Lapwai. No records remain of the subjects that Whitman and Lee discussed, but it takes little imagination to fill in the general outline. Lee must have told Whitman about Slacum's visit and of his strong conviction that the final border must be at the 49° parallel in order to give Puget Sound to the United States. Neither Whitman nor Lee discussed the location of the border in any of their known writings, but it appears that both men were in agreement with Slacum's recommendations. Lee must have told Whitman about the promise of a government subsidy to charter a ship and probably also referred to some "Secret Service" fund mentioned by Slacum. We do know that Whitman in later correspondence referred to Lee's intention to charter a ship, and also then made mention of the availability of financial assistance from a "Secret Service" fund.

A main subject of conversation between Lee and Whitman must have been the former's desire to get a large reenforcement for his mission which would be the nucleus of an expanding American colony in the Willamette Valley. They must have agreed on the importance of the United States securing title to much of Old Oregon, and on the strategy for accomplishing this goal. The method was to secure the presence in Oregon of Americans—thousands of them—to outvote any residents who might be under the control of the Hudson's Bay Company when a provisional government would be established. This, Lee must have explained to Whitman, was the primary reason why he was going East. He wanted to persuade the Methodist Missionary Society to send out a colony of missionaries and, no doubt, he urged Whitman to write to the American Board and ask it to do likewise.

Whitman was not only a sympathetic but also an enthusiastic listener. Undoubtedly he told Lee of how, just a few weeks earlier, he had persuaded Tom McKay to send his son, William, to an American school rather than to one in Scotland because of his conviction that Oregon would surely belong to the United States. No doubt Whitman reminded Lee of the fact that he and Spalding had taken their wives over the Rockies. The overland gateway to Old Oregon had been opened for women; they did not have to be sent by sea around South America. In this respect, the United States, because of its proximity to Oregon, had a great advantage over Great Britain if the Oregon emigrants would take the overland route. With the exception of a few colonists entering Oregon from what is now western Canada, British subjects would have to take the long sea voyage around Cape Horn.

Having won full and sympathetic support for his plan from Whitman, Lee went to see Spalding. He arrived at Lapwai either late Friday evening, April 20, or early the next day. After explaining his plan to Spalding, Lee found him as enthusiastic about the desirability of securing American sovereignty over Oregon as Whitman had been. Spalding agreed that an appeal should be made to the American Board to send a colony of missionaries to the upper Columbia River Valley.

On Saturday, April 21, 1838, Spalding began what was evidently intended to be a joint letter from him and Whitman to the American Board, for he opened his letter by writing: "We, the undersigned... " After reviewing the length of their residence on the field, their acquaintance with the country, the promising outlook for work among other tribes, and the favorable reception which had been given them by the natives, Spalding then made the following amazing request: "To occupy these fields immediately, we ask as the least possible number which God & our conscience will admit us to name, for *30 ordained missionaries, 30 farmers, 30 school teachers, 10 physicians, & 10 mechanics, with their wives*.²¹ This meant a reenforcement of 220 adults!!!

As to the route such a reenforcement should take to go to Oregon, Spalding suggested that they go either by sea around Cape Horn "or the Mountain route, as you may think proper ... with all possible dispatch." In long involved sentences and with his characteristic flowery language, Spalding fortified his request with pious sentiments about the thousands who would "take their leave of this world & pass beyond the borders of hope, leaving the blood of their souls in the skirts of somebody, before the laborers can arrive on the ground..."

Regarding the expected return of Gray that fall, he wrote: "We expect that a good number of these laborers are now, or will be soon on their way with brother Gray." On that date, April 21, Gray with his bride, three other newly-wedded couples, and a single man were at Westport, Missouri, waiting for the American Fur Company's caravan to start for the Rendezvous.

Being completely ignorant of the fact that the United States had experienced a minor financial depression in 1837 which left the American Board with a debt of over $40,000.00, in spite of greatly curtailed activities, Spalding unrealistically suggested: "You have only to make the request known & the men & money are at your command at once." ²²

The total number of missionaries under appointment by the American Board in 1837 was 360.²³ Spalding was asking that this number be increased by two-thirds and all of the new appointees be sent to Old Oregon! Jason Lee had oversold his project!

As to where these new missionaries were to serve, Spalding listed tribes to the north of Lapwai including the Coeur d'Alenes, and others to the west as far as Puget's Sound, and then looking to the east and southeast, he mentioned the Snakes, the Bannocks, and the Utahs. The whole appeal of the letter was based on the importance of evangelizing the red men. Nothing was said of any political aspirations or of the Oregon boundary or of Lee's ambitious designs to establish a large American colony in the Willamette Valley.

THE REQUEST FOR SUPPLIES

This letter of April 21, 1838, included a long list of supplies which were then needed for Waiilatpu and Lapwai and possibly for some of the expected reenforcement of 1838. With the exception of some items needed to be given as compensation for Indian labor or for trade, the list was reasonable. Requested items of clothing included: "6 pr female shoes, No. 7; 6 pr. male shoes, No. 8, 9 & 10; and 12 palmleaf hats." [24] Household needs were: "2 cook stoves, 6 box stoves,... 12 candlesticks;" and an assortment of dishes and crockery as "4 doz dining plates," and other kinds of dishes in proportion, "1 doz chambers with covers," tools, kitchen utensils, knives, forks, spoons, lanterns, and kettles.

The request for two cook stoves indicates that both Narcissa and Eliza were still cooking over an open fire in a fireplace. When an archaeologist examined the soil where the Whitman house once stood, he found fragments of chinaware, "at least half of which is beautiful English pictorial ware—Spode, Staffordshire, Copeland and Garrett there was very little plain undecorated earthenware or utility china. What must have been the everyday ware had an attractive blue border." [25] Since Narcissa had no opportunity to go shopping for chinaware after leaving Fort Vancouver in the fall of 1836, such patterns must have been selected for herself by others from the stores at the Fort, or possibly secured by an order placed by the American Board through an English firm. It may be assumed that the Spaldings had similar dishes.

Supplies needed in their contacts with the Indians included: "Five hundred yards of striped or checked cotton for shirts to be made by native girls," and books and school supplies "for two English schools of 50 scholars each." Evidently, Spalding was still dreaming of teaching the natives the English language. Spalding also asked for machinery and tools for a blacksmith shop and a gristmill. Needed for the blacksmith shop were "several tons" of iron and steel. Spalding wanted to make hoes, hundreds of them, for the natives. A gristmill would have saved money for the missionaries, as they were paying $10.00 per hundred pounds of flour purchased from the Hudson's Bay Company. A gristmill could also have given encouragement to the Indians to raise wheat.

Spalding also requested "50 gross Indian awls" which were much desired by the natives in sewing their buckskin garments, but "50 gross" totaled 7,200 awls!

Another amazing request that Spalding made was for: "2,000 gunflints... 100 doz scalping knives," and for a quantity of powder and ammunition. The scalping knife was a utility tool used for many purposes, all perfectly legitimate. Greene honored most of the requests for supplies contained in this letter, but not for tons of iron and steel, the excessive number of awls, gunflints, scalping knives, and ammunition. Regarding the latter items, Greene wrote on March 31, 1839: "Our Committee have never... consented to send to any mission... [such items as] balls, powder, gunflints, scalping knives, etc., nor does it seem to me proper to send them [to you] to be used in trade with the Indians. Would you feel satisfied to see one tribe for some slight provocation, or perhaps in a war party got up for the sake of plunder, using the balls, powder, & flints which you sold them, upon their unhappy neighbors? What would be said of you & the cause of Christian missions, should it be known that you traded with the Indians in such articles as these?"[26] Undoubtedly Spalding was thinking more of the Indians' needs for the hunt for wild game than for war.

Whitman's Involvement

Spalding went with Lee on his return trip to Waiilatpu on Monday and Tuesday, April 23 and 24. We have no contemporary evidence to show just what Whitman thought of Spalding's extravagant request for 220 additional workers except a statement in his letter of May 8 to Greene: "I have had the pleasure of signing a joint letter to yourself prepared by Brother Spalding & of filling a blank with supplies..." Whitman added a request for "three hundred hoes & fifty ploughs." There is some mystery about Whitman's statement about "filling a blank with supplies." The original correspondence in the Board's archives in Boston shows that the letter of April 21, including the request for supplies, is in Spalding's handwriting.[27]

About two years later, when strained relationships existed between Whitman and Spalding, Whitman wrote to Greene repudiating the letter of April 21, 1838, which he had signed with Spalding. He stated: "I feel to regret the joint letter sent by Mr. Spalding & myself in 1838 as containing a forced view of things calculated to excite hopes not to be realized. This I have wished to avoid in all my correspondence. The letter was written in Mr. S's peculiar style for which I do not feel responsible [Letter 74]." Marshall, in his *Acquisition of Oregon* (II:36), accused Whitman of "playing the baby act" by trying to shift the blame for the letter to Spalding.

This joint letter of April 1838 has long puzzled students of the WhitmanSpalding story. The request for 220 additional workers seems altogether unreasonable for such a limited field as that part of Old Oregon not then occupied by the Methodists. Hulbert, in his *Overland to the Pacific* series (VI:302), called it "the notorious joint epistel written by the latter (i.e., Spalding) but signed by Dr. Whitman for some reasons unknown." In my *Marcus Whitman*, M.D. (p. 192), I advanced the theory that perhaps Whitman and Spalding, after learning of Lee's ambitious plans for a large reenforcement, had become envious; not wishing to let the Methodists outdo them, they asked for a reenforcement of 220 for their field. In support of such a view, one could quote from Whitman's letter to Greene of May 8, 1838: "I hope we may not be left unsupported while our Methodist brethren devise so liberal things..."

After reviewing the implications of Slacum's visit to Oregon and Lee's grandiose dreams of establishing a large American colony in the Willamette Valley in order to strengthen the claims of the United States for a large share of Old Oregon, we need no longer say that Whitman signed the joint letter for "some reasons unknown." It is reasonable to believe that he, along with Spalding, had been persuaded to petition the American Board to act in unison with the Methodist Society in sending out a colony of settlers, who could be called missionaries, for political as well as religious purposes. If the two missionary boards would work together, the claims of the United States Government to Old Oregon would be immeasurably enhanced. Since Lee agreed to carry the joint letter of April 21 to Boston with the hope that he might have a personal visit with Greene, Spalding wrote: "Revd. Jason Lee of the Willamette mission, who is the bearer of this, should he visit Boston, can give you more information in relation to this subject, than we can by writing." Here is the suggestion that both Spalding and Whitman felt it wise to refrain from writing about any political matters related to final settlement of the Oregon boundary. Lee was to supplement what had been written by a verbal report.

Neither Whitman nor Spalding added his name to the memorial Lee was carrying which had been signed by the Willamette Valley settlers on March 16, 1838, including all male members of the Methodist Mission. They may have felt that this was something which applied particularly to the residents of the Willamette Valley. Possibly they remembered the advice of Secretary Greene, given in his farewell instructions to them, not to become involved in secular or political affairs. After receiving the joint letter of April 21, Greene answered on October 17, 1838, saying in part: "It is not at all unlikely that a movement will be made by the Government of the United States for taking possession of the Oregon country, and establishing jurisdiction over it." This indicates that Greene had read between the lines of the letter that Spalding and Whitman had signed and also, possibly, that he had talked with Lee. Greene was fearful that if the United States did establish its jurisdiction over a part of Old Oregon, there would be a rush of "speculators & adventurers, making it a theatre for all kinds of wickedness, leading to the corruption and oppression of the Indian tribes beyond anything that has yet been seen on our borders." He strongly advised the two missionaries "from taking any political stand." [28]

DID THE METHODISTS RECEIVE A GOVERNMENT SUBSIDY?

There is evidence that when Jason Lee was at Waiilatpu and Lapwai, he fully expected to obtain a subsidy from the U.S. Government to help pay the cost of chartering a ship, and that the Methodist Missionary Society could be persuaded to recruit a colony of "missionaries." On May 8, four days before Lee left Waiilatpu to continue his eastward journey, Whitman wrote to Greene: "It is expected by him that the Methodists will send a *ship* directly to the Columbia River." [29] Notice those words— "a ship!" Here was news unknown at the time to the Methodist Missionary Society. How could Lee have been so certain that he would be returning by ship unless this was part of the promise made to him by Slacum?

The Hudson's Bay authorities at Fort Vancouver also heard rumors about Lee's expected return to Oregon with a shipload of colonists and merchandise. James Douglas, who was serving as Chief Factor at the Fort during the absence of Dr. McLoughlin, in a letter to the headquarters of the Company in London dated October 18, 1838, wrote: "I fear that the Methodists nourish secret views at variance with your interests. The Revd. Mr. Lee, their superintendent, returns this summer by the overland route to the United States to make arrangements for importing goods. A *vessel* is, therefore, expected in the course of next year freighted by the missionary society, solely or in part, with other adventurers who may be deceived by false hopes of gain." [30]

Here is the second reference to the probability of Lee returning with a company of "adventurers" in a ship. The date of the Douglas letter was several weeks before Jason Lee had an opportunity to meet with the Methodist Missionary Society and present his request for a large reenforcement and a ship. Douglas, sensitive to the exclusive trade privileges then being enjoyed by his Company, was more concerned with the threat of trade competition from the Methodists than with the effect that an enlarged American colony in Oregon might have on political issues.

Douglas also wrote: "It is difficult to anticipate their real intentions and perhaps unfair to question them, but I am naturally anxious about the designs of a body of men, who have the power of seriously injuring our business and whose conduct may justify suspicion. It is my opinion they will engage directly or indirectly in trade and their interference will be more detrimental to our interests than the efforts of the most active commercial body." He made it clear that his suspicions were directed only against the Methodists and not against Whitman and Spalding. "My remarks," he added, "apply solely to the Methodists and have no reference to the Calvinist missionaries, who voluntarily came forward and pledged themselves not to trade furs."

Lee arrived in New York on October 31, having traveled from the frontier by way of Chicago, Detroit, and possibly Boston. One of the Indian boys, Thomas Adams, became ill and had to be left with a kindly family in Illinois. Lee, the second Indian boy, and the three McKay boys, were in Utica, New York, on October 28. Since Fairfield Medical College and its preparatory academy were located about twenty-five miles from Utica, we have reason to believe that Lee took William McKay there and saw that he was properly enrolled. Possibly, Lee then continued on to Wilbraham, Massachusetts, where he left the other two McKay boys. He was then near Boston and perhaps felt it advisable to deliver the letters he had been carrying from Whitman and Spalding to Greene in person. If this assumption is correct, then Lee would have had an opportunity to explain why their missionaries had requested a reenforcement of 220 men and women for the Oregon Mission.

On March 21, 1839, Greene answered the Whitman–Spalding letter of April 21, 1838. "You are quite mistaken, Dear Brethren," he wrote, "when you assert in your letter that the Board have only to make their wants known, and funds & men will be furnished without delay, and only a short experiment in the situation in which the Committee are placed would have led you to seriously modify the language which you use on this point. The Committee have no such control over the churches; or the men or the funds of the Christian community..." As gently and yet as firmly as possible, Greene said that the Board would do what it could to send additional workers but that the expectations expressed in their letter were "too high."[31]

THE QUICK RESPONSE OF THE METHODIST SOCIETY

The promptness and generosity with which the Methodist Missionary Society responded to Lee's request for a large reenforcement for Oregon and a ship would be inexplicable if considered apart from Lee's political designs. Lee called on Dr. Nathan Bangs, Corresponding Secretary of the Missionary Society, in New York as soon as possible after his arrival in the city. Bangs was so impressed with the urgency of Lee's appeal that he called a special meeting of the Board of Managers of the Society for November 14. In a letter to Henry B. Brewer, who was a member of the Methodist reenforcement of 1839, Lee on November 21, 1838, wrote: "Mr. Slacum called on me and seemed very glad to see me."[32] Since Slacum was with Lee frequently during the following months, often appearing with him on public platforms when making appeals for men and money, it may not be idle speculation to suggest that he had been in touch with the Missionary Society before Lee arrived.

According to the minutes of the Board of Managers' meeting for November 14, the proposal of chartering a ship to carry a large reenforcement to Oregon was discussed. At that meeting Lee asked for twenty-six men; if they were married, it would mean a reenforcement of fifty-two adults. A second special meeting of the Board was held on November 21, just a week later, and still a third on December 6. After the November 21 meeting, Lee visited Washington, D.C., where he met several members of Congress including Senator Lewis F. Linn of Missouri and Representative Caleb Cushing of Massachusetts, both of whom were much interested in Oregon. Lee submitted his memorial to Cushing, who had it published, together with other documents, as *House Report, No. 101, 25th Congress, 3d Session.* Here is further evidence of Lee's involvement in politics.

At the December 6 meeting, the Methodist Board made an initial appropriation of $35,000 which was later increased by another $5,000. This totaled more than one-third of the Society's entire budget for one year. Such a relatively large appropriation stands out in sharp contrast to the $1,000 which the American Board had budgeted for its Oregon Mission for 1838.[33] At its December meeting the Methodists authorized the appointment of a reenforcement of thirty-four adults. Never before had any mission board in the United States appropriated so much money and authorized the appointment of so many missionaries for a single mission as this action by the Board of Managers of the Methodist Missionary Society. The fact that the Board held three special meetings in the late fall of 1838 and that it granted practically all of Lee's requests, indicates its recognition of the importance and urgency of Lee's appeal.

The inevitable publicity given to the sending of such a large reenforcement to Oregon raised questions and aroused criticism. Some people asked why so many were being sent to this mission when there were so few Indians in Oregon? Others boldly asked if this were not a colonizing scheme disguised as a missionary enterprise?

Secretary Bangs published an answer to such criticisms in the April 29, 1839, issue of the *Christian Advocate*, in which he declared: "We have nothing to do with planting a colony in Oregon. Our business is to send the Gospel to those who may be there, either now or hereafter, whether native or otherwise." Bang's answer is ambiguous. Although denying that the Methodist Church was sponsoring a colonizing project, yet he admitted that the large company of missionaries to be sent to Oregon would be ministering to settlers who were already there or who might arrive later.

The Lausanne Chartered

Arrangements were made with the P. J. Farnham Company of Boston early in 1839 for the chartering of the four hundred ton *Lausanne*, a three-masted sailing ship. The financial records of the Missionary Society show that the fare for each passenger over the age of fifteen for the nearly eightmonth voyage from New York to Oregon was $250.00, with a smaller sum for younger children. Freight was carried for $25.00 a ton. The *Lausanne* was gone for eighteen months before returning to her home port. The full amount paid to Farnham Company by the Missionary Society was $9,427.55, which seems a small sum for such a long voyage and for a ship with a crew of sixteen in addition to Captain Josiah Spaulding.[34]

Did the United States Government pay a subsidy directly to the shipping firm to supplement what was paid by the Methodist Missionary Society? The best evidence for the affirmative is the testimony of the Rev. Josiah L. Parrish, a member of the Lausanne party, who was interviewed by the historian, H. H. Bancroft, at Salem, Oregon, on July 15, 1878. Parrish testified: "I was told [later] but I knew nothing of it then... I understood after I had been to Oregon seven years [i.e., by 1847] that the Government paid Fry Farnham & Co. 50 dollars a head from the secret treasury... The Government had an eye to the settlement of the boundary question;... I have no doubt that the reinforcement was the settlement of the [boundary] issue."[35]

Bancroft, commenting on this testimony, stated: "Lee kept the secret, and so did those who gave him money, until the boundary question was settled between the United States and Great Britain." After the boundary was fixed at the 49th parallel in 1846, secrecy was no longer necessary; Parrish learned of the subsidy the following year, 1847. According to his figures, the shipping company would have received only $2,500.00 which, when added to the sum known to have been paid by the Methodist Society, still seems much too low for a ship of that size for a voyage of eighteen months.

Another estimate as to the amount of the subsidy supposedly paid is found in the testimony of the Rev. Harvey Kimball Hines, a younger brother of the Rev. Gustavus Hines who was one of the passengers on the *Lausanne*. In 1889, in his *Missionary History of the Pacific Northwest* (p. 201), H. K. Hines wrote: "Such was the impression made by Mr. Lee upon the

Congress, the President and his cabinet... that the government out of the 'secret service fund' assisted in its outfit and expenses to the amount of $5,000.00."

The references made by Parrish and Hines to a secret government fund recalls a similar statement found in one of Whitman's letters. On his return journey to Oregon, after a trip to Washington, D.C., and Boston, Whitman wrote to his brother-in-law, Jonas Galusha Prentiss, on May 28, 1843: "You will be the best judge what can be done & how far you can exert yourself in this matter & whether the *secret service fund* can be obtained. It is now decided in my mind that Oregon will be occupied by American citizens." Endeavors fail to find some record in government archives of such a fund at the time or of such a payment.[36]

The Lausanne Reenforcement

The *Lausanne* sailed from New York on October 10, 1839, with fifty or more members of the Methodist reenforcement for their Oregon Mission. Included were fourteen men, eighteen women, and at least eighteen children. We cannot be certain as to the exact number of children, as the contemporary records are vague. Also on board was Thomas Adams, the Indian boy, and a Presbyterian family—the Rev. and Mrs. S. Dibble and their children, appointees of the American Board, on their way to Honolulu. Among the passengers was Jason Lee's second wife, the former Miss Lucy Thompson, whom he had married the previous July 28.

Only six of the fourteen men, including Jason Lee, were listed as ministers. This does not include two who had been ordained but subsequently had turned to secular pursuits. One of the ministers had an M.D. degree. Among the other eight men were a doctor, two farmers, three carpenters, a blacksmith, and a business manager. The last was George Abernethy who in 1845 would become the first Provisional Governor of Oregon. Four of the five single women were listed as teachers, the sixth was a stewardess. A layman, David Carter, joined the party at Honolulu on April 11, 1840. The *Lausanne* arrived at Fort Vancouver on June 1 where the missionaries were given a cordial welcome by Dr. McLoughlin. A new era in Old Oregon's history began with the arrival of this large reenforcement.

REACTION OF THE HUDSON'S BAY COMPANY

Before Dr. McLoughlin left for England in the spring of 1838, he had encouraged retired servants of the Company to settle at Cowlitz Portage, where several thousand acres of land were available for cultivation. The site is near present-day Toledo, Washington. Since the Hudson's Bay Company was hoping that the Columbia River would ultimately be the border, it was to its advantage to have as many British settlers, including French Canadians, living north of the river as possible. When Sir George Simpson, the top official of the Company in Canada, and Dr. McLoughlin met with the Governor and Committee of the Company in London during the fall of 1838 and the following winter, it was decided to form a corporation, to be known as the Puget Sound Agricultural Company, which would be separate from the Hudson's Bay Company but with an interlocking directorate. The establishment of this Agricultural Company was designed to encourage the settlement of retired servants of the Hudson's Bay Company and other British citizens at the Cowlitz Portage.

When Simpson was on his return journey, he happened to be in New York on October 1, 1839, a few days before the *Lausanne* sailed. There he met Jason Lee and from him learned the size of the Methodist reenforcement. Lee also told him of the activities of the Oregon Provisional Emigration Society, which had been organized at Lynn, Massachusetts, on August 30, 1838, with the primary objective of promoting the emigration of Christian people to Oregon. Beginning in October 1838, the Society published a monthly magazine called *The Oregonian and Indian's Advocate*.[37] The editor repeatedly stressed the advantages of overland travel to the Oregon country as preferable to the long and dangerous sea voyage. The first issue told of Mrs. Whitman and Mrs. Spalding who, as "delicate females," had successfully crossed the Rockies. The June 1839 issue carried an advertisement calling for "two hundred men with whatever families they may have," to make the overland journey to Oregon. By the time the editor was preparing his July number, he had learned of the successful crossing of the Rockies by the four missionary wives who were part of the American Boards' 1838 reenforcement for its Oregon Mission. The editor drove home his argument: if missionary women could cross the Rockies on horseback in safety and comfort, could not "a large company of families, who would move more slowly [and] be better provided... pass from Missouri to Oregon?"[38]

Simpson's reaction to all that he heard and observed in New York was immediate. He looked upon the Methodist reenforcement about to sail on the *Lausanne* as a thinly disguised colonization project. The advertised intentions of the Oregon Provisional Emigration Society were disturbing. Simpson at once notified his superiors in London as to these new developments. On December 31, 1839, the Governor of the Hudson's Bay Company wrote to Dr. McLoughlin: "Governor Simpson, on his way home from Canada this season, saw Mr. Lee, the American missionary at New York on the 1st Oct., who informed him he was then on the eve of sailing for the Columbia River, with about thirty other missionaries and their families, in a vessel called the Lausanne, especially chartered by the Missionary Society of Boston,[39] for the purpose of conveying these people, but without any merchandise intended for trade with natives or others in that quarter."[40] Evidently Simpson had specifically inquired of Lee as to possible intentions of the Methodists to engage in trade.

The Governor's letter to McLoughlin continues:

> Mr. Lee further informed Mr. Simpson that a large party amounting to about 200 souls contemplated migrating from the State of Massachusetts next summer with the view of becoming settlers on the Wilhamet [Willamette] River. We doubt that so large a party will attempt this wild enterprise, but think it is possible many persons may be induced by the flattering reports given of the country to undertake the journey and although the influx of population may not be to the extent spoken of in public report, we are nevertheless apprehensive the settlement on the Wilhamet may be more rapid than desirable for the interests of the Fur Trade, especially so from the miscellaneous and restless character of the people who are likely to migrate thither.

Actually the plans of the Emigration Society to send a company of two hundred men with their families overland to Oregon in 1840 did not materialize, but the publicity that they gave to such a project may have contributed to the numbers who migrated in 1842 and following years. The possibility of a "miscellaneous and restless" people migrating to Oregon was alarming to the Hudson's Bay Company's officials in London. They shared Simpson's fears that if such a migration were realized and if these people combined with an enlarged Methodist colony in the Willamette Valley, the commercial privileges which the Company so long had enjoyed at Fort Vancouver would be imperiled. The Governor and Committee of the Hudson's Bay Company in London comforted themselves by looking upon any overland emigration of large numbers of people from the States to Oregon as a "wild enterprise," most unlikely ever to be realized. These officials failed to realize that after 1836 the Rocky Mountains were no longer the barrier to overland travel they had once seemed.

In addition to the economic threat posed by the Methodist reenforcement of 1839, the Governor and Committee of the Hudson's Bay Company recognized a political challenge. The Governor in his letter of December 31, 1839, to Dr. McLoughlin touched on this when he wrote: "With regard to Mr. Lee and his missionary Brethren, however much they may profess friendship and good will towards us, and notwithstanding the high eulogiums upon us for hospitality and kind offices, it is quite evident that they have promoted the present mania for emigration to the Columbia, which is likely to prove so troublesome and injurious to us; that they are influenced by other *objects of a political nature*, besides the moral and religious instruction of the natives and that they are employed as pioneers for the overflowing population of the New England States, who have it in view to repay us for our good offices by possessing themselves of the fruits of our labors, as soon as they may be in a condition to wrest them from us by main strength."

Whereas Douglas at Fort Vancouver had been concerned about the threat that Lee's proposed reenforcement might offer to the Company's fur trade, Simpson, with keener insight, saw the political implications in the enlargement of the American colony in the Willamette Valley. He communicated his anxiety to the Governor and Committee in Lendo who in turn warned Dr. McLoughlin. Steps had to be taken to offset the threatened American population superiority in Old Oregon. Fortunately for the Hudson's Bay Company, the formation of the Puget Sound Agricultural Company had been authorized late in 1838. Here was a channel through which the Methodist threat could be checked, at least to some degree.

The Governor's letter of December 31, 1839, to Dr. McLoughlin contains the following: "With the view that our Settlement on the Cowlitz may not become overawed by the presence of so large an assemblage of strangers and as a means of protection to the depot [i.e., Fort Vancouver] and trade, we have... directed Chief Factor Finlayson *to encourage migration of Settlers from the Red River Colony to the Columbia River,* and the facilitating such migration by making advances and affording passage to persons... who may feel disposed to proceed thither."[41]

Here is the background story of the migration of a colony of French Canadians, their Indian wives, and half-breed children which left Red River on June 1, 1841, for the Cowlitz Portage.

CHAPTER 12 ENDNOTES

1 Hunter Miller (ed.), *Treaties and Other International Acts of the United States*, Washington, D.C., 1931, p. 660, "Article III. It is agreed that any Country that may be claimed by either Party on the North West Coast of America, westward of the Stone Mountains shall . . . be free and open, for the term of ten Years from the date of the Signature of the present Convention . . ." This Treaty of Joint Occupancy was signed in London on October 20, 1818.

2 Bancroft, *Oregon*, I: 166; Brosnan, *Jason Lee*, p. 147.

3 Kenneth L. Holmes, *Ewing Young, Master Trapper*, Portland, Oregon, 1967, gives a fine biography of Young.

4 *Congressional Record, 25th Cong., 3d Session, House Report, 101*, 60.

5 Dr. McLoughlin resented Kelley's report and wrote: "He published a narrative of his voyage, in which, instead of being grateful for the kindness shown to him, he abused me, and falsely stated that I had been so alarmed with the dread that he would destroy the Hudson's Bay Company's trade that I kept a constant watch over him." McLoughlin mss., 2 and 4, Coll. B.

6 Bancroft, *Oregon*, I:100.

7 A copy of the Hunt memorandum is in Coll. A. Italics are in the original document. Negative reports were also submitted to Edward Bates by Gen. Wm. H. Ashley on Feb. 20 and 29, 1828. Coll. A. See Drury, "Negative Reports on Oregon," *Westerners Brand Book*, No. 13, Los Angeles Corral, pp. 192 ff.

8 Slacum's Report appeared in *Senate Exec. Doc. No. 24, 25th Congress, 2nd Session*, December 18, 1837.

9 Contemporary accounts of when the meeting was held to form the Cattle Company are confusing as to the exact date.

10 Brosnan, *Jason Lee*, p. 84.

11 Bancroft, *Oregon*, I:142.

12 HBC Arch., B/223/c.

13 See ante, fn. 8.

14 Brosnan, *Jason Lee*, p. 84. Edwards served for a time as treasurer of the Methodist Mission. He was one of the cattlemen who went to California in 1887.

15 Slacum's Report, p. 17.

16 Barclay, *History of Methodist Missions*, IV:220 ff.

17 Brosnan, *Jason Lee*, 220 ff., gives the text of the memorial with the list of signers.

18 Mrs. Lee died in childbirth on June 26, 1838. News of her death reached Lee at the Shawnee Mission on the Missouri frontier, Sept. 8.

19 See Appendix I for listing of Whitman letters 42e & 46a, to Young.

20 Both Indian lads had flattened heads and their appearance in the States caused quite a sensation. William Brooks died on May 29, 1839, in Illinois. Thomas Adams returned with the Methodist reenforcement on the *Lausanne* which arrived at Fort Vancouver on June 1, 1840.

21 Italics are the author's.

22 Hulbert, *O.P.*, VI:305.

23 See Drury, *Spalding*, p. 203, for details regarding the financial situation of the American Board in 1837-38.

24 Temperatures in the Lapwai Valley sometimes rise to 1100 or more in summertime. The Walla Walla region is somewhat cooler, but even there 100∞ is not uncommon.

25 Thomas R. Garth, "A Report on the Second Season's Excavations at Waillatpu," *P.N.Q.*, XL (Oct. 1949), pp. 306 ff.

26 Greene to Whitman & Spalding, Hulbert, *O.P.*, VII: 155.

27 See Drury, *Whitman*, p. 193, where on the basis of this statement, credit was given to Whitman for filling out the list for supplies. Whitman may have made such a list which was then copied by Spalding, as the document in Coll. A. is in Spalding's handwriting.

28 Hulbert, *O.P.*, VI:329.

29 Italics are the author's.

30 HBC Arch., B/223/b/20. Italics are the author's.

31 Hulbert, *O.P.*, VII: 133.

32 Original in Coll. W.S.H.S.

33 See circular addressed to Spalding from the American Board, June 23, 1837, Coll. W.

34 These figures were secured by the author from a personal examination of the financial records of the Methodist Missionary Society in New York in the summer of 1966. The volume containing the records of receipts for the years involved in this study was missing. The records of the Bureau of Customs, Record Group 36, National Archives, Washington, D.C., provided information about the crew of the *Lausanne*.

35 Bancroft ms., "Anecdotes of Intercourse with the Indians," Coll. B. Also, Bancroft, *Oregon*, I:177.

36 The Secret Service, as now known, began at the time of the Civil War. Search was made for the existence of some other secret government fund which could have aided the Methodist project in the contemporary records of the Departments of State, Treasury, War, and the Bureau of Indian Affairs, National Archives, Washington, D.C.

37 See Drury article, "The Oregonian and Indian's Advocate," *P.N.Q.*, LVI (Oct. 1965), pp. 159-167.

38 *Op. Cit.*, p. 164.

39 This letter was in error in saying that the headquarters of the Methodist Missionary Society was in Boston; it was in New York. The headquarters of the American Board was in Boston.

40 HBC Arch., B/223/c.

41 Italics are the author's.

[CHAPTER THIRTEEN]

A YEAR OF ADJUSTMENTS
1838–1839

The third year of the Oregon Mission of the American Board was filled with many trials and difficulties for the Whitmans. The experiences of that year ran the gamut of human emotions, from great joy to poignant sorrow. This was a year of painful but necessary adjustments to an ever changing scene.

The summer of 1838 passed swiftly for Marcus and Narcissa. A multitude of demands in the field, in the home, among the Indians, and even from distant neighbors called for their time and attention. Writing to her father on September 28, Narcissa said: "We have had our house full of company most all summer." The comment calls to mind the remark made by her mother when Narcissa was a young woman: "I wish Narcissa would not always have so much company." The time came during the fall of 1838 and the following winter when Narcissa harbored the same wish.

While Spalding was at Waiilatpu with Lee during the latter part of April, he implored Whitman to go to Lapwai to help build a log cabin on the bank of the Clearwater. Spalding's first cabin had been erected on Lapwai Creek about two miles from its mouth. For several reasons, this location had proved unsatisfactory. After listening to Spalding's pleas, Whitman consented to go. A new log cabin was erected at the mouth of Lapwai Creek, and thereafter Spalding referred to the place in his correspondence with the American Board as "Clearwater Mission." Spalding's associates in the Oregon Mission, however, continued to refer to it as Lapwai.[1] To avoid confusion, the author will hereafter refer to Spalding's second location as Lapwai.

Narcissa was unhappy that her husband went to Lapwai to help Spalding erect his log cabin when they needed a new house so badly at Waiilatpu. Writing to her sister, Mary Ann, on September 25, 1838, Narcissa said: "Mr. Spalding persuaded my husband to believe that he needed a house more than we did... He left here the first of June and was gone two weeks." During this time Narcissa was alone at Waiilatpu with the Compo family, possibly one or two Hawaiian single men, and the several half-breed children whom they had received into their home. This was the first of many times that Marcus was called away from Waiilatpu, for business or professional reasons. Usually Narcissa had some reliable person or persons to stay with her, but there were times when she was left alone with no adults except, perhaps, one or two Hawaiians.

During the last week of June, after Whitman had returned from Lapwai, Mr. and Mrs. Archibald McDonald, with four children all under eight years of age, called and spent a week with the Whitmans. McDonald, a Presbyterian, was in charge of Fort Colville from 1836 to 1843, and was friendly with the American Board missionaries, especially those of the 1838 reenforcement who settled at Tshimakian about seventy miles south of Colville. Mrs. McDonald, a half-breed, had been a student in the Red River Mission school and had a good command of English.[2] She had sent a gift of twelve pickled buffalo tongues to Narcissa in January 1838; these were considered a rare delicacy.

Narcissa made two visits to Fort Walla Walla during the summer of 1838, being called there by the illness of Mrs. Pambrun. No doubt she felt a special obligation to go, as Mrs. Pambrun had come to Waiilatpu at the time Alice Clarissa was born. During the first part of August, Dr. Whitman was called to the Methodist Mission at The Dalles, 140 miles distant, to see Mrs. H. K. W. Perkins, who was critically ill. This marked the beginning of the friendship of the Perkins couple with the Whitmans. During Whitman's absence from Waiilatpu, Sarah Hull, the Indian girl who had lived with the Whitmans for more than a year, died on August 11. "If ever I felt the presence of my husband necessary to sustain me," wrote Narcissa, "it was while passing through such a scene" [Letter 52]. During the latter part of August, the Rev. Daniel Lee, a nephew of Jason, called on the Whitmans.

First Mail from Home

On July 11, 1838, when Narcissa was with Mrs. Pambrun at Fort Walla Walla, the westward bound Hudson's Bay express arrived from Canada with letters for herself and her husband. For the first time since they had been married, twenty-seven months earlier, with the single exception of a letter received at Westport, Marcus and Narcissa got letters from home. "You know not with what feelings of inexpressible joy," wrote Narcissa to her sister Jane,"I received your letters dated January and August 1837." It is hard to understand why their loved ones did not write more often. Possibly, they were not sure as to how to address their letters and waited until they had first heard from Oregon. In a letter to her sister Mary Ann, dated September 25, 1838, Narcissa wrote: "You must recollect that three years must elapse from the time of your writing to receiving the answer, if sent by way of the Islands. You cannot be more anxious to hear from me than I am to hear from you." In this same letter, Narcissa expressed the hope that: "When the contemplated railroad over the Isthmus of Darien [i.e., Panama] shall be opened, which is expected within two or three years, communication will be more frequent." The proposed railroad across the Isthmus, however, was not opened until January 1855. If a letter were answered promptly, it usually took two years for a reply to be received; sometimes, as Narcissa indicated, it took three years. This means that Old Oregon was as remote in that day as the planet Mars is in this generation of space travel, if the prognostications of astroscientists are correct.

Financial Matters

As has been stated, the cost to the American Board of establishing its Oregon Mission amounted to about $6,000.00.[3] To this sum should be added the expenses incurred by Parker, Dunbar, and Allis who went out in 1834 to the Missouri frontier; the traveling expenses of Whitman and Parker in 1835; and Parker's expenses for 1836-37.[4] On March 27, 1838, Whitman made out his financial report covering the period after March 18, 1837. He acknowledged receipt of two boxes of goods, shipped from Boston on January 18, 1837, which contained bedding, books, paper, and other supplies. The letters of the missionaries contain occasional references to the arrival of "missionary barrels." These usually contained a miscellaneous assortment of items which were divided according to the needs of individual members of the mission, unless otherwise directed. The books in the boxes Whitman mentioned formed the nucleus of the mission library of which Spalding became librarian.[5]

Purchases from the Hudson's Bay Company were figured in English money. As has been stated, Greene informed Whitman that the Board had to pay $540.00 for every £100. Whitman, in his report of March 27, 1838, summarized his personal expenditures of £63-14-2½ as follows:[6]

Supplies, Clothing & Indian goods to pay for
    Provisions &c, &c, Transportation £29-1-1
Farming Utensils & Building Materials 11-5-9
Clothing &c for a Boy living with me...................... 3-14-1
Bill at Walla Walla for last years
    Seeds & provisions &c 5-8-9
Flour & Seeds & Hogs 10-3-6
One Half of Mr. Grays expenses in the
    Flat Head country & at Rendezvous 4-1-½

From this total, Whitman subtracted £9-19-4½ which was his share of a cash contribution made by the "Society of Honolulu" to the Oregon Mission. Spalding received a like amount. Whitman also reported: "The avails of the sale of salt contributed by the King and his sisters at Oahu (one half), the other being reported by Mr. Spalding £17-5-10." This indicates that King Kamehameha III and his royal sisters were among the contributors for the evangelization of the Oregon Indians. After subtracting these two cash gifts from Hawaii, Whitman found it necessary to draw upon the Board for £130-15-11 to meet his and Spalding's expenses for the year.

To this statement, Whitman added another charge of £58-3-10 to pay wages due the two Hawaiians who had worked for him from September 21, 1836, to June 1, 1838, at £17-0-0 each per annum, and £0-12-0 due some Indians for such services as carrying letters. When we total

Whitman's various expense accounts, we find that up to March 28, 1838, he had drawn upon the Board for £336-18-½. Thus the total cost of the Waiilatpu station was somewhat more than $1,800.00 for its first two years. This included cost of some building materials, wages for laborers, food supplies, Indian goods for trading, tools, some livestock as hogs, and transportation. Neither Whitman nor Spalding received a salary. Considering the fact that prices at Fort Vancouver were double what they were in the States and the high rate of exchange, we can conclude that the total cost to the Board of this station for two years was indeed very modest.

Letters from Secretary Greene

Not all of the letters that the Whitmans received on that memorable July 11, 1838, brought joy. Discouraging word came from Secretary Greene regarding an increasing debt which the American Board was carrying. In 1836, the Board received $176,232.15 but spent $210,407.54. The accumulated deficit then amounted to $38,866.57. This increased by another $2,500.00 in 1837, due in part to a minor financial depression felt in the States. The American Board found it necessary to cut expenses in order to balance the budget and on June 23, 1837, prepared a statement which was sent out to all of its missionaries. One of these circulars addressed to "Rev. H. H. Spalding & Associates" evidently arrived in the packet of letters received on July 11th.[7]

Three letters from Greene also arrived, dated July 6, August 2, and November 4, 1837.[8] Conservative as the expenses of the 1836 mission party had been, they brought dismay to the secretaries of the Board. In a handwritten postscript to the June 23 circular, Greene said: "...no more than one thousand dollars annually can be granted to your mission until you hear further from the Committee... You must permit me here to say that the expenses of your mission hitherto have much exceeded our anticipation... I write also a remark of Mr. Parker, which he made on being informed of the expenses of your outfit and journey, without expressing my opinion respecting its correctness: He remarked that he would pledge himself to outfit a mission of equal numbers, take them across the country, and sustain them in their work three years for the same amount, i.e., about $7,000. We were greatly surprised at your draft of £371 received by Mr. Hill[9] yesterday. It is quite impossible for us to go on meeting such drafts in present circumstances."

Greene urged Whitman to exercise extreme economy. "Your expenses as they stand in your accounts received," he wrote on August 3, "are much greater than anticipated, much beyond what can be allowed to the Mission in future years." What would Greene have written had he known that additional drafts totaling some $1,600.00 were then on their way from Oregon? And what did Whitman and Spalding say to each other when they read the circular of June 1837 and remembered their request of April 1838 for 220 additional workers?

Spalding wrote a long letter to Greene on September 10 in which he vigorously defended the expenditures that he and Whitman had made in order to make their stations self-supporting as soon as possible. The initial expenses were large, he admitted, but these included the costs of livestock, plows, mill machinery, tools, etc. He ventured to assert that he and Whitman could make their stations self-supporting within ten years.

Parker's boast that he could take a mission party of the same number across the country at a cost far below that spent by Whitman and Spalding irritated both men. In answer to that claim, Spalding passed on to Greene some reports of the unfavorable impression that Parker had made on the Hudson's Bay Company's officials.[10] Whitman, in accordance with his milder disposition, did not reply as quickly to Parker's criticisms as Spalding. Writing to Greene on October 30, Whitman said: "I think Brother Spalding & myself will find no difficulty in getting on with $1000 between us & taking that as a guide, the other Brethren [i.e., the members of the 1838 reenforcement] intend to govern themselves by it & not exceed $500 apiece [i.e., per family]." It was not until May 1839 that an incident occurred which moved Whitman to write to Greene to answer Parker's criticisms.

Before receiving the discouraging letters from Greene, Whitman and Spalding had sent a party of six Nez Perces with extra horses and provisions to Fort Hall to meet any possible reenforcement that Gray might be bringing back with him to Oregon. The letters from Greene received in July, however, caused such hopes to fade away. Writing to her sister, Jane, on September 18, after the arrival of the reenforcement, Narcissa explained: "Letters received from Mr. Greene caused our hearts to sink, and we gave up all hopes of a reenforcement very soon joining us." The Whitmans and Spaldings even doubted that Gray himself would be able to return.

The First Presbyterian Church of Oregon

Even before Dr. Whitman had been called to The Dalles to see Mrs. Perkins in her illness, the Whitmans and the Methodist missionaries stationed there had agreed through correspondence to "set aside Tues. eve of each week to pray for the descent of the Holy Spirit upon all the missions in Oregon." On Tuesday evening, July 24, a prayer meeting was held in the Whitman home with Compo and Mungo present. What Narcissa described as "a melting season" was experienced when Compo gave evidence of conversion [Letter 54]. Since the natives at Waiilatpu were then showing an increased interest in Christianity, the Whitmans decided that the time was ripe for a series of evangelistic or "protracted" meetings. Whitman, therefore, wrote to Spalding and urged him "to come & labour with us, & to organize a church, &c immediately." Perhaps also there was a lingering hope that Gray might return during the latter part of August with some associates. In that case, it would be well if the Spaldings were present.

The invitation met with a cordial response from the Spaldings. Although Spalding had made several trips away from Lapwai after they had settled there in the latter part of November 1836, and had been to Waiilatpu with Lee the previous May, his wife had never been away during that period of nearly two years. One problem was the safety of their little flock of eight sheep. Spalding decided that he could leave the premises in care of the Hawaiian, Jack, who had arrived the previous June to help him, but hesitated to give Jack the responsibility of caring for the precious sheep. He finally decided that he would have to take the sheep with them, all the way, 120 miles to Waiilatpu and back. With their eight-month old daughter, the Spaldings left Lapwai with some American milk cows and the sheep on Wednesday, August 8th. The sheep had to be ferried across the Snake River in canoes where Lewiston, Idaho, is now located, and perhaps across some of the smaller rivers such as the Tucannon. The Spaldings spent at least five days in making the journey, arriving at Waiilatpu on or before Monday, August 13th. It was about this time that Whitman returned from The Dalles.

Spalding began his meetings with the Indians on Tuesday, the 14th, and continued them through the following Sunday. By this time he had a sufficient command of the Nez Perce tongue so that the natives could understand him. Possibly Compo, who was present for these meetings, assisted as an interpreter. On Saturday, August 18, 1838, the Whitmans and the Spaldings met in the Whitman home and organized "The First Presbyterian Church in the Oregon Territory."[11] Actually, this was also the first Protestant church to be established on the whole Pacific Slope of what is now the United States, being prior to any similar organization formed by the Methodists in the Willamette Valley. Spalding, acting as clerk for the church, began a record book in which he noted: "H. H. Spalding was elected Pastor & Doct. Marcus Whitman Ruling Elder. Resolved that this church be governed on the Congregational plan, but attached to Bath Presbytery, N.Y." [12] Although Marcus Whitman carried with him his letter of transfer from the Presbyterian Church at Wheeler,[13] and Narcissa had a similar letter from her church in Angelica, Spalding made no reference to either of these documents when writing the report of the organization of the church. He did mention the fact that Joseph and Maria Maki brought letters of transfer from the mission church in Honolulu and on this evidence, they too became charter members of the First Presbyterian Church in the Oregon Territory.

"On the same day, viz 18 Aug.," wrote Spalding in the record book, "Charles Compo, formerly a Catholic, baptized by that church, declaring his disbelief in that faith & expressing a wish to unite with us, was examined & giving satisfactory evidence of being lately born into the Kingdom of Christ, was propounded for admission into the Church at some future time. Mr. Pambrun of Fort Walla Walla, a Catholic present, advised Compo to consider the matter before he left his own religion to join another." On the following day, a Sunday, Compo still declared his desire to join the church. Both Whitman and Spalding felt that first he should be married to the Nez Perce woman with whom he was living and who was the mother of his little boy. Compo willingly consented, and Spalding read the marriage service. He was then, as Spalding noted, "baptized & admitted to our little flock as the first fruit of our missionary labor in this country." Actually, having been baptized by a Catholic priest, there was no need for him to be rebaptized, as most Protestant churches, including the Presbyterian, recognize the validity of Catholic baptism. Spalding, evidently, was not informed on this subject. The little Compo boy, who was "about eighteen months old," was then baptized and given the name John. There is no record that Mrs. Compo joined the church.

On that same Sunday, the seven charter members of the First Presbyterian Church in the Oregon Territory partook of the sacrament of the Lord's Supper. The Rev. Daniel Lee was still at Waiilatpu and joined them at the table. The infant pioneer church had an ecumenical cast with four Presbyterians, two Congregationalists, and an ex-Roman Catholic banned together in a hybrid Presbyterian-Congregational form of government. The church was not only interdenominational, it was also interracial and international; four had come from New York State, two from Hawaii, and one from Frenchs-peaking Canada. Although Pambrun was present at the time the Lord's Supper was served, he was not invited to partake, as he was a Roman Catholic.[14]

THE REENFORCEMENT OF 1838

On Saturday evening, August 18, the very day the First Church of Oregon was organized, an Indian messenger arrived with the exciting news that Gray and his bride were only a couple of days ride away from Waillatpu. Following them was the American Board's reenforcement for its Oregon Mission consisting of three newly-wedded couples and a single man. With characteristic impulsiveness, Gray with his bride had left the other members of the party at Fort Boise on Wednesday, August 15, and by forced marches had pushed on ahead. They arrived at Waiilatpu on the following Tuesday evening, the 21st [Letter 50a].

Spalding was eager to return to Lapwai, as he was concerned about the safety of the premises there during his long absence. He had planned to start back on Monday, but now he felt it necessary to stay and greet the new arrivals. There would have to be a mission meeting. Many important decisions would have to be made. Should one or more new stations be opened? Where would nine extra people live during the corning winter? What new policies of missionary methods should be adopted? Whitman, appreciating the urgency of the situation which Spalding was facing, addressed a letter to "Revs. Walker, Eells & Smith" on August 22, in which he urged them to make all possible speed." Don't delay on account of the animals," he wrote, "but press on and if any are too weak to come, leave them with some of the Kayuses whom you will be likely to see... Do not fail to be here by Sabbath" [Letter 50a].

In this letter, Whitman quoted one of his favorite verses from the Bible. Referring to the joy that he, his wife, and the Spaldings experienced when the Grays arrived, Whitman wrote: "We felt like Paul when he met the brethren from Rome, 'We thanked God and took courage'." This was the same verse that Whitman had quoted in a letter to Narcissa's parents when he described the joy the mission party experienced when, after they had been in danger of missing the Fur Company's caravan, they finally caught up with it at Loup Fork on May 24, 1836 [Letter 24]. In each time of crisis, Whitman felt that they had been "signally blessed" of God. With the return of Gray and the addition of eight more workers, the outlook for the Oregon Mission was indeed bright.

While waiting for the reenforcement to arrive, the Whitmans and the Spaldings plied Gray with questions. Why did Ellis and two of the other Nez Perces return with their horses from the 1837 Rendezvous instead of accompanying Gray to the Missouri frontier? What about the outcome of his venture to drive a band of horses to the States where they would be sold and the money used to buy cattle? Gray told his story. He had started east from the 1837 Rendezvous on July 25 with a small band of horses, probably not more than fourteen, with six Indians including one Nez Perce, The Hat, in advance of the Fur Company's eastbound caravan. Later Whitman and Spalding learned that Jim Bridger and other mountain men had warned Gray that he was courting disaster by venturing to go through hostile Sioux country with so few in his party, but Gray refused to listen.[15]

Disaster overtook Gray on August 7 near Ash Hollow in what is now western Nebraska, when he and his party were attacked by Sioux Indians. All six of the Indians with Gray were killed, his horses stolen, and Gray narrowly escaped death when two bullets pierced his hat leaving a scalp wound. Through the intercession of a French trader who happened to be with the Sioux at the time, Gray's life was spared, and he was permitted to continue his journey.[16] Gray was later accused by the Flathead Indians and the mountain men of cowardice and of abandoning his companions in order to save his own life.

Gray confessed that Secretary Greene was greatly displeased when he learned of his unauthorized return. He told the Whitmans and the Spaldings that he had spent part of the winter of 1837–38 as a student at the Medical College at Fairfield, New York.[17] He also reported that the Board's financial situation had so improved by the spring of 1838 that it felt able to authorize Gray to return to Oregon with a reenforcement.

Personnel of the 1838 Reenforcement

As soon as he was able after his return to the States, Gray called on the young lady to whom he was engaged. According to one report, his fiancée's mother noticed the four bullet holes in his hat and made inquiry as to the cause. Gray told them of the Sioux attack at Ash Hollow and how he had barely escaped with his life, whereupon the mother immediately declared that she could not allow her daughter "to venture upon such a dangerous journey as a trip to the Columbia Valley would be."[18] So the engagement was abruptly terminated.

Early in February 1838, a few weeks before Gray planned to leave for Oregon, he called on Samuel Parker at Ithaca, New York. Since Gray at that time had no prospects of marriage, Parker told him about a young lady in the Dutch Reformed Church of that city, Miss Mary Augusta Dix, 1810–1881, who would make an ideal wife for him. According to a family tradition, William and Mary first met at a church social held in Ithaca on Wednesday evening, February 14. Having already been told much about Mary by Parker, and perhaps by others, William proposed marriage that evening. This was too sudden for Mary who asked for time to think it over. By this time Gray was as anxious to be married and on his way to Oregon as Whitman had been two years earlier. Mary gave her consent on February 20, and they were married on Sunday evening, the 25th. The next day they left for Oregon. For the second time, Parker had played the role of a matchmaker for a couple who were to become members of the Oregon Mission of the American Board.

It so happened that the Board had appointed two clergymen, the Rev. Elkanah Walker, 1805–1877, and the Rev. Cushing Eells, 1810–1893, as missionaries to the Zulus in Africa, but because of a tribal war they were unable to go to that field. Learning that they were willing to have their destination changed to Oregon, the Board authorized them to go with Gray on his return journey. Walker and Eells were married on the same day, March 5, 1838, on the eve of their departure for Oregon; Walker to Miss Mary Richardson, 1811–1897, at Baldwin, Maine, and Eells to Miss Myra Fairbanks, 1805–1878, at Holden, Massachusetts. The two couples met for the first time on Saturday, March 17, when a farewell service was held for them in New York City. They were joined on the following Monday by the Rev. Asa Bowen Smith, 1809–1886, and his bride, née Sarah Gilbert White, 1813–1855.

Asa Bowen Smith

Since the Rev. Asa B. Smith was to become such a troublemaker in the Oregon Mission, special attention should be paid to his background. He and Sarah had become engaged in the fall of 1836 about the time that Asa received an appointment from the American Board with the expectation of being sent to Siam. By advice of the Board, the two postponed their marriage until the way was clear for them to leave for their assigned field. There were many delays including the effects of the financial depression of 1837. Harassed by financial problems, frustrated over the repeated postponement of his departure date for Siam, and eager to be married, Asa was ready to go anywhere if the Board would only give its approval. Psychologically, he was conditioned to make a quick and impulsive decision.

As a faithful reader of the *Missionary Herald*, Asa knew of the establishment of the Oregon Mission in 1836. He had read the lengthy and enthusiastic reports taken from Spalding's letters which appeared in several issues of the *Herald* beginning with July 1837. The October number carried about six thousand words from a letter Spalding had written to Greene on September 20, 1836, and the December issue devoted five pages to extracts from Spalding's letter of February 17, 1837. These letters overflowed with optimism regarding the enthusiastic reception given the missionaries by the natives and the cordial attitude of the Hudson's Bay Company. Spalding was eloquent with both tongue and pen and in these letters his tendency to exaggerate found full expression. To judge by these reports, the whole Nez Perce nation was on the verge of accepting Christianity. Asa Smith found the letters exciting. He decided that Oregon was the field in which he would like to serve.

Smith, despairing that the Board would ever send him to Siam, addressed an inquiry to Greene during the first part of January 1838 about the possibility of going to Oregon. Greene replied on January 15 stating that the Board had authorized the sending of only two ordained men to that field with Gray. Smith waited for about six weeks. He then went to Boston in early March to have a personal interview with Greene. Again he urged the Board to appoint him. He was told that it was rather late for him to join the reenforcement as the Grays were already on their way to the Missouri frontier, and the Walkers and the Eellses were to be in New York for a farewell service on March 18. Smith showed such eagerness to be included that he was told he would be appointed if he could get married and be in New York by the 18th.

The evident need for quick decisions was breathtaking. Asa was back in Sarah's home at West Brookfield, Massachusetts, by March 10. He found Sarah much interested, but she wanted a few days to think about this sudden development. Two days later, Asa wrote again to the Board saying that they had decided to go, and asking for final confirmation of their appointment. Greene's letter confirming their selection arrived on the 14th. Asa and Sarah were married the next day and left at once for New York City. Not wishing to travel on Sunday, even when faced with an emergency, they stayed over in New Haven and continued their journey to New York on Monday, the 19th. They were one day too late for the farewell service, but were in time to join the other two couples when they started for Westport the next day.

It is interesting to note that the three men who became focal points of dissension and controversy within the Oregon Mission—Spalding, Gray, and Smith—each made a spur-of-the-moment decision. Spalding and his wife had been on their way to the Osage Mission when Whitman caught up with them at Howard, New York, and persuaded them to accept a change of destination. Gray had not asked for an appointment until February 17, 1836, and by the time he was notified that he could go, had settled his affairs, and made preparations for the journey, the Spaldings and the Whitmans were some twelve days in advance of him. Perhaps no couple went through such a period of turmoil when such life-shaping decisions had to be made in so short a time as the Smiths. Yet this was not of the Board's choosing, but rather due to the impulsiveness and impatience of Smith. He was so eager to be appointed to some mission field so that he could get married and enter upon his life's chosen work that he was incapable of a balanced judgment.

Cornelius Rogers

The seventh and last member of the 1838 mission party was Cornelius Rogers who likewise made a sudden decision to be a missionary in Old Oregon. When the three couples were in Cincinnati, March 29–April 4, they met Rogers who was then twenty-two years old and unmarried. He was a member of the Second Presbyterian Church of which Dr. Lyman Beecher was pastor. Not waiting for any official appointment from the American Board, Rogers decided to join the reenforcement on a volunteer basis. Even after his arrival in Oregon, Rogers remained on an unofficial basis for about two and a half years, or until he left for the Willamette Valley in May 1841.[19] He was a likeable, well-mannered young man who caused no trouble within the mission. Including Rogers, the personnel of the American Board's Oregon Mission grew to thirteen. It was never any larger. Of this number the Whitmans, the Spaldings, the Grays, and Rogers were Presbyterians; the other three couples were Congregationalists.

"A Strange Company of Missionaries"

The three couples and Rogers arrived at Liberty, Missouri, on April 15 where they met the Grays for the first time. The united party had about a week at Liberty to complete their arrangements for the long trek to Waiilatpu. They left on April 23 and joined the American Fur Company's caravan on the 28th. Their livestock included twenty-five horses and mules, and nine head of cattle including two milk cows. They took a light wagon with them as far as Fort Laramie where it was abandoned. In general the members of the 1838 reenforcement endured all of the hardships and privations experienced by those of the Whitman-Spalding party two years earlier. The four women rode side-saddle as Narcissa Whitman and Eliza Spalding had done.

The four-month close association on the Oregon Trail, beginning at Liberty and continuing across the plains, the mountains, and the desert to Oregon, was a most trying experience for all members of the reenforcement. The physical hardships inseparable from their mode of travel, combined with serious clashes of personalities, created deep animosities which later disrupted the life of the Oregon Mission. As will be told, the Whitmans and the Spaldings were unavoidably drawn into the unhappy dissensions which began while the mission party was still at Liberty Missouri.

Since Gray had been to Oregon and back and since he was the one who was largely responsible for the American Board's decision to send a reenforcement that year to Oregon, it was logical that he should have considered himself to be in charge. The responsibility inflated his ego. An evidence of this is found in the fact that soon after the arrival of the three couples and Rogers at Westport, Gray informed them that he was to be called "Dr. Gray." This claim to the title of Doctor was based on the fact that he had attended medical lectures for a few weeks at the College of Physicians and Surgeons at Fairfield, New York, during the winter of 1837-38; however, he had not taken enough work to be licensed to practice medicine. Mary Walker, in her very personal and revealing diary, made several references to him as "Doctor Gray." Shortly after the reenforcement arrived at Waiilatpu and Whitman learned of this, he quickly eliminated the use of the title.

Gray had been listed in the *Annual Reports* of the American Board for 1836, 1837, and 1838 as a mechanic. The 1839 *Report*, however, listed him as "Doctor Gray," no doubt at his request. Whitman was irritated when this came to his attention. On October 22, 1839, he wrote to Greene: "I cannot conceive how you have been so much imposed upon to report him a Physician. What can a man learn in sixteen weeks of public lectures (which is barely all he can boast) to entitle him to that distinction?" The Board thereafter listed Gray as "Mechanic and Teacher."

Much of the trouble which Gray had with his associates arose out of the fact that he was too parsimonious in the purchase of supplies and in the hiring of assistants. In his eagerness to induce the Board to send out a reenforcement in 1838, Gray claimed that he could take a party of ten through to Old Oregon for $3,000.00. Having committed himself to a policy of strict economy, Gray felt obliged to maintain it even though this meant privations and extra work for his associates. For instance, the mission party of 1836 had had two hired men and three Nez Perces to assist with the animals and with packing and unpacking. Gray, with a party almost twice the size, hired only two men. This meant that the five men of the 1838 reenforcement, three of whom were clergymen, had to endure much physical labor in addition to taking their turns with the men of the caravan standing guard at night. Smith, in a letter to Greene dated April 29, 1839, complained: "I have not indeed worked my passage on board a vessel to a foreign port, but I can say in truth, I worked my passage across the Rocky Mountains."

Although Smith had been assured by Greene that he and his bride would have the sole use of a small tent while crossing the country, such was not the case.[20] Gray, remembering how the five members of the 1836 party shared their one tent, refused to buy enough canvass at Westport to make four small tents, to give one to each newly wedded couple. Instead only two tents were made, each measuring 8 x 10 feet. This permitted each couple to have a bed four feet wide, seven feet long, and with three feet at one end for storage space. A sheet was hung in the center to separate the two beds. The Smiths shared their tent with the Walkers, and the Grays and the Eellses were together. The Smiths and the Walkers especially found the arrangement very unsatisfactory. Smith complained about it in one of his letters to Greene, and Mary Walker made mention of it in her diary. Both Cushing and Myra Eells were of the uncomplaining kind; they made no mention of the inconvenience; nor, of course, did the Grays.

On April 27, only four days after the mission party started on their overland journey, Mary wrote in the privacy of her diary: "Some of the company feel disposed to murmur against Moses [i.e., Gray]." Undoubtedly the complainant was Smith. The 1838 party had been gone from the frontier less than two weeks when Smith wished he had never started, but there was no turning back then. Mary Walker penned another caustic sentiment on May 6: "Some of our company expressed regret that they have undertaken the journey. I suspect more from aversion to the toil than real dread of sin." By May 27, personnel animosities were so sharp that Mary wrote: "We have a strange company of Missionaries. Scarcely one who is not intolerable on some account."[21]

The Rendezvous of 1838 was held at the junction of the Popo Agie and Wind Rivers on the east side of the Continental Divide, near present-day Riverton, Wyoming. While there, Smith on July 10 unburdened himself in a letter to Greene:"What I am now to write I whisper in your ear, but would not say it to the world. We have not found Mr. Gray such a man as we hoped to find. I presume you are already aware, & I should judge so from the letters he read from you at Independence, that he is not judicious in all his movements. He is rash & inconsiderate & not at all calculated properly to fill the station he now does. He has assumed a great deal of authority over us, & talked to us in a very harsh & unbecoming, & I may say abusive, manner, regardless of the feelings of others, even of the ladies. This has often rendered our situation very unpleasant." [22]

At the Rendezvous the mission party met Jason Lee who showed Gray the joint letter of Whitman and Spalding of April 21, 1838, in which they had asked for 220 additional missionaries. Even Gray was surprised at the magnitude of the request. Writing to Greene on July 10 from the Rendezvous, Gray said that he thought Whitman and Spalding "were somewhat premature in forwarding it, at least till they had heard something farther from yourself or from Me."[23]

On Thursday, July 12, the mission party took leave of the caravan of the American Fur Company and joined a party of about twenty men of the Hudson's Bay Company under the command of Francis Ermatinger who was to escort them to Fort Hall. The missionaries rode through South Pass on July 15, thus bringing the number of white women who rode horseback over the Rockies to six. This fact, when made known through the public press in the States, further increased interest in the possibilities of emigration to Old Oregon.

Upon their arrival at Fort Hall on July 17, the missionaries were heartened to find a party of six Nez Perces with horses and provisions waiting there for them. This was an indication that Whitman and Spalding were expecting Gray to return that year with a reenforcement. By this time the members of the reenforcement were discussing various possibilities for their future locations. In a letter to her parents, Mary Walker wrote: "Mr. Walker is expecting to settle with Dr. Whitman. Dr. Gray [sic] among the Flatheads, Mr. Smith & Eells, I know not where, but unless some one should like Mr. S. better than at present, he will have to settle alone. He is as successful in gaining universal ill will as Mr. Walker good."[24] Here is evidence that by this time Gray was dreaming of establishing a separate station and that neither of the other two couples was willing to live with the Smiths.

This was the "strange company of missionaries," as Mary Walker described the reenforcement, which the Whitmans and the Spaldings were waiting to welcome with such high expectations. For two years, these two couples had worked together in harmony, but with the arrival of the 1838 reenforcement, things were to be different. Of course, when the Grays arrived at Waiilatpu on August 21, they probably said little or nothing about the personality clashes which had been engendered along the way. For a short time the Whitmans and the Spaldings were overjoyed with the prospects of an enlarged mission. They soon became disillusioned as they were made aware of the personality conflicts which existed within the reenforcement.

Introducing Captain John A. Sutter

John A. Sutter of Switzerland, who was on his way to California, traveled with the Fur Company's caravan to the Rendezvous, and then with the mission party after it left that place. Mary Walker mentioned him several times in her diary. Eager for the members of the mission party to arrive at Waiilatpu as soon as possible, Whitman sent a second note to them on August 28, urging them to press forward with all possible speed [Letter 50b]. He sent fresh horses and suggested that the Indians follow with the packs. Having been informed by Gray that Captain Sutter was with the party, Whitman wrote: "Please give our compliments to Capt. Sutur & invite him to come on with you & let his packs come slowly with yours."

In a letter dated from Fort Vancouver on October 18, 1838, Douglas informed the officials of his Company in London that: "A party of Calvinist missionaries and Captain Sutter, a Swiss gentleman, with a suite of 8 men travelled with our people from rendezvous to Fort Hall; from whence they took the lead to the Columbia." According to Douglas, Sutter "draws his title from a commission formerly held in the French Army, and has no connection whatever with the United States Government." [25]

On Saturday, August 25, as the missionaries were crossing the Blue Mountains, a baby girl was born to the Nez Perce wife of James Conner, a mountain man who had been hired by Gray at the Rendezvous to assist in the packing. According to an entry in Mary's diary for that day, the Indian woman was able to resume riding within a few hours after giving birth. On August 27, Rogers was thrown from his horse and received an injury which further delayed the travelers. The Smiths volunteered to stay with him while the Walkers and the Eellses with the Sutter party pushed on ahead.

On Wednesday, the 29th, the two couples with Sutter rode thirty miles in seven hours and arrived at Waiilatpu at 2:00 p.m. They were warmly greeted by the Whitmans and the Spaldings. The Grays were absent because they had gone to Fort Walla Walla. Mary wrote in her diary: "We were feasted on melons, pumpkin pies & milk. Capt. Sutor was with us. Just as we were sitting down to eat melons, the house became thronged with Indians & we were obliged to suspend eating & shake hands with some 30, 40, or 50 of them. Towards night we partook of a fine dinner of vegetables, salt salmon, bread, butter, cream &c. Thus our long toilsome journey at length came to a close."

The next day the Smiths, Rogers, and the Conners arrived with the baggage. Also on that day, the Grays returned from Fort Walla Walla. Thus, for the first and only time in the history of the Oregon Mission, all thirteen members were together. Just when Captain Sutter left for Fort Vancouver is not known, evidently shortly after his arrival at Waiilatpu. Before saying goodbye to his missionary friends, he gave his leatherbound French-English and English-French pocket dictionary to the Walkers. On the flyleaf of this volume, now on display at the Whitman Mission National Historic Site, is the following inscription in Mary Walker's handwriting: "Elkanah Walker. Presented by Capt. Sutor who crossed the plains with our party in 1838. He gave us this book as a parting memo when we parted at Dr. Marcus Whitman's mission among the Cayuses in Oregon. He afterwards settled in Sacramento, Ca. & was the first to discover gold in Cal. in 1848. He died in June, 1880. His funeral was in Washington, D.C. M.R.W.".[26]

THE FIRST MISSION MEETING

The members of the reenforcement spent Friday, August 31, in unpacking, paying off the hired men, and getting settled. Before the reenforcement arrived, the Whitmans had thirteen living with them, either in their adobe house or in Indian lodges on the grounds. This included the three Spaldings, the three Compos, the two Hawaiians, Margaret McKay, Mungo Mevway, a sick half-breed boy (Xavier Foier), and two Indian helpers. With the three Whitmans, this made sixteen. Then suddenly the Whitmans had to provide accommodations for the nine members of the reenforcement plus the three Conners, thus bringing the total to twenty-eight. Since the total area of the house, including the lean-to, was about 1,500 square feet, this meant that some would have had to sleep in tents or Indian lodges. Possibly some sleeping accommodations had been arranged in the halfstory of the main section of the house for the children. All cooking was done over an open fire in the fireplace of the leanto with the exception, perhaps, of that done out-of-doors by the native wives of Compo and Conner.

Because Spalding was becoming increasingly eager to be on his way back to Lapwai, the first business meeting of the enlarged Oregon Mission began on Saturday morning and, after the Sunday intermission, continued through Monday. Spalding served as moderator and Walker, clerk.[27] Rogers had not received a commission from the Board; hence he was not invited to take part in the deliberations. Neither were the women. On a few rare occasions in following years, some of the women were invited to attend the official meetings of the Mission, but even then they were not permitted to take part in the discussions or to vote. It was a man's world. There is evidence, however, that a husband often voiced his wife's opinions.

The first and most important question which confronted the six men was the assignment of the reenforcement. Gray wanted to open a new station among the Spokane Indians, then sometimes called Flatheads.[28] However, it was the unanimous judgment of the other five men that Gray was not qualified to do independent missionary work. Spalding, in a letter to Greene, October 15, 1842, stated: "At the first meeting after Mr. Gray and his party arrived, the three clergymen who accompanied him said respectively and decidedly they would not be associated with Mr. Gray." After a lengthy and sometimes heated debate, which surprised Whitman, the majority voted that Walker and Eells would be assigned to the Spokane field. The question then arose, where was the unhappy Gray to be sent? Finally, Spalding agreed to let the Grays live at Lapwai.

The next perplexing decision which had to be made was the assignment of the Smiths. Eells and Walker made it clear that they did not want them at the Flathead station. Spalding had already consented to take the Grays. Since it was clearly impossible for the Smiths and the Grays to live in the same station; therefore, by elimination, the Smiths would have to live with the Whitmans at Waiilatpu. This compromise settlement, accepted at the first Annual Meeting of the Oregon Mission, was to give rise to four years of growing dissension. Gray was never happy with the decision affecting him and repeatedly tried to gain permission during the following years to start a new station. And, as we shall see, Smith, likewise unhappy and ill-adjusted, withdrew to Kamiah in the summer of 1839.

Other actions taken at this business meeting included the following: (1) That all members of the mission apply themselves to the study of the language of the place where they lived and reduce it to writing; (2) That the natives be taught primarily in their own language, but as far as possible they should also be taught some English; (3) That the offer of a printing press by the Hawaiian Mission be accepted; (4) That a corn and gristmill and a blacksmith shop be established at Lapwai; and finally (5) That Dr. Whitman go to Fort Vancouver for supplies. Nothing was said as to where Rogers was to live. Evidently, he could go where he pleased. It was also agreed, although not so recorded in the minutes, that Walker and Eells should leave soon for the Spokane country to select a site for their station, and that a new and larger house was to be erected at Waiilatpu.

On Sunday, September 2, all business was laid aside, and the day was spent in rest and worship. Services were conducted by Spalding for the natives. All nine of the incoming party joined the Mission Church, raising its membership to sixteen. Walker was asked to deliver the sermon. He chose John 15:8 for his text: "Herein is my Father glorified." The very words suggest the outline of his thought. They had left their comfortable homes in the States and had endured the hardships and perils of a long journey across the country, not for personal glory but for the glory of God. The sacrament of the Lord's Supper was served, after which Spalding explained to a group of curious Indians, who were watching the proceedings, the meaning of the service. After the meeting was over, Mary Walker wrote in her diary:"We had an interesting & I think a happy season, notwithstanding all the hardness that has existed among us."

THE COLUMBIA MATERNAL ASSOCIATION

On Monday, September 8, while the six men were still in their business meeting, the six missionary wives met and organized the Columbia [River] Maternal Association, which has the distinction of having been the first club organized by American women west of the Rockies. It was modelled after similar organizations quite common at that time in the East and could be likened to various forms of mother's clubs of our own generation.

The original record book, now in the archives of Whitman College, shows that Eliza Spalding was elected president; Narcissa Whitman, corresponding secretary; Mary Gray, recording secretary; and Mary Walker, vicepresident. The records begin with the following statement of objectives in Mary Gray's handwriting:[29]

Sensible of the evils that beset the young mind especially in a Heathen land, & confident that no arm but God's can secure our children or those committed to our care, from the dangers that surround them, to bring them early into the fold of Christ & fit them for usefulness here & glory hereafter, we the subscribers agree to form ourselves into an Association for the purpose of adopting such [methods] as are best calculated to assist us in the right performance of our Maternal duties.

At that time only Narcissa and Eliza were mothers but Mary Walker was in the sixth month of her pregnancy and Mary Gray, who gave birth to a son on the following March 20, had reason to believe that she also was pregnant.

Even the women of the mission had their disagreements. It appears that soon after the arrival of the reenforcement at Waiilatpu, Mary Gray was questioned by Narcissa. Regarding this, Mary on February 23, 1839, wrote from Lapwai to Mary Walker who was then at Waiilatpu:"The second day after our arrival at W[aiilatpu], Mrs. Whitman in conversation with me commenced questioning me relative to my situation. I evaded her first question but she continued her questions until I could no longer evade them without hurting her with rudeness. This I was unwilling to do, & supposing I might place some confidence in her, told her some circumstances but she drew her own conclusions. I told her I wished her to keep her views to herself—for I felt uncertain—she said she must tell her husband—to this I made no reply, for I supposed it would be of no avail, but thought he as a physician would feel it out of place to publish such things—but I found that my favors were soon spread abroad, and how could it come but through Mrs. W.?"[30] The report of Mary's pregnancy was soon known throughout the mission, to her great embarrassment.

On February 22, 1839, following the visit of the Whitmans and Eellses at Lapwai, Spalding wrote in his diary:"Mrs. Whitman & Mrs. Gray do not succeed in settling their difficulties. Mr. Gray in all probability was the first person that made known the fact in this country that his wife was pregnant, but wishes to make himself & wife think that Mrs. Whitman pumped the secret out of Mrs. Gray & then communicated it to Mrs. Spalding & she to me, whereas Mr. Gray communicated the fact to me long before. A very little matter to cause such a difficulty."[31]

In the spring before the arrival of the 1838 reenforcement, Narcissa and Eliza had agreed to observe a certain hour each day in prayer for each other and their little daughters. Eliza in her diary for March 28 and 29, 1838, wrote:"I have received a note from Mrs. Whitman this evening in which she informs me that she has fixed upon the half past eight or nine o'clock in the morning of each day to be observed by us as a season of special and united prayer... Resolved, to observe daily at nine in the morning, a season of reading some select portion of scripture & prayer, in unison with Mrs. Whitman, to seek divine assistance in discharging the responsible duties of mothers & for the early conversion of our children."

Never again after that initial organization meeting were all of the charter members of the Columbia Maternal Association able to meet together at the same time. The women, following the example of Narcissa and Eliza, agreed to observe"the second & last Wednesday of every month" as a Maternal Association meeting, each in her respective station even though she might be alone at the time. Mary Walker kept the fullest diary of any of the missionaries for the full mission period. One has but to look through this remarkable document for the entries for the designated Wednesdays to see with what regularity she observed the days. Sometimes she met with her neighbor, Myra Eells, in their lonely station at Tshimakain, and sometimes she was alone.[32]

Narcissa was active in securing subscriptions for the *Mother's Magazine*, the national journal of the movement, not only from the women of the Oregon Mission but also from the wives of the officials of the Hudson's Bay Company and from women who lived in the Willamette Valley. The archives of the American Board contain two orders for subscriptions sent by Narcissa for *Mother's Magazine* and for the *Youth's Companion* in 1843 and 1845. The 1846 volume of the former published a letter from Narcissa dated April 16, 1846. The minutes of the Maternal Association show that during the nine years of its existence, the membership increased to thirteen, including the wives of the five independent missionaries who arrived in Old Oregon in 1839 and 1840 and the native wives of two Company officials, Archibald McDonald and Archibald McKinlay. The names of twenty-seven children are listed, including fourteen of the sixteen born to the women of the Oregon Mission during the years 1837–47 inclusive.[33] The minutes also record the deaths of several of the children. These records are undoubtedly the first vital statistics kept in Old Oregon.

Departures and Arrivals

On Tuesday morning, September 4, 1838, the Spaldings with their cows and sheep, the Grays, and the Conners left for Lapwai. Spaiding had hired Conner to work for him through the coming winter. Compo also accompanied the party to help with the packing and the care of the animals.

The six Nez Perces, who had taken supplies to Fort Hall for the reenforcement, preceded the Spalding party back to Lapwai. They carried the news of the disaster which had overtaken Gray and his party at Ash Hollow where The Hat had been killed. They also reported that the horses, owned by the Nez Perces, which Gray had driven east with the hope of exchanging them for cattle, had been stolen. Hence, Gray was returning with no cattle. This news angered the formerly friendly Nez Perces. They blamed Gray for the death of one of their number and for the loss of their horses. Spalding was also censured as the Indians felt that he had encouraged Gray in his project.

Evidently Spalding and Gray had a bitter confrontation with some of the most belligerent of the Nez Perces as reflected in an entry in Mary Walker's diary for September 20:"In the afternoon letter from Mr. S. informing that they were in trouble. Dick [Possibly Jack, the Hawaiian] & Conner so alarmed they can neither eat nor sleep. He [i.e., Spalding] does not dare part with Compo." In order to appease the anger of the Nez Perces, Spalding had to give them some of his precious cows.[34] Although the incident was evidently temporary in character, it was a harbinger of more trouble which both Whitman and Spalding were to have with the Indians. When Rogers heard of the trouble at Lapwai, he left on September 20 for that place to be of any assistance possible.

Mission Site at Tshimakain Selected

On September 10, Walker and Eells left for the Spokane country to select a mission site. The two men reached the ford on the south bank of the Spokane River on Friday evening, the 14th, where they met a number of Spokane Indians. With the aid of someone who could interpret to a limited degree, Eells read from his New Testament. "They seemed to know what it was," wrote Walker,"and said that Garry had read the same. While he was reading, tears came into their eyes. I never so much desired the gift of tongues as at the present time that I might communicate religious truth."³⁵ Although both Walker and Eells knew about Spokane Gary and that he had been at the Red River school, they did not meet him on this their first trip to the Spokane country.

On Saturday, the two men crossed the Spokane River and followed a northern tributary taking the trail that led to Fort Colville. About seven miles from the mouth of this creek, they rode across a plain which they were later to select to be the site of their mission station. This was about seventy miles south of Fort Colville and about twenty-five miles northwest of present-day Spokane. The place was called Tshimakain or Chimakain, "place of the springs," referring to a spring which still flows on the site where Walker and Eells built their cabins. The name, now spelled Chamokane, has survived as the name of the creek flowing through this valley.

On that Saturday afternoon, the two missionaries met the local chief called Big Head or Old Chief. Later he was known as Cornelius. He was to figure prominently in the Tshimakain story. A son of his, Spokane Berens, had been sent to the Red River Mission school in the spring of 1830 when only eleven years old. He was one of the five Old Oregon Indian boys taken to the school when Spokane Garry and Kootenay Pelly returned there after their visit to their people during the winter of 1829–30. Spokane Berens died at the school and was buried on July 21, 1834. Walker wrote that Chief Big Head "referred to the case of his son who died at the Red River. Said he mourned much at his death. Not because he was dead but because he did not return to teach him about the way to heaven."

Old Chief was most eager to have missionaries settle in his vicinity. He had visited Lapwai shortly after the Spaldings went there in the fall of 1836, and had met Gray in the Spokane country in the spring of 1837. He had visited Waiilatpu at the time the reenforcement arrived, or shortly thereafter, in order to plead that some of the missionaries go to his people. His keen interest, therefore, gave great promise for the success of the Spokane mission.

On Monday, September 17, Walker and Eells arrived at Fort Colvile, where they were given a warm welcome by Archibald McDonald, the Hudson's Bay Company's trader in charge.³⁶ The missionaries spent several days at the Fort during which time they sought the advice of McDonald as to the best place to establish their station. He recommended the Tshimakain site and promised to furnish tools and supplies to help them erect their cabins. The two men returned to Tshimakain on Tuesday, the 25th, at which time they met a member of Old Chief's band whom they called Solomon "from the sagacious look on his countenance." He proved to be a good man and a friend of both missionary families.

After selecting a building site near the spring Walker and Eells, with the willing help of a number of Indians, raised the walls for two log cabins, each about fourteen feet square and separated by about twenty feet. The season being too far advanced for them to finish the buildings and move their wives to the location, they decided to return to Waiilatpu and complete their work the next spring. They were back at Waiilatpu on Saturday, October 13.

On the Saturday following the departure of Walker and Eells for Spokane, Whitman left for Fort Vancouver to get supplies. Mary Walker's diary for September 17 contains the following note: "We rose early. I churned and wrote to Mrs. Perkins[37] &c. In the P.M. began to work on husband's coat. The Dr. hurried & bustled just as my husband does. Finally he got in such a fret that his wife began to cry which brought him to himself; he went on more calmly until he got ready to start." Whitman returned to his home on Monday morning, October 15.

ROMAN CATHOLIC MISSIONARIES ARRIVE IN OLD OREGON

The first Roman Catholic missionaries to arrive in Old Oregon were Fathers Francois Norbert Blanchet and Modeste Demers who were given free passage across Canada with the Hudson's Bay Company's express in the spring and summer of 1838. In a letter dated October 31, 1838, from the Governor and Committee of the Company's office in London to James Douglas at Fort Vancouver, we may read: "Those missionaries were permitted to go to the Columbia on the express condition that they were to locate themselves on the Cowlitz Portage, or wherever the Company's representative at Fort Vancouver might determine on the north side of the Columbia River, as we were unwilling to facilitate the formation of a Settlement on the South Side, which in all probability, will in due time, become United States Territory, but Mr. McLoughlin is of opinion that advantage may arise from allowing one of them to seat himself down among such of the Company's retired Canadian servants on the Wilhamet [Willamette], as may determine on not removing to the Cowlitz river portage." [38]

Although at the time, Dr. McLoughlin was not a member of the Roman Catholic Church, he was sympathetic and cooperative with it. He had been born of Catholic parents who had him baptized by a priest when he was fifteen days old. Later he had become a communicant member of the Church of England.[39] When Jason Lee and his companions first arrived at Fort Vancouver in September 1834, McLoughlin asked Lee to baptize a number of women and children at the Fort, including Mrs. McLoughlin. This Lee did.[40]

When the members of the Whitman-Spalding party were at Fort Vancouver in the fall of 1836, Narcissa noted in her diary that Dr. McLoughlin was conducting religious services on Sundays for the Catholic employees at the Fort. Using the French language, the Doctor would read a chapter from the Bible, a sermon, and offer prayers. Writing from Fort Vancouver to Samuel Parker, Narcissa said:"They have been expecting a Roman Catholic priest by the express this fall, but no one has come [Letter 36]. Anticipating the arrival of a priest, Dr. McLoughlin had a log church erected in 1836 at Fairfield on French Prairie near Champoeg in the Willamette Valley. There Father Blanchet celebrated the first mass in what is now the State of Oregon on January 3, 1839.[41] Father Demers was assigned to work with the French Canadians at the Cowlitz Portage.

The arrival of these two Roman Catholic priests at Fort Vancouver in the fall of 1838 opened another chapter in the complicated story of the contest then taking place between the United States and Great Britain over the location of the Oregon boundary. Dr. McLoughlin was no doubt primarily interested in meeting the spiritual needs of the former employees of the Hudson's Bay Company, yet he was astute enough to appreciate the services that Father Blanchet could render as a liaison between the Company and the French Canadians living in the Willamette Valley.

Prior to the arrival of Father Blanchet, the former servants of the Company had been drawn into the orbit of the Methodist missionaries. Some of the French Canadians had signed the petition of 1837 which Slacum took East with him in which a plea was made for the United States to extend its jurisdiction over Oregon. Likewise, nine Canadians signed a similar memorial in 1838 which Lee carried East. The attitude of the British Government, as expressed through the Hudson's Bay Company, was firmly to the contrary. The formation even of a provisional American government in the Willamette Valley was viewed as a threat to British territorial claims in Oregon.

After the arrival of Father Blanchet, Dr. McLoughlin was able to exercise a tighter control over the French Canadians in the Valley. Thereafter for four years, or until a provisional government was formed in May 1843, the Canadians refrained from joining the American settlers in their endeavors to establish a local government or to petition the United States to extend its jurisdiction to Oregon.

In 1840 a third memorial was drawn up by American settlers which boldly stated: "And your petitioners represent, that the said Territory, north of the Columbia, is an invaluable possession to the American Union; that in and about Puget Sound are the only harbors of easy access, and commodious and safe, upon the whole coast of the Territory... For these and other reasons, your petitioners pray that Congress will establish its sovereignty over said Territory."[42] This was signed by sixty-seven American settlers who were either citizens of the United States or were desirous of becoming so.[43] No French Canadians signed this memorial.

CATHOLIC PRIESTS SUBSIDIZED BY THE HUDSON'S BAY COMPANY

The archives of the Hudson's Bay Company in London contain a copy of the 1857 *Parliamentary Report, Notes from the Select Committee* which contains an account of the investigations of this Committee of the British Parliament into the activities of the Hudson's Bay Company in Oregon. On February 26, 1857, when Simpson was being cross-examined, he stated that his Company was paying £100 a year to the Roman Catholic bishop in Oregon. Since the international border had been settled by treaty in 1846, this statement surprised members of the Committee. One asked: "What do you mean by Oregon? Oregon is in the United States. Do you give religious instruction to the inhabitants of the United States?" Simpson's answer was somewhat ambiguous: "No, there is a Roman Catholic bishop who was taken across by us a good many years ago to Oregon, and he remains there on the promise that he should be allowed 100 £ a year."[44] Just how long that subsidy continued after 1857 is not known to the author.

An interesting parallel may be drawn between what appears to be, on strong circumstantial evidence, the payment of a subsidy by the United States Government to the Methodist Church to assist in the cost of sending a colony of missionaries to the Willamette Valley in 1839–40 and the free passage given two priests by the Hudson's Bay Company to Oregon in 1838 and the annual subsidy of £100. Mention will be made later of the assistance given by the Company to a colony of settlers from the Red River sent out to Old Oregon in 1841. After the provisional government was established in the Willamette Valley in 1843, the political influence of Bishop Blanchet[45] was minimal.

The coming of the Roman Catholic priests into Oregon brought many complications for the Protestant missionaries and especially for the Whitmans. Mary Walker in her diary commented on a minor problem which the Protestants at Waiilatpu faced when they were invited to go to Fort Walla Walla to meet the incoming Catholic priests. Under date of November 3, 1838, Mary wrote: "Last night Mr. Pambrun sent us a quarter of beef. He was expecting some Catholic priests to visit him & so he slew the old cream colored cow, which was 23 years old. He also sent the tripe, so that I had the job of cleaning it. Mr. P. also invited the gentlemen to call over and make his guests a visit. They hardly knew what to do about accepting it, but finally concluded that it was best." The fact that the men were hesitant about accepting Pambrun's invitation to pay a social call in order to meet the priests reflects the intolerant spirit towards Roman Catholics of the communities in which each was born and reared. During the early decades of the nineteenth century, there were very few Catholics in New England and upper New York State. This lack of knowledge and of personal contact with Roman Catholics explains much of the prejudice the missionaries displayed. According to Mary's account, Whitman, Eells, and her husband finally decided to go to meet the priests, but Smith refused saying "that it looked too much like countenancing Romanism." Mary added: "Hope our husbands will manage discreetly." The men returned on Monday with the news that the expected Hudson's Bay express had been delayed and the priests had not arrived.

If the Protestant missionaries had known that the Hudson's Bay Company had paid the traveling expenses of the priests and was giving an annual subsidy of £100 to the bishop who was to settle in the Willamette Valley, surely they would have had reason for concern. These facts were not known to Spalding even in 1865 when he began his attacks through the press on the Roman Catholic missionaries in Oregon nor by Gray who wrote several tirades against the Hudson's Bay Company [See Appendix 3].

Whitman's Second Adobe House

Fortunately for all members of the Oregon Mission, both Whitman and Spalding had a bountiful harvest in the fall of 1838. In a letter dated September 15, 1838, Smith told of Whitman's success. "My first business here has been to assist in securing the crops," he wrote. "Dr. W. has about 17 acres in all under cultivation. His crop of wheat was very fine. It is not threshed but he thinks there will be from 75 to 100 bushels from 2½ acres. Nicer wheat I never saw. His crop of corn was good. No frost touched it... The corn is all gathered in & put in big cribs—near 300 bushels of it. Potatoes do well here. Dr. has about 6 (?) acres, all in the field yet thinks there will not be less than 1000 bushels. He has about 2 acres of turnips, & garden vegetables in abundance. We have had an abundance of melons all the time since we have been here.

"The labor of gleaning the crops is done considerably by the natives. The women do most of the work. They have harvested the corn almost entirely. Some of it was brought from the field to the house in bags on the backs of the women. We have no vehicle of any kind for the transportation of articles. No cart, sled, or corn dray. Much of the corn was cut up & drawn to the house by the oxen on brush. This was very hard dragging." Several years had to pass before Whitman was able to obtain a wagon.

Smith's account continues: "We labor to great disadvantage in many respects. We are in great want of tools of most every kind. Dr. has two ploughs but neither of them very good... We labor under disadvantage in respect to building. There is no good building timber nearer than 20 miles. On the mountains there is a great abundance of excellent pine & spruce but at present it is very difficult getting it. There is a limited supply of cottonwood (a kind of poplar) on the streams near us & scarcely any other timber... We build our houses here with *dobies*, or clay dried in the sun in the form of brick 20 inches long, 10 wide & 5 in thickness.

This is the best of anything we can use."[46]

When Walker and Eells returned from their first visit to the Spokane country, they made a detour in order to call on the Spaldings at Lapwai. Walker was much impressed with Spalding's potato crop and claimed that three acres produced 1,500 bushels, or 500 bushels to the acre. Walker wrote: "I never saw any that turned out so well."[47] This marks the beginning of Idaho's fame as a great potato raising state. It should be remembered that both Whitman and Spalding used their produce in trade with the Indians, sometimes in payment for labor, and also for seed for themselves and for the natives.

After gathering the harvest, the next important task at Waiilatpu was the erection of another house. The first adobe building was pitifully inadequate. On September 4, 1838, Sarah Smith wrote the following description of the Whitman house in her diary: "We are arranging our things, begin to feel a little at home. The Doctor's house would be considered in the States a very rough one. Part of it is log & part dobie or dried clay. One side of it has partly fallen down & [is] propped up with large poles. Some of the floors are nailed & some of them loose boards & all unplaned. But we are glad to find a home in so comfortable a place. Our room is the Indians meeting house, school room, wash room & store room, so you may well suppose [how] it is furnished." We have no floor plan of Whitman's first house but from the above description by Sarah, we may assume that the room she and her husband occupied was the largest in the main part of the 30 x 36 foot building.

Asa Smith, in a letter written to his parents about the middle of October, throws further light upon Whitman's first adobe house when he stated that it contained only "3 rooms & 2 bedrooms."[48] From one of Narcissa's letters [No. 39] we learn that the 12 x 36 lean-to had two bedrooms and a "very pleasant kitchen in the middle." If Smith was referring to the two bedrooms in the lean-to, then the "3 rooms" would have included the one in the lean-to and only two in the main part of the house. It is possible that some sleeping accommodations were in the upper half-story of the main structure. Even so, the prospect of housing about twenty people in such cramped quarters during the winter months was not appealing. The crowded conditions brought difficulties, as we shall see.

PLANS FOR A NEW BUILDING

Following the flooding of the basement of his first house during December 1837 and the following March, Whitman saw the necessity of building another house located on higher ground and further back from the river. Narcissa's letter of May 2, 1840, contains a drawing of the floor plan of this second house. The outline of the foundations of this house as laid bare by the excavations of archaeologists at the Whitman Mission National Historic Site shows that the house which was actually erected differed in many respects from what was originally planned. [See the illustration in this volume for the actual floor plan, page 363.] Whitman selected a site about ninety feet to the north of the first adobe structure. He sent men into the mountains some twenty or more miles from Waiilatpu to whipsaw boards during the winters of 1837–38 and 1838–39 [Letter 39]. Occasionally there was enough snow during the winter months so that lumber could be drawn to the mission site on sleds. Some boards were packed on horses. Information is lacking as to how much Whitman had been able to accomplish towards the erection of the new house before the reenforcement of 1838 arrived.

Whitman planned the erection of a "T" shaped building with the main axis of the top of the "T" running north and south, and with the stem of the "T" joining on the east side. Evidently the building was laid out with a compass, as the axis of the top of the "T" was oriented approximately with the magnetic north. This part of the new building was to be a story and a half high and to contain a bedroom, a living room, and an Indian room. A stairway leading to the attic was in the central part, or in the living room. The drawing made in 1840 by Asahel Munger indicated a fourth room at the south end of the top of the "T" (room "A" on his drawing) but it is evident from the uncovered foundations that this was never built. According to the archaeologist, the top of the "T" measured 19' 3" by 60' 10", and the stem of the "T" measured 22' x 80'.

In a letter to his parents written about the middle of October 1838, during the temporary absence of Whitman, Walker, and Eells, Smith stated that he was laying adobe bricks for the new house and that the walls had been raised "nearly to the chamber floor." This indicates that the unit on which he was working had an upper story or a half-story. We have good reason to believe that the top of the "T" was the first section of the building to be erected. Smith was able to finish one room by December 4, 1838, for on that day he and his wife moved out of the crowded adobe house near the river into the new building.

Evidence is lacking as to when the other units of the building were erected, except the room marked "H" on Munger's drawing, which was built near the end of 1843. This room was erected over a cellar and, according to the rough sketch made of the Whitman home by Paul Kane in 1847 [see the illustration on page 363], was a story and a half high. A room was being built at the east end of the stem of the "T" at the time of the massacre in November 1847.

The adobe bricks uncovered by the archaeologist measure roughly 5 x 10 x 29 inches and, according to one estimate, about six thousand were needed in the erection of this building.[49] Spalding in his description of the building found in the inventory of the Waiilatpu property compiled after the massacre, stated that the roof was constructed of "split timber, grassed earth [i.e., sod]."[50] With the possible exception of the first roof on the lean-to, the roofs at Waiilatpu seem to have been efficient in shedding the heavy winter rains; no complaints about leaky roofs have been found in the writings of those who lived for varying periods of time at this station. Evidently the main Whitman home was built in segments over several years as time and manpower were available. Although one room was finished in December 1838, about a year and a half passed before the Whitmans were able to move into their new quarters.

"Such Folks Right in My Kitchen"

The news that Henry and Mary Gray carried to the Whitmans and the Spaldings on August 21, 1838, that a reenforcement of seven (in addition to Mrs. Gray) for the Oregon Mission was about to arrive, lifted their spirits to the heights. As Whitman wrote: "They thanked God and took courage." It was a time of rejoicing—a day of triumph! But within a few days after all had arrived at Waiilatpu, the Whitmans and the Spaldings became aware that the tensions, which had developed within the reenforcement during their overland journey, were being forced upon them. Circumstances were such that they too became involved in personality clashes.

The fact that these people were missionaries did not mean that they were saints. They were first of all human beings, subject to all of the inherent weaknesses of human flesh. Indeed, the fact that they were missionaries is evidence that each was an individual with strong convictions, else they would not have ventured on such a journey. The hardships endured while traveling, and the primitive conditions under which so many lived in the cramped quarters of the Whitman home, made it easy for strained relationships to arise. Perhaps no sharper test of Christian forbearance has been devised than that of making two or more families live under the same roof and share the same kitchen. This becomes especially trying when such families are surrounded by peoples of another culture, race, or language, thus forcing them all the more upon each other's society. Modern-day missionaries who have lived in the same compound on some foreign mission field can testify to the truth of this statement.

The change which took place in the minds and hearts of Marcus and Narcissa when their initial joy was changed to disappointment can easily be traced in the writings of the missionaries themselves, especially in Mary Walker's diary and in some of Narcissa's letters. On the whole, this is an unpleasant side of the Whitman story, but in the light of later events, it is too important to be omitted. The friction which developed within the mission had important consequences.

Mary Walker opens many windows in her diary through which we can look into the Whitman household. In strict conformity with the custom of that day, she always referred to the other members of the Mission, even to her husband, with the title "Mr.," "Mrs.," or "Dr." as the case might be. She never used the given name alone. Mary noted a number of incidents which involved Asa Smith. On September 18, she wrote: "Mr. Smith came to pantry & found nothing but milk & melons. Didn't like it... At supper Mr. S. said he was very hungry, had had no dinner. In forenoon Mr. S. sent out to give a melon to some boys for pounding [i.e., washing clothes]. Mrs. W. countermanded." On October 13, she noted: "Mrs. Whitman quite put out with Mr. Smith because he was unwilling to let her have Jack [the Hawaiian] help her." Even mild-mannered Dr. Whitman had difficulties with Smith; on November 30, Mary wrote: "Dr. W. quite out of patience with Mr. Smith."

A difference of opinion arose over the question whether women should pray aloud in the mission prayer meetings. Narcissa grew up in communities in western New York where women took part with men in public prayer. Hers was an emotional religion. As a girl and young woman, she took part in revivals and gloried in seeing sinners weep when under conviction of sin. These were for her "melting times." The three couples from New England were more restrained in giving expression to their inner feelings. In their home communities women did not pray aloud in the presence of men. During the absence of Walker and Eells on their trip to Spokane, Mary ventured to pray aloud in the Whitman family worship. But this troubled her, for she wrote in her diary on October 2: "I wish I knew whether my husband likes to have me pray before folks or not. When he comes home I will ask him."

Narcissa, in a letter to her father dated October 10, 1840, wrote:"We have none in our mission of as high-toned piety as we could wish, especially among those who came in the last reenforcement. They think it wrong for females to pray in the presence of men, and do not allow it even in our small circle here. This has been a great trial to me, and I have almost sunk under it." And again on October 6, 1841, she wrote:"In all the prayer meetings of this mission, the brethren only pray. I believe all the sisters would be willing to pray if their husbands would let them... My husband has no objection to my praying, but if my sisters do not, he thinks it quite as well for me not to."

Still another irritant was the fact that Elkanah Walker chewed tobacco and, no doubt to Narcissa's great disgust, used the open fireplace in the kitchen as a spittoon. Also at least one of the New England men liked his wine, and this too was objectionable to the Whitmans. In wet and cold weather, the men sought the warmth of the kitchen where Narcissa and the other women would be preparing their meals. All this is background for the following comment taken from Narcissa's letter to her sister, Jane, dated March 23, 1839: "We need help very much, and those who will pray, too. In this we have been disappointed in our helpers last come, particularly the two Revs. who have gone to the Flatheads. They think it not good to have too many meetings, too many prayers, and that it is wrong and unseemly for a woman to pray where there are men, and plead the necessity for wine, tobacco, etc.' and now how do you think I have lived with *such folks right in my kitchen for the whole winter.*" [51]

The endless household duties, multiplied by the presence of so many in her home, added to the nervous strain under which Narcissa was living. In addition to such daily tasks as cooking for twenty or more over an open fire in the fireplace, were the repeated duties of washing clothes, making soap, and dipping candles. On January 29, 1839, Mary Walker mentioned that she, Mary, had that day "dipped 24 doz candles." Narcissa also had the care of her little girl whom she was still nursing. A remembrance of these facts helps us to appreciate the following extracts from Mary's diary: "Nov. 16. Worked about house all day. Got very tired. Mrs. W. appears to feel cross at everybody... She seems in a worry about [something]. Went out & blustered round & succeeded in melting over her tallow." "Friday 23. Mrs. Whitman washing. Cross time of it." And "Friday 30. Mrs. W. washing. Think she has less help from the other ladies than she ought."

On Sunday, November 11, less than a month before her baby was born, Mary wrote: "Oh! I wish I had a little chamber where I could secrete myself." On the 18th, she added: "My husband seems to think I expose myself more than is necessary, but what can I do? There is no place where I can be."

Asa Smith, eager to have a private bedroom for himself and his wife, worked hard to complete one room in the new adobe house. The Smiths were able to spend the first night in the new house on Monday, December 3, although Mary did not refer to them as actually moving out of the old adobe until the next day, December 4. On Monday evening, according to Mary's diary, the three couples—the Whitmans, the Walkers, and the Eellses—sat up "till midnight talking about Mr. S[mith] & Mr. G[ray]." Evidently Narcissa was deeply moved by what was said, for Mary added: "Mrs. W. gets to feeling very bad, goes to bed crying." And on the 4th, Mary wrote:"Mrs. W. in a sad mood all day, did not present herself at the breakfast table." Then comes the saddest entry to be found in Mary's diary: "[Mrs. Whitman] went out doors, down by the river to cry." Since she could find no privacy in her home, Narcissa had to seek some lonely spot in the outofdoors where she could weep.

As soon as the Smiths had moved, Elkanah erected a board partition in a corner of one of the rooms in the main section of the adobe house thus giving his wife a private bedroom. Mary was able to move into it on the 5th. On the 6th, for some unknown reason, Elkanah found it necessary to ride to Fort Walla Walla and hence was not present when his son was born. Early on the morning of the 7th, Mary's labor pains began.

She called the Whitmans who made such preparations as were necessary. About nine o'clock the pains increased. Later, looking back upon her experience, she wrote in her diary: "Felt as if I almost wished I had never been married. But there was no retreating, meet it I must. About eleven I began to be quite discouraged. I had hoped to be delivered ere then... But just as I supposed the worst was at hand, my ears were saluted with the cry of my child. A son was the salutation. Soon I forgot my misery in the joy of possessing a proper child." They called the boy Cyrus Hamblin after one of Elkanah's classmates who was a pioneer missionary to Turkey.[52] Inevitably the birth of the baby meant extra work for Narcissa.

Camping on the Tucannon

Perhaps the nearest to a vacation that the Whitmans ever experienced came during the latter part of January and the first part of February 1839 when they rode to the Tucannon River, about fifty miles distant, with their little girl and spent about two and one-half weeks camping. The occasion for the outing arose out of some special meetings Spalding had conducted at Lapwai for the Nez Perces during December 1838. The meetings were first held in a 20' x 40' log schoolhouse which Gray had built. This soon became too small to accommodate the numbers who came, so that Spalding had to conduct the meetings outofdoors. With his characteristic tendency to exaggerate, Spalding, in a letter to Greene dated March 3, 1839, reported that "several thousand" Nez Perces were in attendance and the "probably two thousand have made a public confession of their sins."[53]

Spalding's Success with the Nez Perces

Both Spalding and Gray were eager to have a millrace dug so that a gristmill could be erected at Lapwai. The presence of so many natives on the mission grounds suggested the idea of enlisting their aid in the project and paying them with potatoes. The Indians were encouraged to assist in digging the millrace by being told that they would benefit by having a gristmill available for the grinding of their wheat. So with the enthusiastic help of several hundred Indians, a ditch was dug about half a mile long, four feet wide, and in some places fifteen feet deep. They had no other tools than two shovels, a few hoes, some axes, tomahawks, and sharpened sticks. The Indians worked in the mornings and early afternoons and then attended Spalding's meetings in the latter part of the afternoons and evenings. The outline of the millrace can still be traced at the Spalding mission site which is now a part of the Nez Perce National Historical Park.

One of the secrets of Spalding's success with the Nez Perces was the fact that he won the support of several influential chiefs. Among those who seemed to have experienced a spiritual awakening during those December meetings were two chiefs, Teutakas and Timosa. Spalding had the custom of bestowing upon his converts Bible names and to these two he gave the names of Joseph and Timothy. Teutakas is mentioned in Parker's *Journal of an Exploring Tour* when his interpreter, Kentuc, once had occasion to compare the sincerity of Teutakas with that of another chief called Charlie. According to Parker, Kentuc said:"Charlie prayed with his lips, but Teutacus prayed with his heart." [54]

Teutakas is also known as Old Joseph to distinguish him from his son, also called Joseph, or Young Joseph, who was to be a leader in the Nez Perce uprising of 1877. Among the few natives who became members of the First Presbyterian Church of Oregon, there was none more sincere and faithful in the profession and practice of the Christian faith than Timothy. He figures prominently in the history of the Oregon Mission of the American Board and also in the history of the Indian wars following the Whitman massacre. He was always a faithful friend of the white men. On the other hand, Tackensuatis, who had manifested such eagerness to have at least one missionary couple settle among the Nez Perces, lost interest in the white man's religion. For some reason he had become disillusioned within a year or so after the Spaldings went to Lapwai. Writing to Greene on February 6, 1840, Smith said: "People at home may think from what was written of him that he is a christian, but he is far from it. Instead of being settled with Mr. S[palding], he has become his enemy & proves to be a very wicked man." [55]

Whitman Visits Spalding at Lapwai

When Whitman learned of the stirring events taking place at Lapwai, he decided to go and see for himself. He left Waiilatpu on January 1, 1839. According to a letter Narcissa wrote to her sister Jane, dated May 17, 1839, he wanted "to attend a protracted meeting" which Spalding was holding for the natives. Judging by subsequent events, however, it is possible that there were other reasons for the trip. Spalding was having some difficulties with Gray at Lapwai and may have asked for Whitman's presence to discuss the problem. Also, it is possible that Whitman wanted to talk with Spalding about problems which had arisen at Waiilatpu with Smith.

Whitman made the 120-mile ride to Lapwai in less than four days. After seeing the response the natives were giving to Spalding, Whitman found himself deeply impressed. Never again during the mission period was Spalding going to be able to attract so many natives to the mission site and keep them there for so many days as was the case during the winter of 1838-39. Whitman admired Spalding's ability to use the native language and felt somewhat conscience stricken at his failure to be as proficient.

Evidently Whitman and Spalding discussed the need for Whitman to get away from Waiilatpu for a time and live with the natives in order to have a better opportunity to learn the language. A plan was evolved. Whitman would return to Waiilatpu, get Narcissa and Alice Clarissa and then the three would return to the place where the Lapwai-Waiilatpu trail crossed the Tucannon River. Timothy agreed to meet the Whitmans there with some of his band and do what he could to teach them the Nez Perce language.

Whitman left Lapwai on January 10 and was back at his home by the 15th. When he told Narcissa of his plan, he found her not only willing to endure whatever hardships they might encounter at that time of the year, but even enthusiastic. Writing to her sister Jane, Narcissa said: "He had no difficulty to persuade me to accompany him, for I was nearly exhausted, both in body and mind, in the labour and care of our numerous family." She explained that the purpose of their going to live with the Indians was "for the benefit of having free access to the language and be free from care and company" [Letter 63].

With the Nez Perces on the Tucannon

The Whitmans with their daughter, then nearly two years old, left Waiilatpu on Tuesday, January 22. Cushing and Myra Eells, Mary Walker, and Margaret McKay rode with them for the first three miles. The following extract from Mary's diary reflects a continuing tension in the home: "Mrs. W. has dealt so largely in powder and balls of late that perhaps her absence will not detract much from our happiness."

If such an excursion could be called a vacation, then this was the first that Marcus and Narcissa had enjoyed after their marriage. The weather was mild, even quite warm for that time of the year. After a leisurely journey of three days, they arrived at the Tucannon where they found an encampment of Nez Perces with Timothy. Soon after their arrival, the weather turned cold and snow fell. The Whitmans were sheltered in a tent. In order to keep warm, Marcus built a small fire inside the tent but the smoke caused the child to cry. Marcus then moved the fire to the entrance and erected a "lodge" around the fire to carry off the smoke. This proved to be a better plan.

Narcissa's account of the worship services her husband conducted on Sunday shows not only Whitman's participation in teaching Christianity but also the religious receptivity of the Nez Perces. She wrote:

> Sab. at Tukanon. Jan. 27, 1839. This has been a day of peculiar interest here. Could you have been an eye witness of the scenes you would, as I do, have rejoiced in being thus privileged. The morning worship at daybreak I did not attend. At midday I was present. Husband talked to them of the parable of the rich man and Lazarus; all listened with eager attention. After prayer and singing, an opportunity was given for those who had heavy hearts under a sense of sin, and only those, to speak if they wished it. For a few moments all sat in silence; soon a prominent and intelligent man named Timothy broke the silence with sobs weeping. He arose, spoke of his great wickedness, and how very black his heart was; how weak and insufficient he was of himself to effect his own salvation; that his only dependence was in the blood of Christ to make him clean and save his soul from sin and hell.
>
> He was followed by a brother, who spoke much to the same effect. Next came the wives of the first and of the second, who seemed to manifest deep feelings. Several others followed; one in particular, while confessing her sins, her tears fell to the ground so copiously that I was reminded of the weeping 'Mary who washed her Saviour's feet with her tears.' All manifested much deep feeling; some in loud sobs and tears; others in anxious and solemn countenance. You can better imagine my feelings than I can describe them on witnessing such a scene in

heathen lands. They had but recently come from the meeting at Brother Spalding's.

Narcissa liked the Nez Perces. She told Jane that: "Most of them were not so hardened in sin; or, rather, they were not so proud a people as our people, the Wieletpoos, are." Both Marcus and Narcissa experienced a deep feeling of joy and satisfaction when they witnessed these evidences of the acceptance of Christianity by the natives. This was a moment of triumph for the Whitmans, an experience which made them feel that all of the hardships they had endured were eminently worthwhile. God was blessing their labors!

While sitting in the door of her tent on that Sunday evening, Narcissa continued her letter to Jane: "O, my dear Jane, could you see us here this beautiful eve, the full moon shining in all her splendor, clear, yet freezing cold, my little one sleeping by my side, husband at worship with the people within hearing, and I sitting in the 'door of the tent' writing, with my usual clothing except a shawl, and handkerchief on my head, and before me a large comfortable fire in the open air. Do you think we suffer? No, dear Jane; I have not realized so much enjoyment for a long time as I have since I have been here."

The Whitmans stayed at Tucannon into the third week and returned home on Saturday, February 9. Mary Walker mentioned this in her diary and added: "Adieu to peace and order."

Growing Dissension Within the Mission

The winter of 1838–39 and spring of 1839 was a time of growing dissension within the Oregon Mission. A focal point of trouble at Waiilatpu was Asa Smith, who soon realized that the life of an Oregon missionary was far different from that which he had imagined. His deep unhappiness is reflected in a letter to Greene dated April 29, 1839, and a longer one of some six thousand words of August 27.[56] For one thing, he was amazed to realize how much time the missionaries had to spend in manual work and secular activities just to keep alive. He Wrote: "I feel that it is a great calamity that we are under the necessity of spending so much time in providing for our temporal wants. But necessity is laid upon us & we must do it or suffer."

Soon after his arrival at Waiilatpu, Smith began to have doubts over the wisdom of the endeavors that Whitman and Spalding were making to settle the Indians. Here was a fundamental difference of opinion. In his letter of April 29, Smith wrote: "Much has been said about furnishing the Indians with cattle, ploughs, sending out farmers, mechanics, &c. With regard to this I must say that it appears to me to be departing from the object which the Board has in view. A few cows are important for our comfort & support but to think of furnishing a nation with them, it would I believe defeat our object in coming. I feel that there is very great danger of introducing the habits of civilized life faster than the natives are capable of appreciating them." Smith felt that the enthusiasm the Indians manifested at the coming of the missionaries was not a reflection of their eagerness for the truths of Christianity but rather for their "hope of temporal gain." Over and over again, he emphasized what he considered to be the selfishness of the natives. Writing in his diary on September 1, 1839, Spalding commented: "Mr. Smith preaches against all efforts to settle the poor Indians, thinks they should be kept upon the chase to prevent their becoming worldly minded."

In recalling the circumstances which led to his application to be included in the 1838 reenforcements, Smith blamed Spalding for the over enthusiastic reports which the latter had sent to the Board during his first year in Old Oregon and which had been published in the *Missionary Herald*. Smith felt that he would never have volunteered for the Oregon Mission had he not been misled by Spalding's exaggerations. Blaming Spalding for his predicament, he became increasingly critical of him. Writing to Greene on February 6, 1840, Smith said: "Before I left the States this mission seemed to absorb the attention of Christians, I often thought, more than all others, tho' in fact it was one of the very least in its relative importance." And in his letter of August 27, 1839, he declared:"Had I known what I now do before I left the States, I can not say that I should have come here."

Friction arose between Smith and Whitman during the winter of 1838–39; details are lacking as to its causes. Smith became extremely unhappy, and by February was determined to leave Waiilatpu. He wanted a station of his own. The idea occurred to him that he might move to Kamiah in the heart of the Nez Perce country, about sixty miles up the river from Lapwai. During the winter of 1838–39, Lawyer had spent some time at Waiilatpu tutoring Smith in the Nez Perce language.[57]

Lawyer's home was at Kamiah; in all probability it was he who told Smith about the advantages of studying the language there.

Special Mission Meeting of February 1839

The decision had been made at the first mission meeting held at Waiilatpu in September 1838 to establish a gristmill at Lapwai. As has been stated, Spalding was successful in securing the aid of the Nez Perces in the digging of a millrace. The next requirement was to quarry the millstones. Walker was asked to go to Lapwai to help Gray, Spalding, and Rogers in this undertaking. When Smith learned of Walker's intended journey, he decided to go along, with the intention of continuing on to Kamiah to explore the country for a mission site. The two men left Waiilatpu on Monday, February 11, and arrived at Lapwai the following Wednesday afternoon.

The arrival of Walker and Smith at Lapwai brought five of the seven men of the Mission together. Smith emphatically told his four associates that "he would leave the Mission rather than be connected with Dr. Whitman."[58] The situation was so serious that the men agreed a special meeting of the Mission should be held as soon as possible. Spalding, therefore, sent word the next day, February 14, to Whitman asking that he and Eells come to Lapwai at once. In the meantime, Walker, Gray, and Rogers set out to see if they could cut out some millstones, and Smith, with an Indian guide, left for Kamiah to explore for a possible mission site.

When Narcissa learned of the special meeting, she decided to go with her husband to Lapwai. Accordingly, the Whitmans with their little girl and Eells left Waiilatpu on the 19th, and arrived at Lapwai at noon on the 22nd. By this time the three men who had gone for millstones had returned, but without having any success; and Smith was back from Kamiah. Thus all members of the Oregon Mission were present except Mary Walker, Myra Eells, and Sarah Smith.

The Mission meeting began on Saturday morning, the 23rd, with Spalding serving as moderator. A number of minor items of business were first considered. Some time before this date, Spalding had officiated at the marriage of Richard Williams, a mountain man in his employ, to a Nez Perce woman with whom he had been living. It had been the common practice in the heyday of the fur trade for the traders and trappers to live with native women without benefit of clergy. There had been no other course, when no clergy or authorized law officials were available. This was looked upon as a shocking situation by clergymen of various denominations who came into contact with this custom. Anglican ministers at Red River, Chaplain Beaver at Fort Vancouver, and the Methodist missionaries in the Willamette Valley, all encouraged the white men to legalize their common law relationships by having a marriage service performed. This would give valuable legal rights to the offspring of such marriages. Spalding acted entirely in line with accepted ecclesiastical practice when he married Williams and the Nez Perce woman, yet someone protested, no doubt the overcritical Smith. After reviewing the facts of the case, the Mission voted that in the future no member of the Mission should perform such a marriage unless the white man was a candidate for church membership.[59]

After some other lesser issues were settled, a resolution was introduced to authorize the transfer of Smith from Waiilatpu to some undesignated new location. Spalding, in his diary, noted that this precipitated "a long debate." Not being able to reach a decision on Saturday, the question was carried over until the following Monday when, after further deliberation, the resolution was rejected. Smith was not authorized to leave Waiilatpu.

Then a second resolution was introduced which called for Dr. Whitman to leave Wailatpu and open a new station on the Snake River near the mouth of the Palouse River. Such a location, argued Spalding, Walker, and Eells, would put the doctor in a more central location, thus making him more quickly available in cases of severe illness in the more distant stations. An implication of this resolution was that Smith would take charge of the Waiilatpu mission. To the surprise and dismay of both Marcus and Narcissa, this motion carried. Narcissa was of the opinion that Spalding was the one most responsible for the vote. Looking back on that meeting, Narcissa in a letter to her father dated October 10, 1840, wrote: "Every mind in the mission that he had had access to, he has tried to prejudice against us, and did succeed for a while, which was the cause of our being voted to remove and form a new station."

Another important action was taken when full charge of the blacksmith shop, gristmill, and framing operations at Lapwai was given to Gray, with the understanding that Spalding, relieved of such duties, would be able to give full time to his religious work. Such an assignment of duties to Gray was in harmony with the original intention of the Board, but the action of the Mission, as will be seen, did not prove satisfactory. The Mission also voted that the printing press, which was expected to arrive that spring from Honolulu, be located at Lapwai. It may be that this decision was based in part on the fact that Spalding, as a student in Lane Theological Seminary at Cincinnati, 1833–35, had worked in a printing shop.

The business meeting closed on Tuesday noon, February 26. Walker, Eells, and Smith left at once for Waiilatpu. Previous arrangements had been made with the Spokane chief, Cornelius, to escort the Walkers and the Eellses to Tshimakain, leaving Waiilatpu on or about March 5; thus the men felt a special urge to be on their way back to Waiilatpu. They made the return journey in two and one-half days, and upon their arrival, found Cornelius waiting for them. Evidently Elkanah gave Mary a discouraging report of the Lapwai meeting, for she wrote in her diary that the men "had a bad time."

SMITH CONSIDERS LEAVING THE MISSION

The Whitmans tarried at Lapwai for a few days because of the illness of little Eliza Spalding. Eager to be back at his home before the two couples left for Tshimakain, Whitman left Lapwai on Saturday, March 2, after making arrangements for the Spaldings to escort his wife and daughter to the Tucannon River where he would meet them on the 8th. Whitman wanted Spalding's advice in the selection of a site for the proposed new station. Even though pressed for time, it appears that Whitman obeyed his conscience about not traveling on Sunday. After remaining in camp on that day, he continued his journey early Monday morning. He had a hard ride all day Monday and perhaps through all of Monday night. Mary wrote in her diary for Tuesday, May 5: "About sunrise Dr. W. reached home & about noon we left W[aiilatpu]." A residence of about six months for the Walkers and the Eellses in the crowded Whitman home had come to an end.

Rarely in the eleven-year history of the Oregon Mission was Whitman so dejected as he was during those days. To begin with, there were the letters from Greene received in the summer of 1838 with the criticisms of Whitman's expenditures made by Samuel Parker. Then came the tensions and personality conflicts which grew out of the crowded living conditions at Waiilatpu during the fall of 1838 and the following winter. The blunt declaration that Smith had made to the members of the Mission that he refused to live in the same station with him and Narcissa must have been hard to take. But the final blow was the vote that the Mission had taken that he should turn over Waiilatpu to Smith and start a new station. Of all members of the Mission, no one was less qualified for the responsibilities of Waiilatpu than Smith and no one realized this more than Whitman. The hasty and ill-considered vote of the Mission calling upon the Whitmans to leave Waiilatpu and start a new station was devastating to his morale. His heart failed him as he thought of the work, the privations, and the difficulties attendant upon establishing a new station in the wilderness. The outlook was so discouraging that Whitman seriously considered leaving the Mission.

When the Walker-Eells party left Waiilatpu at noon on March 5 for Tshimakain, Whitman traveled with them to their first encampment on Mill Creek, five or six miles east of Waiilatpu, on what is now a part of the campus of Whitman College. Mary Walker wrote that day in her diary: "We talked with him all that time would allow & he left us feeling much better than when he came home." For the time being, Whitman tried to accept the decision of the Mission with Christian forbearance. At least he would make an effort to investigate the possibilities of a new location.

Riding in advance of the Walkers and the Eellses, Whitman met the Spaldings and Narcissa at the crossing of the Tucannon River on the 8th. Because of Eliza Spalding's feeble health, she remained in camp the next day while her husband, their daughter, and the Whitmans with their little girl rode the trail following the Tucannon to where it emptied into the Snake River. The Whitmans and Spalding met the Walker-Eells party, who had taken a different trail from that followed by Whitman, at the Snake River crossing on March 9. Mary Walker mentioned the meeting in her diary and added: "Had not a remarkably pleasant interview with them." This was the last time the two women en route to the Spokane country were to see any of the other four women of the Mission for over a year. With the passing of time, the strained relationships, evident at Waiilatpu, disappeared.

While the four men were together, they again discussed the advisability of the Whitmans leaving Waiilatpu. By this time Narcissa was voicing her strong opposition. When Spalding, Walker, and Eells began to realize more of the problems involved, they began to doubt the wisdom of their vote. On Saturday, February 9, the Walker-Eells party bade farewell to the Spaldings and Whitman, crossed the Snake, and continued their journey to Tshimakain. A few miles below the mouth of the Tucannon was the place where the Palouse River, coming in from the north, also emptied into the Snake. The trail which led to the Spokane country followed the Palouse and its tributaries for about fifty miles before striking across the country to the Spokane River. [See map in this volume.] Spalding wrote in his diary for that day: "Doct. & myself examine the Paluse, not favorable for a location." After spending Sunday with a band of Nez Perces on the Tucannon, the Whitmans and Spaldings separated on Monday to return to their respective stations.

Back at Waiilatpu, Whitman and Smith debated the pros and cons of the prospective move. Out of the discussions came a compromise suggestion, perhaps made by Whitman: Smith would move to Kamiah on a temporary basis in order to study the language, and the Whitmans would remain at Waiilatpu. Then at the Annual Meeting of the Mission scheduled for September, the whole question would be reconsidered. Feeling the necessity of Spalding's approval for this plan, the two men journeyed again to Lapwai where they arrived on March 23. On the 25th Spalding wrote in his diary: "Doct. Whitman & Mr. Smith wish advice as to their future course but after long consultation, came to no conclusion." Whitman and Smith started back to Waiilatpu on the 25th. This was the third time since the beginning of that year that Whitman had ridden the 240-mile round trip from Waiilatpu to Lapwai.

On March 28, the day after their return to Waiilatpu, Smith wrote to Walker: "It is very evident that the Dr. & his wife were not so willing to leave this place as was pretended at the meeting. He told me that he did not expect that such a decision would have been made. So it seems that neither of us have been suited by the arrangement. I lament that I ever consented to remain here [i.e., at Waiilatpu]. Indeed my heart never has consented to it & I do not expect ever to be satisfied or contented with my present situation. *I lament the day that connected me with this mission.* Why it is that I am here, I know not... Should this mission be broken up, I should not be disappointed. At any rate I doubt whether I have any connection with it for a long time to come."⁶⁰

On April 1, Spalding wrote in his diary: "Last eve letters arrived from Doct. Whitman & wife. Doct. remains at his old station. Everything seems to be settled." During the latter part of that month, Spalding went to Waiilatpu to get the printing press. On the 27th, he wrote: "Mr. Smith & the Doct. on good terms for which I am truly thankful. Also Mrs. Whitman & Mrs. Smith are on good terms which is a matter of much joy. Doubtless they have all prayed more & talked less."

On April 30, the Smiths left for Kamiah. For the first time in eight months, the Whitman household was back to normal size. After tarrying a few days at Lapwai, the Smiths moved on to Kamiah arriving there on May 10. Gray accompanied them in order to help in the erection of a rude cabin to serve as a temporary shelter for the summer. The cabin had no floor except the earth and no windows. Sarah wrote in her diary that they really did not need windows as "the many cracks furnish us with sufficient light." None of the other couples in the Oregon Mission lived in such an isolated place and under such primitive conditions as the Smiths at Kamiah. Moreover, none of the six missionary wives was in such poor health as Sarah Smith.

Smith and Gray, who had not been on speaking terms with each other at times when crossing the country in the summer of 1838, now discovered that they were in full agreement in their criticisms of Spalding. In the lonely isolation of Kamiah, the unhappy and ill-adjusted Smith had plenty of time to brood on his misfortunes and to write long letters to Greene. Thus, while at Kamiah, Smith's discontentment became a greater threat to the harmony and success of the Oregon Mission than it ever was at Waiilatpu.

OTHER EVENTS OF THE SPRING AND SUMMER OF 1839

On April 17, 1839, Spalding learned of the arrival at Fort Vancouver of Mr. and Mrs. Edwin O. Hall, members of the Hawaiian Mission of the American Board, with the small printing press which that Mission was giving to the Oregon Mission. Hall informed Spalding that he expected to accompany a Hudson's Bay party under the command of Francis Ermatinger up the Columbia to Fort Walla Walla with the hope of arriving there on or about May 1. He suggested that Spalding meet him at the fort with horses to carry the press to Lapwai but that a canoe be provided for Mrs. Hall as she was then unable to ride horseback. She was suffering from a chronic illness of the spine and was able to sit up, as Narcissa wrote, "but very little" [Letter 63]. We are amazed to read of the long sea voyage and then the travel in Old Oregon under primitive conditions which Mrs. Hall ventured to undertake in her handicapped condition. Moreover, she was pregnant and gave birth to a daughter at Waiilatpu on November 5, 1839. Even Whitman, however, felt that the travel would improve her health and that she would gain much by a change of climate [Letter 62].

The Spaldings with their little girl left Lapwai on April 24 and arrived at Waiilatpu on the 27th. Word came from Pambrun on the 29th that the Halls, with the press, were at Fort Walla Walla. The next day, the Whitmans and the Spaldings rode to the fort. Spalding was delighted with the press and the supplies which came with it. Writing in his diary, he said: "Rev. Mr. Bingham says the press, type, paper, binding materials, sugar, molasses & salt which his church & congregation purchased & sent as a donation to this Mission amounted to about $400." This was the first American press to be established on the Pacific Coast of what is now the United States. In the years following, seven items in the Nez Perce and one in the Spokane language were to be printed on it.[61]

WHITMAN REPORTS TO GREENE

The Spaldings and Edwin Hall, with the pack train carrying the press and supplies, left Fort Walla Walla on May 6. Mrs. Hall made the journey to Lapwai in a canoe manned by friendly Nez Perces. Whitman was at the Fort to see them off. During this visit to the Fort, Whitman had opportunity to talk with Ermatinger, who passed on to him some gossip regarding the unfavorable impression that Samuel Parker had left on Company officials at Fort Vancouver. Such information revived unhappy memories of letters which he and Spalding had received from Greene about a year earlier quoting Parker as saying that he could have taken a party of missionaries of the same size as the 1836 party to Oregon at far less expense than that incurred by Whitman and Spalding. Whitman had replied to those letters in October 1838, but in a mild way.

Some of the things which Ermatinger told raised Whitman's ire. He was doubly sensitive of criticism because of recent events within the Mission; for instance, the vote calling upon him to leave Waiilatpu. There is reason to believe that the Whitmans had considered the possibility of leaving the Mission and moving to the Willamette Valley. Whatever may have been the psychological background, this we know; on May 10, 1839, Whitman wrote a 3,000-word letter to Greene which is the sharpest of all of his extant letters. In it he reviewed his experiences with Parker while crossing the plains and the mountains in the summer of 1835. He cited incident after incident to show Parker's ineptness, his lack of good judgment, his refusal to do his fair share of work, and finally his failure in Old Oregon to prepare the way for the mission party of 1836.[62] Regarding this last point, Whitman wrote:"We cannot say how much good Mr. P's tour will do others, it has done us none, for instead of meeting us at Rendezvous as he agreed, he neglected even to write a single letter containing any information concerning the country, Indians, prospects, or advice of any kind whatever" [Letter 62].

In this letter of May 10, Whitman made only a brief reference to the action of the Mission regarding his possible removal from Waiilatpu:"It was expected that I should have gone to join a new station in a more central location, but it has been deferred for the present." Whitman also gave a financial report for the year ending on the date he wrote. The total expense incurred by the Oregon Mission was £595-1-0, which was less than an average of £100 for each of the six families. When we remember that prices at Fort Vancouver were about double prime cost, the total expense for the year was most reasonable. Whitman assumed £118-19-10 as his share, which included the cost of taking care of three couples of the reenforcement during the winter of 1838–39. His itemized statement follows:

> Family supplies, building materials, farming (tools) provisions, medicines, Indian goods, transportation £67-8-4
> One-sixth General Expense for Black Smith shop, Mill Irons, Steel for ploughs, hoes, chains, etc, bolt cloth, hire of Smith, transportation £17-17-2
> Labour.. £21-3-4
> Passage of an Hawaiian & wife from the Sandwich Isls. ... £12-10-0

ALICE CLARISSA WHITMAN

About four months before Narcissa received her first mail from her family in New York State, she wrote a letter to her "Very, Very Dear Parents," under date of March 14, 1838. This was her thirtieth birthday and the first of her daughter, Alice Clarissa. The letter begins with the lament: "More than two years have passed since I left my father's home and not a single word has been wafted hence, or, perhaps I should say, has greeted my ears to afford consolation in a desponding hour. This long, long silence makes me feel the truth of our situation, that we are far, very far removed from the land of our birth and Christian privileges."

This letter, like others written by Narcissa to her loved ones during the two years her daughter was alive, is sprinkled with tender references to her. The proud mother listed the words the one-year-old could say, as "Papa," "Mama," and "pussy." The last word shows that the Whitmans had a cat. From other references, we know that they also had at least one dog. The little girl was then learning to walk. Narcissa wrote: "She is as large and larger than some of the native children of two years old. Her strength, size, and activity surprise the Indians very much. They think it is owing to their being laced on their tecashes (as they call the board they use for them), motionless night and day, that makes their children so weak and small when compared with her."

On April 11, 1838, Narcissa wrote again to her parents and again made mention of her little girl. "My Clarissa is my own little companion from day to day, and dear daughter." Again: "She is her mother's constant companion, & appears to be very lonely if she is out of sight but for a few moments... Dear child, she is a great solace & comfort to her mother in her lonely hours & God grant she may live still to continue so."[63] In this letter Narcissa requested that some flannel dresses, shoes, and other clothing items be sent for her daughter. She also requested that "the name of Alice Clarissa Whitman, born Wieletpoo, O. Territory, March 14, 1837, be placed in father's family Bible."[64]

On September 18, 1838, shortly after the arrival of the reenforcement, Narcissa wrote another long letter to her sister Jane, from which the following is taken: "Yes, Jane, you cannot know how much of a comfort our little daughter, Alice Clarissa, is to her father and mother. O, how many melancholy hours she has saved me, while living here alone so long, especially when her father is gone for many days together. I wish most sincerely that her aunts could see her, for surely they would love her as well as her parents. She is now eighteen months old, very large and remarkably healthy. She is a great talker. Causes her mother many steps and much anxiety. She is just beginning to sing with us in our family worship. The moment singing commences, if she is not in her mother's arms, she comes to me immediately and wishes me to take her, especially if it is a Nez Perce hymn[65] that we are singing. We have but three or four of them, and sing them every day, and Alice has become so familiar with them that she is repeating some part of them most of the time."

As Narcissa was writing this letter, Alice Clarissa happened to lay a dirty hand on the upper left-hand corner of the page. Since Narcissa had nearly finished filling the page when the incident took place, she decided not to rewrite that part of her letter but to send it as it was with the explanation: "You see, Jane, Alice has come & laid her dirty hands on this paper & given it a fine mark. I send it as it is so that you may have some of her doings to look at & realize perhaps that there is such a child in existence." [See illustration in this volume, page 346.]

The original letter was included in the collection of Narcissa's letters given by her sister, Harriet, to the Oregon Historical Society sometime before 1891. When I was gathering material for my *Marcus Whitman, M.D.*, I visited the Oregon Historical Society and asked to see this letter, as I wanted to see the little girl's smudge marks. I then learned that the letter had mysteriously disappeared. Years later, while examining the Whitman letters in the Coe Collection at Yale University, I discovered this letter, and there on one page were the marks of Alice Clarissa's dirty hand. A copy of this page is included as an illustration in this book. Just how the letter got into the Coe Collection is not fully known.

ALICE CLARISSA DROWNED

As has been indicated, the Walla Walla River flowed a few feet from the first Whitman home. Both Marcus and Narcissa were aware of the danger of the stream as they saw their little girl learning to walk and watched her active feet carry her about the house and dooryard. Marcus was unable to construct a fence around the dooryard for lack of suitable materials. On the Friday before the tragedy, the parents were working in their vegetable garden with Alice who, in her baby ways, was trying to be of assistance. Marcus happened to pull up a radish which the child took and ran away with it. After awhile the parents, missing her in the garden, searched for her and found her washing the radish in the river. They were "horrorstricken," to use Narcissa's term, to find her alone by the stream [Letter 67].

Being more aware than ever of the danger of the stream, the parents repeatedly sought to warn Alice of its dangers. Some weeks before the final tragedy, Whitman found it necessary to drown a sick dog, called Boxer, with which Alice had often played. Feeling that this might be a good object lesson, Alice was permitted to watch the drowning of the dog. That evening after her mother had again repeated the warning about going near the river, the child said: "Alice fall in water; Alice she die like Boxer—Mama have no Alice" [Letter 67].

The events of the last day of Alice's life are described in detail by the sorrowing mother in a letter sent to her father dated September 30, 1839. On Sunday morning, June 23, Narcissa awakened her daughter with a kiss. The child slowly opened her eyes and, then seeing her mother, stretched up her pudgy arms for an embrace. Although only two years and three months old, Alice was able to sing a number of hymns frequently used by her parents in family worship. That morning she asked for "Rock of Ages." Later the grieving mother remembered how, after singing the first stanza, Alice asked: "Mama, should my tears forever flow." That was her way of calling for the second stanza where these words occur.

Later that morning the Whitmans took their daughter with them when they conducted a worship service for the Indians in their vicinity. Here again at the close of the service, "Rock of Ages" was sung. Of this, Narcissa wrote: "She united with us again, with a clearness and distinctness we shall never forget, and with such ecstacy as almost to raise her out of her chair. And no wonder for what words could have been more appropriate to her mind than these:

> *While I draw this fleeting breath,*
> *When my eyelids close in death;*
> *When I rise to worlds unknown,*
> *And behold Thee on Thy throne,*
> *Rock of Ages, cleft for me,*
> *Let me hide myself in Thee.*

Dear father, when you sing this hymn, think of me, for my thoughts do not recur to it without almost overcoming me... This was the last [time] we heard her sing."

About two-thirty on that fateful Sunday afternoon, Margaret McKay set the table for the Sunday evening meal. Both Marcus and Narcissa were absorbed in reading. Later Narcissa had a dim recollection that Alice had said: "Mama, supper is almost ready; let Alice get some water" [Letter 68]. Taking two cups from the table, the child left the house. "This was like a shadow that passed across my mind," wrote Narcissa." [It] passed away and made no impression."

Soon Narcissa realized that the child was gone and asked Margaret to look for her. Margaret went out and not seeing Alice, went to the garden for some vegetables instead of returning at once to report. Then Mungo went out to look and soon he came back saying that he saw two cups in the river. "How did they get there?" asked Narcissa. "Let them be," said Marcus, "and get them tomorrow, because of the Sabbath." But Narcissa, becoming uneasy, again asked: "How did they get there?" Then Marcus replied: "I suppose Alice put them there." Laying aside his book, he went out to investigate. Narcissa followed. At first they went to the garden. Then after a flash of memory crossed her mind about Alice getting the cups, Narcissa ran to the river. Marcus joined her.

In a letter to her mother, Narcissa described their frantic search: "We ran down on the brink of the river near the place where she was, and, as if forbidden to approach the spot, although accessible, we passed her, crossed a bend in the river far below, and then back again, and then in another direction, still further below, while others got into the river and waded to find her, and what was remarkable, all entered the river below where she was last found."

When all hope passed of finding her alive, the despairing parents turned towards their house. Then, according to Narcissa: "We saw an old Indian preparing to enter the river where she fell in. I stopped to see him swim under water until he passed me, and just a little below me he took her from the water and exclaimed 'She is found.'"[66] Dr. Whitman grasped the body and did what he could to restore breathing but it was in vain. The child was dead. In the depths of her sorrow, Narcissa "flew to the promises of God's holy word," where she found the strength to say: "Thy will be done, not mine" [Letter 68].

The Funeral

A messenger was sent at once to notify the Spaldings and others at Lapwai. He made the 120-mile trip in twenty-five hours. E. O. Hall, the printer, left at once for Waiilatpu. He rode all Monday night and arrived at Waiilatpu in twenty-four hours. Spalding was recovering from an injury received as the result of a serious fall, perhaps from a horse, and was unable to ride horseback. Therefore, the Spaldings made the trip to Fort Walla Walla by canoe down the Clearwater, the Snake, and the Columbia Rivers. The log canoe was manned by Nez Perces. They traveled all Monday night, and during the day on Tuesday and Wednesday, arriving at Fort Walla Walla about 8:00 p.m. on Wednesday. The next morning, June 26, they rode out to Waiilatpu, arriving there about 10:00 a.m. Pambrun accompanied them. Spalding noted in his diary: "Riding caused considerable pain in my side... Mrs. S. much fatigued." It may be assumed that the Spaldings took their little girl with them.

During the three-day interval following the child's death, Narcissa had prepared a shroud for the body while Marcus supervised the making of a coffin and the digging of a grave at the foot of the hill to the northeast of the mission house. Spalding took for his text words found in II Kings 4:26: "Is it well with the child?" Only a few were present for the funeral service. These included the Whitmans and the members of their household, the Spaldings, Hall, Pambrun, and possibly a few Indians. In a letter to her mother dated October 9, 1839, Narcissa wrote that although the grave was in sight every time she stepped out-of-doors:"I seem not to feel that she is there." The spirit had gone to God who gave it.

Because of the slowness of the mails, we may assume that for the next two years letters from the States carried references to Alice Clarissa. Perhaps also in time came the clothing that Narcissa had requested in her letter of April 11, 1838. Such references and articles of clothing would have been poignant reminders of the little child no longer with them.

Sometime after the funeral, Dr. Whitman constructed a picket fence around the grave which a visitor to Waiilatpu saw in May 1843.[67] In the late 1930s, a construction crew working on the road at the base of the hill, uncovered some short boards which might have been used for a coffin and bones judged to be of a two-year-old child. Because of a belief

CHAPTER THIRTEEN *A Year of Adjustments, 1838–1839* 387

that these remains were those of Alice Clarissa, a marker was erected on the site and dedicated on May 8, 1969.

RECONCILIATION AND REDEDICATION

An old adage proved again to be true: "A joy shared is a joy increased; a sorrow shared is a sorrow decreased." The hearts of all in the Mission were touched by the great bereavement which had come to the Whitmans. For the time being, at least, old animosities were forgotten and a kindlier feeling was manifested. Whitman began to reproach himself for his reluctance to abide by the decision of the Mission to move. Terrible questions haunted his mind. Was the death of his little girl a judgment of God for his hardness of heart? Was this tragic event a sign from heaven telling him not to leave the Mission but to remain at his post? In a letter dated June 30, 1839, and directed to Elkanah Walker, Whitman wrote: "It is sufficient to say I could not, see any hope of a reconciliation in the Mission & *had concluded to take the consequences of leaving the Mission*[68] at the (next) annual meeting but God in his wise & holy Providence has seen fit to stay me from such a course. I feel satisfied nothing but his hand has done it. I was set upon an opportunity of self justification but God, I trust, has shown me that I should exercise a different spirit."

Whitman gave Walker further details regarding his change of attitude: "On Sabbath, the 23rd instant, I was lead to read Henry on Meekness[69] which so softened my feelings for the time at least as to lead me to desire that Grace & to resolve to exercise it toward the Brethren of the Mission, which was the first lucid moment of reason I had seen. But this was God's method to prepare me for a severe chastening stroke. In the afternoon of that day, he saw cause to take from us our much loved Alice Clarissa." Matthew Henry's small volume on *Meekness* may have been the book he was reading when little Alice got the cups and left the house for the river. Whitman was moved to ask the forgiveness of all in the Mission "for the spirit of hardness & stubbornness which they have seen in me at any time." Whitman added, in this letter to Walker: "I find my pen quite too stiff to express the feelings of my heart. I no longer wish to make conditions of peace with my brethren... I feel to confess that I have been to blame at every step of difficulty in the Mission." Humbly, he asked the forgiveness of the Walkers for everything he might have done to offend them. In this confession, Narcissa joined and likewise asked forgiveness.

Narcissa, in a letter to her father dated October 10, 1840, mentioned that her husband had been about to leave the Mission "had not the Lord removed from us our beloved child." She wrote that the affliction had not only softened his heart, but also "had a great effect upon all in the mission; it softened their hearts toward us." In a letter that Whitman wrote to Greene on October 15, 1840, he stated that he had planned to leave the Mission "had not the Providence of God arrested me in my deliberate determination to do so by taking away our dear child in so sudden a manner by drowning."

More Trips to Lapwai

The Spaldings remained at Waiilatpu for a week following Alice Clarissa's funeral, thus giving Spalding time to recover from his injury. Since Spalding felt the need for a conference of all working in the Nez Perce language to decide on an alphabet, he induced the Whitmans to return with him and E. O. Hall to Lapwai. The party left Waiilatpu on Thursday morning, July 4, and, in order to avoid traveling on Sunday, rode on the average forty miles a day. They arrived at Lapwai late on Saturday, the 6th. On the following Monday, the Whitmans, the Spaldings, and Hall left for Kamiah, sixty miles distant, to consult with Smith. This trip took them two days. Spalding noted in his diary that the Smiths were living "in a very open house without floor or windows, much to the injury... of Mrs. Smith's health. Their food, pudding & milk is quite too simple, I think."

Now that a printing press was at hand and Hall from Honolulu was present to help with any printing that might be done, it was necessary to decide upon a system for reducing the Nez Perce language to writing. Spalding had worked on this problem and had devised an alphabet in which he used some consonant letters of the Roman alphabet, not needed in the Nez Perce language, to represent certain vowel sounds: e.g., "b" was used as "a" in"hawk". [70] Spalding's alphabet proved to be too inaccurate to be used. Even though Smith had been on the field for less than a year, he had already mastered the language to such an extent that even Spalding deferred to his judgment. Sometime previous to this meeting at Kamiah, Greene had sent to the Oregon missionaries an essay by John Pickering on "The Adoption of a Uniform Orthography for the Indian languages of North America,"[71] which proved to be a helpful guide. The four men—Whitman, Spalding, Hall, and Smith agreed on taking the twelve letter alphabet which was being used in the Hawaiian Islands to which were added the letters "s" and "t." Other letters, as "b, d, f, g, r, v, and z" were to be used in foreign words. The alphabet thus worked out was formally adopted at the mission meeting held the following September.

The Whitmans spent the following Sunday, July 14, at Lapwai and left on Tuesday for Waiilatpu where they arrived on Friday, the 19th. That very day word came from Tshimakain that Mrs. Eells was seriously ill. Her husband, desparing of her life, begged Whitman to come at once. Marcus was reluctant to leave his wife alone when the loss of their daughter was still so fresh in their minds, but duty called. Narcissa had to pay the price of being a doctor's wife. "It was then," she wrote, "that I fully realized the full reality of my bereavement" [Letter 68].

Marcus was able to return in about two weeks. During the third week in August, the Whitmans were pleasantly surprised when William Geiger, Jr., of Angelica, New York, suddenly arrived at Waiilatpu. With him was a D. G. Johnson. Both men were on their way to the Willamette Valley with the expectation of settling there. They were the first of a long procession of Oregon immigrants to stream past the Whitman mission. A few years later [as will be mentioned], Geiger entered Whitman's employ.

On Sunday, August 25, little Eliza Spalding got an obstruction in her throat which so alarmed her parents that they sent for Dr. Whitman. By riding all night after receiving word, he was able to reach Lapwai on the 28th. He found the little girl recovered. This was the fifth time since the first of that year, 1839, that Whitman had made the 240-mile, round trip, ride to Lapwai. During those same eight months, he had also ridden twice to the Tucannon River, once to Kamiah from Lapwai, and once to Tshimakain, making a total of about 1,800 miles. If on these trips, Whitman had averaged riding thirty miles a day, this meant that he would have spent a full two months in the saddle! Under such circumstances, we marvel how he was able at the same time to direct farming activities at Waiilatpu, tend to the growing administrative duties of the Mission, continue his study of the language, and carry on his professional and missionary activities for the natives.

Since the Annual Meeting of the Mission was scheduled to be held at Lapwai during the first part of September, Whitman made plans, before he left Waiilatpu, for Narcissa to follow. On the evening of August 30, when Narcissa was expected to arrive, Marcus mounted his horse and with little Eliza Spalding rode down the trail on the south side of the Clearwater to meet his wife. Narcissa and those with her happened to have crossed the Snake River at Alpowa and had gone up the north side of the Clearwater, so they missed each other. Narcissa arrived at Lapwai at sunset while Marcus returned after dark.

CHAPTER 13 ENDNOTES

1 Strictly speaking, the name Lapwai applied to the whole valley and also to the site of the first Spalding home. Today the name Lapwai has been given to a small settlement several miles up the valley. In 1897 the mission site on the bank of the Clearwater was named Spalding when a post office was established there.

2 From Spalding letter of October 9, 1837, in *Hawaiian Spectator*, I:367: "Mrs. McDonald ... with more or less native blood ... has no native appearance, has spent some time with Rev. Mr. Cochran of Red. R., reads and speaks English very correctly." Narcissa called her "quite an intelligent woman" [Letter 50].

3 See, also, discussion of finances in section "The Men at Fort Vancouver," Chapter Nine, and Appendix 2.

4 Although Dunbar and Allis founded the mission for the Pawnee Indians, at first they were appointed for the Oregon work.

5 See Drury, *Walker*, pp. 254 ff., for an account of the author's experiences in receiving from Sam Walker, the youngest son of Elkanah and Mary Walker, many items such as letters, books, etc., which had belonged to his parents. Included in the lot were eight volumes from the Columbia Mission Library. Most of the items then received are now in Coll. Wn.

6 The financial reports of the Oregon Mission are in Coll. A. Photostats of certain relevant sections are in Coll. Wn.

7 See Drury, *Spalding*, p. 203. The copy Spalding received is now in Coll. W.

8 Hulbert, *O.P.*, VI:284 ff.

9 Henry Hill was Treasurer of the American Board, 1822–54.

10 Drury, *Spalding*, 205 ff. Also, McLoughlin ms., Coll. B., p. 6: "The Rev. Mr. Parker... is very unpopular with the other Protestant missionaries in this country for which I see no cause."

11 The original record book is in the Presbyterian Historical Society, Philadelphia. An inaccurate transcription appeared in the 1903 *Minutes of the Synod of Washington* which was republished in the *Minutes* for 1936. Spalding included in the records of the church a brief biographical sketch of each of the charter members.

12 See Chapter Four, fn. 3, for reference to the division of the Presbyterian Church in 1837 into the Old and New School branches. The latter was closely affiliated with the Congregational Church. Bath Presbytery was a part of the New School. At the time of the organization of the First Presbyterian Church of Oregon, the missionaries were unaware of this division in their home church. No record has been found in the minutes of Bath Presbytery to this Oregon church. Spalding possibly had forgotten to report its organization. Actually, the polity of the Oregon Mission Church was more Congregational than it was Presbyterian.

13 Original in Coll. W.

14 Writing to Greene on Sept. 11, 1838, Spalding asked: "Did I do right in baptizing Compo, who had before been baptized by a Catholic priest, & did I do right in refusing our friend Mr. Pambrun, a Catholic, a place at our table?" No record of Greene's reply to these questions has been found.

15 Drury, *Spalding and Smith*, p. 72, quoting from Smith's letter to Greene of July 10, 1838.

16 *W.C.Q.*, xvi (1913), No. 2, gives Gray's journal of the trip. Josephy, *The Nez Perce Indians*, pp. 166 ff. points out that Gray's conduct in this skirmish brought lasting

disgrace to him among the mountain men when they heard about the fight.

17 According to the records of the Medical College, Gray gave his home address as "Columbia, Oregon."

18 Mowry, *Marcus Whitman*, p. 86.

19 The *Annual Reports of the American Board* listed Rogers as a member of the Oregon Mission for three years under the following classifications: 1840—Mechanic; 1841—Teacher; and 1842—Printer & Teacher.

20 Drury, *F.W.W.*, III:239, quoting from Gray's letter to Greene written at the Rendezvous July 10, 1838: "Please inform me in your next letter whether you told Mr. Smith while in N. York that he would be furnished with a separate tent, travelling cases, cooking utensils &c &c for the journey or what suggestion you made to him on the subject of traveling from Independence to Walla Walla." Evidently Smith had complained to Gray regarding his failure to provide what Greene had promised. Greene's answer to Gray's question has not been found.

21 Drury, *F.W.W.*, II:87. Hereafter when name of person quoted and date of diary entry are given, no further reference will be given in endnotes.

22 Drury, *Spalding and Smith*, p. 72. Josephy, in his *The Nez Perce Indians*, p. 176, in commenting on Smith's evaluation of Gray, wrote: "Smith was a master at character assassination, but in the case of Gray, he reported facts."

23 Drury, *F.W.W.*, III:238.

24 Drury, *F.W.W.*, II:109.

25 HBC *Arch.*, 2/223/b/20.

26 See ante, fn. 5 of this chapter. This volume was one of the items received from Sam Walker on July 15, 1939. A few months after these items were obtained, the Walker home with all of its contents burned. Mr. and Mrs. Walker escaped.

27 No record book containing the minutes of the Annual Meetings of the Oregon Mission has been located. Copies of actions taken were sometimes included in letters sent to the American Board by individual members of the Mission. In Walker's letter to Greene dated October 15, 1838, we find a summary of actions taken at the September 1838 meeting. See Drury, *Spalding and Smith*, p. 90.

28 The term Flathead is nowadays confined to a tribe in western Montana, but in the time of the missionaries, the name was used more widely to include some other tribes, such as the Spokanes, who spoke closely related Salishan dialects.

29 See Drury, "The Columbia Maternal Associations," *O.H.Q.*, XXXIX (1938), pp. 99ff.

30 Drury, *F.W.W.*, I:245. Original letter in Coll. Y.

31 Drury, *Spalding and Smith*, p. 255. Hereafter references to diary entries of either Spalding or Smith will be to this volume, thus no endnotes will be needed.

32 Drury, *F.W.W.*, I:244 gives a letter written by Mary Gray to Lapwai on Sept. 29, 1838, in which she stated: "We have observed the M[aternal] Association but in order to do this we were last Wednesday obliged to resort to a grove to find a place sufficiently retired from public gaze.

33 Through some oversight, the two younger daughters of the Spaldings were not listed. For a list of the children born to the five women, see Drury, *F.W.W.*, I:22. The Smiths had no children. Descendants of the Walkers, the Spaldings, and the Grays still live in the Pacific Northwest.

34 Drury, *Spalding*, p. 201, quoting from a letter Spalding wrote to Greene on July 12, 1841: "I have already disposed of a few young cattle on this score."

35 Walker to Greene, Oct. 15, 1838. See also, Drury, *Walker*, p. 101.

36 Fort Colville stood in the middle of a prairie about one and one-half miles wide, and about three miles long on the east bank of the Columbia River. The site is now covered with waters backed up by the Grand Coulee Dam.

37 Mrs. Perkins, neé Elvira Johnson, was a schoolmate of Mary Walker's in 1834 when both attended the Maine Wesleyan Seminary, Kents Hill, Maine. Miss Johnson was a member of the first 1837 Methodist reenforcement. On Nov. 21, 1837, she married the Rev. H. K. W. Perkins, who arrived in Oregon with the second reenforcement of that year.

38 HBC Arch., A/6/25. According to a letter from the Hudson's Bay Company in London to Douglas, Nov. 15, 1837, the initial idea of sending priests to Old Oregon for the French Canadians came from the Bishop of Juliopolis, the Roman Catholic primate of Canada. The letter stated: "One important objection to our compliance with the Bishop's request . . . is that when the boundary line shall be determined, the southern side of the Columbia River may become United States Territory, and we are unwilling to become instrumental in forwarding the views of the American Government and establishing for them a Colony of British Subjects, who in due time might become dangerous neighbors." HBC Arch., B/223/c carries a reference to a recommendation of Dr. McLoughlin's that a priest be sent to the Willamette Valley. In Oct. 1838, the adult male population of the Valley was 51, including 23 French Canadians, 10 Methodist missionaries, and 18 other Americans. *McLoughlin's Vancouver Letters*, III:XXXIV.

39 Frederick V. Holman, "Biographical Sketch of Dr. McLoughlin," *O.H.Q.*, VIII (1907) 312.

40 *W.H.Q.*, XXIV (1933):56, quoting from a letter written by Cyrus Shepard which first appeared in *Zion's Herald*, Boston, Oct. 28, 1835.

41 This log church was the forerunner of the Roman Catholic church at St. Paul, Oregon. A brick building, which replaced the log church, was dedicated Nov. 1, 1846. It is still in use.

42 Gray, *Oregon*, pp. 194 ff., gives the text, quoting from *Senate Document, TwentySixth Congress, First Session, No. 514*.

43 Bancroft, *Oregon*, I:231.

44 HBC Arch., *1857 Parliamentary Report, Notes from the Select Committee*, pp. 1102 ff.

45 There were four priests with the Blanchet surname in the Old Oregon country. The first was Francois Norbet Blanchet, consecrated Bishop of Philadelphia in Partibus Infidelium (name later changed to Bishop of Drasa) at Montreal on July 25, 1845. A younger brother, A. M. A. Blanchet was made Bishop of Walla Walla shortly before the Whitman massacre in 1847. A nephew of these two, Francis Xavier Blanchet, and George Blanchet, O.M. (relationship unknown) later went to Oregon. Information furnished by kindness of the late Father W. J. Davis, S.J., of Spokane.

46 Drury, *F.W.W.*, III: 159.

47 Elkanah Walker's diary; original in Huntington Library, San Marino, Calif.

48 Drury, *F.W.W.*, III:162.

49 Richardson, *The Whitman Mission*, p. 49.

50 *Ibid.*, p. 150.

51 Italics are the author's.

52 Cyrus Walker was the second son born of white American parents in Old Oregon, but the first to live to maturity. The first was Joseph Beers, a son of a Methodist missionary couple, Mr. and Mrs. Alanson Beers, born Sept. 15, 1837, in the Willamette Valley.

53 A long part of Spalding's letter appeared in the *Missionary Herald*, XXXIII (1839):473 ff.

54 Parker, *Journal*, p. 288.

55 Drury, *Spalding and Smith*, p. 127. Sections of Spalding's letters to Greene, written in 1836 and 1837, which referred to Tackensuatis, had been published in the *Missionary Herald*.

56 *Ibid.*, pp. 96 ff.

57 Whitman's letter, No. 59a, carries reference to a request for a supply of corn and potatoes to be paid to Lawyer, perhaps for his services in teaching the Nez Perce language to Smith.

58 Drury, *Spalding*, p. 217, quoting from Spalding's letter to Greene, Oct. 15, 1842.

59 Drury, *Spalding and Smith*, p. 173, for reference by Smith to the marriage performed by Spalding.

60 *Ibid.*, p. 95. Italics are the author's.

61 See articles by Howard M. Ballou, *O.H.Q.*, XXIII (1922): 3952; 95-110, for history of the press.

62 Much information from this letter has been used in a previous chapter of this book where the travels of Whitman and Parker to the Rockies in 1835 were reviewed.

63 This letter of Narcissa's was published in *T.O.P.A.*, 1891: 101 ff., but with about 1,000 words being omitted. The quotation here given is from the part not published.

64 All efforts to locate the Prentiss family Bible have failed. The Whitman family Bible is in Coll. W.

65 Spalding translated a number of gospel hymns into the Nez Perce language, some of which are still being used by the Christian Nez Perces. It may be that the Nez Perce hymns used by the Whitmans were some Spalding had translated.

66 In a letter to me dated May 13, 1960, Helen L. Shaffner of Dillon, Montana, wrote: "I wish I could have recorded all the stories told me by my Father and GreatUncle. One of my favorites, though, concerns the son of the man who found Alice Clarissa's body. For years his picture hung on the wall in the basement of my Great Uncle's home. The picture showed him in the bright shirt that had been given his Father by Whitman as a reward for finding the body." She identified the Indian who found the body of Alice Clarissa as Chief Umtippe.

67 Hines, *Wild Life in Oregon*, p. 176.

68 Italics are the author's.

69 Matthew Henry's *Discourse on Meekness* was published at Plymouth, Mass., in 1828. This volume may have been included in a shipment of books sent to the Oregon Mission by the American Board which arrived during the summer of 1838. The following quotation from p. 12, might have been read by Whitman on that fateful

June 23:"When the events of providence are grievous and afflictive, displeasing to sense, and crossing our secular interests; meekness, doth not only quiet us under them, but reconciles us to them; and enables us, not only to bear, but to receive evil as well as good, at the hand of the Lord."

70 *O.H.Q.*, XXIII (1922) carries illustrations of some pages printed by Spalding at Lapwai which illustrate the alphabet which Spalding first devised.

71 Published in *Memoirs of the American Academy of Arts and Sciences*, Vol. IV, Part I, Cambridge, Mass., 1820.

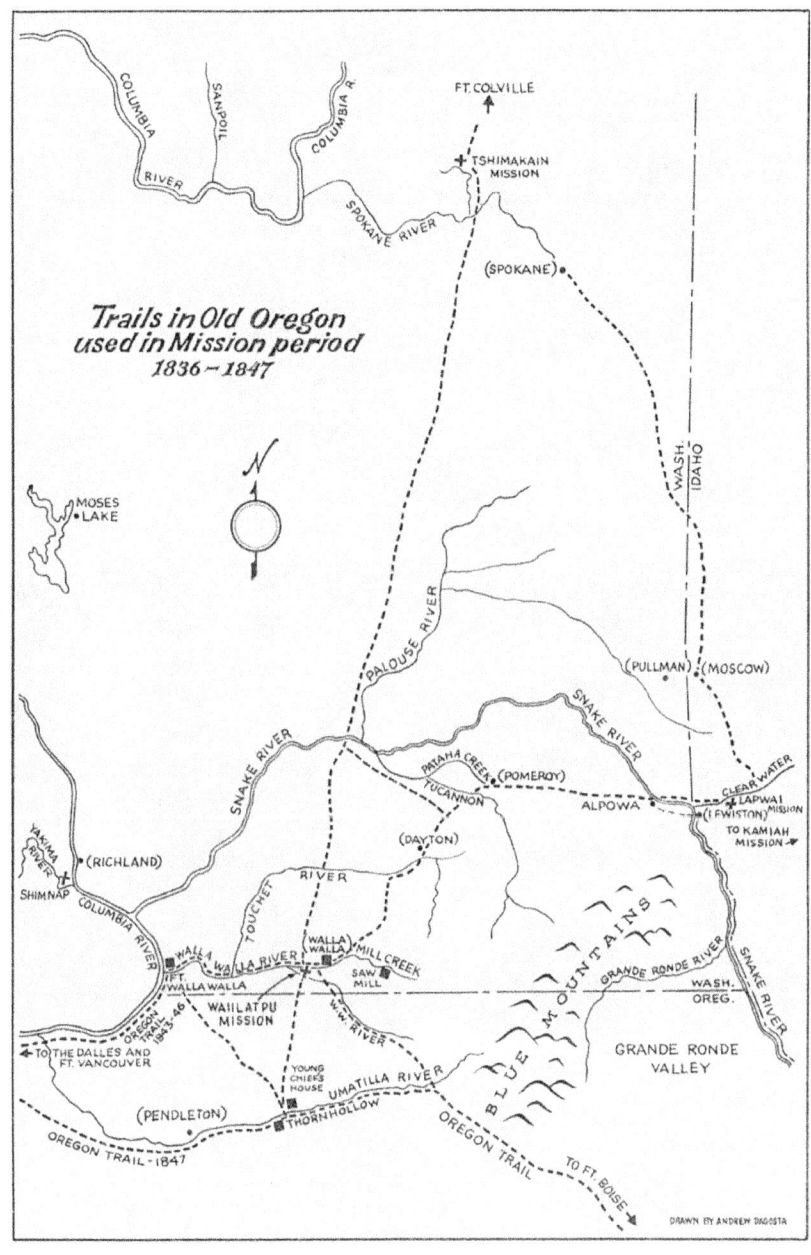

LETTER OF NARCISSA WHITMAN
This last page of the letter to her sister Jane, September 18, 1838, shows the smudge of her little girl's hand. Alice was eighteen months old. The final two sentences read: "You see Jane, Alice has come & laid her dirty hands on this letter & given it a fine mark. I send it as it is so that you may have some of her doings to look at & realize perhaps that there is such a child in existance." Courtesy and permission, Houghton Library, Harvard University.

[CHAPTER FOURTEEN]

FOURTH YEAR OF THE OREGON MISSION
1839–1840

The fourth year of the Oregon Mission of the American Board was marred by growing dissension among its members; long letters of criticism about Spalding were sent to the Board. The two troublemakers were W. H. Gray and Asa B. Smith, both being unhappy in their respective stations within the Mission. The fact that both men had made spurofthemoment decisions to go as missionaries to Old Oregon reveals a certain instability of character and lack of good judgment. Some of the blame must also rest on the secretaries of the Board who approved their appointments with so little investigation of suitability.

Gray Demands a Station for Himself

The Annual Meeting of the Oregon Mission for 1839 was held in Spalding's home at Lapwai September 2–5. Whitman, Spalding, Gray, and Smith were present. Walker and Eells were unable to attend. Hall and Rogers were made corresponding members. Spalding was again elected moderator and Smith, clerk. The first action taken rescinded the vote of the special meeting held the previous February, which called for Whitman to start a new station in a central location. Now he was permitted to remain at Waiilatpu, and Smith was authorized to open a station at Kamiah. "I do not approve of this," wrote Spalding in his diary. "There should be a mission in the Cayuse tribe & the physician should be near the centre of the field."

Gray argued for a station of his own. After considerable heated discussion, the majority reluctantly granted permission for him to explore for a station, but again Spalding disapproved. This particular action of the Mission caused much subsequent trouble because Gray interpreted it to mean that he was authorized to establish a new station, and not merely to explore the possibility. In a letter to Walker dated October 15, Whitman wrote: "I thought it was clearly expressed by the meeting that he was not to locate for the year to come but make his home at Clear Water for that time."

As soon as possible after the Mission meeting closed on September 5, the Grays started on their tour of exploration. After being away from Lapwai for more than a month, they returned on October 18 and informed Spalding that they had selected a site "about a day above Walla Walla on a small stream putting in from the S.W."[1] Gray began immediate preparations to move. Spalding, with his characteristic bluntness, told him that the Mission had not authorized the establishment of a new station, but had only given him permission to explore. The argument became heated. Gray, thoroughly discouraged and smarting under what he felt was his inferior status in the Mission, decided to investigate the possibilities of finding employment elsewhere.

Gray left for Fort Vancouver on October 21 with the hope of finding some employment in the Willamette Valley and even possibly with the Hudson's Bay Company. Dr. McLoughlin refused to hire him as he could not produce satisfactory evidence that his withdrawal from the Mission met the approval of his associates. This rebuff by Dr. McLoughlin accounts in part for the caustic remarks which Gray later made on the Hudson's Bay Company. Also, Spalding's attitude explains Gray's severe criticism of him in several letters written to Greene during the winter of 1839–40.

Disappointed in his endeavors to find employment elsewhere, Gray returned to Fort Walla Walla and sent word to his wife at Lapwai to join him. Gray was so angry with Spalding that he refused to return to Lapwai. Mary Gray, with her seven-month-old baby left Lapwai on November 11 with only an Indian escort. During Gray's absence, Spalding wrote to Walker and Eells to find out how they would interpret the action of the Mission regarding Gray. Both replied expressing full agreement with the position that he and Whitman had taken; thus the judgment of the four was unanimous against Gray moving. Had Gray been able to find employment elsewhere, the subsequent history of the Mission would have been far different.

Early in the week of November 10, Whitman left for Lapwai to attend Mrs. Spalding who was expecting to be confined about the middle of November. He reached the sandy beach on the Clearwater River, opposite the Spalding home, on Thursday night, the 14th, but being unable to attract Spalding's attention, had to spend the night sleeping on the sand. The little beach is still there.[2]

While Whitman was at Lapwai, word came from Gray demanding a special meeting of the Mission to clarify his status. Both Whitman and Spalding felt that this was impractical because of the cost and trouble involved. They wrote a joint letter, dated November 25, to Gray in which they pointed out the difficulties in holding such a meeting and "respectfully requested" him to proceed to Waiilatpu where Whitman was to provide him with living quarters and where he was to assist in the erection of buildings and such other work as "Doct. Whitman shall direct." Gray was infuriated when he received the letter. He replied on December 2, saying:

In regard to your orders or request, I have only to say: Gentlemen, I shall not yet nor shall I put myself under the control of any Committee of our Mission to answer individual demands any further than labor properly coming under the care and control of the Mission. The proposition to which you refer was gratuitous and does not relate to Doct. Whitman in any way except that he is bound equally with myself to assist the ordained Ministers (not Doct. Whitman) in building and furnishing their permanent houses... I protest against your right as a Committee of this Mission to order me to obey the private order or direction of any member of this Mission, or any body else in any way, shape, or manner.[3]

Whitman, on December 3, wrote to Walker: "What is to be the course of Mr. Gray, I know not. He is with his family at Walla Walla. I invited him here & offered to arrange a house for him... but he objected to all we propose..." Although Gray was embittered against Spalding, he was even more aroused over the "request" that he go to Waiilatpu and work for Whitman. In another letter to Walker, dated December 27, 1839, Whitman wrote that Gray "has spent six to eight weeks at Walla Walla, much of the time... in playing chequers with Mr. Payette while I had no door to my house & of course, no chairs or any thing of furniture or windows but what Mr. Pambrun sent me." Finally, Gray decided that returning to Lapwai was for him the lesser of two evils. Although Gray and his family arrived at the Spalding station on December 28, he sulked during the winter months, criticizing the constructive efforts Spalding was making, and in other ways causing trouble.

The First Independent Missionaries

When Whitman had arrived at Lapwai on August 28 to attend the Annual Meeting of the Mission, he brought news of the expected arrival that fall of two missionary couples who were venturing into the Oregon country on a "faith" basis, without the support of any missionary board. Whitman had learned this from William Geiger, Jr., who had traveled with them as far as the Rendezvous and had then pushed on ahead. The couples were the Rev. and Mrs. John Smith Griffin and Mr. and Mrs. Asahel Munger. Spalding knew Griffin, for Griffin had helped him attach a top to the Dearborn wagon Captain Levi Hart had given his daughter and son-in-law in July 1835 before they started for their mission field which they then thought would be among the Osage Indians.[4] The Griffins and the Mungers expected to establish a selfsupporting mission among some tribe of Oregon Indians—a highly impractical idea which at once aroused grave misgivings among all members of the Oregon Mission. They foresaw trouble and indeed trouble came.

Asahel Munger, a carpenter, had been a member of a colony of religious zealots who settled at Oberlin, Ohio, in 1833. John S. Griffin had entered the newly established Oberlin Theological Seminary in 1836, graduated in 1838, and shortly afterwards was ordained by the Congregational Church. Sometime in the summer of 1838 Muriger and Griffin had attended a meeting of the Oberlin Missionary Society when a speaker presented a thrilling report on missionary activities in Old Oregon. References were made to the Lee Party of 1834 and to the Whitman-Spalding party of 1836. Griffin was stirred by the message as he knew the Spaldings. According to Gray, Griffin decided shortly afterwards to go to Oregon as a missionary and persuaded Munger and his wife, Eliza, to go with him.[5] At that time Griffin was unmarried.

The two men applied to the American Board for appointments. But the Board had just authorized the 1838 reenforcement, and was also in financial difficulties, so the applications were therefore rejected. Munger then applied to the Congregational Church in Oberlin for an endorsement of his plan to go to Oregon as a missionary but the church refused to give any funds saying: "Under present circumstances the church can not feel justified in recommending to Br. & Sister Munger to embark on their proposed missionary expedition."[6] As will be told later, Munger became insane after his arrival in Old Oregon; it may be that the Oberlin church was aware of some mental instability and for that reason refused to endorse or support his proposed mission.

Griffin and Munger then turned to the Congregational Association of North Litchfield, Connecticut, which agreed to furnish funds to buy their outfit. With this assistance, the two men decided to go out to Oregon in 1839 on an independent basis, foolishly believing that the Lord would provide. Out of their abysmal ignorance of conditions in Old Oregon, they cherished the hope that once there, they could establish a self-supporting mission, without any outside financial assistance.

While passing through St. Louis on their way west, Griffin, in February 1839, met Miss Desire C. Smith. After a whirlwind courtship, they were married on April 10. The four crossed the plains to the Rendezvous with a small caravan of the American Fur Company. Mrs. Griffin and Mrs. Munger were the seventh and eighth white American omen to cross the Continental Divide. Like the six who had preceded them, they rode horseback on sidesaddles from the Missouri frontier to the Columbia River. After leaving the Rendezvous, the two couples had the good fortune to travel with a small Hudson's Bay party to Fort Walla Walla under the command of Francis Ermatinger.

From several sources we learn that Griffin and Munger quarreled, especially after they left the Rendezvous. According to one report: "Munger blamed Griffin for the diet which made Mrs. M. unwell." Evidently Griffin was doing the cooking. Munger, who kept a journal his overland travels, made the following brief note for Monday, July 29: "This day we divided our mess."[7] There were other points of friction also. The dream they had cherished at the beginning of their journey that the two couples would live and work together in one station was shattered. By the time they had reached Fort Boise, they were scarcely on speaking terms.

The missionaries learned much from Ermatinger. As they drew near Fort Walla Walla, they became increasingly aware of the realities of their precarious situation. Munger's journal reflects the uneasiness he felt regarding his future. How would they be able to support themselves without funds in a wilderness? In the Grande Ronde Valley, they learned from the Cayuse Indians that the Whitmans were at Lapwai attending a Mission meeting. After obtaining some directions regarding trails, the Griffins struck out alone without a guide for the Spalding mission. On September 9, Spalding noted without enthusiasm in his diary: "Mr. Griffin & wife arrive unexpectedly." He had no alternative but to receive them.

On his way back to Waiilatpu, following the Mission meeting, Whitan stopped over at Fort Walla Walla where he met the Mungers. On the morning of September 10, he entered into an arrangement with Munger by which he agreed to furnish board and room for the couple and pay Munger $8.00 a month until March 1, 1840, for his services as carpenter. Whitman needed help as Compo and his family had left for the Willamette Valley the previous May. Being able to hire a carpenter was one bright aspect of the unexpected burden of taking care of indigent missionaries so suddenly thrust upon the members of the Oregon Mission. Whitman was in urgent need of a qualified workman to assist in the erection of his new house, especially after Gray had refused to help; Munger seemed to be an answer to his prayers. The Mungers moved into the room which the Smiths had occupied, and within a month Munger finished a room for the Halls.

Edwin O. Hall, who had been at Lapwai to set up the printing press, returned to Waiilatpu after the Mission meeting. His wife, being an invalid, was taken down the Snake River in a canoe and carried from Fort Walla Walla to Waiilatpu in a hammock. On November 5, she gave birth to a baby girl. The Halls remained at Waiilatpu until March 1, 1840, when they left to return to Hawaii.

Secretary Greene Advises Regarding Independent Missionaries

When Secretary Greene heard about the intentions of Griffin and Munger to go out to Old Oregon on an independent bases, he wrote to Spalding on October 15, 1838, saying: "You should conduct [yourselves] toward them, as of course you will be disposed to do, with all Christian courtesy & kindness... But do not permit the affairs of your mission & theirs to become entangled, so that you shall in any manner be deemed responsible for what they do." [8] Although the members of the Oregon Mission had pronounced differences of opinion regarding some policies, they were unanimous in deploring the coming of the independent missionaries and were in full accord with the advice Greene had to give.

In a letter to Greene dated September 13, 1839, Smith wrote: "The least that can be said is that they have brought themselves & the cause of Christ into disgrace... We must feed them for the winter, or the H.B. Co. must have mercy upon them or they will starve." [9] Spalding expressed himself in a similar way in his letter to Greene of October 2 when he wrote: "We shall probably furnish them with labor enough for their support this winter. But I am sure they cannot succeed in their proposed self supporting Mission." [10]

The straitened circumstances in which the Griffins and the Mungers found themselves is further revealed in a letter written by Sarah Smith to Mary Walker and Myra Eells dated from Kamiah on December 18, 1839. She wrote: "What is best for us to do about giving to Mrs. Griffin? What they can do I know not, or how they can get things to make them comfortable I know not, unless some one gives them. I would give with all my heart if it is right. Mr. Smith, Mr. Hall & others say that they have come in opposition to the Amr. Board & ought not to be assisted. But the poor woman has come without a sheet or pillow case, & how they will get them I don't know. Mrs. Spalding while I was there gave her three *broken plates*... & enough wide striped cotton to make a pair of sheets. If husband will consent I shall give her some things... She has more neck dresses than she will ever need & all *very pretty*. Mr. G. has enough. But *sheets, pillow cases, paper & crockery*, they need. Would you give them: Shall you do it?" [11]

When Munger's term of service ended on March 1, 1840, Whitman rehired him for another six months and raised his wages to £3 per month. "He is a good house carpenter," wrote Whitman to Greene on

March 27. "In that time I hope he will finish our house & make us some comfortable furniture & some farming implements." Writing on May 2, Narcissa said: "It seems as if the Lord's hand was in it in sending Mr. and Mrs. Munger just at this time, and I know not how to feel grateful enough." Mrs. Munger was able to help Narcissa with the housework. On June 25, 1840, she gave birth to a daughter. The Mungers continued to live at Waiilatpu until the spring of 1841 when they moved to the Willamette Valley. More will be said of them in a later chapter. As also will be indicated, three more independent missionary couples arrived at the Whitman mission in August 1840.

First Native Converts

Should the success or failure of a mission to American Indians be judged by the number of baptisms recorded? If so, then the Oregon Mission of the American Board could not be called a success, especially when its record of baptisms is compared with that of the Roman Catholic missionaries who, during the same years, were baptizing natives by the hundreds in the upper Columbia River Valley.

Of the four ordained men in the Oregon Mission, only Spalding reported any baptisms. Walker and Eells lived at Tshimakain for nine years without having had a single native convert. The records of the First Presbyterian Church in the Territory of Oregon show that during the years following its organization to the time of the Whitman massacre, Spalding baptized twenty-one native adults, of whom one was a Cayuse, and fifteen were children.

A fundamental difference in the theology of baptism separates the Roman Catholic Church from most Protestant denominations and this, in part, explains why the Catholic priests, working in the same general area as the missionaries of the American Board, were able to baptize so many more natives than did Spalding. To the Catholics, baptism is necessary for salvation, even for infants, whereas for the average Protestant, baptism is the initiation rite into church membership. For Protestants, infants are baptized on the announced faith of one or both Parents; later these children become full church members on their own confession of faith. The Roman Catholics would baptize adult natives after they had received, what the Protestants considered to be, minimal religious instruction. The American Board missionaries, on the other hand, expected evidence of a change of hearts and a good understanding of Christian doctrine.

According to Presbyterian polity, the pastor of a church together with one or more of his elders constitutes the session, which has the authority to receive and dismiss members. Spalding, taking advantage of the presence of Whitman at Lapwai during the middle of November, called a session meeting and presented two Nez Perce chiefs, Joseph and Timothy, and a mountain man, James Conner, as candidates for church membership. Joseph and Timothy had been converted in the revival meeting held at Lapwai the previous January. Spalding entered the following record in the minute book of the church: "Nov. 17, 1839 [Sunday], on profession of their faith in Christ & by the decision of the Pastor & Elder the following persons were admitted to the First Presby. Church in Oregon Territory, having been examined as to the grounds of their hopes some 10 months before, viz. Joseph Tuitakas the principle Nez Perce Chief some 37 years old. Timothy Timosa[12] a native of considerable influence, some 31 years of age, And James Conner..." Eight years had to pass following the arrival of the Nez Perce delegation in St. Louis before the first natives made public confession of their faith and became members of a Christian church. James Conner was the mountain man who had been hired by the 1838 reenforcement to assist them in traveling from the Rendezvous to Waiilatpu.

On that same Sunday, the jubilant Spalding copied into his diary the prayer that he evidently had used at the baptism of the two Indians and the mountain man: "Oh Lord thou knowest the hearts of all men, thou knowest the hearts of these three, who now stand before thee to take the solemn vows of God upon them. I know they are not sheep, but I would hope they are lambs. Feed them, O thou kind Shepherd." Following the reception of the new members, the sacrament of the Lord's Supper[13] was served. "Oh what a glorious thought," wrote Spalding, "that we have lived to see two of the sons of the Red men brought into the fold of Christ. To God be all the praise forever & ever. Amen."

On the following Sunday, Spalding baptized the two sons of "Timothy & Tamar Timosa" and three daughters and a son of "Joseph & Asenath[14] Tuitakas." On Sunday, April 12, 1840, Spalding recorded the baptism of his son, Henry Hart; a son and a daughter of James and Mary Conner; and another son of Joseph and Asenath, age "3½ months" whom Spalding christened "Ephraim." Since Young Joseph, one of the leaders in the 1877 Nez Perce uprising, claimed that he was born in 1840, it is possible that he is the one whom Spalding baptized and called Ephraim. Of the first two native converts, Timothy was more faithful in his endeavors to live according to Christian principles, both during the mission period and in after-years, than was Joseph. Old Joseph lost faith in the white man when the United States Government in 1863 excluded his beloved Wallowa Valley in creating the Nez Perce reservation. He then reportedly renounced his Christian faith.

Several years after Conner became a member of the church, Spalding added this note after his name: "James Conner was suspended from the church for the sin of Sabbath breaking, neglect of religious duties & fighting, Febr. 4, 1843. It has since [been] proven that he has been guilty of polygamy, sending a challenge to fight a duel, and vending liquor."

The Visit of Thomas J. Farnham

After returning from the fall Mission meeting of 1839, Whitman wrote a report of the year's activities for the American Board. He mentioned the death of his little girl; the action taken regarding Smith's move to Kamiah; the coming of the two independent missionary couples; and acknowledged the arrival of twenty-eight boxes of goods for the Mission which were then still at Fort Vancouver [Letter 70]. In this letter Whitman objected to the dual role he was obliged to play at Waiilatpu. He wrote: "I do not think it proper for me to hold the most difficult & responsible station in the mission where all contacts with Traders, Catholics, Travellers & adventurers of every description come in immediate contact & where I have to discharge all the duties of Minister & Physician to the Mission." When Whitman selected the Waiilatpu site in the late fall of 1836, he was only dimly aware of its strategic location. Now, three years later, a fuller realization of its importance was apparent. Narcissa in her letter of May 2, 1840, to her mother, after emphasizing the fact that their home was on "the highway between the States and the Columbia River," added: "[it is] a resting place for weary travelers, consequently a greater burden rests upon us than upon any of our associates."

Those who visited Waiilatpu in the fall of 1839 were but the vanguard of a great host who followed. Geiger and Johnson were the first to arrive and then came the Mungers. On September 23, Thomas J. Farnham arrived with three companions—Robert Shortess, Sidney Smith, and A. M. Blair. The Farnham party had started from Peoria, Illinois, with at least fourteen young men who had the avowed intention of establishing a settlement in the Willamette Valley. The expedition was torn by dissensions with the result that only the four here mentioned reached Old Oregon. This shows that the missionaries were not the only ones who quarreled while making the difficult overland journey. Shortess entered Whitman's employ for the winter of 1839–40 for $6.00 a month; Smith continued on to the Willamette Valley with Farnham; while Blair went to Lapwai where Spalding hired him.[15]

After Farnham returned to the States, he published in 1841 his *Travels in the Great Western Prairies*, which contained the first printed description of Waiilatpu and of the multitudinous duties being carried on by Dr. and Mrs. Whitman. Farnham found Waiilatpu bustling with activity when he and his companions dismounted on that Monday morning, September 23. He found Whitman shouting at the top of his voice "to some lazy Indians who were driving their cattle out of his garden." A team of oxen was being yoked preparatory to being driven to the mountains to get timbers for the new house. Hall appeared with an axe on his shoulder. Munger came out of the house which was being constructed, pulling the shavings out of his plane. Farnham wrote of his welcome: "All seemed desirous to ask me how long a balloon line had been running between the States and the Pacific." The reason for such an inquiry remains a mystery.

Farnham's narrative for September 24, after mentioning the parched earth, so dry and dusty, says: "And yet when the smoking vegetables, the hissing steak, bread white as snow, and the newly-churned golden butter graced the breakfast table, and the happy countenances of countrymen and countrywomen shone around, I could with difficulty believe myself in a country so far distant from, and so unlike my native land, in all its features. But during breakfast, this pleasant illusion was dispelled by one of the causes which induced it. Our steak was horse-flesh! On such meat this poor family subsist most of the time. They do not complain."[16]

Following breakfast, Whitman took his guests on a tour of the mission grounds. "The garden was first examined," wrote Farnham, "its location on the curving bank of the Wallawalla; the apple trees, growing thriftily on its western border; the beautiful tomato and other vegetables, burdening the grounds."

After inspecting a new house being built, Whitman took the party to his corral where they saw "a fine yoke of oxen, two cows, an American bull, and the beginning of a stock of hogs." After that, Whitman proudly escorted his new friends to his mill. Of this Farnham wrote: "It consisted of a spherical wrought iron burr four or five inches in diameter, surrounded by a counterburred surface of the same material. The spherical burr was permanently attached to the shaft of a horizontal water-wheel. The surrounding burred surface was firmly fastened to timbers, in such a position that when the water-wheel was put in motion, the operation of the mill was similar to that of a coffee-mill. It was a crazy thing, but for it the doctor was grateful. It would, with the help of himself and an Indian, grind enough in a day to feed his family a week, and that was better than to beat it with a pestle and mortar."

Farnham, as an impartial observer, had great praise for what had been accomplished at Waiilatpu. Of the doctor, he wrote: "The industry which crowded every hour of the day, his untiring energy of character, and the very efficient aid of his wife in relieving him in a great degree from the labors of the school, are, perhaps, circumstances which will render possibility probable, that in five [sic] years one man without funds for such purposes, without other aid in that business than that of a fellow missionary at short intervals, should fence, plough, build, plant an orchard, and do all the other laborious acts of opening a plantation on the face of that distant wilderness; learn an Indian language, and do the duties, meanwhile, of a physician to the associate stations on the Clear Water and Spokan." That was high praise indeed, especially when we note that Farnham thought that the Whitmans had been there for five years when in reality it was only three.

Farnham attended a session of the school and then wrote: "Forty or fifty children between the ages of 7 and 18, and several other people, gathered on the shady side of the new mission-house at the ringing of a hand-bell... The Doctor then wrote monosyllables, words, and instructive sentences in the Nez Perce language, on a large blackboard suspended on the wall, and proceeded first to teach the nature and power of the letters in representing the simple sounds of the language, and then the construction of words and their uses in forming sentences expressive of thought." Whitman did not believe in trying to teach the natives the English language. Rather, he concentrated on teaching in the native tongue. Farnham noted that the pupils were using a Nez Perce primer which had been printed on the Mission press at Lapwai the previous May. This little eightpage booklet was the first to come from the American press on the whole Pacific Slope of what is now the United States. Farnham called Mrs. Whitman "an indefatigable instructress."

Farnham also described the manner in which Whitman conducted his worship services. On Saturday evening, Whitman would call one of the most intelligent of the Cayuses into his home and go over a passage of scripture with him and explain in detail the doctrines involved. He would ask the Indian to repeat what he had been told to make sure that he understood. "This was repeated again and again," wrote Farnham, "until the Indian obtained a clear understanding of its doctrines." At ten o'clock Sunday morning, the Indians assembled in the open air for their worship service. Farnham wrote: "The exercises were according to the Presbyterian form; the invocation, the hymn, the prayer, the hymn, the sermon, a prayer, a hymn, and the blessing; all in the Nez Perce tongue. The principal peculiarity about the services was the mode of delivering the discourse. When Dr. Whitman arose and announced the text, the Indian who had been instructed on the previous night, rose and repeated it; and as the address proceeded, repeated it also by sentence or paragraph till it was finished."

Farnham gave A. B. Smith the credit for translating or composing the Nez Perce hymns which were sung. As has been stated, Spalding was also working on this project. "Everything," wrote Farnham, "was conducted with much solemnity."

On the whole, Marcus and Narcissa were pleased with the response of the Cayuses during the winter of 1839–40. The school was continued through the winter although Whitman reported that the average attendance fell to ten. In the spring the attendance went up to about fifty when many of the Indian families returned to Waiilatpu to prepare for the spring planting [Letter 74]. Both Whitman and Spalding found it extremely difficult to carry on school work when the Indians were so much on the move. Whitman was encouraged to see an increased number of natives planting crops in the spring of 1840. The more they depended upon cultivation for subsistence, and the less upon the hunt, the easier it would be to educate and evangelize them.

The New Mission House

Farnham's description of the new house shows that Whitman had been able to make considerable progress in its building after Smith had finished the first room during the first week of December 1838. Farnham's account follows: "Then to the new house. The adobe walls had been erected a year. These were about 40 feet by 20, and one and a half stories high. The interior area consisted of two parlors of the ordinary size, separated by an adobe partition... Above were to be sleeping apartments." Farnham was describing the top arm of the T-shaped building which, in addition to the two "parlors," contained a bedroom for the Whitmans. This was the room at the south end that the Smiths had used. A larger room, located at the north end, was the Indian room, to be used as a schoolroom or for such other purposes as religious services. The center room was the Whitmans' sitting or living room. "To the main building," wrote Farnham, "was attached another of equal height designed for a kitchen, with chambers above for servants. Mr. Munger and a Sandwich Islander were laying the floors, making the doors, etc. The lumber used was a very superior quality of yellow pine plank." When Munger began his work on the building during the first week of September, he noted in his diary that Whitman had on hand a supply "of good pine timber seasoned and piled up in the house ready to finish it off." [17]

In her letter of April 30, 1840, to her carpenter father, Narcissa said: "We still live in the house we first built although we built one of adobe the year our reenforcement arrived. Various hindrances prevented our getting into it, or attending to finish it. Indeed, there was no one to do it until last fall. The Lord sent us a good mechanic from Oberlin, Mr. Munger... A part of the house is nearly finished and will be a very comfortable and clean house to what this has been. Father cannot realize the difficulty and hardship we have had in getting what timber we must have for doors, floors, shelves, etc., for our house. No durable wood near us of any kind except alder, which we are trying to make answer for our tables, bedsteads, etc... All our boards are sawed by hand with a pit saw, which dear father must know is very hard work, and besides this, the smoothing, daubing, and whitewashing of an adobe house is very tedious work and requires much time and labor. Husband is now engaged in it, preparing it for painting. We feel ourselves highly favored that we could obtain oil and paint enough and at a reasonable price, to paint the wood work and floors, so as to save my strength and labor."

Since the window glass which Whitman purchased from the Hudson's Bay Company was thin and expensive, he made shutters (referred to as Venetian blinds) to protect the windows. The shutters together with outside woodwork were painted green, thus giving the building with its whitewashed walls some resemblance to the neat colonial-type buildings in New York State which were usually painted white and trimmed in green. Regarding lime, Narcissa wrote: "There is no lime stone to be obtained near us and our alternative is to burn clam shells" [Letter 75].

After living for about three and one-half years in the first adobe house, Narcissa was eagerly looking forward to moving into the new house with its promise of more space, greater warmth in the winter time, and much desired privacy. In her letter of May 2, 1840, to her mother, she commented: "Could dear mother know how I have been situated the two winters past, especially winter before last, I know she would pity me. I often think how disagreeable it used to be to her feelings to do her cooking in the presence of men sitting about the room. This I have had to bear ever since I have been here—at times it has seemed as if [I] could not endure it any longer. It has been the more trying because our house has been so miserable and cold—small and inconvenient for us—many people as have lived in it. But the greatest trial to a woman's feelings is to have her cooking and eating room always filled with four or five or more Indians—men—especially at meal time."

She reported that when they would move into the new house, the Indians would not be permitted to go into their private quarters but would be restricted to the Indian room which had its own entrance. "They are so filthy," Narcissa wrote, "they make a great deal of cleaning wherever they go, and this wears out a woman very fast. We must clean after them, for we have come to elevate them and not to suffer ourselves to sink down to their standard. I hardly know how to describe my feelings at the prospect of a clean, comfortable house, and one large enough so that I can find a closet to pray in." Narcissa complained about the fleas and lice which the Indians always brought into her home.

"They are exceedingly proud, haughty and insolent people," she wrote, "and keep us constantly upon the stretch after patience and forbearance. We feed them far more than any of our associates do their people, yet they will not be satisfied. Notwithstanding all this, there are many redeeming qualities in them, else we should have been discouraged long ago. We are more and more encouraged the longer we stay among them." How interesting! Narcissa called the Indians "exceedingly proud, haughty." Following the massacre, H. K. W. Perkins claimed that the Indians considered her to be "haughty" and "very proud" [See Appendix 6].

The Whitmans Journey to Tshimakain

In May, when Dr. Whitman was called to Tshimakain to attend Mrs. Walker, Narcissa decided to go with her husband. This was her first visit to the Spokane station. Tiloukaikt, the principal chief living in the vicinity of Waiilatpu, could not understand the consideration that Whitman gave to his wife. "Why do you not go alone?" he asked. "What do you make so much of her for?" This gave Whitman a chance to explain the Christian conception of marriage. "This has often been brought up by them," wrote Narcissa, "the way I am treated, and contrasted with themselves; they do not like to have it so; their consciences are troubled about it" [Letter 76].

The Whitmans reached Tshimakain on Thursday, May 14. Mary Walker gave birth to a daughter on Sunday, the 24th, who was named Abigail.[18] The Whitmans began their return trip on the 26th. During their visit at Tshimakain, the Whitmans rode to Fort Colville which was the first time either had been there. Upon their return to Waiilatpu, they moved into their new home to Narcissa's great joy [Letters 78 & 76a]. The old house remained standing for nearly two years and was sometimes used by visitors. It was torn down early in 1842 and the adobe bricks used to build a blacksmith shop.

Second Arrival of Home Mail

On the first of June 1840, an Indian messenger from Fort Walla Walla arrived at Waiilatpu with letters from home for the Whitmans. These were the first they had received from the States since the memorable July 11, 1838, to which reference has been made. Although the

Whitmans had retired when the Indian arrived, they quickly arose, lighted a candle, and read and reread the letters from loved ones so far away in both time and distance. The news the letters brought was then about a year old. One letter was from Narcissa's mother, the first she had received. Narcissa was overjoyed. "It was enough to transport me in imagination to that dear circle I loved so well," she wrote in reply, "and to prevent sleep from returning that night... O, could my dear parents know how much comfort it would be to their solitary children here, they would each of them fill out a sheet as often as once a month and send it to the Board for us" [Letter 78]. It is hard to understand why there was an interlude of about two years between these two deliveries of home mail. Since the letters that Marcus wrote to his family are not known to be extant, we cannot tell how often they wrote.

"The Man who Came With Us"

Would that it were possible to write the history of the Oregon Mission of the American Board without describing the discord within it. The problems came to a focus in 1840, but the effects were not felt until the early fall of 1842. There were many reasons for the dissension including honest differences of opinion regarding mission policies, personality clashes, frustrated hopes, and the physical hardships connected with their primitive living conditions. Also involved was a certain feeling of resentment which Spalding harbored toward Narcissa because of her rejection of his proposal for marriage. Although Spalding, before he left for Old Oregon, had reassured Judge Prentiss that he harbored no ill will toward Narcissa, the hurt feelings remained. The consequences of the dissensions which troubled the Oregon Mission of the American Board, especially during the years 1839–41, were too far-reaching to be overlooked.

The members of the 1838 reenforcement soon became aware of the strained feelings which existed between the Whitmans and the Spaldings after their arrival on the field. Why had the two couples established separate stations 120 miles apart? When asked, Spalding tactlessly replied: "Do you suppose I would have come off here all alone a hundred & twenty miles if I could have lived with him or Mrs. Whitman?" [19]

On July 9, 1840, Spalding wrote in his diary regarding a quarrel that broke out at the Mission meeting: "...the Doct rose in great agitation

& said that either himself or me must leave the mission. That the root of all the difficulties in the Mission lay between us, viz, in an expression I made while in the States respecting his wife before she was married to Doct. Whitman, viz, that I would not go into the same Mission with her, questioning her judgment, but which we had certainly settled four times before."

Smith, in a letter to Greene dated September 3, 1840, referred to this incidence and claimed that Whitman had accused Spalding of publishing "from town to town before he left the States that he would not go on a mission with Mrs. Whitman."[20] Gray, likewise, in his letter of October 14 to Greene, wrote: "Dr. Whitman stated that he thought, or believed, that the whole difficulty originated between him and Mr. Spalding before they left the States... He felt that he had been injured by Mr. Spalding by the reports he had circulated from town to town in the United States."[21]

Narcissa blamed Spalding for the action taken by the special meeting of the Mission held at Lapwai in February 1839, when the Whitmans were asked to turn Waiilatpu over to the Smiths and open a new station in some central location. At first the Whitmans indicated a willingness to consider moving but after some investigation, decided not to do so. Several years passed after her arrival in Oregon before Narcissa felt free to tell her family of the difficulties they were experiencing with Spalding. In a letter to her father dated October 10, 1840, Narcissa wrote:

> Our trials, dear father knows but little about. The missionaries' greatest trials are but little known to the churches. I have never ventured to write about them for fear it might do hurt. *The man who came with us is one who never ought to have come.*[22] My dear husband has suffered more from him in consequence of his wicked jealousy, and his great pique towards me, than can be known in this world. But he suffers not alone the whole mission suffers, which is most to be deplored. It has nearly broken up the mission.
>
> This pretended settlement with father, before we started, was only an excuse, and from all we have seen and heard, both during the journey, and since we have been here, the same bitter feeling exists. His principal aim has been at me; as he said, 'Bring out her character,' 'Expose her character,' as though I was the vilest creature on earth.

At the end of this letter, Narcissa added: "Part of the contents of this sheet, ought not to be circulated; it may do hurt. I do not wish to make it public, for any one to make ill use of it." This is the only reference in Narcissa's extant writings to her rejection of Spalding's suit and here the reference is indirect.

OTHER CRITICISMS OF SPALDING

For a variety of reasons, Spalding became the object of criticisms from all of the other members of the Mission except Walker and Eells. Of these, Gray and Smith were the most caustic in their letters of complaint sent to Greene. When the reenforcement of 1838 arrived at Waiilatpu and plans were made as to where each couple was to live, no one wanted to live with the Grays. He had been too overbearing on the overland journey. It was Spalding's misfortune to have had the Grays assigned to live with him at Lapwai. As has been mentioned, Gray became unhappy because he was not permitted to establish a separate station for himself. Gray blamed Spalding for the decision of the Mission. After spending some weeks during the fall of 1839 in idleness at Fort Walla Walla, and after refusing to assist Whitman in building at Waiilatpu, Gray returned to the Clearwater with his family during the latter part of December. Hall warned Spalding about receiving him back again "as his disposition rendered him unfit to be associated with any one." [23] But there was no alternative for either Gray or Spalding, so Spalding let him return.

Spalding's diary for the first half of 1840 contains repeated references to his difficulties with Gray. On April 2, for instance, Gray suddenly informed Spalding that "by the authority of the Mission," he was taking possession of the premises and even forbade Spalding "to cultivate any of the land." After a little more than two weeks, on April 19, Gray turned the premises back to Spalding and indicated his readiness to work with him as "an associate."

As has been noted, Smith blamed Spalding for writing such optimistic letters about the eagerness of the Nez Perces to receive Christianity, lengthy extracts of which had been published in the *Missionary Herald*. Smith claimed that such reports had been the main reason why he had volunteered so suddenly to join the 1838 reenforcement. Spalding had no critic more bitter than A. B. Smith.

All this is the background of the Annual Meeting of 1840.

Annual Meeting of 1840

The Annual Meeting of the Oregon Mission for 1840 was held at Lapwai beginning on Saturday, July 4. All of the men were present and three of the women—Narcissa Whitman, Mary Gray, and Eliza Spalding. Spalding's diary throws much light on the strained feelings which existed even before the business meetings began. Walker and Eells were always a moderating influence and never caused trouble. They arrived on the 1st. Gray had by this time erected a log cabin for himself and his family and was thus prepared to receive guests. Walker was invited to stay at the Grays while Eells was entertained by the Spaldings. The Whitmans with Chief Joseph came on the 2nd. The Whitmans were also received by the Grays as were Rogers and Smith who arrived the following day.

With the majority of the voting members of the Mission in the Gray home before the meeting was officially opened, it may be assumed that several decisions were agreed upon in the absence of Spalding. It is evident that Gray was adamant in his demand that he be permitted to open a separate station. He had selected a site, called Shimnap,[24] located near the mouth of the Yakima River where it flows from the northwest into the Columbia. Some of the Walla Walla Indians lived in that vicinity. The site is near present-day Richland, Washington. It is probable that Gray laid down an ultimatum: either he be allowed to move or he would leave the Mission. One of the first items of business on Saturday, the 4th, was to grant Gray permission to locate a mission at Shimnap.[25] No doubt Spalding disapproved.

Another action taken, which was aimed directly at Spalding, was that no Nez Perce be received into the First Church of Oregon except by vote of all missionaries working in that language. Here a point of ecclesiastical polity was raised. When Spalding and Whitman had met as a session on November 17, 1839, and voted to receive Joseph and Timothy on confession of their faith, they were acting in strict accord with Presbyterian polity. Smith, who was a Congregationalist, had strongly objected. He felt that the two natives were not sufficiently indoctrinated to become church members. According to Congregational polity, all members of a congregation had the right to vote on the reception of new members. Smith's views were accepted; this implied a censure, especially for Spalding. Although Spalding had a number of natives he felt were ready for church membership, he felt obligated to postpone suggesting their names for consideration.

On Sunday, Spalding conducted religious services for what he called a "great number" of Indians who had assembled on the plain near his home. No doubt with the hope that the testimony of Joseph and Timothy would impress his associates, he invited the two chiefs to speak. Spalding wrote in his diary that they spoke "with much feeling." Instead of receiving words of commendation from his associates, Spalding became aware of a spirit of hostility. That day he wrote in his diary: "There seems to be a labor. I know not what it means."

Spalding Criticized

Spalding's entries for July 7 and 8[26] indicate that the Mission was in a crisis which threatened its continuance. On the 7th, Spalding wrote: "It was proposed to have a conference, quite unexpected but not unacceptable. I perceive that the brethren feel that I am some what in their way. A strange doctrine was advanced, viz. that if one did not agree with the multitude he of course is in error & should be dealt with. I objected & said that God was always right, but not the multitude." Before going into the meeting of that day, Eliza, knowing that her husband would be the object of much criticism, urged him to hold his temper. "My dear wife," wrote Spalding in his diary, "had furnished me with several portions of select scripture on which I kept my eye almost constantly." Thus he sat in silence as one after another poured out criticisms of what he had said or done. Spalding closed his entry of the 7th with the words: "I went home with a sick soul."

On Wednesday, July 8, Spalding wrote: "Confessions again. [The meeting] had scarcely opened when the Doct. rose in great agitation & said that either himself or me must leave the mission." Whitman, beginning with Spalding's statement made before they left the States for Oregon regarding not wanting to go into the same mission with Narcissa because he questioned her judgment, rehearsed the history of their quarrel. "During the whole talk which [was] long," wrote Spalding, "I kept silent with my eyes on my portion of scripture. After several had spoken, plainly betraying their object, I was requested to speak, but I saw clearly that the time had not come & consequently kept my eye fixed on my paper, a long silence ensued. Doct. Whitman's storm began to abate. He thought a reconciliation could be had, & began to admit that he might sometimes have said things that he should not have said. Mr. Eells said the object of this interview was to have every thing settled forever. I, for the first time, inquired, do I understand you to say forever? My inquiry was understood, as the matter to which Doct. W. referred had been settled several times. The Doct. saw his nakedness & apparently melted & declared he would henceforth strive with me & all the brethren in our common work." Whitman's spirit of penitence moved others to express similar feelings, with but one exception. Smith remained unrepentant and unforgiving. Spalding closed the entry of that day in his diary by writing: "I feel that our sins are the greatest obstruction to our work & for the honor of the cause we ought to be united. After several prayers, we separated."

Walker, Eells, and Smith left for their respective stations before the week closed but the Whitmans decided to remain at Lapwai over Sunday to avoid traveling on that day. On the following Monday, July 13, the Whitmans with Gray and Rogers left for Waiilatpu. After the turbulent meeting, the Spaldings were glad to be alone; Mary Gray was their only guest and she was living in her own cabin. After arriving at Waiilatpu, Gray made some preliminary investigations regarding the possibility of establishing a station at Shimnap that fall and decided that it was too late to do so that year. He would have to wait until the following spring. In the meantime Gray made a second attempt to enter the employ of the Hudson's Bay Company, applying by letter to Dr. McLoughlin for the position of schoolteacher. According to Spalding's diary, Gray received a reply on August 26. There was no opening for him at Vancouver. This second rebuff only increased Gray's feeling of hostility to the Hudson's Bay Company.

Griffin's Failure to Establish a Mission

When the Whitmans returned to Waiilatpu, they found Mr. and Mrs. Griffin there. The Griffins had left Lapwai on March 16, with six animals carrying supplies obtained from Spalding, for the Snake River country where they hoped to establish a self-supporting mission. They suffered incredible hardships while crossing the mountains which separate what is now northern Idaho from its southern part. The snow was still deep at the higher elevations so early in the season.

Writing to Mary Walker on July 25, Narcissa said: "On our arrival we found Mr. and Mrs. Griffin here & were rejoiced to see them alive, for we had given up nearly all hope of it. It would be in vain to attempt to describe the dangers of the way through which they forced themselves. We can only say that they have escaped with their lives." In a letter dated November 16, 1840, Griffin described his experiences for a friend in Honolulu: "Our Indians left us in the mountains where we were obliged to remain alone without seeing a human form but once for about sixty days & not until I [we] was able to escape by crossing the mountains upon 15 ft. of snow in the last part of May, & travel a hundred miles or more through a most dreadful region of mountain & glen & swollen rivers which threatened our lives daily, were we permitted to behold the face of even a savage." [27] Thus ended Griffin's attempt to establish an independent and self-supporting mission. He finally realized how impractical and impossible was the venture he had so idealistically envisioned. He had evidently planned to establish a mission among the Snake Indians somewhere in the vicinity of Fort Boise.

More Independent Missionaries

On August 8, the faithful Joseph Maki, the Hawaiian, died of "inflammation of the bowels," evidently appendicitis [Letter 78]. This was a great loss to the Whitmans as he had been a most faithful assistant. Another grave was dug in the little mission cemetery at the foot of the hill to the northeast of the Whitman home. Marie Maki was sent back to Honolulu in December of the following year.

About the middle of August 1840, six more independent missionaries unexpectedly arrived at Waiilatpu. They were the Rev. and Mrs. Harvey Clark, Mr. and Mrs. Alvin T. Smith, and Mr. and Mrs. Philo B. Littlejohn. Narcissa had known Mrs. Littlejohn before leaving for Old Oregon as Adeline Sadler [Letter 217]. Of all the missionaries, Mrs. Littlejohn was the only one whom Narcissa referred to by her given name. As has been mentioned, the custom of the time among educated people was to refer to others by the proper title and the last name. There is no evidence that even in the hours of closest fellowship, either of the Whitmans ever called Mr. Spalding, "Henry," or Mrs. Spalding, "Eliza." The formalities of their Eastern training forbade such familiarities. The fact that Narcissa referred to Mrs. Littlejohn as Adeline indicates a former acquaintance of a friendly nature.

Nothing definite is known as to why these three couples, who hailed from Quincy, Illinois, decided to go to Oregon as independent missionaries. Since they are believed to have been members of the Congregational Church, they would have been readers of the *Missionary Herald* and therefore influenced by the optimistic reports of the Oregon Mission which appeared so frequently in that publication during the years 1837–39. The three couples crossed the prairies and the Rockies during the spring and summer of 1840 under the protection of the caravan of the American Fur Company. The rendezvous that year was held again on Green River and was the last of the series which began in 1825. The mission party took two wagons with them as far west as Fort Hall.

The three women of this party also deserve special mention; their feat in crossing the Continental Divide opened the doorway to Old Oregon a little wider for the countless emigrants who were to follow. Altogether eleven missionary women—six under appointment by the American Board and five on an independent basis—had crossed the Rockies before the great Oregon emigration of 1843 rolled through South Pass.

Introducing Father Pierre Jean De Smet, S.J.

Among those present at the 1840 Rendezvous was the Belgian Jesuit priest, Father Pierre Jean De Smet, who was on his way back to St. Louis to obtain associates for a mission he had established among the Flathead Indians in what is now western Montana. In a letter addressed to the Hon. J. C. Spencer, who served as Secretary of War in President Tyler's cabinet, dated March 4, 1843, Father De Smet gave the following account as to how the Jesuit mission to the Indians of Old Oregon was started:

> It is now about 24 years ago since the Indians of the Flatheads acquired a slight knowledge of the civil institutions of Christianity through the means of four poor Iroquois Indians who had wandered beyond the Rocky Mountains. Anxious to obtain instructions, they sent about 20 years ago [i.e., in 1823] a deputation of three of their chiefs to St. Louis. They were carried off by sickness. As their Deputies did not return, they appointed five others who were massacred in passing through the territory of

the Sioux. In 1834 a third delegation arrived, an Iroquois accompanied it bringing with him his two children over a long and dangerous route. Owing to a want of means and members connected with the University of St. Louis to which application was made, their urgent request for proper persons to return with them could not be complied with.

In 1839 they deputed other missioners to communicate their wishes. It was on this occasion that I was requested to accompany the deputies on their return in order to ascertain the disposition of the nation.[28]

After spending several months with the Flatheads and after selecting a site for his mission station in the Bitter Root River Valley, De Smet was on his way to St. Louis for reenforcements when he attended the 1840 Rendezvous. His account of the various delegations sent to St. Louis by the Flatheads makes no mention of the 1831 Nez Perce delegation which gave rise to the Protestant missionary thrust into Old Oregon.[29]

Although the three independent missionary couples were at the same Rendezvous with Father De Smet, there is no evidence that any of the mission party actually talked with the Catholic priest, due to a strong antiCatholic spirit rampant in that day throughout the Middle West among many Protestants. The Jesuit order was especially suspect.[30] Without a doubt, however, the three couples would have informed Whitman of what they had heard at the Rendezvous of Father De Smet's intentions.

THE FIVE INDEPENDENT MISSIONARY COUPLES AT WAIILATPU

Also at the 1840 Rendezvous was the mountain man, Robert or "Doc" Newell, with whom Whitman had traveled from the Rendezvous to the States in the summer of 1835. With the discontinuance of the Rendezvous and the break-up of the American fur trade, the mountain men were forced to scatter. Several, including Newell, decided to migrate to the Willamette Valley. Since the mission party needed an escort, they entered into an agreement with Newell to take them to Fort Hall. By the time the party reached there, the horses pulling the two wagons through the dense sage were so exhausted that the missionaries found it best to abandon the wagons and continue their journey on horseback.

Instead of receiving cash for his services, Newell agreed to accept the discarded wagons and the harness and to trade some fresh horses for the worn-out animals of the missionaries. Mention will be made later of Newell taking these wagons through to the Columbia River Valley. In company with the Joel P. Walker emigrant family, the three missionary couples continued their journey to Waiilatpu.

The Walkers and the missionaries arrived at Waiilatpu about the middle of August, shortly after the arrival of the Griffins from their ill-fated attempt to establish a mission in the Snake River country and after the return of the Whitmans from the Lapwai meeting. The Whitmans were now the reluctant hosts for all five of the independent missionary couples at the same time. Also present at Waiilatpu were the Grays who had moved there from Lapwai during the first week of September. A baby girl, named Caroline, was born to the Grays on October 16. No wonder that Narcissa in her letter to her mother dated October 9 said: "We are thronged with company now and have been for some time past and may be through the winter... As we are situated, our house is the missionaries' tavern, and we must accommodate more or less the whole time." Fortunately for the Whitmans, the new house was ready to receive some of the visitors so that they could still enjoy the privacy of their own quarters. The first adobe house was also still being used.

Secretary Greene had warned the members of the Oregon Mission against being too friendly with the independent missionaries; however, when these people arrived destitute, what else could the Whitmans and Spaldings do but receive them? Narcissa explained to her mother something of their problem: "We cannot sell to them, because we are missionaries and did not come to be traders; and if we did, we should help them to establish an opposition Board [i.e., a competing mission]. But we can give to them, and report to the Board, which is not agreeable to them." One solution which appeared acceptable was to hire the men as day laborers.

Although the last three couples to arrive exercised poor judgment in believing that they could establish self-supporting missions in Old Oregon without the financial backing of an established mission board, otherwise they seemed to have been sensible Christian people. None of the three men had the instability of Munger or the fanaticism of Griffin. "They are excellent people," wrote Narcissa, "and we wish they were under the Board, for we need their labours very much."

Faced with the necessity of making some provision for the new arrivals to tide them through the coming winter, it was finally agreed that the Littlejohns and the Clarks should remain with the Whitmans, and the Alvin Smiths should go to Lapwai. When the Smiths left Lapwai in August 1841, Spalding wrote to Greene regarding Alvin: "His kindness & patience & industrious habits & good judgment & ardent but consistent zeal, I have never seen combined in one man before." Not one of the five couples was received into the membership of the Mission church, perhaps because of Greene's advice regarding the treatment of the independent missionaries. The women, however, were made members of the Columbia Maternal Association.

"SOME DIFFICULTIES FROM THE CATHOLIC PRIEST"

No history of the Oregon Mission of the American Board and no biography of Dr. Marcus Whitman would be complete without references to the conflicts and tensions which existed between the Protestant and Roman Catholic missionaries working in the same field in Old Oregon at the same time. We must consider the religious rivalry which existed then, not in the spirit of the interfaith tolerance which is so common in our generation. In that generation the Protestants in the eyes of the Roman Catholics were heretics doomed to eternal damnation, while the Catholics were to the Protestants bigoted teachers of error. The claims and counterclaims were most confusing to the natives. As will be shown, this religious rivalry was one of several causes of the Indian unrest which preceded the Whitman massacre.

For two years the Protestant missionaries in Old Oregon had worked with the natives without any competition from the Roman Catholics. When Fathers Blanchet and Demers arrived in the fall of 1838, the situation began to change. Whitman in his letter of May 10, 1839, to Greene commented: "The prospects of [doing] good to the Indians are as favourable as ever if we are permitted to labour without molestation from the Catholics." Here is the first indication in Whitman's letters of his concern regarding the presence of the Catholic missionaries in Oregon.

During the summer of 1839, Father Demers spent a month at Fort Colville and vicinity and two weeks at Fort Walla Walla teaching and baptizing the natives. On September 19, Spalding wrote in his diary: "Doct speaks of *some difficulty from the Catholic priest*. He is now at Walla Walla calling the Indians & telling the Indians that we are false teachers because we do not feed & clothe the people; that we have wives as other men, & wear pantaloons as common men & not frocks as he does. The people are told not to come near the Doct as he is a bad man, & has made no christians as yet but he [i.e., the priest] will fix them all for heaven soon." [31]

In his letter of August 27, 1839, to Greene, Smith had the following to say about Father Demers' visit to Walla Walla: "Catholicism is now making its appearance, & the errors of that church are beginning to be diffused among this people. As this very moment, the Catholic priest is at Walla Walla instructing the people & the Indians are gathering together there to listen to the false doctrines which he inculcates. Already has the priest denounced us because we have wives & the people told that they are going to hell because they are unbaptized." [32] Narcissa wrote in one of her letters: "A Catholic priest has recently been at Walla Walla and held meetings with the Indians and used their influence to draw all the people away from us. Some they have forbidden to visit us again, and fill all their minds with distraction about truths we teach, and their own doctrine; say we have been talking to them about their bad hearts long enough, and too long—say we ought to have baptized them long ago, etc., etc. The conflict has begun what trials await us we know not" [Letter 68].

An echo of Father De Smet's work among the Flatheads and Nez Perces in the Bitter Root Valley is found in Smith's letter to Greene of October 12, 1840:

> A Catholic Priest from St. Louis has been in the buffalo country this season & from the accounts of the Indians, the Lawyer especially, he has already accomplished ten times as much as has been effected from the opposite quarter [i.e., by Father Demers]... A considerable number, the Indians say, a great many children both Flat Head & Nez Perces have been baptized & have been presented with the image of the cross or other emblems of Popery.
>
> The Lawyer saw him two days & he says they tried to get the cross on him. He heard considerable from the priest & says the priest inquired of him about the mission [i.e., Spalding's] & according to his account, he defended the mission very well... When they pretended that the cross was God, he said it was only

Kiswi, like the ring on his finger. He denied to the interpreter the saving efficacy of baptism, & when the priest said it was bad for us to have wives, he in a sarcastic manner asked the interpreter how the priest came into the world? If it was not by means of a father & mother? When the priest pretended that when he got established, he should give the people a plenty of food, he said to the interpreter: "I am very glad, my servant, I will come here & do nothing & load my horses with provisions & go home again." So the Lawyer tells his story.[33]

Whitman in his letter to Greene of October 15, 1840, also referred to Father De Smet's activities but felt that the natives in the vicinity of Waiilatpu and Lapwai were "better prepared now to understand the truth than at any former period." Since by that date, Father Demers had returned to the Cowlitz and Father De Smet had gone back to St. Louis, Whitman added: "We shall now have another year without further interruptions from the Catholics."

Both Nez Perce Ellis and Spokane Garry, who, as his been stated, had been students at the Red River Mission school, joined Lawyer in his opposition to the coming of the Roman Catholic priests among their respective tribes. On December 12, 1841, Walker, writing from his station at Tshimakain to the Rev. William Cochran at the Red River school, stated: "Spokane Garry, though a most profligate wretch, has ever opposed the priests & they tried hard to bring him under their influence but cannot succeed."[34]

In Summary, 1839–1840

Marcus and Narcissa had their share of difficulties and heartaches during their fourth year of residence at Waiilatpu. The dissension within the Mission became so distressing that Whitman again seriously considered leaving. The coming of the uninvited missionaries brought problems which involved the Whitmans more than it did any of their associates. Also during the year under review came the first conflicts with the Roman Catholic priests which aroused fears of greater difficulties to come.

On the other hand, Marcus and Narcissa could look back upon a number of achievements which gladdened their hearts. The new house which had been completed provided them with more room, greater comfort, and above all more privacy than they had previously enjoyed. The observations of the visitor, T. J. Farnham, tell much about the material improvements at Waiilatpu. In spite of the wandering habits of the natives, real progress had been made in the school where now a Nez Perce primer was available for use. Religious services were conducted regularly so long as natives were available. The Indians continued to be friendly and cooperative.

Perhaps the brightest aspect of the year's work was the increased interest the natives were showing in farming. It is a mistake to think of the Cayuses of that day as herdsmen. They had no herds before the white man came except their horses. Neither were they farmers, but they quickly learned that it was far better to depend upon the products of the soil than to follow their age-old custom of depending exclusively on hunting, fishing, and digging for roots. On March 27, 1840, Whitman wrote in a letter to Greene: "There is no abatement in [their] interest in cultivation. A spirit of independence is manifesting itself among them which is seen in a desire to purchase ploughs & hoes for themselves, if they could be obtained." Then he added the following significant statement: "They appear not to feel now as they used to formerly that it was to accommodate *us* that they plant & cultivate their lands."

CHAPTER 14 ENDNOTES

1 Drury, *Spalding and Smith*, p. 277.

2 A son, Henry Hart, was born to the Spaldings on Nov. 24. When I first began my researches in the history of the Oregon Mission in the summer of 1934, I called on the widow of Henry Hart Spalding, who was then living at Almota, Washington. I secured from her at that time eight original Spalding letters, dating back to 1833, which are now in the Presbyterian Historical Society, Philadelphia.

3 Copy in Coll. O.

4 See section "Spalding Appointed by the American Board," Chapter Seven.

5 Gray, *Oregon*, p. 185, states that Griffin was "the getter-up" of the mission.

6 Information from Robert S. Fletcher, "Oberlin, 1833–1866," ms. in Oberlin College Library, pp. 98 & 216.

7 Munger's overland journal appeared in *O.H.Q.*, VIII (1907): pp. 387-405.

8 A copy of Greene's letter to Spalding is in Coll. A.

9 Drury, *Spalding and Smith*, p. 111.

10 *Ibid.*, p. 276, fn. 72.

11 *Ibid.*, p. 117. Italics in the original.

12 A painting of Timothy by Rowena Lung Alcom, made from a photograph, was reproduced in color in Drury, *Spalding*, p. 214. A collection of Mrs. Alcorn's portraits of Nez Perces, painted in the 1930s, including this of Timothy are now on permanent display in the Indian Exhibit at Rocky Beach Dam, a few miles north of Wenatchee, Washington. Mrs. Alcorn painted a second portrait of both Timothy and Lawyer which are now at Whitman College, Walla Walla.

13 For reference to the communion silver, see Chapter Seven, fn. 46.

14 Asenath was the name of the Egyptian woman who became the wife of Joseph, Gen. 41:45.

15 Spalding to Greene, April 22, 1840: "Last. Oct. a miserable old man came to me, apparently in a state of starvation. On inquiry he proved to be one of a party of 16 who left Missouri last spring for this country." Blair proved to be a skilled workman and helped Spalding build both a sawmill and a gristmill during the winter of 1839–40. In addition to Blair, Spalding had Gray, Conner, and Griffin assisting him. Perhaps during this winter, Gray built a log cabin for himself.

16 Thomas J. Farnham, *Travels in the Great Western Prairies*, Cleveland, 1906, I:336.

17 Munger's journal, *O.H.Q.*, VIII (1907):404.

18 A reproduction of the painting of Abigail made in November 1847 by John Mix Stanley is in Drury, *Walker*, p. 202. Abigail was married on Sept. 14, 1868, to James A. Karr. They became the parents of twelve children. One of her daughters, Mrs. Ruth Karr McKee, served as regent of the University of Washington, 1917–26.

19 Walker to Greene, Oct. 14, 1840. Coll. A.

20 Drury, *Spalding and Smith*, p. 164.

21 Original letter, Coll. A.

22 Italics are the author's.

23 Spalding to Greene, Oct. 15, 1842, Coll. A. Spalding quoted Hall as saying: "A man may do very well as a mechanic who would not do at all as an equal or associate."

24 The name Shimnap has variations in spelling as Chimnapums, mentioned by Lewis and Clark; Chamnapum in Ross Cox, *Adventures on the Columbia River*, 2 vols., London, 1831; A. J. Allen, *Ten Years in Oregon*, 1850, p. 211, speaks of Tshimnap; Mrs. W. H. Gray spelled it Samnap, Drury, *F.W.W.*, I:254.

25 Drury, *Spalding and Smith*, pp. 155 ff., gives Smith's letter to Greene of Sept. 2, 1840, which contains the minutes of the 1840 Mission meeting.

26 Spalding made a mistake of one day in his entries. His entry, for instance, for July 8 is in reality for the 7th. Corrected dates are here given.

27 Griffin to S. N. Castle, Nov. 19, 1840. Coll. H.

28 Original De Smet letter in Archives of Indian Affairs, Oregon Superintendency, 1842–80, National Archives, Washington, D.C.

29 Father De Smet's statement disproves the much later claim made by Father L. B. Palladino, *Indian and White in the Northwest*, Baltimore, 1894, p. 10, that the Indians who went to St. Louis in 1881 were Flatheads.

30 See Chapter Eight, fn. 2, for reference to antiCatholic sentiment of that generation.

31 Italics are the author's.

32 Drury, *Spalding and Smith*, p. 110.

33 *Ibid.*, p. 193.

34 A copy of Walker's letter to Cochran, in Walker's handwriting, is in the Rosenbach Foundation Library, Philadelphia, Pa.

THE WHITMAN HOUSE AT WAIILATPU
This sketch was drawn by the Canadian artist, Paul Kane, in July 1847. The roof line was irregular as two of the rooms had two stories. The number of chimneys corresponds with contemporary floor plans. Courtesy, Royal Ontario Museum, Toronto, Canada.

W. H. JACKSON PAINTING OF THE WHITMAN MISSION
How the mission may have looked in 1845. The painting is based on descriptions of those who lived at or had visited the mission. By permission of the National Park Service, United States Department of the Interior.

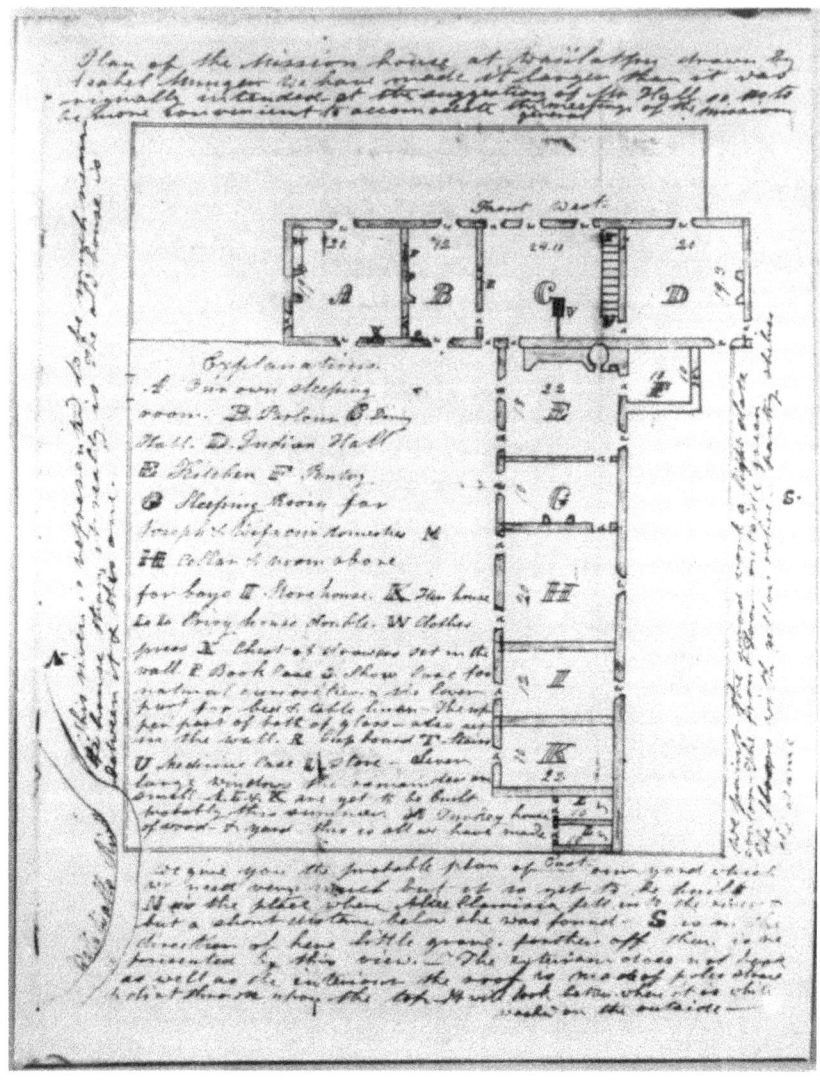

FLOOR PLAN OF THE WHITMAN HOME

Plan of the Whitman Mission House drawn in 1839 by Asahel Munger. Mr. and Mrs. Munger were independant missionaries who arrived at Waiilatpu Mission in the fall of 1839. The Mungers soon realized that establishing a mission would be too difficult without support from a larger organization. They decided to stay at the Waiilatpu Mission. Dr. Whitman hired Mr. Munger as a carpenter to help with projects; Mrs. Munger helped Narcissa with housework. By permission of the National Park Service, United States Department of the Interior.

DRAWING OF WHITMAN MISSION, 1884
The first known picture of the mission, viewed from the northeast. From left: the mill, the immigrant house, blacksmith shop, and the main Whitman home. A branch of the Oregon Trail passed the fence at the north. From Magazine of American History, September 1884.

[CHAPTER FIFTEEN]

THE FIFTH YEAR OF THE OREGON MISSION
1840–1841

Difficulties and discouragements multiplied for the Whitmans during their fifth year's residence at Waiilatpu. Many of the personality conflicts and differences of opinion regarding mission policies, which had disturbed the life of the Oregon Mission during the previous two years, continued. Now a new danger arose. Some of the natives, both Cayuses and Nez Perces, no longer enchanted by having missionaries in their midst, began to make unreasonable demands on their benefactors and even to threaten their lives. Like the low thunder of an approaching storm, these were the warnings of more serious trouble to come.

In response to the repeated pleas for additional workers made by both Whitman and Spalding, including their fantastic request for 220 made in their letter of April 21, 1838, the American Board commissioned two couples for the Oregon Mission in 1840, the Rev. and Mrs. John Davis Paris and Mr. and Mrs. William H. Rice. They sailed from New York in November of that year. Greene in his letter of November 4, 1840, to Whitman suggested that Paris be assigned to Waiilatpu, "as a preacher is so much needed at your station."[1] However, the two couples never arrived in Oregon. When E. O. Hall returned with his family to Honolulu in the fall of 1840, he gave such a discouraging account of the sad state of affairs in the Oregon Mission that when the reenforcement reached the Islands in May 1841, they were detained there.

The failure of the two couples to continue their voyage to Oregon was called by Whitman "a great evil to this mission." In his letter of November 11, 1841, to Greene, Whitman said: "Our situation called only the more imperiously for them to come on... We are in no way unprepared for a reenforcement as we have no secret burnings among us... Nothing could have been more important than for them to come on." No doubt Smith who, as will be mentioned later, arrived in the Islands in the spring of 1841 confirmed Hall's pessimistic report. No further effort was made by the Board to reenforce its Oregon Mission, to Whitman's intense disappointment.

CRITICAL LETTERS AGAINST SPALDING

Several letters critical of Spalding were sent to the American Board in 1840 by Smith, Gray, Rogers, and Hall which had a direct bearing upon the reasons why Whitman went East in the fall of 1842. As one reviews the sequence of events which called forth the letters of criticism, it is well to remember that Spalding never wrote a single letter of complaint against any of his associates until after the Mission meeting of June 1841, when he learned for the first time of the letters which had been sent to Greene about him. Spalding then wrote his defense, but he was handicapped in not knowing exactly the nature of the charges which had been made against him. One must read Spalding's diary to get his side of the controversy.

The sequence of these unhappy events for 1840 began in January when Whitman was called to Lapwai to consult with Spalding, Gray, Hall, and Rogers about the printing of a Nez Perce school book.[2] On January 29, Spalding wrote in his diary: "Very unpleasant & unprofitable talk last night between Messrs. Gray, Whitman, Rogers & Hall on one side & myself on the other." Smith happened to be in Kamiah at the time or he would surely have been among Spalding's critics. According to Spalding, the charges against him were "unfounded." Some of the criticisms were petty. The most serious charge focused on his attempts to settle the Indians. "What the brethren heard was true," he wrote, "& a doctrine which I have always preached, but so far from being a conspiracy against the Mission, I consider it the life of the Mission. I will meet them on this subject before a reasonable world. God in mercy give me grace & wisdom to do my duty regardless of all slanders that grow out of jealousy."

Although Whitman was present at this time, there is no evidence that he joined with the other three men in criticizing Spalding's endeavors to settle the Indians. He and Spalding thought alike on that subject. Possibly Whitman brought up some personal matters. The confrontation made Spalding very unhappy. He felt that he was standing alone.

GRAY RECOMMENDS SPALDING'S DISMISSAL

On March 5, 1840, the Grays left Lapwai for Kamiah where they spent about a week with the Smiths. Gray and Smith had not been on speaking terms at times when crossing the country in 1838; now, however, they became very chummy as they shared their common grievances against Spalding. On March 20, after his return to Lapwai, Gray wrote a twelvepage letter to Greene filled with complaints against Spalding He indirectly suggested that Spalding be recalled: "The [Prudential] committee may yet feel to recall some members of this Mission or to send an agent to enquire into the state of affairs. One or the other I would hope might be done soon." Gray said that it was hopeless to expect the members of the Mission to reach an agreement on Mission policies, and asked: "Do you advise me under such circumstances to remain longer a member of this Mission?"

On April 15, Gray wrote another twelve-page letter to Greene in which he stated: "Let Dr. Whitman and Mr. Spalding or Mr. Lee order as many hundred ploughs, etc., etc., as they please. If they are engaged in teaching the Indians the value of their souls, I am confident they would not think so much about ploughs and mill irons, etc."[3] Here is evidence that Gray and Smith were united in their opposition to the policy that Whitman and Spalding were following in trying to settle the Indians. A third letter from Gray to Greene, dated October 14, 1840, further criticized Spalding. Hall had joined the chorus of disapproval by writing to Greene on March 16, 1840.

SMITH ALSO RECOMMENDS DISMISSAL OF SPALDING

Spalding's most bitter critic was Asa B. Smith. In his lonely situation at Kamiah, Smith had ample time to brood over his misfortunes and write long letters to Greene. During 1840 he wrote seven such letters, dated February 6 and 25, August 5 and 31, September 3 and 28, and October 21.[4] On page after page, Smith went into details regarding what he considered to be the mistakes of Spalding. Smith was the keenest observer of Indian customs of any of the Oregon Mission. Hence his letters contain much valuable information about the customs, traditions, language, and number of the Nez Perces. On the other hand, he was very critical of the natives, calling them avaricious and selfrighteous. In his letter of September 28, he wrote: "...no doubt is left in my mind as to their motives in desiring missionaries. The principal motive evidently is the temporal benefit which may be derived from them." In all fairness to Smith, we should remember that he and his wife were living under conditions more primitive than those of any other family in the Mission and that Sarah was a victim of a chronic illness which was gradually becoming worse. Under such conditions, it was easy for Smith to be pessimistic.

The climax of Smith's embittered feelings is to be found in his letter of October 21, 1840, when he recommended to Greene that "the mission had better be given up to the Methodists & *Mr. Spalding advised to return home.*" He made the same recommendation regarding Gray: "...it would be better that *he should return* home rather than go to another field."[5] As will be seen, the arrival of these letters of criticism caused the Prudential Committee of the American Board to issue its drastic order of February 1842 which dismissed Spalding, Gray, and Smith, and which called for the closing of the work at Waiilatpu and Lapwai. The arrival of this order at Waiilatpu in September 1842 caused Whitman to leave on October 3 for Boston. Of this more later.

FIRST WAGONS OVER THE BLUE MOUNTAINS

Before the Oregon Trail could be opened for covered wagons from the Missouri frontier to the Columbia River, three great obstacles had to be surmounted. It had to be demonstrated that (a) women could cross the Rockies; (b) that wagons could cross the Snake River desert of what is now southern Idaho; (c) and that wagons could be taken over the Blue Mountains of what is now eastern Oregon.

The successful crossing of the Rockies by Narcissa Whitman and Eliza Spalding in July 1836 opened the mountain gateway to Old Oregon. Whitman's stubborn insistence in taking Spalding's wagon, reduced to a cart, as far west as Fort Boise, had opened the Oregon Trail to that point. There remained until 1840 the unconquered and formidable barrier of the Blue Mountains.

Among those who crossed the plains and the Rockies in 1840 with the last caravan of the American Fur Company to go to the Rendezvous was the first non-missionary family to make the overland journey to Old Oregon. They were Joel P. Walker, his wife, a sister, three sons, and two daughters.[6] Also traveling with this caravan were the three independent missionary couples previously mentioned. When Walker and the missionary party arrived at Fort Hall, Walker had one wagon and the missionaries had two. Walker sold his wagon at Fort Hall to Caleb Wilkins, a mountain man, and continued his westward journey, with his family, on horseback. When they arrived at Waiilatpu, the Whitmans were away, attending the Mission meeting at Lapwai. This is probably the reason why no reference to the Joel P. Walker family has been found in the extant Whitman correspondence. After spending the winter of 1840–41 in the Willamette Valley, the Walkers migrated to California in the fall of 1841[7] where Joel was later to play a prominent role in political affairs.[8]

As has been mentioned, the three missionary couples met Robert Newell at the Rendezvous who traveled with them to Fort Hall. There Newell traded some fresh horses for the two wagons which the missionaries had managed to take that far west. Newell had with him his Indian wife and their three sons, the youngest of whom had been born on April 17, 1840, and who was named Marcus Whitman.[9] Newell sold one of the wagons he had obtained from the missionaries to Francis Ermatinger, who was then in charge of Fort Hall. Ermatinger, wishing to have this wagon taken to the Columbia River, hired another mountain man, William Craig, as the driver. Craig and Newell had married Nez Perce women who were sisters. With Craig was his friend, John Larison (or Larrison).

Still another mountain man to join the party was Joe Meek, who had met the Whitmans and the Spaldings at the 1836 Rendezvous. Meek's first wife, a Nez Perce woman, had deserted him after giving birth to a daughter whom he had named Helen Mar after Lady Helen Mar, the heroine of Jane Porter's *The Scottish Chiefs*. Meek took another Nez Perce woman for his wife. Realizing that their trapping days were over, these five mountain men—Newell, Wilkins, Craig, Larison, and Meek—headed for the Oregon country west of the Blue Mountains to begin life anew. The men, with their three wagons, left Fort Hall on September 27.[10] They were several weeks behind the Joel P. Walker party, who had pushed on ahead. "In a few days," wrote Newell in his diary, "we began to realize the difficult task before us, and found that the continual crashing of the sage under our wagons, which was in many places higher than the mules back, was no joke and seeing our animals begin to fail, we began to light up—and finally threw away our wagon beds and were quite sorry we had undertaken the job."[11] The men, however, persisted and succeeded in taking the bare chassis of the three wagons over the Blue Mountains. The party arrived at Waiilatpu sometime during the first week of November. Thus the Oregon Trail had been fully traversed by wheeled vehicles, although three years had to pass before other wagons were taken over the same mountains.

Regarding the reception extended to him and his associates at Waiilatpu, Newell wrote: "In a rather rough and reduced state we arrived at Dr. Whitman's station in the Walla Walla Valley, where we were met by that hospitable man and kindly made welcome and feasted accordingly. On hearing me regret that I had undertaken to bring the wagons, the Doctor said: 'O you will never regret it. You have broken the ice, and when others see that wagons have passed, they too will pass, and in a few years the valley will be full of people."

In all probability one of the wagons was left at Waiilatpu, as Whitman in a letter to Walker dated May 8, 1841, made reference to a "wagon or cart" being at his mission. This is the first discovered mention of a wheeled vehicle being at Waiilatpu. The inventory of the property at Waiilatpu at the time of the massacre listed four wagons. Evidently Whitman had been able to obtain wagons from the immigrants who streamed by his station in great numbers in 1843 and following years. One of the wagons brought by the Newell party was evidently left at Fort Walla Walla and the third was taken down the Columbia River to the Willamette Valley.

While at Waiilatpu, Meek persuaded the Whitmans to take his two-year-old daughter, Helen Mar, into their home to be reared and educated. Narcissa later in a letter to her sister Jane wrote that the child's body was dirty and covered with lice, and that she was half-starved. She found the child fretful, stubborn, and difficult to control [Letter 105]. Narcissa had kept the clothes that Alice Clarissa had worn and now used them. To a certain degree, the little half-breed girl filled the void in the hearts of Marcus and Narcissa, who could never forget their own little girl who had been drowned a little more than a year before.

Craig and Larison did not go with the other three mountain men to the Willamette Valley but instead went to Lapwai, probably because their wives hailed from that area. Craig's wife was a daughter of the principal chief of Lapwai Valley, Thunder Strikes or Thunder Eyes, whom Spalding had renamed James. On November 20, 1840, Spalding noted in his diary that the two men intended to spend the winter at Lapwai and added: "I have seen enough of Mountain men." Craig later settled on Lapwai Creek about eight miles up from the Clearwater mission. He is usually given the credit of being the first non-missionary settler in what is now Idaho. He was unsympathetic towards Spalding and his work and would cause him much trouble over several years.

First Trouble with the Indians

The history of the Oregon Mission of the American Board can be divided roughly into two periods. The first extended from the founding of the Mission in the fall of 1836 to the fall of 1840 when the last of the complaining letters about Spalding was sent to the American Board. These years were marred by dissensions within the Mission which resulted in the Board's drastic order of February 1842 to which reference has been made.

The second period began in the fall of 1840 with the first evidence of hostility to the missionaries on the part of the natives. There seems to be a direct relationship during these years, 1840–1847, between the steadily increasing number of Oregon immigrants and the growing restlessness of the Indians. The first Oregon immigrant family arrived in 1840; a few more came in 1841; still more in 1842; and then in 1843 the first great wagon train crawled over the Blue Mountains bringing about a thousand people. Each year after that the numbers increased, and the Indians became fearful that the white man was engulfing their land, even though none of the immigrants up to 1847 had settled in the upper Columbia River Valley.

The Whitman station, as an outpost on the Oregon Trail, became the focal point of conflict between the red man and the white; between the old life and the new which was being so suddenly thrust upon the natives. The time came when the Cayuses felt that Dr. Whitman was more interested in helping the white man than in helping them. It should be emphasized, however, that had there been no Oregon Mission of the American Board, the changes for the natives would have been just as inevitable. The overflow of white population from the States was a terrible evil for the Oregon Indians which they could not resist. Partly because of the strategic location of the Whitman station, the Whitmans became the object of growing hostility on the part of a small band within the Cayuse nation.

TROUBLE WITH THE NEZ PERCES AT LAPWAI

The first indication of opposition from the Indians came in October 1840, first against Spalding at Lapwai and then against Smith at Kamiah. Spalding's difficulties arose out of two causes. The first had to do with trading, as he explained in a letter to Greene dated September 22, 1840: "Most of our perplexities with the natives, I believe arise from our trading in Indian goods. Our powder measure is not as large as that at Walla Walla... We do not give as much for this thing or that thing..." Spalding was unhappy about the necessity of using ammunition, knives, and blankets as payment to the Indians for any services they might render or in payment for horses purchased, but there was no alternative.

A more serious point of friction was the fact that some of the Indians whom he was encouraging to cultivate the soil—Old Joseph and Timothy, for example—had moved from their respective localities and had begun to farm small acreages in the Lapwai Valley. The Nez Perces and the Cayuses had developed no sense of individual ownership of specific lands at the time the missionaries settled among them; however, tribal bands did claim exclusive possession of certain general areas and resented the intrusion of other members of the same tribe. Joseph and Timothy no doubt moved to Lapwai in order to be near Spalding and, perhaps, to take advantage of farming implements which he freely loaned. Old James, however, whose band claimed the valley, resented this. Smith wrote: "Old James is trying to drive away Joseph & Timothy & all who do not belong there."[12]

One of the tactics used by Old James to harass Spalding was to send two of the young men of his band to disrupt the school that Mrs. Spalding was teaching. According to Spalding's diary, two ìyoung paintedî Indians appeared at the school on October 9. Mrs. Spalding requested them to go away. "They came the nearer," wrote Spalding, "& glanced their hellish looks directly at her. She moved to another part of the room...

They then commenced their savage talk." Eliza called her husband who in turn sent for Old James as the two young men were from his lodge. James refused to call off the men. Among those who protested the outrage was Timothy and another Nez Perce, the Eagle. Spalding was heartsick over the incident as it portended further trouble from James.

TROUBLE WITH THE NEZ PERCES AT KAMIAH

Four days after the disturbance at the Lapwai school, a more serious confrontation took place at Kamiah between Smith and a few dissident Nez Perces. Again ownership of the land being cultivated was the sore point. Smith wrote in his diary for October 18, 1840: "This has been a day of serious trial in respect to the Indians. We have, in the most absolute terms & in the most insolent manner, been ordered by the two principal men of this place to leave the station... They demanded pay for the land. I refused to say anything about it, telling them that the land was given a year ago & they had promised to say no more about it... They pretended that when they gave me the land, they expected that I would give them goods & food, but I had not done it &c... They then ordered me in the most absolute terms to leave on the morrow... I at length told them I would go, but could not get ready so soon. I must have time to get ready." Smith sent a faithful Indian in the dark of the night to Spalding with an urgent plea for him and Whitman to come immediately.

The willingness of Smith to leave caught his antagonists by surprise. When the Nez Perce community at Kamiah learned what had happened, the majority rallied to the defense of their missionaries. Smith does not mention names, except refering to one called Meoway (or Meiway) who boasted of the fact that sometime previous he had "tied Mr. Pambrun & made him a slave."[13] Perhaps Lawyer and Ellis were among those who came to Smith's defense the next day. Smith described an angry confrontation which took place in his house between the two troublemakers and some of the principal men of the tribe. "Much passion was manifested on both sides," wrote Smith to Greene on October 21, "and it seemed to me that our house was filled with demons from the bottomless pit rather than human beings."[14] After several hours of angry debate, the Indians left the Smith home. Sarah was terrified at what had taken place. Asa was both angry and frightened, but secretly may have welcomed the incident as giving them a valid reason for leaving the field.

CHAPTER FIFTEEN *The Fifth Year of the Oregon Mission, 1840–1841*

Spalding received word of the disturbance on Wednesday, October 14, and at once sent a messenger to inform Whitman. Spalding left on the 15th for Kamiah taking several Indians with him, including Joseph. They made the sixty-mile trip in one day. Spalding found Smith extremely discouraged. The Indians were quiet when Spalding arrived. On October 15, he wrote in his diary: "See a proposal coming first from Mr. Walker to Doct Whitman to sell out the Mission to the Methodists. My mind is thrown into confusion." Here was a report, which turned out to be a baseless rumor, which Smith eagerly grasped as being possibly one way out of his situation. On the 17th, Spalding wrote: "The Indians confess their faults & wish Mr. S. to remain, but it seems his mind is made up & he will go." Spalding remained at Kamiah over Sunday, the 18th, and on the 21st started back to Lapwai. He had proceeded but a few miles before he met Whitman with a number of pack animals which would be needed if it were decided to evacuate the Smiths. Spalding returned to Kamiah with Whitman.

Evidently Smith had written such an alarming report of his troubles to Spalding and Whitman that, when Whitman read it, he left as soon as possible for Kamiah fully expecting that it would be necessary to bring out the Smiths. We are not told just when Whitman left Waiilatpu, possibly on October 18, which was a Sunday. The urgency of the call was such that Whitman must have traveled on Sunday if he arrived at Kamiah, 180 miles from Waiilatpu, on the 21st. On October 30, Narcissa, in a letter to her sister Harriet, wrote: "Your brother [in-law] is not at home... Think of him traveling alone [in] this cold weather. The first [day] after he left his warm home the wind blew very hard and cold—he with but two blankets, sleeping on the ground alone; and since, it has rained almost every day, and sometimes snowed a little." Although Narcissa here made two references to her husband traveling alone, she probably meant that no other white man was with him. Since Whitman took a string of pack animals with him, he would have needed some Indian assistants. No comments have been found in any of Whitman's letters regarding his travel experiences when making such long trips on horseback. Did he take a small tent with him? What about his food? Did he cook one or more hot meals each day while on the trail? On this long ride to Kamiah in stormy weather, did he have to sleep each night in wet blankets? Nothing is said of such details.

Smith was still determined to leave Kamiah when Whitman arrived. The question arose as to when. Whitman favored an immediate withdrawal and reminded Smith that he had brought pack animals for that purpose. Sarah, however, was too ill to ride horseback. She would have to be taken down the Clearwater River in a canoe and, since no canoe was available, Spalding recommended that they wait until spring. Possibly those among the Kamiah Indians who wanted to keep the Smiths in their midst deliberately refused to make a canoe available. A favorable factor in the situation was the friendly attitude of the majority of the natives who urged the Smiths to remain. Perhaps it was Whitman who suggested that one of the independent missionary couples then at Waiilatpu, the Rev. and Mrs. Harvey Clark, be sent to Kamiah to give the Smiths companionship and assistance during the coming winter. The Smiths were agreeable to this suggestion as were the Clarks, who left for Kamiah shortly after Whitman returned to his home. In one of the rare instances when Asa Smith had something good to say of others, he wrote in his letter of February 22, 1841, to Greene: "(The Clarks) have been a great comfort to us in our lonely situation."

Should They Sell Out To The Methodists?

Although evidence is lacking as to the exact sequence of events which led up to Smith's proposal that the Oregon Mission of the American Board be turned over to the Methodists, it is probable that this is the story of what happened. When Smith heard of the arrival of the *Lausanne* at Fort Vancouver in June 1840 with the Methodist reenforcement of about fifty men, women, and children, he grasped at the idea of turning the American Board's work in Old Oregon over to the Methodists. They had a surplus of missionaries. Moreover, comparatively speaking, there were only a few natives in the lower Columbia country. He reasoned that the Methodists, under those circumstances, would welcome the opportunity to enlarge their field of endeavor. Indeed, he came to the point of being willing to turn over the American Board's work with or without compensation.

Possibly feeling confident that both Whitman and Spalding would object to the idea, Smith may have broached his plan in a letter to Walker, who then wrote to Whitman. On October 15, 1840, just two days after his confrontation with the two dissident Nez Perces at Kamiah, Smith wrote to Greene suggesting that the Board's work in Oregon be turned over to the Methodists. On that same day, Whitman wrote to Greene and, after reviewing the events of the preceding months and after giving a financial report, wrote: "Mr. Walker writes that he has written you in favour of the Board withdrawing this Mission on account of so many [i.e., Methodist missionaries] coming in among & around us. I feel to say, No: Do not withdraw it. We have not done what we could, & ought to do. It could not be withdrawing the mission, so to speak; but abandoning the cause of the Indians. Rather let us be *reenforced* to enable us to act most efficiently."

As has been stated, when Spalding arrived at Kamiah on October 15 and learned of Smith's proposal, he was shocked. After Whitman arrived, the three men seriously debated the idea. Although Whitman had written to Greene on the 15th of that month rejecting the proposal, he began to wonder whether this might not be a good idea when faced with Smith's despondency and determination to leave. Spalding remained unalterably opposed and said that he would remain at his station even if the American Board abandoned its work and turned it over to the Methodists. The lowest ebb tide in the history of the Oregon Mission of the American Board was reached there at Kamiah when Smith, Whitman, and Spalding debated the proposal to turn their work over to the Methodists. There is no indication that the Methodists ever knew of such a possibility.

After Spalding had returned to Lapwai, he wrote to Walker asking for an explanation of his recommendation to Whitman. Walker replied that he and Eells had no thought of selling out to the Methodists and that ìthe Doct must have misunderstood."[15] Mary Walker wrote in her diary on October 28: ìWe are astonished and somewhat indignant to think they should think of such a thing."[16] The whole incident reflected Smith's despondency. He was looking for what he thought would be an honorable escape from his miserable situation.

On his return trip from Kamiah, Whitman spent the night of October 24 at Lapwai. While there he received a letter from Jason Lee which brought the news that Dr. Elijah White, who had served for three years as the physician in the Methodist Mission, had been dismissed and was to return to the States on the *Lausanne*. Lee expressed his fears that after White had arrived in the States, he would do "all he can to injure them [i.e., the Methodist Mission]." [17] After White returned to the States, he was successful in obtaining from the United States Government an appointment to be the first Indian Agent to Old Oregon. He returned to Oregon in 1842.

"Spalding has a Disease in his Head"

An incident occurred during Whitman's visit with Smith at Kamiah which led W. I. Marshall in his *Acquisition of Oregon* to claim that "Dr. Whitman speaking as a physician as early as September [sic] 1840, had declared that Spalding was suffering from a disease of the head which was liable to make him insane."[18] This needs correction. Marshall based his opinion on a passage in Smith's letter to Greene written at Kamiah on October 21, 1840, following Spalding's departure for Lapwai but while Whitman was still there. Smith wrote: "From what I have seen & know of him [i.e., Spalding], I greatly fear that the man will become deranged should any heavy calamity befall him... The above remarks I have just read to Doct. W. & he concurs in what I have written & says moreover that *Mr. Spalding has a disease in his head* which may result in derangement especially if excited by external circumstances."[19] This comment attributed to Whitman cannot be taken as a professional diagnosis. Whitman was not a co-signer of the letter. Smith's opinion regarding Spalding's mental condition should be read in the light of Smith's own emotional attitude.

Although Whitman was offended by Spalding's occasional references to the latter's broken romance with Narcissa, he never joined Smith, Gray, Rogers, and Hall in writing letters of criticism about Spalding to the Board. In fact, it appears that Whitman was unaware that such letters had been sent; in his letter of October 15, 1840, to Greene, he said: "Mr. Gray has lately informed me that letters have been sent by him & others, setting forth difficulties that have existed in this mission. It was never my intention to trouble you with them."

Whitman's Reaction to the Proposal to Abandon their Mission

After his return to Waiilatpu, Whitman on October 29 wrote a letter of about two thousand words to Greene in which he reported on his trip to Kamiah. He began by saying: "Last evening I arrived home from my trip to Mr. Smith's aid. I left my hired man[20] to make a canoe for them to come down by water in case he still finds it necessary to leave this fall. If he does not leave this fall, he thinks he shall in the spring. Mrs. Smith is indeed very lonely. I think they both suffer much from this cause. I regret that Mr. Smith should have been so anxious to go where he is, as he so easily falls into loneliness & despondency. The Indians, it is true, are very anxious to obtain property, but I do not think we shall be in danger of violence from them."

Regarding the proposal to sell out to the Methodists, Whitman tried to be objective by presenting both sides of the question. In favor of selling, he mentioned Walker's supposed recommendation, the "want of harmony" within the Mission, and finally, Smith's determination to leave. Regarding the latter possibility, Whitman wrote: "In such [an] event, Mr. Gray would leave & also Mr. Rogers and only Mr. Spalding & myself would be left in the Nez Perce language. While all this would be going on, a bad influence would be exerted, & it would not be well for Mr. S. & myself to be left alone under such circumstances."

In arguing against selling, Whitman mentioned such facts as: "An unusual interest & attention has been given to instruction at this station this fall... More people are brought to hear instruction in this Mission than in most of the Missions of the Board... Will it not be abandoning the Indians & in that way western America to the Catholics?" Even should the Methodists be interested in taking over the work, Whitman pointed out that there was certain to be a long interval during which the new missionaries would have to learn the language. As for the missionaries of the American Board, Whitman argued: "The language is acquired; we are on the ground." In conclusion, he wrote: "My feelings are to live & labour for this people... If you sell the Mission, you will be at liberty to send me to any field where I may be needed as Physician, but not as here to fill the place of a Minister, a thing I have [tried] in vain to avoid."

According to a penned notation on the back of Whitman's letter, now on file in the Board's archives, Greene received it on October 2, 1841. On that same day a number of other letters arrived from Oregon, including three long letters from Smith filled with complaints about Spalding. Whitman's letter and the others were laid before the members of the Prudential Committee which met in Boston in February 1842. The Board took no action about turning their work in Oregon over to the Methodists, but did order other changes.

Shortly after writing to Greene on October 29, Whitman heard from Walker, who disavowed any idea of selling out to the Methodists. Walker stated that both he and Eells were opposed to the idea. With this report, all discussions about abandoning the Mission ceased. Whitman, Spalding, Walker, and Eells were determined to carry on even if Smith, Gray, and Rogers left.

The Fall of 1840

Whitman was spared trouble with the natives in the vicinity of Waiilatpu during the fall of 1840 and the following winter. In a letter to Greene dated March 28, 1841, he wrote: "The Old Chief Cut Lip died last winter, which has removed a very troublesome cause." In all probability this Cut Lip was none other than Umtippe, to whom reference has already been made. Possibly also this was the Cut Lip whom George Simpson mentioned as being in league with an interpreter at Fort Walla Walla whom Simpson called a villain.[21] After the death of Cut Lip, or Umtippe, Tilhoukaikt became the head chief of the Waiilatpu band and, as will be told, in turn caused Whitman much trouble.

A few weeks after the arrival of the three independent missionary couples at Waiilatpu in August 1840, Narcissa was taken ill with "inflamation of the kidneys." In her letter to her mother of October 9, she said that she "was brought very low." Whitman, in his letter to Greene of October 15, wrote: "Mrs. Whitman has been sick for nearly two months having first an attack of the kidneys, from which she is not perfectly recovered." Here is the first reference in Whitman's correspondence to Narcissa's ill health. Such references became more frequent in their later letters.

Narcissa was also afflicted with poor eyesight. As early as September 30, 1839, she mentioned this in one of her letters. On March 1, 1842, she wrote again: "My eyes are much weaker than when I left home and no wonder, I have so much use for them. I am at times obliged to use the spectacles Brother J[onas] G[alusha] so kindly furnished me." In those days, long before the development of modern ophthalmology, spectacles were little more than variations of magnifying lenses.

Marcus had his share of ill health during the fall of 1840 as he stated in his letter of March 28, 1841, to Greene: "Soon after I wrote you last fall, I became sick from overdoing in going to Mr. Smith's & from hard labour, after I came home upon the mill race & preparing for winter.

After being recovered a little, I went to Walla Walla at the call of Mr. Pambrun to see one of his men that was sick. While there the water rose very high & in returning, I fell into one of the streams by the stumbling of my horse in crossing & got very wet. Mrs. W. being with me & some Indians at the same time being there in passing [and] having a fire, I was enabled to take off my wet clothes & wrap myself in blankets & so far dry them as to come home by substituting a blanket for my coat." The exposure had its aftereffects which, as Whitman wrote, "held me to my bed for three weeks."

Fortunately, Whitman had been able to harvest his crops before being taken ill. He reported to Greene: "My crops were good having two hundred & fifty bushels of wheat, one hundred & thirty of corn, peas not known, & a good supply of potatoesî [Letter 80]. Because the faithful Hawaiian, Joseph Maki, had died on August 8, and because the Grays did not move to Waiilatpu until September, Whitman was short of help. He welcomed the assistance the three men of the second party of independent missionaries were able to give. Griffin, who had arrived at Waiilatpu with his wife early in July 1840 after making a futile attempt to establish a mission on the Snake River, was surly and uncooperative. Whitman on October 15 wrote about him: "He did not employ himself a day."

The uninvited presence of the five independent missionary couples at Waiilatpu for a short time in the fall of 1840 was an embarrassment for Whitman. "I do not know how to get along with the Free Missionaries," he wrote to Greene. "I do not wish to be a supplier for them & yet I do not see how I can refuse them some grain... It is evident they have no funds to buy of the Company. I dare not oppose them. I dare not sell to them. To give them I am not able, and I cannot let them suffer" [Letter 80]. The most helpful of these independent missionaries was Munger who was hired by Whitman because of his skill as a carpenter. Munger's work made the erection of the main mission house possible during 1840–41.

The Griffins remained at Waiilatpu until sometime after October 15, 1840, and then left for the Willamette Valley where Griffin took up farming on the Tualatin Plains.[22] The Grays remained at Waiilatpu while waiting for spring, when they expected to open their new station at Shimnap. When Whitman first made application for an appointment under the American Board in 1834, he was rejected because of ill health. He then stated that he had suffered pain in his left side from time to time ever since 1830. This condition had seemingly cleared up at the time of his appointment in 1835. The old trouble seemed to have returned during the fall of 1840 and following winter. Writing to Mary Walker on January 19, 1841, Mary Gray said: "Doct. W. has been very sick this winter with his side complaint, [but] is now so as to be about some."[23] The Grays were able to take over some of the responsibilities at Waiilatpu which under normal conditions would have fallen on Whitman's shoulders. Mary taught the Indian school during the winter of 1840-41. Whitman described the attendance as being poor, largely because so few Indians were in the vicinity during those months [Letter 83b].

Cayuses Find Christian Standards Difficult

The Cayuses found the high ethical standards and the Calvinistic doctrines which the Whitmans practiced and preached difficult to accept. It should be remembered that Whitman was not an ordained minister, and had not received training in theology. He taught what he had learned as a youth in the home of relatives and friends in Massachusetts; in the church and school at Plainfield; and in his activities as a layman in the churches at Rushville and Wheeler, New York. His teachings reflected the Calvinistic theology and Puritanical background of his youth. Narcissa's early experiences were much the same as those of her husband.

Narcissa analyzed the problem they faced in a letter dated October 10, 1840, to her father. She explained that the Cayuses were unhappy because "husband tells them that none of them are Christians; that they are all of them in the broad road to destruction, and that worshipping will not save them." In other words, Whitman was telling the natives that it was not enough to observe the outward forms of Christian worship; that there had to be a change of heart. Narcissa's account continues: "They try to persuade him not to talk such bad talk to them, as they say, but talk good talk, or tell some story... Some threaten to whip him and to destroy our crops, and for a long time their cattle were turned into our potato field every night to see if they could not compel him to change his course of instruction to them." According to Narcissa, her husband was not intimidated by the threats of some of the Cayuses and, for the time being, life remained peaceful at Waiilatpu.

Students of Indian life have pointed out that primitive Indians were hedonists, responding to pleasure and pain. They were also pantheistic in their outlook, therefore not overly concerned about contradictions in Oreligious tenets.[24] Such a background, psychologically speaking, made it extremely difficult for the Protestant missionaries to reshape Indian thinking and conduct to make them conform to Calvinist doctrines and puritanical standards.

The Second Flour Mill

The biggest accomplishment made at Waiilatpu during the fall of 1840 was the digging of a millrace and the erection of a gristmill.[25] The millrace tapped Doan Creek, a tributary of Mill Creek, and was about one-third of a mile long and five feet deep in places. Of necessity, the ditch was dug by hand labor. In January 1839, the Nez Perces had voluntarily dug a millrace for Spalding which was longer, deeper, and wider than that at Waiilatpu, because they realized that a mill would be of great benefit to them. The Cayuses, on the other hand, were less cooperative; they refused to work on the ditch unless paid. Of this Whitman wrote: "I cannot give them much powder, as I am so near the Fort. *Tobacco I will not sell* & shirts were not to be had to any extent; so that my labor has had to be either white men or Hawaiians in general"[26] [Letter 80]. No doubt several of the independent missionaries assisted.

On December 7, Whitman wrote to Walker: "Mr. Gray is very busy in building the mill & seems happy. We have finished the race but we may still lower the head of it a few inches. We go for pine for the frame floor & shaft tomorrow. I will not say when it will run but I trust in a reasonable time." The millstones, two feet in diameter, had been sent to Oregon by sea by Greene to replace the first mill with its iron burrs of only four or five inches diameter. Farnham had called the first mill "a crazy thing." In all probability the first mill had been powered by a water wheel set directly in the river. The second mill had an undershot wheel about three feet in diameter set in the millrace. A wooden drive shaft extended up through the platform to turn the stones. Later Whitman installed a small threshing machine to utilize the same power. In his letter to Greene dated March 28, 1841, Whitman wrote: "The power is most complete, ample & safe, being altogether by a race & not requiring any dam... It will grind from one to one & a half bushels in an hour." A milldam with the resultant millpond made a larger mill possible about three years later.

MUNGER INSANE

During the winter of 1840–41, Asahel Munger became insane. Of this Whitman wrote to Greene on March 28, 1841: "Mr. Munger, who has been with us for some time, has become a monomaniac & must be sent home with his family. He has become an unsafe man to remain about the Mission as he holds himself as the representative of the church & often has revelations. He has in mind to cut off the A.B.C.F.M. Mission from all rights to missionate [sic] among the heathen & only allows me to stay in the mission house for a time when he is to take it in some way from me. As he is not connected with any one in the country & having been employed by me & the mission, we must send him home even if it is at the expense of the Board. If he goes by land, it will not cost much, if any thing to the Board."

As Munger's condition worsened, the Whitmans were in a quandary, not knowing what to do. He had to be sent to the States, but how could that be accomplished? Robert Newell and Joe Meek had informed Whitman that the Rocky Mountain fur trade was over. There would be no more caravans of the American Fur Company to the Rendezvous, and there would be no more Rendezvous. Ermatinger of the Hudson's Bay Company, with whom Whitman had discussed his problem, said he knew of a man who was planning to make the overland journey to the Missouri frontier in the summer of 1841; he thought that this man could be hired to take the Mungers with him [Letter 87a]. Whitman grasped at this possibility and obligated the Board to cover the costs involved. Ermatinger agreed to escort the Mungers with their year-old baby to Fort Hall, where he hoped he could turn them over to this unnamed man who would escort them on to the States.

Ermatinger, with the Mungers, left for Fort Hall sometime in the spring of 1841 but, to the dismay of the Whitmans, returned with them in the following August. For some reason, Ermatinger had been unable to make contact with the man he thought was going to the States, and, therefore, had no choice but to return the Mungers to Waiilatpu. We have only our imagination to suggest the anguish Mrs. Munger must have endured with an insane husband and her baby on their long horseback journey twice across the desert wastes along the Snake River. She left no diary or letters to tell of her difficulties and experiences. Narcissa later wrote that Munger was rational enough to be glad to return to Waiilatpu, but "his poor wife did it very reluctantly" [Letter 104].

Somewhere along the way, either at Fort Hall or possibly at the recently established Fort Bridger, Ermatinger met his old friend, Jim Bridger. Bridger persuaded Ermatinger to take with him his five-year-old half-breed daughter, Mary Ann, to Waiilatpu for the Whitmans to rear and educate. Perhaps Bridger had heard of the Whitmans taking Helen Mar Meek into their home. Narcissa never had an opportunity to object to this new responsibility so suddenly thrust upon her, but she seemed to have accepted it in good spirit. Mary Ann was about a year older than Helen Mar. In a letter to her sister Jane, Narcissa wrote: "Mary Ann is of a mild disposition and easily governed and makes but little troubleî [Letter 105]. Indeed with two little half-breed girls in her home, Narcissa found some compensation for the loss she still felt because of the death of Alice Clarissa. "The Lord has taken our own dear child away," she wrote to Jane, "so that we may care for the poor outcasts of the country and suffering children."

The return of the Mungers to Waiilatpu made the Whitmans realize that the Oregon Trail leading east of Waiilatpu was now almost exclusively a one-way road. Traffic was westbound except for a few venturesome men who dared to go through hostile Indian country with little or no protection. Americans in Old Oregon were marooned except for the long and more expensive voyage around Cape Horn.

Sometime during the first part of September 1841, the two independent missionary couples, the Alvin Smiths and the Littlejohns, left for the Willamette Valley. They took the Munger family with them and turned them over to the care of Jason Lee. During the week before Christmas, the deranged Munger committed suicide. Of this Narcissa wrote: "He—after driving two nails in his left hand—drew out a bed of hot coals and burnt it to a crisp, and died four days later" [Letter 105]. In a letter to Mary Walker dated January 24, 1842, Narcissa commented: "What a mercy that we have been spared such a scene as that must have been." As will be noted later, the Littlejohns returned to Waiilatpu in the fall of 1843 when Mr. Littlejohn entered Whitman's employ.[27]

Spring 1841

On January 11, 1841, fire destroyed the Eells home at Tshimakain at a time when the thermometer stood at 8½° below zero. For several weeks, the Eellses had to live with the Walkers. Early in March, Walker traveled to Waiilatpu where he was able to persuade Gray to return with him and assist in the erection of a new cabin for the Eellses. Gray went reluctantly, as he was eager to begin work at his proposed new station at Shimnap. He remained at Tshimakain for about a month.

In spite of the action taken at the 1840 Annual Meeting approving Gray's move, the sentiment within the Mission had by the spring of 1841 gradually reversed itself. Whitman explained to Greene in his letter of March 28, 1841, that the Mission would be overextending itself to open another station. Moreover, if Gray moved to Shimnap, he would be working in a different language and, of all the members of the Mission, he was the slowest in mastering an Indian tongue. Whitman argued that all of the cultivation should be done at Waiilatpu and that even the blacksmith shop, the printing press, and the mills should be centered there. He then could supply the material needs of the other stations, thus giving the ministers more time for their specialized duties. There is evidence that by the late spring of 1841, Gray had come to realize that it would be unwise for him to move to Shimnap. Final action by the Mission, however, was delayed until the Annual Meeting to be held the following May.

Narcissa Seeks Forgiveness

When Walker left for Tshimakain with Gray in March 1841, he carried a letter from Narcissa to Mary. It seems that Narcissa had been going through a period of intensive self-examination. "For two or three days," she wrote, "my distress was very great." Moved by a deep feeling of self-humiliation, she poured out her confession. No one ever condemned her as strongly as she in this letter condemned herself. "Perhaps never in my whole life," she wrote, "have I been led to see so distinctly the hidden iniquity & secret evils of my heart. Of all persons, I see myself as the most unfit for the place I occupy on heathen ground. I wonder that I was ever permitted to come... I see now as I *never* have before wherein I have been a grief to his [God's] children by indulging in unholy passions & exhibiting so little of the meek, lowly & quiet spirit of our blessed Saviour. I have been blind to my own faults & have not known what manner of spirit I was of. Proud & self confident have I been. I do not wonder that brother Spalding, if he saw this trait in my character, felt that he could not come into this field if I did. Neither is it strange that the other members of the Mission should feel that they could not live with us" [Letter 85].

After a full and frank confession, Narcissa begged the forgiveness of the Walkers and the Eellses. Mary made no comment in her diary on her reactions when she read the letter, but a few days after Gray had started back to Waiilatpu, she added this note to her diary: "Would give much to know how & what to do & whether it is I more than others who err. I know that I am a wicked wretch & fear my associates are no better." [28] The mutual exchange of confessions and the willingness to forgive did much to establish the good relationship which thereafter existed between the Whitmans and their associates in Tshimakain.

Agricultural Activities

The introduction of agriculture among the Cayuses brought problems. The growing crops had to be protected from grazing animals. This meant that the fields and gardens had to be fenced or constantly guarded. The Indians would have to settle down in farming communities, abandoning their age-old customs of wandering from place to place in search of food. Another problem which arose among the natives grew out of an increasing appreciation of proprietory rights to the land that was being cultivated. In his letter to Greene of October 29, 1840, Whitman wrote: "I do not think the Indians can be collected together as to make a settlement in any one place on account of difficulties that will arise among themselves." The reasons for this discouraging view were the failure of the Indians to build fences and the conflicting claims of ipretended ownersî to the plots being cultivated.

When the time came for planting in the spring of 1841, Whitman became more encouraged as he found the Indians clamoring for plows. In 1838 Whitman had written to his brother Augustus asking for fifty plows and three hundred hoes. Augustus was authorized to draw upon some of Dr. Whitman's personal funds to the extent of $200.00 to pay for such items. This request stirred the people of Rushville to send twenty-five plows, for on May 24, 1841, Marcus wrote to his brother to acknowledge the arrival of the plows at Fort Vancouver.[29] He also stated that the Board had sent ten. "The Indians are not backward in using them," he wrote. "I help them make collars & harness of good quality & they have plenty of horses" [Letter 89]. The harness had to be made of the hides of such animals as deer, buffalo, and horses, laboriously sewed by hand with awls.

THE SMITHS AND ROGERS LEAVE THE MISSION

After the alarming confrontation with the two belligerent Nez Perces at Kamiah in the fall of 1840, Smith determined to leave the field as soon as possible. Harvey Clark, who with his wife had spent the winter of 1840–41 with the Smiths, told Whitman that Smith had given up all further study of the Nez Perce language and was instead "taking up a course of study in order to prepare himself for preaching in the States" [Letter 86]. The Clarks left Kamiah in early March and returned to Waiilatpu. Smith with his wife, still an invalid, made preparations to follow. He notified Spalding that he would leave Kamiah on April 12.

In the meantime, Eliza Spalding had been taken ill. Spalding wrote in his diary on March 25, 1841: "Last evening my dear wife was attacked with a severe hemorrhage, which soon reduced her to almost a corpse." Henry did what he could to stop the flow of blood and sent an urgent message to Dr. Whitman asking for advice. Eliza's weakness continued through the first part of April. On the 12th of that month, Spalding wrote again: "My dear wife has considerable fever & appears worse." As with job of old, his troubles multiplied as the following diary entries indicate: "[April] 16. Little Henry quite sick last night... 17. Mr. Rogers very sick last night, up with him till late." With three sick people on his hands, Spalding sent an urgent message to Whitman to come at once.

Whitman arrived at Lapwai on Wednesday, April 21, shortly after Asa and Sarah Smith had landed from the canoe which had brought them down the river from Kamiah. Spalding noted in his diary for that day: "Mrs. S. is not able to sit up much; but I am fully persuaded that this is not the principle reason of Mr. Smith's leaving the Mission. He says he will go home in disgrace before he will remain longer in the Indian country. He considers the Indian race doomed to destruction." Smith's letter to Greene, written from Fort Walla Walla on April 29, gives a pathetic picture of his wife's illness and of the intolerable conditions under which they had lived at Kamiah. When the Smith went down the Columbia River, Sarah was still unable to walk; when portages had to be made, she had to be carried in a hammock slung from a pole carried by two Indians.[30] On the other hand, Spalding was probably correct when he wrote that more than the illness of Mrs. Smith was involved in her husband's determination to leave. Even if Sarah had enjoyed robust health, Asa would surely have left about that time since he had become thoroughly disillusioned regarding the prospect of doing anything worthwhile as a missionary among the Nez Perces.

Rogers, sick and likewise discouraged, listened to what Smith had to say to Whitman and Spalding, and confessed that he felt much the same. As early as February 27, 1841, Rogers had written to Greene about his intention to leave the Mission. He then stated: "I will simply say that Mr. Spalding is felt by me to be the principal cause of my course." [31]

Not wishing to see the Smiths make the balance of the river trip to Fort Walla Walla alone, and also realizing that Rogers was not in condition to ride overland to Waiilatpu, Whitman decided to accompany the three down the river in a canoe. The four left Lapwai on April 22 the Smiths in one canoe with one or more Indian boatmen, Whitman and Rogers in another. Gray, with a pack train carrying Smith's belongings and with Whitman's horses, went overland. After a brief stay at Fort Walla Walla, where the Clarks joined them, the two couples continued their travels down the river. They arrived at Fort Vancouver on May 17. There Mrs. Smith came under the care of the Company's physician, Dr. Forbes Barclay. In none of the letters of Whitman or Smith do we find any mention that Dr. Whitman was ever consulted regarding Mrs. Smith's affliction. Since Asa had studied some medicine before leaving for Old Oregon, it may be that he felt himself as well qualified to prescribe for his wife as Dr. Whitman. The Clarks settled in the Willamette Valley where he became active in church and educational work.[32]

The Smiths were obliged to tarry at Fort Vancouver until the latter part of December before being able to get passage on a ship bound for Honolulu. While waiting in the Islands for a ship to take them to the States, Sarah's health so improved that they decided to remain for a time. Asa accepted an assignment under the Hawaiian Mission of the American Board to Waialua on the island of Oahu. After being in the Islands for three years, the Smiths sailed from Honolulu on October 15, 1845, on a ship destined around the Cape of Good Hope.[33]

Asa Smith's greatest contribution to the Nez Perce work during his two and a half years with the Oregon Mission was along linguistic lines. At the time he left Kamiah, Smith had a greater knowledge of the Nez Perce language than any of his colleagues. He had compiled both a dictionary and a grammar, copies of which are now in the archives of the American Board in Boston.[34]

Cornelius Rogers and Maria Pambrun Become Engaged

An unexpected development took place following the return of Rogers to Waiilatpu: he became engaged to Maria, the sixteen-year-old daughter of Pierre Pambrun. In a letter that Whitman wrote to Walker on April 29, shortly after his return to Waiilatpu, he reported that Rogers had suffered a relapse and was then so ill that he was in danger of dying. Whitman's fears proved to be unfounded, for Rogers recovered and was soon well enough to ride to Fort Walla Walla. Since Rogers was not assigned to any particular station, he had been free to travel hither and yon as he pleased. No doubt he had been a frequent visitor at Fort Walla Walla.

It is not known just when he began to notice the teenage Maria and think of her as a wife. Nor is it known whether Pambrun was the one who took the initiative in encouraging the betrothal. We do know that Pambrun was delighted when Rogers asked for the hand of his daughter for he rewrote his will in order to make a generous provision for his future son-in-law. Of this Narcissa wrote: "It was his [i.e., Pambrun's] subject of conversation by day and by night while he was alive, and in his will he appropriated more to her on his account, than to his other children, besides giving him [i.e., Rogers] much of his personal property, and willing him over a hundred pounds sterling" [Letter 96]. The Whitmans felt that Maria was not worthy of Rogers, as she was an uneducated half-breed and knew very little English. Moreover, she was a Catholic. It is not known whether Pambrun told Rogers of the provisions made in his will but in all likelihood he did.

On May 11 when Pambrun and Rogers were riding together, Pambrun was guiding his horse by a rope looped Indian fashion around the animal's lower jaw. Somehow the horse managed to eject the rope and then began to run and buck. Pambrun was thrown repeatedly against the horn of the saddle and finally to the ground. He was so injured in the groin that he was unable to walk and had to be carried to his quarters. Dr. Whitman was summoned at once and upon his arrival discovered that Pambrun's internal injuries were extremely serious [Letter 87d]. Pambrun suffered intense pain for four days. He begged Whitman to give him some medicine which would put him out of his misery, anything to make him die quickly. This Whitman refused to do.

Pambrun died on the 15th, leaving his wife with seven children.[35] Shortly afterwards Mrs. Pambrun with her children left for Fort Vancouver. Pambrun's body was taken to Fort Vancouver for burial. When Rogers left Fort Walla Walla, he also left the Oregon Mission. Since he had never been an officially appointed missionary of the American Board, his departure did not incur the same censure from his associates as was the case with Smith. But Rogers' engagement to marry Maria Pambrun did bring criticism. Spalding, when he heard the news on June 7, wrote in his diary: "I am grieved... Is it possible? What will it profit a man if he gain the whole world & lose his own soul?" After hearing more details, Spalding wrote the next day: "He is to receive considerable property, which is probably the inducement. He leaves the Mission under painful circumstances."

Narcissa, in her letter of October 1, 1841, to her sister Jane, gives further information: "We have since learned that she [i.e., Maria] refused to marry Mr. Rogers, and he has returned the property willed to him. We think he has no reason to regret it on his own account. But the consequence of it all has been, it has taken Brother R. out of our mission, and he has gone to settle on the Willamette." In September 1841, Rogers married Miss Satira Leslie, a daughter of one of the Methodist missionaries. Since Rogers was able to speak the Nez Perce language, his services were soon in demand by the U.S. Government to go with official parties visiting the Nez Perce country. Rogers lost his life in a tragic accident on February 1, 1843, when he, his wife, and several others were swept over Willamette Falls in a boat. Maria married Dr. Forbes Barclay of Fort Vancouver in 1842.

Dr. Whitman to Dr. Bryant

When Whitman returned to Waiilatpu following the death of Pierre Pambrun, he took with him some boxes of goods which had been sent by sea first to Fort Vancouver and then taken up the Columbia to Fort

Walla Walla. These boxes contained supplies and gifts from friends and relatives in Rushville. On May 24 Whitman wrote to his brother Augustus acknowledging receipt of the goods and reporting that the plows which had been sent were still at Fort Vancouver. These plows had been ordered in the spring of 1838. It took three years to secure their delivery.

In one of the boxes, Whitman found some writing paper which had been sent by Dr. and Mrs. Ira Bryant. The gift brought back memories of the days during 1823–25 when he was beginning his medical studies while riding with Dr. Bryant. Thus inspired, Whitman also wrote to the Bryants on that same May 24. He did not know that Dr. Bryant had died sometime in 1840. Whitman began his letter by writing: "For the first time I sit down to write you. I do not see as you will be likely to write me first. You do not know how it seems at this distance to be so much in the dark about old friends... We are cheered by every token of respect. But although the Doctor sent considerable paper, we did not find any which he had written on for us."

In a friendly letter, Whitman gave his former mentor and his wife a quick review of life at Waiilatpu. He commented on the country, the climate, and his activities. "My medical duties call me much from home," he wrote, "as I have to go one hundred & eighty miles to the remotest station." He mentioned the death of Pierre Pambrun, but, strange to say, said nothing of any medical services rendered to the natives. Regarding his own health, he wrote: "In order to get established I have laboured most excessively but I am now so far broken that I cannot expect to accomplish much more manual labor." Here is a reference to the ill health he had suffered during the preceding winter.

He told of the buildings which then stood at Waiilatpu: "In a summary way, let me say we have a good convenient new house. That the old one yet stands & is occupied for a dwelling generally for two families & besides a house for company, that is [for] people who want to stay a while or for passers is nearly finished." The "house for company" was being built by Gray who started it during the winter of 1840–41. This was located about 400 feet east of the main mission house. It measured 32 x 40 feet; was a story and a half high; and was built, like the other two houses, of adobe bricks. Because of its pretentious size, it was first known as the mansion house, and then later as the emigrant house.

Whitman then told Dr. Bryant that: "Cultivation will require the aid of irrigation in order to make a business of it even in this valley." Here is the first mention of irrigation in the Whitman letters. Perhaps the digging of a millrace suggested the possibility of irrigation for his garden. On January 24, 1842, Gray in a letter to Walker drew an outline of the premises at Waiilatpu which showed several irrigation ditches. [See illustration in this volume.] Gray said that the ditches were "4 feet in width, 2 ft deep," and claimed that they had been dug by Indian labor.[36] Because the summers in the Walla Walla area are often dry, Whitman believed that the upper Columbia country was better suited for raising cattle and sheep than it was for farming. Spalding held the same views. Neither ever dreamt that the region would become one of the best wheat raising areas in the nation.

Regarding the future prospects of the natives, Whitman wrote: "It will not be easy to settle the Indians in this region for it will require the recourse & enterprise of White men to develop its resources by means of saw mills in the mountains to furnish timber for fences as well as buildings." [37] Here is the first indication in Whitman's letters of his growing conviction that the Indians could never compete with the white men in occupying the land. Sawmills were needed to produce lumber for fences to protect growing crops, to build granaries for storage of grain, and for houses. The natives had not the resources, the knowledge, or the skills needed for such improvements. Even though Whitman became increasingly convinced that the white man would eventually occupy the country, he never ceased doing what he could to help the Indians make an adjustment to a new way of life which was being forced upon them.

Whitman showed his political interest in this letter to Dr. Bryant by writing: "All forget to tell me who is President or Governor. There seems to be a great fear of saying something that another has said." In the closing paragraph of this letter, he wrote: "I have just heard that Harrison is President." William Henry Harrison was inaugurated on March 4, 1841, but died a month later and was succeeded by the Vice President, John Tyler. Several months had to elapse before Whitman learned of this. Whitman also referred in this letter to Dr. Bryant of the expected arrival in the Columbia River of the United States Exploring Expedition under the command of Lieut. Charles Wilkes. Actually the squadron had arrived at Fort Vancouver about a month before Whitman wrote, but communications were so slow in the Oregon country that he did not hear of it until sometime later.

POLITICAL DEVELOPMENTS

The Wilkes Expedition was the first government party to visit Old Oregon after that of Lieut. William A. Slacum in January 1837. The arrival of the Expedition undoubtedly aroused speculation in Whitman's mind about the future of the Pacific Northwest. What bearing, if any, would such an inspection trip have upon the settlement of the boundary issue with Great Britain? Undoubtedly Whitman knew of the Joint Occupation Treaty of 1818 and that no further official agreement had been reached between the United States and Great Britain regarding the location of the Oregon boundary. Whitman closed his letter to Bryant by writing: "We are all in the dark as to the situation of the U.S. Government about this Country."

Although Whitman was seemingly unaware of the growing concern in official government circles over the boundary question, some important developments were taking place. On February 7, 1838, Senator Lewis F. Linn of Missouri introduced a bill which called for the establishment of U.S. jurisdiction over the Oregon country lying north of the 42nd parallel (i.e., where the California-Oregon border is now located), west of the Rockies, and without specifying where the northern boundary was to be drawn. That was exactly the question—where was the northern boundary to be located? Linn's bill also called for the United States to occupy the territory with a military force. The bill failed to pass the Senate.

On December 11, 1838, after receiving the petition carried East that year by Jason Lee, Senator Linn introduced a second bill calling for the occupation of Old Oregon. This bill, like its predecessor, called for the occupation of the Oregon Territory and the protection of United States citizens residing there. In January 1839, Lee's memorial was presented to the Senate and ordered printed.[38] The Senate delayed taking action in favor of Linn's bill because at that time the United States was trying to negotiate a settlement with Great Britain on several other disputes, including the Maine boundary. On the following December 18, Senator Linn again brought up the Oregon question. A series of resolutions was referred to a select committee which, on March 31, 1840, made a report in which the claims of the United States were again asserted. Bancroft stated that: "The chief feature in these resolutions was a provision for granting to each white male inhabitant over eighteen years of age one thousand acres of land." [39] Such a promised bonanza whetted the appetites of thousands of wouldbe emigrants who were beginning to look with covetous eyes on the Oregon country. In due time Whitman was to hear of these developments. Actually, the United States could not make such land grants as long as the joint Occupation Treaty with England remained in effect. Such unilateral action would have been illegal.

Annual Meeting of 1841

During late April and early May, 1841, when convalescing in the Whitman home, Rogers poured out to Whitman a long list of complaints against Spalding. Even before Rogers had made known his intention to marry Maria Pambrun, he had resolved to leave the Mission because of the "ill treatment" he claimed to have received from Spalding.[40] Gray, who was also living at Waiilatpu when Rogers was there, corroborated much that the sick and despondent Rogers had to tell. After listening to the complaints, Whitman became thoroughly discouraged. Smith had already left the Mission, and now Rogers was planning to do likewise. Writing to Walker on May 8, Whitman said: "I have told Mr. Eells my utter despair of ever cooperating with Mr. Spalding. If you knew as much about this as I do, you would feel as much discouraged, I think, as I am."

The 1841 Annual Meeting of the Oregon Mission was scheduled to begin at Waiilatpu on June 9. Walker, not being in good health at the time, decided to make the trip to Waiilatpu by boat from Fort Colville to Fort Walla Walla. He would then ride out to the Whitman mission. When Walker arrived at Walla Walla, he heard so much news that he wrote two letters to his wife, the first dated May 15.[41] He told of the departure of the Smiths, the death of Pambrun, and the engagement of Rogers and Maria. He learned that Pambrun had willed $1,200.00 to Maria, in addition to the sum given to Rogers, on condition that she marry Rogers. Walker was amazed at these developments and in a burst of sentiment, unusual to his taciturn nature, wrote: "After all, I had rather have my Mary as I took her than Miss Maria with her twelve hundred dollars or more. But every one to his own fancy. It would, I think, take much love to hide all her Indian habits."

Whitman rode to Fort Walla Walla on May 31 to get Walker, and the two rode out to Waiilatpu the next day. On the four-hour ride, Whitman shared with Walker all that he had heard from Rogers and Gray in criticism of Spalding. Eells arrived on June 7, and the Spaldings came the next day with their two little children—Eliza, three and a half, and Henry, one and a half. Mrs. Spalding's presence was unexpected but Walker noted in his diary that it was an "omen for good."

The business meetings began on Wednesday, June 9, as scheduled, with Walker serving as moderator and Eells, secretary. The financial report was first considered. Because of the irregular intervals of time that elapsed between the time a bill was incurred at Fort Vancouver and payment made by the American Board in Boston, it is impossible to compile accurate figures to show the actual annual cost of the Oregon Mission. The best available figures are to be found in the annual reports of the Treasurer of the Board which were published at the close of each fiscal year which came on August 31. According to these reports [see Appendix 2], the Board paid $4,886.14 for the support of its Oregon Mission in 1840 and $3,783.07 in 1841. This meant that the average cost for each of the thirteen adults in 1841 was less than $300.00. These figures do not include the value of gifts sent to Oregon by the Hawaiian Mission; the supplies, especially clothing, sent in missionary barrels; or special gifts such as the plows donated by Whitman or by his relatives and friends in Rushville. To a remarkable degree, the Oregon Mission had become almost self-supporting.

Only routine items of business were considered on Thursday. On Friday tension arose when Whitman repeated some of the charges that Rogers had made against Spalding. Spading wrote in his diary: "I was particularly grieved by being accused by Mr. Rogers through Dr. Whitman of using my knowledge of the Nez Perce language to the disadvantage of the Mission... I think that this charge is entirely without foundation." Once Whitman began to criticize Spalding, he continued by dredging up from the past several incidents including, as Spalding wrote, "one or two small things which occurred in the States & were long since settled." From this we can infer that what Spalding had said about not trusting Mrs. Whitman's judgment had again come up for discussion. Spalding felt that most of the charges made against him "were entirely untrue & have their origin either in Indian reports, misunderstandings, or jealousy." Walker that night wrote in his diary: "Spent most of the day in conversation. It came so sharp that I was compelled to leave. It is enough to make one sick to see what is the state of things in the mission."[42]

On Saturday, June 12, the action of the previous Annual Meeting giving Gray permission to open a station at Shimnap was reconsidered. With the departure of the Smiths and the announced intention of Rogers to do likewise, even Gray had come to realize that such a move was inadvisable. So the proposal which had agitated the Mission for so many months was dropped. Gray agreed to remain at Waiilatpu where a number of projects called for his services including completing the building of the third house, digging more irrigation ditches, erecting a blacksmith shop, and also the building of a sawmill in the Blue Mountains.

At this June 1841 meeting, Spalding learned for the first time that Hall, Gray, Smith, and Rogers had all written to the Board severely criticizing him. He was astounded! "The Lord in great mercy look upon these men," he wrote in his diary, "& forgive their sins & sustain his unworthy servant... under these accumulating trials." Spalding listed Whitman as being one who had also written letters of criticism, but an examination of Whitman's correspondence with the Board shows that his comments were mild. Be it said to Spalding's credit that he never wrote letters complaining about his associates until after he had learned what the others had done.

No business was transacted on Saturday afternoon. Whitman and Spalding took advantage of the day to meet in private to talk out their differences. Subdued and contrite by what he had learned, Spalding wrote in his diary on Sunday, the 13th: "Had a familiar talk with Doct. & Mrs. Whitman, confessed that I had said a great many things which I ought not to have said & asked her pardon." Although Narcissa had been willing to beg forgiveness from the Walkers, she showed no spirit of contrition in dealing with Spalding. Spalding noted in his diary: "Was astonished at self-rightousness manifested by our bro. & sis."

Some good came out of this frank exchange of feelings as is indicated in Whitman's letter to Greene of July 13, about a month after the Annual Meeting had closed. He wrote: "We never had a meeting which promised so much harmony among the members of the Mission as this. We had a most plain talk with Mr. Spalding which resulted in his acknowledging himself to have been in the wrong in the leading causes of complaint & that he had been very jealous... I will not be too sanguine of the future but this much I can say, he has pledged himself that he will not be as jealous & that he will cooperate with the Mission & most especially with Mrs. Whitman and myself."

On Sunday, the Mission family, now reduced to ten, and the Littlejohns observed the sacrament of the Lord's Supper. Even though some bitter feelings had existed, this solemn service, so rarely held in their wilderness isolation, induced a deeper feeling of fellowship. Three small children were presented for baptism; Leverett, the month-old son of the Littlejohns; Caroline, the eight-month-old daughter of the Grays; and Helen Mar Meek, the three-year-old half-breed girl living with the Whitmans.[43] The administration of baptism would normally have been Spalding's prerogative as he was pastor of the Mission church, but, under the circumstances, he asked Eells to officiate.

The business meetings closed on Monday noon, and those who lived at a distance started back to their respective stations. Whitman and Gray rode with Walker and Eells for about five miles. After reviewing the events of the previous five days, the four men felt that the outlook for the future was hopeful. Walker wrote that day in his diary: "At the end, we had reason to say, it was good to be there."

Evidence indicates, however, that all members of the Mission were apprehensive of what the Board might do in response to the letters of criticism about Spalding which had been sent to it. They knew that ordinarily it would take two years for a letter from Old Oregon to reach Boston and for a reply to be received. Greene's answer, therefore, could be expected sometime in the fall of 1842. If only there had been some means of rapid communication, the Board could have been informed of the changed situation in the Oregon Mission following the departure of the Smiths and Rogers and after the Whitmans and Spaldings had settled their differences. Instead, a long year of suspense stretched before them. What action would the Board take?

Some Events of the Summer of 1841

Much to the joy of the Whitmans, Archibald McKinlay, a Presbyterian from the Highlands of Scotland, succeeded Pambrun at Fort Walla Walla during the summer of 1841. In June 1840, McKinlay had married Sarah Julia, daughter of Peter Skene Ogden, a prominent Hudson's Bay official. It had been the custom of Pambrun to buy off the trouble-makers among the natives in order to keep peace [Letter 97]. McKinlay refused to follow such a policy. This removed pressure from the Indians on Whitman, who was financially unable to be constantly giving presents in order to keep their goodwill. Once Narcissa wrote: "From the commencement of this station until the present time, it has constantly been a point with one or more of them to be urging for property to be given to keep them in subjection... It is difficult for them to feel but that we are rich and getting richer by the houses we dwell in and the clothes we wear and hang out to dry after washing from week to week, and the grain we consume in our families" [Letter 97]. Even the family wash drying in the sun awakened envy in the hearts of the natives. Any kind of cloth was expensive to them, and behold what the white people had in abundance!

Asa Smith's letters are sprinkled with references to the cupidity of the natives. The following quotations are typical: "We find here an extremely selfish people, who most of them doubtless follow us more for the loaves and the fishes, then for any spiritual benefit." "They seem to wish to make the stations their trading posts & the most they want of us is to supply their temporal wants." "The temporal favors [we bestow] are not appreciated & only serve to increase the pride & insolence of the Indians." "No doubt is left in my mind as to their motives in desiring missionaries. The principal motive evidently is the temporal benefit which may be derived from them." [44] Even Spalding, usually more charitable regarding this very natural desire of the Indians to secure property, later wrote to Greene, October 17, 1845: "Another cause of excitement is their land. They are told by the enemies of the mission, that people in the civilized world purchase their land & water privileges. This touches a chord that vibrates through every part of the Indian's soul—that insatiable desire for property." [45]

McKinlay's refusal to give presents to the Cayuse chiefs, although applauded by the Whitmans, added to the growing resentment of the Indians against the white man. Here was another cause of the growing unrest among the Cayuses.

Pambrun's friendship with the Roman Catholic priests had also given the Whitmans concern. In his letter to his brother Augustus, Whitman on May 24, 1841, wrote: "There is likely to be a strong Catholic division here for one thing. It has been fostered more or less by our late neighbor, Mr. Pambrun." Pambrun was friendly with a Cayuse chief, Tauitau or Young Chief,[46] who lived on the Umatilla River, about twentyfive miles south of Waiilatpu. Pambrun built a house for Young Chief in the fall of 1840. The site has been located on the north bank of the Umatilla River opposite Thornhollow, a small town about twenty miles east of present-day Pendleton, Oregon.[47] As will be noted, this act of kindness by Pambrun was used by the Catholic priests in the fall of 1847 to gain a foothold among the Cayuse Indians living not far from the Whitman station.

During the latter part of July 1841, Marcus and Narcissa rode to Tshimakain, arriving there on the 21st. On July 27, Myra Eells gave birth to her first child, a son, whom they named Edwin. The Whitmans remained at Tshimakain for almost four weeks. Walker, in his diary, tells of an excursion that he and the doctor made to Spokane Falls, now in the heart of the city of Spokane, Washington. Walker wrote on the 14th: "The Dr. has been as full of Geology as if he had eaten half dozen great volumes on this subject." Evidently the entertainment of guests in their limited living quarters was difficult for the Walkers, for Elkanah wrote in his diary on August 16 when the Whitmans left: "I must say I did not regret to see them depart."

On August 9th, while still at Tshimakain, Whitman wrote to his brother Samuel and discussed a number of items of human interest.

"I am no more of an Abolitionist than I was for years before I left home," he wrote. "I do not feel as much attachment to Illinois as I did & I think it is the last State I would live in on account of its heavy debt & taxes... Tell mother we are eating cheese of Mrs. Whitman's make; that milk & butter are most abundant with us & so will cheese be if we choose to make it. Calves rennet is a scarce article for we value a calf the same as an old cow or ox for it costs nothing to raise them." Rennet was a necessary ingredient for the making of cheese. The missionaries discovered that rennet secured from the stomach of a deer was nearly as effective as that from the calf of an American cow.

Drayton of the Wilkes Expedition Visits Waiilatpu

During the first part of July 1841, before the Whitmans left for Tshimakain, Joseph Drayton, a member of the Wilkes Exploring Expedition visited the Whitmans at Waiilatpu. He was the second person to have his impressions of the Whitmans and of their work published, the first being Thomas J. Farnham. Drayton's report was included in the official *Narrative of the U.S. Exploring Expedition*.[48]

The origin of the Exploring Expedition goes back to the report which Lieut. William A. Slacum submitted to Congress on December 18, 1837. On February 13, 1838, the Senate asked the Secretary of War to submit all the information he had regarding "Oregon" and to have a map made of the territory. Within eight months after Slacum's return, the Navy Department sent a squadron of five vessels under the command of Lieut. Charles Wilkes to explore the Pacific Ocean from the Antarctic to the Oregon coast. The Expedition was gone for about four years.

Lieut. Wilkes with four ships of his squadron arrived in the Columbia River in April 1841. Several exploring parties were then sent into the interior, including one led by Drayton, who was deputized to visit Waiilatpu. Drayton was given a cordial welcome by the Whitmans and the Grays. In his report, Drayton said: "There are two houses, each of one story, built of adobes, with mud roofs, to insure a cooler habitation in summer. There are also a small saw-mill and some grist-mills at the place moved by water." Here is the first mention of Whitman having a sawmill. It may be that Whitman had attached a saw of some kind to his waterwheel. Later, as will be indicated, he erected a larger and more efficient sawmill about twenty miles to the east of Waiilatpu in the foothills of the Blue Mountains.

Drayton's account continues: "All the premises look very comfortable. They have a fine kitchen garden, in which they grow all the vegetables raised in the United States, and several kinds of fine melons. The wheat, some of which stood seven feet high, was in full head, and nearly ripe; Indian corn was in tassel, and some of it measured nine feet in height. They will reap this year about three hundred bushels of wheat, with a quantity of corn and potatoes. The soil in the vicinity of the small streams, is a rich black loam, and very deep." The amazing height of the wheat and corn as reported by Drayton was due, no doubt, to the richness of the virgin soil.

Drayton reported that at the time of his visit there were only fourteen Indians, including men, women, and children, in the vicinity of the mission station. Whitman told Drayton that he had 124 natives on his school roll, but due to the wandering habits of the tribe, the average daily attendance was about twenty-five. Whitman explained that the band living in the vicinity of Waiilatpu would return during the latter part of July from the Grande Ronde Valley. Then after three or four months, they would "move off to the north and east to hunt buffalo." After their return from the buffalo hunt, they would remain another short time at Waiilatpu and then would be off again. It was this wandering, seminomadic habit, which made both schoolwork and religious instruction so extremely difficult for the missionaries. Horatio Hale, the philologist of the Wilkes Expedition who did not visit Waiilatpu, reported that the Cayuses were a small tribe, "not numbering five hundred souls."[49] From other evidence, it is safe to say that Hale's estimate was much too high.

Drayton had been told that the Cayuses were quarrelsome and at times turbulent. Yet he observed that: "These missionaries live quite comfortably, and seem contented; they are, however, not free from apprehension of Indian depredations. Dr. Whitman, being an unusually large and athletic man, is held in much respect by the Indians, and they have made use of his services as a physician, which does not seem to carry with it so much danger here, as among the tribes in the lower country, or further north." Possibly Whitman gave Drayton a too optimistic picture of the lack of danger involved in practicing the white man's medicine among this primitive people. We shall see that this was a factor in bringing on the Whitman massacre.

In the course of his inspection of the mission grounds, Drayton saw the irrigation ditches which were being dug. Whitman told of how some of the Indians, noticing how his gardens and fields had flourished after being irrigated, "desired to take some of the water from his trenches instead of making new ones of their own." Very naturally Whitman objected and told them to dig their own ditches. This they did, but tapped the creek above the outlet for Whitman's ditch and then dammed up the opening Whitman needed. "This," reported Drayton, "had wellnigh produced much difficulty; but finally they were made to understand that there was enough water for both; and they now use it with as much success

CHAPTER FIFTEEN *The Fifth Year of the Oregon Mission, 1840–1841* 473 as the missionaries." W. D. Breckenridge, the horticulturist of the Wilkes Expedition, met Whitman at Fort Walla Walla on July 2, 1841, and wrote in his journal: "Dr. Whitman came down to pay us a visit; found him a very intelligent man."[50]

Farnham's and Drayton's descriptions of the Whitman station have much in common. Both observers had high praise for what the Whitmans and their associates had been able to accomplish.

In Summary

The fifth year of the Oregon Mission of the American Board marked the half-way point in its history. It was a year when a gradual transition was taking place from troubles within the Mission to increasing difficulties from without. Ever since the arrival of the 1838 reenforcement, the Mission had been agitated with personality difficulties and dissensions over Mission policies. With the departure of the Smiths and Rogers, the tensions eased somewhat, but, as will be seen, continued to some extent as long as Gray remained. On the other hand, we find during this year the beginnings of harassments and even hostility on the part of the natives. These were to increase during the following years.

A number of significant events took place during this year, 1840–41, which were portents of things to come. The first emigrant family passed the Whitman station on horseback in the fall of 1840. The first wagons, having been taken over the Blue Mountains, arrived a year later. The presence of the Wilkes Expedition's exploring parties in the interior of Old Oregon was evidence of an awakened interest on the part of the United States government. No one appreciated more than did the Whitmans the strategic importance of Waiilatpu. Sitting astride the Oregon Trail, it was the first outpost of American civilization west of the Blue Mountains. Great events were before the Whitmans in the years immediately before them.

But, a great question haunted their minds. What action would the American Board take in response to the many letters it had received which described the turmoil within the Mission? A year would have to pass before the answer came.

CHAPTER 15 ENDNOTES

1 Hulbert. *O.P.*, VII:207.

2 Douglas McMurtrie, *The American Inventory of Idaho Imprints*, 1839–1890, lists five copies of this primer as being extant.

3 Original letter in Coll. A. See also Marshall, *Acquisition of Oregon*, II: 105.

4 Copies of these letters, containing about 35,000 words, are in Drury, *Spalding and Smith*.

5 Italics are the author's.

6 Bancroft, *Oregon*, I:249. Walker's Reminiscences appeared as Vol. 17, *Early California Travels*, Glen Dawson, Los Angeles, 1951. Joel P. Walker was a brother of Joseph Reddeford Walker, leader of Capt. Bonneville's 1833 brigade to California.

7 The Walker family traveled overland from Oregon to California with the ship's company of the *U.S. Peacock* which had been wrecked at the mouth of the Columbia River on July 18, 1841. The *Peacock* was with the U.S. Exploring Squadron under command of Lieut. Charles Wilkes.

8 In 1878, when Walker was living at Sonoma, California, and eighty-one years old, he dictated his reminiscences. Original ms., Coll. B. Walker was a member of the California Constitutional Convention which met at Monterey in 1849.

9 Reared as a half-breed in a frontier community, Whitman's namesakes, Marcus W. Newell, was often in trouble, once serving a term in the penitentiary for theft. He is reported to have been killed as a young man by the vigilantes. See article by Francis Haines on Robert Newell, Idaho Yesterdays, Spring 1965.

10 Johanson (ed.), Robert Newells's Memoranda, p. 23, gives two dates for Newell's departure August 5 and Sept. 27. The latter date is evidently the correct one.

11 *T.O.P.A.*, 1877, p. 22.

12 Drury, *Spalding and Smith*, p. 193, from letter to Walker, Oct. 12, 1840. The whole subject of the Indian's concept of land ownership at this time is rather vague and needs further study.

13 *Ibid.*, p. 194. Smith, on page 197, identifies Meoway as Atpashwakaiket. This incident of the Indians attacking Pambrun is mentioned in Allen's *Ten Years in Oregon*, p. 175. Josephy, *The Nez Perce Indians*, p. 211, identifies Meoway with Looking Glass, whose son, also called Looking Glass, was a leader in the Nez Perce uprising of 1877.

14 *Ibid.*, p. 201.

15 *Ibid.*, p. 302, from Spalding's diary for Nov. 2, 1840.

16 Drury, *F.W.W.*, II:198.

17 Drury, *Spalding and Smith*, p. 302.

18 *Op. cit.*, II:169. Marshall was in error as to the month when Smith wrote to Greene. It was October not September.

19 Drury, *Spalding and Smith*, p. 203. Italics are the author's.

20 Probably a reference to Jack, the Hawaiian, whom Whitman had sent to Kamiah early in Oct. 1840. See Drury, *Spalding and Smith*, p. 299.

21 Merk, *Fur Trade and Empire*, p. 137.

22 Being a person of strong opinions and fanatical prejudices, Griffin was often involved in controversies in church, community, and political circles. In the

spring of 1849, Griffin ran for Congress on an "anti-monopoly and anti-Jesuit" platform but fell far short of being elected. See George N. Belknap, *McMurtrie's Oregon Imprints, a Supplement*, Eugene, Oregon, 1950, p. 10.

23 Original letter in Coll. Y.

24 Josephy, *The Nez Perces*, pp. 24 ff., gives a good account of primitive Nez Perce religion.

25 Garth, *P.N.Q.*, XXXIX (1948):131: "This mill was of the 'tub' mill type. Such mills had a horizontal wheel set as low as possible to obtain the maximum fall from a low head of water. The wheel was less than 8 feet in diameter, and from its center a wooden drive shaft extended up through the floor of the milling platform to drive the stones."

26 Words in italics were underlined by Whitman. His strong temperance views evidently extended to the use of tobacco. Although Whitman here indicated that he was unable to use Indian labor, Gray in a letter to Walker dated Jan. 24, 1842 (Coll. Y.) stated that some Indians had been hired.

27 A son, Leverett, was born to the Littlejohns at Waiilatpu in May 1841.

28 Drury, *F.W.W.*, II:210; entry for April 11, 1841.

29 The record is not clear regarding who actually paid for these plows. Did all or part of the cost come out of Whitman's private funds, or were the plows paid for by the people of Rushville? We do not know.

30 Smith to Greene, June 2, 1841. Coll. A.

31 Original in Coll. A.

32 Clark organized the First Presbyterian Church at Willamette Falls (now Oregon City) on May 25, 1844, with three charter members, one of whom was the mountain man, Osborne Russell. See Chapter Nine, fn. 13. This church became the First Congregational Church of Oregon City in 1849; is reported to be the oldest Protestant church for white people with a continuous existence on the Pacific Slope of what is now the United States.

33 See Drury, *Spalding and Smith*, pp. 220 ff., for a brief summary of the experiences of the Smiths after they left Old Oregon. Both lie buried in the cemetery of the Congregational Church of Buckland, Mass., of which Smith was pastor from 1848 to 1859.

34 Horatio Hale, *Ethnography and Philology*, first published in 1846, was reprinted Ridgewood, N.J., 1968. This contains a summary of Smith's Nez Perce grammar, pp. 542-61. Hale, who was the philologist for the Wilkes Expedition, met Smith at Astoria shortly before the Smiths sailed for Honolulu and, no doubt, secured his material from Smith at that time.

35 Pambrun was fifty-four years old when he died. He had been in the service of the Hudson's Bay Company for twenty-six years. See fn. 29, Chapter Ten.

36 Original letter in Coll. Y.

37 Hulbert, *O.P.*, VII: 223.

38 Bancroft, *Oregon*, I:372.

39 *Ibid.*

40 Drury, *Spalding and Smith*, pp. 314-5.

41 Originals in Coll. Wn.

42 Drury, *Walker*, p. 158.

43 The names of these children baptized by Eells were not entered in the record book of the Mission church, but Spalding did list their names in his diary.

44 Drury, *Spalding and Smith*, pp. 98, 151, 175, & 184.

45 *Ibid.*, p. 338.

46 See Chapter Ten, section "Three Cayuse Chiefs."

47 Identification of the location of Young Chief's house was made through the kindness of Sister M. Florita, formerly of St. Andrews Mission, Pendleton, Ore. She wrote to me on March 3, 1971: "It is on the hill in Thornhollow. John Shoeship's home is now on part of the property where Young Chief lived." See trail map used as an illustration in this volume.

48 Charles Wilkes, Narrative of the U.S. Exploring Expedition, 5 vols., Philadelphia, 1845. Drayton's report of Waiilatpu is in Vol. IV: Chap. II.

49 Hale, Ethnography and Philology, p. 214. See ante, fn. 84.

50 W. D. Breckenridge, The Breckenridge Journal for the Oregon Country, O. B. Sperlin (ed.), reprint from W.H.Q., 1930-31, Univ. of Wash. Press, Seattle, 1931.

[CHAPTER SIXTEEN]

THE MISSION IN CRISIS
1841–1842

As early as May 1840, Narcissa in a letter to her mother had written: "A tide of immigration appears to be moving this way rapidly. What a few years will bring forth, we know not. A great change has taken place even since we first entered the country, and we have no reason to believe it will stop here. Instead of two lonely American females, we now number fourteen and soon may [be] twenty or forty more, if reports are true. We are emphatically situated on the highway between the States and the Columbia river, and are a resting place for the weary travelers, consequently a greater burden rests upon us than upon any of our associates—to be always ready." The fourteen American women to whom Narcissa referred included the six wives in the Oregon Mission of the American Board, the two wives of the independent missionaries, and six women connected with the Methodist Mission in the Willamette Valley. A few weeks after Narcissa wrote, the *Lausanne* arrived in the Columbia River bringing the large Methodist reenforcement which included eighteen females. Three more independent missionary couples arrived in Old Oregon in the fall of 1840 and one immigrant family. Thus the number of American women in the Old Oregon country rose to thirty-six by that fall.

During the first part of September 1841, a party of twenty-four immigrants from the States passed Waiilatpu bound for the Willamette Valley. Narcissa wrote that included in the number were "two families with small children, from Missouri" [Letter 96]. A larger number had started, but some had branched off at Soda Springs and headed for California. Those who continued on to Oregon left their wagons at Fort Hall and completed their journey on horseback. In this party was a family with six children. "It was very pleasing to me," wrote Narcissa, "to see such a mother with so many children around her, having come so far such a dreadful journey." Included in the 1841 party was a Methodist minister, the Rev. Joseph Williams, who later published an account of his travels. Commenting on his visit with the Whitmans and the Grays, he wrote: "These were kind, friendly people. We heard the doctor hold a meeting on Sunday in a well-behaved congregation of Indians. I tried to preach to them myself that day. Here we had all kinds of garden vegetables, which they gave to us very freely." [1]

Activities of W. H. Gray

During the summer and early fall of 1841, Gray was busy finishing the house he was building for himself and his family. According to a map which Gray drew of the mission premises at Waiilatpu [see illustration in this volume], the new house had two main partitions which crisscrossed the interior, dividing it into four main rooms. Two of the rooms were then subdivided, thus giving six rooms on the ground floor. Whitman was able to hire two men from the 1841 immigration to help Gray place the roof, which was made out of "split timbers of cottonwood... covered with grass and slabs of dirt." By November 11, Whitman reported: "The house was roofed & the walls are being hewed and plastered, & in a short time it will be fit to dwell in" [Letter 100]. The Gray family moved in during the latter part of November.

After finishing his house, Gray built a blacksmith shop, which measured 16 x 30 feet, out of the adobe bricks taken from the original mission house. The shop was located about midway between the main mission house and the emigrant house. On January 24, 1842, Narcissa in a letter to Mary Walker wrote: "The old house is entirely taken down... You will see quite a change in Waiilatpu when you visit us next spring as I hope you will be able to do." In addition to these three main buildings, the premises at Waiilatpu contained a number of smaller structures such as granaries, corn cribs, a smoke house, a hen house, and a corral. These improvements, with irrigation ditches, fenced fields and gardens, the flour mill, the young orchard and the grove of locust trees gave every appearance of a growing and thriving establishment.

Gray was not content to be just a manual laborer. He never forgot that he had studied medicine for a few weeks during the winter of 1837–38 at the Medical College at Fairfield, New York. In a letter to one of his former professors at Fairfield dated February 1841, Gray wrote: "The Doct. [i.e., Whitman] and I differ in some of his professional points, and so far as our practice goes, I do not know as I have lost any more patients than he has. I may not have had as severe cases, I cannot say." [2] No comment by Whitman regarding Gray's practice of medicine has been found, but we may assume that he would have strongly opposed such actions.

THE RED RIVER EMIGRATION OF 1841

The fall of 1841 was noteworthy not only for the arrival in Oregon of the first overland party of immigrants from the States, but also for the arrival of a colony of immigrants from Red River which was sent to Oregon by the Hudson's Bay Company. As has been told in a previous chapter,[3] George Simpson was in New York City a few days before the Methodist Missionary Society sent out its large reenforcement of 1839 on the *Lausanne* under the leadership of Jason Lee. Simpson immediately recognized the political implications in the enlargement of the American colony in the Willamette Valley. As soon as he could, he alerted the officials of the Hudson's Bay Company in London to this threat to the territorial claims of England to Oregon. As a result, the Company decided to send a colony of French Canadians with their families from Red River to settle at the Cowlitz Portage. It is evident that the Company wanted to increase the number of British citizens living north of the Columbia River in order to strengthen British claims to that part of the Oregon territory. The emigrants left Red River on June 1, 1841, under the command of James Sinclair. This was the only emigration of that size sponsored by the Company for Oregon before the settlement of the boundary question in 1846. There is no indication in the writings of any of the missionaries of the American Board that they saw a connection between the arrival of the Methodist reenforcement of 1840 and the Red River immigration of 1841.

Mary Walker in her diary tells of a visit that Sinclair made at Tshimakain on August 21. "He is conducting a company of emigrants from Canada," she wrote. "They expect to settle at the Cowlitz. There are a hundred and twentyfive, 80 of whom are children. The women are mostly halfbloods. Several births have occurred on the way, & since leaving the buffalo country, they have been obliged to kill 8 oxen. An ox only lasts them a day or two. Thus we see Oregon fast filling up."[4] Being French Canadians, it may be assumed that all were Catholics.

The Red River party was at Fort Walla Walla at the time part of the Fort burned on October 3[5] Whitman mentioned the fire in his letter to Greene of October 22, saying that, although the Company's loss was not great, "Messrs. Griffin, Clark, Littlejohn, & Smith were very heavy sufferers;" many of their personal belongings had been left there in storage. Narcissa in a letter to her parents said some property belonging to their mission, such as salt and a few precious plows, were also lost [Letter 97]. Under McKinlay's energetic supervision, the destroyed buildings were soon rebuilt.

According to Spalding, who made the claim in a published article in May 1865,[6] Whitman was called to Fort Walla Walla at the time of the Annual Mission Meeting of September 1842. While there, according to this account, word came of the arrival at Fort Colville of the Red River party, while a number were dining at the Fort. Upon hearing the news, a young priest sprang to his feet and shouted: "Hurrah for Columbia! [Oregon]. America is too late; we have got the country." Spalding claimed that: "In an instant, as by instinct, Dr. Whitman saw through the whole plan, clear to Washington... He immediately rose from the table and asked to be excused, sprang upon his horse, and in a very short time stood with his noble 'Cayuse' [pony] white with foam, before his door; and without stopping to dismount, he replied to our anxious inquiries with great decision and earnestness: 'I am going to cross the Rocky Mountains and reach Washington this winter, God carrying me through, and bring out an emigration over the mountains next season, or this country is lost.'"[7]

Here is one of the main points of the discredited Whitman-Saved-

Oregon story so zealously disseminated by Spalding, Gray,[8] and others. The main fallacy of Spalding's account is that the *Red River colony arrived in Old Oregon in the fall of 1841 and not 1842.* However, there may be a core of truth in Spalding's claim. Whitman may have visited Fort Walla Walla in the fall of 1841 when he heard of the arrival of the Red River colony at Fort Colville. He did comment on this news in his letter to Greene dated November 11, 1841, but said nothing about seeing any political significance in the colony's arrival.

When the colonists arrived at the Cowlitz Portage, they found that the lands made available to them by the Puget Sound Agricultural Company were not well suited for farming. Attracted by the fertile acres and better climate of the Willamette Valley, they soon moved thither. No doubt the presence of a number of former employees of the Hudson's Bay Company in the Valley was an inducement. This was a disappointing development for Dr. McLoughlin and the officials of the Hudson's Bay Company who were eager to increase the British population at the Cowlitz Portage. Bancroft commented: "The failure of the Red River settlers to remain on the lands of the Puget Sound Company defeated whatever political design the formation of that organization favored."[9] But, as will be indicated, the increase of the number of French Canadians in the Willamette Valley gave the Hudson's Bay Company a temporary advantage in its opposition to any move on the part of the Americans to establish a provisional government.

George Simpson estimated the population of the Valley in 1840 to be about five hundred, of whom sixty-five men were Americans and sixty-one French Canadians.[10] Although the number of adult men was about evenly divided between the two groups, the French Canadians had a larger number of children than the Americans. When all or most of the Red River colonists moved to the Valley early in 1842, the French Canadians were in the majority until the arrival of the American immigration in the fall of that year. The annual subsidy of £100 given by the Hudson's Bay Company to Father F. N. Blanchet for his services to the French Canadians in the Willamette Valley has been mentioned previously.[11] This generous assistance to the Roman Catholics in the Valley was not at that time public knowledge. Why was the Company making such a large annual payment? The most apparent reason was that the Company felt a responsibility to provide for the spiritual welfare of its former employees. A second reason was that the presence of a priest in the colony of illiterate but devout Roman Catholics was helpful in maintaining discipline. Lieut. Charles Wilkes, who visited the Valley in 1841, confirms this latter explanation when he wrote: " ...the Catholic portion of the settlement, who form a large majority of these inhabitants, are kept under control by their priests." [12]

The Hudson's Bay Company enjoyed an unexpected benefit on the removal of most of the Red River colonists to the Willamette Valley: it gained a temporary political advantage over the Methodist-dominated American settlement. As has been stated, prior to the arrival of these colonists, the French Canadians had joined the Americans in signing the first two memorials sent to the United States Congress asking for an extension of its jurisdiction over Oregon. When, however, the Americans in the fall of 1842 sought the cooperation of the Canadians in another similar petition to Congress, the Canadians not only declined to sign but actively opposed the idea. Bancroft states that this was "presumably by the advice of McLoughlin and their spiritual adviser, Blanchet." [13] The loyalty of the French Canadians to the Company was such that they could usually be counted on to vote or act en bloc as directed.

The formation of a provisional government was finally approved by a narrow majority of settlers meeting at Champoeg on May 2, 1843. Most of the Canadians on that occasion, still heeding the advice of Father Blanchet, voted against the proposal. However, a few voted with the Americans; thus permitting the provisional government to be established.[14]

War, Diplomacy, or Emigration

The area of Old Oregon claimed by the United States and coveted by Great Britain was that part of the present State of Washington lying to the north and west of the Columbia River. The final settlement of the troublesome boundary question could have been by one of three methods—war, diplomacy, or emigration. The slogan: "Fifty-four forty or fight," referring to the boundary line that far north, was often heard in the United States following the Presidential campaign of 1844,[15] and yet going to war over a wilderness area in faraway "Oregon" was too preposterous to have been taken seriously by either nation. Diplomacy needed a bargaining base before it could be effective, and this is exactly what emigration from the States provided for its diplomats.

As has been stated, Slacum was the first to recognize the strategic value to the United States of the Puget Sound region. He was insistent that the boundary line should be at the 49° parallel. Inspired by the dream that Slacum had imparted to him, Jason Lee had induced Whitman and Spalding to petition the American Board to send out a colony of 220 missionaries. Lee's plan was for the Methodist Church to concentrate on enlarging its colony in the Willamette Valley while the American Board would plant its colony in the interior of Oregon. If this strategy were successful, Oregon would be won by immigration.

When the Joint Occupation Treaty came up for possible consideration in 1837, Senator John C. Calhoun advised Congress to delay. He argued that the whole question of the location of the boundary line would be decided by an influx of American settlers. "Let us encourage emigration," he advocated, "and let the West send off its swarms; fill Oregon with its citizens, and it will become ours as certainly as a ripe peach drops to the ground in autumn." [16]

George Simpson was aware of this strategy when he met Jason Lee in New York shortly before the *Lausanne* sailed in October 1839. As has been mentioned, it was this knowledge that moved the Hudson's Bay Company in London to take steps to counteract the American moves by sending its colony from Red River to Oregon in 1841. Evidently realizing that the number of emigrants who could be sent to Oregon from the Red River settlement would be strictly limited, the officials of the Hudson's Bay Company made plans to send some by sea. We find this plan mentioned in a letter from London to Dr. McLoughlin dated December 31, 1839: "In furtherance of the same object of protection to the fur trade, we have it in view to send by the ship to sail for the Columbia River in the month of September next, about twenty respectable, industrious agriculturists either with small families or single to be taken into the Company's service or placed on the Cowlitz settlement, as may hereafter be found expedient, and we have it in view moreover to increase our numerical strength in your quarter by a regular system of migration from year to year as the means of conveyance may admit." [17] Actually such a plan was never put into effect. If, however, the only practical way to colonize Oregon had been by sea, the Hudson's Bay Company would have had a distinct advantage over any private agency in the United States. If, on the other hand, Oregon was to be colonized by overland emigrations, the advantage lay with the United States.

While in the United States during that fall of 1839, Simpson learned of the proposal of the Oregon Provisional Emigration Society to send a colony of two hundred men "with whatever families they may have" overland to Oregon in 1840. When this was reported to the Company's headquarters in London, the officials called it a "wild enterprise" [18] which was unlikely ever to be realized. The consensus of British opinion seems to have been that, because of the long distance between the Missouri frontier and the Willamette Valley, the high mountains, and the barren deserts, no serious threat to England's claim on Oregon would ever come from any American overland emigration. This view was summarized in the following statement in the July 1843 issue of the *Edinburgh Review*: "However the political question between England and America, as to the ownership of Oregon, may be decided, *Oregon will never be colonized overland from the Eastern States*." [19] Ironically, at the time that issue of the *Review* appeared, the first large Oregon emigration, consisting of about a thousand people, was already moving across the western prairies. In that party were Dr. Whitman and his nephew, Perrin Whitman.

In 1841–42, Sir George Simpson, Governor of the Hudson's Bay Company in Canada, made what he called an overland journey around the world.[20] This included crossing Siberia going west from the Pacific Coast. Simpson began his travels from Red River in June 1841 shortly after the colony left from that place for Cowlitz Portage. Simpson followed after them, passed them, and arrived at Fort Vancouver the latter part of August 1841. There he saw two of the ships of the Wilkes Expedition which were visible reminders of the interest the United States was taking in the Old Oregon country. Simpson sailed from Fort Nisqually on September 6 for Sitka. He wrote in his journal while at the 49° parallel near Point Roberts: "If this parallel, as proposed by the Americans, should become the international boundary... Britain would not only be surrendering all the territory of any agricultural value, but would also virtually cut off the interior and the coast of her own share from each other." [21] As late as 1843, Sir George was still advocating that the boundary dividing the Old Oregon territory be the Columbia River.

By an interesting coincidence, the first emigration to Old Oregon from the States, with twenty-four in the party, arrived at Fort Vancouver shortly before the bateaux came down the Columbia with the Red River colonists. Although Simpson and the officials of the Hudson's Bay Company in London were skeptical that Americans ever could cross the continent in sufficient numbers to threaten England's claim to the heartland of Old Oregon, surely Dr. McLoughlin and James Douglas at Fort Vancouver were not so uninformed. Yet, we may wonder whether McLoughlin and Douglas saw the real significance of the success of the 1841 immigration. All members of the Methodist colony in the Willamette Valley had been sent to Oregon by a mission board, with some possible help from the U.S. Government in the form of a subsidy for the *Lausanne* party. Not one of the Methodist missionaries paid for his or her passage to Oregon. Likewise, all members of the Red River colony had their traveling expenses covered by the Hudson's Bay Company. On the other hand, no private or governmental subsidy helped the members of the 1841 emigration go to Oregon. These were entirely self-supporting. Here was a new factor introduced into the strategy of winning Old Oregon through emigration, which worked exclusively to the advantage of the Americans.

After witnessing the arrival of the second immigration from the States in 1842, consisting of about a hundred men, women, and children, James Douglas recalled the words of Senator Calhoun (previously quoted), who in 1837 had advised Congress not to be in any hurry to renegotiate the joint Occupation Treaty of 1818. In a letter to Simpson dated October 23, 1843, Douglas wrote: "The wily old lawyer is correct, and it would appear from the rush of emigration to this quarter, that his words have produced their effect, and there can be no doubt of the final success of the plan, if the country remains open a few years longer." [22]

During the year that elapsed after the arrival of the Red River immigration in the fall of 1841, Whitman had time to think about the political future of Old Oregon. Nowhere in Whitman's letters do we find him stressing the strategic importance to the United States of securing title to the territory lying south of the 49° parallel. Instead, he was dreaming of a large American population, preferably Protestant, coming into the upper Columbia River Valley to establish homes, schools, communities, and industries. Although consistent in his continuing efforts to civilize and Christianize the natives, he knew that the Indians could never compete with the superior numbers, skills, and industry of the white man. Whitman was only being realistic when he came to the conclusion that the country would eventually belong to the white man.

WHITMAN'S LIFE THREATENED

The first serious trouble that Whitman had with the Cayuses came in September and October 1841, about a year after Spalding and Smith had their difficulties with some Nez Perces at Lapwai and Kamiah. Whitman gave a detailed account of his harrowing experiences, when his very life was threatened, first in a letter to Archibald McKinlay[23] dated September 30 and then in a longer account to Greene on November 11. In the latter he wrote: "The Indians at this station had been very quiet for the last year and a half, but for various reasons causes which have been operating upon them, they were prepared for agitation, thinking that that was the best way to obtain property." Smith had repeatedly referred to the insatiable desire of the Nez Perces for the material things which the white man had, and Spalding had spoken in the same way about the Indians in his vicinity. Now Whitman was referring to it.

One of these "various causes" to which Whitman made reference arose out of a visit a certain Cayuse, called Iatin, had made to the Willamette Valley presumably in the spring or summer of 1841. While there he heard that it was customary for white men to pay for the land they cultivated and to buy the right to cut wood on land owned by another. "He was told," wrote Whitman, "that when a man came on to the white man's land & they wanted him to go off, if he would not, he was kicked off." When Iatin told his fellow Cayuses what he had heard, their cupidity was aroused. Whitman had never paid them for the land he was occupying nor for the timber he was cutting in the Blue Mountains. The fact that they had initially urged Whitman to settle at Waiilatpu in 1836 with every promise of cooperation was overlooked or forgotten.

AGITATION BY HALF-BREEDS

A second source of difficulty arose out of some inflammatory remarks made by Joe Gray, a half-breed Iroquois.[24] According to Whitman, Joe was "for a long time a servant of the H.B. Co.," and lived "in the camp of the Waiilatpu & Walla Walla Indians from April until Sept." Joe, like

Iatin, stressed the idea that the white man should pay for the lands taken from the Indians and became specific when he argued that Whitman should pay for the mission premises at Waiilatpu. Being a Roman Catholic, Joe further complicated the situation for Whitman by encouraging the Cayuses to forsake the teachings of the Protestants and accept the doctrines and practices of the priests.

Three half-breeds figure in the Whitman story. The first was Joe Gray in 1841; then Tom Hill, 1844–46; and finally the archvillain, Joe Lewis, who precipitated the Whitman massacre of November 1847. A half-breed was often an unhappy, frustrated person, frequently rejected by the white people and yet not willing to live as an Indian. Some of the half-breeds who drifted into the Oregon country came from the Eastern States and had first-hand knowledge of how the white men had dispossessed the Indians of their ancestral lands. According to Whitman's report to McKinlay, this was one of the main points which Joe Gray stressed. Whitman claimed that Gray told Tiloukaikt "how the Indians did in his country and [how they] raised disturbances and by that means got property."

The Cayuses listened to Joe and noted that much that was taking place about them confirmed all he was saying. White men were coming into the Oregon country in increasing numbers. Perhaps the day was near when they would take the lands and the horses of the Cayuses. The more Joe talked, the more fearful the Indians became. Iatin aroused the cupidity of the Cayuses; Joe stirred feelings of animosity against the missionaries. The guilt of the wrongs the white men had done to the Indians of the East was focused on Whitman. Disregarding all the good that he had done and was doing for them, Tiloukaikt and his subchiefs finally came to the point of being ready to force the issue; either Whitman was to pay for the land he was occupying or he would have to go. There is no evidence that the Indians ever asked for or received payment from the Hudson's Bay Company for land that it had occupied. However, the Company was powerful and well able to impose its will without fear of reprisals. The missionaries were entirely dependent upon the goodwill of the natives.

First Confrontation with Tiloukaikt

The first confrontation that Whitman had with Tiloukaikt and members of his band came on or before Saturday, September 25, 1841.

In the letters that Whitman wrote to McKinlay and Greene, he gave the names of four of the ringleaders, each of whom was to play a leading role in the massacre which came some six years later. The first was Tiloukaikt,[25] the successor to Chief Umtippe. He and his band had their home camping grounds within a mile or so west of Waiilatpu. Whitman named a second Indian who took part in the disturbance "Sakiaph," believed to be Tamsucky, also called Feathercap.[26] Since the natives were often called by several names and nicknames, a positive identification is not always possible. A third Indian was Tomahas, who has sometimes been confused with Tamsucky as each has been referred to by survivors of the Whitman massacre as "The Murderer."[27] The nickname seems to have been given to one of these individuals because he had killed another Cayuse. The fourth was Ish-ish-kais-kais,[28] also known as Frank Escaloom, a brother of Tomahas.

Tiloukaikt and his band, stirred by the inflammatory statements of Joe Gray, deliberately precipitated a confrontation with Whitman by turning some of their horses into Whitman's fenced corn field. It so happened that Whitman had some Walla Walla Indians working for him who were being paid with Indian goods such as awls, shirts, etc. Even this had become a sore point with Tiloukaikt, as Whitman explained to McKinlay: "There is a great jealousy of the labouring Indians because they get food, shirts, and blankets, in distinction to themselves." When Whitman saw the horses in his field, he ordered one of the Walla Walla Indians to drive them out. Tiloukaikt countermanded the order and told the man that he would be whipped if he obeyed Whitman.[29] With admirable self-control, Whitman told Tiloukaikt that the fence had been erected to protect his crops, not to make a horse pen, "but if he thought [it] good [for the horses] to eat up our crops, I had no more to say about it."

Tiloukaikt replied: "That this was his land, that he grew up here & that the horses were only eating up the growth of the soil; and demanded of me what I had ever paid for the land." Whitman answered that he had paid nothing and that he would never give anything. "He then made use of the word, 'Shame," wrote Whitman. "I spoke to him of the original arrangement made for us to locate here & that we did not come of ourselves but by invitation from the Indians, & that the land was fully granted us. Here I left him" [Letter 100]. The question of property rights had been raised. Whitman refused to press the issue and the horses remained in the field, for the time being, eating his corn crop.

Whitman related to Greene what followed: "In a short time one of the chiefs came to me & asked why I allowed those troublesome horses to eat up the corn? I related to him what had just passed & said I had no intention to remove them. While I was talking Tilkanaiks [Tiloukaikt] came along, having overheard, & came up to me & exclaimed that it was troublesome for me to talk so much & struck me severely twice on my breast & commanded me to stop talking. I simply replyed that I had been in the habit of talking from my childhood & that I intended still to talk." Evidently Tiloukaikt tried to provoke Whitman to strike back, but this he, very wisely, refused to do.

Second Confrontation with Tiloukaikt

A second incident involving Tiloukaikt occurred a few days later. An Indian entered W. H. Gray's kitchen in defiance of a wellknown rule and refused to leave when asked to do so. Maria Maki,[30] who was still at Waiilatpu, called Gray, who also requested the Indian to leave. When he refused to do so, Gray forcibly ejected him. The Indian then went to the corral and roped one of Gray's horses. Gray cut the rope and returned the horse to the corral. Tamuscky then threatened to kill all of the cattle belonging to the mission. Whitman told him: "You have now shown your heart & if you think so, you can kill them."

By this time Gray, realizing that the Indians were spoiling for a fight, withdrew and began to work on the roof of his house. Some Indians followed but remained on the ground. Whitman climbed up to where Gray was working and warned him to say nothing, no matter how insulting the provocation. Tiloukaikt also climbed upon the roof and continued to harass Gray. Tiloukaikt ordered Gray to stop building and to make plans to leave the mission premises the very next day, which was a Sunday. When Whitman interceded on Gray's behalf, Tiloukaikt turned on him and ordered him and his wife to leave also. In Whitman's letter to McKinlay we can read: "I told him we could not consent to move on the Sabbath." So thoroughly had the missionaries stressed the sinfulness of traveling on Sunday that Tiloukaikt under those strained circumstances actually accepted the logic of Whitman's request for a delay.

After both Whitman and Tiloukaikt had climbed down to the ground, Tiloukaikt continued the quarrel. Whitman tells the story: "He complained of my taking the part of Mr. G. He said if he were to go to our country, he should be very careful how he conducted [himself] lest he should be sent off. I told him that if Indians came into Mr. G's or my house & refused to do as we desired, it was right for us to put them out. He then took hold of my ear & pulled it & struck me on the breast, ordering me to hear, as much as to say we must let them do as they pleased about our houses. When he let go, I turned the other [ear] to him & he pulled that & in that way I let him pull first one & then the other, until he gave over & took my hat & threw it into the mud." Whitman asked one of the Walla Walla Indians to retrieve the hat, which he put on his head again. Tiloukaikt then "took it off again & threw it to the same place. Again the Indian gave it to me & I put it on & again with more violence, he took it off & threw it into the mud & water of which it dipped largely. Once more the Indian gave it back to me & I put it on, all mud as it was & said to him, perhaps he was playing." After reading Whitman's detailed account of his terrifying experience, we are amazed at his forbearance and his bravery. He literally obeyed the New Testament injunction to turn the other cheek. Under the circumstances, this was the wisest course he could have followed.

Finally, after realizing his failure to provoke Whitman to some act of resistance, Tiloukaikt withdrew. In Whitman's account to Greene, he added this amazing statement: "On the Sabbath all came to worship as usual." This would have included Tiloukaikt.

When McKinlay received Whitman's letter of September 30 which told of the disturbance at Waiilatpu, he sent a messenger with a stern word of warning to Tiloukaikt. Perhaps the Indians felt that since Pambrun was dead, the new Hudson's Bay official in charge at Fort Walla Walla would be lenient. If so, McKinlay's rebuke would have come as a shock. McKinlay warned Tiloukaikt that any insult to the Whitmans would be considered as a personal affront to himself; that the Company could cut off all trade with the Cayuses; and that if any harm befell the Whitman family, the Company would take immediate steps to avenge the deed. He referred to the fact that the personnel of the Company had but recently been increased by the arrival of the Red River colony which was at that time at Fort Walla Walla. In his letter to Greene,

Whitman referred to the presence of this colony, not as an indication that the British Government was strengthening its claim to Oregon, but rather as an added factor guaranteeing the safety of the American missionary stations.

A Third Confrontation with the Indians

The sharpest part of McKinlay's rebuke was his reference to those who took part in the outrage against the Whitmans as "dogs," a term of reproach particularly objectionable to the Cayuses. Smarting under the lash of McKinlay's hot words, a group of Indians led by Tiloukaikt invaded the Whitman home. When the Whitmans had lived in their first house near the river, the Indians were given free access to the living room and kitchen, but when they moved into the second house, their private quarters were kept locked. This the Indians resented, and no doubt the natural desire on Mrs. Whitman's part for privacy gave rise to the feeling among the natives that she was proud and haughty and "far above them." [31]

When the Indians forced their way into the kitchen, Narcissa called her husband. He persuaded the Indians to move into the living room. Narcissa was then able to lock one of the kitchen doors leading to the outside. For a few moments, all was confusion, as Whitman described in his letter to Greene: "...while we were talking... an old Indian was threatening Mrs. W. with a hammer through the window in order to force open the kitchen door & at the same time Sakiaph [Tamsucky] was trying to open another door in order to throw the house open." The locks were broken with a hammer and an ax "& a horde of lawless savages entered & took possession of the house."

One of the Indians threatened Whitman with an ax. Whitman's account of what then happened follows: "After I took away the ax, he held to my collar & struck me with his fist on the mouth & tore my clothes. Mrs. W. took the ax from me & Mr. G. put both the ax & hammer up stairs & we then sat down again. Sakiaph soon returned with a club and advanced upon me. As I arose to take hold of the club, I avoided the blow he was leveling at my head. For this I was much ridiculed by the Indians as fearing death." Sakiaph then went out and got his gun and threatened Whitman with it. "They persisted in saying," wrote Whitman, "because I said I was not afraid to die that I challenged them to kill me, but I told them no—I did not challenge them nor did I want to suffer pain but still I did not fear to die."

Whitman's amazing coolness cowed his antagonists. They began to weaken by suggesting some compromise terms. Instead of demanding that the missionaries leave, they said that if the Whitmans would not lock their doors, they could live at Waiilatpu in peace. Whitman replied: "...that as long as we lived and occupied our houses, we should order our doors & if they wished to live in peace, they must not oppose the regulations we made." Finally Tiloukaikt exclaimed that "it was impossible to bully us into fright." Tomahas then spoke up and suggested that Whitman give them presents. "I told them," wrote Whitman to Greene, "they would not get the value of a single awl or pin for their bad conduct & if they wanted property in that way, they must steal it." Sensing that he had the upper hand, Whitman then accused them of being made dupes by Joe Gray. Tomahas admitted that Joe had told them of the experiences of the Iroquois who were given "a great deal of money" by the white men and "after that all lived together as brothers."

Whitman added: "They now broke up & went away saying they would go & see if Mr. McKinlay dared call them dogs." Alarmed at the possibility of the Indians attacking Fort Walla Walla, Whitman sent a messenger that night to warn McKinlay. "The next day was the Sabbath," Whitman noted, "& it was a sad day for us. Many stayed away from worship & some went to the fort carrying their arms & others were insolent & reckless of evil. They did many violent acts such as troubling our animals & breaking our windows. We now felt that we had showed the example of non resistance as long as it was called for & as we went to bed, we put ourselves in a state of defence should any thing occur at the Fort & the Indians return upon us. We also resolved to go to the Fort with our families & stay for a time until we could arrange to go away or return as might seem best." Here is the only discovered reference in any of the writings of Whitman of his willingness to use force if he felt that their lives were in danger.

McKinlay Warns the Cayuses

McKinlay was prepared to receive the band of armed Cayuses when they appeared at the Fort on Monday, October 4. Writing to Whitman that day, McKinlay said: "I told them I wished to know their hearts & at the same time tell the state of my own." He informed the Indians that he was about to trade for some of their horses but said he would not do so until he found out whether "we were to have war or not." He stressed the fact that he was well able to defend the Fort and that if any harm befell the Whitmans, Chief Factor McLoughlin "would send up a sufficient number [of men] to revenge the whole and that the plunder of their horses would be considered sufficient payment for the trouble." The threat of losing their horses was something the Cayuses understood, and they at once calmed down. "Let it suffice," McKinlay wrote, "that what one and all of them said expressed deep contrition for what had passed and made many promises that they would conduct themselves well in future... I think you will find it to the advantage of all concerned to forget & forgive the past. But pray put your face against paying them for their bad conduct." McKinlay reassured Whitman that there was "every prospect of your being allowed to keep peaceful possession of your place & that you will not be further molested by the Indians."[32]

When George Simpson had passed through Fort Walla Walla, shortly before this disturbance took place, he met Asahel Munger, who, as Simpson reported, was "grievously disappointed with the country." Simpson, who was always cynical regarding any good that missionaries might be able to do for the Indians, then added: "But the ministers of the Gospel, moreover, had a grievance peculiar to themselves, for, instead of finding the savages eager to embrace Christianity, as they had been led to expect, they saw a superstitious, jealous and bigoted people. They soon ascertained that they could gain converts only by buying them; and they were even reproached by the savages on the ground, that, if they were really good men, they would procure guns and blankets for them from the Great Spirit, merely by their prayers. In short, the Indians, discovering that the new religion did not render them independent of the traders, any more than their old one, regarded the missionaries as mere failures, as nothing better than imposters."[33]

"Among a People of No Law"

Following the receipt of McKinlay's letter, Whitman had a meeting with Tiloukaikt and his followers on October 5. "We told them plainly," Whitman reported to Greene, "that unless they were ready to protect us— & enforce good order we would leave them, that we did not come to fight but to teach them." The Indians appeared to be contrite and promised that they would not make further trouble. However, Whitman did tell Greene: "From the commencement of this station to the present time, it had constantly been a point with some one or more to be urging for property to be given them to keep them in subjection to order... I do not think we shall again be molested on these points very soon."

Whitman had no more trouble with the Indians until his confrontation with Young Chief in November 1845. The unhappy episodes of October 1841 put a damper upon the educational and religious activities of the Whitmans. A bond of sympathy had been severed which made it much more difficult for the Whitmans to receive the cooperation of the natives.

Whitman's bravery in standing up against the threats of the Indians even when his life was threatened was no doubt the reason why H. K. W. Perkins was able to give the following appraisal: "Though they feared the *Doctor*, they did not *love* him... And *knowing him* as I *knew him*, you would not need to be told that an Oregon Indian & he could never get along well together... I need hardly tell you he cared for no man under heaven—perfectly fearless and independent." [34]

Several years later, on April 10, 1846, Narcissa, in a letter to her father, made the following comment about the difficulties white settlers in the Willamette Valley faced: *"To be in a country among a people of no law, even if they are from a civilized land, is the nearest like a hell on earth of anything I can imagine."* [35] If such were her feelings regarding the more stable society in the Willamette Valley, how much more did her words apply to the situation that she and her husband faced when living among the lawless and uncivilized Cayuses.

More Disagreements Within the Mission

On October 13, about a week after Whitman had settled his difficulties with the Cayuse chiefs, Spalding arrived at Waiilatpu for supplies. A few days later Eells came on a similar errand. As would be expected with four of the five men of the Mission present, certain items of business came up for informal discussion. Again some things that Spalding had either said or done aroused the ire of Whitman. In the August preceding, Spalding had received two letters from Greene which made him feel that the Board fully supported the views he had advocated regarding the policies to be followed in evangelizing the natives. These letters may have given Spalding too much confidence, and he may therefore have spoken too boldly in his criticism of others.

Another factor to be remembered is that the Grays had been living with the Whitmans for about a year, and no doubt Gray's prejudices against Spalding had to some degree influenced Whitman. The Coe Collection in the Yale library contains several letters from Gray to Walker, written during the fall of 1841 and the following winter, which reveal Gray's animosity towards Spalding. Over and over again, Gray accused Spalding of "duplicity." The following quotation taken from his letter of March 28, 1842 is typical: "Duplicity you are well aware is one that holds a prominent station in all his correspondence & actions."

Whatever the cause, this we know: Whitman had become deeply discouraged. No doubt his recent unpleasant experience with Tiloukaikt contributed to his depression. On October 22, a few days after Spalding and Eells had left for their respective stations, Whitman wrote to Greene saying that a Mission meeting would be called as soon as possible to settle their differences or else they would "mutually divide & leave the Board to fill our places with others more suitable." He also wrote: "When I last wrote you, I thought we were prepared to cooperate together—but more recent facts have shown that hope to be vain, for Mr. and Mrs. Spalding have proved it otherwise

He has again expressed a full desire to be reconciled to all in the Mission but as Mrs. Spalding was not present & wishing not to make reconciliation to be so soon broken, or of partial understanding, we did not go any farther than to agree to act as being under covenant [i.e., Christian] fellowship."

From Spalding's diary we learn that Whitman with a Mr. Cook, who was evidently in Whitman's temporary employ, arrived at Lapwai on the evening of November 26, 1841, to help Spalding build a flour mill. The day happened to be Spalding's thirty-eighth birthday. Spalding had been conducting another series of what he called "protracted meetings" for the natives and was giving special instruction to a number he felt were ready for church membership. On Sunday, the 28th, Whitman addressed the people.

On the following Wednesday, December 1, Spalding wrote in his diary: "Examine Five Crows who has been here since the commencement of the protracted meeting & is surprisingly attentive to religious instruction & his book. Attends school regularly every day. I think he indulges a hope. Oh Lord, grant he may be really a child of thine."

Five Crows was a Cayuse chief, a half-brother of Old Joseph and a brother of Young Chief. Spalding also called him Hezekiah. Five Crows and his band lived along the Umatilla River. His interest in Christianity had induced him to travel to Lapwai sometime in the fall of 1841 and become a member of a class that Spalding was preparing for church membership.[36]

When Spalding presented Five Crows and a number of Nez Perces to Whitman as candidates for membership in the Mission church, Whitman, to Spalding's great surprise, objected. Whitman allowed his personal pique to block Spalding's laudable objective of receiving several Indian converts into the church. An entry in Spalding's diary for December 8 tells the story: "Doct. W. is not willing that these persons who have been examined & who give satisfactory evidence that they are new creatures in Christ should be received into the church till our difficulties are settled. He read over a long list of charges against me, many of which were true & for which I told him I was willing and anxious to make any concessions, or do any thing he wished, if he would let me know his wish... but though he did not directly say what he wanted, still he gave us plainly to understand that nothing short of excision from the Mission would satisfy him & Mr. Gray. Many of the charges were facts perverted. And many of them were direct falsehoods got up by somebody."[37] Spalding's mention of Gray is evidence that Gray was the one who was keeping old disagreements alive. As long as Whitman objected to the reception of Five Crows and the others whom Spalding had prepared for church membership, there was nothing that Spalding could do at that time.

When Whitman started back on December 7 for Waiilatpu, accompanied by Cook, he took with him the blacksmith equipment which had been at Lapwai. This was to be placed in the new shop which Gray had erected. Spalding kept the printing press and, at the time of Whitman's visit, was working on a translation of the Gospel of Matthew into the Nez Perce tongue. Whitman took the first ten chapters of Spaldling's work with him to review. Since Rogers spent some time at Fort Walla Walla and Waiilatpu during the winter of 1841–42 and the following spring, while working on a dictionary of the Nez Perce language, it is possible that he too went over Spalding's translation.

THE AMERICAN BOARD TAKES DRASTIC ACTION

Secretary Greene was stunned when he received four long letters from A. B. Smith on October 5, 1841. When these were added to previous letters that Smith had written, each of which contained criticisms of Spalding, and also to the letters of criticism written by Gray, Rogers, and Hall, Greene felt that the situation in the Oregon Mission was far too serious for him to settle alone. He decided to wait until the Prudential Committee would meet on the following February 15.

A major difficulty faced both by the American Board in Boston and by its missionaries in faraway Old Oregon were the long delays in the transmission of the mails. Since Greene had the custom of noting on the letters received the date of their arrival in Boston, it is easy to ascertain the time which elapsed between the time of writing and the time each arrived in Greene's office. Letters carried by the Hudson's Bay Company's express across Canada were delivered in about seven months. Letters that went by sea often took twice as long. For instance, the letter which Smith wrote on February 24, 1840, did not arrive in Boston until October 5, 1841, about nineteen months later. This was longer than usual. On the average, it took about two years for an exchange of letters. This long interval made it impossible for the Board to write to Spalding and get his side of the controversy before taking decisive action.

The members of the Prudential Committee met in Boston as scheduled on February 15, 1842, and Greene laid before them the series of complaining letters. The Committee was faced with a distressing situation. The Oregon Mission had received extensive publicity through the *Missionary Herald* as being one of the most promising of all the missions of the Board. Any action to dismiss any of the members of that mission or to close any of the three stations would have been most painful. No account has been discovered of the agonizing discussions of the Committee which must have occurred as they debated what should be done.

On February 25, a day or so after the Prudential Committee had adjourned, Secretary Greene addressed a letter to "The Members of the

Oregon Mission" which summarized the actions taken. His introductory sentences reflect his heaviness of heart. He noted that the Committee had hoped that "the Stations at Waiilatpu and Clear Water" might have been continued "with the expectation of their being prosperous and highly useful, both to the Indian race, and as planting and nourishing the seeds of Christianity and Christian institutions in a country into which a white population will be pressing at no distant day." Now those hopes seemed doomed to failure.

Greene then listed the five following resolutions passed by the Prudential Committee:

1. To discontinue the southern branch of the Oregon Mission.
2. To recall the Rev. Henry H. Spalding and wife, with the expectation that they would return to the United States by the earliest suitable opportunity.
3. Expressing the decided opinion that it is expedient for Rev. Asa B. Smith and wife and Mr. William H. Gray and wife also to return to the United States by the earliest suitable opportunity.
4. Transferring Doct. Marcus Whitman, and Mr. Cornelius Rogers, if he should be disposed to continue in the missionary work, to the north branch of the mission, to cooperate with Messrs. Eells and Walker.
5. Appointing Doct. Whitman and Mr. Rogers to dispose of the mission property connected with the south branch of the mission, to the Methodist mission, or in such other manner as they might deem advisable, in order to bring the affairs of those stations to a close more speedily and with the least loss to the Board.

The Prudential Committee did not know that the Smiths were in Hawaii at the time the above actions were taken or that Rogers had severed his connections with the Mission. The actions to close Waiilatpu and Lapwai and recall the Spaldings and the Grays were tantamount to closing all stations of the Oregon Mission, for it is extremely doubtful that the Whitmans would ever have consented to move to Tshimakain where they would have had to learn a different Indian language. Had the resolutions of the Prudential Committee been implemented, in all probability the Whitmans would have left the Mission by moving to the

Willamette Valley. The Walkers and Eellses, under those circumstances, would have been stranded at Tshimakain and no doubt would also have left the Mission. Thus the fate of the whole Oregon Mission was involved in the drastic action taken by the Board's Prudential Committee.

In the closing paragraph of the letter addressed to all members of the Mission, Greene wrote: "It is a cause of much grief and disappointment, as you may well suppose, that a mission which seemed to promise so great and speedy results, as did yours for years, should be brought to such a close, and that too owing to disaffection among its members. The Christian community, when the catastrophe becomes known, will also be grieved and disappointed. And we fear that in the eyes of many... the missionary work will be dishonored and prejudiced." [38]

On that same day, February 25, 1842, on which Greene wrote a general letter to all members of the Oregon Mission, he addressed a personal note to Whitman. "In everything that relates to Mr. Spalding," he wrote, "you will need to act with much discretion and kindness." Greene recommended that the Spaldings, with their two small children, return to the States by the overland route since this would be much less expensive than going by sea around Cape Horn. Evidently Greene did not know that the fur trade was over and that there were no more caravans going to a Rendezvous. Nor did the Committee know of the Annual Meeting of the Oregon Mission held in May 1841 when most of the personality differences involving Spalding had been brought out in to the open and amicably settled.[39]

Greene's two letters of February 25, 1842, were entrusted to Dr. Elijah White for delivery. White, who, as has been stated, had been dismissed from the Methodist Mission in 1840, had returned to the States and had received an appointment as a sub-Indian Agent for Old Oregon. White was planning to make the overland journey in the spring and summer of 1842 with a party of emigrants. Learning of this, Greene asked White to deliver the letters to Whitman.

A few days after the letters of February 25 were on their way to Oregon, Whitman's letter to Greene of July 13, 1841, and also one from Spalding of the same date, reached Greene. Whitman gave an optimistic report of conditions then existing within the Mission which reflected the conciliations worked out at the Annual Meeting held in the previous May. Whitman wrote: "We are prepared so far as we can, to labour together in harmony with the exception of some that may be waiting to see the result of the communications to the Board." By that date, conditions within the Mission had greatly changed because of the departure of the Smiths and Rogers. Greene hastened to send another letter to Whitman to countermand the directives given in his February 25 letter to the Mission. Writing on April 28, Greene said that if the Committee had known what Whitman had reported in his July 13 letter, "they would almost necessarily [have] decided differently." Since it was then impossible to call the Prudential Committee together on short notice, Greene suggested to Whitman that he ignore the actions taken and continue to carry on as before. Unfortunately for all concerned, Greene's letter of April 28 failed to reach Whitman before he left for Boston on October 3 of that year.

Fall 1841–Spring 1842

After depending upon horseflesh for their meat for about five years, the Whitmans were able in the fall of 1841 to butcher their first beef and hogs. Of this Narcissa wrote in a letter to her parents dated October 6, 1841, "We killed a very fat beef a short time ago, fed upon grass only, which yielded 148 pounds of tallow after it was tried." She also reported that her husband had on that day butchered seven hogs. Since by that date, Whitman had a smokehouse, he could have thus preserved both pork and beef.

The winter of 1841–42 passed quietly at Waiilatpu with the Whitmans experiencing no serious difficulty with the Indians. The Walkers were expecting their third child in March, and Whitman was requested to be present. Whitman left Waiilatpu on Tuesday, March 1, and arrived at Tshimakain the following Saturday. Mary Walker gave birth to a son on the 17th and they named him Marcus Whitman.[40] This was the fourth boy to be named after Dr. Whitman during his lifetime. Whitman did not start back to Waiilatpu until the 23rd. He arrived at his home on the 26th, having been absent for about four weeks.

A great feeling of loneliness swept over Narcissa after her husband left for Tshimakain. She began a letter that day addressed to her sister Jane and her brother, Edward, in which she gave intimate glimpses into her home life and also into her own mind and heart. She added postscripts on each of the eleven following days so that the letter became a diary and grew until it contained about 6,000 words. After referring to the departure of her husband, she wrote: "I am once more left alone in this house with no other company than my two little half-breed girls, Mary Ann Bridger and Helen Mar Meek." The Grays were in their new house nearby. Living in an Indian lodge on the grounds was a friendly half-breed, who may have been the "Mr. Cook" who accompanied Whitman to Lapwai a few weeks earlier. "He is the man," she wrote, "who attends to my wants, such as milking, getting water, wood, etc." The drinking water used by the Whitmans was dipped up out of the Walla Walla River. There was no well on the mission grounds.

Narcissa yearned for the company of her sister and brother "to enjoy my solitude with me," and then she added: "Jane, I wish you were here to sleep with me, I am such a timid creature about sleeping alone that sometimes I suffer considerably, especially since my health has been not very good." She again referred to her weak eyes and mentioned using the spectacles that her brother, Jonas Galusha, had given her. "I do not know what I could do without them," she commented.

DAVID MALIN RECEIVED INTO THE WHITMAN HOME

On March 2, 1842, two Indian women called on Narcissa bringing with them "a miserable looking child, between three and four years old, and wished me to take him. He is nearly naked, and they said his mother had thrown him away and gone off with another Indian." The little boy was the son of a Spaniard by the name of Cortez, who was once in the employ of the Hudson's Bay Company, and a Walla Walla Indian woman. According to Narcissa's account in her letter to Jane and Edward, his parents had deserted him and his Indian grandmother had cared for him for a time. "My feelings were greatly excited for the poor child and [I] felt a great disposition to take him." She hesitated, however, to accept the responsibility of having a third half-breed child to rear. Of this she wrote: "I, however, told them they might take him away and bring him again in the morning, and in the meantime I would think about it. The care of such a child is very great at first dirty, covered with body and head lice, and starved—his clothing is part of a skin dress which does not half cover his nakedness, and a small bit of skin over his shoulders."

The forlorn and forsaken boy was returned to Narcissa the next day. Of this she wrote: "I could not shut my heart against him. I washed him, oiled and bound up his wounds, and dressed him and cleaned his head of lice. Before he came his hair was cut close to his head and a strip as wide as your finger was shaved from ear to ear, and also from his forehead to his neck, crossed the other at right angles. This the [Indian] boys had done to make him look ridiculous. He had a burn on his foot where they said he had been pushed into the fire for the purpose of gratifying their malicious feelings, and because he was friendless." In a letter to Maria Pambrun, Narcissa told how some of the boys had gratified their evil hearts "by burning his naked body with sticks of fire" [Letter III].

When cleaned up, Narcissa saw that the boy was not more than two years old. The hardships through which he had passed had made him appear to be older. Having accepted the child, Narcissa wondered what name should be given to him. In memory she went back to her school days at Prattsburg and thought of a schoolmate, David Malin,[41] who had married her friend, Mary Porter. So she called the boy David Malin.

The boy's grandmother, delighted to know that Mrs. Whitman would take the lad, called on her a few days later and asked for food and clothing, "because I had got the child to live with me." "So it is with them," Narcissa wrote, "the moment you do them a favour, you place yourself under lasting obligation to them and must continue to give to keep their love strong towards you." David proved to be a lovable child, much easier to handle than Helen Mar "who was so stubborn and fretful and wanted to cry all the time if she could not get her way."

More from Narcissa's Letter

On March 4, 1842, Narcissa added another note to her growing letter when she wrote about high winds and stormy weather. She thought of Marcus on horseback working his way some 140 miles to the north towards Tshimakain where the weather would in all probability be even more severe. "He has never been obliged to encounter so much snow before," she wrote, "and I do not know how it will affect him." Whitman had the foresight to take with him a pair of snowshoes so that if the snow became too deep, he could dismount and walk. "He is a courageous man," wrote Narcissa proudly, "and it is well that he is so, to be a physician in this country. Common obstacles never affect him; he goes ahead when duty calls. Jane and Edward, you know but little about your brother Marcus, and all I can tell you about him at this time is that he is a *bundle of thoughts*."[42] Actually, as Narcissa later learned, Whitman did meet with deep snow, but the top crust was so hard that it supported both horse and rider.

In the same entry for this day, Narcissa wrote: "I am blessed with a lovely sister and an excellent associate in Sister Gray, and I trust that I am in some measure thankful, for I have found by experience that it is not good to be alone in our cares and labors." Mary Gray, already the mother of a boy and a girl, was expecting another child at any time. Since her husband had attended her on the two previous confinements, the Grays were not concerned about the absence of Dr. Whitman.

According to Narcissa's entry in her letter of March 11, she became ill that day. She wrote: "Dear Jane, I am sick tonight and in much pain— have been scarcely able to crawl about all day." She missed her husband and felt that if only he were present, "all the gloom that creeps over the mind in spite of efforts to the contrary," would disappear.

On March 12th, she wrote: "Before I could get to bed last night, I was seized with such severe pains in my stomach and bowels that it was with difficulty that I could straighten myself. I succeeded in crawling about until I got something to produce perspiration, thinking it might proceed from a cold, and went to bed. About two o'clock in the morning, Sister Gray sent for me, for she was sick and needed my assistance. When I waked, I was in a profuse perspiration. What to do, I did not know. Neither of them knew that I was sick the day before."

Narcissa felt it her duty to respond to Mary Gray's call, so arose and got dressed. She called for Cook who made a roaring fire in the fireplace in her room. This warmed her, for the night was cold. "I bundled myself pretty well," she wrote, "and went with Mr. C's assistance, for I felt but very little better able to walk than I did the evening before, yet not in so much pain. When I arrived the babe [a girl] was born, and Br. Gray was washing it... I took the babe and dressed it, and have been there all day with my children, although I have not been able to sit up all day."

On March 14, Narcissa noted the arrival of her thirty-fifth birthday and what would have been the fifth birthday of her own little girl had she lived. As far as she was able, Narcissa helped in the Gray household. For a time she took the two older Gray children, one three years old and the other eighteen months, to her home to be with her three half-breed children. After telling of her experiences, she gave the following advice to her brother Edward, who was thinking of becoming a minister or a missionary:

"You would do well to write a sermon on the word PATIENCE every day." This was a virtue much needed in the mission field of Old Oregon.

On Saturday, March 26, to Narcissa's great joy and relief, Marcus returned home. Eells was with him in order to get some supplies which had been shipped from Vancouver to Fort Walla Walla. "We are cheered," Narcissa commented, "with an occasional visit from one and another, which is a source of comfort to us in our pilgrimage here."

Death of Cayuse Pitt

From time to time references to one or more of the seven Oregon Indian boys who had been sent to the Red River Mission school occur in the correspondence of the Hudson's Bay officials or of the missionaries of the American Board. On February 5, 1842, Whitman wrote to Walker and told of some difficulties he had experienced while trying to mediate a dispute between some Nez Perces and some Cayuses resulting from the death of Cayuse Pitt, possibly at The Dalles or in the lower Columbia River area. According to a statement in a letter Narcissa wrote to Jane on February 2, 1842, Cayuse Pitt could just as well have been called Nez Perce Pitt, for it appears that he was part Nez Perce. According to Whitman's letter to Walker, the Cayuses blamed the Indians of the lower Columbia for the death of Cayuse Pitt and, therefore, demanded payment. Whitman wrote: "They have caused the Indians below to give them a great deal of property on account of Pitt's death... [including] 10 horses, 2 blankets, 15 or 20 shirts, many kettles, besides guns & muskets, food, etc." According to Narcissa, the trouble arose out of the Indians' superstitious faith in the medicine man, the "te-wat" [Letter 104]. Evidently, the Cayuses felt that because the te-wat had failed to cure Cayuse Pitt when he was summoned to do so, the River Indians would have to pay a penalty. The Cayuses, a much stronger and more warlike tribe than the River Indians, threatened severe reprisals if payment were not made. Whitman reproved the Cayuses for what they had done, and this aroused their anger against him.

The Nez Perce chief, Meiway, who had made trouble for Smith at Kamiah and who claimed that he was a brother, or half-brother, of Cayuse Pitt, visited Waiilatpu and demanded a share of the loot received from the River Indians. When Whitman tried to arbitrate the dispute, "twelve or fifteen" Indians crowded into his home in a menacing manner, one with a war club, and threatened his life [Letter 102a]. Finally Whitman was able to soothe the ruffled feelings. Narcissa's comment on the blind faith of the Indians in the power of the tewat "to kill or make alive at pleasure," reveals the dangerous situation in which Whitman was constantly being placed whenever he, a white te-wat, ministered to the sick and dying among the Cayuses.

After the death of Cayuse Pitt, only two of the seven Indians who had been sent to the Red River Mission were still alive: Spokane Garry and Nez Perce Ellis. Perhaps the one who had been the most sincere in his efforts to introduce Christianity among his people was Cayuse Halket, who returned from the school in the fall of 1834 when he was fifteen years old. He returned to Red River in the spring of 1835 or 1836 and died there in January 1837. On the whole the experiment of sending the Oregon Indian boys to the Red River school to be educated was not a success, although there were some benefits. Both Spokane Garry and Nez Perce Ellis had learned English, and become useful in their respective tribes as leaders of their people in their contacts with the whites.

Roman Catholic Activities

When Joseph Drayton of the Wilkes Expedition visited Waiilatpu in the summer of 1841, he described a picture that he had seen in Dr. McLoughlin's home at Fort Vancouver. According to Whitman's account in a letter to Greene, the picture represented "all Protestants as the withered ends of the several branches of Papacy falling off down into infernal society & flames." Whitman was told that the priests gave copies of the picture to the Indians with an explanation of its meaning. "The possession of one of these manuscripts by an Indian," wrote Whitman, "binds him not to hear any more instruction of Protestants so far as my observation can prove" [Letter 100].

Both the Protestants and the Roman Catholics discovered that the use of pictures was an effective way to teach religious doctrines. Gray tells how Spalding, wishing to emphasize the divine importance of labor, had his wife paint a picture of Adam with a hoe and of Eve with a spinning wheel.[43] Sometime during the summer of 1839, Fathers Blanchet and Demers devised a plan of teaching Christian history by marking off the centuries on a board and then painting symbolic pictures in the separate sections. Father Demers is reported to have had a board ten feet tall which was called a "ladder" because of the horizontal lines drawn across it to indicate the centuries.[44] At the bottom were forty such lines to indicate the forty centuries before Christ; then came thirty-three dots to symbolize the years of His life on earth; and then eighteen more bars and thirty-nine dots to bring the chronology down to 1839. In the representation of the key events of the sixteenth century, the departure of such "heretics" as Luther, Calvin, and Henry VIII from the Catholic Church was shown by their being cast into hell.[45]

To counteract such teachings, Spalding devised a Protestant ladder which showed Luther leaving the broad road leading to destruction which the Catholic Church was following and taking the narrow way leading to salvation. Spalding showed "the Man of Sin," i.e., the Pope, as the one being cast into hell.

Since the Indians looked upon pictures with an almost superstitious awe, the use of them in teaching by both the Protestants and the Catholics was most effective. Narcissa explained this in one of her letters: "The influence of Catholicism adds much to distract their minds. They are constantly told by the followers of the priest that all who attend upon our instructions are in the sure way to Hell—& all who go to the priests' worship will go to heaven. They are certain of it for they have seen the road with their own eyes & see us & all who follow us falling off into Hell. They have a representative of this kind given them by the priests & they need nothing more to make them positive that it must be so" [Letter 114].

A letter from Whitman to Walker, dated April 14, 1842, contains two references to the efforts of the Catholics to win over to their faith some of the followers of the Protestants. "Richard has just come in from the Papist station above," he wrote. "He appears well & disposed to stay with us." Richard, one of the two lads Whitman took East with him in 1835, proved to be uncooperative and no doubt was a great disappointment to Whitman. Yet, Richard refused to turn Catholic. On the other hand Whitman passed on the surprising news to Walker: "Tackensuatis & Kansut [two Nez Perce chiefs] & their wives have been baptized." Evidently this was done by Father Demers. As has been stated, Tackensuatis was one of the Nez Perces who gave the mission party such an enthusiastic welcome in 1836 and who was so eager that the Spaldings settle among his people. Spalding's early letters carried many laudatory references to this chief, yet by 1840 Tackensuatis had lost his zeal for the white man's religion. Smith, writing to Greene on February 6, 1840, called the chief "a very wicked man."[46] The baptism of Tackensuatis and his wife by the Catholics must have caused dismay to both Spalding and Whitman.

Another convert won by the Catholics in 1842 was Dr. John McLoughlin. Reared as a Church of England communicant, Dr. McLoughun from his earliest days at Fort Vancouver was accustomed to read the Anglican service on Sunday mornings at the Fort. He was a deeply religious man and personally gave every encouragement to the Protestant as well as to the Roman Catholic missionaries. Following the arrival of the Catholic priests, Dr. McLoughlin reexamined his own religious convictions and on November 10, 1842, after his "abjuration of heresy," became a communicant member of the Roman Catholic Church.[47] Nine days later, Father Blanchet solemnized the sacrament of marriage for "John McLoughlin and Margaret Wadin." Mrs. McLoughlin, as has been stated, was the widow of Alexander McKay and the mother of Thomas McKay. In 1846, Pope Gregory XVI honored Dr. McLoughlin by making him a Knight of St. Gregory.

THE ANNUAL MISSION MEETING OF 1842

After his return from Tshimakain on March 26, Whitman turned to his spring planting which had to be completed before the annual meeting of the Mission was held in May. To his great satisfaction, more of the Cayuses were cultivating the soil that spring than ever before. In her letter to Mrs. Parker of July 25, 1842, Narcissa wrote: "The success of the Kayuses in farming is pleasing beyond description. There is scarcely an individual of them but what has his little farm some where & every year extending it farther & farther. A large number of the Walla Walla tribe are doing the same... The Nez Perces are a labouring people, far more so than the Kayuses. Mrs. S. has succeeded very well in teaching several girls to spin & weave, knit & sew some but the Kayuse ladies are too proud to be seen usefully employed. Those who labour for us are Walla Wallas principally. One has learned to spin & knit some & others to sew." After giving further news of their situation, Narcissa wrote in the concluding paragraph of her letter: "Do not think me unhappy or discontented—neither would I murmur. No, in no wise—I would not change places with any one so long as we may be permitted to remain & do good to these benighted Indians."

In his letter to Greene written on the eve of the 1842 Annual Meeting, Whitman gave the following optimistic report: "The natives at this station never appeared better & more quiet than at present. They have gone on with the cultivation with their usual energy & are gradually enlarging their little farms, with the assistance of the plows, hoes &c. &c, furnished by the Mission & the H. Bay Company." Here is evidence that the Company was cooperating with Whitman in making agricultural tools available.

Whitman, in this letter of May 12, 1842, to Greene gave a hint of more trouble with Spalding by writing: "Mr. Spalding has notified us that he shall not be present at the coming meeting... In relation to the internal affairs of the mission, there is no change, at least all things remain as they were last fall & no better understanding with Mr. Spalding." Looking into the future, Whitman added: "There will probably be a large party of immigrants coming to this country in the spring of 1843. Some young men are now returning with the expectation of bringing out a party next spring." Little did he dream that he himself would be with the 1843 migration.

Narcissa also was conscious of coming immigrations. In her letter to Mrs. Parker written on the following July 25, she said: "A party of military and scientific men are expected across the mountains this fall. What the effect will be upon the Indians, we know not. The rumor of it may have a worse effect upon them than the reality." Such quotations from the Whitman letters show their awareness of the inevitability of Oregon emigration. One could no more hold back the surge of Oregon-bound Americans at that time than he could sweep back the incoming tide on some ocean beach. Also, the Whitmans were beginning to wonder what effect these immigrations would have upon the Indians and particularly upon the volatile Cayuses.

VISIT OF THE REV. JOSEPH WILLIAMS

Among the visitors at Waiilatpu during the week beginning May 8, 1842, was the Methodist minister, Joseph Williams, who had arrived in Oregon in the fall of 1841 and who was with the company of young men, of whom Whitman wrote, returning to the United States. In his *Narrative of a Tour*, Williams told of his second visit to Waiilatpu. "I lodged with Mr. Gray, my old friend," he wrote, "who was very kind to me, as was also his wife." On the 13th, when Walker and Eells were expected to arrive at Waiilatpu to attend the mission meeting, Williams with others "galloped out, about four or five miles into the plains," to welcome them.[48] The Walkers had with them their three children, the youngest but two months old, and the Eellses had their yearold son. The two couples were obliged to drive a fresh milk cow with them on the long 140-mile journey from Tshimakain. One night they had to camp in the snow. Because of some unexpected delays, the trip took longer than usual, as they were eight days on the road.[49]

Since the missionaries had the rare experience of having a visiting minister with them, he was invited to preach on Sunday, May 15. Of this Williams wrote: "I tried to preach to the people there." The expression "trying to preach" was often used by ministers of that day who wished to avoid giving the impression of excelling as pulpit orators. Williams throws further light on the day's religious exercises: "They had with them a coarse violin, which was poor music on Sunday." He was referring to the bass viol which Eells owned and which he cherished enough to take the trouble of packing it all the way from Tshimakain. Williams' use of the word "coarse" in this connection is archaic and refers to an instrument larger than the ordinary violin and one that had six strings instead of the usual four. Williams also commented: "They [then] read two sermons, which was all the preaching that was done. They appeared very dull in religion." Perhaps as a Methodist, Williams expected more emotion than the four missionary couples were accustomed to display.

Another Unhappy Mission Meeting

The four men of the Oregon Mission—Whitman, Gray, Walker, and Eells—opened the meeting as scheduled on Monday, May 16. Walker and Eells were reelected to their respective offices as moderator and clerk. Spalding was not present. His absence may have been due to some resentment he felt against Whitman for not agreeing to the reception of Five Crows and some Nez Perces into the Mission church the preceding December. Possibly there were other issues also which accounted for his absence. Spalding did send word to Whitman that he was too busy to attend. The four men found his reasons for his absence unacceptable and sent a messenger to Lapwai requesting his immediate attendance. They then adjourned to await his coming. Spalding appeared on Thursday, May 26, and the Mission resumed its meetings the next day.

Since Spalding made no entries in his diary after April 28, 1842, except for a short section in March 1843, we do not have his side of the story. Both Elkanah and Mary Walker kept diaries for those days and from them we get many glimpses into what took place.[50] After clearing such routine business as reading the most recent correspondence from Greene, the men turned their attention to the differences which had arisen between Whitman and Spalding. The women were invited to be present for the discussions. All members of the Mission were present except Mrs. Spalding who had remained in Lapwai.

Walker, in his diary, noted that it was decided to have each man present write out what he considered to be the chief difficulties within the Mission and then each was to give specific suggestions as to how the difficulties could be settled. This took all of Friday. No business sessions were held on Saturday and Sunday. When these were resumed on Monday, the individual specifications were read. That night Mary Walker wrote in her diary: "Hear much to make our ears tingle." On Tuesday the discussions continued; many bitter words were said. Walker that night wrote: "Had a hard session today and there was so much bad feeling manifested that I said that I thought it was an abomination for us to meet and pray."

Walker, according to his diary, placed most of the blame for the unhappy condition existing within the Mission on Whitman. Cornelius Rogers, who had been at Fort Walla Walla working on his Nez Perce dictionary, was invited to sit in on the discussions; evidence shows that he shared Walker's views about Whitman's unforgiving spirit. On Wednesday, June 1, Walker and Eells took a long ride in the rain. Walker wrote that they "felt that all hope was gone." The Mission was on the verge of complete disintegration. The next day the men frankly faced the stark reality of what the consequences would be if a reconciliation were not reached. Walker wrote in his diary: "I felt much and said considerable, and hope that it was not in vain. I think there was a better state of feeling than there had been since the session began."

However, Friday, June 3, was another unhappy day. Walker confessed: "My feelings have been anything but calm. I have been much moved by some threats the Doctor made, that if he was not allowed to pursue his own course, he would leave the Mission. The Doctor asked to be allowed to go on in his own way without being checked." Walker could scarcely sleep that night because of worry. His wife's diary for the same day stated: "Soon after the opening of the session, Dr. W. began to call Mr. Spalding to account. Mr. Rogers thought Dr. W. wrong. Much talk followed and the Dr. was allowed to proceed... If any restraint is laid on the Dr. or if he suspects he is not to have his own way entirely, he immediately threatens to leave the mission."

On Saturday Whitman and Spalding had a private conference, after which they asked all to assemble. Spalding began with a confession which Mary Walker described as being "as humble as could be wished." When Whitman was questioned as to his threats about leaving the Mission, he replied that he did not mean for them to take his remarks seriously. According to Mary's diary: "He said he saw nothing why he & Mr. Spalding could not come to a settlement. The minds of all were relieved." Thus another crisis in the Oregon Mission passed. An enduring understanding had finally been reached by Whitman and Spalding.

Mission Moves to Forestall Action by the Board

After Whitman and Spalding had settled their differences, the Mission turned to other items of business which kept them busy for the next two days. The possibility of the Board taking some drastic action on the basis of the complaining letters about Spalding which had been sent to the Board in 1840 was discussed. To forestall any order disastrous to the welfare of the Mission, the men decided that if such an order arrived, the Prudential Committee should be informed of the new developments before implementing any such order. On June 8, Walker, Eells, and Spalding signed a letter addressed to Greene which stated that all difficulties had been settled and that they then had reason "to hope for permanent peace & harmony."

This letter of June 8 also contained the following statement which, as later events proved, was of utmost importance to Spalding: "It was the unanimous opinion at the close of the investigation that, should the Prudential Committee have taken any action on any communication yet unanswered, that the Mission ought to wait until this communication can be answered."[51] This, in effect, nullified the yet unknown order of the Board of the previous February. By an interesting coincidence, Elijah White, who was carrying the Board's letter, left the Missouri frontier on May 16, the very day the 1842 Annual Meeting of the Oregon Mission began its sessions.

Before the meeting was adjourned on June 1, the men passed a strange motion which called for Whitman and Spalding to exchange stations. This action was taken on the insistence of Gray. Eells, in his letter to Greene of October 3, 1842, said that "a rather hesitating assent was given to the resolution." In July when both Walker and Spalding happened to be at Waiilatpu for supplies, they agreed with Whitman that no exchange should be made. For some reason Gray was adamant in his insistence and when he learned that the exchange had not been made, he expressed his regret "that he was connected with a mission which had not the courage to carry out such a vote."[52]

Gray, still unhappy with his place within the Oregon Mission, seized upon this incident as an excuse to resign. Before doing so, he felt it necessary to find a job in the Willamette Valley. He left Waiilatpu on September 1 to see what could be found. While in the Valley, Gray was successful in securing an appointment as Secular Agent and General Superintendent of the Oregon Institute, a Methodist school which later became Willamette University.[53] Gray was back in Waiilatpu by September 21 and began making preparations to move his family to Salem.[54]

DR. ELIJAH WHITE AND THE 1842 EMIGRATION

When Dr. Elijah White returned to the States in April 1841, he found a growing public interest in the possibilities of emigrating to Oregon, an interest which he assiduously promoted. By this time it was well known that white women had crossed the Rockies, and White was aware of the fact that Meek and Newell had taken their wagons over the Blue Mountains in 1840.

President John Tyler, in his message to the Twenty-Seventh Congress, which sat from December 6, 1841, to August 31, 1842, voiced his approval of the recommendation made by John C. Spencer, then Secretary of War, for the establishment of "a chain of military posts from Council Bluffs to some point on the Pacific Ocean within our limits." This, he said, would benefit those engaged in the fur trade and be the means of establishing safe intercourse "between the American settlements at the mouth of the Columbia River and those on this side of the Rocky Mountains."[55] President Tyler was assuming that all of the country south of the Columbia would become U.S. territory.

No member of Congress was more interested in extending United States jurisdiction over Oregon than Senator Lewis F. Linn of Missouri. Beginning as early as February 1838, he introduced a series of bills calling for that action. Congress for several years failed to act, but Linn's bills did focus attention on what was coming to be known as the "Oregon question." In January 1842, Senator Linn tried once again to induce Congress to act by introducing another bill which called for the extension of United States jurisdiction to all of Old Oregon south of the 49th parallel and for the granting of a section of land to every settler. Speaking in favor of his bill, Senator Linn in April 1842 said: "There should be no dispute about the right of the United States to all the region south of the Columbia River, a right which Great Britain had fully conceded. The only question was to the right of the United States to the territory north of the Columbia River."[56]

The arrival in the United States of Lord Ashburton from England on April 4, 1842, to negotiate a treaty caused Congress to postpone action on the Linn bill until after the treaty had been signed. The Webster-Ashburton Treaty was concluded on August 9, 1842. Even though Lord Ashburton had been instructed by his government to deal with the Oregon boundary, the Treaty had nothing to say about it. It dealt only with the boundary between Maine and Canada. Daniel Webster, then Secretary of State, felt that the time was not opportune to settle the Oregon question and deliberately kept this subject out of their discussions.

In January 1842, Elijah White, with letters of testimony from persons of note, visited Washington, D.C., and called on President Tyler, Secretary Webster, Secretary Spencer, and Senator Linn. The White file in the Old Indian Bureau records in National Archives, Washington, D.C., contains a number of letters written by him which reveal his intense interest in the Oregon question. White was politically minded and asked for an appointment as sub-Indian Agent for Oregon which he succeeded in getting on January 27, 1842. His salary was fixed at $750.00 a year with the understanding that if the Linn bill passed, it would be raised to $1,500.00. White thus had the distinction of being the first person to be appointed to some official position in Oregon by the United States Government.

Some Details of the 1842 Emigration

After receiving his appointment, White issued through the public press a call for families to go out with him to Oregon that year. His call was successful for he left Independence, Missouri, on May 16, 1842, with a party of 105 emigrants. White had with him the two sons of Tom McKay, John and Alexander, who had been taken East by Jason Lee in 1838 to be educated. Writing to the Commissioner of Indian Affairs from Fort Hall on August 15, White stated that the number in his party had increased to 112.

The members of this migration left the Missouri frontier with nineteen wagons, none of which was taken west of Fort Hall. From that point all, including women and children, rode horseback. White's letter of August 15 refers to certain funds that he had received from the Government to cover some expenses incurred by the emigration of that year.[57] Such a subsidy lends support to the theory that Jason Lee also had received financial aid from some Government fund to help pay the costs of sending the *Lausanne* company to Oregon.

White left the main party of emigrants on August 23 and pushed on ahead. He arrived at Waiilatpu on September 9 and delivered Greene's two letters of February 25 to Whitman. White spent the weekend of September 11 at Waiilatpu and left the next Tuesday for the Willamette Valley. Mary Gray noted in her diary that during those days she copied two letters from Greene which White had brought.[58] These letters she gave to White with the request that, if on his way down the Columbia River he met her husband returning from the Willamette Valley, he should give them to him.

The 1842 emigration broke up into small groups. One of these parties arrived on Wednesday afternoon, September 14. In this group was Medorem Crawford who wrote in his journal that he was never more pleased to see a house or white people in his life. He reported that the Whitmans treated him and his fellow travelers with the utmost kindness and sold provisions on "very reasonable terms."[59] Here is the first reference to Whitman selling supplies to the emigrants. He was later accused of charging exorbitant prices for supplies and Elijah White was one of his critics. Yet for the most part, this service was greatly appreciated.

Another member of the 1842 immigration who visited Waiilatpu and recorded his impressions was the lawyer, Lansford Warren Hastings. He wrote in his journal: "...the next place of note, at which we arrived, was a presbyterian mission, in charge of which, is a Dr. Whitman, who is a very kind and hospitable gentleman. He received us with the utmost kindness and attention, and insisted upon our remaining a few days with him, in order to obtain some relaxation of both body and mind." Hastings spent a Sunday at Waiilatpu and attended religious meeting where Whitman "delivered a discourse to the Indians in their own language." He also commented: "The doctor is not only a very kind and hospitable gentleman, but he is no doubt, a very good man, and a devoted Christian. He appears to be rendering a great service in christianizing and civilizing the natives."[60]

WHITE'S ARRIVAL IN OLD OREGON BRINGS DISMAY

The unexpected arrival of Dr. White in the Willamette Valley in the fall of 1842 as an officially appointed Indian Agent brought dismay both to the colony of Methodist missionaries and to Dr. McLoughlin and his associates at Fort Vancouver. White's return was an embarrassment, especially to Jason Lee, as he had been dismissed from the Methodist Mission in 1840. Now he was back again.

Dr. McLoughlin was disturbed but for different reasons. He at once informed Gov. Simpson, who on June 21, 1843, writing from Red River, stated: "I shall be glad to learn that the 100 emigrants you speak of as having accompanied Dr. White from St. Louis have proceeded to California as the rapidly increasing vagrant population in the Willamette is becoming too numerous for the safety of the Company's interest in its immediate neighborhood." Dr. McLoughlin had evidently reported that Hastings and some others were planning to move on to California, but Simpson's hope that all of the 1842 party would do likewise was nothing more than wishful thinking.

When Dr. White arrived in the Willamette Valley, he notified Dr. McLoughlin of his appointment by the United States Government by letter, which the latter forwarded to Simpson. Simpson called the letter "a curious specimen of impertinence," and wrote: "We cannot recognize Dr. White's commission as sub-Indian Agent nor any other commission of the U. States Government assuming authority in the country pending the adjustment of the Boundary question."[61] Simpson advised McLoughlin to notify all "gentlemen" in charge of the various Company's posts in Oregon "that they are not to receive nor extend their hospitalities, nor afford any facility or assistance to strangers of any description assuming authority, unless you be perfectly satisfied that such authority is founded on an amicable adjustment of the Boundary question." Simpson was still confident that the Columbia River "from its outlet to the source in the mountains by the northern branch [i.e., the Snake River], or Lewis & Clark's route will become the boundary."[62]

When the London headquarters of the Company heard about White's arrival in Oregon, the Governor and Committee wrote on September 27, 1843, to Dr. McLoughlin saying: "...no authority emanating from the Government of the United States is to be recognized west of the Rocky Mountains until the boundary questions shall have been settled."[63] Legally the Hudson's Bay Company and the British Government stood on solid ground. The appointment of Dr. White as an Indian Agent for Oregon was a unilateral act which contradicted the spirit of the joint Occupation Treaty of 1818. The fact that Dr. White confined his activities to the country lying to the south and east of the Columbia River did not, in the eyes of the British, lessen the seriousness of what they considered to be his illegal appointment.

The Special Mission Meeting of September 1842

We have no contemporary document which would reveal Whitman's reactions when he read Greene's two letters of February 25, 1842. We may assume that he was not surprised to read of the dismissal of the Spaldings but the recall of Smith and Gray may have been unexpected. Surely the order to close both Waiilatpu and Lapwai and for him to move to Tshimakain would have brought dismay to his heart. The southern stations were far superior in regard to agricultural possibilities than Tshimakain, as each had irrigation ditches, mills, fenced fields, and other improvements. With members of the 1842 immigration still streaming by his door, Whitman realized anew the strategic importance of Waiilatpu. To him it was unthinkable that his station and Spalding's should be abandoned. The Board simply did not understand the situation. Moreover, conditions within the Mission had changed. A reconciliation had been effected between him and Spalding which gave promise of enduring. Smith and Rogers had already resigned and Gray was preparing to leave. The Board's order was out-of-date. Then, too, how impossible was the order for the Spaldings with two small children to return to the States by the overland route. There was no longer any Fur Company's caravan going to the Rockies. How could a family cross the plains unescorted?

We learn from Mary Gray's diary that Whitman received Greene's letters on September 9, yet Elkanah Walker in his diary stated that he and Eells did not receive notification, of the call for a special meeting of the Mission until September 20.[64] If we allow five days for a messenger to carry Whitman's letter to Tshimakain, it is apparent that Whitman waited until September 15 before issuing his call for the special meeting. Why this delay of about six days when the issues to be decided were so urgent? A probable explanation for the delay is that Whitman wished to consult with Spalding before calling a special meeting. If he had sent a messenger to Lapwai, the round trip would have taken about six days. If this had been done, then Whitman would have learned that Spalding and his family were not at Lapwai. No one seemed to know where they were. Thinking that perhaps the Spaldings had gone to Tshimakain, Whitman sent Greene's letter addressed to Spalding to Tshimakain, along with other correspondence received from Greene, with the request that he, Walker, and Eells leave as soon as possible for Waiilatpu.[65]

The next piece of this jigsaw puzzle, which is now being put together, is found in Medorem Crawford's journal. As has been mentioned, Crawford was a member of the 1842 immigration. After spending the night of September 14 at Waiilatpu, Crawford and his party continued their journey, going overland to The Dalles. On September 20, when Crawford was forty-five miles below Fort Walla Walla, he wrote: "Mr. Spalding & Lady overtook us at noon... Mr. Gray called at camp on his return from Vancouver." Just why the Spaldings with their two little children were at that place at that time remains a mystery. On September 21, Crawford noted: "Parted with Mr. & Mrs. Spalding who in consequence of some intelligence from Mr. Gray resolved to return."[66] Evidently Gray had met Dr. White en route to the Willamette Valley and had received from him the copies of the letters sent by his wife, including Greene's letter of February 25. Thus Gray learned of the action of the Board dismissing both him and Spalding, which information he had passed on to Spalding. Since Gray had already taken steps to leave the Mission, the order did not strike him with the same force as it did Spalding. Both, however, hastened to Waiilatpu, where they arrived on Thursday, September 22.

On Tuesday, September 20, Walker wrote in his diary: "Just as we were about to sit down to breakfast, the long looked for express came in with some letters from the Dr. & from Mr. Greene... The Dr. requested us to come down immediately." Walker and Eells left the next day and arrived at Waiilatpu on Monday, the 26th, where they found the other three men of the Mission waiting for them.

Gray Resigns

The Special Meeting of the Oregon Mission opened that Monday evening. Greene's letter of February 25, together with copies of communications sent to him giving the actions of the May–June meeting, was read. The men were thus reminded of the action taken which suspended the implementation of any order that the Board might send until it could be informed of the changed situation. Thus, neither Spalding nor Gray was in any immediate danger of being dismissed. Nevertheless, Gray presented his resignation.[67] He informed his associates that he had found work in the Willamette Valley and was planning to leave with his family as soon as possible. Walker and Eells, with a high sense of loyalty to the commission each had received from the American Board, opposed the departure of Gray. They felt that it was a disgrace to resign. An appointment from the Board was for life. This had been their attitude when Smith left in the spring of 1841. Whitman voted in the affirmative with Gray. Strange to say, Spalding voted in the negative with Walker and Eells. Gray threatened to leave with or without formal acceptance of his resignation, and so, two days later, the action of Monday evening was reconsidered and a unanimous approval was given to his request. Thus ended Gray's six-year connection with the Oregon Mission of the American Board.[68]

Whitman Proposes Going to Boston

According to Walker's diary, nothing special happened at the Mission meeting on Tuesday, September 27. On Wednesday morning, when Walker, Eells, and Spalding were making preparations to return to their respective stations, Whitman suddenly proposed that he go to Boston to intercede with the Board for the revocation of its drastic order of February 25. Walker and Eells with their customary reluctance to make any move without deliberate thought, were hesitant. They wanted time to think about it. Whitman urged the need for immediate action. If he could leave that fall, then he could return with the 1843 emigration. If he should wait to go East in the spring, he would not be able to return until the fall of 1844. Whitman stressed the fact that if he were to leave for the East that fall, the sooner he got started the better in order to cross the mountains before winter.

Walker and Eells brought up the question of care of the Waiilatpu property during his proposed absence. Finally, they gave their consent for Whitman to leave on condition that some satisfactory arrangements be made for the care of the station. Whitman assured them that he would get somebody to live at Waiilatpu during his absence. He then hastily wrote out the following:

> Resolved: That, if arrangements can be made to continue the operations of this station, That Dr. Marcus Whitman be at liberty & advised to visit the United States as soon as practicable to confer with the Committee of the A.B.C.F.M. in regard to the interests of this mission.
>
> Waiilatpu, September 28th, 1842

This was signed by E. Walker, Moderator; Cushing Eells, Scribe; and H. H. Spalding.[69] Here in Whitman's handwriting is the first statement given to explain why he wanted to go East. He was to go on mission business.

Motives for Whitman's Ride

Whitman's reasons for suddenly deciding to cross the Rocky Mountains in the late fall of 1842 and to travel on to Washington and Boston have been debated for over one hundred years. The subject is complex and the evidence in some particulars conflicting. We can list three apparent motives, but it would be unhistorical to say that any particular one took priority over the other two.[70]

On Mission Business

Before Walker and Eells left Waiilatpu, it was agreed that each would write a letter to Greene which Whitman would carry should he go East. It was understood that Whitman would wait until the two had returned to Tshimakain, had time to write the letters, and then send them to Waiilatpu. By forced marches, Walker and Eells were able to return to their homes by October 1. They delayed in writing their letters, however, for Mary's diary states that the letters were not sent until October 12. Since Whitman had become restless and had left for the East on October 3, the letters were mailed to Greene and arrived in Boston months after Whitman had been there.

The letters that Eells and Walker wrote are illuminating, as they throw light on what was discussed at the Special Meeting of the Mission. Eells in his fourteenpage letter dealt especially with the Gray case. Walker in a longer letter of sixteen pages reviewed the reasons why Whitman wanted to make the journey. He wrote: "If necessity demanded that one branch of the Mission be abandoned, the north part could have been given up with far less disastrous consequences both as respects white settlers and the natives..." He also stated: "We do not approve the hasty manner in which this question was decided. Nothing it seemed to us but stern necessity induced us to decide in the manner we did. It seemed death to put the proposition in force, and worse than death to remain as we were." [71] There is nothing in either of the letters that Walker or Eells wrote which indicates that the main reason, or even a secondary reason, for Whitman's sudden decision to go East was anything other than mission business.

News of the Whitman massacre, which began on November 29, 1847, reached the offices of the American Board in time for the editor of the *Missionary Herald* to make a brief mention of it in the July, 1848, issue. Regarding the reasons for Whitman's journey east in 1842–43, the editor wrote: "He made a visit to the Atlantic States in the spring of 1843, *being called hither by the business of the mission.*" [72]

To Promote Oregon Emigration

The text of the Resolution adopted by the Mission, which was carried to Boston by Whitman, and the letters of Walker and Eells do not give a complete answer as to why Whitman was moved to leave for the East on such short notice in the fall of 1842. The unhistorical and often perverted explanations of Whitman's motives, as found in Spalding's later Whitman-Saved-Oregon story, must be rejected; yet there were some motives which moved Whitman to make the journey which had political overtones [see Appendices 3 & 4]. When Mary Walker noted the return of her husband on Saturday, October 1, she wrote that day in her diary: "Messrs. W. & E. had much trouble with Gray & Co. The Mission have concluded to send Dr. W. to the States to represent the Mission & *obtain a reinforcement or settlers or do something.*" [73] Here is contemporary evidence that Whitman was concerned about other issues beyond mission business.

Ever since Jason Lee's visit to Waiilatpu and Lapwai in the early spring of 1838, at which time Whitman and Spalding sent in their amazing request for 220 additional missionaries, we find evidences of Whitman's growing interest in the political future of Old Oregon. The limits of that interest need to be defined. As previously stated, he never seemed concerned about the exact location of the boundary line which would divide Old Oregon. Rather, his political interests centered on (1) the promotion of the emigration of American citizens to Oregon, especially those of the Protestant faith, and (2) the extension of the jurisdiction of the United States over whatever part of the Oregon territory would be granted it by treaty.

The arrival of the first wagons at Waiilatpu, which had been taken over the Blue Mountains by Meek and Newell in the summer of 1840, prompted Whitman to remark to them that the day was coming when other wagons would follow, and "in a few years the valley will be full of people." Even though the emigrants of 1841 and 1842 had abandoned their wagons at Fort Hall, and had completed their journey on horseback, Whitman believed that the emigration of 1843 would take its wagons over the mountains into the Columbia River Valley. By the late spring of 1840, both Marcus and Narcissa realized the importance of Waiilatpu as an outpost on the Oregon Trail. Little, however, did they dream of the demands which would be made upon their hospitality and resources by the hungry, the weary, the sick, and the destitute in the years just ahead.

On May 2, 1840, Narcissa wrote in a letter to her mother: "A tide of immigration appears to be moving this way rapidly. What a few years will bring forth, we know not. A great change has taken place ever since we first entered the country, and we have no reason to believe it will stop here." Writing to Greene on July 13, 1841, Whitman said: "It has been distinctly my feeling that we are not to measure the sphere of our action & hope of usefulness by the few natives of the country, but, by all that we can see in prospect, both as it relates to a white population & [to counteract a] Catholic influence."

According to Dr. White's biographer, White and Whitman had much to tell each other when they were together at Waiilatpu, September 9–13. "The visit was very agreeable to both," wrote Miss Allen, "as he had much to tell Dr. White of Oregon affairs, and Dr. him of his two years' residence in the States."[74] Undoubtedly White would have told Whitman of Lord Ashburton's visit to the United States, of the expected settlement of the boundary in Old Oregon, and especially of Senator Linn's bill which offered to give a section of land in Old Oregon to every emigrant including children. White would certainly have reported that all signs pointed to a large emigration in 1843. At the time the two men were together, they did not know that the Webster-Ashburton Treaty had been signed without containing any mention of the Oregon boundary and that Congress had adjourned without taking action on the Linn bill. Like a dry sponge soaking up water, Whitman's mind avidly absorbed all that White had to tell him about the political prospects for the future of Old Oregon.

Another member of the 1842 immigration who visited Waiilatpu was a lawyer, Asa Lawrence Lovejoy, 1808–1882, with whom Whitman also discussed certain political matters relating to the Pacific Northwest. Lovejoy with a small party of immigrants arrived at the mission on Monday, September 19, when both of the Whitmans for some unknown reason were absent.[75] Since Lovejoy was Whitman's companion on his ride over the Rockies in the late fall of 1842 and the following winter, special attention must be given to his recollections of this journey. Lovejoy wrote three accounts describing his travels with Whitman, two of which have been published.[76] Some minor differences are to be found when the three accounts are compared. When we note that Lovejoy wrote the earliest letter twenty-seven years after some of the events described had taken place, allowances should be made for the fallibility of human memory. On the whole, Lovejoy was a reliable witness and became a highly respected citizen of Willamette Valley after returning to Oregon with the 1843 emigration.

In Lovejoy's letter of 1876, we may read: "I crossed the Plains in company with Dr. White and others, arrived at Waiilatpu the last of September, 1842. My party camped some two miles below Dr. Whitman's place. The day after our arrival [i.e., on September 20], Dr. Whitman called at our camp and asked me to accompany him to his house, as he wished me to draw up a memorial to Congress to prohibit the sale of ardent spirits in this country. The Doctor was alive to the interests of this Coast, and manifested a very warm desire to have it properly represented in Washington; and after numerous conversations with the Doctor touching the future prosperity of Oregon, he asked me one day in a very anxious manner, if I thought it would be possible for him to cross the mountains at that time of the year. I told him I thought he could. He next asked, 'Will you accompany me?' After a little reflection, I told him I would. His arrangements were rapidly made."

After spending a day or so in the vicinity of Waiilatpu, Lovejoy moved on to Fort Walla Walla. Whitman visited him at the fort shortly before the Mission opened its meeting on Monday, the 26th, and it may be that it was then that Whitman secured Lovejoy's consent to accompany him across the mountains that fall. Lovejoy's testimony indicates that Whitman was already planning the journey before he gained a reluctant consent from his associates to go. We have no indication that Whitman ever mentioned the possibility of Lovejoy going with him to his associates. Without that assurance, it is doubtful that Whitman would have attempted making the journey. The combined testimony of White's biographer and Lovejoy's accounts is evidence that Whitman was concerned with certain political issues involved in the future of Old Oregon. As later events indicated, he was deeply interested in promoting emigration to Oregon. Hence, his visit to Washington, D.C., before going to Boston.

To Counteract the Roman Catholics

A third reason which moved Whitman to make his sudden decision to go East was his concern over the growing influence of the Roman Catholic missionaries in the Northwest. This, to Whitman, was a threatening situation especially in view of the possible abandonment of the Oregon Mission of the American Board and the uncertain future of the Methodist Mission in the Willamette Valley. As has been stated,

Jason Lee wrote to Whitman in the early fall of 1840 telling of Dr. White's dismissal from the Methodist Mission and of his intention to return to the States. Lee expressed his fears lest White might do "all that he can to injure them [i.e., the Methodist missionaries in the Valley]" after he got back to New York City. Lee's fears were well founded; White did appear before the Methodist Missionary Society and declared that Lee was not qualified "for the important trusts which had been committed to him." [77] White's charges were reenforced by two other disgruntled returned Methodist missionaires, Rev. W. W. Kone and Dr. John P. Richmond. As a result of these criticisms, Lee was superseded by the Rev. George Gary in September 1843. Gary was sent out to Oregon in 1844 with instructions to close the Methodist work and dispose of the property. Just as the Oregon Mission of the American Board had its critics—Smith and Gray—so the Methodists had theirs—White, Kone, and Richmond. Thus the Methodist Mission in Oregon functioned for only ten years, 1834–44.

We have reason to believe that White gave Whitman a detailed account of the dismal prospects of the Methodist Mission. Such information would have been alarming to Whitman; if both the American Board's Mission and the Methodist Mission in Old Oregon were abandoned, organized religious activities in the country would be monopolized by the Roman Catholics. We have already noted that the Belgian Jesuit, Father Pierre Jean De Smet, was at the 1840 Rendezvous on his way back to St. Louis after a visit to the Flathead country. In 1841 he returned to the Flatheads with a reenforcement of two priests and three lay brothers. With these assistants, De Smet established St. Mary's Mission among the Flatheads in Bitterroot Valley, in what is now western Montana, in the fall of 1841.

After Narcissa had learned of the founding of St. Mary's Mission, she wrote to her sister Jane on October 1, 1841: "Now we have Catholics on both sides of us and, we may say, right in our midst, for Mr. Pambrun, while he was alive, failed not to secure one of the principal men of this tribe [Young Chief] to that religion and had his family baptized." Nearly a year later, Narcissa wrote again: "Romanism stalks abroad on our right hand and on our left, and with daring effrontery boasts that she is to possess the land. I ask, must it be so?... The zeal and energy of her [priests] are without a parallel... Two are in the country below us, and two far above in the mountains. One of the latter is to return this fall to Canada, the States and the eastern world for a large reenforcement" [Letter 115].

Father De Smet visited Fort Vancouver in the spring of 1842, where he consulted with Fathers Blanchet and Demers about the future of Roman Catholic work in Oregon. En route to Vancouver, he visited Tshimakain in April 1842, at which time he had some discussion with Elkanah Walker over the proper Flathead term to be used to express the idea of the Trinity.[78] De Smet left Fort Vancouver on his return trip up the Columbia on June 30. He was back at St. Mary's Mission about July 25.

There is a strong possibility that while going down or returning up the Columbia River, Father De Smet saw Dr. Whitman at Fort Walla Walla. For several years, the Oregon Historical Society displayed a copy of the Roman Catholic English translation of the Bible, known as the Rheims-Douai version, which had been presented by Father De Smet to Dr. Whitman.[79] If the two pioneer missionaries met, Whitman would have learned of De Smet's intention to go to Europe that year to enlist more missionaries for new stations to be established in the upper Columbia River country.

The increasing activities of the Roman Catholic missionaries in the upper Columbia River country gave the Whitmans much concern. What could be done to counteract their influence? Marcus remembered the extravagant request that he and Spalding had made in the spring of 1838 when they asked the Board to send out a reenforcement of 220 missionaries. He later apologized to Greene for signing such a request, but yet the hope of such a reenforcement was revived as he debated what measures could be taken to meet the Catholic threat. Finally, he came to the conviction that the answer lay in getting as large a reenforcement as possible from the Board and then also to recruit colonies of emigrants who would settle in the vicinity of each of the three stations. This seems to be the proposal which Whitman presented to his colleagues and which was reflected in the entry in Mary Walker's diary, previously quoted, which stated that Dr. Whitman was to go to the States "to represent the Mission & obtain a reinforcement or settlers or do something."

Whitman's Statement of his Motives

On April 1, 1847, about four and one half years after the special meeting of the Oregon Mission, held in September 1842, Whitman, in a letter to Greene, looked back on that event and wrote: "From the year 1835 to this time, it has ever been apparent that there was to be a choice only of two things; one of the increase & continuation of British interests here to the easy exclusion of all other acquired rights in the Country; or the establishment of American interests by Citizens [i.e., by emigration]." Whitman then pointed out his conviction that the Roman Catholic interests were deeply rooted in the British establishment, even though he did not know that the Catholic priest in the Willamette Valley was then receiving an annual subsidy of £100 from the Hudson's Bay Company. Regarding the American interests in Oregon, Whitman wrote: "In thirty six [1836] Capt. Wyeth left the Country[80] & with him closed for a long time nearly all of the American interests in the country but the Methodists and our Missions. *In the fall of 1842, I pointed out to our Mission the arrangement of the Papists to settle in our vicinity and that it only required these measures to be completed for us to be obliged to close our Mission operations. This was urged [by me] as a reason for me to return home & try to bring those to carry on the affairs of the Mission stations and to settle in the Country who would stand on the footing of Citizens & not as missionaries.*[81] It may not be inappropriate to observe that at that moment [i.e., September 1842], the Methodist Mission as well as our own was on the point of dissolution."

Two questions arise: (1) If the Oregon boundary had been settled before Dr. White left for Oregon and if he had carried such news to Whitman, would Whitman have made his journey merely on the need to correct the Board's order of February 25, 1842? In my opinion, the answer must be No! (2) If the Board had never issued its drastic order and if Dr. White had informed Whitman of pending treaty negotiations which involved the Oregon boundary, would Whitman then have made his ride? Again, in my opinion, the answer would be NO!

In other words, there was a combination of motives which, taken together, prompted Whitman to leave for the East, and it is impossible to say which had priority. Whitman did ride on mission business; he did want to get the Board to rescind its order dismissing Spalding and closing the work at Waiilatpu and Lapwai. He was eager for the extension of United States jurisdiction over the disputed Oregon territory, although, seemingly, he did not advocate any specific boundary line. He was concerned about the future of the Methodist Mission after hearing from Dr. White the story of dissension within its ranks, and he feared for the future of his own Oregon Mission. The failure of either or both of these Missions would, in his opinion, have made it easier for the Roman Catholics to achieve an amazing success in Oregon.

WHITMAN LEAVES FOR WASHINGTON AND BOSTON

Within twenty-four hours after Walker, Eells, and Spalding had left for their respective stations, Dr. Whitman announced his intention to leave for Washington and Boston on the following Monday, October 3. We can be sure that had he proposed such an early departure before Walker and Eells had left for Tshimakain, they would have objected. They wanted time to write their letters and to send them to Waiilatpu. This would have delayed Whitman's departure by about two weeks. To Whitman, it was far more important for him to be on his way before winter came to the Rockies than to wait for letters which could be sent by other means. Therefore, it is possible that Whitman deliberately kept his intentions secret while Walker and Eells were still at Waiilatpu.

On Thursday, September 29, the day after the Mission meeting was adjourned, Narcissa wrote to Jane and Edward: "I sit down to write you but in great haste. My beloved husband has about concluded to start next Monday to go to the United States, the dear land of our birth; but I remain behind. I could not undertake the journey, if it was considered best for me to accompany him, that is to travel as he expects to. He hopes to reach the borders [of Missouri] in less than three months, if the Lord prospers his way. It is a dreadful journey, especially at this season of the year." Narcissa made no direct comment regarding the purpose of her husband's journey except to say: "He wishes to reach Boston as early as possible so as to make arrangements to return next summer, if prospered. The interests of the missionary cause in this country calls him home." The wording of the last sentence is sufficiently ambiguous to include all three of the motives for Whitman's ride discussed above. Jane and Edward Prentiss were then associated with one of Narcissa's former Prattsburg teachers, the Rev. William Beardsley, in the Mission Institute at Quincy, Illinois. Jane may have been a teacher, while Edward seems to have been studying for the ministry. Narcissa begged her sister to return with Marcus the next spring.

Since Narcissa fully expected Marcus to call on her parents and other members of her family, she wrote to them on September 30: "You will be surprised if this letter reaches you to learn that the bearer is my dear husband, and that you will, after a few days, have the pleasure of seeing him. May you have a joyful meeting. He goes upon important business connected with the missionary cause, the cause of Christ in this land, which I will leave for him to explain when you see him, because I have not time to enlarge. He has but yesterday fully made up his mind to go, and he wishes to start Monday, and this is Friday."

Narcissa returned to the object of her husband's journey by adding: "As much as I do desire to see my beloved friends once more, yet I cheerfully consent to remain behind, that the object of his almost immediate presence in the land of our birth might, if possible, be accomplished. He wishes to cross the mountains during this month, I mean October, and reach St. Louis about the first of Dec., if he is not detained by the cold or hostile Indians... He has for a companion, Mr. Lovejoy, a respectable, intelligent man and a lawyer, but not a Christian, who expects to accompany him all the way to Boston, as his friends are in that region, and perhaps to Washington. This is a comfort to me..." It is significant that Narcissa here indicated her husband's intention to visit Washington.

Narcissa mentioned that she expected to be "quite alone at this station for a season," as the Gray family expected to leave for the Willamette Valley within a few days. She did not indicate that she was concerned over this as she had been left alone on a number of previous occasions when her husband was called away on professional business. The other men of the Mission also at times had left their wives alone at their stations for ten days or even longer.[82] Narcissa did say in her letter to her parents that Marcus had asked Gray to see if he could secure the services of Mr. and Mrs. Rogers or the Littlejohns to take charge of activities at Waiilatpu until he could return. "Next spring," she wrote, "I intend going below and spending some time in visiting for the benefit of my health."

For the third time, Narcissa returned to the reasons why Marcus was going: "He goes with the advice and entire confidence of his brethren in the mission, and who value him not only as an associate, but as their physician, and feel, as much as I do, that they know not how to spare him; but the interest of the cause demands the sacrifice on our part; and could you know all the circumstances in the cause, you would see more clearly how much our hearts are identified in the salvation of the Indians and the interest of the cause generally."

Narcissa's love and wifely concern for her husband is revealed in the following: "Forgive me, dear mother, if he is the sole theme of this letter; I can write about nothing else at this time. He is inexpressibly dear to me." After explaining that she did not have time to write individual letters to each member of her family, she added this postscript: "...all others must receive my dear husband as my living epistle to them and write me by him." Nowhere in any of the letters Narcissa wrote for her husband to carry east with him is there any hint of any question being in her mind as to the necessity of her husband's journey. She was in full accord with his views.

Evidently Whitman rode to Fort Walla Walla on Thursday or Friday, September 29 or 30, to complete arrangements with Lovejoy and to inform McKinlay of his plans.[83] No doubt McKinlay assured Whitman of his readiness to stand by and render Narcissa any assistance that might be needed, even though he was twentyfive miles away. Whitman has been censured for his willingness to leave his wife alone with the Indians for an indefinite period. His willingness to do so can only be explained by what he considered to be the great urgency of his mission. Whitman made such provisions as were possible under the circumstances. In addition to talking with McKinlay, Whitman had asked Gray to find someone to go to Waiilatpu and take care of the premises. However, it would have taken weeks for any party to arrive at Waiilatpu from the Willamette Valley. Whitman also confided in the Indians who lived nearby. Both Tiloukaikt and Tamsucky solemnly promised that they would protect both Mrs. Whitman and the mission property.

Like other ordinary human beings, the Whitmans were sometimes guilty of procrastination. The archives of the American Board contain copies of two questionnaires filled out by Marcus and Narcissa which gave information about their early lives, education, and spiritual experiences. The fact that they are dated October 3, 1843, the day Marcus left for Boston, shows one of them suddenly remembered their failure to answer the Board's request for such information.[84] The Spaldings received like questionnaires which were filled out and dated May, 1840.

The two questionnaires were carried east by Whitman along with the other letters that Narcissa had written.

Believing that McKinlay and Gray would find someone to go and live with Narcissa at Waiilatpu, and lulled by the promises of Tiloukaikt and Tamsucky to protect his wife and the mission property, Marcus kissed his wife goodby on Monday morning, October 3, 1842, and started his long journey to Boston [Letter 119]. With him were Lovejoy and at least one Indian by the name of Aps. The men had with them several pack animals and a dog, called Trapper, which had once been a pet of Alice Clarissa's.[85] With a brave but heavy heart, Narcissa stood watching her husband and his companions ride up the trail that led to the Blue Mountains until they were lost to view. She then reentered the house knowing that about a year would pass before she would see her husband again. She was alone except for the three halfbreed children—Mary Ann Bridger, Helen Mar Meek, and David Malin—and the Hawaiian, Jack. The Grays were still living in the emigrant house but they were planning to leave for the Willamette Valley the next day. Tiloukaikt and his band of about fifty men, women, and children had their lodges about a mile away.

END OF THE FIRST VOLUME

CHAPTER 16 ENDNOTES

1 Joseph Williams, *Narrative of a Tour from the State of Indiana to the Oregon Territory*, Cadmus Book Shop, reprint, New York, 1921, p. 48.

2 O. Larsell, *The Doctor in Oregon*, Portland, 1947, p. 114.

3 See Chapter Twelve, section, "Reaction of the Hudson's Bay Company."

4 Drury, *F.W.W.*, II:220.

5 Marshall, *Acquisition of Oregon*, II:61, quoting from *Seattle Daily Intelligencer*, April 28, 1881.

6 See Appendices 3 & 4 for a discussion of the *Whitman-Saved-Oregon* story. Spalding, writing some twenty-four years after the arrival of the Red River colony, made several errors in his series of articles which began appearing in the San Francisco *Pacific* with its May 23, 1865, issue.

7 Spalding, *Senate Document*, p. 20. Also, Marshall *Acquisition of Oregon*, I:62, quoting from the San Francisco *Pacific*, Oct. 19, 1865.

8 Gray, in his *Oregon*, p. 288, embellishes Spalding's fanciful account of what was supposed to have happened at Fort Walla Walla in the fall of 1842, by saying that after Whitman heard the taunt of the priest at the dinner table about the Americans being too late, he hastily withdrew, mounted his horse, and rode the twenty-five miles to Waiilatpu in two hours! Gray, who was at Waiilatpu in the fall of 1842, also stated: "I saw in a moment that he was fixed on some important object or errand." Gray's personal testimony gave weight to Spalding's version as to why Whitman left for Washington so suddenly in the fall of 1842.

9 Bancroft, *Oregon*. I:252.

10 *McLoughlin's Letters*, III:XXXIV.

11 See Chapter Thirteen, section "Roman Catholic Missionaries Arrive in Oregon."

12 *O.H.Q.*, XII (1911):292.

13 Bancroft, *Oregon*, I:97.

14 Accurate figures as to how all present at this historic Champoeg meeting voted are not available. Some writers claim that the Americans had a majority of two; others say six out of a total vote of over 100. A good account of the meeting is to be found in John A. Hussey, *Champoeg*, Portland, 1967, p. 154.

15 See Edwin A. Miles, "Fifty-Four Forty or Fight—An American Political Legend," in *Mississippi Valley Historical Review*, Vol. 44: (Sept. 1957), pp. 291 ff.

16 *McLoughlin's Letters*, III:XXXIV.

17 HBC Arch., B/223/c.

18 See Chapter Twelve, section "Reaction of the Hudson's Bay Company."

19 *Op. cit.*, p. 191. Italics are the author's.

20 George Simpson, *An Overland Journey Round the World During the Years 1841 and 1842*, Philadelphia, 1847. A later edition of this work under the title *Narrative of a Voyage to California Ports*, San Francisco, 1930, also appeared.

21 Simpson, *Overland Journey*, p. 110.

22 *McLoughlin's Letters*, III:XXXIV.

23 Narcissa copied her husband's letter to McKinlay in her letter to her father of Nov. 18, 1841.

24 Possibly the same John Gray, a half-breed Iroquois, who deserted Ogden's Snake River brigade in Utah in 1825. See Josephy, *Nez Perces*, pp. 68 & 216.

25 See Chapter Ten, "Three Cayuse Chiefs." In Whitman letters Nos. 100 & 101, the name is given as "Tilankaik."

26 Cannon, *Waiilatpu*, p. 103, identifies Sakiaph as Tamsucky and also as Feathercap. Cannon gives five different ways by which this Indian's name was spelled.

27 Clarke, *Pioneer Days*, II:526, and Gray, *Oregon*, p. 467.

28 Also spelled Isai-shal-akis, Tsai-ach-alkis, or Isai-ashel-uckas.

29 Here is evidence that some of the chiefs would use this form of punishment on members of their bands. Hudson's Bay Company's officials also used the whip as is noted in letters from James Douglas to Angus McDonald, Jan. 25, 1842, and Feb. 23, 1842, *Fort Vancouver Correspondence, Outward to 1845*, Provincial Archives, Victoria, B.C. In the latter letter Douglas advised: "Never apply the whip unjustly or without the clearest proof of the person's guilt." There is no evidence that Whitman ever used the lash in punishment. See Chapter Eleven, "Let Them Feel the Lash."

30 Maria Maki, the wife of Joseph Malin, who died at Waiilatpu on August 8, 1840, remained at the mission until the fall of 1841 when she was sent to Fort Vancouver. There she joined the A. B. Smiths and returned with them to Hawaii in December of that year.

31 See Appendix 6 for text of the H. K. W. Perkins letter from which this quotation was taken.

32 McKinlay's letter to Whitman was copied and sent to Greene [Letter 100].

33 Simpson, *Overland Journey*, p. 99. Simpson's views on the avarice of the natives harmonized with that which A. B. Smith had written on that subject.

34 See Appendix 6. Words in italics are underlined in the original.

35 Italics are the author's.

36 Drury, *Spalding*, p. 273.

37 Drury, *Spalding and Smith*, p. 326.

38 Hulbert, *O.P.*, VII:253 ff.

39 *Ibid.*, pp. 258 ff.

40 See Chapter Twenty-Four, section "Other Memorials" for reference to name-sakes of Dr. Whitman.

41 This David Malin, 1805–85, was pastor of a church in Philadelphia when Spalding visited him in 1870. Drury, *Spalding*, p. 391.

42 Italics are the author's.

43 Drury, *F.W.W.*, I:218 if; Gray, *Oregon*, p. 110.

44 Clarence Bagley, *Early Catholic Missions in old Oregon*, Seattle, 1932, p. 70; Carl Landerholm (translator), *Notices & Voyages of the Famed Quebec Mission to the Pacific Northwest*, Oregon Historical Society, 1956, pp. 44 ff. An original Catholic ladder in Coll. B. is reproduced in this latter work.

45 An original painting of a Protestant ladder by Mrs. Spalding is in Coll. O; copy reproduced in Drury, *F.W.W.*, I:218. Landerholm, *op. cit.*, p. 45, quoting Bishop Blanchet as saying: "Protestant ministers stop at nothing in sowing tares in

the field of the family father. They have fabricated an imitation of our historic ladder, and have not hesitated to place a mark on it at the sixteenth century to indicate the rise of their religion."

46 Drury, *Spalding and Smith*, p. 127.

47 Record book labelled "Baptisms, Marriages, Interments," St. James Cathedral, Vancouver, Wash., 1842–56.

48 Williams, *Narrative of a Tour*, pp. 70–1. See ante, fn. 1.

49 Drury, *F.W.W.*, II:229 ff., from Mary Walker's diary.

50 Elkanah Walker's diary covering these days in 1842 is in Coll. O.

51 Marshall, *Acquisition of Oregon*, II:118.

52 *Ibid.*, II: 180.

53 *Ibid.*, II: 126.

54 Drury, *F.W.W.*, I:262–5. Information from Mary Gray's diary.

55 Dorothy O. Johansen and Charles M. Gates, *Empire of the Columbia*, Harper, 1957, have a chapter on "The Boundary Question" which gives a fine review of the activities of Senator Linn and others in behalf of the U.S. claims to Old Oregon.

56 Marshall, *Acquisition of Oregon*, I:212.

57 White file, Old Indian Records, National Archives, Washington, n.c.

58 Drury, *F.W.W.*, I:264.

59 *Sources of the History of Oregon.*, Vol. I, No. 1 (F. G. Young, ed.), Univ. of Oregon, Eugene, 1897, "*Journal of Medorem Crawford*," p. 20.

60 L. W. Hastings, *A New Description of Oregon and California*, Cincinnati, 1857, p. 21.

61 HBC Arch., B/223/c/7.

62 *Ibid.*

63 HBC Arch., B/223/c/210a.

64 Drury, *F.W.W.*, II:236.

65 Walker could not understand why Whitman had sent letters addressed to Spalding to Tshimakain. Marshall, *Acquisition of Oregon*, II:128, gives a transcription of this section of Walker's diary.

66 See ante, fn. 59. *Crawford's Journal*, p. 21.

67 Marshall, *Acquisition of Oregon*, II:126–7 gives a copy of Gray's letter.

68 After serving two years as General Superintendent of the Methodist Oregon Institute, Salem, Oregon, Gray moved first to Oregon City and then to Clatsop Plains, south of Astoria. He took an active and often stormy part in the political, community, and church affairs of the different localities in which he lived. Following the completion of the transcontinental railroad in 1869, the Grays visited their old homes in the East. In 1870 Gray published his biased, but still important, *History of Oregon*.

69 Original in Coll. A. Reproduction in Drury, *Whitman*, p. 269.

70 This modifies the position taken in my Spalding biography, published in 1936, where I stated that Whitman rode primarily to save Spalding and the Mission. I now feel that there were other motives as well as that of concern for the Mission.

71 The original Eells and Walker letters are in Coll. A.

72 *Op. cit.*, p. 237. Italics are the author's.

73 Italics are the author's.

74 Allen, *Ten Years in Oregon*, p. 166. Miss Allen was mistaken about the time Dr. White spent in the States. He arrived in April 1841 and left the Missouri frontier in May 1842.

75 Drury, *F.W.W.*, I:265, quoting from Mary Gray's diary for Monday, September 19: "Mr. Smith & family, Mr. Lovejoy & several other Americans arrived today. Mr. S. [identity unknown] said they were starving—wanted to buy food. As the Dr. was gone, I sold them some flour—took one dollar for it. Gave him some butter & cheese." Feeling that he had not paid enough for the food received, Smith returned the next day and gave another dollar.

76 Lovejoy's earliest account, a letter addressed to W. H. Gray dated Nov. 6, 1869, appeared in Gray's *Oregon*, pp. 324–6; Spalding included a paraphrase of this letter in his *Senate Document*, p. 23. Lovejoy's second account, also a letter, was sent to Dr. G. H. Atkinson, a pioneer Congregational minister of Portland, February 14, 1876, and was published in *Pioneer and Historical Society of Oregon*, pp. 13 ff., and in Nixon, *How Marcus Whitman Saved Oregon*, pp. 304 ff. His third account, still unpublished, was written for the historian H. H. Bancroft, June 18, 1878, is in Coll. B, with photostats in Coll. O. Reference to any of these three accounts will be indicated by the abbreviations (L1), (L2), and (L3) used in the text, thus referring to the documents in their chronological order.

77 Barclay, *Early American Methodism*, II: pp. 234, 254.

78 Drury, F.W.W., II:226. Walker, in a letter to Chamberlain in Honolulu, Sept. 6, 1842, wrote: "I had some conversation with De Smet on the language. He remarked that as our belief was the same in regard to the Trinity, he thought we had better adopt one common phraseology. He gave me some of his phrases & my knowledge of this language would not allow me to adopt them."

79 Hiram M. Chittenden and Alfred T. Richardson, *Life, Letters, and Travels of... De Smet*, New York, 1905, I:129, fn. 1: "There is now in the possession of George H. Hines of Portland, Oregon, a 'Douay Bible' dated Belfast, 1839, with the following inscription in Father De Smet's hand: 'Presented to Dr. M. Whitman by P. J. DeSmet.'" I recall seeing this volume on display in the museum of the Oregon Historical Society in the spring of 1954. Present location of the Bible is unknown.

80 Fort Hall, founded by Capt. N. J. Wyeth in 1834, was sold to the Hudson's Bay Company in 1836.

81 Italics are the author's.

82 See Drury, *Spalding*, pp. 317 ff., for an account of Spalding leaving his wife and year-old baby girl alone at Lapwai for several weeks in the summer of 1845 while he made a trip to The Dalles for supplies.

83 Archibald McKinlay to Dr. W. F. Tolmie from Lac La Hache, Dec. 9, 1884: "He came to Walla Walla a few days before his departure, not on a professional call but to bid me farewell. He was in my opinion a very superior man, his whole soul was devoted to christianizing and civilizing the Indians." Also McKinlay to Myron Eells, Jan. 4, 1884: "Whitman did say to me before his departure that his objects in going east were to frustrate unfavorable reports sent the Board by discontented

members of the mission." Original letters owned by descendants of McKinlay; copies in Kamloops Museum, Kamloops, B.C.

84 My attention was directed to these questionnaires by Ross Woodbridge of Pittsford, N.Y., who evidently was the first student of the Whitman story to discover them in the archives of the American Board.

85 I received this story about Trapper, the dog, about thirty-five years ago from the late Mrs. Edmund Bowden of Seattle who in turn heard it from the Rev. Cushing Eells.

www.ingramcontent.com/pod-product-compliance
Lightning Source LLC
Chambersburg PA
CBHW022054150426
43195CB00008B/130